41025

FIELDS OF PRAISE

The National Ground, 1980

FIELDS OF PRAISE

The Official History of The Welsh Rugby Union 1881-1981

David Smith and
Gareth Williams

Cardiff
University of Wales Press
on behalf of the Welsh Rugby Union
1980

© The Welsh Rugby Union, 1980

Published October, 1980

The University of Wales Press
6 Gwennyth Street, Cathays
Cardiff CF2 4YD

British Library Cataloguing in Publication Data

Smith, David Burton
  Fields of Praise.
  1. Welsh Rugby Union — History
  I. Title   II. Williams, Gareth W
  796.33' 3' 062429   GV945.55.W/

ISBN 0 7083 0766 3

Frontispiece: © Terence Soames Ltd.

Printed in Wales by CSP Printing of Cardiff

FOREWORD

by

HERMAS EVANS

Chairman, W.R.U. Centenary Publications Committee

———

I T is often stated that Rugby Football in Wales is more than a national game — it is a way of life; it is a religion; it is a political activity — and throughout the last hundred years the game has permeated all walks of Welsh life. Any history of the Welsh Rugby Union, and hence, the game, must therefore be more than a mere description of great matches, famous players, and the administration; it must also attach itself to the social, industrial and religious life of Wales during the period. This was to be the broad term of reference within which such a history would be written.

The quest for an author would be one for a person whose love of rugby football was matched by a knowledge of Welsh history. Who better than the University of Wales to supply an author? — a University which has always been a source of great rugby talent in players and administrators and one which obviously specializes in the history of its native land. My first contact in the University was with Professor Glanmor Williams of University College, Swansea. He was enthusiastic about the whole idea and without hesitation recommended *two* young lecturers whom he thought would admirably and efficiently do the necessary researching and writing.

In my early discussions with them I realized that in David Smith of University College, Cardiff, and Gareth Williams of University College, Aberystwyth, the writing of the History of the Welsh Rugby Union would be in very capable and enthusiastic hands. They immediately responded to the suggested approach and their introductory illustration of how the subject matter should be covered convinced the W.R.U. that here was a new and enlightened approach to writing a history of the game.

As the history was to be more than a descriptive exercise and would have academic status, it was felt that the University of Wales Press should be invited to publish the work. Following discussions on the nature of the project the Press accepted the undertaking and I would pay tribute to their ready co-operation and advice throughout the whole period of negotiation and publication.

The authors have produced a most absorbing account of the evolution of the Welsh Rugby Union during the first one hundred years of its existence. The mystery surrounding the formation of the Union has been unravelled in clear terms; the drama and excitement of the first quarter of the century has been revealed in a new form to all rugby enthusiasts; the controversies surrounding team selection, the dominance of certain individuals, the background and attitude of great players, the scenes of great matches, and the whole period leading up to the Second World War have all been vividly described.

The later period of the hundred years has been given pride of place by the authors in a narrative that indicates the greatness of Wales in the rugby world. The building of the National Ground, the famous players of the great Triple Crown and 'Grand Slam' teams, and memorable matches when Wales floated in a euphoric sea of triumphs, have now been placed on permanent record for many to relive those scenes, and others to enjoy reading about them in the future.

In a single-volume work of this nature, it is impossible to include all the interesting facets of Welsh rugby. Space did not allow detailed praise of the many, many enthusiasts who week after week, year after year give their wholehearted endeavour and loyalty to the service of the game they have grown to love and enjoy. To these unpublicized persons, to the many rugby clubs in Wales, to the Schools and Youth XVs, Welsh rugby will be forever grateful and this excellent History of the Welsh Rugby Union must surely be dedicated to these great servants of the game.

Baron de Coubertin rekindled the Olympic torch in the spirit that the important thing was not to win but to take part. I am sure that when you have completed reading the vivid reminiscences and accounts in this book you too will feel that you have taken part in a magnificent century of Welsh rugby football.

PREFACE

SOMETIMES one of us kicked and the other ran. Other times, one of us swerved and the other went straight. Now and again, one of us, in breaking through, would leave our defence exposed, and the other had to race back and save. At all times we went in search of the ball together, and this book is as integrated a piece of work as we could make it.

Our intention was clear from the moment the Welsh Rugby Union took the decision to invite two professional historians to write its history. We had no doubt of the special role that sport — and in the Welsh case this means, above everything, rugby — had played in industrial society over the last hundred years, and we wanted to show that relationship clearly. At the same time much of the sociology of sport that we had read seemed to carry with it an inevitable reductionism by which the game described emerged only as illustration of something else, usually thought of as more important, that was going on in the 'real' world. This view we rejected since it expressed neither appreciation of the intrinsic value of our game's history nor understanding of the interlocking aspects that intrigued us. In his superb book on cricket, *Beyond a Boundary*, the West Indian writer C. L. R. James had said in 1963 that he could 'no longer accept the system of values which could not find [in most history books] a place . . . for the best-known Englishman of his time . . . W. G. Grace'. To accept the implications of that remark is one thing; to breathe back life into the portrait of a dramatic performer, the player, is another. Athletic style and prowess cannot be truly reflected by a catalogue of games, a litany of victories, a string of statistics or a scatter of similes. We have tried to argue, through the style of our prose and the structure of our book, that both the tension between sport and society and the fleeting unrepeatability of thrilling rugby play can be, if not recaptured direct, at least suggested by historical writing that is sensitive to the needs of its subject-matter.

Since the history of Welsh rugby has been neither chronologically straight-forward nor a linear progress we have tried in places to capture the flux of the time and the game by darting hither and thither. This is especially the case in the early chapters, where the unformed nature of the game precludes a blow-by-blow account. We have been selective, as all historians must, in our choice of material from the enormous amount that we have garnered. This is a hefty volume; it would have been even bigger had we not decided, sometimes reluctantly, where, when and what material could be rejected as only incidental to our main purpose: to present the history of rugby in Wales in the context of the progress and administration of the game in Welsh society. The reader can refer to the appendices for some of the basic data which the form of the book precluded us from incorporating wholesale into our narrative. In addition, of course, we have been fortunate in being able to write as we wished because of the indispensable work of others. The extent of our indebtedness can be gauged from our bibliography at the end, but without the pathfinding works of J. B. G. Thomas and the prodigious labour expended by John Billot in compiling his irreplaceable *History of Welsh International Rugby* (2nd ed. 1971) and its companion volumes *All Blacks in Wales* (1972) and *Springboks in Wales* (1974), our research would most certainly have taken longer and our life expectancy become shorter. Peter Corrigan's *100 Years of Welsh Soccer* (1976) was another book to which we found ourselves constantly referring while, amongst the scores of club histories we consulted, the standard accounts of D. E. Davies on Cardiff, Jack Davis on Newport, and Brinley E. Matthews on Swansea also became much thumbed.

It would be impossible to list all those — players, administrators, referees, spectators, journalists, club officials, local historians — who by word and deed both assisted us in our task and confirmed Aneurin Bevan's opinion that 'politics in Westminster are in their infancy compared with Welsh rugby'. The international fame of those former players whose memories and scrapbooks we have ransacked is secure enough to transcend our gratitude to them, and we trust they will forgive us for not listing them here: their exploits litter the text like stardust. There are also many other people who have corresponded with us or been interviewed by us, whom we cannot acknowledge individually: we hope they will accept this book as a full proof of their co-operation. Some, however, must be mentioned by name for their special help. From the beginning, Centenary President Cliff Jones was an enthusiastic source of encouragement and practical assistance. Among the W.R.U. Office staff, W. H. Clement, Ray Williams, Brian Kempson, Malcolm Lewis, Len Matthews, and Avril Power met every request with endless helpfulness and courtesy. Alun Richards and Onllwyn Brace, at work on the B.B.C.'s W.R.U. Centenary Film, freely exchanged information and ideas with us. We discovered that no one concerned to unearth biographical details of international players past and present can afford to neglect the assistance of Timothy Auty of Leeds, an indefatigable compiler of rugby facts and figures to whom we frequently turned. The technical knowledge of Howard Goodfield of Pontypridd R.F.C. converted neighbourliness into a rescue operation when the book stalled in mid-1979; similarly, the constant readiness of Tony Lewis, historian and secretary of Kenfig Hill R.F.C., to supply us with material from his enviable rugby library places us heavily in his debt. Barrie Morgan (gratefully, he says) used some of his sabbatical term at the University of Canterbury to research New Zealand papers for us. Gwyn Roblin saved us from error about rugby in North Wales. Bill Jones of Cardiff gave us titbits of information uncovered in the course of his own research and went on to take time off from Clwb Rygbi Caerdydd to prepare a meticulous index. Others whose patience we never seemed quite to erode but without whose help and accommodation, sometimes in a literal sense, this book would never have been completed include R. J. Boulton and Brian Chappin of Cardiff; Ivor Edwards of Mountain Ash R.F.C.; Graham Evans of Maesteg Celtic R.F.C.; Mrs Janetta E. Evans, widow of former W.R.U. Secretary Eric Evans; Geoff Hughes of Cross Keys R.F.C.; Dan James of Brecon R.F.C.; Tom Lodge of Neath R.F.C.; Alan Watts, grandson of W. J. Bancroft, of Swansea; the staff of the Newspaper Reading Room of the National Library of Wales, and Brian Lile, in particular, of the Department of Printed Books; Roger Padfield of the Cardiff Central Reference Library; Mrs J. Gibbon of Usk, who put us on the track of Richard Mullock; the Headmasters of many schools in and beyond Wales; the Secretaries of the English, Irish and Scottish Rugby Unions, and particularly, the ever-helpful and painstaking archivist of the R.F.U., Alfred Wright. Glanmor Williams of University College, Swansea, has been behind so many historical enterprises in Wales that it will come as no surprise to those who know of his energy and his sympathies to find his name among our acknowledgements: its inevitability does not dim the warmth of our appreciation. Hermas Evans introduced us to the inner sanctum of the W.R.U. and proved to be a constant support as well as a firm friend. Both he and Kenneth Harris undertook to read the entire manuscript so that it has much benefited from their constructive comments. Our typists Pam Matthewman and Buddug West deserve our thanks for scrupulously decoding the cryptograms that we called drafts, and for turning them into a final and polished typescript; Margaret White, too, provided much appreciated secretarial assistance. And as the book entered its final stages we were very grateful for the understanding and patient advice of John Rhys and Alun Treharne of the University of Wales Press.

Our greatest debts, though, must be to our families. In Aberystwyth, Mary, Daniel and Tomos patiently bore much domestic deprivation, and in Pontypridd, Norette, Owen, Aled and Daniel wondered if the work would ever end. It has, for now, and we hope that they, and everyone else, will think this book was worth it.

David Smith
Gareth Williams

1 March 1980

ACKNOWLEDGEMENTS

Thanks are expressed to those who have given permission to quote from particular publications, as follows:

His Honour Judge Rowe Harding, *Rugby Reminiscences and Opinions*, London, 1929; Terry McLean, *Great Days in New Zealand Rugby*, A. H. & A. W. Reed, Wellington; Sioned O'Connor, copyright owner of the works of Cynan; Ray Williams, *Skilful Rugby*, Souvenir Press 1976; Llys yr Eisteddfod Genedlaethol (the National Eisteddfod Court) and Dic Jones, for an extract from '*Parc yr Arfau*'; John Ormond, 'Salmon', from *Definition of a Waterfall*, © Oxford University Press, 1973.

CONTENTS

ABBREVIATIONS

A.A.A.	Amateur Athletic Association.
A.F.C.	Association Football Club.
A.G.M.	Annual General Meeting.
C.C.P.R.	Central Council for Physical Recreation.
F.A.W.	Football Association of Wales.
F.F.R.	Fédération Française de Rugby.
I.B.	International Rugby Football Board.
I.R.F.U.	Irish Rugby Football Union.
N.U.	Northern Union.
N.W.R.U.	North Wales Rugby Union.
R.F.U.	Rugby Football Union (of England).
R.F.C.	Rugby Football Club.
R.L.	Rugby League.
S.R.U.	Scottish Rugby Union.
S.W.F.C.	South Wales Football Club (1875-1878)
S.W.F.U.	South Wales Football Union (1878-1881)
U.A.U.	Universities' Athletic Union.
W.F.U.	Welsh Football Union (1881-1934)
W.R.U.	Welsh Rugby Union
W.S.R.U.	Welsh Schools Rugby Union.
W.S.S.R.U.	Welsh Secondary Schools Rugby Union.

'THE ONE GREAT PASTIME OF THE PEOPLE'

THROUGHOUT the afternoon of 8 March 1879, the Newport telegraph offices of the *Monmouthshire Merlin* were besieged by urgent enquirers seeking news of the game in Cardiff. At Sophia Gardens, 'the sister ports', as contemporaries called them, were engaged in the final tie of the South Wales Challenge Cup. The game had aroused great interest in both towns, and a thousand Newport supporters had travelled to Cardiff on one of the first football excursions to be run in South Wales.

'On its becoming known that Newport had won', reported the *Merlin* later, Cardiff having gone down by one goal and two tries to nil, 'the news was circulated through the town and received by many with almost frantic excitement. Boys and youths were running wildly through the streets shouting "Newport has won!"' By the time the team were due at Newport station by the 9.30 mail, 'a dense crowd had assembled and a band of music engaged to play the conquering heroes through the main streets'. A pair-horse brake was ready to receive the team, and as the train pulled in 'a deafening cheer was given. This was taken up by the crowd outside the station until the town was ringing with the cheers of the multitude, intermingled with the occasional strains of the brass band which for a time was literally overpowered.' One of the brake-horses began prancing excitedly in the milling crowd until one of the players, Teddy Jenkins, jumped on its back and rode it western-style. At Cardiff Road a halt was made, 'followed by renewed cheering, shaking of hands with the members of the team, a general waving of hats and tremendous confusion'. The team was led to the King's Head Hotel, 'where a speech was demanded from the captain and cheer after cheer greeted him as he arose to address the multitude'.

The era of football enthusiasm had arrived, not only in Newport but throughout South Wales. In February 1880 Swansea beat Lampeter College in the Cup Final at Ystrad, near Carmarthen. On their arrival back in Swansea, the victors were greeted by a band and cheered through the streets to the Workingmen's Institute, to which most of the team belonged. When Cardiff captured the trophy the following year, they, too, were met at the station by a band and a huge crowd who carried the players shoulder-high to the Queen's Hotel. For enthusiasm, Llanelli could outdo them all. Having been runners-up on two previous occasions, they beat Newport in the 1884 final at Neath, where the 5,000 spectators included eighteen carriage loads of supporters who had paid the 2s. 4d. excursion return fare from Llanelli. Arriving back, the team, given a rapturous reception by a jubilant throng of 2,000 led by a Rechabite band, were preceded on a triumphant procession through the town by a tramcar of torch-bearers. 'Torches burned, houses were illuminated, coloured lights flared', reported the *Llanelly and County Guardian,* 'an election victory paled before it'. After a repetition of the same scenes when Llanelli beat Newport in the 1886 final, to be greeted by thousands of rockets and coloured lights, 'Touchstone', one of the new species of sporting correspondent, mischievously suggested in the *Western Mail* that Harry Bowen, the Llanelli captain, be memorialized in a tin-plate statue or ran for Local Board honours — 'extremists advocate both'.

The Cup competition had been launched at a meeting of the South Wales Football Club at the Cardiff Arms Hotel on 23 October 1877, when it was decided to institute a challenge cup of the value of fifty guineas, open to competition by any club subscribing two guineas. After applications had been received, the draw was made:

Carmarthen v. Cardiff, to be played at Neath
Talgarth v. Merthyr, at Merthyr
Brecon v. Monmouth G.S., at Cardiff
Cowbridge G.S. v. Llanelli, at Neath
Carmarthen G.S. v. Lampeter College, at Carmarthen
Glamorgan 10th Rifle Volunteers (Cardiff) v. Llandovery College,
at Swansea
Pontypool v. Newport, at Newport
Llandeilo v. Neath, at Neath
Swansea v. Abergavenny, at Brecon

And it was Newport, after dismissing Pontypool, Llanelli and Carmarthen, who defeated Swansea by a goal to nil in the final on 2 March 1878 at Bridgend, to become the first holders of the South Wales Cup.

For the next ten years the South Wales Challenge Cup was keenly, sometimes literally, fought for, to become the pivot around which early Welsh rugby revolved; and the competition acquired extra spice by the decision in September 1880 to divide the contesting clubs into eastern and western districts, thus ensuring an East - West final. It played a formative role in the emergence of Welsh Rugby and in its growth as a spectator sport. It attracted large crowds; in 1883 the final between Swansea and Newport was watched by 6,000. It thus provided the financial basis for the transformation of 'open' into 'gate-taking' clubs. It generated intense local rivalry and brought excitement and spectacle into the routine lives of congested, industrial towns. It also raised the standard of football played. But these gains were won at some cost, for the disputes and bitterness caused by the Challenge Cup eventually led to its abandonment.

Sometimes these disputes were protracted. In 1879 Newport had to play another two Cup matches *after* winning the final. Swansea and Neath had been drawn together in the first round, but having played six drawn games without being able to reach a conclusion, they were disqualified by the match committee of the competition, who decided that the two sides who had progressed furthest in the competition, Newport and Cardiff, should compete in the final. Newport won, but aware of the dissatisfaction of Neath and Swansea, allowed them to settle their tie and then offered to play the winners. Neath and Swansea played a seventh game, which Neath won after two and a half hours play, by the narrowest possible margin of a minor (forcing the opposition to touch-down in self-defence), which counted as a score if there were no goals or tries. Newport then played and beat Neath 49 - 0, and to meet Swansea's complaints, met and beat her 48 - 0; the sort of remarkable consistency only a club in its fourth invincible season could attain.

Another cause of friction was the accusation that clubs were importing players from other areas, in contravention of the stipulation that only *bona fide* residents could play in Cup matches. After they had played a draw with Newport in the 1882 final, Llanelli lodged an official complaint that Tom Clapp had played for Newport, as he lived forty miles away and had gone to live in the town only a few days before the match; another two Newport players, it was also alleged, had violated the 'twelve-mile radius' rule. For the replay, Llanelli threatened to invite down some players from Blackheath, the champion side of England, to stay for a few days among them. In the event they were beaten, but went down proclaiming that at least all their team were residents 'within a mile of the parish church', as opposed to Newport's 'picked team'. Llanelli were quick learners though. At the 1884 annual meeting of the Welsh Football Union it was reported that one of Cardiff's international players, 'Buller' Stadden, had received a letter from Llanelli offering him a situation for five days a week so that he could play for them. This was denied by Llanelli and the matter dropped, but competitive rugby meant increased working-class participation, and already there were allegations of incipient professionalism in the game. Competition was certainly an incentive for many clubs to go into 'strict training' for cup-ties. The committee had the Llanelli team out running, boxing and practising several evenings before the 1881 final, and Newport believed they were beaten in 1886 because Llanelli had been training for six weeks. In 1886 Cardiff hired a room in Quay Street 'where the players two nights a week donned the mittens and indulged in other exercises, and Geo. Lewis was employed at 6s. a week to rub them down.'

Competition also sharpened the desire to win. Following a heated exchange in the *Western Mail* over 'disdainful and rough tactics' like holding opponents on the ground and butting in the 1883 cup-tie between Cardiff and local rivals Cardiff Wanderers, the ubiquitous 'Admirer of Fair Play', making an early appearance, lamented that 'it is a most unfortunate thing connected with football in South Wales that there are so many objections raised to the ruling of umpires, especially by the team who comes off second best, and it is high time the Welsh Football Union did interfere in the Challenge Cup matches.' Later that year, at the W.F.U.'s annual meeting in Swansea, Tom Williams of Neath proposed that the Cup be withdrawn from competition, 'its object having been accomplished, the creation of sufficient interest'. The proposer had found several club captains in agreement, including H. J. Simpson of Cardiff, who had told him, 'I endorse your views. To my mind the Cup only causes dissension, strife and hard feeling'. Llanelli and Newport successfully advocated retaining the competition, but thereafter the numbers of clubs entering for it declined. In 1883-4 only eight competed, in 1885-6, seven, and it was decided that the 1887 final should be the last. Efforts were immediately made to revive it, but 'Old Stager', the sports writer of the *South Wales Daily News,* for one, did not miss it. 'For the present', he wrote in 1888, 'that trophy is laid on the shelf. Is it too much to hope that it may be permitted to remain there?'.

It was, but when it was brought back in 1889, it was for competition among second teams and minor clubs, and lasted only another eight years. In the first of the new-look finals in March 1890, Penygraig, symbol of the gathering strength of the valley sides, beat Llanelli 'A', without having conceded a point in the five rounds of the competition. But 'Old Stager' was determined to write the epitaph of the South Wales Cup — 'Poor old pot! Put up once more to be wrangled over among the second teams, it can scarcely be said to attract the attention it excited in days gone by'. That may have been, but in truth the Cup was a victim of its own success, for it had stimulated such an interest in competitive rugby that local cup competitions had mushroomed all over South Wales. From 1885 the Monmouthshire Challenge Cup, worth thirty guineas, was the prize most sought after by Gwent clubs, in Cardiff a District Challenge Cup, in Swansea, soon, the Llewellyn Cup, while the Llanelli club instituted its own competition for local sides in 1885, the *Guardian* Cup, sponsored by the *Llanelly and County Guardian*.

It was in that paper that the social significance of the Challenge Cup competition in the wider context of South Wales life was most clearly recognized. 'The question', wrote a correspondent on the eve of the 1881 final, 'is not one merely of beating fifteen picked men from each of the other towns in the western district of South Wales. It means much more. It means vindicating the honour of Llanelli against her many detractors, the editor of the *South Wales Daily News* included. It means raising her name and her fame amongst the towns. It tends to bring more trade, a more vigorous public spirit, and a healthier social life'.

From the early 1880s, East Walians were prepared to concede that Llanelli enjoyed greater public support than any other club in Wales. The Llanelli *Guardian* not only fuelled the local enthusiasm, but frequently fanned the smouldering grievances of the town's rabid rugbyites. This was due in no small measure to its proprietor, editor and sports correspondent, J. Allen Williams, who was also a Llanelli committee-man and frequent delegate of the club at meetings of the W.F.U. The pride, partisanship and petulance of the *Guardian's* constantly informative coverage of rugby affairs reflected the intense involvement of the community in the game, as if the town's distinctive geographical location made its inhabitants more self-conscious and sensitive to the merest slight on their club. When only one Llanelli player was selected for the Welsh team to meet England in 1884, he was urged by the *Guardian*, 'Don't play. Better that than an inadequate representation. Llanelli ought to challenge the pseudo-Welsh team and ignore the Union'.

The *Guardian* took especial pride in the sporting behaviour of Llanelli followers. 'I never saw such a fair lot of spectators in all of my life', it

5

gleefully reported a supporter of the visiting Hull side in February 1885. 'Our spectators in Yorkshire have much to learn from yours. Why! they cheered us more than they did their own men.' Other clubs had a lot to learn from Llanelli. When Dewsbury went on from Llanelli to Neath in April the same year, the *Guardian* followed them, and reported that 'their reception at Neath supplied a striking contrast to that which they had experienced at Llanelli. The Neath players were exceedingly disagreeable to them; and the few spectators who were present, excepting a few Llanellyites, conducted themselves as they usually do'. Swansea fared no better, being 'richly endowed with well-dressed rowdies', and was disliked for its 'bounce and conceit'. As for Cardiff, Llanelli found it difficult to squeeze a fixture out of them, as 'they [Cardiff] are engaged for the greater part of the season in waging warfare with second-class teams against whom they pile up abnormally large scores'. When Llanelli did get to the Arms Park in January 1888 and lost, the *Guardian* concentrated on the boorishness of the crowd. 'The gentlemen of Cardiff have yet to learn some of the elements of good breeding, even on the football field . . . We feel more proud than ever of our ground, our stand, our team and our spectators'. With rugby exciting such emotions in the community, few would have felt disposed to argue with the *Guardian's* self-gratifying reponse to the news that Stradey Park was about to host its first international in 1887: 'Where has football found a more congenial soil than at Llanelli? Where in South Wales is the town in which the winter pastime has become so interwoven with the social life of its inhabitants?'.

For the tastes of some, in Llanelli and beyond, it was becoming so closely identified as to constitute a threat to morality and clean living, in the way that those abstractions were perceived by the Welsh nonconformist conscience at its most puritan. Its associations with the demon drink — in default of any better facilities teams invariably changed at a local 'arms', and clubs often had public houses as their headquarters, while the interest of brewers and publicans was a continuing legacy of their traditional involvement in pre-industrial games — its apparent incitement to disorderly and uninhibited behaviour, its secular, alien connotations, meant that many a player dared not confess at home that he was a member of a football side. For every hundred who were discouraged from playing by the ghoulish warning that they were kicking the head of John the Baptist — a prevalent and widespread belief — another hundred sought to cover their traces by concealing their football clothes at the bottom of the garden, or where they could.

Not all religious denominations were so horrified. The Church, like the publicans, had for centuries patronized popular recreations and extended its support into the industrial period. Several English soccer clubs — Everton, Aston Villa, Bolton, Wolverhampton — grew out of church sides, and some junior Welsh rugby teams had similar origins, like Dowlais St. Illtyd's and Penydarren Church Juniors in Merthyr, and St. Peter's Silver Stars, encouraged by Parson Howell Howells on horseback, in Blaina; while the Irish community near Aberavon Beach formed the nucleus of St. Joseph's R.C. Church team, founded in 1887 to become the renowned Aberavon Green Stars. There were three future Anglican clergymen in the first ever Welsh XV of 1881 (Newman, Peake and captain Bevan), a tradition maintained up to and beyond the First World War. The Revd Alban Davies captained the 1914 Welsh XV, whose ferocious pack was known as 'the terrible eight'. Alban was one of the eight and he led by example; when asked whether he ever found the rich language of the other seven offensive, he explained to his inquirer that he always wore a scrum-cap. Just after the War, W. T. Havard, later Bishop of St. Asaph and St. David's, won a cap at forward; and for many in South Wales the Church Militant meant no more than the Lampeter College XV, whose brawling ordinands were once headlined in the *Carmarthen Journal* as 'Fighting Parsons'.

The Nonconformist churches, too, overcame their scruples in time, but in the early years of Welsh rugby the opposition of the chapels was bitter. In 1881 Llanelli's Allen Williams spoke publicly of 'a certain few prejudiced to the game' but why he could not say, 'as what was religion but the teachings of the principles of forebearance, patience and good feelings towards one another, and these football matches encouraged to an eminent degree'. In 1886 a clergyman bardically signing himself 'Taborfryn' protested to the Llanelli *Spectator* that the game was 'unsuitable for young ladies of both sexes.'

In the upper Swansea valley, the Ystradgynlais club was founded in 1890 in the teeth of what was described as 'unprecedented opposition' from the local clergy who sought to prevent it. The controversy was to be settled by a vote taken after a public debate between the spokesmen of the rival factions, where Dr Fraser for the footballers, faced the Revd W. M. Morgan of Sardis. It was a confrontation recalling the historic clash of T. H. Huxley and Bishop Wilberforce, for it was the apes versus the angels, a Welsh monkey trial with its own Clarence Darrow and William Jennings Bryan: Oxford 1860, Ystradgynlais 1890, Tennessee 1925. The apes won by three votes and proceeded to arrange fixtures for their new club, but the 'sêt fawr' refused to take this lying down, and before the first game was due to take place, chapel representatives overnight removed the goal posts to the police station. Bloodied but unbowed, next morning players and officials of the new club cut replacement posts from a nearby wood, and the game went on.

The Canute-like stance of a Revd W. M. Morgan could avail little against the rising tide of rugby football that by 1890 had engulfed the whole of South Wales. The facts, and especially the conclusion drawn from them, would be unpalatable to some, but the *South Wales Daily News* put the situation in a nutshell. 'Football in South Wales, which in this connection means Wales,' it observed in 1891, 'has steadily gained in favour during the last few years, until it has now become the one great pastime of the people. For one club that existed ten years ago, there are now twenty, and that the influence the game has exercised on the youth of the country has been all for the good cannot be gainsaid, occasionally denunciating utterances from the pulpit notwithstanding'.

The attention devoted to rugby in the press, and the growth of a distinct sporting journalism, was an index of the ever-increasing popularity of the game. Local and provincial newspapers, and from the late 1880s their sporting editions, enlarged their readership with lively football reports, illustrated pen-portraits of leading players, and devices for testing popular opinion, as when 'Old Stager' took a readers' poll to find the best Welsh XV in January 1889. He received 2,102 lists, one from the continent, with Evan James of Swansea heading the poll with 1,946 votes. The speed with which the telegraph could convey results invested the sporting editions with a still greater urgency. The Scotland v. Wales international at Edinburgh in February 1889 had kicked off at 3.00 p.m. The final score was handed in at Edinburgh Post Office at 4.21 p.m. and by 4.45 p.m. the *Evening Express* was on sale in Cardiff with the result.

If the rise of the popular press mirrored increased consumer power in one way, the growth of rugby reflected it in another, as thousands of people paid to travel to games, gain admission, and acquired the necessary equipment for playing themselves. The Cup competition heralded not only the take-off of rugby in South Wales, it brought financial prosperity to the leading clubs as large crowds became an attendant feature of the game.

Newport's first home game with Cardiff in December 1876 had attracted 200 people; three years later 5,000 watched them play the crack English side, Blackheath. Cardiff often drew between 3,000 and 4,000 spectators during the 1881-2 season; 7,000 watched Newport at the Arms Park in February 1888. It was the 1890s that saw rugby become a mass spectator sport, but well before then it paid clubs to charge admission. The 200 who saw Cardiff play at Newport in December 1876 had been charged sixpence admission, so the 'gate' was around five pounds. Cardiff charged gate-money for the first time when they played Newport in the Cup Final at the Sophia Gardens in 1879, and several people wrote indignantly to the papers expressing their disapproval of this innovation. But rugby, like most other entertainment, cost money, and the £72 taken went on the costs of roping off the ground and advertising the match.

Only the principal clubs had enclosed grounds. Newport had an enclosure, grandstand and committee rooms; Llanelli, an enclosure and pavilion. In 1881 admission to Stradey was sixpence, working-class threepence, and ladies free; season tickets cost 5s. to the ground, 10s. 6d. to ground and pavilion; in 1884-5 a 2s. season ticket was introduced for schoolboys under thirteen.

By the mid-1880s, the principal clubs were thus able to defray players' expenses, whereas a decade before, as the *South Wales Daily News* pointed out in 1886, 'a very different state of things prevailed. Football as far as the masses were concerned was only just beginning to make itself known. The crowds who now flock to see a match on any of our leading Welsh grounds, and pour much treasure in the shape of gate-money into the coffers of the various clubs, were then represented by a mere handful of people who would not have come at all were it proposed to impose even the smallest charge. Men who played had to pay for their sport. There was no assistance from outside'.

The facilities that clubs could offer also determined the rate for admission charged for internationals. Three hundred pounds was taken in gate-money at Rodney Parade when Wales played Scotland in February 1888 and 7,000 paid admission of sixpence or a shilling according to their situation in the ground. Prices at Cardiff were higher. When a record crowd of 10,000 paid £500 to see Wales play Scotland in February 1890, the W.F.U. had imposed admission charges of 1s. to the field, 2s. to the enclosure and 3s. to the grandstand, which could accommodate 600. Cardiff had erected its first stand, seating 300 people, 'for the convenience of the spectators and the ladies in particular', in 1881-2 at a cost of £50, which was soon covered by the consistently good gates Cardiff was getting that year. Then, such was the phenomenal success of the Cardiff side under

Frank Hancock in 1885-6, when it won twenty-six of its twenty-seven matches, a new stand was built, costing £362, a steel rope put around the ground in place of the previous hempen one, and footboards laid. Again gate-money paid for these, for where in 1880-1 Cardiff took £69 11s. 0d., in 1885-6 the figure was £720 3s. 9d. The following season it was able to put up another temporary stand for the increasing number of spectators and in 1888-9 launch an insurance scheme at a cost of £25 4s. 0d. to cover accidents to its players. By 1890-1 Cardiff's gate receipts totalled £1,223 16s. 10d., further income coming from the sale of 299 season tickets and 968 workmen's tickets. On the expenditure side, £260 was given to local charities, the first in a long history of charitable donations.

Sport mirrored a society where market forces predominated: if supply was to keep pace with demand, the spectator appeal of rugby needed to be sustained by making the product more interesting. The provision of increased facilities was one way of obtaining this end; the extension and diversification of fixture-lists was another. In the seventies, the season ran from late November to early March; by the mid-eighties it extended from early October to mid-April. In its first season, 1876-7, Cardiff played three fixtures, with Newport, Swansea and Merthyr; in 1881-2 nineteen; in 1886-7 thirty; in 1889-90 thirty-five. As early as 1884-5 they were playing sides as geographically disparate as Wakefield Trinity, Clifton, Harlequins, Queen's College Cork, Moseley, Weston, Gloucester and the London German Gymnastic Society. From the early 1880s, according to a sporting journalist writing in 1886, 'the Cardiff men found that there was a better, a more skilful game than the heavy forward one at that time in vogue in South Wales and which even now has not altogether disappeared', to be found among English clubs. Thus, of Cardiff's thirty-one fixtures in 1888-9, twelve were with English clubs; Newport's thirty fixtures the same season included games with Blackheath, Richmond, Cambridge University, Guy's Hospital, Gloucester, Moseley, Oldham, Bristol, United Hospitals and Weston. Sporting links with the crack north of England teams were first forged in 1884 when Wakefield Trinity visited Newport and Cardiff. At Christmas 1884, Llanelli became the first Welsh side to tour in Yorkshire, where they played Dewsbury, Hull, Bradford and Halifax; they went back every Christmas for the next three years. From 1884 Dewsbury, Hull and Batley came down to play Newport, Cardiff, Neath and Llanelli. By 1886 the novelty had worn off and the press, at least, was becoming blasé in reporting the activities of northern tourists; in April that year Castleford were 'our latest lot of visitors from Yorkshire'. As far as Welsh inter-club rivalry was concerned, fixtures were acquiring something like their modern appearance. By 1886 Llanelli and Neath, and Cardiff and Swansea were playing each other four times a season; by 1887 Newport was playing Cardiff and Swansea four times each; by 1889 Swansea was meeting Llanelli four times. London Welsh, founded in 1885, inaugurated its traditional Christmas tour of South Wales that year.

But rugby was far from being the preserve of a handful of prosperous coastal towns. By 1880 at least thirty clubs had been formerly established, mostly in Monmouthshire and East Glamorgan, from Abergavenny (1877), Blaenavon (1877) and Ebbw Vale (1879) to Merthyr (1876), Mountain Ash (1875), and Penygraig (1877), as well as in Brecon (1874), Felinfoel (1876), Carmarthen (1875) and Cardigan (1876); in the next decade they were joined by another thirty, from Newbridge (1888) in the east, to Bridgend (1878) and Maesteg (1882) in mid-Glamorgan, and Gowerton (1884) and Neyland (1886) in the west. The 1890s saw a whole clutch of valley clubs emerging, like Tonna and Ystalyfera in 1890, Ferndale and Llwynypia in 1891, Gilfach Goch in 1894, Pontyberem in 1895, Glais in 1896, Trebanos and Tumble in 1897, Talywain, Ynysybwl and Brynamman in 1898, Abercynon in 1899, as much a narrative of the industrial development of South Wales as of the irresistible growth of its rugby. By the end of the century at least seventy, perhaps a half, of the member clubs of the Welsh Rugby Union in its centenary year, had been formed.

Yet this serves only as the roughest indication of the amount of rugby being played, for within the interstices of the network of formal clubs that criss-crossed South Wales were scores of informal sides: countless townships had their school, street and works teams, nearly every village its scratch selections. In the 1880s Cardiff was the home of Roath Star, Cathays Wanderers, St. Margaret's Collegiate, Ely, and Bute Dock Rangers, soon to be joined, or replaced by, Cardiff United, Cathays Star, Cardiff Rangers, Adamsdown Rovers, Canton Rovers, Eldon Rangers, Llandaff Juniors, Talbot Stars, Clare Rovers, and Rennie Stars. Swansea sides, around 1881, could boast rather more exotic designations: Melbourne, Trinity Rose, Nil Desperandum, Goat Street, as well as its East Side Rovers, Brynymor, Victoria and Alexandra Club, and Danygraig Rovers. By the middle of the 1880s a tropical abundance of local sides had sprouted in the rugby hot-house of Llanelli: Gower Road, Seasiders, Morfa Rangers, Prospect Place Rovers, Wern Foundry, Copper Mills Rangers, New Dock Strollers, Vauxhall Juniors, Moonlight Rovers,

Gilbert Place Rangers. But for sheer proliferation, the blooms of the valleys took some beating. Merthyr in the 1890s had its Thursdays, Stars, Excelsiors, Cyfarthfa Juniors, Georgetown Rovers, Dowlais Harlequins, Dowlais Hibernians, Dowlais proper, Gellifaelog Stars, Penydarren Excelsiors, Penydarren Rifles, Troedyrhiw Searchlights, Merthyr and District Police, and Merthyr White Stars. In Pontypool and district there flourished the Ironsides, United Friends, Tranch Rovers, Garn and Varteg Pride, Cwmffrwdoer Rovers, Panteg Harlequins, Cwmbran Black Watch, Pontymoil Wanderers, Pontnewynydd Lilies of the Valley, Talywain Red Stars, Trosnant White Stars, Varteg Dark Blues, Panteg Artillery, Cwmbran Harriers, Cwmffrwdoer United, Abersychan Albion, to name but a few. While some sides adopted names that hinted at hidden virtuosity, like Rhymney's Salmon Tin Dribblers and Pig's Bladder Barbarians, others opted for intimdating names that hinted at ill-concealed violence, like Carmarthen's Diamond Skull Crackers, Dervishes, Shin Slashers, and Rough and Tumble Boys. Nick-names were bestowed with gusto and proved ineradicable. Glais were 'the Bluebirds', Tumble 'the Magpies', Kenfig Hill 'the Mules', Penclawdd 'the Donkeys', all-black Neath 'the Mourners', Mountain Ash 'the Old Firm'; one exception was Cardiff, early on, but eradicably, known as 'the Pirates'.

Rivalries took imaginative forms. A defeat in a derby match would be announced in the local papers framed in black edging, to resemble an obituary notice. Supporters took mourning cards to distribute among rival factions, sympathizing with them on their defeat, a practice imitated beyond the confines of South Wales, as dejected Newportonians found on an unsuccessful visit to Kingsholm in the early 1890s. They were handed obituary notices by the exultant rivals bearing the following legend:

In loving memory
of the Newport team
who fell asleep on the
Gloucester Football ground

Nov. 28, 1891

'Not dead but sleepeth'

This practice remained highly popular in the Welsh-speaking areas of the western coalfield, like the Amman, Dulais and Gwendraeth valleys, up to the First World War, and local poets like Amanwy, brother of James Griffiths, were often sought after, and always ready, to put their intricate muse at the service of the community.

Rivalries were not always so good-humoured. Amiability could be at a discount when ritual derbies provoked fighting among players, among spectators, and between both: the referee, too, suffered frequent abuse and assault from enraged followers who symbolically regarded him as some sort of scapegoat for the rent-collector or whipper-in.

In December 1883 Llanelli received advance warning of the dire results that would follow upon beating Neath in their forthcoming clash. The committee discussed at length whether to fulfil the fixture, went to Neath, and won. The prophecy was fulfilled. At the end of the game, the Llanelli players, reportedly, 'were faced by an infuriated mob. Surrounded by some scores of youths and men, not boys, they were hustled and pushed, hooted and pelted with clods, mud and even stones,' and had to fight their way to their hotel. When Llanelli visited St. Helen's in January 1886, Swansea's 'well-dressed rowdies' were apparently there in full force, and 'their gross and ill-usage of the Llanellyites', according to the *Guardian*, 'was in the highest degree unwarrantable . . . The referee, Mr Norman of Neath, had a decidedly strong taste of Swansea courtesy . . . Contumely was heaped upon his head, and personal violence offered him, . . . the crowd's behaviour was perfectly disgraceful'. Clearly, the litany of outraged sensibility was already familiar, for when Carmarthen had played Llandovery College in 1881, then, too, 'the conduct of the mob was disgraceful'. When Carmarthen went to Neath in November 1885, 'the team was greeted by hissing and groaning and some players were unlucky recipients of the compliments of the crowd in the shape of sods and other missiles'.

Sometimes violence escalated into wanton destruction. The derby matches between Llangennech, Bynea, Burry Port and further afield, Tenby, were notorious for being hardly kid-glove affairs. After a game at Tenby in the 1890s, Llangennech's players and supporters were hounded and fought all the way to the station and into the carriages, some of which were severely wrecked. When Llangennech, twenty-eight years later, applied to the G.W.R. for travelling facilities to Pembroke, they were refused, because the previous excursion had been the costliest on record.

Rugby in the South Wales of the late nineteenth century was as coarse and violent as the raw frontier society which nurtured it, but its growth cannot be dissociated from wider movements in Wales and Britain as a whole. Britain, having pioneered the industrial revolution, became in the third quarter of the nineteenth century the first to introduce a pattern of sport for an urban population. Sporting bodies were organized by the middle class whose preserve, initially, they were: the first Open Golf Championship was held in 1860, the Football Association was founded in 1863. The Amateur Athletic Club was established in 1866 to become the Amateur Athletic Association in 1880. By 1870 all but four English counties had formed cricket clubs and two English touring sides had visited Australia. In 1871 the F.A. launched its Challenge Cup competition; in 1873 the Scottish F.A. was formed; in 1877 the Welsh F.A., founded the year before, launched its own cup competition.

In rugby, the first ever county match was played between Lancashire and Yorkshire in 1870 and the Rugby Football Union established in 1871. The first Varsity match was played in 1872, the Scottish Football Union formed in 1873, the Yorkshire County Football Club in 1874. The following year the Irish Football Union came into existence, and the Yorkshire Challenge Cup inaugurated in 1876. It was of a piece with these developments that the South Wales Football Club was formed in 1875, that it should launch the South Wales Challenge Cup competition in 1877, that it became the South Wales Football Union in 1878, and that the process culminated in the formation of the Welsh Rugby Football Union in 1881.

The rise of organized games in Britain amounted to nothing less than a sporting revolution, but the popularity and spread of these games among the mass of the population depended on a number of preconditions. Increasing free time, thanks to the shortening of working hours by successive measures since the 1847 Factory Act, and the campaign for a five and a half day working week, fought and won between 1850 and 1870; mass literacy with the provision of compulsory state education from 1870; greater popular consumer power with the upturn of the business cycle between 1850 and 1880; the development of national and municipal transport services — all these factors contributed to the rise of organized spectator sports. But what were in conception middle-class games soon attracted wider audiences, for the last quarter of the nineteenth century were the years in which the working class forged its collective identity, to assert itself in politics, in industry, and in sport, particularly a mass participation sport that supplied the social and cultural needs displaced by industrialization. Sport provided pleasure where work did not, and the more strenuous the physical labour the more strenuous the physical release it demanded. Organized sport provided both, and its whole ethos of rules and controlled competitiveness was consonant with the needs and interests of industrial society which depended on those same qualities of order and discipline. This is not to say that sports were the unwitting tool of a

14

prevailing economic order, but merely that both the sport and the society were the products of similar circumstances.

Nowhere was this more true than in South Wales, where the arrival of rugby coincided with the greatest industrial explosion Wales had seen. Between 1880 and 1900 some 200,000 people moved into Glamorgan alone. In the decade which saw the foundation of the W.R.U., the Welsh coalfield was expanding at a far greater rate than any other in the kingdom. The ports of Newport, Cardiff and Swansea grew and prospered as they exported the unprecedented amounts of coal being dug in the industrial valleys to the north. South Wales in the late nineteenth century was a society for which the sands were running *in;* its relationship to the rest of Wales gave the country the appearance of a gigantic egg-timer. It was a nervy society, its nerves one jump ahead of its architecture, but it was the nervousness that is the subtle complement to confidence, for the last third of the nineteenth century also saw the emergence of a new awareness of Welsh nationality. Wales came to be regarded as a distinct entity. A newly created regiment, the South Wales Borderers, fought in the Zulu Wars of 1879; for the first time in history the Imperial Parliament introduced separate legislation for Wales, even if it was to prohibit Sunday drinking, with the Welsh Sunday Closing Act of 1881; the Welsh educational system was given unique attention. The five decades following the election year of 1868, when Henry Richard's spectacular Liberal victory at industrial Merthyr Tydfil symbolized the breaking of the age-old domination of landed families over the political and social life of the countryside too, saw the emergence of modern Wales; and the institutions expressive of that modernity, of Welsh nationality, of the determined resourcefulness of the new leaders of Welsh society, were created and conceived in the 1870s and 1880s. It was in 1872 that the first University College of Wales was founded at Aberystwyth; Cardiff opened in 1883 and Bangor in 1884, to enable the new federal University of Wales to be set up in 1893. The idea of a national library and national museum was first mooted in the 1870s. In 1880 the National Eisteddfod Society was formed to coordinate the affairs of that cultural gypsy, give it a central organizing body and determine the form which it would retain for at least the next hundred years. In 1881 it was decided 'to consider the question of forming a Welsh Rugby Union,' to perform a similar function for rugby football.

The founding of the Welsh Rugby Union was part-and-parcel of the movement for national institutions. It would have a distinct role to play in the new chapter that was opening in the history of Wales, a Wales characterized not only by self-awareness, but a wider awareness: the transport revolution brought Wales closer to England as well as bringing together parts of Wales itself. The definition of the merits of rugby, as perceived by the chairman of the Llanelli club on the occasion of a wedding presentation to one of the players in 1884, was received with applause by his audience. Rugby, he said, was 'of material aid in the formation of character and it had a great deal to do with the development of those characteristics which have made England a nation — determination and perseverance'. The Welsh ideal was to be recognized as a consequential part of the British political and social structure and for a specific Welsh identity to take its place in the Empire. In 1881 J. Allen Williams of the Llanelli *Guardian* urged his club to greater efforts: '"Onward" be your motto', he cried, 'Play as Britons'. Rugby, after all, was 'the grand old British game'. Or so it was thought.

FRIENDS, ROMANS, COUNTRYMEN

EVERY society seeks to establish links with its past, just as the first act of the parvenu is to invent himself a pedigree. There was no concealing the disconcerting newness of the South Wales society of the last quarter of the nineteenth century, but adjustment to it might be eased by showing that apparent novelty did not necessarily involve a radical break with the past. Rugby football was unknown in Wales before 1870, yet in the 1880s it was often hailed by many of its most active propagandists as 'the grand old game'. In the context of the dramatically expanding industrial South Wales of the last quarter of the nineteenth century, the pretence of maintaining a continuity between past and present may have been psychologically a comfort; historically, it was a distortion.

Bloodhounds roaming the centuries on the scent of the pedigree of Welsh rugby ever since have detected a number of exciting aromas, but they have managed to establish little more than that ball games have been a feature of the Welsh countryside for well over a millenium. We would be ill-advised to attach much credence to the dubious claims of Iolo Morganwg, eighteenth-century Glamorgan's forger extraordinaire, when he regales us with a description of a 'traditional' eisteddfodic olympiad that occurred regularly at Llangyfelach, near Swansea, where football was sandwiched between animal-baiting and old-women's grinning matches. Nor can the twelfth-century testimony of that peripatetic gossip, Gerald of Wales, be regarded as exactly conclusive. He has much to say about many things, but aside from the tantalising observation that the men of Gwent did not compete at archery because they were concerned not to shoot great distances but to kill people, nothing about sport. Even Romano-Celtic Britain has been ransacked for evidence of football, with laurels being jointly awarded to the Welsh chronicler Nennius's account of a fifth-century ball game between youths of noble birth, and, inevitably, to *harpastum*, the recreation of Roman legionaries as they did violence to an inflated balloon in the Caerleon region, when they were not doing violence to the Silurian tribesmen of the vicinity. The last word on the fatuity of these forays into the past was said as long ago as 1894 by the English International Charles Marriott. 'Football is undoubtedly an ancient pastime', he wrote. 'Among the carvings on the walls of Egyptian buildings there frequently occurs the representation of one gentleman passing to another in approved fashion what may be a football of the period or a plum pudding. If the former, it proves without a doubt that the early inhabitants of the Nile Valley played under the handling code'.

But when in late-nineteenth century Wales, rugby was hailed as 'the grand old game', the game in mind was one that had first been noticed in West Wales under the Tudors, and therefore redolent of Welsh and British associations. This was *cnappan*, brought to life for us even today by George Owen's racy account of it in his *Description of Pembrokeshire* (1603). The cnappan was a ball made of wood boiled in tallow to make it slippery and was the name of the game played between neighbouring parishes on feast days like Shrove Tuesday by anything up to 2,000 men on foot and on horseback. There was no goal as such; the game was won when the ball had been carried so far away that it was beyond return.

These dissimilarities to the rugby game, however, were more than compensated for by some striking similarities. It engendered a vigorous community involvement and fierce inter-village rivalry; it was a game of throwing, tackling and kicking, played in the best spirit of amateurism — 'they contend not' wrote Owen, 'for any wager or valuable thing but strive to the death for glory and fame which they esteem dearer than any worldly wealth'. There were even some technical prefigurations, like the maul which developed when one of the players 'happening on the cnappan clappeth the same against his belly, holding it fast with his hands. Another of his company clappeth him about the middle, they face to face. So then is the cnappan in fastness between both their bodies. And then cometh more of the same side and layeth grips on them, round about them both, so that you shall see a hundred or six score clustered together as bees when they swarm are knit together, the ball being in the midst of them, which the other party seek to open or undo by heaving and pulling'. Nor was traditional Welsh guile at a discount. Twentieth-century tricksters at the base of the scrum — Dickie Owen, Brace, Rowlands, let us say — were the lineal descendants of George Owen's 'young gallant, who not being able to get hold of the *cnappan* started off at a gallop as if he had the ball in his possession. A detachment of horsemen readily taken in followed him in hot pursuit and in time he was overtaken, but alas!the heady youth had not counted on the result . . . ' It required the legal refinements of the late nineteenth century to pronounce those horsemen offside for having been outwitted by the stratagem of the heady youth.

Of course, all ball games will inevitably share some characteristics, and to recognize *cnappan's* kinship with Cornish hurling and Irish *cad*, French *soule* and plain English *foot-balle,* is not to invalidate the claims made on its behalf: it remains, to a limited extent, Welsh rugby's most plausible forebear. This is not because of its suggestive anticipations of later developments, but because local variants of it were from the seventeenth century sufficiently resilient to survive the successive assaults Puritans, Methodists and enclosing farmers made upon it until well into the nineteenth century. Allowing that the ball was now a bullock's bladder encased in leather, adaptations of *cnappan* were practised as far north as Dolgellau and as far east as Glamorgan. Amazingly, as late as 1884 the town of Neath became a Shrove Tuesday Pamplona as 'all shutters are put up and the principal thoroughfare is given over to the players'.

But if the traditional sports of rural Wales would not meekly yield to the new imperatives of industrial society, what Neath heard in 1884 was the last defiant shout of the old order. Three years previously in the Castle Hotel of the same town the Welsh Rugby Union had been formed to direct the affairs and regulate the expansion of a game that was sweeping South Wales. Sentimental, if calculated, evocations of 'the grand old game' notwithstanding, this was a whole new ball game, tailor-made for and increasingly tailored by the demands of a new society. This game, in intention at least, was shorn of the violent disorderliness of its rural forebears. Thanks to an accumulating complexity of standardizing rules and regulations, it was no longer diffuse and informally organized, its unwritten conventions governed only by local custom without limit of territory, time or participants. This game was subject to formal and elaborately written laws, limited in duration and played in a confined area by a fixed small number of players. In Wales this game was rugby football, and we would do better to seek its origins not in the ritualistic pastimes of the countryside but in the loutish violence of the great public schools of England.

In the first half of the nineteenth century, when the traditional bastions of political power and wealth were being challenged by the profound social changes which were already transforming England into the first industrial nation, the public schools were subjected to agonized re-appraisal. Socially and educationally, they were severely wanting. Indiscipline and disorder, the hallmarks of rural sports which according to contemporary commentators were in retreat in the face of agricultural modernization and urban growth, were to be found alive and kicking in those historic pedagogic institutions which had long since cheerfully disowned their 'public' obligation to provide for poor scholars, and were now narrow enclaves of private privilege. Recreation within their cloistered walls too frequently found expression in organized riot and rebellion.

For a cluster of reasons — anti-aristocratic hostility, genuine concern for moral reform, and the rising demands and expectations of the proliferating commercial and professional bourgeoisie — progressive headmasters like Arnold of Rugby (1828-42) and Thring of Uppingham (1853-87) perceived the advantages that could accrue from harnessing the traditional lawlessness of public school sports. The channelling of athletic energies into organized games would, through instilling self-control, respect for legality and authority, unselfishness and manliness, reinforce the discipline they were seeking to impose on the school community as a whole. Physical recreation was incorporated into the curriculum as an integral component of an enlightened education. Games, especially football, cricket and athletics, became moral correctives, instruments of character formation and social control. Such was the success of Arnold in particular at Rugby School, so insistent the middle-class demand for a greater provision for the proper education of their sons, that old schools took on a new lease of life: new schools from the 1840s — Cheltenham, Marlborough, Wellington, Tonbridge, Llandovery — multiplied; and old endowed grammar schools — Uppingham, Monmouth, Brecon, Cowbridge — transformed themselves into boarding establishments and were remodelled according to Arnoldian civilizing precepts in conscious emulation of the more prestigious public schools.

In the late 1830s Arthur Pell and other Rugbeians at King's College, Cambridge, introduced the game they had learned at school into the university. But other schools, conditioned by different physical environments and traditions longer than Rugby's, played according to different conventions. When Pell and his associates sought to play a group of Old Etonians in 1840, 'the Eton men howled at the Rugby men for handling the ball'. For meaningful fixtures to take place, a common set of rules needed to be agreed upon, and to this end successive attempts were made at the university between 1842 and 1863 to arrive at a consensus. The Cambridge rules of 1863 were adopted as a working basis by the Football Association, which was established later that year, under the aegis of a group of ex-public schoolboys spearheaded by Etonians and Harrovians. The Rugby School faction, whose banner was upheld principally by the Blackheath club, withdrew to form the nucleus of the Rugby Football Union which was established nine years later in a restaurant off Trafalgar Square. But the point at issue between them in 1863 had been 'hacking' — Rugby men regarded the deliberate kicking of an opponent on the shin as character-building, though the R.F.U. would, ironically, abolish it at its formation in 1871 — rather than handling and passing, which were not legitimate till the 1870s.

Whether the evolution of the rugby game owes anything at all to William Webb Ellis must be doubtful. The legend that it was Ellis 'who with a fine disregard for the rules of football as played in his time first took the ball in his arms and ran with it' in 1823, was first circulated in 1880 by a man who had left the school in 1820. Nor is it without significance that the plaque commemorating the alleged exploit was laid in 1895, the year when the rupture between the amateur ex-public schoolboys of the south of England and the non-public school manufacturers who were professionalizing the game in the industrial north became absolute. In the face of repeated attempts to outlaw it by law-makers at the universities, Rugby School's stubborn adherence to 'running in' with the ball instead of kicking it back to the opposition, owed less to the insubordination of a day-boy than the school's search for some identifying characteristic. For whatever Ellis did or did not do in 1823, being a day-boy he was of inferior social status and more likely to have been punished for his contravention of the rules than praised as an inspired innovator; in any case, 'running in' was not legalized even at Rugby till 1841. Far more crucial in the context of the times is that Rugby School was a relatively recent foundation and anxious to assert itself at the public school high table. Because of its middle-class sympathies it lacked the impeccable aristocratic credentials of Eton and Winchester, who could incorporate the old kicking game into their reformed football without any qualms. Middle-class Rugby could not afford the risk of being contaminated by the lower orders, and carrying the ball became its distinctive feature.

The division of football into two codes was a product, then, of the third quarter of the century. By 1850 the acceptance of civilized and civilizing sports by the great educational institutions of England had bestowed respectability on team games like football. They were a form of recreation socially permissible for young gentlemen, including young Welsh gentlemen. The new model sports reached Wales in 1850 with the arrival in Lampeter of the Revd Rowland Williams as the Vice-Principal and Professor of Hebrew at St. David's College, established in 1828. For the previous fourteen years, Rowland Williams had been at Cambridge, first as an undergraduate, then as a Fellow and tutor at King's, when Arthur Pell had arrived at the college and introduced the Rugby School game to the university. It was now to be introduced to Lampeter. The new Vice-Principal made an immediate impact on the sporting life of the College. From 1850 a college rule stipulated that 'whatever time a student may require for relaxation should be spent in healthful exercise rather than in clownish lounging about shops or market places'. Forthwith, athletics, cricket, croquet, fives and football were introduced to St. David's College.

Lampeter could only claim to have the first established rugby side in Wales after they had found other sides to play against. It became possible to find opponents within reasonable reach as the skeleton of the rail network which had been laid in the 1840s was filled out during the next two decades. The spinal chord was the line that snaked in from Gloucester to Newport initially, then on to Fishguard, ultimately, the familiar route of the old G.W.R., which is what it became in 1863. It had been linked up with tracks already connecting Hereford, Abergavenny, Brecon and Merthyr by the late 1850s, and the valley lines joined it and each other in the 1860s. The Llanelli railway reached Llandeilo in 1857 and Llandovery the following year; the mid-Wales line connecting Llandovery and Swansea had been completed in 1868; Lampeter had access to the whole of South Wales now the line from Carmarthen had reached it in 1866; the completion of the track from Swansea via Neath to Brecon in 1875 added final confirmation that the midwives at the birth and immediate growth of rugby football in Wales would be arriving on the scene together.

Naturally Lampeter College's first fixtures were with old schools now cautiously accessible. From the late 1860s there were games of an undefined football nature with the grammar schools at Llandeilo, Cardigan, Ystrad Meurig (a combination of Maynooth Seminary and a farmhouse, in Rowland Williams's withering view) and, particularly, Llandovery College. Llandovery had been founded in 1847, its object being, according to the Trust Deed, 'the dissemination of useful and practical knowledge in Wales, and raising both morally and intellectually the character of its people'. Organized games were to play a central role in this ambitious programme of national moral refurbishment. Football of a sort had been played at the College since the 1850s and its rivalry with neighbouring Lampeter had since the mid-sixties taken the form of a hybrid twelve-a-side game played at a point midway between both places. The adoption of rugby rules occurred in the early 1870s, on the initiative of the Revd W. P. Whittington, a master who had learned the Rugby School game at Fettes in Edinburgh. The game developed apace at Llandovery during the wardenship from 1875 of the Revd A. G. Edwards, who frankly conceived of its becoming 'a great English public school'. To this end, he leased a large field, laid it out for football and cricket, and erected the school pavilion. Rugby received a further impetus when Charles Prydderch Lewis returned from Jesus College, Oxford, to join the staff of his old school in 1877. Lewis, a triple athletics Blue, captained the South Wales side many times between 1878 and 1886, won five international caps between 1882 and 1884, and frequently turned out for the school XV.

In 1879 Llandovery played its first match against Christ College, Brecon, a school which had seen rapid expansion from the 1850s when the endowments of the Cathedral had been diverted to the College. Since the 1860s the College was already playing pick-up teams with the town, but this, according to the recollections of a participant, was 'a somewhat feeble game, being a kind of soccer with very stringent rules with regard to hands'. The switch to rugby was made in 1875, but it is likely that town-gown encounters lost none of their needle — 'the town can seldom or never indulge in a game with their classic young friends over the water without some unpleasantness arising', complained an aggrieved townie — and it did mean that fixtures could be regularized, as they were from 1879, with rivals from further afield, like Monmouth School. Monmouth had been re-founded from its early seventeenth-century origins as an independent boarding school in the early nineteenth. It had 'played the dribbling game in a somewhat casual way' with neighbouring towns like Hereford, Ross, Usk and Monmouth itself, but from 1873 adopted rugby football, a decision for which Newportonians would be immensely grateful. At Cowbridge Grammar School, rugby was introduced during the headship of the Revd J. C. F. Morson (1870-1875), a graduate of Jesus College, Oxford; the newly formed Cardiff club's first ever away fixture was against Cowbridge Grammar School, in 1876. A. F. Laloe left Cowbridge in 1874 to become headmaster of Queen Elizabeth Grammar

School, Carmarthen, where he introduced rugby; the following year a club was founded in the town.

This initial thrust of rugby football into Wales was sustained by less prestigious, but within their communities no less influential, educational establishments. Examples abound. The Abergavenny club owed its inception in 1875 to the presence there of Faithfull's Army and Navy training college, and Abergavenny played its first match under rugby rules against Monmouth School in 1877. Wales's first two captains, James Bevan and Tom Clapp, were Abergavenny men. The Chepstow club was formed in 1878 by former pupils of Chepstow Grammar School and its innovative headmaster George Dewdney. At Llandaff, St. Michael's Theological College received graduates from Oxford and Cambridge and had ties with Llandovery and Lampeter; under its auspices the Llandaff club was founded in 1876, with Cambridge blue as its predominant colour. Farther to the west, the same year, Oxford blue was the colour adopted by the Cardigan club, founded by old boys of the local collegiate school, and as if further to confirm that civilization had arrived in lower Ceredigion, one of the club rules read: 'Players will please use boots with as few nails as possible, and no iron plates must be worn on the toes of the boots'.

While old boys comprised the bulk of the founder players of Welsh clubs, their ranks were stiffened by the ever-increasing self-confident class of solicitors, doctors, clerks, and engineers, the service lubricators of an expanding South Wales, who were much taken by the codes of conduct of the public schools and appreciative of the social relevance of the values they were seeking to transmit through sport. The Neath club was founded in 1871 by a consortium of ten: a doctor, a surveyor, a mining engineer and a veritable plague of solicitors, in the chambers of one of whose number, Lewis Kempthorne, an old Llandoverian, the club's first meetings were held. The doctor — T. P. Whittington — was its first captain, educated at Merchiston Castle, Edinburgh, and capped for Scotland in 1873; his brother taught at Llandovery. That Neath's earliest players were not short of a penny can be gauged from the fact that when E. V. Pegge — a Briton Ferry doctor and International — missed the departure of the team for their tour of Devon in 1887, he chartered a special train to catch up with them.

The Cardiff club grew out of an amalgamation in 1876 of the Glamorgan, Tredegarville, and Wanderers Football Clubs. The Tredegarville side was mostly made up of old boys of Monkton House School which had adopted rugby rules in 1872, while well to the fore in the

Glamorgan Club was S. Campbell Cory, a solicitor with a name redolent of the dynastic wealth which was thrusting Cardiff to the forefront of the British economy. Cory's principal lieutenants in setting the Cardiff club on its feet were the headmaster of a local private school, and another teacher, James Bush, father of the later, greater, and irrepressible Percy. The unmistakable blue and black were adopted as they were the colours worn in 1877 by T. W. Rees, a Cambridge student whose presence was highly valued.

Cardiff played its first game in 1875 against Newport, a club that was a year older, having been founded at the instigation of the recently arrived brewing family of Phillips. (The Hancock family of brewers would arrive, fatefully, in Cardiff within the decade.) The intention at the foundation meeting at the Dock Street Brewery was to get an Association side going, but being unable to find opponents locally, the members were persuaded, irreversibly, to embrace the rugby game, by H. W. Peill, a master at Monmouth School. The Newport club was launched by a powerful alliance of forces: the financial initiative of the Phillipses, the playing expertise of a phalanx of Old Monmouthians — Charles Newman, Tom Clapp, George and Theo Harding, Baker-Jones, George Rosser, H. M. Purdon — and the attentiveness to legal and constitutional niceties of its solicitor playing-members Horace Lyne, Babbington-Jones (ex-Oxford), and A. V. Julius of Abergavenny.

By the mid-1870s, therefore, the rugby game was already moving out from the progressively minded schools of Wales to the wider community, the nakedness of its underpinning ideology of social control concealed by the fig leaves of moral propriety. The cult of national recreation was ready for common consumption; the so-called 'condition of England question' had been debated for a generation, just as the concern over bodily health as a Christian obligation had, since the 1840s at least, engaged the minds of moralists and social observers alike. It was by now an axiom of faith that in the provision of facilities for outdoor recreation lay the key to social responsibility and rectitude, and with foreign powers making ominous noises from across the Channel, the admixture of sport with piety and patriotism made for a powerful chemistry. The provision of sports facilities in the way of municipal parks, football and cricket fields and running tracks complemented, on the one hand, improving — if less energizing —amenities like museums, libraries and galleries, and also provided an alternative outdoor counter-culture to the physically and morally damaging attractions of the beer-hall and gin-palace.

It was a logical progression therefore that football clubs often grew out of cricket clubs. The Cardiff Cricket Club (established in 1842) had been playing since 1845 on an area behind the Cardiff Arms Coaching Inn known as the Cardiff Arms Park. In 1876 the Cardiff Football Club joined forces with the cricket club because there was an overlap of personnel, they played on the same ground, and it was a convenient way of continuing an association during winter. Similarly, the Swansea Football Club grew out of the local cricket club; it was cricketers who converted some sandhills within a drop-kick of Swansea Bay into an eight acre enclosure that became the circus maximus of the west, St. Helen's.

It was natural too, because of its sound credentials as an education in commitment, co-operation, and obedience to authority, that football should early on be patronized by the captains of industry. When in 1879 the *Chepstow Weekly Advertiser* made an overt appeal to the local gentry to patronize the newly formed local football club ('as there is considerable expense in connection with the game, it would be very advantageous if gentlemen of the town and neighbourhood would become honorary members and aid the funds so as to sustain an efficient team to keep up the prowess of Chepstow in this, the now recognized national outdoor game') the industrial areas could already testify to the sort of beneficent sponsorship the newspaper had in mind.

The Neville family had moved from Worcestershire in the early years of the century to become copper and coal entrepreneurs in the Llanelli area. The Felinfoel club owed its inception in 1876 to the generosity of the Nevilles of Felinfoel House, and the Johns of Felinfoel brewery. William Neville had gone to Oxford; on coming down he inherited the directorship of the Wern Engineering Works and founded the Llanelli club in 1875. Another prominent founder member was a young industrialist who had been at Rugby School; this was John D. Rogers, heir to the South Wales & Cwmbwrla Tinplate Works. Llanelli's first captain, Buchanan, was another old Rugbeian. He was also a Scot, and the impact of newly immigrant Scotsmen in establishing rugby in South Wales can hardly be exaggerated: Llanelli was steered through its early years by a clutch of Caledonians, Buchanan, R. V. Innes, John Brown and Gavin Henry, as was Neath by its Whittingtons and Gordons, while Duncan McGregor, a draper mad with rugby, was a pioneer of the Pontypridd club in 1876. In the late seventies key industrial workers from Llanelli migrated to the tinplate township of Blaina in the Monmouthshire valleys. They were especially welcome for they brought a knowledge of rugby with them, and in 1875 players from local sides had amalgamated to form a club which played on a ground made available to them by the Lancaster Company whose manager, Mr. Sidney Lancaster, was chief patron and founder.

Traditionally the most popular game in Glamorgan had been bando; the historian of the culture of the Vale, Griffith John Williams, has claimed that 'it held the place occupied in the twentieth century by rugby football'. We are indebted to a native of the Vale, the great Methodist minister Edward Matthews of Ewenni (1813-92) for our knowledge of the game and how sides of twenty or thirty players, selected, naturally, by committee, mostly in the team colours of its finest exponents and fiercest rivals Pyle, Kenfig and Margam, squared off against each other on the sands at Margam, attracting great crowds from all over. The fate of bando in that district was sealed in the 1870s with the building of the Mansel tinplate works. Its proprietors, Col. D. R. David and Sir Sidney H. Byass, encouraged the formation of the Aberavon club in 1876 and the conditions for spectacular expansion had been created. History repeated itself in the 1950s when the expansion of the local steel industry saw Aberavon R.F.C. enter the most successful period in its existence.

Yet another industrialist was William Gilbertson, who had come to Pontardawe in 1860, the year the first passenger train came up the valley from Swansea, and built a tinplate works which his Cowbridge and Brecon-educated son, Arthur, inherited in 1882. The Gilbertsons, as they continued to be till after the Second World War, proved to be notable benefactors of the community, inaugurating music festivals, establishing reading-rooms and providing a recreation ground and cinder track on which Pontardawe's sportsmen could play rugby and run. Here was a classic example of the middle class seeking to shape working class choice by providing an alternative world of reformed recreations to protect the worker from the degeneration of his own culture; of recreational athletic activities being equated with moral edification. That so many of the early Welsh sides have names like Tredegar Harriers, Cross Keys Harriers, Burry Port Harriers and that Llanelli were in the 1880s referred to as the Scarlet Runners, betrays their origins. Several of the first generation of rugby stars were track champions. The greatest of them was undoubtedly the immortal Arthur Gould; the rugby career of the Revd Edward Peake of Chepstow, a member of the first Welsh XV, was cut short by a hurdling accident at Oxford; and Welsh rugby's first recorded fatality was suffered, 'in consequence of his collar being broken and the lung penetrated' by Neath's Richard Gordon, the quarter-mile champion of Wales, in a game with Bridgend in March 1880.

The interest that captains of commerce and industry in Wales took in the encouragement of the new model athletic sports was not, therefore, mere altruism. Their readiness to provide sporting facilities was based on their perception of the sound credentials of those sports; physical fitness for the individual, an education in self-discipline and team-work, even readiness for the armed service. At the annual dinner of the Llanelli club in March 1887, one of its principal benefactors spoke of 'the preference of young ladies for men of buoyant and vigorous physical development to sleepy decrepit young men', and added, 'that the dash and courage which they had wielded in the game was one and the same as shown by our army in the past, and that if necessary they would be ready to wield the bayonet as they had the ball'. The speaker was newspaper proprietor J. Allen Williams, who saw to the club's printing and publicity, an involvement reminiscent of gentry patronage of popular pastimes in the pre-industrial countryside: football like cricket, carried with it associations of an idealized past, of social harmony and the fraternity of all classes in sport.

The society that was taking shape in South Wales in the last thirty years of the nineteenth century was one in need of sentimental myths, for those years witnessed the transformation of Wales. Within a few convulsive decades the steam that had built up around earlier, but isolated pressure points in the iron and coal industry around Merthyr Tydfil and settlements at the heads of the Monmouthshire valleys, or around sea-ports like Swansea, was diffused throughout South Wales. The release valve was the development of the sale coal collieries in the Aberdare valley for naval purposes, and then, by the 1860s, the mining of hitherto inaccessible coal seams, especially in the central steam-coal areas. The point is quickest made by visualizing the statistical graph for South Wales in this period — in 1840 four and a half million tons of coal were mined in the area, by 1913, the peak year, almost fifty-seven million tons were produced; between 1890 and 1910 the South Wales export trade in coal amounted to one-third of total world exports; there were two self-made millionaires in South Wales in the first half of the nineteenth century and five in the second; for every decade after 1851 the population of Glamorgan and Monmouthshire had a net gain through migration.

Insofar as the history of Welsh rugby is concerned, this is the most vital statistic. The coal had to be cut and transported on railway lines that had to be built to reach docks that had to be constructed so that men could unload it onto ships. This meant the supply of a growing labour force who, in turn, required to be housed, fed, instructed, and entertained. Initially people flocked in from a depressed Welsh countryside to earn relatively high wages — they came from the north and from the west bringing their language and culture with them. For the most part they came to intermingle with an equally Welsh society which was becoming less and less a peasant world, more and more an urban, industrial whirlpool. The Welsh, unlike their Irish counterparts, had no need to emigrate overseas. Wales kept her own population in these years and still managed to suck in immigrants at a rate higher than any other country except the United States. Increasingly these migrants would come from further afield, especially the English border and West Country. They became Welsh, but it was a different Welsh world from any that had existed in the past. The language itself would become a victim of this sea-change. By 1911 the population of Wales had increased in forty years from one and a half million to two and a half million, and two-thirds, the entire total for 1871, were clustered together in the southern industrial belt.

As the Welsh economy took off, so also did Welsh rugby football. Within those populous industrial valleys, each cwm *culach na cham ceiliog,* ('more narrow than a cockerel's step') the rural games like *cnappan* which swept over vast tracts of countryside and lasted all day, perhaps several days, were now quite impracticable. There was neither the space, nor the time. Leisure, like life itself, had to be reconstructed according to the rhythms and demands of a new environment governed by whistle, clock and machine. Industrial society could degenerate into anarchy if it were not organized, and whether interpreted in the literal sense that it recreated energies for the next day's work, or the mythical sense of recreating associations with an idealized past, recreation, too, needed to be organized. Institutional arrangements were soon made for its occupation in the form of brass bands, choral societies, pigeon and greyhound racing, darts clubs and football clubs, and the enthusiasm generated by these activities revealed an affirmative quality which argues against seeing them as merely compensation for the frustrations of work.

The popular appetite for sport in Wales was not extinguished by deficiencies of diet, time or space, and the fact that football was practised by respectable people made it legitimate for the lower orders. With its empahasis on regulation and discipline, it was particularly congenial to a labour force whose lives were characterized by those same qualities. But it was not merely a knee-jerk response. While the new codes of play and conduct were the work of middle-class administrators who were able to secure for them almost immediate widespread recognition, innovations in play would come from working men themselves, determined to adapt the new games to the circumstances and needs of their own culture. The new game of rugby football would become an integral part of that culture; with its urgency, excitement and physical commitment it was peculiarly attuned to the rigours and privations of working-class life, itself so devoid of physical grace. It offered opportunities for an expression of group and community loyalties, for the achievement of personal recognition and the settling of grudges, for collective endeavour and common aspiration. But for it to be an effective agent for social cohesiveness, it required to be organized, to be established on a systematic footing, to be co-ordinated and controlled by a central governing body.

For eight years after 1863, when the Football Association was founded and the dribbling code tabulated into fourteen rules, forms of rugby continued to be played in a confused limbo of local variations. It was to check this accelerating process of fragmentation from sliding into total anarchy that the first of the national controlling bodies, the Rugby Football Union, was established in London in 1871, and the Rugby code clearly differentiated from the Association game in a legislative over-kill of fifty-nine rules. These did not become uniformly adopted overnight, even where they were fully understood, and they required continuous modification for the next twenty years before the game began to resemble its modern form. The need for systemization is clearly to be seen from accounts of a hybrid football game, neither dribbling fish nor handling fowl, played at Abergavenny in 1867. The visitors were a Newport team including in the persons of Joseph Gould, Charles Lyne and H. C. Lloyd, fathers of subsequently greater rugby sons of Newport and Wales. It appears that this fifteen-a-side mongrel game contained a good quota of hacking, yet players could not pick up the ball and run with it, nor pass from hand to hand, and while there was running and dodging, there was also dribbling. The evidence of town v. town games of the early 1870s confirms that the distinctive features of the rugby and association codes were not immediately clarified by the cumbersome commandments of 1871, though the abolition of hacking was rapidly welcomed by leading groups in society that viewed the practice as repugnantly uncivilized. Some old-boys regretted its disappearance, and well into the 1870s held a five-minute 'Hallelujah' at the end of a match for unrestrained hacking.

This, though, was an idiosyncrasy of public school men. At the beginning of the 1870s, it did seem that Association, with its fewer rules, was simpler and could be easily grasped by men who had not played at school. This might explain why some of the earliest Welsh rugby clubs, Swansea, Newport and Cardiff, were formed with the original intention of playing soccer. Neath and Llanelli had a more pronounced public school flavour, and Newport soon felt the impact of its ex-Monmouth school arrivals. The decision to play Association was early abandoned in favour of rugby partly because the leading schools in Wales were adopting a game becoming more familiar after the systemization of 1871, partly because of the simple fact of the proximity of South Wales to the West of England, where Herefordshire, Gloucestershire, Somerset and Devon were strongholds of the rugby game. For those progressively-minded Welsh clubs that wished to include English fixtures in their programme, the twin considerations of communications and travel costs dictated that those fixtures would be with the nearest England had to offer.

Thus, when in September 1875, in Brecon, the South Wales Football Club was formed, it was 'with the intention of playing matches with the principal clubs in the West of England and the neighbourhood. The rugby rules will be the code adopted'. The founding fathers were local men, Major T. Conway Lloyd as president, and H. W. Davies of the town club as secretary and treasurer. The match committee included Campbell Cory of Cardiff, Tom Whittington of Neath, and Swansea's captain, C. C. Chambers. Gentlemen who wished to be considered for selection were to send five shillings to the secretary, and six fixtures were arranged for 1875-6. These were not all fulfilled, but the first ever representative team in Welsh rugby history sauntered onto the Castle Green, Hereford, in black and white colours in December 1875, and beat Hereford by a try, scored by A. H. Richardson of Swansea, to nothing. For the next few seasons, the S.W.F.C. provided an opportunity for Welsh players so minded to combine against West Country opposition, with more than moderate success. Players with formidable club and international reputations ahead of them — Chambers, Richardson, F. F. Meager of Swansea, C. P. Lewis and T. A. Rees of Llandovery, C. H. Newman and W. Phillips of Newport — represented the S.W.F.C. in January 1876 against Clifton at Cardiff and in December 1876 beat Hereford at Hereford. The following month Hereford was again defeated at Brecon, and Clifton at Newport; Swindon and a West of England combination were played later that year, and in January 1878 a draw was registered with Clifton at Newport.

The conviction that the standard of Welsh football could only but benefit from outside contact was not confined to the South. Identical preconditions of geography and east-west communications determined that North Wales was drawn increasingly closer to soccer-playing Merseyside. Rugby in North Wales would be the limited preserve of a few schools: in the 1870s these were Ruabon, Ruthin, and Beaumaris. North and South moved apart from 1876. In January of that year a letter appeared in *The Field* magazine from a London Welshman, G. A. Clay-Thomas. His impression, from a distance of two hundred miles, was that 'football in Wales is not of common occurrence', and that it might be encouraged by raising a team of Anglo-Welshmen to play Scotland or Ireland, 'since an English twenty would be much too formidable a body to encounter, at least at the first onset'.

It was the advocates of the association code from North Wales who took up this idea, when an enterprising Ruabon solicitor named Llewellyn Kenrick convened a meeting at Wrexham to raise a team to play Scotland 'according to Association rules'. When it was announced that a Welsh eleven had been selected for such a fixture in March in Glasgow, a flurry of angry exchanges promptly enlivened the correspondence columns of the *Western Mail*. C. C. Chambers, captain of Swansea and a committee member of the S.W.F.C., claimed that this was the first South Walians had heard of the arrangement, and that neither the self-styled Football Association of Wales nor its team could pretend to be representative of Welsh football. Furthermore, he affirmed, 'I shall be happy to produce from these parts a team who shall hold their own against any team from North Wales either at the Association or Rugby Union games — the latter preferred'. H. W. Davies, secretary of the S.W.F.C., confirmed Chambers's point: the F.A.W. was a misnomer because it ignored the claims of players 'south of a line drawn from Cardigan through Llandovery to Brecon'.

Kenrick gave them a tart reply. If the S.W.F.C. had failed to notice his previous announcements, that was their affair, 'although Welsh gentlemen residing in different parts of England and Wales, including Dorset, Cheshire, Oxford and Cambridge Universities, Montgomeryshire, Cardiganshire, Merionethshire, etc., were aware that the match was arranged'. Lest the S.W.F.C. entertained pardonable suspicion that the fledgling Welsh F.A. was anxious to keep *South* Wales in the dark, Chambers and Davies were invited to attend the May meeting of the F.A.W. in Shrewsbury. They never did, and it was nearly thirty years before soccer began to make any headway against the massive domination of rugby football in South Wales.

That domination was due to accidents of time and place. Of time, because the second phase of the industrial revolution arrived in Wales later than it did in England, so that the handling and dribbling codes had already begun to reflect and project different social values; of place, because the proximity of the West Country enabled a two-way influence to operate. From the 1880s, many thousands of immigrants from the rugby strongholds of Gloucestershire, Somerset and Devon poured into a spectacularly industrializing South Wales. Hancock, of the four three-quarter system, was a Somerset man, and so were the Biggs brothers, and, soon, Boucher, Sweet-Escott, Brice, Vile; Harry Uzzell came from Gloucester, Dick Hellings from Tiverton; Harry Packer was another Devon man. Others who wore the scarlet jersey with distinction came from further afield: Tom Graham from Newcastle, Bert Winfield from Nottingham, 'Boxer' Harding from Lincolnshire. But it was from the West Country that Welsh rugby derived its greatest stimulus, and there was enough poetic justice to compensate for its historic irony in the tribute paid by 'Old Stager' of the *Western Mail* on the death in 1939 of the great Gwyn Nicholls, born in Westbury-on-Severn, Gloucestershire: that *'in everything except birth*, he was a true rugby son of Wales'.

APPOINTMENT IN NEATH

I N 1878 the South Wales Football Club was superseded by the South Wales Football Union, a new body called into existence by the ever-increasing expansion of rugby football in South Wales to regulate competition among the clubs and to select representative teams direct from club sides themselves. It was appropriate that the last game of the old S.W.F.C. should have been played at Newport, for Newport not only dominated the early years of the Challenge Cup competition inaugurated by the S.W.F.C. and taken over by its successor, but was the agent of change which saw the S.W.F.U. itself, in three years' time, succeeded by the Welsh Rugby Football Union. The years 1879-81 were crucial to that change, and Newport the hinge on which it turned.

Since 1877, the rugby section of the Newport Cricket, Athletic, Football and Tennis Club had been playing at Rodney Parade, its new ground which had been opened with sports events during which 'Mr J. Hooper, jun. and Master A. J. Gould were attired in motley and amused the crowd with their droll capers'. Considerably more would be heard of Master Gould's capers, on that ground and elsewhere, in later years. For the present, the Newport XV, which won the South Wales Cup in its two first years running, contained in its ranks young men whose cosmopolitan and restless outlook crystallized the bursting vitality of an expansive South Wales: A. J. Moggridge, a crack three-quarter, was a Tonbridge-educated army officer who went to India in 1879; Josiah Richards became manager of the Pontymister Iron Foundry, then held the same position in Cape Breton, Newfoundland; T. M. Phillips was a barrister who died in China; A. V. Julius went to Ceylon to become a solicitor in Colombo; William Phillips went ranching in Texas, returning after twenty years to die of sunstroke after following Dorando's 1908 marathon on a bicycle. The energies disfiguring the whole face of South Wales were forcefully concentrated here, at this south-eastern ear, geographically attuned to external influences and innovations. Newport had the strongest fixture list of all the Welsh clubs. It was the first of them to be given a fixture by one of the most prestigious north of England sides, Manchester Athletic, in 1878; that year Newport also played Birmingham, Clifton, Gloucester and Swindon.

With a fixture list worthy of the S.W.F.U. itself, the Newport club was nothing if not progressive in play and administration. In 1877-8 they were already playing eight forwards and seven backs, in anticipation of the four three-quarter system. In October 1879 the first electric light flickered in South Wales when an evening match with Cardiff was played on an erratically floodlit Rodney Parade.

It was the visit of Blackheath a few weeks later that plunged Newport into gloom. Newport was undefeated on Rodney Parade; in fact, she was undefeated anywhere since her second game ever in 1875. Richard Mullock, the resourceful Newport secretary, challenged the champion club of England, Blackheath, to meet the champion Welsh club. The Heathens accepted and came down to Rodney Parade like wolves on the fold. On 20 November 1879, before a record 5,000 spectators who paid an unprecedented £103 in gate money, Blackheath devoured the wearers of 'the mustard and blacking' by four goals and eight tries to nil. When all allowances had been made — that Newport were below strength through injury, that they had played two matches in the previous five days, that Blackheath had imported outside players for the occasion — Newport, the best in Wales, had received a lesson in rugby methods, dispensed by a side with eleven English Internationals in it, including the England captain, Stokes, as well as two of the creative thinkers of the contemporary game, Arthur Budd and H. H. Vassall. They were among the first to appreciate the significance of the new law of 1878 concerning putting the ball down in a tackle, for this, they saw, made for a looser forward game. To counter it, Blackheath introduced new methods of attack, which involved moving the ball away from the forwards to the open side of the field. And not only from scrummages. While their first-half tries against Newport were the result of combined play with the halves playing virtually as link-men, they scored all their second-half tries from the long throw at the line-out over the heads of the Newport forwards bunched on the touch-line in the formation customary at the time.

Newport were not so demoralized by their drubbing that they ceased to be the leading Welsh club: they appeared in every Cup Final between 1882 and 1886, winning it another three times. But that November night at Newport had repercussions that reverberated for well over a year; in particular they haunted the mind of Richard Mullock, and it would be March 1881 before they were finally exorcized.

Mullock, whose bovine rotundity matched his name, belonged to the family firm of Henry Mullock & Son, printers by steam power, Commercial Street, Newport. He had been secretary of the Newport Athletic Club since 1874; he had seen the S.W.F.C. metamorphose into the S.W.F.U. without any appreciable widening of its horizons; in his spare time, which was little, he painted. He knew that only through contact with the best opposition could the standard of Welsh rugby be raised, at club as well as representative level. Thus, when the S.W.F.U. announced in September 1879 that it intended playing Oxford University, the West of Scotland, Blackheath and a South of Ireland team in the forthcoming season, Mullock stole a march on it by securing the Blackheath fixture for his own club, and the S.W.F.U. never did get to play them. The games with Oxford and the West of Scotland never came off, but a South Wales XV did play a touring South of Ireland team; so also did Newport on 18 November 1879, *the day before* they played South Wales.

Two months later, on 12 February, South Wales went to Gloucester, and lost. Not for the first time, through their own short-sightedness, the S.W.F.U. found themselves the victims of a fixture clash. In November 1878, when South Wales had played Monmouthshire at Sophia Gardens, fourteen of the South Wales team were Cardiff men since Swansea and Neath had a cup-tie that day; this time, the South Wales side was weakened by the fact that Cardiff were playing Lampeter College in a cup match. At the representative level, South Wales rugby was going nowhere fast. Its governing body, the S.W.F.U., was apparently lacking in energy and purpose when it came to translating vague intentions into firm fixtures, and planned those with scant attention to putting truly representative teams in the field.

Mullock was nothing if not energetic and purposeful, and it was with a view to improving the situation, to casting the representative net wider by contacting Welshmen recently or currently playing in English schools and in the universities, and to discussing the feasibility of assembling a genuinely representative Welsh side to meet the national representative side of England, that Mullock met with various interested parties at the

36

Tenby Hotel, Swansea, in March 1880. What transpired at that meeting, who attended it, even who was represented there, must remain conjectural. The talks were informal and, quite deliberately, no details were released. Richard Mullock can certainly be presumed to have been present. He left it under the impression that he had been given a cautious mandate to open direct negotiations with the English R.F.U. to arrange a full international fixture between England and Wales, and to raise a Welsh XV for that purpose. That match took place in February 1881; caps were awarded for it, and once fixtures between them were regularized, both countries came to acknowledge it as the first encounter of the series; as such it has always been officially recognized. Not surprisingly, therefore, if its legitimacy were not to be seriously impugned and the validity of the caps won for it not to be called in question, it became convenient for the W.F.U. in its first anxious years to ignore the uncomfortable fact that the match had preceded its own foundation by a month, and to locate an earlier founding-meeting at Swansea in March 1880.

The origins of the Welsh Rugby Football Union can plausibly be traced to the Tenby Hotel, Swansea, but without a doubt its foundation occurred at the Castle Hotel, Neath, a year later. Nevertheless, and irrespective of incidental asides in the South Wales press of the late 1880s that 'the Welsh Union was formed in season 1880-1', once the Union's own invention was given the stamp of authority by the Revd Frank Marshall's respected *Football — the Rugby Union Game* in 1892, the myth of 1880 as foundation year became a truth, an accepted fact. It became another accepted fact that at the Swansea meeting, the S.W.F.U. was dissolved. That was wrong too. Accepted facts, because they are accepted, tend to become fictions.

It has always been held that the clubs represented at the Tenby Hotel in March 1880 were Cardiff, Chepstow, Haverfordwest, Llandaff, Llanelli, Neath, Newport, Pontypridd and Swansea. The evidence demands careful consideration; but there is no evidence, only a poor substitute — repetition. As it stands, it is an odd list, though no odder than the list of actual founder clubs who met at Neath the following year. It was, of course, inconceivable that the major coastal clubs could be absent from any discussion regarding the future of Welsh rugby; but some of the others were as much on the fringes of Welsh football as they were of its geography. They had never competed for the Challenge Cup, nor, with the exception of Pontypridd's fixture with Cardiff, had they played the leading clubs. What *is* significant is that Chepstow, Haverfordwest, Llandaff and

Pontypridd were all represented in the first-ever Welsh XV that played England at Blackheath in February 1881. One of that side was Richard Summers of Haverfordwest. If Mullock wanted to find a team composed of players with experience of English football, Summers would have been recommended to him by Cardiff men, because Summers was currently playing for Cheltenham College, whom Cardiff had played the previous year. Summers had gone to Cheltenham in May 1879 from Cowbridge Grammar School, and Cardiff might have noticed him then, for Cowbridge was also on their fixture card. They had certainly spotted Treharne, who was still at Cowbridge when he played for Wales in February 1881. Summers left school in July 1880 and returned to Haverfordwest. Treharne lived in Pontypridd. They appear in the Welsh team list in 1881 as Summers (Haverfordwest) and Treharne (Pontypridd). Edward Peake of Chepstow, another member of that first Welsh XV, would have been familiar to Mullock because that club twice played Newport's Second XV in 1879-80. The Tenby Hotel talks had more to do with contacts than clubs: the discussion among Mullock and some others from the leading clubs centred on individuals, names, persons. The personnel of a potential Welsh XV was under review, and the clubs, in some cases merely the place of residence, of members of the XV who represented Wales at Blackheath in February 1881 were later projected backwards to be credited with what can best be called retrospective representation at Swansea in March 1880. Founder-clubs of the Welsh Rugby Union they were not.

Not least, of course, because that was not the founding. Apart from the fact that the Tenby Hotel meeting, held at some unspecified date in March 1880 was unrecorded, uncorroborated, and made no claim to be forming a new union — whereas the Castle Hotel meeting at Neath on 12 March 1881 *was* recorded, *can* be corroborated by other evidence and was convened *specifically* 'to consider the question of forming a Welsh Rugby Union' — apart from these difficulties in the way of investing the 1880 meeting with more significance than it can bear, there is the stubborn fact of the continued activity of the S.W.F.U. *after* March 1880. Not only is it very much in existence, it is spurred by the Tenby Hotel ginger group to adopt a more purposeful and decisive posture.

On 27 April 1880, the S.W.F.U. appointed a new, youthful secretary, S. S. Clarke of Neath. On 15 September it met at the Queen's Hotel, Cardiff, with representatives from Newport, Cardiff, Neath, Swansea and Llanelli in attendance, and it was resolved to invite Mr J. T. D. Llewellyn of Neath to become president. Nine days later the S.W.F.U. held its annual meeting, again in Cardiff, where the draw for the Cup competition was made, and a letter read out from Mr J. T. D. Llewellyn stating his willingness to undertake the presidency of the S.W.F.U. 'and to do what he could to further the effectiveness of South Wales sports'. Fixtures were then arranged for the forthcoming season, with the South of Ireland at Swansea in November and two fixtures with Gloucestershire at Cardiff in November and Gloucester in January. Not only were these fixtures fulfilled, but other games were played, with Old Monmouthians and with Somerset, at Newport in December.

This was an unusually hectic programme for the S.W.F.U. to undertake, but it does suggest that it was only too well aware of the informal meeting at Swansea in March, and that it needed to adopt a more positive, forward policy if it was not to have its authority undermined from within. An indication of its determination to head off the Tenby Hotel Turks at the pass was the choice of an active new secretary and a new president, well-known for his involvement in the sporting life of South Wales. The S.W.F.U. was given a new Neath-based facelift.

But the momentum generated at the Swansea meeting in March was not easily deflected. The momentum was Mullock. On 30 November 1880, the R.F.U. in London discussed a letter from 'Mr R. Mullock of Newport, Monmouthshire, proposing a match with Wales'. The challenge was accepted, 'after considerable discussion'. The game was fixed for 8 January 1881, and Mullock arranged a trial for late December in Swansea, where the respective sides would be captained by R. L. Knight of Oxford University and J. A. Bevan of Cambridge. 'Judging from the number and quality of the names sent in to play in this trial match', announced Mullock, 'visitors to the ground will see one of the best games ever played in Swansea, or even in Wales. The proceeds will go towards the expenses of the London match'.

In the event, the trial was not played, and the players who eventually took the field against England were selected in a rather more arbitrary fashion; so haphazard, in fact, that Wales turned up short of two players, for whom substitutes had to be found from the field. One of the missing players was J. E. Brooks of Pontypridd, who later recalled, 'There was no organization or committee assisting in 1880 to select players. All that would happen was that some individual would have a conversation with you, take your name and address, and pass on. That happened to me after I had played for Pontypridd against Shewbrook's School at Sophia Gardens,

Cardiff. It was mentioned to me that Treharne and I had been chosen to play for Wales against England in that first international. I had no definite instructions from anyone to play in that match, but I heard afterwards that I had been expected to play'.

On such a casual selectorial basis, worthy of the S.W.F.U. itself, did Mullock's private army take the field against England. Ironically, Mullock's own plans were thwarted by the sort of fixture clash that had always irritated him under the old union. Because the R.F.U. had found the date originally agreed on, 8 January, to be inconvenient, a new date, 22 January, was fixed. This was mutually acceptable but again had to be postponed because of frost. Eventually, the only remaining date the R.F.U. could offer was 19 February, and Mullock, determined not to relinquish the fixture, accepted, even though that was the day fixed for the semi-final cup-tie between Swansea and Llanelli at Neath.

The historic, scholastic, geographically diverse, but scarely representative first Welsh XV that eventually took the field at Blackheath in 1881 was: C. H. Newman[1] (Newport), R. H. B. Summers[2] (Haverfordwest) — fullbacks; J. A. Bevan[3] (Cambridge Univ. and Newport) (capt.), E. Peake[4] (Chepstow and Newport) — three-quarters; L. Watkins[5] (Llandaff and Cardiff), E. J. Lewis[6] (Llandovery) — half-backs; F. J. Purdon (Newport), G. F. Harding[7] (Newport), T. A. Rees[8] (Llandovery), B. E. Girling (Cardiff), B. B. Mann (Cardiff), W. D. Phillips (Cardiff), E. Treharne[9] (Pontypridd), G. Darbishire[10] (Bangor), R. D. Garnons Williams[11] (Brecon and Newport) — forwards.

'So far as the strength of the visiting team is concerned it is possible that had the decision of the contest been possible at an earlier period, the Welsh executive would have had more material at their command. As it was, England were set an easy task'. Mullock, with a sudden awful awareness that *he was* the Welsh executive, could do little but sadly agree with *The Times*'s sniffy post-mortem. Seven goals, a dropped goal and six tries to nil as well as eleven touch-downs in self-defence, *was* a crushing defeat.

---

1. Educ. Monmouth School & St. John's Coll., Cambridge. 2. Educ. Cowbridge Grammar School and Cheltenham Coll. 3. Educ. Hereford Cathedral School & St. John's Coll., Cambidge. 4. Educ. Marlborough & Oriel Coll., Oxford. 5. Educ. Sherborne & Exeter Coll., Oxford. 6. Educ. Llandovery & Christ's Coll., Cambridge. 7. Educ. Monmouth School. 8. Educ. Llandovery, Sherborne & Jesus Coll., Oxford. 9. Educ. Cowbridge G.S. 10. Educ. Rugby and Balliol Coll., Oxford. 11. Educ. Magdalen C.S., Oxford, Trinity Coll., Cambridge, & R.M.C. Sandhurst.

Within a few days, an anonymous correspondent imaginatively signing himself 'A Welsh Football Player' was finger-stabbing the editor of the *Western Mail* with the demand, 'Could you or any of your readers inform me whether the members of the Welsh XV who played against England were selected by responsible persons appointed by the committee of the South Wales Football Union? Or was it a private team got up by Mr Mullock, Newport, to do battle for Wales?'

Writing on behalf of the S.W.F.U., secretary Sam Clarke's reply was curt: 'I beg to inform your correspondent that the team which represented Wales was not elected by the committee of the South Wales Football Union; neither had they anything to do with it. As your correspondent assumes, Mr Mullock was one of the committee who selected the Welsh team and will, no doubt, be pleased to give any information required'. Clarke's assumed air of disdainful indifference was understandable. History was repeating itself: just as the S.W.F.C., five years previously, had been upstaged by the wily Ruabon solicitor, Llewellyn Kenrick, now the same fate seemed likely to befall the S.W.F.U. That Wales had lost, that Mullock refused to provide 'Welsh Football Player' with the information required, was small comfort: Clarke knew in his bones that he and his Union had been abandoned to stumble among the foothills as Mullock's advance party scaled the heights of Parnassus to deal with the Olympians of the R.F.U. direct.

When he saw in the 24 February 1881 issue of *Athletic World* that 'The Welsh are, I understand, about to form a Union', he knew the writing was on the wall. Three weeks later, he was reading it himself, for nearly every newspaper from the *Star of Gwent* to the *Carmarthen Journal* carried the same story. The report ran as follows:

Welsh Rugby Football Union

A meeting was held at the Castle Hotel, Neath, on Saturday last (12 March, 1881), the following clubs being represented: Swansea, Lampeter, Llandeilo, Cardiff, Newport, Llanelli, Merthyr, Llandovery, Brecon, Pontypool and Bangor, to consider the question of establishing a Welsh Rugby Union. The chair was taken by Mr. Richardson, captain of the Swansea club, and after considerable discussion it was proposed by the Chairman and seconded by Mr. F. Meager, Swansea, that a Welsh Rugby Football Union be formed. This resolution was carried unanimously. It was then proposed by Mr. Mullock, Newport, and seconded by Mr. Margrave, Llanelli, that Mr. C. C. Chambers, president of the Swansea Football Club, be elected president of the Welsh Rugby Football Union for the season 1881-2. The next proposition by the Chairman and seconded by Mr. Mullock, was that Mr. E.

C. Fry, Cardiff, and Mr. C. P. Lewis, Llandovery, be elected vice-presidents of the Welsh Rugby Union for the season 1881-2. Carried unanimously. The election of a committee, which will in all probability consist of a member of each club in the Union, was left until the next meeting which will be held during this month. Mr. Forester, Merthyr, proposed and Mr. Knill, Swansea, seconded, that Mr. Richard Mullock be elected hon. secretary to the W.R.U. The hon. secretary was instructed to prepare for the next meeting a draft copy of proposed bye-laws to govern the Welsh Rugby Union. The annual subscription was fixed at £1 1s., with an entrance fee of £1 1s.

The Union was born. It was not an immaculate conception, nor did it result from a fit of absence of mind. Neither the timing nor the location of the meeting of 12 March, 1881, was accidental. That Saturday, in Neath, the Challenge Cup Final was down for decision between Cardiff and Llanelli. The occasion provided a convenient opportunity for a meeting of club representatives. The leading clubs of Newport, Cardiff, Swansea and Llanelli had, in the wake of the Tenby Hotel talks of March 1880, sanctioned Mullock's proposal to arrange a full international match with England; at the same time, they were careful to retain their membership of the S.W.F.U., which was still the governing body of the game in Wales. Nevertheless, they could not but commend Mullock's resourceful enthusiasm.

It was the Swansea club who gave Mullock's initiative the most positive backing, who saw also the importance of allowing him freedom of expression within manageable — preferably formal — constraints, and who recognized that if Mullock was prepared to be accountable to the collective decisions of the other clubs, he would have won the argument. The indications were that Mullock had fully appreciated the advantages of this approach himself. It was shrewd of him to have started the ball rolling at Swansea in March 1880, because thereby he could not be cast in the role of Newport lone wolf, or East Wales plotter. Moreover, in flying his kite at the Tenby Hotel he was recognizing Swansea's current status as the champion Welsh club, for a month previously they had defeated Lampeter College in the final round of the Challenge Cup.

Now, a year on, Swansea were repaying the compliment, for the 1881 Neath meeting pivoted on a Swansea-Newport axis. The strategic proposals were made and the principal offices taken by Messrs. Chambers, Richardson and Meager, respectively president, captain and secretary of the Swansea club. It is highly probable that it was they who had actually convened the meeting. Certainly it is they who create the scenario and set the temper of the gathering; Mullock is commended rather than censured for his Blackheath initiative, and formally elected as secretary. Mullock returns the favour by proposing Chambers for president, and by looking after Swansea in the arrangements he makes for the Union's fixtures. Wales's first ever home international would take place in December 1882, at St. Helen's; the first ever Welsh inter-county game, between Glamorgan and Monmouthshire, was played there in November 1881; the W.F.U. would hold its first A.G.M. in Swansea — though at the Mackworth Hotel, not that conspirators' cave in Walter Road, the Tenby.

If the new Union was born under the pole stars of Newport and Swansea, the presence of some of the other clubs represented at Neath is less easily explained. Some were there through good fortune, others out of careful calculation. The port towns excepted, the clubs in attendance were representative of neither the numerical nor the playing strength of Welsh rugby. Nevertheless, it was not wholly coincidental that Brecon, Llandeilo, Lampeter College, Llandovery College, Merthyr and Pontypool had helped inaugurate the South Wales Cup competition in 1877-78, and still enjoyed occasional fixtures with the big clubs. Bangor was there thanks to its links with the college at Brecon. In 1879 the headmaster of Friars School, Bangor, the Revd D. Lewis Lloyd, had moved south to take up his new appointment at Christ College, Brecon, and brought most of his pupils with him. It was on the recommendation of the Bangor-Breconians that Godfrey Darbishire had been chosen to play at Blackheath. The Darbishires, a well-known family of Caernarvonshire quarry-owners, lived in Penmaenmawr, and sent Godfrey to the cradle of the game, Rugby itself, where he played for the school team. The fact that in 1881 he had not played a match for two years was not regarded as a drawback. What is unlikely is that there was a Bangor club in existence then, and it is most probable that the spokesman for rugby in that area was a Breconian of Bangor origin. Certainly it was gratifying that a northern delegate was present at the founding of a national union for Wales, just as Darbishire's selection for the Blackheath game had given the first Welsh XV the truly representative, national flavour that Mullock aimed at. Appearances mattered in these early years. That was why at the Neath meeting of 1881, the colleges of Lampeter, Llandovery and Brecon were represented, for if the English Union owed its inception to old boys of Rugby and Marlborough, and the Scottish Union was founded by former pupils of Fettes and Loretto, then the Welsh Union must enlist its public schools as well. In any case, the colleges had a respectable record in the South Wales Challenge Cup with Lampeter College reaching the final in 1880. On the other hand, it is more than likely that the college delegates were joined in upholding the interests of their localities by representatives of their town sides; there was as much a sense of mutual interest, arising from an overlap of personnel, as there was the inevitable town-gown rivalry, in those bustling market townships. C. P. Lewis of Llandovery, elected vice-president of the W.R.U. at the 1881 meeting, was as well-known in the town as in the college where he taught; and not only in Llandovery, for he often played for neighbouring Llandeilo, and it was his influence that secured that club's place at the founding meeting. Similarly, it is almost inconceivable that there were not representatives of the Brecon town club at Neath, with the delegation from the college. Brecon Football Club had played a formative role in Welsh rugby in the 1870s. The S.W.F.C. had been founded and spearheaded by Breconians: its first president, Major T. Conway Lloyd, and secretary, H. W. Davies, were Brecon men (and former collegians), while the town club, even if its star was rather less in the ascendant by now, had also participated in the early years of the Challenge Cup.

There was one club, however, a leading club in Welsh rugby, which was quite strikingly conspicuous by its non-attendance at the Castle Hotel. Distance or communication difficulties can hardly have explained its absence, for that club was Neath itself. The moves culminating in the formation of the W.R.U. had not merely taken the wind out of the sails of the S.W.F.U. The tacit involvement of the other clubs in these manoeuvres meant that the crew had deserted as well. There were just two people left aboard the *Marie Celeste* of the old union, secretary Sam Clarke and president John Llewellyn. Both were from Neath. Smarting from the indignity of the other clubs' collusion with Mullock, Neath declined to attend the foundation meeting which was taking place on its own door step. Clarke, in particular, quite understandably had no intention of lifting a finger to dig a pit into which he was being invited to jump. But the wound soon healed: Neath were mollified by being awarded the final trial of October 1881; Clarke would be awarded two international caps by the Union which had deposed him; and Llewellyn would in time become its President. Neath did not compete for the Cup in the 1881-2 season, but re-entered the lists in 1882-3, and at the end of that season D. J. Price of Neath became a western district representative on the W.R.U. match committee. From 1883, Neath never failed to be represented at Union meetings, and in the persons of Walter Rees and Eric Evans, would make the greatest individual club contribution in the history of the W.R.U. by monopolizing the secretaryship from 1896 to 1955.

The transition from S.W.F.U. to W.R.U. — or W.F.U., as the Union called itself until 1934 — was a delicate operation, but it was effected with little shedding of blood. The incision made on 12 March 1881 was clean and decisive; the S.W.F.U. never met again. The W.F.U. assumed its functions, and held its spring and annual meetings in the same places as its predecessor. It continued to arrange fixtures for a South Wales team, which played, for instance, an Irish Rovers XV at Newport in November 1881, and met Oxford University in an annual 5 November away fixture until 1886. The drama implicit in the palace revolution that was enacted at Neath on 12 March 1881, made little impact on the wider rugby community; in the late 1880s the press could still be found referring to the W.F.U. as 'the South Wales Union'.

But the new union did not run off with all the clothes of its predecessor. The S.W.F.U. had played in black vests, with a white leek slashed boldly across the front. Mullock, for reasons of diplomacy as well as distinctiveness, had clad his Welsh XV at Blackheath in scarlet jerseys emblazoned with the Prince of Wales feathers. It was under the Tudors that the three white ostrich plumes, enfiled by the words 'Ich Dien' (I serve), had become the exclusive heraldic emblem of the Prince of Wales. Since then it had been adopted by prestigious bodies like the Welch Regiment, in 1719, and the London Cymmrodorion Society, when the Prince of Wales, son of George II, became its patron, in 1751. The W.F.U. would hardly have been guilty of a lapse of taste had it reverted to the S.W.F.U.'s audacious vegetable, for the other national unions had already opted for the traditional floral emblems of their countries. But it had to be admitted there was something peculiarly satisfying about the appearance of Mullock's men in scarlet, and the defiant white leek on black circumspectly deferred to the princely plumes on red.

The Union's drive for respectability was further advanced in September 1881 by its decision to appoint as President, the Earl of Jersey. C. C. Chambers of Swansea had fulfilled his historic role as charter-president; he had guided the Union through an awkward transitional period, and as a founder-member of the old S.W.F.U. had been a necessary link with the past. His obvious successor as figurehead was J. T. D. Llewellyn, but it was considered indecently soon after the interment of the S.W.F.U. to ask him to legitimize what was virtually its usurpation by the W.F.U. The choice of the Union fell on a man who would not have been out of place adorning the hierarchy of the R.F.U. itself: one of the greatest peers of the realm. Victor Albert George Child-Villiers, 7th Earl of Jersey (1845-1915), educated at Eton and Balliol, was a grandson of Robert Peel and a descendant of Henry VII. The founder of his line, the first Earl, had distinguished himself in the Civil War of the seventeenth century, and it was unlikely to have been on behalf of Cromwell. He owned 19,400 acres, a half of which were in Glamorgan, where his estates provided him with an annual rent-roll of £18,000. He was a generous benefactor of the Briton Ferry and St. Thomas districts where he spent £60,000 in providing a variety of public amenities from roads to libraries and sports facilities: he had a particular interest in amateur athletics. He would become Paymaster-General of Lord Salisbury's Conservative government in 1889 and Governor-General of New South Wales from 1890 to 1893. Such was the aristocrat who presided over the humble fortunes of the W.F.U. from September 1881 to 1885.

And humble fortunes they were. In its first years the Union lived a hand-to-mouth existence, the hands belonging chiefly to Mullock and Alex Duncan of Cardiff. The Newport and Cardiff clubs were prevailed upon to loan ten pounds each to the Union in its first few weeks, Mullock breezingly allaying any doubts his own club might have entertained about repayment by explaining that the money would be paid off with the takings next year from matches Wales would play with England, and perhaps an Australian team. The Challenge Cup, he added, would be competed for in future by teams from North Wales as well as South.

Impatient of narrow horizons and minor difficulties, Mullock was talking the only language he knew. From his experience with the Newport club, he also knew it brought results. He was dissatisfied that the governing body of the game in Wales, the S.W.F.U., was content with being a provincial union, dealing amicably but unambitiously with its English and Irish counterparts, the Yorkshire County Union, Gloucestershire, Munster. Mullock was anxious that a *national* body representing the whole of Wales should be able to meet the national unions of the other countries on equal terms. It was not mere high-mindedness, therefore, but a critical section in the scaffolding of his ambition that he should want the Challenge Cup competition extended to embrace the whole of Wales; not a fantasy, but a hardnosed assumption, that representatives of Australia would want to play the national

46

representatives of Wales. In the event, no Australian tourists materialized, nor did the R.F.U. wholly enthuse over Mullock's blueprint for the future, and felt unable to offer the W.F.U. more than a fixture with the North of England in 1882. But at least, where in November 1880 he was referred to as 'Mr. R. Mullock of Newport, Monmouthshire', from September 1881 he appears in the minutes of the R.F.U. as 'Mr. R. Mullock, Secretary of the Wales Union'. And after, on successive Saturdays at Rodney Parade in January 1882, seeing the Welsh narrowly go under to the North of England (in front of 4,000 spectators and followed by an excellent dinner provided by the W.F.U. at the King's Head Hotel) and thoroughly trounce a Midland Counties combination (where W. F. Evans ran in five of Wales's six tries: typically, Bill Evans, the son of a Rhymney clergyman, was an old Breconian who taught at Cheltenham College and played for Newport) — after seeing these things, the English Union was prepared to renew fixtures with Wales in the 1882-3 season.

From now on the W.F.U. might continue to look somewhat scruffy, but it never looked back. In September 1882 its officials were confirmed: the Earl of Jersey in his presidency, Fry and Lewis as vice-presidents, Duncan of Cardiff and C. E. Parsons of Newport as auditors, and Mullock as Secretary and Treasurer. In addition the Union resurrected a scheme first adopted by the S.W.F.U. in 1880, of dividing the teams entered for the Cup into eastern and western districts, 'Bridgend being the centre'. It was on this basis, with its in-built invitation to east-west tribal warfare, that the Match Committee was chosen, and the Union's first national selectors were Mullock (Newport) and Duncan (Cardiff) for the eastern district, and H. Ray Knill (Swansea) and T. A. Rees (Llandovery) for the west.

The financial position of the Union deteriorated. At the end of the 1882-3 season, Mullock, whose cavalier attitude towards the presentation of a balance-sheet would be his eventual undoing, reported that while the Union's receipts had come to £96 11s. 4d., expenditure had totalled £215 10s. 0d. It appears that nearly a quarter of this had been deployed at the Mackworth Hotel, Swansea, to impress the R.F.U., on their first visit to Wales in December 1882, that their Welsh equivalents no longer ate with their fingers. Various individuals had advanced money to assist the Union — Mullock himself was seventy pounds out of pocket — but it was Horace Lyne of Newport who summed up the situation: the accounts were 'in a regular mess'. However, when it was suggested that the Union could no longer afford to pay train fares, it was Lyne, too, who smartly replied that 'if that was the case, the sooner the Union was dissolved the better. If every player had to pay his own train fare, the teams would be teams of gentlemen and not representative teams'. Lyne's egalitarian standpoint — from which he never wavered until his death in 1949 — failed to carry the day and it was hoped that players' clubs would pay their travel expenses. In any case, as the request to each club to donate the proceeds of one game to the Union in the following season recognized, club rugby in the 1880s was in a far sturdier state of health than its impoverished governing body.

By the end of 1884 the debt had been reduced to a more manageable £46 6s. 2d.; thereafter, the Union's finances crept gingerly into the black. It was in 1885 that the Union felt sufficiently confident to rejig its administrative structure. The Match Committee was increased to six: Mullock, Duncan and William Wilkins of Llanelli were the stable components of this committee during the first decade; in addition, Wilkins, a future Treasurer of the Union, replaced Duncan as co-auditor with C. E. Parsons. Of greater long-term significance, while a proposal to promote the vice-presidents in succession to the presidency was defeated in principle, it was actually implemented that year, for the absentee landlord Earl of Jersey was succeeded as President by J. T. D. Llewellyn, who had been made a vice-president in 1884.

Pound for pound, John Llewellyn (1836-1927) was a few divisions lower than his heavyweight baronial predecessor, but he could boast some impressive credentials nonetheless: his education — Eton and Christ Church, Oxford; his social standing — he had married the daughter of Sir Michael Hicks-Beach, Disraeli's Colonial Secretary; his wealth — 15,000 acres; and his known and active involvement with Welsh sport — he was a former captain of the South Wales Cricket Club. It was especially gratifying that, as the son of J. D. Dillwyn Llewellyn, F.R.S., the eminent scientist, and Emma Maud Talbot of Margam, he was Welsh, and a gentleman to boot. Knighted in 1890, Sir John Llewellyn of Penllergaer, Conservative M.P. for Swansea from 1895 to 1900, served as President of the W.F.U. from 1885 until 1906, and as Horace Lyne, who would succeed him, observed in 1888, 'they had been singularly fortunate in getting a gentleman like Mr. J. T. D. Llewellyn to act in that capacity'.

There was general agreement on the choice of Llewellyn as President, but the annual meeting of 1885 was then enlivened by competing claims for the staging of the one home international of the forthcoming season, against Scotland. W. H. Treatt of Cardiff said Cardiff should get it since

48

Newport had it last. The Llanelli representative would support him so long as Llanelli was awarded the next match after that. Temperatures rose when the chairman said they could not promise Llanelli anything and another speaker pronounced Llanelli 'an out of the way place', which was hotly denied by the partisans of Stradey. Regional rivalry had raised its head early in the history of the Union.

Llanelli maintained a tetchy wariness towards the W.F.U. in its early years, frequently professing themselves puzzled by what they regarded as 'the marked hostility of the executive towards our local organization', and its 'studied and continual slighting of Llanelli'. In particular they were less than happy with Richard Mullock, partly because of his alleged high-handedness, partly because he came from Newport. These misgivings were not confined to Llanelli. Mullock's handling of Union affairs came under increasing scrutiny in the late 1880s, and the first murmurs of the ground-swell of opposition which would topple him in 1892 were heard in 1886.

At that year's A.G.M., the Pontypridd representative opined that 'it was possible for a secretary to get stale just as a player got stale', and proposed Wilkins of Llanelli to stand against Mullock, who offered to retire. This provoked protests from some quarters, to the effect that they were indebted to him for setting up the Union and promoting international matches, but Wilkins was urged by others not to stand down. A vote was forced and Mullock survived, ten-six.

By the end of 1887 Mullock, for the first time in the history of the W.F.U., could report a credit balance; all of twenty-three pounds. This was due less to the Treasurer's vigilant book-keeping than an eight thousand crowd at Stradey in January for the English match. That figure would have been larger had Mullock not bungled the pre-match arrangements. The new year had been severely cold and Mullock was uncertain whether the Llanelli ground would be playable. As a precaution, on the morning of the match he sent a telegram to Swansea concerning the state of St. Helen's. The Swansea people informed him that their ground was fit to play and awaited his reply. Mullock never did reply and while the game went ahead in Llanelli, many hundreds of people in Swansea, hearing of the rumours, assembled at St. Helen's. Various other sins, of omission mostly, were laid at Mullock's door that year, but he again survived an attempt to unseat him.

From 1887, he, Lyne and Duncan were the Welsh representatives on the newly formed International Board. The first full international season, where each of the four countries played the other three, had been 1883-4, when a disputed try in the England v. Scotland game at Blackheath led to the suspension of fixtures between those two countries for a year. It was on Irish initiative that a preliminary meeting was held in Dublin in February 1886, where representatives of the four international unions, including Horace Lyne from Wales, considered the formation of an International Board to settle such disputes. The I.B. was formally established at Manchester on 5 March 1887, when Lyne and Mullock gave Welsh assent to its four inaugural resolutions.

Of these, it was the third — 'that the International Board shall have absolute and exclusive jurisdiction over all disputes arising in international matches played under their rules' — and the fourth — 'that the Board shall consist of three representatives from each of the Unions' — that the English Union found unpalatable. Although the Board adopted as international rules the R.F.U.'s rules of 1885, the R.F.U. was unwilling to accept the possibility of the Board's becoming the sole law-maker and felt in addition that the English Union deserved greater representation than the other countries because it represented ten times the number of clubs.

The R.F.U. complicated its position by in 1886 altering the scoring rule and in 1887 proposing that international matches in England should be played under their rules rather than those of the I.B. At a meeting of the Board in Newport on 4 February 1888, England was again invited to join it on the basis of equality of representation with the other countries, but declined. It was at this first meeting of the Board on Welsh soil, with Horace Lyne in the chair, that the twelve original bye-laws of the I.B. were formally established, resolutely reiterating the principles of equality of representation and exclusive international jurisdisction. The interpretation of a secondary clause in Bye-law 5 — 'it [the I.B.] shall have no power to interfere with the game as played within the limits of the different Unions' — would, at the height of the Gould affair in 1897, present the I.B. with the gravest crisis in its history; but for the moment stalemate prevailed, and because of her refusal to recognize the jurisdiction of the I.B., the other three countries did not play England in 1888 and 1889.

The W.F.U. was unhappy with this situation and was prepared to be flexible in its attitude to constitutional forms by seeking a compromise. Anxious to see the resumption of fixtures, Wales expressed a readiness to play England in 1889 under the rules of the country in which the game took place. It required a tap on the shoulder from the I.B. in December 1888, in the form of a directive drawing the attention of the W.F.U. to the agreed constitution that all international matches be played under rules approved by the Board — because 'the significance of its terms may not have been fully appreciated' by the W.F.U. — to dissuade the Union from going ahead. In the event, fixtures were resumed in 1889-90 when the R.F.U. agreed to resolve the deadlock through arbitration. When the arbitrators' decision was announced in April 1890, it recommended that all international matches should be played under one code of laws and that the International Board should consist of six representatives from the R.F.U. and two from each of the other countries. Mullock's opinion that the I.B. 'had had the best of it with England' was a somewhat tendentious view of the decision and not till 1948 was English representation reduced to two.

Of the founder-members of the Board, Horace Lyne alone lived to see it. Though no longer a member of the I.B. by that date, his unbroken service on the Board, from its inception in 1887 to 1938, was historic and remarkable. The holder of six Welsh caps between 1883 and 1885, graduating into administration straight from the field of play, Lyne was held in high esteem from the earliest days in national and international rugby circles because of the judicious fairmindedness with which he appraised each situation. As a delegate to the R.F.U. in October 1886, he sought to temper its more rabid outbursts against professionalism by advocating the payment of compensation for loss of time to working men. At a W.F.U. meeting in April 1887, he voiced ultimately prophetic fears that if the I.B. took too firm a line with the recalcitrant English, the north of England would be driven into forming a separate union, for northern opinion was strongly in favour of joining the Board, contrary to the view held in the south. From 1887, too, Lyne invariably took the chair at the annual meeting of the W.F.U. and steered its deliberations with a quiet authority. Among the delegates he welcomed to the 1888 meeting was the secretary of Neath, though Lyne could not then have known that together they would regulate the affairs of the Welsh Rugby Union for the next sixty years. The secretary of Neath was Walter E. Rees.

Their partnership commenced the following year, 1889, when they were both elected to the Match Committee. Mullock was confirmed as Secretary and Treasurer, but from now on, as his opponents found ever new grounds for complaint, he would be subjected to an increasing fusillade of criticism. Mullock had learned to live with his critics, as an ox lives with flies, by ignoring them. But his insensitivity only served to inspire his critics to new piques: 'I know he makes a boast of it that he never reads what the papers

51

say of him', smarted 'Cestus' of the Llanelli *Guardian* in January 1886. Others knew more than they were prepared to divulge. 'I am continually hearing of one or other of his sins of omission', confessed the sports correspondent of the *South Wales Daily News* in January 1887, but he preferred to keep them 'locked in the innermost recesses of my bosom'. By 1890, even that paper was finding the quality of mercy increasingly strained, and had to report that 'matters have not been working smoothly in the Union for some years, the secretarial question has divided members into factions'.

Typical of the grievances raised against Mullock's inefficient execution of his duties were those expressed at Llanelli's A.G.M. in April 1891, when Gavin Henry, the club secretary, complained that following the international match with Ireland at Stradey in March, he had written several times to Mullock 'concerning payment for the men who had erected stands, posted bills, etc.' Mullock had apparently taken all the 'gate', and Henry had had to find some of the money out of his own pocket. Mullock did not answer letters, and Gavin Henry, for one, 'really thought that the sooner Mr. Mullock was deposed of his office the better it would be for South Wales football (applause)'. Clearly it was not just dereliction of duty that was being called in question.

At the end of that season, delegates to the annual meeting of the W.F.U. itself voiced their disquiet, with W. H. Gwynn of Swansea attacking Mullock on the grounds of financial mismanagement. As ever, Mullock had failed to provide a balance-sheet for members — as far back as 1884 Tom Williams of Neath, a member of the W.F.U. committee, had complained of this irritating habit, and since the circulating of the printed balance-sheet was required under Clause 15 of the Union's constitution, he had formally moved 'that the attention of the Secretary be called to the bye-law' — but this time Gwynn had discovered that Mullock had actually prevented the accounts from being properly audited. Gwynn conceded that 'he [Mullock] is a jolly good fellow and he is in many regards a capital representative of the Union, to build up which he has done so much, but he does not pay that attention to his duties which the members of the Union have a right to expect'. So saying, Gwynn promptly proposed Walter Rees as Secretary in Mullock's stead. After W. D. Phillips of Cardiff and Lyne reminded members that at one time Mullock 'had financed the Union', Rees withdrew and Mullock, while renouncing his position as Treasurer in favour of William Wilkins of Llanelli, retained the secretaryship for what he said would be his last year.

And it was. During the winter of 1891-2 a Swansea player, Thorogood, had been involved in an incident in a game at Exeter. The matter was taken up by the R.F.U., who prevailed upon Mullock to instruct Thorogood to apologize in writing. It was felt, especially in Swansea, that Mullock had grovelled. In September 1892 the knives finally came out. It was the end of an era, but the future was rosier than even the bold former Secretary would have dared paint it ten years earlier. Mullock, incontestably the father of the Welsh Rugby Union, had seen his sickly brain-child develop into a sturdy infant. By 1892 the Union's receipts totalled £1,270 10s. 0d., when in 1882-3 they were less than £100. The Union had been born under the sign of the public schools; now new constellations clustered in the firmament. By the early 1890s no longer were Lampeter, Llandeilo, Llandovery and Brecon represented at W.F.U. meetings; of the founder members, only Newport, Cardiff, Swansea and Llanelli continued to be regularly represented, but they were joined by delegates from clubs such as Penygraig, Llwynypia, Treorchy, Ferndale, Abercarn, Mountain Ash, Ogmore Vale, Morriston and Pontarddulais. In 1891 the Match Committee was enlarged from six members to seven, to accommodate the representative of the new Rhondda Division. This striking redistribution of the social geography of Welsh rugby was an indicator of the shuddering economic changes which were propelling South Wales into position at the hub of the world economy. A further index of the accelerating expansion of the W.F.U. in money and members was its ready acceptance of two proposals made by Walter Rees in 1892: that a hundred guineas be donated to the Tondu disaster fund (over a hundred lives had been lost at the Park Slip Colliery in August) and that before clubs became affiliated to the Union, they should be approved of and recommended by the Committee. Whether this mood of buoyant optimism could be translated into results on the field of play remained to be seen. In 1891 Wales had lost all three fixtures with England, Scotland and Ireland in dismal celebration of what had been, overall, an inauspicious first decade at international level. But it had been a decade of momentous development, too.

'To compare the rugby football of 1881 with the game as we know it', noted 'Old Stager' in 1893, 'would be about as absurd as instituting a comparison between the old Snider rifle of the period and the up-to-date magazine death-dealer'. Had 'Old Stager' pushed his analogy back into the 1870s, he would have needed to invoke the blunderbuss. For rather than science and sophistication it was the colour and carnival of the community virility tests which passed for club matches that captured the imagination of the sporting public of South Wales. It could hardly have been the spectacular nature of the play, for in its early days rugby was quite dull to watch.

The effect of the abolition of 'hacking' in 1871 had been to make scrummages longer and the game less fast and open. For lengthy periods now the ball disappeared entirely from view as play, lurching from one ten-minute maul to another, consisted mostly, according to one early witness, of 'a quarter of a hundred of heavyweights leaning up against each other'. In the 1870s sides varied in number from ten to twenty, the more-round-than-oval ball was caught on the bounce before it could be carried, and handling movements were unknown. Once a player was 'collared' he might hand the ball on, but he never passed it. Players gathered round to form a 'scrimmage', but the scrum in its modern form was not legislated for until 1892. When the ball went into touch it was not followed by a line-out; instead, the forwards of each side formed a line with their heads down and the ball was thrown into the tunnel, the aim being to 'force it through'. The object of the game itself was to kick goals direct, or take the ball over the line to earn a 'try' for a kick at goal; and the most highly cultivated art of all rugby skills was drop-kicking, for this was the means by which goals were scored.

The first international, played at Raeburn Place, Edinburgh, between Scotland and England in March 1871, had been contested between two sides of twenty each: seven backs and thirteen forwards. It was Oxford and Cambridge who played the first representative fifteen-a-side game in the Varsity match of 1875, and the idea was adopted at international level from 1877, the fifteen generally deployed as nine forwards, two half-backs, two three-quarters and two full-backs. Various permutations of this combination were practised over the next decade, from ten forwards to one or three three-quarters, but essentially the halves played an attacking role by standing five to six yards behind the primitive scrum, waiting for the ball to be kicked through. When they gathered it they burst upfield, but never passed, which was to 'funk'. The three-quarter hoped for the occasional wild ball to be kicked through in his direction, giving him a snap chance at goal; it was he who was expected to do most of the scoring, especially with the advent of the linking, passing half-backs from the early 1880s. Meanwhile, back at the last line of defence were the full-backs, whose function was to find touch through drop-kicks — punting was 'bad form'.

From 1878 the introduction of the 'down-rule' requiring a player to release the ball when tackled undermined the former prolonged trial of strength between opposing heavyweights, for the nine or ten forwards now had to scrum with their heads down to see where the ball was in order to control it. This led to 'foiking', or hooking the ball out of the side of the scrum; the development of the wheel as a counter-move, first perfected by Yorkshire sides but soon to become a speciality of the great Newport pack of the early 1890s; and to a premium on fast, heavy forwards adept at breaking away in a loose foot-rush.

It took at least two decades from the formulating of the first Rugby Union rules in 1871 for the game to progress from a rough draft to a fair copy. Those years saw the laborious process of standardizing regional variations into a national and then an international code of playing; of converting goals and tries into points, as the I.B. sought from 1889 to establish a scoring-system acceptable to all four countries;* of regularizing the dimensions of the playing field, and of the ball; of making dress more uniform; and not least, defining the powers allowed the referee.

Expediency became the mother of invention. In the early days, players, ordinarily attired, just took off their coats. In one of Cardiff's first matches, some players did not even discard their bowler hats, and one player took part in evening dress; but such eccentricities became rarer as packed scrummages became a feature of play. In an early fixture on a wet afternoon at Llandovery, Swansea played in mackintosh coats, but expanding fixture-lists soon diffused the idea of tight-fitting, rough-knit sailors' jerseys, Welsh-wool stockings fastened below the knee under tight knickerbocker trousers, and pit boots with a bar of leather tapped on the sole. The need for a stricter definition of the playing area was vividly illustrated by Newport's game against Rockleaze in November 1877 on Clifton Downs, when C. B. Cross is reported to have chased a rolling ball for five hundred yards before touching down; not until 1891 was the dead-ball line fixed at twenty-five yards maximum. Then, too, the game was being played, increasingly in South Wales, as in the north of England, by players who, in social status at least, were obviously not gentlemen, though they had their own ideal of respectability, expressed more in style and appearance than in a set of beliefs and attitudes. They preferred to jettison the arch vocabulary of the public school game, with its collaring, sneaking, rouges and squashes, in favour of the more practical tackling, offside, minors and scrums. Growing working-class participation and the

---

* See Note on Scoring in Appendices (ii) and (vii).

competitive atmosphere generated by cup and derby matches soon exposed the gentlemanly fiction that any breach of the rules was unintentional and that it was impolite to assume anything else; in 1882 it became necessary to introduce penalty and free kicks for foul play, obstruction and off-side. In the 1870s the settling of disputes had been left to rival captains, and umpires were only appointed if desired, but arguments between players and umpires often incited violence among spectators, until in 1881 neutral referees were appointed for big matches. Gradually they were invested with increasing powers: in 1885-6 the referee was given a whistle, which spared him the indignity of breathlessly yelping 'Man down!' or 'Held!' as he chased after play, while umpires became regulated to patrolling the side lines with flags. The W.F.U., like the other countries, had its own rules early on — while there was a general conformity of rules for international games from the 1880s, only in 1930 was it finally decided that 'all matches [in domestic rugby as well] shall be played under the Laws of the International Board' — so that in Wales the practice of allowing appeals to the referee was abolished some time before the R.F.U. followed suit in 1893, and long before the I.B. decided in 1896 that 'the referee shall be sole judge in all matters of fact'.

But, in most respects, Welsh rugby in its first years was not so much innovative as imitative of the methods and techniques of the foremost exponents of the game in the other countries, and, with one striking exception, this was particularly true of Wales's first decade at international level.

Wales's hundred years of international rugby kicked off at 3.10 p.m. on Saturday 19 February 1881 at Blackheath, against an England team that had lost only two games since the original international ten years earlier. The Welsh XV, purposely chosen to represent all parts of Wales, from Chepstow to Bangor, was in fact representative of little more than the determination of Richard Mullock, the restless impresario who had collected the curious consortium together. Merely to state that this first Welsh international XV was defeated would be to elevate understatement to an art-form. It was decimated.

There were some mitigating circumstances: there always are. When the team were changing in a small old-fashioned inn near the ground, where maybe they lingered too long, it was discovered that two of the invitations to play had gone astray, and a couple of Varsity men with Welsh qualifications were picked up from the small crowd lined three-deep around the field. This required a last-minute re-arrangement, so that

Charles Newman played the only game of his life at full back and Treharne, a half-back, had to go into the pack, where his speed made him the most prominent of the Welsh forwards. To add injury to ill-luck, Lewis, at half-back, and Mann, a forward, were crocked after ten minutes, and eventually had to go off. Unsurprisingly, in the second half the ball hardly moved out of Welsh territory, for Wales had elected to play nine forwards and six backs against ten forwards and five backs, and England's numerical superiority up front began to tell. The Welsh forwards were beaten for weight, speed and skill, and England's backs revelled in the possession they were getting, none more than captain of the English side and architect of the Welsh downfall, Lennard Stokes, whose swerving runs and powerful left-footed kicking had already earned him the sobriquet of 'the bloody snipe' from his own Blackheath crowd.

The London papers were naturally quite scathing at England's 'ridiculously easy victory' of eight goals and six tries to nil, and collectively gave their readers the impression that Wales were lucky to get nil. Nevertheless, at the dinner following the match, Stokes had told the chastened men in scarlet, 'I have seen enough to know that you Welshmen will be hard to beat in a few years' time, when you get together'. Some of the Welshmen, chosen on hearsay or past reputation, did not intend staying around that long. Before the end of the year, Darbishire emigrated to Florida; soon afterwards Summers left for India, and Leonard Watkins took off for the Argentine.

They were thus unavailable to witness, let alone participate in the first international played in Wales, which was also against England, at St. Helen's in December 1882, when Wales again failed to make any reply to six tries. Whereas the sniping Stokes had been the menace the previous year, this time it was Richmond's Gregory Wade who gave Wales, in *The Field*'s words, 'a heap of trouble', and scored three tries. Fore and aft, Welsh deficiencies were cruelly exposed. The backs held on too long, ran into trouble, passed recklessly, failed to support each other and tackled too high. The forwards were completely bemused by the Englishmen's sophisticated ploys, entering scrums in wedge formation, fanning out in a line interpassing carefully, following up kicks and punts where Wales held back. It was also noticeable that the England players knew each other by name — nine of them came fom the Blackheath and Richmond clubs alone — whereas the Welsh players had never played together before. But familiarity alone was not enough, for Wales included eight Newport players in the side that played Scotland for the first time in Edinburgh in

57

January 1883, and still it did not save her from defeat by three converted tries to one.

It was in 1883-4 that Wales first played the other three countries in one season, and if she was still not properly a team, at least individual ability could plainly be detected. Against England at Leeds in January 1884, Welsh efforts 'received constant applause' from a small crowd resentful that there was not a single Yorkshireman in the England XV. The efforts were mostly those of new cap W. H. Gwynn of Swansea, a future Secretary of the W.F.U. and Welsh representative on the I.B., who was the first to open and enter the portals of the pantheon of the Welsh glory spot: outside-half. Initially Gwynn had been an association player, and in the late 1870s had been for two seasons captain of the undefeated Battersea College XI, but he had already switched to rugby before returning to Swansea in the early 1880s. Like so many great Welsh backs of later years, Gwynn not only owed his football skills to a flirtation with soccer, but his keen eye and safe handling to his prowess at cricket. As a member of the Swansea Cricket Club, he acquired the reputation of being a reliable bat and wicked fast bowler; between 1881 and 1884 he headed both the bowling and batting averages. Like other players who skirted greatness without quite becoming enfolded by it, Gwynn was prone to the occasional alarming error that was the despair of his fellows and admirers alike: against Scotland in 1884, he dummied the defence, raced through the gaping hole he had created, then paused to look around for support and dropped the ball when he was over the line.

Also making his début against England that year was Charles Taylor at three-quarter, whose drop-kick nearly won the match. He, too, was originally a soccer player and it showed in his rugby: an athlete of some note, like many early Welsh players, he was also the champion pole-vaulter of Wales. He learnt his rugby at the Royal Naval Engineering College at Portsmouth where he was noticed by a brother of Horace Lyne, who was himself winning his second cap in the game at Leeds. Taylor had been asked to play in a South Wales team against Oxford University in 1883 and had 'a clinking game', scoring two tries. Immediately afterwards he was chosen for Wales where his penchant for fly-kicking the ball, a legacy of his soccer days, disconcerted his own team as much as the opposition. His presence continued to give the Welsh side a truly national flavour, consistent with Mullock's dream, and Taylor, from Ruabon, was not the only North Walian in the side, for Wales's first ever try against England was scored by the ex-Rugby Oxford Blue, Charlie Allen from Beaumaris.

58

Against Scotland a week later in Newport, Gwynn, in sparkling form, shared the limelight with Charles Newman, who survived the Blackheath débacle to win a total of ten caps. He was always a Rodney Parade favourite despite having moved to Durham in 1883. Like Gwynn, Newman's coolness reflected an inner but secure confidence in his own ability; he would often mesmerize an opponent by stopping dead, looking him in the eye, and accelerate past. It was the art, or perhaps the science, of combination that Wales still had to learn. 'On many occasions when the ball might have been passed,' noted one observer, 'it was hugged for personal distinction's sake. The Scotsmen throughout had more dash, pluck, decision, cohesion and science in their play, the Welshmen being selfish and indecisive.' All the same, the margin of the Scottish victory — a dropped goal and a try to nil — suggested that Wales were becoming less of a push-over.

The Times thought this was worth pointing out to the English team that travelled to Swansea in 1885. 'Within the past few years,' it noted, 'the Rugby Union game of football has made rapid strides in Wales, and the southern part of the Principality is now noted for the keen enthusiasm shown by the players themselves and the spectators'. If the implication was that enthusiasm is one thing, winning another, England's conclusive victory bore it out. It also confirmed the baleful suspicions of the West Walians, who regarded the inability of the Welsh Match Committee to recognize any player from Llanelli as treasonable, and who therefore greeted the result with some satisfaction. 'To leave the cup-holders out in the cold may be gratifying to the self-love of Newport,' sulked the Llanelli *Guardian*, 'but detrimental to the interests of the Union.' Ironically, two new caps from Newport scored all Wales's points, Arthur Gould at full-back launching a legendary international career by converting one of the two début tries by H. M. Jordan, the smallest player to appear on an international field to date, and the fastest. Overall, however, the Welsh backs were outpaced and outclassed by the likes of Wade, Stoddart and Alan Rotherham, who had introduced the concept of the outside-half as link-man, and Gwynn did not help by shirking tackles and erratic passing. But the forwards had scrummaged well, and this was no mere flash in the pan: a week later, the Scots were held to a no-score draw in Glasgow.

Wales appeared to have taken to heart the criticisms made of their ineffectual tackling against England; they harassed like dervishes, baulked the Scottish footrushes, and backed up intelligently. The press never ceased to be intrigued by the striking, even ludicrous, disparity in size between the big-boned, burly Scots and the seemingly diminutive, wiry Welshmen. Muscular, powerfully-built Scottish backs like Don Wauchope and Grant Asher were physically indistinguishable from their forwards, and it would take Wales a few years to discover that only through nimbleness of mind, sleight of hand and foot, and the sudden unexpected manoeuvre, could they occasionally be confounded: it was necessity, rather than any ethnic quirk, that gave rise to the celebrated cleverness of Welsh back play. On this occasion Wauchope was kept on a tight leash by Charlie Newman; only once did he slip it, and then he was held up on the line, like Benoit Dauga in similar circumstances nearly ninety years later, by the man he least expected to meet, W. H. Gwynn, the Barry John of the 1880s. The real revelation of the 1884 Glasgow match was the heroic performance of the Welsh pack. At last, Wales seemed to have hit on a forward combination that gave away nothing in weight or speed to its opponents, spearheaded by the young Goliath, W. H. Thomas of Llandovery College, the prototype of C. B. Nicholl, A. M. Rees and Rees Stephens, and welded into a scrummaging pack by the redoubtable Tom Clapp, who had not missed a game since 1882.

This pack was the mast to which the Match Committee decided to nail its colours in a bold move when Scotland came south in 1886. The date was 9 January; the place, Cardiff Arms Park. The previous week had been fiercely cold, and while the precaution was taken, at a cost of fifty pounds, of covering the ground with straw, the pitch still looked like a transplant from the tundra. Scotland scored two goals and a try to nil, though for Wales 'Stadden, Douglas, Gould and Taylor were most pertinacious in their attempts to get away with the ball,' but '. . . beyond the points mentioned, nothing else of a distinct character occurred,' — thus *The Times*. Not in its whole history, even its notorious nineteenth-century history of grotesquely misunderstanding Welsh affairs, could 'The Thunderer' have been more wrong. For that day in Cardiff, Wales played four three-quarters, her most enduring contribution to rugby football, and the greatest.

With so many of its practitioners coming to the game fresh and without any rigid assumptions and preconceptions as to how it should be played, Wales had from the first adopted a flexible, empirical approach to the relative numbers of forwards and backs. Against England in 1881, she had unwisely pitted nine forwards against ten; in 1882, eight against nine, with the backs deployed in the unusual formation of two full-backs, three-quarters and two half-backs. As it became apparent that one of the two full-backs could be better employed elsewhere, most clubs put him back in the forwards; but not all, not Cardiff.

Crucial to the innovation was an Englishman, F. E. Hancock, who, twenty-two years old in 1883, was drawn from his native Wiveliscombe in Somerset to work in the expanding coal-exporting town of Cardiff. Having previously captained his club and county sides, he was anxious to continue his rugby in South Wales, and at the end of 1883 played for Cardiff Seconds v. Newport Seconds. On 9 February 1884 he was promoted to the first team, when Cardiff needed a third three-quarter for a tough away fixture with Cheltenham College, and he scored the only two tries of the game. Reluctant to omit him for the next match, but equally unwilling to drop any of the current three-quarters, the Cardiff selectors, in a stroke of improvisation, retained Hancock as a *fourth* three-quarter for the next game on 23 February against Gloucester, and the combination was continued for the rest of the season. During the 1884-5 season, Cardiff alternated between the four and three three-quarter systems, and Neath, Swansea and Llanelli began adopting it. In the 1885 Cup Final, Neath played four against Newport's three. It was in 1885-6 that it came to be copied by most of the first and second class clubs in Wales, and that it was established as the Cardiff game, because that season, captained by Hancock and playing the new system throughout, Cardiff won twenty-six consecutive matches out of twenty-seven. Cardiff's line was crossed only four times during the whole season, but they scored one hundred and thirty-one tries themselves, with Billy Douglas on the wing getting twenty-three of them. Douglas, Hancock, Gould and Taylor were Wales's four three-quarters against Scotland in 1886.

Frank Hancock, whose chunky 5 foot 9½ inches and 12 stone 7lb. English frame fixed the paradigm proportions of the classic Welsh centre, had been first capped for Wales against Ireland in 1884, and retained for the two matches of 1885. Had he played against England in 1886, he would have been on the opposite side to his brother, P. Froude 'Baby' Hancock. Now settled in Cardiff, Frank came to the notice of the Welsh selectors through his dodginess and proverbial 'corkscrew runs' which more than compensated for his relative deficiency of speed. As captain of Cardiff when they were 'the Welsh invincibles' of 1885-6, he was a strict disciplinarian but a skilful and unselfish player, who believed in scoring tries rather than dropping goals, and who had a keen eye for spotting a weakness in the opposition. He was the obvious choice to captain Wales on the international baptism of the four three-quarter, or two-centre, system.

But the Siberian conditions were against the swift passing necessary to show the new combination to advantage, and the Welsh pack was not one to play a subordinate role to the men behind. As the game developed, the Scottish forwards threatened to swamp the Welsh eight, and Hancock was forced to try Gould at full-back in order that Harry Bowen might reinforce the pack. This move came in for acid criticism from Llanelli, whom Bowen captained and where he was an idol ever since his first appearance for them at fifteen years of age. It was the *Guardian*'s opinion that 'to please Cardiff, four three-quarters were played with disastrous results. When room had to be made for a Cardiff man, a Llanellyite, of course, had to make way for him.' But is was not only a Llanelli viewpoint that 'the Hancock business spoiled the Welsh team,' for Newport thought so too, and, influenced by Gould, refused to adopt four three-quarters until 1887-8. Gould also persuaded the Welsh selectors to revert to the traditional system; and when Wales next risked putting four three-quarters in the field, in December 1888 against Joe Warbrick's native-born New Zealand tourists, misleadingly known as 'The Maoris', Gould was absent. But if the effectiveness of the four three-quarter system would not be denied neither could Gould's own genius, and in the next decade he became as great an exponent of the new system as he had been of the old. No movie star made the comparable transition from silent films to talkies with such devastating success.

It was 1888 before Wales recorded her first win against Scotland. It might not have been unconnected that the team for this game was picked after the first effective trial that the W.F.U. had managed to stage. There had been trials, of sorts, since the first at Neath in October in 1881, but there was general agreement that they were all 'miserable fiascos', like that arranged in 1884 between East and West at Bridgend, for which only one player from the west turned up. It was not merely the victory of a Welsh side including seven new caps against a Scottish XV averaging 13 stone a man that was so totally unexpected, but that the victory was based on careful thought beforehand. The plan was to concentrate on wheeling and heeling back to avoid prolonged confrontation with the mountainous Scots, 'to whom,' according to a local journalist, 'an hour's knocking about was a matter of no consequence.' The hero of the hour, in front of his own admiring crowd of 7,000, was Gould, covering, smothering and tackling in the greatest defensive display of his illustrious career. 'Those who saw the game', waxed the exhilarated correspondent of the *Western Mail*, 'will remember how cheer followed cheer as the Welshmen — their backs manifesting a surprising vim and vigour and chucking the leather with no little daring — swept down the ground; how the enthusiasm was mightily moved as they surged around the Scottish half-way flag; how it fairly bubbled over as Pryce-Jenkins took the ball from 'Buller'. Pryce-Jenkins did a preliminary hop through the 'thistle men' swarming around him, shook off Duncan, fairly flummoxed Cameron, and went tumbling over the line. Then arose a multitude of noises that blended into Wagnerian sweetness, and faces grew flushed and voices hoarse and husky.'

It was the only score of the match, and the finest Welsh performance of the decade, but it was followed by a disappointing defeat in Ireland, Gould reportedly declining to travel because he was refused the captaincy. Unhappily, nearly all of Wales's fixtures with Ireland in the first ten years were clouded by mishap and controversy. Wales's first ever international victory was registered at Lansdowne Road in January 1882, 'in the presence of a large and fashionable assemblage, including many ladies, two of whom came over with the Welsh team.' Newport men scored all four tries, with solicitor Tom Baker-Jones crossing for Wales's first international try after twenty-six minutes. But thereafter the occasion was disfigured by arguments and walk-offs, and the home team finished what the *Irish Times* called 'this wearisome game' with only eleven men. In 1883 the Irish Union was unable to raise a team prepared to travel to Cardiff, and when the game was eventually played in April 1884, the Irish team was still two players short so that a couple of Welsh players stood in for them. Relationships between the two countries broke down for the next two years, though Mullock and Lyne refereed successive defeats of Ireland by England in 1885 and 1886 respectively. This still rankled with the acerbic Irish critic Jacques McCarthy, renowned for substituting vitriol for ink, when he reported in 1886 that 'Wales are most anxious to arrange a match with Ireland this year and have written to Mr McAllister [the Irish Secretary] to that effect. It is to be hoped that no such proposal will be entertained for an instant. It is bad enough for us to lose internationals with England through the instrumentality of Welsh referees, without meeting fifteen of these Heathen Chinese. Once bitten, twice shy'. Fixtures were resumed in 1887, but then at the neutral venue of Birkenhead, to save the Irish Union expense.

Wales ended her first decade with just five wins from nineteen games, but international rugby was beginning to assert a powerful hold on the popular imagination. The opening game of the 1890s drew the largest crowd yet seen in Cardiff for the visit of Scotland in February. Thousands saw the match from rooftops, windows and vehicles of every description in

Westgate Street, and such was the pressure of the 10,000 inside the ground that a section of the wire fencing collapsed and spectators surged over the touch-line. It marked the début of W. J. Bancroft, who came in at the last moment for the injured Tom England to make the full-back position his personal property for the next eleven years; but with Evan James 'a failure of the deepest dye' without his brother at half-back and the forwards unable to stem the Scots' dribbling, the new decade opened with a defeat; ironically, at the hands of a team who had decided to imitate Wales by fielding four three-quarters for the first time.

It was very much as underdogs, therefore, that Wales went up to play England at Dewsbury two weeks later. Odds of 5 to 1 against were being laid on the Cardiff docks. The day of the match it rained all morning and turned to icy sleet by afternoon so that after five minutes of play both sides were unrecognizable. Incredibly, in conditions least suited to it, the four three-quarter system came into its kingdom. Wales short-passed with speed and skill, while the long passes of England's three three-quarters came to grief in the swamp. Ten minutes after half-time, a line-out was formed not far from the England line and the Englishmen grouped in midfield as Stadden, playing now on his home ground, made as if to execute a long throw. He did throw, but not to the Englishmen, or even the Welshmen, but to himself, re-gathered and swerved past two opponents over the line. Long, raking kicks by Bancroft and tenacious tackling by the three-quarters ensured there would be no reply, and Wales had beaten England for the first time.

But the *Yorkshire Post* detected a still wider significance in the result. 'It was not only a defeat but a disaster for the English team who were beaten at all points of the game', it adjudicated. 'It must now become an open question whether as the game is now played the proper number of three-quarter backs should not be four, instead of three. For our part, we should not be surprised if in this country in the near future a free trade of the system were by common consent established.'

Wales had pioneered the four three-quarter back division. Its recognition was now secured, and it would be bequeathed to the world as rugby football's richest legacy.

CHAPTER 4

MONKEY BUSINESS

THE second decade in the history of the Welsh Football Union did not have an auspicious start. There were problems in the administration of the game at all levels, from the inner circles of the Union to the control of impassioned crowds, from the nature of Welsh refereeing to the problem of professionalism, whilst success at international level, despite the winning of the first Triple Crown in 1893, remained dauntingly elusive. However, there were observers acute enough to notice that the growing power and popularity of club rugby was connected to Welsh perseverance with the four three-quarter game, since this was both more likely to yield results and more attractive to watch. This was a combination well suited to a bustling, confident society in South Wales. It was personified by the collective discipline of Newport R.F.C. and the individual skills of the man who now established beyond any lingering doubt that he was the greatest exponent of the game hitherto seen.

Ironically enough, A. J. Gould was absent for the opening season of the 1890s. This did not prevent Newport, for the second year under the captaincy of T. C. Graham, from continuing with an enviable run of success that echoed their pre-eminence of the late 1870s and early 1880s. They were soon to have as profound an impact on the 1890s. There were sound reasons for this. Newport, whose population was only 2,346 in 1811 would have rocketed to 115,450 by 1901. Through this period of unprecedented industrial growth in Wales, Newport could rank as one of the most spectacular examples of a new urban presence. Men flocked to build its new docks, to service its ships, to work in its shops, and to develop its thriving commercial life. We have seen how Monmouthshire in these years proved an exchange mart in progressive ideas that was as dependent on its geographical proximity to England as it was on sheer economic dynamism. It would be from Monmouthshire that the dissatisfaction with the old, valley-based miners' unions would cohere into a movement to found a South Wales Miners' Federation in 1898, and go on to ally it to the British Federation; it would be in Newport in 1896 that David Lloyd George's attempt to fuse nationalism with liberalism in the *Cymru Fydd* movement would founder when the South Wales Liberals speaking, they said, on behalf of the cosmopolitan population of South Wales' towns, rejected 'Welsh domination'. Lloyd George fumed that the meeting has been packed with 'Newport Englishmen'. In his campaign of 1895, Lloyd George had been gratified by the support he discovered in West Wales, Aberdare and the Rhondda but had written to his wife that he was not pleased with the reception at Tredegar, where the people had 'sunk into a morbid footballism'. This complaint against football by aspirants to either political or moral or social or religious control, would recur. Lloyd George, himself, would see his first game in 1907 when, as President of the Board of Trade, he received the freedom of the city of Cardiff. On this occasion the rising politician reflected, after Cardiff had beaten Blackheath, 'It's a most extraordinary game. I never saw it before and I must say I think it is more exciting than politics.' After 1905 even Lloyd George knew where to apply Welsh flannel. For both the inhabitants of those terraced rows of Pennant sandstone houses and those semi-detached villas, tricked out in yellow and red brick, the importance and excitement of football were well established by the 1890s.

As with so many of the other collective activities in late-Victorian Wales, football acted more as a social cement than a divisive force. Even sectional interests in the society argued for their own communal role. How much more of a unifier of a raw world was a game that could focus the attention of both east and west ends, of Maindee and of Pill, in a town consciousness that gave local patriotism the added spice of civic pride? Whereas it was, in towns like Newport, very much middle-class initiative that launched and sustained various forms of athletic activity, including rugby football, the whole ethos of South Walian society, albeit layered in widely divergent social classes, was against social exclusiveness in the public domain. Its politics were 'progressive'; its union leaders were 'labour' men with 'liberal principles'; its rugby clubs were 'open', socially inclusive; its dynamic was vital enough to convince many that its adolescent energy could take mature, and settled, shape.

Nonetheless, it was not a shape that fitted in easily to the pattern of the Welsh past. The 1890s could be seen, in the eyes of those Welshmen who recognized the fostering of a national consciousness undertaken in the nineteenth century, as the apogee of those particular achievements upon which the Welsh political and social élites prided themselves — the National University was firmly established after the rocky days of the 1870s and 1880s; Welsh influence within the British Liberal Party, despite frustrations, was stronger than ever and the advances would be sustained in the first decade of the twentieth century by bills for a National Museum and National Library along with a Welsh Department in the Board of Education for which Owen M. Edwards, scholar and ex-Liberal M.P. for Merioneth, was made Chief Inspector for Schools. The idea that rugby was in any way connected with these developments in Welsh life was, for a long time, treated with as much contempt as the notion that it was the material expansion of Welsh society which fed her 'spiritual' aspirations. It was only hindsight (and a few victories) which placed rugby in the centre of Welsh life. Certainly, in the early 1890s, it occupied only an ante-room of Welsh culture. O. M. Edwards, a product of the unlikely rugby nursery of Llanuwchllyn who had played the game as a student at Aberystwyth in the early 1880s, was the greatest popularizer of Welsh history and culture of his day and, like many other Welsh patriots, was deeply troubled by the concentration of population in the South that followed the rural exodus and influx of non-Welsh. Theories allying race to other qualities of body and mind were common in late nineteenth century Europe, so it made perfect sense for Edwards to try to explain the dis-unity of Wales in these terms when he wrote his new history of Wales in 1892. The Welsh were, he argued, originally of Iberian descent, now inter-mingled with the Celt but still distinctive:

> The Iberian was short and weak; dark of countenance, black hair and eyes; narrow forehead and long head . . . but . . . there was a strange life within him; the weakness of his body made his soul active. Britain was once his. He came over the shores of the Mediterranean from Egypt and Arabia. He is the Silure of Gwent and Morgannwg and may be seen on Saturday nights at Cardiff and Newport, is the adjudicator at the Eisteddfod, and not unfrequently met at Jesus College, Oxford . . . The spirit of the Iberian still battles with the spirit of the Celt (who came after) . . . Every religious movement is a victory of the Iberian. The discovery of coal and of precious metal is due to the Celt . . . In every new song is heard the voice of the Iberian; in the history of the chase or of football you hear that of the Celt.

This species of academic nonsense was not without purpose. For Edwards, and others, it meant that the essence of Wales could still be detected in those flocking to work in the South Walian hill districts ('Blood and language are secondary matters') whilst the true anti-Welsh tendencies remained isolated in the towns ('A capital town would prevent the development of the nation'). Later the string of victories of the first Golden Era would see these warring tendencies fused as the players would be hailed more for their inherent qualities as Welshmen than for their technical skills. In the early 1890s, it was by no means certain that matters would move this way. Nothing is more symbolic of the conflict, and its eventual outcome, than the night of Easter Monday 1897. In Denbigh, Lloyd George was at a testimonial meeting for Thomas Gee, radical publisher and polemicist for all the great causes of nineteenth century Wales, in the Capel Mawr; in Newport's Drill Hall, where A. J. Gould was being given a house to mark his retirement from rugby at the age of thirty-two, D. A. Thomas, the coal-owner M.P. for Merthyr Tydfil and arch-opponent of the *Cymru Fydd* movement of the previous year, told the audience that he 'was glad that the prejudice against football and athletics was dying out, and that a discriminating public were beginning to see what the nation owed to this national characteristic'. To all intent and purpose a century died that night and another came of age.

Arthur Joseph Gould cannot be held solely responsible for these great shifts. On the other hand his career exemplifies the lineaments of change and of achievement more than any other. He would be the first to go beyond local fame, regional renown, even national recognition, to earn both meanings of the word 'an international'. Gould had received the plaudits of his admirers long before 1897. At the Albert Hall, Newport, in June 1890, Gould was honoured at a smoking concert given by the club and attended by the Mayor. He was presented with a cheque for fifty guineas and a 'handsomely chased' gold ring. Gould was off to the West Indies to join his elder brother, the ex-international Bob Gould, in contract work on water and bridge works. It was not so much to the hills as to the oceans that this society looked. Expertise was exported along with coal. It did not dwell on the past or live off sentiment. And yet it was already enmeshing itself in the spider's web of its own, enticing culture. A. J. Gould in reply, 'made a manly little speech, in which there was no trace of affectation or forced sentiment and . . . hoped he might return some day and have the pleasure of once more donning the old "mustard and blacking". He almost dreaded the coming October when the football season would commence, and hoped the blacks under his charge would not have a bad time of it in his inclination to kick off with something. (Laughter) . . . if by a miracle he found his fortune was made when he got out to the Indies, he should take the first steamer back again'. Within eighteen months he *was* back, to play rugby again for Newport and Wales.

Gould was born in Newport, in 1864, into a large and boisterous athletic family. His father, Joseph, had come from Oxford to work in the brass foundry business in Newport. He himself was a notable local cricketer and ardent supporter of the rugby club. Bob Gould, a year older than Arthur, won eleven Welsh caps at forward between 1882 and 1887; Bert Gould, a centre or a wing three-quarter, was capped three times in the 1890s; Wyatt Gould would captain Newport in the early twentieth century whilst two other brothers, Harry, the eldest, and Gus, played for Newport. Arthur Gould, starting young and finishing late, would span two eras of rugby history. His exploits were recorded in countless pen portraits, his handsomely chiselled features and lithe form as familiar to sportsmen and even to mere newspaper readers as the more portly frame of the best known Englishman of the day, W. G. Grace. Indeed Gould's striking good looks — dark curly hair, deep brown eyes and a frame of 5 foot 10½ inches that hovered around 11 stone — account, in part, for the admiration he received from spectators of both sexes. There was something penetratingly attractive about the man and his manner of play. Small boys would follow him in droves, even after he retired, as he went about his business (as a brewery representative) in Newport. They sold matchboxes with his face on the paper covers. His opinions would be sought on any and every subject. To all and sundry he was 'Monk' Gould, from the nickname 'Monkey' that he had picked up in school because of his general agility and his constant habit of climbing trees.

Gould captained the Newport Junior side when he was fourteen. At sixteen he was drafted into the First XV as an emergency full back against Weston-super-Mare. Despite orders to kick he scored twice by running through the entire opposing team. He was, thereafter, never dropped from the First XV, moving up to play as one of the three three-quarters in his fourth season. First capped, at full-back, in 1885, he captained Wales against Ireland in 1889. By that time he already had unparalleled experience. This stemmed, in part, from Newport's boldness in taking on the best rugby sides in England, notably Blackheath, whose Lennard Stokes, in the 1879 game which Gould saw, impressed him by kicking to touch on the attack instead of running. Gould, who was naturally left-handed and left-footed, practised assiduously until he could punt and drop-kick with either foot. In 1885-86 Gould dropped 20 goals. He was now, in association with his brother, working as a public works contractor and so travelling the country. The railway train turned A. J. Gould from a local phenomenon into a nation-wide sensation. Before 4,000 spectators at the 1885 Whit Monday meeting of the Newport Cricket, Football, Athletic and Lawn Tennis club, Gould won the open sprint, the hurdles, the high jump and 120 yards; in June 1885, on business in London, he ran in the open invitation 100 yards of the Private Banks Sports at Catford Bridge, and won from a field of fifty-nine. When in the West Country he continued his winning ways on the running track and by playing rugby for Southampton Trojans; back in London he played for the newly-formed London Welsh and, from 1887, more regularly for Richmond. Gould also played for Hampshire, for Middlesex, and for South Wales. In 1885-86 he travelled almost 4,000 miles by rail in order to play football. When Gould left for the Indies in 1890, he had won over £1,000 in foot races alone, been Midland Counties Hurdles champion, and he had played in invincible sides with Richmond (1886-7) and Middlesex (1887-8). W. J. Townsend Collins (later 'Dromio' of the *South Wales Argus*) recalled seeing Richmond play Blackheath during the 1888-9 season when both sides kicked accurately, tackled well and prevented any breach of their lines until, late in the game, 'there was a hush, a shout, a triumphant roar — a three-quarter in an amber, red and black jersey — graceful, swift, elusive — swerving left, dodging right, went through the defence without a hand being laid upon him, and by the try he scored Richmond won. This dazzling player was Arthur Gould . . . So I saw for the first time the man whom I regard as the greatest rugby player who ever took the field'.

Collins wrote that in 1948. Contemporaries back his judgement of Gould and of his dodging, quick-silver runs. For the Revd F. P. Marshall in 1893 Gould was 'the central figure, in the football world . . . the greatest centre three-quarter that has ever played.' When he went overseas in 1890, it was thought that his game was declining, yet in 1896 the Northampton *Herald* would declare that thousands watched rugby only to see Gould, whose play was marked by its deadly surety and speed but above all by its gracefulness — 'This lithe, sinewy grace Gould possesses in a marked degree, and having been well favoured in face and form by Dame Nature, his wonderful popularity is easily understood. What he has done for Welsh football . . . cannot well be over-estimated.' The journal *St. Paul's* intoned from London — 'When a history of the Welsh game comes to be written, one thing is certain, the central figure will be A. J. Gould.'

Gould undoubtedly put rugby in Wales onto a different plane of expectation even before 1890. Nonetheless, as he was the first to argue, it was the fact that after 1890 the theory of the game, the execution of play, and a combination of skill and experience in key players, all came together, which allowed his gifts their finest expression in a team game. Once more it was Newport who provided the platform.

The club had been more reluctant than Swansea and Llanelli in following the lead of Cardiff in playing four three-quarters; in part, no doubt, because of Gould's capabilities as a kicker of the ball and snapper-up of trifles. When he came to play for them fully once more in 1891 the virtues of combination in play had won the day in Wales. Exceptional skill would no longer be seen only in flashes of individual genius, rather the game would be designed in such a way as to provide constant channels down which genius such as Gould's could flow. There were particular reasons why this philosphy should have its first flowering in Newport. Since Blackheath's first visit to Newport, there had been a desire to imitate the London club's forward strength. Newport appointed a succession of forwards as captain at the same time as they moved slowly to accept the four three-quarter game. They played and learned from a wide variety of clubs outside Wales. They welcomed working-class players into their ranks. Above all else, perhaps, they thought about concerted moves and practised them to perfection. So much so, in fact, that they were accused by opponents of being a professional side. In so far as their approach is concerned, the adjective can stand. Newport possessed a gymnasium in which for at least one night a week the team would now train regularly. This mostly involved the use of athletic apparatus, but passing and re-passing of the ball at speed amongst forwards and backs was an essential element. Self-denying ordinances over social dances and the use of alcohol were taken for granted. This unusual level of discipline was initiated and maintained by the leadership of a player whose considerable skills as a forward were only surpassed by his capabilities as a captain. T. C. Graham, who later became a minister, had come from Tyneside to work in Newport. He would play 12 times for Wales between 1890 and 1895, but be remembered above all for his captaincy of Newport in 1891-92, their invincible season, when 29 games were won, 4 drawn and 72 goals, 95 tries scored against 3 goals, 5 tries. W. J. T. Collins wrote of him that he, in addition to constant practice, 'called for the study of theory and the understanding of tactics; the dressing room became a school for footballers on the lines of a Workers' Education class where, in the give-and-take of discussion, tutor and students make a co-operative effort'.

Graham exerted his tact, his sympathy and a sardonic brand of humour over an exceptional pack of forwards — Jim Hannan, his vice-captain, was a fourteen stone boilermaker, capped 18 times between 1889 and 1895, and a masterly tactician who could wheel a scrum at will to let his back row dribble the ball away; Wallace Watts, exceptionally fast and adept with foot or hand, was a native of Chipping Norton who had come on a business apprenticeship in Newport, returned to play in 1891 and won twelve caps between 1892 and 1896; Arthur Boucher, (13 caps 1892-1897), a native of Somerset who became a shipping executive, was an amazing all-round footballer who was selected as a forward for Wales but also named, on more than one occasion, as reserve for either centre position. The muscle of Harry Day (5 caps 1892-94) and the science of Harry Packer (7 caps 1891 to 1897 and later a national selector) ensured a very strong presence, in all the Welsh packs of this period, of forwards who conceived their job as releasing their backs but who were willing and able to pass and inter-pass amongst themselves as well as with the three-quarters. The result, then, was speed, skill and science to an extent then unknown in rugby football. Matches with other Welsh clubs, especially against a Swansea side that could boast of W. J. Bancroft and the James Brothers, were titanic struggles. Victory meant brass bands, speeches and cheering crowds.

On 26 March 1892 Newport travelled to Swansea knowing that if they won, their record would be almost unassailable. They had the Gould brothers, the speedy C. J. Thomas, and, behind that formidable pack, their well-matched halves, the frail but deceptive Percy Phillips and the resolute F. C. Parfitt. Tom England, at full-back, had only missed his cap in 1890 because of injury. He was now destined to see Billy Bancroft of Swansea win thirty-three consecutive caps in the position. Swansea had Bancroft, Evan and David James at half, and internationals past and future in the pack, in William Bowen, Mills and Deacon. The ground was dry, for the elements had retreated before this human spectacle and there was no wind, rain or sun. A stern unrelenting game of cut and thrust was broken up just before half-time when Gould swayed through to dodge over for a try which was converted. He then dropped a goal, but Swansea still turned round with grim determination — Cole scored a try that Bancroft converted and now the Whites pressed hard for the equalizing drop goal worth four points. Townsend Collins in 1914 recalled the absorbing contest of mate and check-mate:

> The great 'W. J.' could drop goals from any angle on the Swansea ground, and the game was to heel to David James, so that he might pass to Evan, and

his brother should transfer to Bancroft, who was close up for the purpose of dropping a goal . . . In the main the closing stages of the game resolved themselves into a contest between the Brothers James and Bancroft on the one side and Parfitt, Phillips and Arthur Gould on the other. Immediately David James had the ball, Parfitt went for him and put him down. Generally the ball was gone, but never once did Parfitt fail to get his man. As he passed Phillips dashed at Evan and forced him to transfer while Arthur Gould dashed up between Bancroft's foot and the goal, forcing him to swerve away in the effort to get in his kick, whereupon he was met on the other side by Percy Phillips who left Evan James, immediately he had passed, to support Gould in circumventing Bancroft.

Newport won the day; Swansea were not disgraced. Yet only three weeks before in Dublin, Wales, fielding six Newport players and five from Swansea, had crashed to her third defeat of the season for the first time. Achievements at club level were not reflected in the national side. The James brothers were not available for the opening game at Blackheath's ground against England which Wales lost by three goals, one try to nothing but their presence at St. Helen's for the first visit by Scotland brought a crowd of some 12,000 and unprecedented numbers of visitors on excursions from Newport, Cardiff and Llanelli which matched, said the booking clerks of the Great Western Railway, the numbers present in National Eisteddfod week. Wales lost, more narrowly, yet again. The value of playing eight forwards against nine to accommodate four three-quarters was examined minutely in the press. The overwhelming opinion, surely inspired by what could be seen at club level in Wales, was that it was not the system that was lacking but its lack of application by the particular men chosen, who could not reach the consistency of club players in a one-off game.

Either way, the year 1892 was marked by problems. At the Scottish game in Swansea, the English referee so irritated the crowd by some of his decisions that he was physically attacked. Mr. Hodgson had gone so far as to disallow a penalty taken by Evan James. He only reached the Mackworth Hotel by coach because Gould accompanied him. When the Match Committee met to choose the team for the Irish game they formally regretted the behaviour of the Swansea crowd but went on to request the R.F.U. to 'appoint competent men to act as referees in international matches'. It was not an isolated incident for a week later at Rodney Parade when Swansea played, the referee, William Wilkins of Llanelli (the Treasurer of the W.F.U.) was snowballed by the spectators. Mobbing of referees along with verbal abuse increased in the early months of the new season. Nor was the W.F.U. at one with itself in its treatment of referees. At the Swansea - Cardiff game on 7 November 1892 which Cardiff won by a try, the referee was attacked after a very rough game in which he first gave and then, upon appeals from Cardiff, disallowed a drop goal. That night in Swansea hotels the result was chalked up as 'Cardiff won by one referee and one try to a drop goal'. Newspaper offices were attacked for printing the 'correct' score. Stones thrown at the referee took out the eye of a by-stander. Swansea's appeal to the W.F.U. was, later that month, upheld by the Committee who reversed the referee's decision on the grounds that he should not have changed his mind once made up; in February 1893, after a great deal of East-West bitterness, a Special General Meeting restored the position. In the course of 1893 a Referees Society under the auspices of the W.F.U. was formed and given, after a year, slightly more independence. But the short supply of able officials who were, in any case, generally associated with the game in some other capacity did not diminish accusations of partisanship nor lessen the violent behaviour of supporters whose clubs were severely warned for not controlling them. Referees intent on avoiding trouble sometimes used their authority instead of rules. Thus when Cardiff beat Pontypridd at the latter's ground before 2,000 spectators the Pontypridd half-backs persistently fed the balls crookedly into the scrums: the referee, instead of penalizing them, put the ball in for them himself. But then this referee was Arthur Gould.

The game's growing popularity (crowds of 10,000 to 12,000 at needle matches between the big clubs or to see English visitors) amongst the public was outstripping the haphazard control enjoyed by the W.F.U., and not only on the playing field. As early as April 1892, the James brothers were rumoured to have left Swansea and to be settled in West Hartlepool. They played a trial for Swansea in September for all that, yet in October were certainly in the north playing for Broughton Rangers. The Swansea club claimed they had left without a proper transfer after demanding, and being refused, payments of £1 10s. 0d. a week. The W.F.U. were annoyed at the Lancashire Rugby Union's cavalier treatment of their own rules and appealed to the R.F.U. who, after exhaustive enquiry, partially exonerated Broughton Rangers whilst at the same time declaring the brothers to be professionals for requesting money in Wales. It would not be the last that was heard of the James', although they were now placed in a limbo world until January 1896, when the R.F.U. relented. The R.F.U. was soon to have its own problems over 'broken-time' payments amongst the northern clubs turned into the biggest crises in its own history. For the W.F.U. the issue of overt or covert professionalism was also a sore one; on this occasion, since the James' did not benefit to any extent, they were soon arguing that the technical infringement of the transfer rules, which they codified more strictly in 1893 anyway, should not damn the brothers everlastingly and that the punishment meted out was sufficient. Besides, at the A.G.M. in May 1892 W. H. Gwynn, of Swansea and a representative on the International Board, had declared that the professional rules in existence were not only 'totally unnecessary' but also 'unsuitable to the game as played in Wales'. Their existence, he argued, did not alter the fact that they 'had been constantly broken by the majority of Welsh clubs' and 'had never been enforced'. Times were to change. At that time it must have seemed hard to working men like the James' that the successful Newport side of that year were each given a 'handsome gold watch' raised by public subscription and £5 per man by *Pearson's Monthly* for being the best side in the kingdom. In 1893 Gould was made Clerk of Works at Newport.

At an early stage the James' defection pinpointed the link between gate money and entertainment, for they had not only built upon the advances of earlier half-backs, they had initiated tactical ploys which were effective *and* crowd pleasing. They were the Merlins of Welsh rugby and their lineage has proved as long as that of the graceful 'King' Arthurs begotten by Gould. *His* party piece after a game was 'Sister Mary walked like that', but Evan and David James clowned *on* the field, literally walking on their hands from touch flag to goal post for the assembled crowd. Rugby in Wales was a popular game not merely because of some success or local patriotism, but because it displayed an excellence that was not confined in spirit, that was questing for a rounded presentation of physical and mental agility. The James brothers were, literally, a marvel. The music halls were packed with Chinese wrestlers, fire-eaters, strong ladies and illusionists of all kinds. In a world hemmed in by pressing realities the release of fantasy held a strong appeal. Rugby had become people's theatre and the James' were aware of their dramatic qualities. During the cold, rainy winter of 1893 the sports reporter of the *South Wales Daily News* reflected with more accuracy than he realized:

> Oh this terrible fascination of football . . . notwithstanding the weather . . . the multitude flocked to the different grounds just in the old sweet way, and stood patiently out in the open . . . utterly heedless of the falling rain and slush under the foot. This, as we know, is nothing new but how is it to be accounted for? To any sport, amusement or pastime, indoor or outdoor, bar

football, bad weather simply spells no gate and empty benches. People who will hang back from visiting a well-lighted theatre or concert room in moderately bad weather will yet rush eagerly to damp, slushy football fields in torrents of rain to witness even a second rate match and bravely dare possibilities in the shape of rheumatism and incipient consumption. Truly football is a wonderful game!

The people of Swansea, for whom the reinstatement of the brothers as amateurs was signalled by a searchlight playing over the town, recognized that the play of their 'curly-headed marmosets' was designed to please. Their first game for Swansea after this was held up until they had both taken a bow from both touchlines. They were the Swansea jackanapes of the football field, exasperating staider traditionalists because of their inventiveness and trickery. They were physically as well as figuratively an extension of the individual player, working the scrum alternatively, passing to each other at speed, never releasing the ball until they had left their opposing halves in their bewildering wake, shaking their curls from side to side as they ran to confuse further the unfortunate enemy. They were also, of course, in their occupation as labourers in Swansea's copper works, direct representatives of the people who flocked to see them. Their father had worked in tin mines in Cornwall where he married before returning to the town which was one of the metal centres of the world. Swansea was a much older town than Newport. Its growth around tinplate, steel, copper, zinc, nickel, coal and the docks created the sprawling settlements on the hills around the bay and in the lower Swansea valley. This town, of some 120,000 people by the turn of the century, was highly conscious of its role as the metropolis of West Wales. Here, too, rugby provided a focus for community involvement that did not reject all classes and occupations in the locality. Evan James was born in 1869 and David in 1867. They were, respectively, 5 foot 7½ inches, 10½ stone and 5 foot 6 inches, 10 stone. Together they progressed from the Harlequins of St. Thomas, the downtown district by the banks of the Tawe where they lived and worked, into Swansea Seconds and by 1888-9 into the Firsts. Behind a large and effective pack, they were 'like squirrels behind the forwards', able to practice and perfect their technique until by 1891 their tackling, passing and general quickness were legendary. When Swansea beat their great rivals from Tinopolis, Llanelli, in March 1891, by five goals and two tries to nil, 'their tricks with the ball and with their bodies remind one more of circus performances than of football contests,' whilst a Cardiff reporter wryly observed of a club match 'I admired very much their adroitness at putting the ball into the scrummage. They always take care to swing it in . . . well under the back rank of their forwards'. Arthur Gould, who played with and against them, reflected more soberly that they had thought out many moves and were clever enough to bring them off in attack as well as being deadly tacklers in defence. They would use every ounce of the muscles developed in carrying red-hot copper ores about in confined spaces. Gould, in his own retirement, commented sympathetically on their final move to professional rugby, but his own experienced view of their combination of skill and resolution removes a little of the magic these rugby alchemists sprinkled on the history of the game:

> From some reports . . . one might be led to think the Jameses were not a bit like ordinary players, but that they played some marvellous, bewildering sort of game, with conjuring or legerdemain introduced into football. They are not conjurors but they are an exceptionally clever pair of halves who . . . have brought half-back play to a state of perfection . . . They never wrangle, they hardly speak on the field, and no matter how much they are knocked about they go on playing as if they were proof against injury.

It was precisely the elevation of artisanship to artistry through the application of constant practice to inborn talent that marked the James brothers as, in a different way, it did Gould. Later there would be Welsh half-backs who would represent one or other strain; rarely would both elements coalesce in one body and mind. Here, at the start of the game's first great period in Wales, these brothers began a tradition whose very centre revolves around fact and fantasy until what is real is what human ingenuity creates, not what is given or merely accepted. What was expected of the game in the wake of such players often dictated satisfaction or frustration, and always the stories that embroidered possibility into the fabric. After the 1904 game in which Wales defeated Scotland at Swansea a reporter on the crowded trains where past matches and players were being discussed overheard a Swansea man advising a Cardiff supporter to make their half-backs practice more as they always did in Swansea — ' "There was the brothers James for instance — they was always practising. If they hadn't a ball to practice with, they practised on anything that was handy — kettles, pots, pans, copper ladles. They played the passing game with the baby sometimes, and although the poor nipper was often dropped they kept on practising. They was terrors for practising," — "Oh, you beautiful liar" said a Plasmarl man'.

If such wit, within and around the game, were to flourish after the early 1890s in a society whose size and pretensions were altering dramatically as people continued to pour in to man those industries which were making South Wales a central hub of the British Empire, then the organization of rugby in Wales required stricter control. In a nutshell, the cavalier days of a Richard Mullock could not survive the increasingly structured world of corporate associations and social hierarchies that were knitting together a society of diverse interests and tastes. For rugby the codifying activities of the International Board defined the body of law against which the contingencies of play could operate; the administrators of the game in Wales had allowed it to find its feet in the 1870s and 1880s, now closer supervision was required. Mullock was a victim of this process. Always an impetuous man, he had not always managed affairs smoothly in his tenure of office even if he had always responded generously when the Union was in financial difficulty. To an extent they now reciprocated for at the A.G.M. held in the Angel Hotel, Cardiff on 10 September 1892, they voted the retiring Secretary, Richard Mullock, a testimonial of 100 guineas. The ex-secretary informed the meeting that he would continue to take a great interest in Welsh football and thanked the members for their courtesy during his years of office, but he also hoped 'before he left that all bygones should be bygones and that they would all bury the hatchet'. The question of his resignation had been broached previously as William Wilkins, the Treasurer from Llanelli, reminded the meeting, adding that he knew 'there was a feeling that Mr Mullock had been a little dilatory . . . but they would all agree that if it had not been for Mr Mullock's services they might never have had a Union today'. Horace Lyne, on the other hand did not, despite Newport connections, mince his words when he declared that it was time the Union had a new secretary for although Mullock's 'heart was in his work and . . . he did his work to the best of his ability . . . A paid secretary was a man they could handle in a much better way than an Honorary Secretary (laughter) — and they had a much better chance of things being properly done (Hear, hear, and laughter)'.

Nevertheless, when voting began Richard Mullock was still elected to the Committee as one of the three Committee members to represent the East; there were three from the West, and one from the Mid District serving Aberdare, Rhondda and Merthyr areas in addition. H. S. Lyne was one of four vice-presidents also elected on a geographical basis (Lyne and W. D. Phillips of Cardiff for the East; E. V. Pegge of Briton Ferry and Gavin Henry of Llanelli for the West). The new Secretary was to be the former half-back W. H. Gwynn of Swansea who just pipped W. H. Treatt of Cardiff by 28 votes to 26. This momentous A. G. M. which had, therefore, dropped its original pilot without too much regret went on to discuss the advisability of a league system. This was defeated amidst complaints that the smaller clubs who had been joining the Union did not always possess the enclosed grounds and experience they should have before pushing for changes. The voices would echo and re-echo on these themes down to the present but the voice of one of the W.F.U.'s moving spirits would not be heard much longer. In February 1893, a couple of weeks after Wales's first great triumph in international rugby, Mullock resigned from the Committee. Our glimpses of him after this are desultory, and, indeed, melancholy. He is declared a bankrupt in April 1893 though appears to continue in the printing business since it is his firm which binds the testimonial book that he illuminated personally for A. J. Gould in 1897; in 1902 he is sued in court for £3 worth of goods and pleads that he had been a commercial traveller until 1900 when he gave up. He was selling black-and-white drawings which earned him £1 a month with which he found difficulty in supporting a wife and six children; then he emigrated, to Africa. The enterprise Mullock had helped found voted his successor a stipend of 50 guineas a year from 1894 when the pre-fix Honorary was dropped from the office of Secretary.

Of more pressing concern to the W.F.U. in 1892 and 1893 was the ordering of those features of rugby which would encourage the type and development of the game in Wales. As early as March 1892 they decided to propose to the I.B. that a try's value be increased from 2 to 3 points (with 5 for a goal) and that the penalty goal be 3 points with 'any other goal' at 4 points. When the I.B. in July ratified their new rules, some were to the advantage of the Welsh game, especially the penalizing of obstruction of opposing half-backs. Wales's proposed alteration of scoring values was thrown out. However, for club games the W.F.U. decided to go ahead anyway from September 1892, with the upgrading of the try. At that meeting which saw Mullock's resignation, the 'South Wales Union' (as they still called themselves on occasion) declared a credit balance of £794 11s. 8d. but also congratulated themselves on 'not having the low status of Association football in playing for money'. There is no doubt that a crucial factor in keeping Wales within the amateur fold during the next few years of crisis was the determination of the Welsh administrators to give rugby in Wales as high a social status as possible. Given the uncertain, kaleidoscopic nature of South Walian society, this meant, in practice, having a peer group outside Wales with which to compare. At the same time it required a broad definition of 'Welsh' for rugby purposes, so that from 1892 on to 1894 the W.F.U. pressed for a continuation of the right of any home Union to play in international teams those who represented club football, irrespective of birth or original residence, in that country. Welsh rugby was already distinctive in its own right. Now in the hinterland of the coastal towns and ports, valley clubs were beginning to add their own ingredients. The final trial for December 1892 was held in Pontypridd, twelve miles north of Cardiff at the confluence of the Rhondda, Cynon and Taff valleys, in order to encourage 'the rising Rhondda valley club'. It is perhaps a sign of the relative ignorance of the geography of this hinterland, whose population was swelling beyond that of the coast, that the press should refer to a club very conscious of its town-status, in the same manner as a Neath or a Llanelli, as a Rhondda club. The full impact of working-class participation in the game was still a few years away. When it came, the accusations against Welsh inventive ploys as 'cheating' would be allied to slurs on the gentlemanly status of Welsh footballers. But by that time the openness of the Welsh game in its mirror image of Welsh society (both, from the 'populist' Lloyd George to the idea of a 'progressive' community, decidedly more American than English) would have produced a success which could ignore such sour grapes. Few can have believed the first taste of wine would come in 1893.

Apart from the score-less draw in Llanelli in 1887 and the try sneaked by 'Buller' Stadden at Dewsbury in 1890 to bring a victory, England had beaten Wales seven times since 1881, never re-crossing the Severn undefeated. Doubtless, but for the years of 1888 and 1889 when no match was played, the sequence would have been longer. Sports commentators in the London press were not too convinced of the efficacy of Welsh back play, nor the new-fangled forward play designed to serve it. They complained that Welsh clubs engaged in 'scraping in the scrums' instead of the old-fashioned 'hard work'. This was victory 'through the miserable tricks of one or two men in the front ranks of the pack'. Besides, in the English trial the North had attempted the four three-quarter game ('the Welsh abortion') and failed at it. In general the English side were thought superior in physique and ability. The London *Star* took 'the representatives of the Rose' — including Stoddart, the captain, and five other renowned Blackheath players — to defeat 'the Taffies' and vindicate 'the old system'. Budd, the leading English commentator, was not quite so sanguine nor quite so gratuitously insulting as to refer, as did so many others of this era, to 'Taffyland' for he pointed out that the Welsh 'are going to play the game according to their own ideas, and have taken three men outside the scrimmage and five forwards from the ever victorious Newport team. Here we shall have a much better idea as to the real value of the tactics Wales invented, and the followers of the rugby code of rules will await the result of the game at Cardiff . . . with much more curiosity, than the international game with "gallant little Wales" has usually provoked'.

The Match Committee had indeed decided to rely heavily on Newport, for in addition to Gould at right centre they played Newport's Percy Phillips and the new cap, Parfitt, at half-back with Graham, Hannan, Watts, Day and Boucher in the pack. On the other hand, the playing of the club pair at half-back was partly dictated by the enforced absence of the James brothers, whilst advocates of club combination objected to playing Conway Rees of Llanelli and McCutcheon of Swansea as left centre and wing, instead of Bert Gould and T. W. Pearson of Cardiff. The respective demands of East and West Wales had to be met! Percy ('Sparrow') Phillips had won his only previous cap in 1892 (his sixth and last would come in 1894) and was, for all his elusiveness in attack, neither bold in defence nor an effective kick. He was baled out by Parfitt, the first of whose nine caps this would be, who made up for his partner's deficiencies in tight play, but Phillips's real contribution, unlike the absent James', was that he could link with his backs. And this meant, for Newport and Wales, the incomparable Gould who would run with Phillips, one or other having made a break, shoulder to shoulder, bewildering defenders with their inter-passing or feinting at speed. Gould was at the height of his powers, a sinuous, deceptive runner, all bone and sinew, able to do 100 yards in 10.2 seconds and capable of lasting the pace of a hectic game. His description of centre play necessities given to the Revd Marshall a month after this game describes the theory that lay behind the scintillating application and why the presence of his Newport half-backs proved a key factor:

> The first essential is that the centre should be able to 'snap' the pass from the half-back at speed . . . It is never any trouble to me. I can get the ball anyhow and take it on the run . . . The pass should be swift and low . . . 2 or 3 feet from the ground. The centre can then take the ball on the move . . . and baffle the opposing centre, for if in motion he can wriggle about and the opposing back does not know what to do . . . by snapping the ball quickly the centre is past the pack and the half back before they know he has the ball.
>
> Speed is not so desirable as cleverness and judgement in knowing in which direction the centre should run. By cleverness I mean being able to take your opposing men off your wings . . . never run wings on to the touch line . . . should always carry the ball in front of him in his hands and never tuck it under his arm . . . should keep looking at each side, watching the favourable

moment to pass. If the tackler does not come to me, I go on till he does come, and then I pass . . . only to a man in a better position than myself.

On his right wing Gould had Norman Biggs, member of a Cardiff rugby family, with two caps to his credit and five more to come in 1893 and 1894. He was a good, all-round athlete who had played for Cambridge and Richmond. He was twenty-three years old, destined to die aged thirty-eight when, as a superintendent of police in Nigeria, he was ambushed. His brother Selwyn Biggs would win eight caps at half-back between 1895 and 1900. Inside the Welsh captain was the stocky Conway Rees, capped once in 1892, 1893 and then 1894 when he would also captain Oxford University.

The left wing, W. McCutcheon was a Swansea boy, capped in 1891 and 1892, who went to play rugby union for Oldham and won the last of his seven caps in 1894. The three non-Newportonians in the forwards were all experienced — A. F. Hill of Cardiff had won the first of his eight caps in 1885 and would add now another six. He was a burly man of considerable dash. C. B. ('Boomer') Nicholl was capped from Llanelli in 1891 and captained Cambridge in 1893, when he was described as 'The most distinguished member of the least distinguished college . . . fond of smoking and a connoisseur of exhilarating beverages, in which strength rather than delicacy of bouquet is a predominant feature'. This did not prevent him winning fifteen caps by the time he finished with international rugby in 1896 using his height and reach as a complement to strength (6 foot 2 inches and 14 stone 8 lb) in the lineout. Frank Mills, born in Mountain Ash, and in his twentieth year, was an ever-present in Welsh packs from 1892-95. He played first with Swansea and then Cardiff, winning the last of his 13 caps against England that year.

Behind this impressive pack, winning his tenth cap, in what would go on to be an unbroken sequence of thirty-three caps from 1890 to 1901, was the first of the exceptional full-backs that Wales has produced. W. J. ('Billy') Bancroft had taken his first cap when he stepped up as second-choice for his injured rival T. W. England, but by 1893, despite criticisms of his 'Gallery' tactics, he was immovable. Bancroft was born in Swansea in 1871 and moved, when quite young, to live with his grandfather, groundsman of St. Helen's, in a cottage in the ground itself. Like Gould in Newport, Bancroft practised, kicking the ball from all angles of the field, even replacing corner flag with ball to kick inswinging goals from there. His prowess as a place and drop kicker was unequalled in his lifetime. Cool, dapper and astute, never seeming to hurry, never troubled in fielding high balls, Bancroft was an infuriating opponent who loved to tease lumbering forwards to catch him as he side-stepped (often laterally) out of their annoyed clutches before, on the run, he would kick for touch with heart-breaking accuracy. Bancroft sometimes paid for his tantalizing runs by being roughly handled but it was mostly very rare for this little man (5 foot 5½ inches but over 11 stone) his hair brilliantined and centre-parted, to be ruffled in his role as the Fred Astaire of Welsh rugby. He had graduated through junior grades of rugby to play at the age of seventeen in the Swansea First XV. Before he finished he had been the first Welshman in two Triple Crown sides and he had captained his country twelve times. A cobbler by profession, W. J. Bancroft went on to play as wicket-keeper and batsman for Glamorgan before they attained first class status in 1921. Naturally, he opened the batting.

The players, insured for £1 10s. 0d. a week by the W.F.U., assembled only on the morning of the game. A series of excursion trains were to run from Llanelli in the west and Bristol across the Severn, to arrive before 2 p.m. Reserved seats were 4s. each and hard to obtain. The winter weather of the week before had been so severe that there were doubts about the playing surface up to the eve of the match. Frost had penetrated the ground even through a protective covering of straw but the Cardiff groundsman had the idea of thawing it out by constantly burning coal in a 'fire-devil' or brazier made from buckets pierced with holes and mounted on bricks. Iron boiler plates were spread on the ground around the 500 fire-devils which, burning over 18 tons of coal through Friday and up to 11 a.m. on Saturday, softened the ground sufficiently to play. There was, of course, no shortage of coal in Cardiff, for the phenomenal rise of the town to its position as 'Coal Metropolis' of the world was still on an upward curve. At the turn of the nineteenth century Cardiff's population of some 2,000 were gathered in a small market town around their ancient castle; by 1891 there were 130,000 scattered in a 3 mile radius of divergent communities ranging from shipowners and coal merchants and shopkeepers to coal-trimmers, tippers, seamen and railwaymen, from Welsh and English to segregated streets of Irish, Lascars and Chinese. From the 1880s the wide tree-lined avenues of Cardiff suburbia were taking the well-to-do away from the city centre into which the Taff Vale railway line and lesser valley branches poured coal in an endless stream. The population of both Glamorgan as a whole, and Cardiff in particular, rose by over three times the British national average between 1861 and 1911. In that year Cardiff's population had risen to 182,000 and the town had become a Welsh Chicago that hummed and thrived around its traffic in coal, timber and money. At the pierhead around Mountstuart Square the Coal Exchange, built in the 1880s, clustered around itself banks and offices, for ships and coals, who bought, with the money they turned over more rapidly than any money had been turned over before in Wales, the architectural appurtenances, from columns and gables to balconies and staircases, that a dozen cultures and ages had spawned. With its enticing arcades and swelling hotel and shop fronts, as well as the self-conscious dignity of its municipal buildings, Cardiff was engaged in showing a public face that could indicate its importance. Chicago staged a World's Fair in 1893 which was another way of pointing out the daily fair the meat-packing centre of the West had become; Cardiff, with its 18 tons of burning coal to save a mere football match, was a spectacle in itself. Only it was more, already, than a *mere* football match. Many, then and now, have tried to account for the grip of the game on the imagination of the people by seeing it as a form of escapism. A. J. Gould, writing in 1898, was keen to defend rugby against the allegation that it interfered with work and careers (after all his was a society produced by the sale of labour and its proceeds), since he saw it as an addition — 'The life of the toiling thousands is hard and uninteresting enough, the mind of the professional and business man is vexed with the cares of his occupation, and it is good that football should come once a week to take them out of themselves'. This was to sell football short for, just as the outward shape and design of the Welsh metropolis was not an incidental to its growth but an intimate part of its inhabitants' attitudes to and perceptions of life, so the game had moved beyond provision of sensible or rational recreation for gentlemen of all classes. Instead of escape it was, at its highest levels in Wales, about intense involvement. Rugby was an arena now for the display of excellence. Players once on the field might become self-absorbed to the point of being oblivious of their audience just as an actor may sink his own personality into his part, but the presence of spectators is not an incidental either for those who, like the James', played to the crowd or, like Gould, played for it in a manner whose self-possession made him an individual extension of the crowd's collectivity. His own man, and therefore everyone's. *The Northern Athlete* in 1894 told its Newcastle readership: 'If you want to see Gould in all his autocratic glory, go to an international. He walks on the field of battle with the pomp of an Emperor, and thrusting his hands deeply into his trouser pockets, surveys the cheering crowd with that equanimity born of supreme confidence'. The virtues of rugby, and hence its crowd-pleasing, were not, for the mass, the moralists' exhortation to the lessons of hard-knocks, exercise and fair play (though these would grow in assumed value as clubs and schools spread) but the dazzle of something done supremely well, the acceptance of risk in an ordered world, the imaginative unity forged between participant and spectator in triumph or defeat or struggle. Above all else the ability to see that it is not 'only a game' but that games are, in modern industrial societies, key framers of man's need for physical expression. Rugby in Wales (as with other sports in other countries) was not a diversion from 'real' life, it was a playing-out of true capacities and real aspirations. No art flourishes in a vacuum. Welsh rugby derived its essential features from the interaction, in the 1880s and early 1890s, of a rather rough-and-ready traditional sport and the needs of its society to refine the game in the interests of the mutual satisfaction of player and spectator. Rugby was innovation, improvization within rules, it was a finished product in a society that had moved a long way from the satisfactions of craftsmanship, it was a successfull blend of individual and co-operative effort and it was a vehicle for patriotism that would come to stand for the name of the new Wales alongside its primary economic products and consequent political clout. Rowe Harding, Welsh wing and captain of the 1920s, wrote in 1929 in a way that, despite the string of defeats of the 1920s, explains the path down which Welsh rugby would move:

> The Rugby player during the course of a game is living life at its most intoxicating. There is movement, energy, grace, strength, fear, intelligence, competition, everything. When our economists have settled the problem of living, what remains but to live? Like all fascinating things, however, Rugby has its dangers . . . To say that Rugby is good for the health is wrong. It is played above the natural pace of living and imposes a tremendous strain upon every organ in the body . . . So many of the greatest exponents of Rugby have fallen into an early grave.

Rowe Harding would have appreciated the tension that was gathering around the game on 7 January 1893. Once more Wales had a chance to turn parochial pleasures into a national gratification. The national side had not yet emerged as a team from the shadows of patronizing toleration. The biennial English incursion was still a jaunt to foreign parts inhabited by excitable, rather amusing, natives. The correspondent of the London *Morning Leader* captured the tone of mingled superiority, disdain and puzzlement in his journey down on the English team's train on the Friday afternoon:

> We had a saloon to ourselves, or at least what the Great Western Railway were pleased to call a saloon, but what others would have dignified with the

name of a horse-box with seats . . . At Gloucester a crowd peered in to see the men who would beat Wales but Gloucester people are of a melancholy cast and we got no fun out of them . . . At Newport the crowd was much more aggressive and entertaining . . . one of them . . . with prophetic insight brought down the house by remarking that 'Wales would win by one Gould to nil'. On arrival at Cardiff we were literally mobbed by the excited populace, and it was wearing on for midnight too. On our way round to the Angel Hotel a strange, weird uncanny sight presented itself. The ground on which the match of the morrow was to be played was like a scene from Dante's *Inferno*. Imagine if you can an acre or more of ground heaped several feet high with live coals from 500 fires blazing far up into the dark night. Dozens of dark, ghoul-like figures were threading their way about the fires, heaping on fresh fuel, while the falling snow rendered the scene one of the most unique and romantic ever seen on a football field. Like Wellington at Waterloo your reporter walked over the field at midnight, and found it in a fairly good condition.

The day broke cold with no snow but a keen, slicing wind. The crowd that milled around the streets by mid-day would provide a Welsh record of perhaps as many as 20,000 crammed into the grandstand and adjacent terraces, with others packed in on the make-shift terrace that ran the field's length opposite. The teams came out before 3 p.m., lined up and kicked off without any further ceremony. The English side, playing with the wind, were noticeably taller and heavier. On a slippery ground the English pack of nine forwards carried some early scrums and when Stoddart, after a good run, went into touch on the Welsh 25, Sammy Woods, the great Wellington forward, took the ball from the lineout. He was tackled on the line but gave to Lohden of Blackheath who went over. Four minutes had not passed. Woods failed to convert, but it was to be the only respite Wales would have in the half as the English forwards pinned them to their own line. The Welsh pack were, at times, being lifted off their feet in the scrums. Tom Graham anxiously consulted Gould and was told to hang on. The English halves, Marshall and de Winton, snapped away behind a rampaging pack who rushed irresistibly through the Welsh team. Marshall scored after a heel in the Welsh 25 and Lockwood the Dewsbury right-wing converted. At half-time Wales were 7 - 0 down. Nonetheless a couple of Welsh passing bouts and a run by Bancroft had given some heart to Welsh supporters.

Early in the second half England, though now against the wind, surged ahead when Marshall dodged over the line from close in after the English forwards stormed through once more. The conversion was missed, but there can have been few who gave Wales any further chance. The tide of the game now turned at forward, however. The big English forwards could not maintain the game at the pace they had set, whilst an early penalty goal and two conversions had been missed. Now 'Boomer' Nicholl first disconcerted them by urging his team, in Welsh, to even greater efforts (it must have disconcerted the Welsh as well since few of the pre-1900 teams spoke Welsh) and then, breaking through a line-out with the ball, raced away until transferring to Hannan who gave to Gould on the half-way line. The Welsh captain darted away from Alderson, dodged Lockwood and, outpacing Field, the full-back, put the ball between the posts. Bancroft kicked the goal. At last the guile of Phillips was seen in teasing little runs that opened up the field. Gould took such a pass on the Welsh 25 and moved the ball smartly to Conway Rees who slipped a high tackle by Stoddart and transferred to Biggs who had, at his speed, a clear run-in from the half-way line. Once the ball was moved in this fashion by the Welsh backs the hopelessness of the three three-quarter defence was exposed. Bancroft failed to convert. The score was now 7 - 9 against Wales. A Welsh reporter crowed 'Now came what we had all been looking for. Finding themselves getting worsted, the Englishmen who had beforehand proudly announced their intention to stand or fall by the three three-quarter game, brought Woods out of the scrummage'. Almost immediately Gould dribbled the ball to the English line from half-way only to miss the touch-down. From the ensuing drop-out, with Woods restored to the pack, the English forwards managed a foot-rush, picked the ball up and Marshall went over in the corner for his third try. It was unconverted yet surely decisive, at 11 points to 7 with less than ten minutes of play remaining. Welsh resolve refused to crumble. The most exciting international game seen to that date swung yet again. Phillips took a swift heel, broke away and found the inevitable Gould waiting for his superbly timed pass. Gould, 'gliding snake-like through the thickest throng', swallowed up the distance and scored his second try in a position easy for Bancroft's conversion attempt. Inexplicably the Swansea full-back failed. To the end the Welshmen pressed as they had been pressed earlier until an infringement gave Bancroft a penalty attempt, on the English 25 and at a wide angle, near the touch-line. There would be no more chances. Accounts of what now happened differ. Some believed they saw Gould trying to place the ball for Bancroft on the frozen ground and failing to keep it upright so that Bancroft, against his captain's orders, decided to drop-kick for goal. On the other hand Gould, in his recollections in 1898, stated categorically 'The ball was given to Bancroft to drop. With a grand kick he dropped the ball over the centre of the bar'. For an encore Bancroft screwed the ball away four yards from the English line from outside his own goal-mouth and Wales had won by 12 points to 11, though the first defeat of England on Welsh soil would have been a 14 - 14 draw under Welsh scoring values.

The pitch was invaded. Gould was carried shoulder-high back to the Angel Hotel, cheered all the way by supporters and girls waving from windows and balconies. The streets and the hotels were packed with celebrators re-living the palpitating effect of the drama. For cooler heads the significance of the game was attributed to the superior combination of the Welsh four three-quarters, though many observers believed the number of Newport men in the team had swayed victory in Wales's direction. Others blamed the English backs for not feeding sufficiently off the undoubted superiority of their forwards. Gould, himself, credited the victory to the nature of South Wales football, and, in essence, he was right:

> . . . our men down here are far more keen upon footballing than you are in the South. Welshmen keep themselves in strict training . . . None of us have an ounce of superfluous flesh . . . Our men don't try to push their opponents. Their game is simply to hold the scrum and heel out to the half-backs. We practise this in our gymnasium at Newport once a week . . . English individual excellence far exceeds our own. With perhaps one or two exceptions we have no brilliant men; the whole secret of our success lies in our combination. We have thought that matter carefully out, and time is beginning to show that the four three-quarter system is the better one. We have not many clubs to choose our players from but that is not greatly against us, for we understand each other's play better and today we have vindicated the contention that combination amongst moderate players is superior to any amount of individual brilliancy.

The remainder of the international season seemed to bear out the centre's words. On 4 February 1893 the same Welsh team, with the replacement of the injured Conway Rees by Bert Gould, took their open, short passing game to Raeburn Place, Edinburgh where on a firm turf on a sunny day they beat Scotland by a penalty goal and three tries (nine points altogether) to nil. More importantly, each of the three tries (Bert Gould, Norman Biggs and McCutcheon) was scored by swift, precision handling amongst the backs. The Welsh press informed its readers that the crowd of 10,000 was 'essentially a well-dressed' one since Scottish football was 'almost exclusively dependent on ex-public schoolboys'. If anything it was the spectacle more than the win, down to Bancroft's kicking of the ball on the full and even fisting it away from him, not to mention his running from defence, which gave Welsh supporters the conviction that the principles of their play had finally triumphed. Gould declared that the other countries' clubs and national sides would be compelled to adopt Welsh methods — 'It will now be the object of the other nations to get into line with Welsh football, and this they will not do until they practise and play the four three-quarter game. It is the game of the future'.

The player of the future upon whose shoulders Gould's mantle would fall had turned out that day in the centre for Cardiff against Bristol. The young Gwyn Nicholls struck an observer not fortunate enough to be in Edinburgh as a 'very promising youngster' who 'kicks well . . . his tackling is good . . . while he passes with precision'. From all sides the sustenance, by such men, of Welsh back play became the rallying cry. W. H. Gwynn, in Marshall's volume on rugby published in 1892, and practically all the Welsh backs, in articles or interviews, set out the technicalities of four three-quarter play as if they were in possession of a rugby rosetta stone. Not quite the thermodynamic intricacies of later coaching manuals but complex enough for those critics who still considered the 'pretty' Welsh a trifle effete.

Sam Lee, the Irish captain and centre who at Llanelli in March, like the English before him, would deposit and withdraw forwards amongst his three-quarters with all the doubtful trust placed in banks by a W. C. Fields, was uncomplimentary enough to his own pack, after the game they lost by one try to nil, to opine 'A pack of good forwards will beat four three-quarters any day'. Admittedly, with Gould nursing a shoulder injury and brother Bert just scraping in at the flag, it was not a convincing display of 'the game of the future'. Even so, an enthusiastic crowd of around 20,000, some at the lowest admission price of 1s., had seen Wales win her first Triple Crown. The Llanelli town band who entertained the assembly between halves were so unwilling to put that future at risk after Bert Gould had scored his first-half try that the Welsh captain had to ask them to stop playing so that the Irish might have a chance to redeem their fortunes.

By the time the following international season had come round, yet another Gould, (Bert this time), had gone to Barbados as a civil engineer, but the foundations of Welsh fortunes that his try had apparently laid now proved shaky yet again. In the following three seasons Wales only managed one victory a year, against Scotland in 1894 and 1896 at home, and Ireland at home in 1895. England crushed Wales 24 points to 3 in 1894, 14 points to 6 at Swansea in 1895 and, worst of all 25 points to nil (7 tries) at Blackheath in 1896. This last game took place after the Northern Union split that was supposed to have weakened English forward play, and all of them under the new ruling of a try being worth 3 points which the I.B. adopted after the 1893 season. The England side had moved to four three-quarters for the 1894 game, after which the prospect of a superior side *and* a superior system came to haunt Welsh minds. There were moments of relief from the gloom such as Pearson's try against Ireland in 1895 which Bancroft converted to win the game: the try, after some bewildering passing and feinting within the Welsh 25 amongst all the three-quarters and the Welsh outside-half, sent Pearson in from half-way. Then there would be the first cap of Gwyn Nicholls, just under twenty-one years old, 6 foot and 11 stone 6 lb., in January 1896 when Wales beat Scotland 6 points to nil. Nicholls acted as a perfect foil to Gould who was everywhere in defence and attack. He scored one of the two tries on the day he equalled the old cap record of McLagan of Scotland. Nicholls would play two more games with Gould before the greatest centre of the three three-quarter game finally gave way to the player who would take the 'game of the future' where Gould felt it could go.

Until that happened, the strange limbo position of the Welsh international game attracted much comment. The essence of it came to centre not so much on back play as the role and nature of Welsh forwards. Gould himself had confessed after the Scottish victory in 1893 that it was the first time Welsh forwards had managed to hold their own sufficiently to allow the backs free rein; now others worked on the 'mechanical' weaknesses of Welsh play. Admittedly the Irish who won their first Triple Crown when they beat Wales by a penalty goal to nil at Belfast in 1894 owed a great deal to a quagmire of a pitch that neutralized Welsh skills, but their deployment of Rooke and Forrest as winging marauders was an effective counter in its own right, especially since the Welsh three-quarters inclined, in a number of games, to over-elaboration or too much running. Arthur Budd, a fervent advocate of the merits of the old-style English game, delighted in using English victories to extol the merits of physique amongst forwards who were not 'merely utility men to understudy their backs'. The Welsh were dismissed as supreme opportunists in attack yet defensively suspect once their forwards were broken. The Welsh victory of 1893, in this perspective, could be seen as more to do with English forward fatigue than Welsh play. When Wales reeled away from her 25 - 0 drubbing in 1896, the loss of Owen Badger, the Llanelli centre, with a broken collar-bone, after only ten minutes, was seen as no excuse for these apparently ingrained Welsh deficiencies in size and determination. The critics all agreed that Welsh 'science', however enjoyable at club levels, did not translate into the international arena where it was overwhelmed by a modicum of skill allied to 'strength and dash'. Budd now had a field day. 'The game' he asserted 'will be a landmark in history for two reasons. It has proved that in these times, when people are discussing the advisability of making the game more theatrical, in order to please the onlookers, good, sterling forward play is as efficacious as ever, and that the forward, despite every innovation is still the pivot of the situation'. He deepened his cut by adding that the Welsh manner of playing one half-back away from the scrum was a mere frippery. Even within Wales, the earlier optimism was shrouded in the horrific feeling that whatever humiliation England had visited upon the uncertain Welsh in 1881, they could do to the more cocksure team who had visited the Rectory Field in 1896. If this, a copying of England, was required for victory, then Wales, it was felt, might as well give up — 'We cannot' said 'Old Stager' in the *South Wales Daily News*, 'expect to meet our opponents at their own style of play. We do not breed the type of men required to do so'.

What rescued Welsh rugby from the doldrums was a combination of sticking fast to a vision of the game irrespective of victory and a whittling away of that stasis of traditionalism that has so often, then and since, slowed down developments in the game. The first point was carried quite readily by those who believed being 'overwhelmed by sheer force' was no disgrace and that the advancement of the game as game overode consideration of international victories. Tom Graham who played his last international against Scotland in January 1895 when, on an icy pitch, the Scots skated to victory as the Welsh slipped, had thought about forward play as hard as anyone of his generation and in February 1895 he entered the current controversy by airing his views. Graham spoke out against the picking of heavy men merely for their weight, as well as the 'ornamental' wing-forward. He advocated a settled scrummage pattern, a combined shove and light, 'slingy' (12 to 13½ stone) forwards who could run and pass as well as dribble and tackle. The ex-international was describing the kind of light pack, well-versed in wheeling and following up, that Newport had drilled so well. The ideal of the all-round forward sounds, in many ways, remarkably prescient but it neglected two things that were to assume importance both in the interests of sustaining Welsh style and of playing winning rugby — the need for specialist forwards just as there were backs, and the possibility of finding skill in big men. In turn this led to an internal debate on the merits of clubs outside the existing leaders. The spread of club football in the coastal hinterland brought into the open the question not only of fervent working-class support for rugby but also the wider selection of working-men players. Perhaps the different Welsh needed a different type of player. The suggestion was indignantly refuted in the press which saw mere parochial sentiment in the notion that 'an entire pack be seriously picked from the Rhondda valleys'. The spur of defeat plus an ageing pack saw the selectors begin to ring the changes until into the January 1897 pack to face England came Dick Hellings of Llwynypia and Jack Rhapps of Penygraig to join P. C. Dai Evans of Penygraig. The day of the 'Rhondda forward' had dawned. Even the twice-capped Jack Evans of Llanelli was now playing for Llwynypia.

Nothing could be more suitable than that these harbingers of Wales's 'golden era' after 1900 should figure in the last game of Wales's first 'golden boy'. Gould was, in fact, thirty-two when, in the midst of the biggest crisis the W.F.U. has ever faced at international level, he led his team out to meet England on his own home-ground, Rodney Parade. The ground was packed with over 17,000 people despite a blowing, cold rain to see the veteran win his twenty-seventh cap. His defence, never his strong point, was infallible on this occasion as he stiffened Welsh nerves by hurling himself into tackles. The new forwards were equally effective in the tight and the loose; when they tired Gould gave his halves (Biggs of Cardiff and the new cap from Aberavon, Dan Jones) instructions to nurse them by kicking. All three Welsh tries came about after the forwards rushed the ball up in loose play. Appropriately enough Gould gave Dan Jones the last of the three tries, by which Wales won 11 - 0, when, with the English centres converging on him as he went for a loose ball, they hesitated, fatally, waiting for his direction after he had gathered. Gould played the ball with his foot to the scrum-half, who went over unopposed.

It was only the third victory against England but, with it, Wales gave new indications of her capacity to build rugby teams as startlingly novel as the world around them. The *Morning Leader* from London made no bones about it — 'The Rhondda valley forwards won the match . . . They gave the Welshmen what they have always wanted — Wales can always win behind; on Saturday she won everywhere,' and the *Daily Chronicle* suggested the win marked 'a new epoch'. 'Monkey' Gould had already undergone a metamorphosis in rugby terms equal to the social one underway in South Wales. The knowing, subdued theatricality of his play had burst into the open the previous January in Cardiff when, after Wales had beaten mud and Scottish forwards, the Welsh captain, black from head to foot, had stood surrounded by cheering admirers in the Queen's Hotel. He had 'never seemed in happier mood' and, after praising the fowards (there were already miners and ex-miners in the pack) he turned, threw his arms open and shouted 'Why, *I'm* like a collier, look at me!' — 'and amid the hurrahs of the assembled crowd in the hall, Mr Gould ran up the stairs to his dressing room'. The butterfly had embraced the caterpillar. The admiration that butterflies like Gould evoked in South Wales would mean that after the 1896 game events would occur which led to no international fixtures for Wales between January 1897 and March 1898. This was the Gould affair.

By January 1896 A. J. Gould had played in more first class matches, scored more tries and dropped more goals than any other player on record. On the Monday after the game 'Dromio' wrote in the *South Wales Argus* that 'as Arthur Gould is as pre-eminent in football as W. G. Grace is in cricket, the footballing enthusiasts of Wales might recognize his services to the game . . . by some national testimonial'; a leader in the *South Wales Daily News* had urged the same. The response, from other sections of the press and the public, was instantaneous. W. J. Orders, an ex-Newport sportsman now a shipbroker, organized a collection on the floor of the Cardiff Coal Exchange and floated a public testimonial of 1s. Within weeks it was soaring into hundreds of pounds, truly a 'national' response to Gould's fame although it was a novel 'nation' of which Gould was a representative son — in his happy mood after the 1896 Scottish game he greeted everyone with 'Cymru am byth!' and then added 'I don't know what it means, but I've been told to say it', until Gavin Henry, the W.F.U. Vice-president from Llanelli, told him it meant 'Wales for ever!', adding 'that it was rather good . . . for a Scotsman to teach a Welshman his own language'. Nonetheless the question of a *national* testimonial, organized by an independent committee and subscribed to by many people, prominent in public life and otherwise, outside Newport itself, was vital to the W.F.U.'s subsequent argument that Gould could not under their rules be 'professionalized' by being a recipient of the fund. This was because their Rule 2 on professionalism read:

> A professional is . . . any player who shall receive from his club or any member of it any money consideration whatever, actual or prospective, for services rendered to football for the club of which he is a member.

For the R.F.U., and subsequently the I.B., the Welsh interpretation of the rule amounted to casuistry, but by the time, in late January 1897, that these views were expounded, the W.F.U.'s willingness to tell the I.B. that it had not been formed 'for the purpose of dealing with the rules as to professionalism, but merely to settle the laws of the game and disputes arising between the different Unions' had been pushed to the point of no return by extreme indignation in Wales itself.

In April 1896, the W.F.U. had sanctioned a subscription of 1,000 shillings from Union funds to the Gould testimonial; in September 1896, after complaints from the R.F.U. and a suggestion from the I.B. that a gift of plate, to the value of £100 only, be given to Gould or else Wales would lose her international fixtures, the W.F.U. withdrew their subscription to and sanction of the fund. This action was greeted as weak-willed pusillanimity in Wales and anyway did not satisfy the I.B., and Scotland in particular, who demanded to know what was to happen to the money subscribed and would Gould receive it, retrospectively, after retirement? Gould himself, though retired at the start of the 1896-97 season, had not been able to resist turning out for Newport and for Wales, too, before the I.B. met for a final consideration on 25 January. The W.F.U. argued that Bromet, the Richmond captain and English international, had been given £50 worth of plate for his services to his club (and so would be a 'professional' in Wales), so why not £500 in the form of a house as proposed by the Testimonial Committee for Gould? The upshot was that the W.F.U. in late February 1897 withdrew from the I.B. in more a spirit of hurt, angry pride than sorrow. The I.B.'s legalistic analysis of the affair was answered point for point in a lengthy statement which in its ending showed the W.F.U. to have come of age in this baptism of fire:

> Leaving out . . . all points as to jurisdiction, and as to the intention of the arbiters or the powers of the International Board, we would ask . . . whether any reasonable man can suggest that because £500 has been subscribed by the admirers of an International football player . . . he is therefore to be called a professional; and . . . that we could have done anything more than we have without sacrificing our principles and our independence.

> We have fought hard against encouraging professionalism amongst our players under more trying circumstances . . . than any of the other Unions and . . . with greater success than the English Union . . . until . . . reconciliation is brought about we intend to do all we can to foster the Rugby game of football in Wales, which has made such extraordinary headway during the last few years from a purely amateur and practical standpoint.

Within Wales this was applauded as a correct assertion of 'Home Rule' in the face of 'impertinent meddling' and, total masters of their own destiny now, the W.F.U. restored their money and their approval in the shape of Sir J. T. D. Llewellyn, their President, who had cabled the Testimonial Committee in March 1897 'Am heartily with you; will send subscription', and followed it up with 100 shillings. It was Sir John Llewellyn, too, who delivered the main speech the Easter Monday night in 1897 when Arthur Gould was given a handsome detached villa in his native town. Two hundred and fifty diners, M.P.'s, civic dignitaries, a string and reed orchestra, the band of the Fourth Battalion of South Wales Borderers, and public galleries that overflowed, paid their tribute to the extraordinary Arthur Gould. His gifts, as referee and national selector, would be in use after that night until his sudden death, upstairs in his gift-home, in 1919 at the age of fifty-four. His contribution to rugby in Wales, at the most critical of times for the game, is immeasurable in terms of the characteristics he brought to bear. If anyone injected a feeling of grace that could be transmitted beyond the field through the collective participation of his watchers it was A. J. Gould, of whom a contemporary parodist of the poet-historian Macaulay's rollicking *Lays of Rome*, wrote:—

> But hark! the cry is 'Monk Gould'
> And lo! the ranks divide
> And the great crack of Newport
> Comes with his stately stride
> He shakes his lissom shoulders
> And dodges his foes with ease
> And in his hand he holds the ball
> And swings his wiry knees
>
> And now his name sounds stirring
> Unto the men of Wales,
> For his prowess has given them victory
> And his resource never fails.

T HE willingness of the W.F.U. to risk lasting international ostracism over the Gould affair speaks volumes for that 'extraordinary headway' of the game in Wales. So far and so fast was it travelling, on the domestic level, in the 1890s, that the Union sometimes give the impression of men trying to hold their footing on a juddering cakewalk. The stand they take over such matters as Gould's house and the related question of overt payment for playing signalled the acceptance that the popularity of rugby in Wales would automatically convey a certain status, and maybe 'social' reward, on some players, and that at the same time they would fight tooth and nail to preserve that pristine amateurism which in other countries served, through its assumed virtues of unique sportsmanship, to mark out the rugby fraternity (the only sport to suffer a split in the late nineteeth century) but which, in Wales, worked as a unifying factor within the community. There would be severe stress put upon it, just as the community was, by no means, free of internal political and social conflict. On the other hand, down to 1914 anyway, what is noticeable about South Wales is the general acceptance of common notions of what is desirable in human behaviour, and since there was hardly any tradition to conserve, this consensus grouped around liberalism in politics, the dignity and respectability of labour, and, above all, a free-wheeling progressivism that proved open to many influences. Amateurism in Wales was a means of holding together a community in which there were steep gradations of wealth and expectation; it was also a yardstick for measuring the cream of the country's sporting talent against those of other nations. Hence, the split of the gate-taking Northern clubs into a separate Union in 1895 held little attraction for the W.F.U. who had no wish to recede to the old S.W.F.U. position of competing against regions and who had not reached the established stage of rugby in the north where 'broken-time' payments seemed, to the industrialists and businessmen from non-public schools, so essential to retain working-class participation. In Wales the administration of the game was similarly in the hands of a socially-aspiring middle class, but part of their aspiration was the need for 'acceptance' within the more prestigious world of rugby outside Wales that the northerners did not feel, whilst their patronage of the game inside Wales was never based on social exclusiveness. If they had adapted the latter course, full professionalism would have come as night follows day: the trick was to balance various factors in such a way as to keep the game one for the whole of the community. This meant a mixture of rigidity over their own rules and a compromise, as over Gould, in the face of a social reality very different from that elsewhere. It was, paradoxically, the shifting sands of life in late nineteenth century Wales that allowed them to sidestep their way into an immediate rugby future which, once passed, weighted the sport for evermore with an inescapable tradition.

Through the 1890s the W.F.U. began, with more decisiveness, to fashion itself into as much a governing as a co-ordinating body. This process was, in the context of a mushrooming society, not that dissimilar to the one undergone by the Monmouthshire and South Wales Coalowners Association who struggled towards a joint policy from their foundation in 1873 or, indeed, that of the South Wales Miners' Federation founded in 1898 to give the workmen a more effective say than had seven separate district unions. The geography of South Wales, with the fingers of the valley joining the coastal plain's palm, required such organizations to knit together towns and villages with a distinctive sense of their own special identity. Communication between valleys was, until the linking road schemes of the 1920s, much more difficult than a glimpse at a map would suggest: the consequence was that the existence of professional clubs within valleys was always a slight chance since the support was thick and voluble enough to sustain a local side but not to provide enough gate-money. As early as 1893 those players who had trekked north under the inducements of advertisements offering first-class expenses, meals and accommodation as well as superior employment ('Buller' Stadden who had settled in Dewsbury became a butcher and then a publican) would face the W.F.U.'s injunction that if they had not had permission (as did McCutcheon of Swansea who ended as a prominent referee in the union code in Lancashire) they would be labelled 'professional'. Soon the

W.F.U. would require notification of transfer of players from clubs under its own jurisdiction. This was regarded as an insupportable interference by some of the 'old school' but an essential brake on inducements to good players to become covert professionals by a Committee faced with an influx of new clubs. It now became compulsory for all clubs to apply to the Society of Referees, itself firmly under the Union's control, for referees in all inter-club games. Local rivalry could spill over not just into the physical berating of referees (the proximity of many fast-flowing streams gave some officials an early bath) but also more dire accusations such as that of the indignant Dowlais player who was ordered off in 1892 for telling the referee, 'You have been bought by Merthyr'. The nearness of Dowlais to Merthyr was, it seems, no guarantee of fraternity between players — it was reported that in their traditional Boxing Day match in 1895, 'most of the Merthyr players were maimed' — so to place referees slightly out of the firing line expenses were covered in 1896 to the tune of second class rail fare within a twenty mile radius plus five shillings and, thereafter, the luxury of first class travel plus 7s. 6d. If fraternity remained an ideal of the W.F.U.'s second rule — 'to promote . . . a greater amount of sociability and good fellowship between the various clubs' — hard-headedness dictated that the General Committee take the role of arbiter in inter-club disputes. This, too, they did in 1896, a year that was a milestone in the history of the W.F.U. in another respect.

W. H. Gwynn, the Union's first paid Secretary, had suffered a mental breakdown, so that William Wilkins, the Treasurer, had taken up his duties in 1895. It was felt that Gwynn had to be replaced, and indeed he died in 1897 when in care. Once more W. H. Treatt of Cardiff came near to election but, on a second ballot at the 1896 A.G.M., Walter E. Rees of Neath took over the office he was to hold until he retired in 1948 at the age of 86. He was born in Neath in 1862. His early career was in the local building trade. He became secretary of Neath R.F.C. from 1888 and promptly revived the fortunes of the club by improving its fixture list and finances. Walter Rees was elected onto the W.F.U.'s Match Committee in 1889 and though, unlike most of the other administrators of that era, he had not played the game, his astuteness and attention to detail soon brought him to the fore. He was only thirty-four-years-old when appointed Secretary and conducted himself with 'rare tact and courtesy' so that Horace Lyne, himself only thirty-five in 1896, would tell the 1897 A.G.M. that Walter Rees was 'the most efficient secretary the Union has had'. His autocratic procedure, the perfect foil to the elevated aristocratic stance of Horace Lyne, would, spreading out tentacles from his house 'Norwood', Victoria Gardens, in Neath whence the Union's business was now concentrated, come to attract as much resentment as admiration but there can be no doubt that here, at the start of his term of office and for long thereafter, his forceful will and determined views were a boon to the expanding organization.

No longer dependent on its Secretary dipping into his own pocket for funds, the W.F.U. was, in the mid-1890s, in receipt of enough money in fees (£1 1s., as a club's annual subscription), gate money from trials (separate district trials, inter-district trials *and* final trials) and from internationals, that they were embarrassed by the money in their possession into setting up a committee to investigate ways of disposing of it. They had already given donations to those disaster appeals which peppered their Wales like freckles on a face (100 guineas for the Albion Colliery Fund, near Pontypridd, where 294 men and boys were killed in 1894). Now in 1895 they decided to divide all money surplus to running costs amongst hospitals, asylums, orphanages, nursing institutions and other such charities in addition to contributions to those perennial disasters. The W.F.U.'s view of itself at this time as an integral part of only one geographical section of Wales can be seen in the proviso that this money be shared out only in South Wales and 'that a subscription of £100 be given to the National Eisteddfod whenever held in South Wales'.

However admirable this philanthropy, in an age when most social services relied heavily on such largesse, there were voices within the W.F.U. which were arguing for an older adage — the suggestion came from Aberdare, Merthyr and Rhondda that the money be distributed amongst the junior branches of the game in order to encourage it. The Committee rejected this out of hand as beyond their powers and desire. They also kept the representation of the populous Mid-District down to one on a committee of seven until, in 1896, that District's representation was, after strong pressure, increased to two. This was a result of the phenomenal spread of clubs, now able to compete successfully, in the inland areas.

Not that this success was a total one. Although rugby would become a touchstone of Welshness, especially in the eyes of the non-Welsh world, it was lacking any such unequivocal lineage in the 1890s. Rugby, in the eyes of those who thought they were leading a national renaissance in politics and in the arts, was of foreign origin and dubious influence. The W.F.U. authorized itself to close grounds in the light of continued crowd misbehaviour, erected warning placards and even distributed copies of the rules amongst the crowd, but it was still associated with violent scenes. This was, in itself, a cause for concern at a time when boisterous crowds of working-men were seen as a threat to public order: troops patrolled the coalfield during the strike of hauliers in 1893 and, with the more usual large forces of police, would do so again in the five stormy decades that were to follow. The social conflict spawned by an industrial Wales was presented, quite unhistorically, by the leaders and commentators of Victorian Wales, as something alien to Wales; for a while rugby, another manifestation of the new society, received the same treatment. It was, anyway, associated with that other 'non-Welsh' pastime — the public consumption of alcohol.

No matter how moderate or teetotal the individual player might be, (and a Gould or a Bancroft, both of whom frequently stressed their almost complete lack of interest in 'the weed' and drink, would hardly have played so long at their level had they had not been so), it remained true that even leading clubs often still changed and met in public houses or hotels: Cardiff at the Queen's Hotel; Pontypridd in the White Hart or The Greyhound; Aberavon moved with bewildering pace from the staidness of the Castle Hotel to the exotic delights of the Hong Kong Hotel; whilst Dowlais would have upset any sensible purveyor of social morality by not only meeting in the Bee Hive Hotel but also changing their appropriately subdued colours of Chocolate and Slate, which had the additional merit of blending into the surrounding environment, to a shockingly daring Electric Blue and White. No wonder that those Welsh exiles in America who nurtured their eisteddfod and gymanfa as delicate memory-plants to be watered in an American cultural desert could not, no matter how gratifying national victories, quite fathom or bless the new Welsh obsession. Thus, in their influential newspaper from New York State, *The Cambrian*, they could read, in 1893, of Wales's strictly pyrrhic victories:

> Athletics beget a healthy, vigorous race of men but it is sadly open to abuse and there are tendencies observable in its popularity which point to a national danger . . . The football season . . . has just concluded, with great relief to many persons in Wales. Very few have objections to the game itelf, but under the concomitant conditions, it has not, on the whole, a healthy influence on young people. Everything is given up to its pursuit. The only advantage derived therefrom is the fact that Wales has been successful . . . There is increased respect for the little country outside.

Inside, notwithstanding great 'popular rejoicing', perhaps in some ways *because* of it, there was censure to dampen joy. Late nineteenth century Wales prided itself on its religiosity, but there is considerable evidence to suggest that neither the influence nor the numbers of the predominantly nonconformist churches were quite so sacrosanct as adherents would have liked. At Pontypridd in 1894 it was claimed that almost one-third of all families attended no place of worship. The Revd John Rees of the Rhondda railed: 'Were the churches what they professed to be why should their young men seek their pleasures in play-houses and on football fields? Football, he declared, to be the dullest and most senseless game the world had ever seen (Laughter). Even an ape . . . would not disgrace itself by seeking its pleasures in kicking a football. If their young and middle-aged men wished to frequent pubs, theatres and football fields then let them, in the name of the living God, remain outside the Christian pale'. Strong words, but ones sustained in 1896 when Congregational chapels objected to the Rhondda School Board that some elementary schools were allowing the pupils to play football despite its 'demoralizing effects'. Nor could they play in the streets without letters in the local press complaining of a lack of police prosecution. A leading magistrate, T. P. Jenkins of mid-Rhondda, wrote urging direct taxation of the working-class so that they could attain 'full, responsible citizenship'. On the night of 8 November 1910 when, during the Cambrian Colliery dispute, the high street of Tonypandy was selectively wrecked by colliers and their womenfolk, the shop of the unbending Mr. Jenkins, a magistrate, was the first to be smashed; the chemist's shop of Willie Llewellyn who, from 1899, was to play right wing for Wales was untouched by the social blast. Clearly the effects of rugby on popular morality had not been negligible at all. 'Football . . .' in the words of a contemporary critic in 1895, 'at all events in South Wales . . . has become a popular institution.'

It was the institutionalization of the game, which settled clubs could alone provide, that turned them into beacons of progress as surely as the chapels had been. Rugby clubs were able to satisfy the demands of men for democratic participation in an organization of their own choice. And the demand was an insistent one. From 1892, with 'numerous applications' from clubs of doubtful status coming in, the Union had begun a vetting process before recommending new members to the A.G.M. Even so the flow did not stop — in 1893 and 1894 clubs like Ferndale and Merthyr, Pontnewydd and Ebbw Vale, were investigated and found to be satisfactory. The 1895 A.G.M. went on to recognize thirteen clubs ranging from Blaina and Risca in the east through the coalfield, via Treherbert and

Maesteg, to Gorseinon in the west; a sign of the times was the inclusion of 'Barry, near Cardiff', a place which was conjured out of sea-air and sand-dunes in the 1880s because the Rhondda coalowner, David Davies, had a bill put through Parliament to allow him to build a railway to bypass Cardiff. With the new docks and the new settlement whose population went from 500 to 30,000 in two decades came a new rugby team. Other clubs had similar pedigrees, albeit with local variations. At Treherbert, in the upper Rhondda Fawr, the new coal seams attracted men from the older towns of Aberdare and Merthyr. They brought their rugby with them, but it took a five month lockout in 1875 to see the infant club establish itself as rugby games were played at the various collieries where the Amalgamated Association of Miners held their meetings. Just west of Swansea, the village of Gower Road had been transformed by the growth of steelworks in the 1870s. In 1885 the parish councillors formally changed its name to Gowerton. In December of the previous year they had established their first rugby side with the owner and manager of the Elba Steelworks prominent in the list of patrons. From 1896 the establishment of the Intermediate and Technical School (later County Grammar) gave notice of the profound effects that the 1889 Intermediate Education Act would have for Wales in its early provision of secondary education. Rugby, as Gowerton Grammar helped show, would reap rich dividends. The year 1896 saw another famous Welsh Grammar School open its doors in Barry where, too, from its origins, the team game of rugby was such an integral part of the curriculum that at the school's speech day in 1909 William Jones, M.P. for Arfon (North Caernarfonshire), could make it the theme of his plea for 'compulsory continuation schools' since 'Wales . . . never had so great an opportunity as the present for giving organized intellect its rightful sway . . . On the football field they achieved great success by organized intellect and alertness, and he appealed for the same spirit of organization in the continued training of boys when they left the elementary schools'. Such were the lines that would run from the 1890s. More common in that decade was the establishment of a village club like Glais in the lower Swansea valley where a local colliery manager organized colliers and metalworkers into a team in 1896. His name was Albert Harding. His son, Rowe, would go to Gowerton Grammar School and win seventeen Welsh caps in the 1920s. There would be many such interconnecting cogs in Welsh rugby.

The 23 clubs 'belonging to the W.F.U.' in 1895 had become 37 by 1896 and 47 at the end of that season. Some clubs drifted out through failure to maintain fixtures or keep their organization together over the next few years, but at the turn of the century the W.F.U. had doubled its club membership, in five years, to reach 50 clubs. The number did not drop appreciably after that down to 1914. This sudden spurt to the first plateau was yet another indicator of the close relationship between the Union and contemporary social developments, since the bulk of these new clubs were formed in the thriving industrial districts whose own say on the W.F.U. had been recognized by the increased representation of 1896.

It is no coincidence that the term 'Rhondda forward' should be generally applied to the working men forwards who stiffen the Welsh international effort from this date for the Rhondda, in its central and spectacular growth, symbolized the overall pattern. The two Rhondda valleys between them had a population of less than 1,000 in 1851; by 1901 it was 113,735 and rising. This was a society of rapid urban ribbon development strung out along the rivers and splattered over the clumpy hillsides. Social amenities were rudimentary even after the formation of the Rhondda Urban District Council in 1897. Early emphasis was placed on leisure activities that took up little time, space or money, whilst providing a heady draught of quick excitement, perhaps violence and certainly exchange of money — foot racing, mountain fighting, cock fighting and itinerant ballad singers laid traditions that were transmuted into cycle championships, open air hand-ball courts (often attached to a public house), greyhound races, boxing booths and, of course, rugby in teams who helped to define the separate identity of similar coal villages striving to have a communal focus beyond the mere, brute existence of the coal pits which had summoned them to life. The number of English migrants to South Wales was, in toto, and Irish and Scots apart, equal to or slightly more than the numbers from Welsh counties in every decade after 1871, though it is only between 1901 and 1911 that the numbers of non-Welsh outnumber Welsh immigrants by almost two to one. Arguably the indigenous Welsh culture which, at the time, was flourishing under the stimulus of new found prosperity was a long-term victim of this pattern. What is not doubtful is the use of such things as rugby to create common ground between the members of this mixed population. Around 40 per cent. of all English migrants between 1861 and 1911 were from south-west England; the number of Rhondda inhabitants born in those counties (Gloucester, Somerset, Devon and Cornwall) was almost 7,000 in 1891 and nearly 9,000 by 1911. Their names would figure amongst those brawny Welsh packs with south western names that would carry on up front what Gould and Nicholls had started behind. Yet it would be wrong to emphasize the major impact of the newer rugby districts as anything other than Welsh, for their popular following now mounted periodic invasions of the coastal towns in such a way as to be a forcible reminder of the internal migration of the Welsh people themselves.

Those who saw Wales beat Scotland at Rodney Parade in February 1894 would have 'delighted . . . Members of the Society for the Utilisation of the Welsh language [established by a concerned educationalist in 1884]' since they would hear 'the sweet Cymric tongue spoken in every part of the ground', and especially in the 'popular' stands from where homing pigeons were released at half time with the score. Already in 1891 the percentage able to speak Welsh in Wales was down to 54.4 per cent. and would decline, in percentage terms, at every subsequent census. At the same time, however, the numbers speaking Welsh rose from the 1891 figure and remained higher in 1921, after which an absolute decline set in. Or, to put it another way, the retreat of the Welsh language into the rural and upland Wales of the north and west had not yet occurred. The percentage of Welsh speakers in Newport and Cardiff in 1901 was only 3.6 and 8.2 respectively, but Swansea had almost a third of its population as Welsh-speakers whilst Merthyr kept 57.2 per cent. and the Rhondda, with a total population second only to that of Cardiff, contained 63.4 per cent. Further west, in the smaller anthracite coalfield of the Dulais, Amman and Gwendraeth Valleys, there was scarcely any admixture of non-Welsh speakers, so when Llanelli came to play Cardiff the press would note 'cosmopolitan Cardiff, the central part of it anyhow, was thoroughly Welsh on Saturday afternoon. Thick-set, sturdy little men talking the tongue of St. Mabon [the reference is to William Abraham, M.P. for Rhondda since 1885 and President of the South Wales Miners' Federation, known by his bardic name of 'Mabon'] and all possessed by "opinions" poured out . . . from the G.W.R. railway stations'. By the mid-1890s Llanelli itself was suffering the effects of the acute trade depression in tin manufacture which followed on President McKinley's 1890 tariff designed to stimulate production in the U.S.A. Over 10,000 were unemployed as works closed. The consequence for a rugby club, as Wales would learn in the 1920s, could be devastating.

Many tinplaters emigrated to the United States. Others moved to the 'American Wales' of the central coalfield where a Glamorgan League was established in 1894 to give a fillip of competitive endeavour to her improving clubs. The moving spirit and first secretary had been 'Teddy'

Lewis, a former captain of Pontypridd, the senior club in the competition, but by no means the strongest side at this time since what were, in effect, village sides like Llwynypia, Mountain Ash and Treherbert were now the match of most leading Welsh sides, with Penygraig and Treorchy not so far behind. In 1895 the Monmouthshire League was organized to improve the standards, interests and finances of that county's mining valleys at the instigation of the Crumlin captain — from the ranks of her clubs, Abercarn, Blaina, Cwmbran, Cwmcarn, Pontnewydd and Pontymister would come a good crop of future players, whilst Abertillery and Ebbw Vale would become clubs to reckon with at any level. The career of an administrator like John Games, the new League's secretary, would not be uncommon: aged twenty-seven in 1897, and playing for the Abercarn side where he had begun as a schoolboy, he was employed in the commercial department at Celynen colliery and was secretary of the Abercarn choir. At the A.G.M. of the W.F.U. in 1897 he was elected to the Match Committee as the first representative for the newly formed Monmouthshire District. The existence of the Referees' Society ensured that leading members of the W.F.U. would come to officiate at the grounds of these clubs and, in turn, began to suggest that the older clubs should give them fixtures on at least an annual basis to find a true assessment of their worth.

Llwynypia, just north of Tonypandy in the Rhondda, was the most meteoric of these clubs, both in its rise and fall. In the 1895-6 season, after past promise had been maintained, they defeated a number of top flight sides and went through the next season undefeated. Their backs were exceptionally speedy and well drilled. Home from his holidays on one wing was the seventeen-year-old Brecon College boy W. M. Llewellyn, who gave and took passes 'with equal facility'. It would not only be Rhondda forwards whose merits the enlarged Match Committee would hear urged by their new members. The brothers P. F. and F. F. Bush played for Penygraig, once the foremost Rhondda valley side, although they were the sons of the Principal of Cardiff Arts School whose own connection with Cardiff R.F.C. was close — 'They are not likely ever to become great three-quarters owing to lack of physical qualifications but they showed some knowledge of the game' reflected an observer of the match of January 1898 when Cardiff won 30 points to 3. Percy went on to captain Cardiff three times. Llanelli, Maesteg, Swansea and Aberavon as well as Cardiff began in the late 1890s to play the 'hill clubs' regularly whilst, in turn, the lack of interest in the W.F.U.'s Cup competition for junior sides (folded in April 1897) was replaced by distinct enthusiasm for the local passions that could be generated when a Llwynypia met a Mountain Ash in the tussles of the Glamorgan League. Crowds big enough to warrant police supervision were now expected to see 'the short, sharp passing which is so popular' and which the valley clubs, by no means just 'bashing' sides, were cultivating. Complaints against the rough play of premier sides was more often heard, with praise for the 'classic' virtues of the smaller clubs alongside lamentations that teams like Newport had once been a team of 'all three-quarters'. This admiration for the emerging generation of players was withheld from spectators whose partisanship did not extend sympathy to visiting referees. The W.F.U. were not tardy in shutting down grounds for a period of matches. More troublesome was the poaching of Northern Union officials who swooped voraciously on the working-men now playing first-class football against sides like Bath and Gloucester (both of whom went down before Llwynypia) and Leicester. These sirens of the north could also receive short shrift. When the whereabouts of Swinton scouts became known, in 1896 in Llwynypia, a crowd ejected them from the hotel and frogmarched them to the station. Whether this was in defence of amateur values or valuable playing assets is debatable. What could not be gainsaid was the exodus to the North that afflicted Welsh rugby (including the unlucky Llwynypia). Not only established names like Owen Badger, the courageous Llanelli centre who played the last of his four games for Wales in 1896 and moved on to Swinton, but also forwards like Jack Rhapps of Penygraig, who played in the only international game of 1897 and then joined Salford. The valley clubs especially could not long sustain the bloodletting that saw eleven Welshmen join Salford alone by 1898. These were more than straws in the wind. Arthur Budd, who often voiced official English rugby opinion, told the metropolitan audience just before the 1897 game: 'I regret to hear that in these mining districts there is a strong leaning towards the adoption of professionalism, and that these clubs may ultimately become powerful enough to bring great pressure to bear on the Welsh Union in this matter'.

What was left unstated was the view that manual workers could not really continue to play amateur rugby. Badger, a tinplater, had taken £75 as a signing fee; Rhapps had £40. These were by no means negligible sums for men in their occupations, but their exit was, paradoxically, a safety valve that allowed the bulk of working men to play at amateur level so long as they chose to remain in Wales. It cannot be said that the W.F.U. responded with alacrity to the claims of footballers playing for less than fashionable clubs, but once they began to detect the merits of such players there was an equivocal welcome in the terms of a society at once 'open' in its attitudes towards achievement in any endeavour and 'closed' in its concept of whether achievement in, say rugby, could alter a man's social status. The W.F.U. drew up a list in late 1896 of all those who had gone to the Northern Union so that they could be listed as professionals whilst, simultaneously, positively encouraging the image of Welsh rugby as not so much a classless but rather an inter-class sport. Without this approach Welsh rugby would have neither reflected its own world nor escaped disintegration, yet it led the W.F.U. further away from the rarified social atmosphere that surrounded its international opponents. The Welsh press, especially that Liberal wing which was the most reliable barometer of majority feeling and opinion, enunciated frequently in the late 1890s principles of play and of selection which, in Wales anyway, were not merely the rhetoric of amateurism. So the *South Wales Daily News'* 'Old Stager' in November 1896 knitted ideas of honour to their actual expression, adding, with typical Welsh pointedness, that rough play would only drive spectators away:

> Class distinctions on the field of play ought always to be ignored, and though many gentlemen by birth and position have been guilty of unsportsmanlike conduct . . . using the word in its broader meaning all players should be gentlemen on the field of play, be they artisans, colliers, tinplaters, members of the recognized professions or fortunate enough to be independent of labour.

There had been working men in the Welsh side hitherto. What the 'Rhondda forward' syndrome was really about was the graphic manner in which it illustrated the basic dependence of this emerging Wales on labour. Sam Ramsay of Treorchy was the only new forward in Wales's defeat by England in 1896. He was born in Scotland in 1874 and came to work, though not as a collier, in the coal industry. He won his second and final cap also against England in 1904 after an eight year absence when he might have noted ruefully the 'Rhondda forwards' who had followed in his wake, though not in his occupation of coal-owner, since then. Dai Evans (4 caps 1896-8) was a native of Pembrokeshire who learned his trade as a collier and as a rugby forward (14 stone, 6 foot) in mid-Rhondda where he played for Penygraig (he had joined the police force in 1892); Evans was capped against Scotland, and for the final match was joined against Ireland by Fred Miller (7 caps in all, 6 of them in 1900-1901), aged twenty-five, 6 foot and 14 stone, and 'a stalwart specimen of the Welsh collier'. Miller had been born in Talybont, near Brecon, and, in 1896, worked for Nixon's

Navigation Colliery from whom the Mountain Ash team rented their ground. For the 1897 game then the selectors brought in Dick Hellings, born in Devon, but a resident for nearly all his twenty-one years of Llwynypia where he cut coal and used his ripping skills and muscles for the local side. Hellings would win nine caps down to 1901 impressing not only with his strength and courage (he played with a fractured arm against England in 1900) but also with his skill and speed. Another first cap was Jack Rhapps, a nineteen-year-old collier from Penygraig, though born in the Penylan pub in Aberaman, near Aberdare, who had worked in the pits since a boy and used his 5 foot 11 inches and 13 stone 10lb. frame very energetically in tight play. Rhapps would play professional rugby until 1910, earning the nickname of the 'Salford Lion'. Jack Evans, though capped twice in 1896 from Llanelli, was playing for Llwynypia in 1897 and, with Dai Evans, made up the fourth 'Rhondda forward' in the side. It was a hard core that might change in name and in geographical origins thereafter yet which, until the changed circumstances of the post-1945 era, would now be a perennial characteristic of Welsh packs as the spectators of the mud-bath game against Scotland realized when at half-time a Llanelli supporter observed 'Welaist ti ddynion debycach i goliars erioed?' ('Did you ever in your life see men more like colliers?') only to be told in reply 'Colliers or not, they are a clinking lot this time'.

That was the last time *that* Welsh side would take the field, for first the disruption occasioned by the Gould affair would have to be repaired. Wales was anxious to put her domestic confidence to the test of the international fray certainly, yet it was England who moved to mend the fallen fences, primarily because the affair was causing a dissension amongst her own remaining clubs that could be ill-afforded so soon after the divorce of 1895. Conversely the W.F.U. had never been in better financial shape. Clubs as small as Mountain Ash and Treorchy were able to spend £350 and £200 respectively on improving their ground facilities in 1896, whilst the draw of Welsh clubs in the English West Country and Midlands was an indication of the gate money regularly received in Wales. When the I.B.'s case against Wales was printed in February 1897 Newport, who enjoyed dual status, withdrew from the English union rather than eject A. J. Gould. That same month the *Newcastle Chronicle* reported a special meeting of the Rockcliff F.C. Committee who, since they had played Newport for some five seasons, wondered if they, too, were to be thought professional — 'They had always found the Welshmen true footballers and perfect sportsmen, and, what was more, unlike many of their matches with other clubs they had no financial loss (Applause) . . . As a club they owed a debt of gratitude to Newport, and if they had to lose their connection with Wales, who were the only people who offered remuneration for their services, it would be a serious matter for them; indeed, it would scarcely be worth the candle to continue the rugby game. As they all knew, Rugby football did not pay in Northumberland'. Pointedly the Rockcliff captain, E. W. Taylor, who was also an ex-English international captain, attended the Gould presentation dinner in April. Only the intervening close season had prevented the W.F.U. from acting to cancel all meetings between Welsh clubs and clubs of the other Unions. This was the suggestion of Ack Llewellyn, a Mid-District representative from Pontypridd, who saw no loss in the senior Welsh clubs turning inwards to play the more junior ones. A. J. Gould himself, in a clear statement of Welsh intentions, was elected at the head of the three East District representatives on the Match Committee when the September A.G.M. was called. If Gould was professional, then so was the entire W.F.U.

As a storm raged against the apparently immovable ranks of the R.F.U. Committee, stalwarts like the Revd F. P. Marshall, who had condemned the 'broken-time' clubs within Yorkshire, defended the right of the English Committee to be elected 'in theory . . . but in practice be confirmed in office since they were not "mere delegates",' whilst 'the Union is concerned about developing the game in the interests of those taking part in it, more than in evolving a system which shall give delight to spectators'. This was a long way from the game in Wales; it was a long way, too, from the wishes of the R.F.U.'s A.G.M. on 16 September 1897 to which G. Rowland Hill (Hon. Sec.) and F. H. Fox (Vice-President) proposed and seconded a motley-worded resolution:

> That Mr. A. J. Gould having accepted a testimonial in a form that the Committee of the Rugby Union has decided to be an act of professionalism, nevertheless under the exceptional circumstances of the case, this Meeting recommends the Committee to allow him to play against Clubs under their management (This proposal does not emanate from the Committee).

In fact, far from bring a Committee proposal, Rowland Hill, in moving it, said that he knew many present disagreed with it, that there was no desire in it to interfere with the I.B. ruling and, further, that it was 'one of the most unpleasant duties that had ever fallen to his lot'. The motivation behind such self-sacrifice was not difficult to discern, however, for he added that if it were not passed there would be a severe strain put on the loyalties of the English clubs anxious for Welsh fixtures. As a spurious afterthought he suggested that this English embrace would preserve sorely-tested Welsh amateurism. Harsh voices spoke for the complete rejection of Wales and all her works, but, on a show of hands, the 'mere delegates' carried it by 'a large majority'. This did not, of course, restore international fixtures nor exonerate Gould himself who would be forbidden to referee in English club games and, when he turned out for Bristol, at that club's invitation on Boxing Day 1897, was, again, labelled 'professional'. This was a species of hysterical mud-slinging not unconnected with the conviction that Welsh rugby, now largely working-class in its players and spectators, was like the centaur, half-man, half-beast and, as an amateur sport, wholly mythical. This definition of amateurism was unreservedly connected to the social status of its adherents so that Wales was guilty automatically. The London *Sportsman* commented on the R.F.U.'s 'sagacious stand':

> It is a matter of common notoriety that Wales has, to put it mildly, a very hard battle to fight with its own clubs. Many of them are gravely suspected . . . of tampering with professionalism . . . There is not anything so difficult to combat as professionalism in a district where the working-class element is so strong . . . Whether Wales can be saved is a moot point. Possibly natural causes will be too strong for them in the long run . . .

Yet this offer of a helping hand cannot be separated from the frenetic complaints of other sections of the English press against the dilatoriness of the I.B. in restoring the W.F.U. to the fold and, thereby, sanctioning the club fixtures which the individual unions had not banned. By early January no decision had been reached. The *Sporting Life* claimed that west of England clubs were chafing at the bit — 'The Welsh Union have a very difficult task in hand; they have succeeded so far in preserving the game as an amateur pastime which is more than can be said in England, and at the same time brought it to its present style . . . if . . .the ultra amateur faddists of the English Union have their way then we shall have the most important clubs in Southern Britain that still play as amateurs driven into revolt'.

The I.B. finally re-admitted Wales in early February 1898. Wales agreed to abide by all the by-laws of the I.B. in future (though she pressed for a uniform application of the laws on professionalism) and Gould was not to play in any future internationals. This stuck in the craw of the Welsh Committee who only agreed to it by a two to one majority, but since he was already an international selector the question did not arise in practice.

Fixtures were arranged between Ireland and England that year but since Scotland, in a hardline stance, refused to travel to Wales, that game lapsed for the season. It was a compromise reached to Welsh satisfaction for the ban on Gould was an incidental, whilst the autonomous character of the sport in Wales, after many vicissitudes, had been asserted. Even so, the Gould affair raised many questions which would return to bedevil rugby administrators. So far as Wales was concerned any overt evidence of professionalism would, now and later, be dealt with summarily, but the W.F.U. gave the lead, which would be consistently followed in Wales, that they could not legislate against admiration for, and reward of, players in this sporting hot-house. Their most exotic bloom to date ruminated, in late 1898, on the implications of the changes he had witnessed. Gould was never one 'to imprison reality in his description of it', as another famous son of Gwent was to put it; he highlighted the ambivalence that had arisen:

> [Twenty-years ago] . . . a few men, many of them old public schoolboys, most of them in good positions, played the game for the love of the game, paying their own expenses, without thought of spectators and gates; now the game is played by all classes and followed by all classes, even in the most prominent clubs players' expenses are paid, and the people who pay to see football demand that the game should be played as well as possible. Out of this demand arose the search for players of special merit which has resulted in the north of England in professionalism . . .
>
> We in Wales . . . desire to play football on an amateur basis; we are paying for our devotion to principle in the loss of players . . . but . . . looking broadly at the whole question as it affects the future . . . professionalism is slowly but surely coming. We in Wales do not want it, but that it is no reason why we should shut our eyes to the tendency; we are not ripe for it, but that does not prevent the thoughtful among us looking ahead. It would be suicidal of Wales to adopt professionalism at this stage, but the body of public opinion is changing . . .

The principle of amateurism was not erected into a moral fetishism in Wales but, as Gould had shrewdly noted, the half-way house of 'broken-time' payment would isolate Wales from both professional and amateur codes. Only the latter had the prestige of national competition at the highest level whilst the former would have created a divided rugby community in Wales and would scarcely manage to finance its outlay anyway. The W.F.U. therefore agreed with the R.F.U. in late 1899 on a set of rules against allowing any payment for playing rugby or training or losing time at work or, as their own resolution of 1898 had it, offering 'employment as an inducement to leave a particular club.' A similar I.B.

resolution of April 1900, after their own investigation, was fully accepted. From September 1898 the W.F.U. had declared as banned professionals not only any Welsh player who had joined the Northern Union but also any who played alongside them in any other match. Players would receive mementoes, such as the gold medals of less than two guineas in value given to the 1900 Triple Crown side, but international jerseys (from Messrs. Gardiner & Fulford of Manchester) were not to be supplied for each match — 'All players must return old jerseys before obtaining new ones'. This was scarcely open-handed generosity; it was the action of a Union tightening its control over all aspects of the game.

It did this, in a sense, by becoming more 'professional' in its approach. Walter Rees' salary was increased, to £100 p.a. in 1898, partly because of the additional duties he undertook since the Referees' Society was abolished and its powers vested in the W.F.U. Committee. Control of referees was not remote from control of the conduct of players and clubs. Penalties grew harsher. When in March 1899 a 'disorderly mob' pursued the referee at Aberavon the ground was closed until November; exactly twelve months later Stradey Park was shut down for four consecutive Saturdays because of the Llanelli crowd's misconduct. Those who were selected for Wales were, from 1899, not to play a week before an international without permission and could be suspended from club rugby for the wrong word to the wrong committee man (Dick Hellings offended on both counts!). As the squeeze of central control grew tighter so did the tentacles spread — the representation of the Monmouthshire District was doubled to two members and a new seat on the Match Committee found for 'West of Llanelly' which brought them to eleven, practically double the size at the start of the decade. As the old century waned, the W.F.U.'s importance in administering what were now the multifarious branches of rugby waxed stronger. They remained aware, though, of that provision of a spectacle for the people which had fostered their own vitality. In the last year of the nineteenth century they decided to propose to the I.B. that the value of a drop goal be reduced to three points and of a penalty to two, but the upgrading of a try's value that this implied would have to wait until well into the twentieth century, as indeed would the provision of an International Ground for Wales which the Committee discussed at length in April 1899 at the end of yet another disappointing season for the Welsh national team.

It had been disappointing chiefly through the continued failure to fulfill such a great deal of promise. Resumption of international games, in March

1898 against Ireland, with Bancroft as captain in Gould's stead, proved a happy occasion with victory by 11 points to 3 despite seven new caps, five in the pack alone. The game was memorable, too, for being played in Limerick in the far west of Ireland so that the team had to arrive in Dublin on Thursday. They practised in the capital on the Friday, catching a train in the afternoon to arrive in Limerick at 7.45 p.m. This was the longest journey ever undertaken by a Welsh team, so appropriately enough they were greeted by a big crowd and a brass band who escorted them to their hotel where, rather less appropriately, they were entertained that evening by a 'smoking concert with the cream of local talent organized by the town Athletic and Bicycle Club'. It seems, from the victory which followed, that the officials were right to stress that the Welshmen had taken care 'to preserve their form despite Irish temptations'. The report for home consumption concentrated as much on this aspect of the trip as on the game itself for it was not just Welsh playing ability that was being scrutinized:

> The side contained more bona fide hard-working men than ever before. Their conduct put to blush those who have ridiculously contended that the spreading of the game outside professional classes has introduced the rowdy element . . . There was no need for the unenviable duty of espionage . . . On the contrary, every man proved a gentleman in the truest sense of the word . . . and there was no fear that excesses had in any way injured the prospects of this team, as undoubtedly and regrettably happened in 1896.

By boat and train, via Chester, they arrived back in South Wales on the Monday morning to be cheered by waiting crowds. Some Welshmen had crossed from Milford Haven, despite rough weather, to watch their heroes and, as expected, packed excursion trains despite the start of a bitter coalfield strike took more to Blackheath two weeks later to see the delayed English game. In 1898 'Hen Wlad fy Nhadau' was only a rousing part of 'appropriate musical selections', not yet universally known as the National Anthem, but the Naval College Band did welcome Bancroft's side with the equally popular 'Men of Harlech'. It would seem their rendering of 'Hearts of Oak' was more inspiring for England tore into the Welsh backs to win 14 - 7. They outscored Wales by four tries to one. The Swansea captain clearly wished that the James', restored at Swansea but not for Wales, had played instead of the sluggish Cardiff pair of Selwyn Biggs and Elliott, and perhaps there was a divine hint delivered to Walter Rees to remind the selectors of the Swansea marvels for when he attended, with the Welsh team, P. T. Barnum's Mammoth Hippodrome at the Prince of Wales

113

theatre, the Welsh Secretary was 'seized with sudden sickness and forced to retire'.

When Wales met England in the first match of the new season, it would be with the James' at half back. It was their last game for Wales and the start of twelve years of defeat for England who would not beat Wales again until Twickenham opened in 1910. Admittedly Wales would tumble before the vigour of the Scots and Irish forwards in the next two games so that the merits of the 'conservative stylists' in vigorous forward play (Bancroft was caught by the Ryan brothers in the Irish game and thrown into the record-breaking crowd of 40,000, who spilled over the Arms Park touch-line, with the result that he broke a rib after twenty mintues) were put forward once more. Had England only been beaten through the loss of her forward power after the northern split? Mechanical passing amongst the backs was not enough, the press wailed, and, in a familiar sounding accusation (at least in Wales) — 'The Union and conservatism are synonomous'. However, with hindsight the game at St. Helen's on 7 January 1899 was, in all its circumstances, a much more significant indication of Welsh rugby in the twentieth century.

This was the first international at St. Helen's since 1895. The ground, magnificently situated on the curve of Swansea Bay, would alternate with th Arms Park until 1954. Its international tradition reached back seventeen years in 1899 to the first home international with England in 1882, so neither the expected crowds nor the importance of this game would overawe the jostling town of winding streets that mediated their commercial way between the pressing hills and open sea. There were five Swansea men in the side. The ever-present W. J. Bancroft as captain had kept away, as he always did, from 'the fragrant weed' for a week before the match, and was confident the return of Evan and David James would ensure victory, though if they were too closely penalised by sterner refereeing he might swing it himself. A twenty-nine year-old veteran of 328 first class games, Bancroft had already that season converted 43 goals, dropped 2 goals, kicked 3 penalties and scored 5 tries. His play was reported to be as vigorous as ever, still enlived by a readiness to throw the ball to himself from line-outs and to run from behind his own goal (in the Irish game that March an encroaching crowd would limit his space for manouevre and hundreds of forwards, some of them Welsh, would cheer to hear the Swansea imp had gone down). The James' were opposed by the skilful Livesay of Blackheath and the captain, Arthur Rotherham of Richmond, who would complain of their play during the game. The

Swansea forwards were the new caps, Fred Scrines, a fast spoiling forward (3 caps in all, the last in 1901) and Parker (both caps that year), who were part of a formidable All Whites team that would sweep the Welsh honours for that season. The new Cardiff forward, joining Tom Dobson (4 caps, 1898-99), was the dribbling Jerry Blake, a policeman (9 caps, 1899-1901), who joined Salford, whilst W. H. Alexander (7 caps, 1898-1901) and D. J. Daniel (8 caps spread from 1891 to 1899) represented respectively the new and the old, in Llwynypia and Llanelli. The two remaining forwards would be amongst those who took Wales to glory upon glory in the next few seasons. Arthur Brice (Aberavon, and later Cardiff) would win another 17 consecutive caps after this game, ending in 1904. Brice, a policeman, was a solid scrummager who would show his versatility when he replaced the injured Bancroft in March after the Ryans had mistaken him for the ball. Another new cap that day was a twenty-two year-old Newport forward J. J. Hodges who won 23 caps from 1899-1906. Jehoida Hodges was a club player who took on fresh powers in an international. It was said of him that 'he could do everything a Rugby player should be able to do, whether he is a full-back, three-quarter, half-back or forward'. On this occasion he would not be needed on the right wing where the Cardiff pair, Viv Huzzey (5 caps, 1898-1899) and Gwyn Nicholls (winning his sixth cap) looked a sound combination. Doubts were expressed about the left-hand-side pair for both were new caps — R. T. Skrimshire, speedy but inclined to ignore his wings, who would win all his three caps that season and, on the wing, the twenty year-old W. M. Llewellyn who had turned out for Llwynypia as a seventeen year old on vacation from Christ College and helped them rocket to fame and those Glamorgan League Championships and Cups. He scored 50 tries in 1897-8, and had figured for the Glamorgan County side on a number of occasions, including 3 against Somerset when Forrest, the English right wing, had opposed him. But Willie Llewellyn, at 5 foot 8 inches and 11 stone, was considered light and inexperienced with much to learn. His final, and twentieth cap, would be against New Zealand in 1905.

A team of seven new caps in all, then, and short of match practice because very heavy rain washed out club games and turned others into mud heaps in early January. A game between the Monmouthshire and Glamorgan Leagues was called off at Newport, so Skrimshire and Llewellyn could not even oppose each other let alone combine. The James brothers had not played with any of the Welsh three-quarters before. Prognostications were gloomy, and apparently did affect the W.F.U. who took the unprecedented, and to their critics dubious step ('too businesslike for amateur sport' warned 'Old Ebor' of the *Yorkshire Post*), of calling 'the selected Welsh team' for practice in Cardiff on the Thursday before the game. The Match Committe stressed it was not a match — 'only a general sort of practice', but T. C. Graham, the ex-international, 'has promised to attend and coach the forwards'. Those fierce English forward rushes were still feared but enthusiasm prevailed again, and on the Saturday, the sleet driving in from the Bristol Channel gave way, abruptly, to a brave sunshine. The now customary brass band blared away before the first international match on Welsh soil for two full years started promptly at 2.45 p.m. The crowd had been pouring into Swansea all day. The G.W.R. alone was running fifteen day excursion trips from Cardiff to Swansea, leaving at 10.00 a.m. to return at 6.00 p.m., their usual fare of 7s. 7d. slashed to 3 shillings; the Taff Vale Railway Company had joined forces with the Rhondda and Swansea Bay Company, whose trains rattled through the mountain wall that had once blocked off the top of the Rhondda, to offer a day trip for half a crown and with a later start for morning workers. Over 20,000 people were expected. The gate receipts totalled £1,500, which made it the largest crowd at a Welsh international. The newly wed Walter Rees (now on the Neath School Board and to be Mayor in 1905) was much pleased, though less so by those other entrants on the rugby scene, the ticket touts, who were selling three shilling tickets for a sovereign.

From the railway station in the town, disgorged from carriages where they had been packed in up to 20 at a time, grey-white engine smoke billowing around them before blowing up to join the white pall of the copper works, the rugby fans hired horse cabs or caught a tram or, more often, walked the couple of miles to the ground in a jostling, chattering, stream of bowlers and ulsters, cloth caps and mufflers, brown polished brogues and black shiny lace-up boots with clattering nails for long wear. It was a scene that was already taking on the shape of familiarity for participants and onlookers. Old friends, favourite eating-houses, a bagful of chestnuts so hot they burned your frozen fingers, a white china bowlful of spiced faggots and peas, a hotel foyer, the grandiose Mackworth's perhaps, echoing to opinions on the state of the coal trade after the strike's end or the tense political situation in South Africa (the Boer War would break out in October 1899). An ambience piquant with the smell of warmed whisky and mulled wine mingling into the heady fumes of cigars and oil lamps lit against the winter gloom that would soon lift outside just

116

as the glint of brass fittings and gilt scrolled mirrors inside seemed to promise. Lots of watering-holes on the way to St. Helen's would fill and empty with successive thirsty travellers slapping coppers on a curving mahogany bar, scraping the light snow from their shoes on the bar rail while waiting for frothy pints of amber-coloured ale to slip down throats and slop on the scuffed sawdust floor where the dented spitoon yawned tirelessly for the attention of hawking clay-pipe smokers.

All the small noises of these packed spaces then flowed on into the main procession flattening out down King Edward's Road or along the sea-road swerving between town and the far Mumbles lighthouse, switchbacking over the humped up streets that fell over each other down from the Uplands, like conscious lemmings anxious for their fate, to St. Helen's. Newspapers of the day, their right to visual entertainment not denied by film and television, spelled out the full flavour of the crowds by positioning reporters in various parts:

> On the one side the grand stand was packed, and a large proportion of seats having been taken by ladies, their sporting favours lent enchantment to the view. On the other, standing high up above a natural terrace, which was like a sea of faces, is a large row of villas, and all the windows of these houses were filled with interested occupants who, considering the chance of rain, were envied by the less fortunate people who had failed to gain admission to the stand by the spirited competition which had bought up every inch of available room. A long range of seats inside the ropes had been reserved for old internationals . . .

> We were outside the ropes, standing about the cinder path where of old time Swansea had a cycling track, and like herrings in a barrel we were pressed, squeezed, jammed on that sloping vantage ground which rises above the green level on the northern side of the enclosure. This odd 15,000 or so were representative of the masses, and they talked and smoked and expectorated and swore, according to their ability and inclination . . . I gathered that the vast majority favoured shag for smoking and Wales to win. Rhondda colliers, Swansea copper workers, Landore steelworkers, Llanelly tinplaters . . . in abounding multitude . . . argued about the respective merits of the Welsh three-quarters whether playing or not . . . for man is much the same whatever chapel he does not go to.

The game itself was a triumph for a Welsh football combination that revealed club form after their coaching session in the week. Bancroft's men were praised for their willingness to vary the passing game with cross-kicks, screw-kicking to touch, punts and short bursts near the line. They added to that the unexpected thrusts of the James', 'Banky's' elusive runs from suicidal positions and Llewellyn's opportunism, to swamp a plucky English side which only managed a consolation try near the end. Before that, Wales had plundered 26 points. In the first half, Llewellyn scored twice — first he charged down a clearance kick, gathered and darted in, then, as the Welsh pack pushed their counterparts, the James' stole away 'on the short side' to send him in. The Welsh pack were disciplined throughout, holding or heeling when required, nursed from time to time by Bancroft 'the great one who did what everybody expected he would do'. And sometimes what they did not.

At the start of the second half his kick-off astonished everyone by going to touch in goal. Shortly after, receiving the ball from David James on his own line, he ran, causing 'a great deal of uneasiness', until it was cleared. Viv Huzzey's first try came when the Welsh forwards wheeled the scrum on the English 25 and Evan James, despite a split finger and dislocated shoulder, scurried away, feinting a pass left to his brother, throwing right (was Dickie Owen watching?) to Gwyn Nicholls who swerved past Royds, the English centre, and gave to Huzzey who left his opposing wing to score. Huzzey had had his second try before Llewellyn, when a rare English attack was repulsed, picked up in the open, passed to Scrines who threw to Parker who gave the trainee pharmacist his third. From a cross kick by Bancroft that Nicholls and Stout, the Richmond centre, contested the young Llwynypia captain scored a record four tries. Bancroft goaled four of the Welsh six tries. It took thirty minutes to clear the crowd from the pitch when the final whistle went.

Nicholls was hailed as another 'Monk' Gould, the deceptions of the James' in their variety of feints and quickness were praised as much as Llewellyn and Bancroft himself, but the constant theme in all comment, was the wonder of 'scientific play' that had made them all play like a club side. English eyebrows were raised at the 'drill by experts' which had perhaps achieved the result and certainly marked 'a departure in the methods of International procedure'. Other English observers more accurately attributed the crushing Welsh victory to the long-awaited results of the loss of Yorkshire and Lancashire forwards, though 'Old Ebor' did remark that Wales had suffered too. It was the *Morning Leader* who laid the wreath at the door of the R.F.U. itself and, implicitly, pointed to the divergent paths that different societies had caused rugby to follow:

> For many years the Rugby Union has been a close corporation, composed of men with the mistaken idea that only public schoolboys and University men could play the game. The middle class and working man footballer was barely

tolerated. And yet it is the latter class rather than the University player that furnishes the majority of the best footballers today . . . I can imagine a meeting of the Rugby Union five years hence. The selecting Committee meet to choose the Rugby XV to meet Wales. 'Let me see', says Rowland Hill . . . 'We will have four men from Oxford, four men from Cambridge, four from Blackheath and three from Richmond'. Carried nem. con. Enter a telegraph boy who hands R. H. a message. 'Gracious alive!', he exclaims. 'Wales declines to meet us, and prefers to play the rest of England'.

Those 'professionals', the James' and Gould, must have enjoyed a wry smile reading that. 'Taffyland' was buried that day in Swansea. The setting for the burial was quite appropriate, too, for there were criticisms amongst Welsh rugby watchers of the 'decadence' that had affected the game in east Wales where it was not as 'entertaining for the spectators as previously' whilst Swansea R.F.C. almost managed an unbeaten season which they ended by becoming the first Welsh club to play outside the British Isles. Their chairman was Mr. Livingston, a vice-president of the W.F.U., who had business interests in the patent fuel trade then being rapidly promoted in Europe by anthracite coal dealers. Swansea met a representative French XV at the Stade Française on 16 April 1899. They won, before 2,000 spectators, by 30 points to 3. What was more they had won on a Sunday when, at home, the ministry denounced them for bringing a disgrace on Wales, 'the land of the Bible and the Sunday School', for desecrating the Sabbath in a foreign land. The W.F.U. promptly banned Sunday football in a fitting bow to ruling sentiments. The sentiments altered before the rules did.

As 1899 ended the James brothers had fled nineteenth-century Wales for the last time. They were picked to play against Scotland in March but first one, then the other, had cried off through injury. Shortly after, they were back with Broughton Rangers for £200 down, £2 a week and jobs as warehousemen. They took the whole family, from grandmother to children, with them, but *hiraeth* for Bonymaen was too strong for David's Welsh-speaking wife. Evan contracted tuberculosis. The 'Greek gods', as their Jewish mother proudly called them, came back to twentieth-century Wales. David toiled in the copper works once more until he died in 1929. Evan died of tuberculosis in 1902, aged thirty-three. David, a voracious reader about the American West, had named one son Jesse, and wanted to call the other Frank. His wife insisted on Llewellyn. It was a good compromise between past and future.

BODY AND SOUL

THE twentieth century began in Wales to a chorus of thanksgiving for
the previous century. Wales, it was proclaimed on all sides, had been
transformed into a prosperous, advanced country freed from a static
rural economy with an inward-looking people. At the same time the spread
of literacy, the growth of a Welsh press and the success of a political
leadership based on the social and religious grievances of the Welsh people
ensured that this material wealth had a spiritual or cultural tip to its iceberg.
The adherence of the Welsh to the nonconformist faith may have been
exaggerated in strictly religious terms but its general influence throughout
society had been as intense as its association with the Welsh language and
rural life had been its path to glory. Despite a new wave of non-Welsh
immigrants in the century's first decade, the bulk of the industrial
population in South Wales had had direct experience of this 'traditional'
Welsh culture. Their own lives, however, and certainly those of their
children were moving away from it, so that the later geographical and
linguistic divide in Wales can be observed, in the early twentieth century,
as a form of tension *within* the people themselves. In some ways it led to a
more determined rendering of a separate Welsh identity (though, often, in
different form) whilst it could also just lose older characteristics. From this
perspective the great religious revival of 1904-05 which the collier-
blacksmith turned lay-preacher, Evan Roberts, spread through Wales was
not only the last such phenomenon in Wales but can be interpreted as a cry
of anguish from a people torn between two cultures. Rugby, itself a child
of urban Wales, would fall partial victim to its accusatory finger.

Nor did the difficulties remain within the cultural field, for the Welsh economy, devastatingly dependent on single industries like slate, copper, iron or tinplate which were all, already, in varying degrees of recession, was, even in the heyday of King Coal, by no means secure. D. A. Thomas, later Lord Rhondda, argued in 1901 that the export coal trade was heavily dependent on overseas, especially European, markets that might diminish; further, the enormous increase in population was, in essence, there to hand-cut and haul coal. This made it the biggest single charge on the industry and in turn ensured that the falling productivity from deeper and more difficult seams would lead to conflict over wages that would erode the liberal consensus within society. These were, in 1900, only straws in the wind but the election of Keir Hardie, the Scottish miner's leader as Wales's first socialist M.P., showed that a wind was blowing. Hardie was elected as the second member for the two-member constituency of Merthyr Boroughs (with Aberdare); D. A. Thomas, great Rhondda coal-owner, was the first, and Liberal, member. Their enforced tandem ride, with the Liberal clearly in front, may be taken as a symbol of industrial Wales down to 1914. Once again rugby, however innocent of any direct commitment one way or the other, would, by virtue of its enormous attraction, play a vital, sometimes shaping, role in this whirling society. In particular, any lingering view, as expressed in 1901, that all sport was 'degrading' and that 'football especially is an abomination' would, by 1914, be replaced by a wish to see rugby as a social unifier in an increasingly divided community. Clergymen who played rugby would be praised and the game itself seen as a primary national trait.

The W.F.U. itself has to be understood at this time within the context of a Wales at once confident of the future within the British Empire as one of the jewels in that crown and, though fiercely loyal, in charge of its own proud destiny. When they were not acting within the strict boundaries of *Welsh* football, the W.F.U., like most of the Welsh people, chose to emphasize their Britishness. It has entered mythology that the Welsh were pro-Boer and identified themselves with a small nation fighting an Imperial bully. Historians have been more inclined to note widespread Welsh support for this war. Certainly the W.F.U. gave £250 in 1899 towards the support of the dependents of South Walians who volunteered to fight and followed this up, in 1900, with a handsome donation to the 'Welsh hospital' in South Africa. That January in Swansea the crowd of almost 40,000 who had come to see Scotland sang 'God Save the Queen' with some feeling — the immediate news of the war had been of General

Warren's bloody retreat from Spion Kop. When Victoria died in early 1901 Welsh clubs at the W.F.U.'s request called off their Saturday games, and did so again for the state funeral, 'as a mark of respect'. In every other way, too, the W.F.U. took its duties as an influential organization seriously. From 1903 players who were 'reported for acts of brutality' would be suspended for at least three months, whilst when Alfred Brice, a policeman, refused to apologize, at the I.B.'s request, to Crawford Findlay, Scottish referee of the Ireland - Wales game in 1904, 'for a thing I never said', he was suspended from April to November. The principles of 'fair play' might be thrust upon recalcitrant players; spectators were another matter. The raucous behaviour of the early crowds spilling over into mock and real violence had not entirely vanished, even from distinguished citadels of the game like Rodney Parade where a notice went up in November 1900 requesting spectators 'not to shout at or dispute the decisions of the referee ... Such conduct is neither fair nor sportsmanlike'. Arguably the acceptable code of behaviour, unknown to those 'ignorant of the rules' as that notice put it, might be inculcated in two other ways. First, by encouraging more to play the game; so in 1901 the Challenge Cup was restored 'in the interests of local Junior Rugby football' and in 1902 clubs in both the Monmouthshire and Glamorgan Leagues received money from the W.F.U.; secondly, there was an emphasis upon maintaining the game's attraction for those who had originated it. Thus London Welsh F.C., from the late nineteenth century, received monetary aid along with the inducement that Welshmen, in business or studying in the South East, who played for them rather than other London clubs would have preference for international consideration (Aberdare, on the other hand, were told in 1904 that they could not have a grant since the W.F.U. did not have the constitutional power to help individual clubs). The potential for rugby amongst the rapidly developing Welsh public schools (elementary and higher) was not neglected either, for in 1903 a sub-committee was set up to investigate the nature of schools rugby under the Welsh Schools Rugby Union whose inaugural meeting had been held in Cardiff in March 1903. They reported that there were five leagues (Cardiff with 23 schools, Newport with 14, Swansea with 7, Llanelli with 6, and Pontypridd with 6) all, with the exception of Swansea which also catered for Association, 'purely in the interests of Rugby football'. Equipment varied, as did support from senior clubs, but most were in credit. The W.F.U. in September 1903 gave the Schools Union £200 for 'a good start free from care' and accepted their direct affiliation. This was a policy that, despite some dissension later, would bear rich fruits.

The W.F.U. looked to the future as their credit balance soared from the £2,000 mark to over £4,000 by 1905: they bought the Secretary a new-fangled typewriter and, on the retirement of William Wilkins in 1903, resolved that all future Treasurers should be Bank Managers. T. R. Griffiths of Pontypridd was elected and, soon after, the accumulation of a reserve fund to reach £10,000 was started. Their response to colliery disasters and requests from hospitals continued to be open-handed but the increased money in the game caused problems especially when allied to a fierce competitive spirit amongst clubs looking to make their mark. Aberaman's offer of payment to two Mountain Ash players if they trans-ferred led to the club's expulsion in 1901 but it was, in essence, the same kind of issue that led to the third abandonment of the Challenge Cup in 1904 as 'veterans' from further and further afield were drafted in to supply the taste of victory. In some ways Arthur Gould had, in his playing days, been as important for Welsh rugby as the W.F.U. itself, but no player would ever be in that position again nor would the W.F.U. fly in the face of international censure, so that when W. J. Bancroft, still playing club rugby in 1905, received a testimonial of £322 from his admirers, he was promptly suspended. Formally the W.F.U. was beyond reproach in the eyes of others whilst, at home, the idea of rugby was becoming pervasive in these early years of the century, figuring in music hall songs, in advertisements and, most significantly, in areas of Welsh life where it had no immediate relevance — politicians were depicted in rugby contests in cartoons and when, in 1903, a new wages agreement was reached in the coal industry, the *Western Mail*'s cartoonist depicted the bearded Mabon (President of the South Wales miners) holding the ball, marked 'Negotiations', that Sir W. T. Lewis, the Coalowners' Chairman, kicked over a rugby cross bar, plastered 'Agreement', whilst Dame Wales and an audience, labelled 'South Wales coalfield', cheered wildly. This was a more effective depiction than acres of words. Rugby had become a short-hand code whose image could be taken up outside the sport itself.

Within the sport, at least outside Wales, that image had to be constantly defended in the light of attacks whose hostility was thought to bear a direct relation to Welsh playing success. Scotland, in losing 12 - 3 at Swansea in 1900, suffered her fourth defeat in six exchanges with Wales. Welsh commentators smugly declared that the Scots could accept defeat 'by her sister country Ireland' and 'for the sake of sport . . . by England' but that 'Wales has got upon the national nerves'. The Scots would prove a thorn in the side after that, winning Triple Crowns in 1901 and 1903 with a fiery pack of skilled forwards led by Mark Morrison of Edinburgh University, upon whose team, including the great 'Darkie' Bedell-Sivright, they were based. Defeat, especially away from home, was acceptable but not the attentions of the Scottish referee, Crawford Findlay who, in the 1904 English game that was drawn 14 - 14, penalized Wales so much that England had eleven penalties, most of them kickable, in the first half. Dickie Owen grew so frustrated that he refused to put the ball into the scrums after an infringement (the side in possession then put in). He handed it to his opponent instead. Hamish Stuart, a respected Scottish critic, admitted that the referee was anticipating events on the basis of 'past repute'. Worse followed when in the last minute Rhys Gabe's pass to Teddy Morgan, who crossed the line, was ruled forward. Gabe, who 'always deprecated the tendency to blame referees . . . could forgive and forget everything the referee did that day, but not that final decision'. Mr Findlay, after Wales beat Scotland 21 points to 3, met the Welsh side again in Belfast before a meagre crowd of 3,000 (a soccer international with England was taking place). This time he allowed an Irish try which the Irish players later admitted to be forward and disallowed, for the same offence, Dick Jones's otherwise winning 'try'. Mr Findlay did not seem to appreciate the finer points of the Welsh game nor, perhaps, their structure, for he had informed the school teacher Rhys Gabe ('Scotland's attitude at the time was interesting') at a dinner in 1903 'that he was surprised that Wales selected miners, steelworkers and policemen for their international teams and suggested that these players should join the Northern Union'.

It was exactly this old notion, in its inverted form, that so infuriated the Welsh XV in both 1905 games against England and Scotland, the latter being the first victory at Inverleith, Edinburgh, when the London papers insinuated that the W.F.U. ran the game 'on commercial lines'. It was true that some Swansea players, of whom there were five in the side, were employed by men whose connection with the club induced them to release their employees, on occasion, for practice, but this was no different from Morrison's students practising on their playing fields. The objection was, again, a social one as rugby football in the other countries became more entrenched in a definition of amateurism that pirouetted around the advantages of a man's status for the nature of the game. 'It is' said a Welshman made irate by the Scottish querying of the amateur position of Dan Rees, the Swansea centre, 'because in Wales we have government on democratic lines, and our players are mainly of the artisan class'. Indeed within Wales in 1905 there were a number of attempts to reduce the powers of the W.F.U. Committee in favour of club delegates whilst at Swansea, in 1906, Fred Scrines led a players' revolt that altered the club's rules so that First XV players whose nomination papers had been turned down should be allowed on the committee on the same, 'reserved' basis of that section which paid a guinea. Scrines called it 'class distinction'. In Ireland it was held that Welsh working men, by virtue of their hardy occupations, had an unfair 'class distinction', in reverse, on the field of play.

These were precisely the arguments used against the northern English clubs before their split and which were, in the early twentieth century, widespread outside Wales — that working men, either through their innate toughness or through covert professionalism, were enjoying an unequal advantage. The international dinner in Dublin on 8 March 1902 was not, in the wake of Wales's 15 to nil victory and third Triple Crown, a pleasant affair — 'References were made by prominent Irishmen from which the only possible inference was that professionalism is being winked at by the Welsh Union. Other nasty observations which provoked immediate resentment were that Welsh internationals were able to get into better condition . . . being workmen'. Once more the Welsh concept of the game as open to all was spelled out in reply — 'the gentleman in sport is not born. He is the man who plays the game whatever his station in life. The aristocrats in sport are the men like the Rhondda colliers who play the game they have taken up with a higher than average degree of skill. It is certainly not playing the game to attempt to gloss over severe and unexpected defeat by attacking the status of opponents'. Twelve thousand, including 800 excursionists from Wales, saw the all-ticket game whose reverberations echoed at the 1903 A.G.M. of the I.R.F.U. in Cork when their treasurer introduced his balance sheet by pointing out that the proposed rise in admission prices would keep out the roughs, and continued:

> Last year, the Welsh fellows broke in all over the ground and smashed up everything they could lay their hands upon. They would notice that over £50 had been paid for a dinner to the Scotsmen and only about £30 for a dinner to the Welshmen. The reason for this was that champagne was given to the Scotsmen and beer only (but plenty of it) to the Welshmen. Whisky and porter were always good enough for Welshmen, for such were the drinks they were used to. The Scotsmen, however, were gentlemen, and appreciated a dinner when it was given to them. Not so the Welshmen.

Wales had a long way to go before the distinctive features of her rugby football were fully accepted in their own terms. At home, with a slight shift in emphatic indignation, the festivities associated with rugby were roundly condemned by many people no matter which type of drink was consumed. When it reached the newspapers in 1896 that deacons of Libanus Baptist Chapel, Treherbert, had threatened instant excommunication to anyone connected with rugby, the 'sêt fawr' was highly embarrassed since two of the diaconate were vice-presidents of Treherbert R.F.C. This belief that rugby must be greeted with howls of moral dismay reached a high-water mark during the religious fervour that swept parts of Wales from the autumn of 1904. Admittedly there were some evangelists who saw sport as an antidote to a 'liverish, flabby-bodied set of Christian men and women' but as George Clarke, English preacher and athlete, observed, the trouble with South Wales as opposed to England is that lots of people only watched the game — 'It is this which is doing harm . . . if I were in South Wales, and the football had got too wrong with swearing and gambling I'd start a club of my own. In it there should only be churchgoers, and, if possible, only teetotallers'. Arthur Gould, a future representative for a brewery company, insisted that 'most of the men who played . . . for Wales' were 'teetotallers, and moral, clean fellows' but innocently added, no doubt with the famous 'diabolic twinkle' in his eyes, 'I believe it is pretty bad in some of the smaller teams. I mean the language and the rough play. There is also a good deal of drinking after the games, and betting about them also, I'm told though I don't know anything about it really, save hearsay'.

The Revival, in fact, infused new hope and vigour in a Welsh nonconformity badly shaken by the growing secularism that accompanied the enormous changes that had visited late nineteenth-century Wales. Temporarily, the individual grace through salvation that Evan Roberts promised would follow on recantation of guilt assuaged many tormented souls and converted hundreds of others. Chapels, throughout the industrial valleys especially (Roberts refused to visit 'English' Cardiff though he did, right at the end of the revival in winter 1905, visit 'Welsh' Liverpool) were packed to hear the evangelist and his lady singers. The Welsh press reported these emotional, often colourful, meetings with the same degree of detail and fascination that they normally reserved for rugby football. This was not mere chance. Wales was a society in the making. All of its works intrigued the Welsh themselves. The Revival singled out rugby as a rival deserving of condemnation. It had some success. International tickets were ostentatiously torn up in public by their repentant possessors; football jerseys ceremonially burnt by ardent converts. In the wake of Evan Roberts' crusade through the valleys of east Glamorgan in November

1904, Noddfa Chapel, Treorchy, suddenly found its Sunday School increased by the addition of a 'footballers class', which included the captain of Treorchy R.F.C. who had renounced rugby for ever. At Ynysybwl, the entire team was baptized and all sporting activities were rejected for three years. After hearing Evan Roberts preach at Kenfig Hill, veteran footballer Jenkin Thomas announced to a startled congregation, 'I used to play full-back for the Devil, but now I'm forward for God'. In West Wales, rugby was suspended at Morriston, Penygroes and Crynant for four years. The Revival killed off rugby in Evan Roberts' home town of Loughor till 1909; it 'spelt doom to Ammanford rugby' till 1907. Ammanford R.F.C., a product of two successive waves of industrialization in West Wales, founded in 1889 by migrants from the Swansea and Neath valleys and Llanelli come to labour in the tinplate works, then strengthened in players and support by the opening of coal mines that made Ammanford a frontier boom-town, resigns from the W.F.U. as players and officials disband their 'sinful' club. Such actions demonstrate the depth of feeling that could be aroused in a migrant society (and small Welsh villages or towns were highly susceptible) in the throes of industrialization.

France, herself embroiled in political turmoil over the separation of Church and State, was keenly aware of the Welsh dilemma. The Minister of the Interior commissioned Jacques Rogues de Fursac to visit Wales in 1906 to examine this mystical phenomenon for himself, especially as it affected the populace. De Fursac's book, published in Paris in 1907, contains a brief, cool, outsider's report of Welsh rugby and religion:

> . . . although quite recently introduced, football may be considered today as the national Welsh game. Welsh youth have given themselves to it, body and soul. This enthusiasm has been rewarded with success. Within a few short years the Welsh have equalled and then surpassed their original teachers, the English, so that, during the tour of the New Zealand team, it was Wales alone who saved the otherwise lost honour of the British Isles . . . but . . . football was strongly abused at the height of the Revival . . . certain Revivalists waged implacable war against it with the result that players stopped a game to go to church, cancelled fixtures, dissolved their teams or transformed them into prayer clubs. This antagonism between the Revival and the game, prayers and football, is a marked dislike of spirituality for sports that, at first sight, is one of the least attractive traits of the movement. Mr John D . . . [a Pontypridd wholesaler active in the Revival] . . . explained . . . that it was not against football as such that objections were raised . . . but rather that the present state of the game amounted to a religious and social danger. To begin with, clubs met in public houses which

offered the chance to drink, then, take the case of youths playing on a public park on a Saturday and attracting a crowd of onlookers who would soon reach a pitch of unhealthy excitement that had no physical release. Bets were laid, men would take their wages . . . just as at the race-course. The players appear to have the benefits of physical exercise . . . but they become impetuous, being young, and football threatens to become more and more brutal and degrading as violent activity and language go beyond not only the bounds of Christian behaviour but even threaten respect for human beings and bodily safety . . . Mr John D. added . . . from personal experience that sports, like all pleasure, empty you leaving nothing for the service of God. The true formula for life should be God first, work after, and pleasure last. If the reins on the appetite for sport are slackened this is overturned: games first, only the necessary amount of work, and almost nothing for God . . .

De Fursac concluded that the Welsh temperament swung wildly from one extreme to the other. More accurately it was, without becoming quite as Godless as some suggested, exercising a choice. The youth of Ammanford anyway formed a junior team to rise from the sacrificial ashes of their predecessors whose name they took in 1907 and which, by 1912, via practice, training, moonlight jogs and tactical discussions had become, in the words of the club's historian, 'a team in the truest sense . . . each player of equal merit, with but one objective — the team's success and no individual glory'. A collective bid for Paradise rather than an individual dash for Heaven was what came, more and more, to characterize this developing community. It was what, too, despite superb individual talents in the ranks, marks the Welsh XVs who dominated the international world. They were public heroes because they rose above individual weakness, and often subordinated individual strength, for the sake of a collective victory that reflected their society's profoundly Romantic view of itself.

No one elevated the game, in the pursuit of a perfection beyond self-attainment, more than Erith Gwyn Nicholls. His career in international rugby spanned ten years (1896-1906) during which he won twenty-four caps and captained Wales ten times. Aside from a part-season with Newport in 1901-02 when he began a laundry business there with Bert Winfield, his brother-in-law and fellow international, Nicholls was a Cardiff stalwart who graduated via the local club, Cardiff Stars, and then the Cardiff R.F.C. reserves, into the First XV in 1893. As with Gould, whose mantle he inherited, this 'prince of three-quarters' would serve as a Welsh selector (1925-31) before his early death aged sixty-four in 1939. Nicholls had supreme gifts as an individual player, being able to leave his opponents with a delicate twist of his body or burst past them in a surge of power; he was adept at fielding a loose ball for a quick return to touch or snap drop goal, his covering behind the full-back was instinctive and his head-on tackling, using a solid frame to good effect, was invariably punishing. Nicholls was primarily recognized as a truly great player by his contemporaries for two other, related, features of his play — that he brought the four three-quarter game to perfection by interpreting the centre's role as, fundamentally though not mechanically, to set his wing free and, secondly, he made time and space for others by taking and delivering a ball with an exquisite nuance of judgement which made mockery of mere physical attributes. This brought many tries for those who played with him yet, more importantly, instilled a confidence, by his ubiquitous presence, in any team he served. Nicholls' bearing, a restrained yet menacing power, needed nothing added to it for show and was, perhaps, the reason why those who saw him or knew him, talk of his play (and indeed his life) as being noble. Rhys Gabe, whose own career blossomed in Nicholls' care, and who in 1949 officially opened the Gwyn Nicholls Memorial Gates through which thousands have found entry to the Arms Park, wrote in 1939: '. . . he was the complete centre three-quarter . . . In attack he always ran straight as he lived, and his abiding passion was to make things easy for his confrères to carry on — the very antithesis of selfishness . . . His own defence was impregnable — this the spectators saw, but what they did not see was his unfailing support of every man on his side'.

Gwyn Nicholls brought precision to Welsh back play. In his early days, playing for Cardiff against Newport, he had been warned 'watch Gould' but confessed the task was 'as difficult as trying to catch a butterfly in flight with a hat-pin'. Much as he admired this dazzling elusiveness, Nicholls respected the inherent qualities of the game more. He sunk his own genius into the performance of his side so that this spirit infused the team with a life of its own for, he argued, 'if any player in any position in a rugby game stands out head and shoulders over his fellows then is that player inevitably *the* weak point of his side' Nicholls turned his own reputation into a strength by advising his co-centre Gabe to exploit the opportunities that might come from opposition concentration on Nicholls himself whose concept of 'the Welsh or modern game' involved the elimination of all unforced error. His influence on the free-flowing pattern adopted by Wales became paramount since, without rejecting advanced strategy or innovatory tactics, he argued for an understanding of the game's inner

workings that no amount of applied method could bring by itself —
'Elsewhere in the United Kingdom it appears to me that the Welsh
arrangement alone has been adopted without the *idea* being fully grasped'
whereas 'In an ideal Welsh game you really see fifteen great chess masters
working in partnership and without consultation, each man intuitively
knowing not only the best thing to be done but that all the other fellows
know it also'.

This is the diametric opposite to automatic play. It takes the vision that a
few players had grasped for themselves and translates it to a principle for
all. The clash with the New Zealand 1905 side was magnificent in prospect,
and in fulfillment, because complementary philosophies were enacting the
drama in a unity of opposites. A great deal of Gwyn Nicholls' beliefs as a
rugby player are re-echoed in the purple patch that comes to Welsh rugby,
briefly in the early 1950s, and again after 1969. Neither era neglected the
basics, or the subtleties, of the game's moves but both achieved more than
victory because they glimpsed that discovery of its joy (for players
especially, yet not they alone) which happens when self is immersed. There
is nothing mystical about any of this for the experience is lived, seen and
felt as it happens; it is the heightening of reality which gives power of
expression and influence to all national games played in this way, or as
Gwyn Nicholls put it, when asked to think of the needed 'system' for
rugby, 'there isn't one. The one thing necessary is love for the game — to
realize that it is the grandest, most glorious and most scientific of all games,
and that if one cannot play it with all one's heart . . . and for its own sake
one had better devote one's energies to croquet'.

Wales was fortunate that although Nicholls, through injury or
premature retirement, only played in 12 of the 19 internationals played
from 1900 to 1905, there were very sound centres to play with him or in his
place. Dan Rees (5 caps, 1900-05), a speedy three-quarter with a deceptive
action, partnered his Swansea colleague George Davies against England in
1900. Davies, a sound dependable player, was with Nicholls for the next
three games and then joined for one game R. T. Gabe who was generally
thought the perfect foil for the Cardiff man. Davies won nine caps (three of
them at full-back in the 1905 home internationals) and, like Rees, could
consider himself unlucky to be playing in Nicholls' day. This was
particularly the case in that Rhys Gabe's entry on the international stage
gave the ageing Nicholls a tailor-made greyhound to release. No-one was
more conscious of this than Gabe who later paid tribute to his master by, in
his declining days as a player, emulating the finesse in passing whose

grateful recipient he had once been, Rhys Gabe (24 caps, 1901-08), born in 1880 at Llangennech, played his rugby, after village sides and Llanelli Intermediate School, for the Scarlets as right centre in place of the crash-tackling Owen Badger. He had seen Gould's first ever Triple Crown side at Llanelli in 1893 and had played against Gwyn Nicholls before leaving for Borough Road Training College and a few seasons with London Welsh who, with the help of Wallace Watts, Willie Llewellyn and E. T. Morgan, were re-gaining lost prestige. Gabe became a schoolteacher in Cardiff in 1903 and began a long association with the Blue-and-Blacks, playing regularly from the 1903-04 season onwards. He had won his first cap, against Ireland, on the left wing when W. J. Trew pulled out through injury; his second came when a collision between himself and George Davies, at a London Welsh - Swansea Game, put the Swansea centre out of action for weeks. Of such accidents are teams sometimes made, for Gabe moved to left centre for Wales and Morgan filled his place on the wing to complete the famous Llewellyn-Nicholls-Gabe-Morgan line. Rhys Gabe was then 5 foot 11 inches and 12 stone 10 lb., very hard to stop as he ran straight, elbows and knees pounding, or changed direction with a rapidity unexpected in such a big man. His own style fitted in to Nicholls' scheme of things making the two of them greater as a pair than Gould and Nicholls had ever been. Outside them their wings, when available, were Willie Llewellyn (of Llwynypia and London Welsh) and 'Teddy' Morgan whose sixteen caps came between 1902 and 1908. Morgan, born in 1879 near Aberdare where his father was a colliery engineer, had been educated, like Llewellyn, whom he joined at London Welsh when studying medicine, at Christ College, Brecon. Not so full of guile as the ex-Llwynypia flyer who had met and learned from stern treatment on Rhondda slopes, Morgan was as full of courage despite his small frame. There were, besides, none faster than Teddy Morgan in his prime. The two wings made, thought Townsend Collins, 'the perfect complement for the perfect centres'.

The blessings in talent showered on Wales did not end there, for halves of immense skill abounded to the extent that D. R. Gent, who had a Welsh trial from Gloucester, opted for England and T. H. Vile of Newport, a British tourist in 1904, would wait until 1908 for the first of his twelve caps. The departure of Evan and David James allowed Llewellyn Lloyd, the Newport solicitor, to return for the two remaining games (and defeats) of 1899, after his first cap as a nineteen-year-old in 1896. He would win nine more down to 1903, playing mostly in harness with his club partner Lou Phillips and for the last five with the incomparable R. M. Owen whom the selectors generally preferred with his Swansea clubmate, Dickie Jones. It says a lot for Lloyd that he played with a variety of international partners at both inside and outside half. Lou Phillips, a swift and orthodox player, who alternated with Lloyd at the scrummages, broke down through knee trouble in 1901 which allowed Owen and Jones in as a club pair. But for that, Lloyd's fame might have been greater. Certainly Gwyn Nicholls thought him the greatest half-back he had ever played with since he would always expedite the work of others, never running too far or passing too soon or late. His pluck in defence was as renowned as were his knife thrusts in attack. Lloyd was a rounded footballer, sturdily built (5 foot 6 inches, 10 stone 6 lb.) and in that Welsh tradition, established through Newman and Gwynn, of providing a speedy channel for his backs. Not that Dickie Owen was against that, only that he brought to the scrum-half position the extra refinement of the totally unexpected which the James' had given to Swansea with such effect that an Irish team in the early 1890s were instructed 'Go for the Jameses; never mind whether the varmints have got the ball or not. By the time you reach them one of 'em's sure to have it'. Since Dickie Owen did not have an illusionist with him he just left the ball where it was, — in the last minutes of the 1902 game at Blackheath, with England leading 8 - 6, and a scrum formed on the '25' in front of the English posts, Owen, bending down as if to pick up the ball as it came back told his forwards in Welsh to keep it in. Oughtred, the eager English scrum-half, sped round to find Owen empty-handed and was penalized for being off-side. Strand-Jones kicked the goal and Wales had won 9 -6. To Gwyn Nicholls' chess game which Owen, utterly obsessed with the possibilities of rugby, was prepared to serve on a good day, he added the bluff of stud poker that could bring sudden death to the fainthearted. Owen was never less than a very singular player who revelled in the deadpan wit that made up for his lack of inches and weight (5 foot 4 inches, 9 stone 10 lb. in 1907) but it would be a mistake to conclude that this great creative rugby thinker was a one-string player for he, too, paved the way for others to show their paces. His views on scrum-half play given in 1927, only five years before his doleful suicide in the Swansea pub he kept, pick out the scarlet thread of thought he stitched into Welsh play:

> My advice to a scrum half is to do away with kicking to touch; or, in fact, any kicking at all. That should be left to the stand-off . . . who, however, should not forget that the game of football is intended to be played inside, and not outside, the touch-lines . . . My idea is that the scrum-worker, directly the ball is heeled, should pass direct and as swiftly as possible to the stand-off man . . . to run or kick before the opposition is on top of him. To

do this . . . a swift and accurate pass should be given from a stooping position . . . If you're going to pass do so at once, and from the very spot where you get the ball. If you decide to run, also do so at once, and keep thinking as you run.

This again is not to say that mixing up your game by means of ruses that keep the opposition guessing is not of service. I can tell you of one that combined with good passing . . . waist high and a foot in front of the running man with the opposition drawn up to you before actually parting with the ball — enabled Teddy Morgan to score in 1905.

Owen, according to D. R. Gent, 'revelled in talks of the theory of the game'. In the Swansea of the early twentieth century the tactical manoeuvres of the James' and Bancroft would now be taken further by a scrum-half who looked like a man-boy. Photographs show Owen, whose height and weight in 1902 were given as 5 foot 1½ inches and 9 stone 7 lb., as sunken-chested and scrawny, almost a mascot put at the feet of other athletes as an after-thought. No advantage was ever taken of Owen's physical deficiencies for he never allowed any. Opponents quickly lost all the complacency that a first sight of this unlikely looking footballer aroused because, with a ball in his hand, it was the Welsh Pinocchio who pulled all the strings. He played for Wales, though not consecutively nor without moments of controversy, from 1901 to 1912, winning a record thirty-five caps. One problem was that he never really managed to hit it off with the irrepressible Percy Bush, regarded by many as the finest attacking outside-half of his time, but then Owen's rugby was Swansea rugby at a high-point in the club's history.

Richard Morgan Owen was born in Swansea in 1876. A steelworker, his early football was with the town side, Hafod Rovers and then, as the century turned, with the All Whites where he would forge a link with Richard Jones that would give Jones fifteen Welsh caps with Owen to serve him. These were the 'Dancing Dicks' but, fine player that Jones could be, it was Owen, with his lightning delivery (the 'Bullet') and reverse passes from all positions and angles, refined so that he gave them in a standing position (the 'Mighty Midget'), shattering the best laid plans by combining in unknown intricate moves with his wing-forwards (the 'Swansea Marvel') and even predicting the scores he would conjure up (the 'Pocket Oracle'), who was proudly boasted as the greatest scrum half in the world. Whatever he tried on international fields had already been manufactured at St. Helen's.

Swansea were consistently to the fore in club rugby in the early twentieth century. They were unofficial Welsh champions for four consecutive seasons from 1898-99 to 1901-02 with their greatest triumph still to come for, under Frank ('General' or 'Gennie') Gordon's captaincy at centre, in 1904-05 they proved invincible. Indeed they were unbeaten from December 1903 (when Newport won at Rodney Parade) to October 1905 (when Cardiff lowered their colours at the Arms Park). Gordon would be unlucky not to win a cap. Other Swansea players, like Sid Bevan at forward and Jowett on the wing, would prove one-cap wonders but the talent for a club side was very rich. Furthermore, in addition to Owen and his capped outside-halves, Jones and Phil Hopkins, (4 caps, 1908-10), there was the man who captained them six times between 1906 and 1913 and can lay claim to being the most complete rugby player of his era. William John Trew, however, was not just a utility player: he was a natural.

Trew, a boilermaker by trade and later a publican through fame, was born in Swansea in 1880. He had played for various junior sides in the area before appearing for the Swansea First XV in 1897. On his début he dropped a goal and spent the rest of the season shuttling from position to position behind the scrum. By 1900 Trew's vociferous supporters were wondering how a man who had outscored everyone in Wales with 33 tries in 1898-99 and 31 in 1899-1900 could be kept out of the Welsh side. At last the selectors brought him in on the left-wing against England in January 1900. The twenty-year-old, 'bright-eyed youngster, "Trewee"', would be thirty-three when he finished with 29 caps to his credit. Twenty-one of those were won after 1906 because W. J. Trew's tremendous gifts did not always click easily into the formation Wales built in the first part of the decade. Willie Trew, a wraith-like 5 foot 8 inches and 10 stone 9 lb., drifted through Welsh rugby like the ghost in the machine. No one was in any doubt about his other-worldly skills. His conventional attributes at twenty were those of a sprint champion whose 'rapid swerve could double opponents up' but there were already other things noticed — 'near the touch-line he is very resourceful, and if in difficulties can often put in most judicious kicks and extricate himself with ease. He invariably receives the ball in an upright position and rarely mulls a pass. It is not very often that Trew is baffled — and now . . . he has a complete control over his body at whatever speed he gets up . . . indeed, he has at times been seen to jump bodily over one of his opponents and score'.

Trew played for Wales at wing, outside-half and centre three-quarter. He captained Wales fourteen times which, with five consecutive seasons for Swansea (stepping down for Dickie Owen to have the honour, for Swansea and Wales, in 1911-12), is proof enough, beyond the inspired changes in tactics he would ring on the field of play, that he was a natural as a leader too. So many things were done with such a minimum of fuss that Trew's contribution could be missed, apart from a sudden filigree flashing passage, yet those who played with him, or saw him, give Trew his own place of special fame. Rhys Gabe in 1946 still thought him 'the most complete footballer who ever played for Wales' and D. R. Gent, in 1932, wrote that Trew was 'easily the finest Rugby player I ever saw . . . to look at his genius seemed to have terribly inadequate physical support, for he was small, slight and always looked sickly'. Trew received many batterings by more robust men which, it seems, contributed to his death, aged forty-six, in 1926 but this slim, rather delicately built man, an ungainly long neck thrusting up from his buttoned-down jersey was, in motion, 'graceful, speedy, a joy to watch for the ease and finish of his play'. Townsend Collins gave Trew his own supreme accolade of 'unfailing judgement' which that critic believed few players possessed. Trew had it in abundance since 'brain and body, fine thought and perfect physical judgement were at one in him'. Trew and Owen together made heroic qualities from what looked like very common clay. It was rugby that allowed them to rise above the ordinariness of their bodies to attain a magical presence which crackled and danced from inside their own resolve onto the fields of praise and into the imaginations of those other ordinary humans who watched. These were men, by upbringing, occupation and demeanour with whom it was a satisfying, simple matter to identify. Huge forwards were, for most working-men patrons anyway, singled out for awesome wonder by their sheer unusual size. They could be objects of pride only. The Swansea pair could have come off those terraces which their admirers packed.

And what they saw has been described, again by Gent, who added to his Welsh birth and English representation the gifts of acute critic, as 'the most perfect form of rugby I have ever seen'. Gent applies this to Welsh clubs and national XVs of this period who, he says, had 'team-telepathy . . . baffling sequences of passes very different from the monotonous passing runs so common today [1932]', because of the freedom to manoeuvre given the backs by forwards who heeled quickly and, concentrating on a close scrummage game, did not interfere in the open play of the backs. Forwards packed down generally, sometimes in differing formation, on the principle of first there first down. They were wanted for their ability to tackle and obtain the ball in the line-out, with an occasional fierce foot-rush, but handling ability was not a paramount consideration nor were marauding wing forwards quite the disruptive influence on well-oiled back play that they would later become. The image of the Golden Era of Welsh rugby is, in essence, of the servicing of superb backs by faithful, dogged packs, and, to the extent that the idea of the game was to give those backs the dimension in which to execute their joint and individual skills this image will serve. And yet it does an injustice not only to the more complex patterning of the Welsh game but also to the forwards whose role was considerably more than servants who kept their heads well down.

The 'Rhondda forwards' drafted in since the late 1890s continued to supply a core of hardness in the pack which kept Wales steady in tight play. These were men like W. T. Osborne of Mountain Ash, a twenty-year-old collier, 5 foot 11½ inches and over 13 stone, who won 6 caps in 1902 and 1903 and then went to Huddersfield Northern Union; or, David 'Tarw' Jones of Treherbert, also capped in 1902 as a twenty year old, and with 12 more caps to come in the next four years. Dai Jones, a collier turned policeman turned collier, was one of the heaviest men to have played for Wales. He was, it was said coyly, a 'robust player'. With almost 16 stone distributed over a 6 foot 1 inch frame, this moustachioed collier giant could afford to be. In that 1902 season Harry Jones (6 foot and 13 stone 7 lb.) (2 caps) of Penygraig joined his tackling skills to their efforts, and to his double, in weight and size, the Swansea man, Will Joseph whose 16 caps for line-out foraging and tight play ended in 1906 when Dai 'Tarw', with whom he started, also ended. Even more specialized in his skills was George Travers of Newport who, lean and indefatigable (6 foot and 12 stone), could, and did, play anywhere in the heart of the scrum but went, with a frequency that signified his mastery, to hook. Travers was a pivotal part of Welsh success with his clean lunges for a quickly returned ball. He won 25 caps, from 1903 to 1911, the first coming, such was his fame as a twenty-four-year-old, from Pill Harriers, the minor club who kept his services for many years before he transferred across town to Newport. There were others — Harry Watkins of Llanelli (6 caps, 1904-6) and the great taker of tail-end ball, Cardiff's Billy Neill, like Travers a dock-side worker (11 caps, 1904-8, and many more if he had not joined Warrington N.U.) — who lend credence to the argument that ball-winners gave it to ball-users in a separation of functions that was designed to let the aesthetics of the game proceed.

Nonetheless it was Tom Graham, who had coached the raw pack of 1899 that helped defeat England, who, with that mobile 1890s Newport pack in his mind, had pointed out that the four three-quarter game, assumed by its critics to turn forwards into mere machines designed to heel out, in fact gave the forward more opportunities, when the ball was out, to do 'less laborious work' in backing up:

> I have often asked myself, Why cannot a forward handle and pass the ball as accurately as a half-back or a three-quarter? . . . From experience I am convinced that all that is needed is practice, also that not very far in the future a forward who aspires to . . . International honours will have to be, not only an effective dribbler and tackler, but also able to gather and pass the ball.

Graham did not neglect tight play (though he suggests variations of push and shove) but he did refer continually to the ball itself — in line-out it, not the opponent, should be the object of attention, and be taken cleanly; scrums should be turned with skill in order to retain the ball — and, in a typical forward's plea, he warned backs against too great a readiness to give orders. Anyway, if forwards kept their 'eye on the ball' this was unnecessary since they, as much as halves and three-quarters, had it 'in their power to elevate . . . the character of the game' above 'the level of the prize-ring'. Even the hard-core forwards in Welsh XVs of the early twentieth century were often described as 'fast' or 'speedy'. The forward who caught the eye in a 1904 East versus West game for his play in the open was the Treherbert man-mountain, Dai Jones, back 'in his best form'. Of course men like Miller of Mountain Ash were 'vigorous and strong rather than clever', but Graham's line of thinking had not been forgotten.

Besides, beyond these heavy men, Welsh packs carried the leaven of the Newport legacy. This was literally true in the case of George Boots, who won two caps in 1898 and then played in fourteen consecutive internationals until 1904, a schemer able to co-ordinate attacks from a forward base. His forte, though, was a spoiling game to smother the attacks of others. Against the brilliant Swansea team of 1903-04 it was Boots, at Newport, who kept them out by clamping down on Owen and Jones. Boots first played for the Black-and-Ambers in 1895; he still turned out occasionally in the first few seasons of the 1920s, chalking up 365 games for the club. Hodges, whose versatility behind the scrum was quite remarkable, played in the same packs as the flying Boots (Newport captain 1903-04) and A. F. Harding (Cardiff and London Welsh, 20 caps 1902-08) whose own leadership qualities would be used for Wales and for an Anglo-Welsh touring side in 1908. Harding, an ex-captain of Christ

College, Brecon, in succession to Willie Llewellyn, was no heavyweight but quick about the field and a good kicker of the ball as was J. F. Williams (London Welsh, 4 caps 1905-06) who, it was said, 'could pick up like a half, pass like a centre and run like a wing'. All of which sounds remarkably like the kind of forward in the sort of packs that T. C. Graham had so eloquently advocated in 1895. Welsh power-house scrummagers, too, it needs to be remembered were men whose occupational skill was, as colliers or tinplaters or boilermakers, not based on sheer strength but on a dexterity of hand and muscle which was akin to that of an apprenticed craft. The notion that they were only deliverers of the ball is a part-myth that needs to be revised.

Certainly accounts of games and types of play confound the simplifier. Swansea, for example, took up Newport's mantle in encouraging a pack with swift destroyers like Fred Scrines and enormously constructive back-row men like Ivor Morgan (15 caps, 1908-12) to work in concert with their darting half-backs or to run away with the ball themselves. It was backs who would serve *them* as, throughout the 1906 season, Willie Trew, taking Owen Badger's cross-kick for the wing a stage further, would run the ball away from his pack only in order to cross-punt it back for them in pre-determined collusion. At St. Helen's in January 1900 when Scotland went down by four tries to one, an irate Scottish supporter in the stand yelled, in traditional style, 'Feet, Scotland' and the cry, in return, was 'Brains, Wales'. Throughout the second half the Welsh forwards when taking the ball in open field would spin it out. Harry Bowen, Match Committee-man from Llanelli, observed afterwards — 'The game proves that the superiority of the Scottish forwards over the Welsh is a thing of the past, and this together with a knowledge of the passing game is bound to put Wales in the forefront of future matches. The passing not only originated from the halves and the three-quarters, but from the forwards as well, and this seemed to non-plus the Scotsmen'. This was no flash in the pan. It was a feature of Welsh sides at their best. The Welsh team who bounced back after a Scottish defeat in 1903 to outscore Ireland by six tries to none at Cardiff — Alfred Brice, the burly constable got one, and did so again, from open play, against Scotland in 1904 — had a hard scrummaging pack, who shone everywhere. The leading Welsh sportswriter, W. J. Hoare, reported gleefully — 'The days when they served the backs are gone'.

In strict statistical terms the record of the Welsh XVs between 1900 and 1905 would be bettered by the sides who played from 1907 to 1912, yet it is impressive enough even stated coldly — 15 victories from 19 games and three Triple Crown seasons in 1900, 1902 and 1905. Oddly enough contemporary opinion was, despite these obvious glories, willing to bewail the 'decadence' besetting the game at the slightest suggestion of over-vigorous play, a declining gate, or a club in trouble. This happened in 1904 to Llwynypia who had so recently shot into the first rank but who had neither the playing nor financial resources to sustain a sudden loss of players to professional or major club rugby. When success dwindled, support transferred elsewhere. At the start of the 1905 season the club was temporarily disbanded. They were not the only club to struggle after the first wave of enthusiasm. Soccer, it was feared, was spreading with the advent into the schools of soccer-orientated teachers trained at Bangor Normal College. The elements conspired to dampen spirits when at Swansea in 1903 the skies opened and poured their rain into the brass instruments whose rendering of the anthem was decidedly soggy as a result. Neither gales, such as the one that blew Wales out of contention at Inverleith before 9,000, nor worries about a team of veterans who might 'blow up', seriously affected the stately progress of the Welsh XV nor the ardour of the public who, at a time when in the other countries, a gate of over 10,000 was a cause of congratulation, were filling St. Helen's and the Arms Park with well over three times that number.

For the 1902 game against Scotland their patriotism was to the fore. This time they drowned the Tongwynlais Band's lively rendering of a polka by singing 'Hen Wlad' in part-harmony from various sections of the field. The crowd at Cardiff that day was another record. Over 40,000 people paid £2,178 to see the game, and their numbers would not drop below 35,000 a game for many seasons yet. There had never been anything like this in rugby football. Hamish Stuart tried to explain to his readers, who did not travel down in any numbers to Wales, what seemed to overcome visiting Scottish sides — 'Playing on a Welsh field' he wrote in 1905 '. . . is like playing in the arena of a circus. That at least is the effect of a vast crowd upon players not used to Welsh grounds but accustomed . . . to play on grounds where the sense of a wide horizon is constant, and the people do not seem to overtop the players tier upon tier like the folk in the ancient tournament or a modern circus'.

Stuart was concluding that the loss of this crowd would deprive Wales, as it had in 1901 and 1903, of victory in Scotland. Willie Llewellyn's team upset the calculation by two tries to one, the captain scoring both. Owen had passed the ball out along his own goal line as the Welsh forwards made the Scottish forwards forsake a rampaging game by scrummaging them ceaselessly. Trew had darted down the touchline like an electric eel and all the telegraph wires hummed with the inadequate description of Welsh exploits. All the more reason to see the stars in their true firmament in either or both of the home games. This made every home international a gala day in Wales. The crowds hurled themselves into a mixing bowl of activity and excitement. A game sucked the diversity of South Wales into a momentary whirlpool, brash and voracious for incident, dotted with parochial partisanship yet immersed in a collective appreciation of those whose seeds they had locally nurtured for just this blossoming. The *South Wales Daily News* cast a Dickensian eye:

> A patient, peevish, amiable, sarcastic, nervous, confident crowd; but above all . . . good fellowship and sport's best spirit. John Jones of Treorchy is here, with immaculate bell-bottomed pants, fiercely-coloured tie, and his sturdy 'Henry Clay'. He scorns the idea that the English pack is going to give the Welshmen 'fits'. 'Why', he explains, 'it will take three Englishers to hold Dai Jones', but he finds fault with the Welsh Union in not selecting more forwards from the Rhondda, just to give the pack all the grit and robustness necessary to swamp the proud 'Saesneg' [the band had welcomed the English XV with the sedate 'A Fine Old English Gentleman', and the crowd's champions with the brisk 'Men of Harlech']. John Jones . . . has a host of friends from Llwynypia and Treherbert, Mountain Ash and Penygraig . . . who know how to cheer and sing . . . their language seems to warm the atmosphere. 'Lawr â fe' yells an Abergwynfi John Jones as Raphael is seen bursting from the 'thin red line' . . .

> I squirm and wriggle to another part of the field. Here are girls with feathers in their hats and silver lockets and fringes, and every bit of ribbon they possess. Not Welsh girls — Cardiff factory girls, and they have come out to cheer Wales. As they can't see very much of the game they try to keep themselves warm by humming 'Dolly Gray', 'The 'orse the missus dries the clothes on', and, of course, 'Bill Bailey'. A peripatetic vocalist gives in a subdued, painful sort of way, 'After the Ball'. I finance him, others finance him, and no sooner is he financed than he hurries away. The martial, soul-stirring strains of 'Sospan Fach' reach me from a group of aggressively enthusiastic Llanellyites, who jeeringly ask a few Swansea friends — 'What is Joseph doing? . . . Harry Watkins is playing the eight Scottish forwards all by himself!' A man with a check trousers, well-coloured clay poised upwards and hands dug deep in his pockets gives the Llanellyites a painful look — more of sorrow than of anger. It needs no stretch of the imagination to see that his nose is red — ''Arry Watkins! Bill Joseph . . . They ain't in the same class as our boy Travers. Just keep your peepers on him, and then you'll see things'. 'You'll see things, if you ain't careful' mutters a Cardiffian. And so it

goes on, but good temper always comes out on top, and the cheers for the Englishmen are often loud and long. Your Welsh footballer loves a good game. He likes to see his 'pets' win, but he loves a good game . . . above mere victory.

He saw both that day in January 1905. Owen kept Jones supplied all afternoon for the outside half to make openings for his backs by running or feinting or kicking over the heads of the English centres. Behind a Welsh pack that swept all before them, the Welsh backs, passing at speed, let Teddy Morgan in for two tries, Llewellyn (with Newport since 1904), Rhys Gabe and Dick Jones took one each whilst Harry Watkins and Arthur Harding brought in two for the pack. George Davies only converted twice but did enough to hold the full-back berth through this Triple Crown season. Davies played that final game, against Ireland, in March 1905 on his own Swansea ground yet the Welsh fans began the game by jeering. A twist of fate had removed three Swansea men from the side — Dickie Jones had not played against Scotland through injury so Trew, who had refused to play in the centre for the trials prior to the English game, had taken his place at outside-half; now, with both crocked, Wyndham Jones of Mountain Ash came in, for his one and only cap, to score under the posts after dummying through. He went on to make Wales's second try by stealing the ball from an Irish foot-rush. A cap was elusive enough in this era of all the talents; the jeering at St. Helen's was reserved for Gwyn Nicholls who had, at the urgent insistence of the Welsh selectors, come out of his retirement from international rugby, to replace the Swansea centre, Dan Rees, who had taken the position that Trew could have had against England and who had withdrawn to give the Swansea captain, Frank Gordon, a cap. Nicholls' return botched a Swansea predilection to choose themselves or others for Wales that would recur this decade. The luckless Gordon never had a cap. Nicholls tackled the 14 stone white-gloved Irish centre, Basil Maclear, out of the game and 30,000 stayed to cheer him off.

With such seasoning was Welsh rugby now flavoured. Triumphs and disappointments came in equal measure. W. J. Bancroft had not retired willingly from the Welsh XV after a lucky one point victory over Ireland at Swansea, in 1901, from an offside Welsh try (one of two by the Llwynypia forward Billy Alexander). He had not played so well in February against Scotland when Morrison's team crashed through the Welsh defence to catch the slowing full-back, nor at Cardiff in January where a 13 -0 defeat of England was received grudgingly by a public and press not content to win badly. Bancroft's departure saw endless speculation over his successor, until the selectors plumped for Jack Strand-Jones of Llanelli whose unorthodox play, a slow, hesitating crab-like run upfield followed by a searing forward dash, baffled many intending tacklers and reminded others of a larger version of Bancroft himself. Strand-Jones, then twenty-four, had gone from St. David's College, Lampeter to Oxford (5 caps, 1902-03) and must be the only Welsh rugby player to end up as a Chaplain in Lahore. The press printed the names of the selectors who by 6 votes to 5 voted Strand-Jones into the 1902 side. To his credit Harry Bowen of Llanelli cast his vote for the rival from Cardiff, Bert Winfield, whose hanging touch-line kicks that could spin, whether to the right or the left, had Gabe rate him as 'the best kicker I ever saw'. Winfield's touch of glory would come, too. As well as fifteen caps, one against New Zealand, and a Welsh captaincy in 1908, H. B. Winfield would enjoy, as did the other two full-backs who filled Bancroft's shoes, Strand-Jones and George Davies, a Triple Crown.

There had been none sweeter than Bancroft's in the season that began over a decade of success. At Gloucester, where England played for the first time in the West Country, Tiverton-born Hellings scored a try despite carrying a fractured arm, for Wales to win 13 points to 3. At St. Helen's, Nicholls came back after his tour of Australia to score one of four Welsh tries after Scotland had been first prised open by 'such brilliant back play as has seldom been witnessed even in the annals of Welsh club matches when . . . from a scrum a little way on the Welsh side of the half-way Lou Phillips had the ball heeled to him, and while the two opposing half-backs were watching him under the impression that he would endeavour to break past them, he threw directly to Lloyd . . . who . . . passing to Trew, the Swansea three-quarter with a feint to travel along his wing, passed to George Davies who threw to Nicholls, and the Cardiffian making that magnificent swerve for which he is famous, gave Llewellyn the ball just over the half-way line. The fleet Llwynypian with a splendid effort beat all . . . and made a grand try'. After that it was a tight 3 - 0 slog in Belfast to win the prize that Llewellyn's try with all the backs handling, one way then the other, deserved so richly.

George Davies had been concussed in scoring Wales's winning try in the final game of 1900; Rhys Gabe fell over the line in the same state when he scored in the opening game against England in 1902 — Strand-Jones had deceived the English defence by circumventing the pack and carrying on through the team before passing to Gabe who had only to round Gamlin the full-back. He did so at the cost of a blow to his solar plexus from an outstretched arm, stumbled on, scored, and passed out. Gamlin, over 6 foot and 14 stone was compared variously to an octopus and to a boa-constrictor; he did not so much tackle a man as crush him. If his deadly tackles were evaded there were still arms which seemed to reach out after he had been passed to do the necessary evil. Exactly one year later in Cardiff, he caught the thirty-one-year-old Tom Pearson, Wales's captain and no lightweight on the left wing, after about twenty-five minutes play and so badly bruised his ribs that Pearson had to retire. The Bombay-born winger had been called in after Nicholls, Llewellyn and Morgan were injured, for his first cap since 1898. His first had come in 1891. Pearson, in his heyday a winger of pace and determination, must have thought the thirteenth was to be the unluckiest although he had already scored Wales's first try. The accident occurred after Gabe, perhaps unconsciously remembering Gloucester, had passed early, leaving Pearson to face 'Octopus' Gamlin. Gabe now made up for it in the best possible way for, with Jehoida Hodges brought out onto the wing and the ball still streaming out from the seven-man pack, Gabe delayed each pass he gave until Gamlin was committed to him. The Cardiff centre came off 'as sore and bruised as if I had been mauled by a bear'. And Hodges, the Newport forward, scored three tries in a Welsh victory of 21 points to 5.

The inner eye of the Welsh rugby spectator was regaled with passages of play to keep the memory warm in match after match. For some it was perhaps the long, raking strides of Gwyn Nicholls tearing the fabric of Irish defence aside in the 18 - 0 (six tries) crushing of Ireland at Cardiff in March 1903. This was, perhaps, Nicholls' best game as the Triple Crown halves and three-quarters of 1902 were re-united to produce the most spectacular bouts of combined passing, with the forwards well in on the act despite the loss of George Boots at the half with a broken collar-bone. Or it might have been the Welsh swamping of Scotland in Swansea in February 1904, by 21 points to 3, where it was the uncanny interaction of Owen, a 'needle at the base of the scrum', and Jones, who scored one of the four tries, that proved unforgettable — 'the Welsh pair, by long association, not only understand each other's play but everything they do is done with a purpose, while there is nothing that the one does that the other cannot anticipate. Jones is always where Owen knows he ought to be, and Owen does what Jones expects him to do . . . they have developed clever methods . . . dodges . . . that are the reverse of conventional, and all extremely bewildering to halves used to the orthodox in half-back play'.

When March 1905 ended, and another Crown had been won, two very open and attentive eyes had been needed to register how far and how quickly Wales had moved. The debates of the 1890s on the four three-quarter game were over. Wales no longer had a pack that instilled no fear. Indeed those who only saw the Welsh game sporadically now confused scintillating back play with the banishment of the forwards to the engine-house. In reality, gifted players egged on to achievement by an appreciative, and critical, following had knitted together different strands to make a whole that was unsurpassed in its integrated power and beauty. Those eleven selectors had overcome that geographical scatter, hardly conducive to concentrated thinking on a player's virtue, which would bedevil later years. Admittedly they did not always convince those who believed them to be congenitally one-eyed in their selection and, once, they literally proved it. This was during a rough sea-voyage to Ireland in 1902 when all eleven of them, notoriously bad sailors, were assured that if they bandaged up one eye they would not suffer; it worked like a charm — until one of them spotted a distressed traveller with an artificial eye. Hopefully their victorious return was a smoother passage. Either way they, and the assiduous, brilliant XVs they had assembled, took Wales to the forefront of rugby-playing nations. And there they were poised when black thunderclouds from New Zealand scudded across the horizon to darken skies that only forked lightning could clear.

LIFE, DEATH AND THE AFTERNOON

T HERE would be later games between Wales and New Zealand that would be brimful of tension, there would come moments of joy, instances of perfection, innumerable errors and a fair measure of bitter feeling, yet nothing that was not prefigured in 1905 when Wales first faced New Zealand on a rugby field. This was a complete meeting of peoples. It was, perhaps, the first time that each country saw in the other that utter dedication to the sport which, they had discovered for themselves, was a function of its greatness. They clashed as two superb teams, both conquerors of all that was in sight; the aura of mutual invincibility was a major factor in the making of this epic encounter. That does, not, however explain the expectations that swelled the afternoon of 16 December into a contest with reverberations beyond that year, or, indeed, beyond rugby itself. The two XVs were, in a way perhaps impossible to repeat now, and partly because of them, directly representative of a manner of life as well as styles of play, of a dominant social philosophy as well as of rugby thinking, of a permeation of one sport through the interstices of their respective societies. They both were offering up their 'deaths' for the prize of 'life'. It was not victory or defeat that turned the 1905 game into a seedbed that saw the final, ineradicable identification of these two countries, now as nations, with rugby football. For both that was, in the important sense, an incidental of the contest whose deeper meaning is not about the arrogance of superiority but the necessity of pride.

They were very different societies at the start of this century. Both had in common a desire to define themselves in their own terms to the outside world. Football, early on in New Zealand came, like cricket in Australia, to serve as a vehicle for testing that world. New Zealand was a place less encumbered with the deadweight of hierarchies and traditions, even in sport. There was experiment, innovation, success. And with success came lessons handed out to those in 'the old country' towards whom loyalty as a dominion within the Empire was a creed of faith, but who should not, and would not, look down on the raw 'Colonials' from the Antipodes. It was a feeling that 'Taffs' could understand. They could not surround *their* victories, though, with Antipodean mythology about sporting prowess. Wales equated her progress in football with her being a 'progressive' society until, in the aftermath of 1905, an inlay of basic 'Celticism' was discerned in the sport. At stake also, however, was the 'honour' of the Mother Country, challenged by the brawny youngster overseas and defended, in default of any other British hope, by 'gallant little Wales' who might derive great kudos from the outcome. From the late nineteenth-century social surveys of one kind or another in Britain had indicated, often exaggeratedly, a decline in the health, physical standards and moral behaviour of an increasingly city-bred population. It came home to governments, at least in the physical sense, when the minimum required height of the needed recruits for the Boer War had to be lowered to 5 foot 4 inches. Out of this was born the Boy Scout movement and a stress on the life-enhancing force that might be re-discovered in the fresh lands, the colonies, of the far-flung Empire. People were enticed, by extensive propaganda drives, to Australia, to Canada, to make South Africa less Boer (at one point the Patagonian Welsh almost left *en masse* for the Transvaal), and to New Zealand which, in common with the others, was concerned over the debate in Britain about free trade and tariffs that could disturb relationships. Sporting ties were a way of strengthening those links and, for the colonies, a chance to advertise the potentially better life they had to offer. It was a vision of a rural Arcadia long familiar in literary concepts of the ideal life but long gone in British reality and nowhere more so than in Wales, where the switch to an industrial life had so recently transformed a people's culture.

The New Zealand touring side arrived in Britain in September 1905. To the surprise of those who had not anticipated any great skill they began their triumphant sweep through English clubs and counties by crushing the championship county, Devon, by 55 points to 4. Leonard Tosswill, ex-English International, thought they combined all the best features of British sides and asked:

> Is the Colonial born and bred on a higher mental and physical scale nowadays as compared with that at home, as is so frequently urged by some travelled

146

Britons? It would really seem to be the case . . . The writer has seen the New Zealanders play several of their matches, and the conclusion is irresistibly borne in upon him after every match that they are not only better men physically, but quicker in conception, possess much more initiative, and, moreover, a greater amount of resolution . . . what is the reason? Has the decadence of the English athlete really set in?

Such views were not only commonplace, they were meat-and-drink to those sections of British public opinion who were agitating on behalf of the imperial possibilities of the Empire. The *Daily Mail* was one such voice. They cabled the New Zealand Premier, Richard Seddon — 'Why do the New Zealanders win?' — and that gentleman was, on 12 October, happy to oblige by reference first to the victories already achieved against the British touring team in 1904 and, then, through a Darwinian explanation:

> . . . information of the contests taking place in Great Britain is awaited almost as eagerly as news of the late war in South Africa. The results have been received with great enthusiasm. The natural and healthy conditions of Colonial life produce the stalwart and athletic sons of whom New Zealand and the Empire may be justly proud.

Football was moving in a rarefied atmosphere now. The Hon. W. Pember Reeves, ex-Canterbury footballer and High Commissioner for New Zealand, advised the *Daily Mail,* deeply concerned by 'the future of the race' as defined by its proprietor, Alfred Harmsworth (the future Lord Northcliffe), that 'the climate is a great factor . . . brisk, breezy and bracing with a combination of sea and mountain air. Our country is peopled with a race inheriting the sporting instincts of British stock, with vaster opportunities . . . Even in the four most populous cities . . . the inhabitants do not live packed together, house touching house.' Add, as Reeves did, plentiful food, ample leisure, universal education and small, healthy families and you have not only a Paradise Down Under but also a recipe for human perfection which the attainments of the All Blacks proved — 'These clear-witted intelligent people are apt to use their brains as well as their muscles . . . there is nothing mystical about our team's success. They play . . . with both ends — their heads and their feet'.

Their hands were quite useful too, for what disconcerted their opponents was the speed and agility with which the whole team moved the ball as if 'everyone was a three-quarter'. Arthur Gould noted, in October, after they had already registered 429 points to 10 in nine matches, that their trained combination tended to move more smoothly once the opposition began to crack under relentless pressure. He speculated that though they

147

might come to Cardiff 'with an unbeaten certificate' that the Welsh XV who had lifted the Triple Crown earlier in the year would also have had no difficulty in winning the matches so far won. In the meantime the All Black juggernaut rumbled on. Their playing methods attracted the attention of keen-eyed observers like Gould but the dazzle of individuals was what impressed the public. Their captain, Dave Gallaher, who caused controversy because of his role as a wing-forward detached from his pack, had served as a scout throughout the South African war and he led his team with all the daring he must have brought to his military role. He was subject to considerable abuse by press and crowds for the way in which he allegedly spun the ball into the scrums. That theory was roundly dismissed as nonsense by Gwyn Nicholls who saw the rapidity of New Zealand heeling as due to a better pack formation of 2-3-2. More worrying was Gallaher's equally legitimate obstruction of opposing halves. Wales would need to counter both. Even if they did, there were outstanding forwards like Charles Seeling and Glasgow to combat, whilst behind them came the tricky Hunter, the hard-running Deans and the incomparable W. J. Wallace who, as a utility back, was this high-scoring team's top-scorer. Billy Wallace could rifle goals over from almost anywhere; his dropped goal against Swansea would win the match; but his nickname, 'Carbine', was taken from a famous New Zealand race-horse. Wales would remember Wallace's running.

Some of the Welsh players knew in advance what to expect. Gwyn Nicholls, the single Welshman who went on the British tour of 1899, had been to Australia only. The 1904 tourists visited both Australia and New Zealand. Nicholls was not there this time though his fame in Australia, where three of the four Tests were won, lingered on. Bedell-Sivright of Scotland captained twenty-four men, eight of them Welsh. Selection, then, was more on the basis of availability for a long journey by sea and rail than on ability itself. However, six of the eight were already Internationals (A. F. Harding and T. S. Bevan at forward; Jowett, Llewellyn, Teddy Morgan and Gabe behind) whilst Bush and Vile, the halves, would both be capped by Wales and five of them would face Gallaher's men in Cardiff. They won every game, including three Tests, in Australia before going on to New Zealand. A fatigued, injury-struck team lost three games here, including the one Test game. The All Blacks side was skippered by Gallaher, who would also defeat the British Isles at Auckland, and contained many of those who would face Wales. At Wellington in 1904 Harding kicked a penalty goal, as had Wallace, to make it 3 - 3 at half-time; the second half brought two McGregor tries and a 9 - 3 victory. What was noticed, however, even in this defeat was the speed and thrust of Gabe and Llewellyn and Morgan of whom the New Zealand *Herald* said 'In the flashes of passing . . . we can form an opinion of how dangerous they can be in attack.' All over the southern hemisphere Bush had been dropping a prankster's bricks and a gifted player's goals. He was the 'scoring-machine' of the tour. As yet uncapped, Bush had already given hints of the promise in his play. Only a month before he had sailed away he had played for East Wales against the West in an end-of-season game that many had taken to be the Welsh international backs from the East (Nicholls, Gabe, Morgan and Llewellyn) plus the untried Bush and Vile, against the Swansea champions. In fact twelve of the West's side, and everyone behind the scrum, were from Swansea with Owen and Jones as the halves. To the surprise of most the East won by 18 points to 9. The feature of the day was Bush's kicking; once he fielded a ball on his left touch-line just beyond the half-way line and, without pause, dropped for goal — 'the crowd rose at this, and the Western players joined equally with the spectators in applauding'. Bush returned from New Zealand with his reputation at its zenith. Of the Wellington Test, the New Zealand *Times*, a future pattern of rugby encounters buried in its words, commented:

> It was a struggle between the clever and fast forwards of New Zealand and tricky, resourceful, hard-striving British backs; and one man stood in strong relief from all the others — the little Welshman P. Bush. Whenever the ball reached him in the second spell there would be seen a rush of New Zealand forwards to fall upon him lest he might . . . turn his side's probable defeat into victory.

P. F. Bush would win only eight caps for Wales. Nonetheless the superlative control of outside-half play that he achieved at his best brought him some spectacular international games. More vital than those, perhaps, was the effect that this twisting, scurrying, sidestepping maestro ('Trix' to his friend Rhys Gabe who said many could sidestep one way or the other but that Bush did it both ways 'all the time') had on the New Zealanders. Nothing is more indicative of the wiles of R. M. Owen than the way he would scheme to beat the All Blacks by not using the man they feared, and with whom he played only three times. The first was when Bush came into the Welsh side as the only new cap in December 1905 having been ignored in all three games of the 1904-5 season.

That side had taken a lot of thought. The Welsh Union had known the date they would meet the New Zealanders as early as 23 June 1904. Only the winning ways of Gallaher's men, however, induced any hint of preparation. In early October it was decided that the Match Committee should all travel to Gloucester to observe the rugby phenomenon that threatened Welsh supremacy. The burning question was how to oppose their style of 7 forwards, a wing-forward, a scrum half, 2 five-eighth backs, 3 three-quarters and a full-back. Should Wales withdraw a man from the pack and risk being over-run by heavier forwards? Would 5 three-quarters impede Welsh attacks no matter how useful the extra man was in defence? Would an ageing Welsh side match the hard, fast runners in black? How could the swift heel and quick break-up of the scrum be countered? The New Zealanders had no obvious weaknesses as cover-defenders, kickers or supporters of the man in possession. The atmosphere in Wales grew decidedly despondent.

The debate centred on the arguments as to whether Wales should adopt New Zealand style or keep her set patterns of play. After New Zealand defeated Scotland, despite vigorous play from a driving Scottish pack, by 12 points to 7, the consensus grew that Wales must at least hold them at forward and then play intricate football with her clever half-backs within the '25'. Even so, authorities amongst press, selectors and players, were firmly of the opinion that Wales would not be able to make the All Blacks scrum nor win by attempting to stem the flood of expected attacks. T. H. Vile who had partnered Bush in Wellington warned of the need for thoughtful scrummage formation against the two-man only front-row but thought, rather glumly, that Wales should stick to tried ways for the backs to attack 'if they . . . get possession'.

Within the selectorial ranks the discussion proceeded until the first trial teams were picked to play on 20 November. There is no doubt that the views of those who had toured were heeded, especially by the most influential selector of the day, Tom Williams of Llwynypia. He was then forty-five years old and had been caught up in rugby as a player (with Cardiff; capped against Ireland in 1882), referee and administrator for over twenty-five years (Williams served as a Mid-District representative from 1899 to 1910 when he was made a life vice-president; he died in 1913). This solicitor, the son of a Rhondda farmer, was also Willie Llewellyn's uncle and inclined to listen not only to the advice of his illustrious nephew but also to others connected with London Welsh. It was Tom Williams who announced to the press that the Probables in the trial game would play eight backs, though not the contentious wing-forward — 'I was in favour at first of . . . the old style, but this I now know was only sentiment. It is easy to advocate the eight forward game on the grounds that this will make the Colonials scrummage, but it has been clearly demonstrated that they cannot be made'. He went on to note the advantage of an extra back to disrupt their passing movements — such as Pritchard of Pontypool —and to cite, on the side of the experiment, Harding and Morgan of London Welsh.

The trial was not the required eye-opener. Trew and Owen withdrew because they were not fit; Will Joseph could not have time off from his work in the steel mills; Nicholls had intimated at the end of the previous season that he had retired from international rugby; Morgan was too busy with his studies in medicine and Pritchard was 'on the injured list'. This was a common fate for trial matches but could be ill-afforded for this one. When it was over and the Probables had lost by 18 points to 9, Ted Lewis (the Secretary of the Glamorgan League) concluded that New Zealand would beat all thirty players. All they could do was call another trial for early December, and hope.

The second trial took place on the day the All Blacks routed England by five tries to nil. Their forwards had been absolutely dominant, giving no chance to Dai Gent, the new English scrum-half who had actually played for the Welsh Probables on 20 November. On this occasion the Probables won 33 to 11. Pritchard tackled effectively and even scored a try but the seven forward experiment was still scorned. Besides, Owen was still out of action so that Bush had no rapport with him, and Morgan was absent, replaced by Maddocks of London Welsh who played so well on the left wing that it was proposed he should replace the out-of-form Llewellyn. The selectors were looking for veterans though. Nicholls had been in training after a request to captain Wales once more. His mere presence on the field would seem to presage Welsh glory. With him would be Dai Jones who, though now slower to pick up in loose play, would serve to lock the scrummage and would never be far from the action. Cliff Pritchard had won two caps from Newport in 1904, and now this heavy, hard-tackling centre from Pontypool would win the third of his five caps as 'the extra back', to play up close to the scrum in defence, and serve as an additional prong of attack. Bush, the 'star artiste' of Cardiff during a season where the only defeat suffered by the club would be inflicted by New Zealand, was hardly an unseasoned novice. The rest were already full Internationals. Eleven of them had appeared in the 18 - 0 repulse of Ireland in 1903. Now Cliff Pritchard was playing outside the pack in place of George Boots but another Pritchard, Charles Meyrick, of Newport, would win his fourth cap (10 more would follow before 1910 ended) as a 6 foot 13½ stone forward whose prodigies of tackling in December 1905 would win him special fame. The Welsh pack were considered a vital element; no-one knew how crucial the role of Dai Jones (Aberdare) Will Joseph (Swansea) Charlie Pritchard, Jehoida Hodges (Newport) George Travers (Pill Harriers), Harding and J. F. Williams (London Welsh) would yet be.

Hamish Stuart, and most other critics, were certain that the playing of seven forwards by Wales would bear no dividends since the All Blacks had taken the art of scrummaging to a new level. This apart, he felt, 'their play realizes rather the primary than the secondary qualities of football and does not, in consequence, display the same technical ingenuity and drilled precision which characterizes the Welsh game. Welsh sides alone are the masters of a system: other teams, the New Zealanders included, are merely good or very good natural footballers'. Welsh policy, however, would root itself in the assumption of attack from the very first point of contact so that the 'natural' game would not be able to move into gear. The two-man front row was the primary Welsh consideration. Before a crowded assembly 'on the boards of the Palace of Varieties' in Swansea in February 1906, Dickie Owen informed the audience in a lecture entitled 'Why Wales beat the New Zealanders' that Will Joseph 'had planned and carried out a method by which the Welsh pack was enabled to send the ball out of the scrummage quite as often as the Southerners' who now 'had a taste of play which was agressive, opportune and methodical'; this 'altered their game'.

On Thursday 7 December thirteen of the selected Welsh XV met in Cardiff to practise 'various manoeuvres . . . under the direction of R. M. Owen'. The forwards packed down in differing ways. That Saturday, since Cardiff were playing Blackheath in London, the selectors asked Morgan and Llewellyn to play with Nicholls and Gabe for Cardiff who were joined by Harding in the pack. Nicholls wrenched a shoulder but was fit enough to turn out with the Welsh XV (again without the excused LondonWelshmen, Morgan and Williams) for their second practice on Tuesday 12 December. The first run-out had apparently been satisfying for the backs; this unprecedented second session concentrated on drop-kicking and the scrum. 'Old Stager' darkly told his readers 'there is reason to believe that they have devised a method of formation which is calculated to checkmate the 'hooker's sweep at the ball with outside legs brought in with a swerve.' More accurately, this ploy of Joseph's would be the check to allow Owen's killing checkmate move. The worry was the All Blacks' continuous fighting for the 'loose head' via their two man wedge which had left the third man in British front rows useless. Gwyn Nicholls in 1906 spelled out the plan whose employment in 1905 prevented that steady stream of possession which had overwhelmed other sides: 'In order to circumvent them in "the loose-head" problem we planned that five only of our pack should go down in the first formation of the scrum — two in front —allowing them first of all to get the "loose head"; our two remaining forwards would then pack up — one under the "loose head" and the other to complete the formation. We were thus ensured of invariably having their two hookers' heads in the middle'. For the rest there was Owen's set move with Pritchard, leaving his 'roving commission', to act as an 'extra outside half'. No Welsh team had been so prepared through tactics and manoeuvres as this one. They would need it, coming cold to the new season against a team now playing as one. However, Nicholls was surely right when he concluded that 'the real secret' was Welsh determination 'to do all attacking possible — thus giving them their share of defensive work'. As with New Zealand the means were only a manner of justifying the end, and that was playing rugby to the uttermost limits.

The Welsh team were not the only ones to prepare. For the whole week prior to the game 'Mr. W. E. Rees, secretary of the Welsh Union', it was announced, 'will be at the headquarters of the Union, the Queen's Hotel, Cardiff, between the hours of 12.30 and 6.30 every day, and . . . will there receive all communications'. And a number were issued, too. The match, despite protestations, was not all-ticket. Field and enclosures would be on sale when the gates opened at 12 noon for 1 and 2 shillings respectively. Grand Stand holders (at 3s. a time) and those with 'seats inside the ropes' were to be in place by 2 p.m. The Welsh Regiment's Second Battalion Band was engaged to play a selection ranging from the 'air' 'Hen Wlad fy Nhadau' (at No. 5 on the list) to the march 'Heavy Cavalry' and the daintier 'Primroses of England'. The Union's ideas on musical accompaniment were, however, becoming firmer, impelled, it seems, by the rendition of the Maori War Song with which Gallaher's men regaled the crowds. In a first reference to the first All Black Haka on Welsh soil the *Western Mail*, giving the song's burden as 'be strong and fight to the death', declared 'it is not very musical but it is very impressive' and reported that the earlier suggestion of Tom Williams 'that Welsh players should sing the . . . Welsh National Anthem after the New Zealanders have given the Maori war cry' was accepted by the W.F.U. who hoped that 'the spectators would join in the chorus'.

153

The song composed in 1856 by the Pontypridd weaver-publicans, the father and son, Evan and James James, was thereby assured of the biggest choir it had yet had in its slow ascent to the status of anthem. The choristers would pour into Cardiff on the excursion trains put on by the local rail companies and those that came from Lancashire, the Midlands and London. Over fifty special trains were expected in addition to the ordinary ones. Cardiff docks was to close early, at noon, to allow shipping agents, coal dealers, wharfmen, coaltrimmers and tippers to make their way to the ground in time. Restaurants began to stock up on food, especially bread, and advertise special 1 shilling dinners. Programme sellers were fitted out with Red Dragon badges to prove their official status on the day which the *Western Mail* called 'the most fateful of all . . . in this history of rugby football.'

It was now that the All Blacks came. When they had gone some said they were stale, but they brought with them on a Thursday afternoon their latest scalp, a 40 - 0 trouncing of Yorkshire. The New Zealanders were feted and praised as 'Fernlanders' or 'Maorilanders' in a flurry of Welsh interest that sucked the visitors into the eye of the gathering storm. George Dixon, the team's manager, wrote in his diary: 'We were welcomed by the Lord Mayor and . . . the officials of the Welsh Union and were greeted outside the station by the largest crowd we have yet met. The open space in front of the station was packed with a dense mass of humanity who greeted the team with prolonged cheers . . . with great difficulty a pathway was made for us to the waiting Brakes . . . the streets between the station to the Queen's Hotel were so thickly thronged that much of the journey had to be made at a walking pace . . . on arrival at the Hotel the police had again to make a way for us. It was a somewhat embarrassing and certainly a novel experience to the maori participants in such a royal progress but . . . the greeting to Wales will live long in the memory of every member of the team'. 'We never had such a reception anywhere', Gallaher told the press 'and we have never seen such unmistakeable signs of keeness'. Dixon added they 'had known from the first that they would experience their stiffest game against Wales'. The manager looked after his team with commendable solicitude. In particular he was stung by criticisms of Gallaher's techniques and worried whether referees were influenced by such suggestions. Problems would arise in Wales from crowds who baited the wing-forward, and Dixon first rejected the W.F.U.'s choice of referee for the Glamorgan game after the international. Ironically enough, given the crucial decision made on 16 December, it was Dixon's querying of referees that led to the appointment of Mr J. D. Dallas of Scotland. The four previous officials put up for their approval (2 Irishmen, 1 Englishman and a Scot) had all been refused (three of them had been in charge of previous All Black games). The W.F.U., using I.B. regulations, then asked the Scottish Union to appoint a referee. Their choice was John Dallas, ex-captain of Watsonians, a Scottish international cap as recently as 1903, subsequently dropped because his play was more that of a fast wing-forward than the heavy scrummagers Scotland preferred.

The New Zealanders had a final run-out on the Arms Park on Friday 15 December. They knew that George Smith could not play on the wing so Wallace, otherwise at full-back, went to the left wing and Gillett to full-back. Stead, one of the two 'outside-halves' they normally played, had boils so Mynott, not such a daring player able to work his partner, Hunter, away, was drafted in. Gallaher was there though, to feed in the ball awaited by his scrum-half Roberts in turn ready to feed out to the five-eighths who would be, then, 'protected' by their 6 foot 13 stone captain running across the line of play. Despite Dickie Owen's reputation for cleverness the sight of his puny body, over half a foot shorter and almost 4 stones lighter, pitted against the moustachioed Gallaher could have inspired little confidence in Welsh hearts. Here, surely, was where the battle would be decided. Owen was to be black all over before the end, but not very blue despite a bump which displaced a cartilage in his chest early on in the game. As great a contrast as Owen and Gallaher existed between the thrusting R. G. 'Bob' Deans, the twenty-one year old centre three-quarter, 13 stone 4lb. and 6 foot, christened by the Welsh press as the 'Goliath of the backs', and almost the smallest three-quarter ever to play for Wales, the medical student from Aberdare who would play the role of David. Twice in the game 'Teddy' Morgan would be a central character; before the game began the band had played 'Captain Morgan's War March'. The blood needed stiffening for those All Blacks, standing tall as they always would, a slight breeze from the river Taff rippling their silk shirts ('Did that fabric allow them to escape the clutches of their opponents?' the credulous had asked), had played and won twenty-seven games at that stage, scoring a mountainous 801 points to a mere 22. C. C. Reade, a travelling New Zealand journalist wrote, 'the world's championship in Rugby will be decided in Wales today'.

The pre-match commentators added up physique against skill, forwards against backs, and generally plumped for the former. Outside Wales the opinion was firmly in favour of New Zealand. The Welsh critics were sure

155

it would be a 'titanic struggle', the highpoint of a quarter of a century of football in Wales. Whichever paper the thousands converging on the Welsh metropolis were reading, the intense, stomach-turning excitement was the same. After the technique, the records and the selection of the sides had been pondered with all the arcane knowledge possessed by those who watched so ardently, the irreducible sliver of fear that was also a leaping expectation remained. The outcome was unpredictable. It was life, or death, in the afternoon.

The morning anyway, despite the lateness of the year, was bright, almost spring-like, with no hint of wind or rain to spoil proceedings. The hundreds of ladies who were sprinkled about the grandstands amidst their black-coated escorts would be noticeable for their 'multi-coloured garments', taking advantage of the weather to add their feminine pointilliste touch to this sombre male canvas. The only concession to fashionable accoutrements made by the thousands of men who crushed into the city were a number of Red Dragon flags waved through the streets and the wafted smell of plump leeks pinned to their coats. When the markets sold out of leeks they wore onions as an olfactory, if not visual, substitute. It is estimated that 47,000 saw the game. Thousands milled about outside, no doubt agreeing with one writer after the game that it was one 'which those who have missed must ever lament'. In those pre-ticket-only days most travelled in hope anyway, wending their way down the imposing thoroughfares of St. Mary Street and Queen Street beneath the fantasy architecture of Coalopolis, rich lilting South Welsh accents intermingled with the sharper North Walian nasal tones of migrants from the depressed quarry areas where a three-year long strike had caused the slateworkers' diaspora, and both held in check by the bared-lip vowels of Cardiff that could slice through the winter gloom like wire cutting cheese. Not yet the artificial rosettes and glossy team photographs of the traders who would later live off these captive, committed audiences but plenty ready to offer services to these crowds who moved in and on like the sea from successive waves of trains until they reached the street that fronted the ground. D. E. Davies, President of the W.R.U. 1961-62 and chronicler of Cardiff R.F.C., recalled such occasions at the start of the century:

> Westgate Street would be thronged. There was little or no horse-drawn traffic to hinder the crowds . . . Vendors were . . . selling hot chestnuts and potatoes from their coke fires, their stands the magnet for urchins in winter. Others sold sweets, peppermints, bulls-eyes, brandy snaps and pasties from their baskets, and even Pepsin chewing gum. Their cries were well known on and around the Cardiff Arms Park.

A castellated-like wall about twelve feet high fronted the length of Westgate Street from the Angel entrance to a point opposite Queen Street . . . often used on international days by clambering gate-crashers trying to gain entrance after the gates were closed. From the west side of the ground attempts . . . were made by bold spirits crossing the River Taff at low tide.

Tickets were sold from pay boxes in the street, and entrance to the ground had to be made through tall wooden barriers, at whose openings gatemen would busily cry out: 'Show your tickets *please*'.

Once inside there was the swaying wait until the 2.30 p.m. kick off. Trees lined the far perimeters, their bare branches holding shivering boys. The new stands put up at the start of the season moved dangerously beneath their human weight. They sang 'Boys of the Old Brigade' and 'Tôn-y-botel' and, with feeling, 'Lead Kindly light' as, at ten minutes past two o'clock, a thick mist blotted out the pale sunshine. It hung over the ground for the whole match, not obliterating the play but making distant incidents difficult to see. The drama would not be a showy spectacular, which led some neutrals to express disappointment that two running sides did not entertain the onlookers. This was to misread the afternoon's events in a way no informed observers did. There *was* brilliance, the sparkling, necessarily fitful, brilliance of hammer and anvil. The light was appropriate to the play. The hammer was not always in the same hands.

Gates closed at 1.30 p.m. The press, seated at trestle tables inside the ropes, were surmounted by the biggest rugby assembly hitherto. The noise was constant yet subdued. Townsend Collins was there — 'Excitement was at fever heat. Never before or since have I known anything like it . . . thousands were quivering with excitement — some of us were so affected that we could hardly speak or write. The very air was charged with emotion. Hopes and fears were blended in an aching, choking anxiety . . . To understand why to those who watched it this game stands out pre-eminently it is necessary to recall what was at stake — the invincible record of a touring side who seemed then, and seem still [in 1948] the most brilliant Rugby players, who ever came from overseas, to show what individual skill and combination could achieve'. Collins thought Billy Wallace 'one of the dozen greatest players' he had known and believed that if 'Carbine' had been at full-back Wales would not have won; Roberts at half-back was 'the ideal', whilst Charles Seeling combined, in one body, the best of all forward characteristics — 'physique, fire, skill, endurance and judgement'. The whole XV, as well as these superlative players, were 'so gifted, so versatile, so resourceful'. No wonder hearts were in mouths in anticipation of these giants challenging, and probably rolling over, that Welsh pre-eminence so jealously guarded since the late 1890s. Newspapermen strained to deliver the immediacy of atmosphere; none did it better than 'Old Stager' for the *South Wales Daily News:*

> Now the great crowd sways and heaves; the air has become electric; silence, shod with suspense, rules everywhere. All eyes are upon the lower end of the pavilion. Suddenly the manscape sways to right and left, and at 2.20 the New Zealanders appear — the All Blacks — and from over 40,000 throats goes up a roar of welcome and good cheer, and the band plays 'Men of Harlech'. These Colonials are, indeed, all black. They wear black jerseys, black pants, black stockings, and black boots. They have, however, white faces, white hands and between the end of their pants and the beginning of their stockings there is a strip of white flesh. That stripe fascinates one. It is the oriflamme of the battle. These black marionettes are very lively. In a twinkle they are capering down the field, the ball jumping about them like a familiar imp. On each man's shoulder is a large white ticket with a large black number. . . . Is it a game of human dice or animated teetotums? Whatever it is, it enables the crowd to identify the Colonials. The Welshmen too are numbered. Once more the crowd surge wildly, there's a flash of colour, and the Welshmen, led by Gwyn Nicholls, . . . appear in the arena and the crowd roars itself almost hoarse. The Welshmen form a striking contrast in their scarlet jerseys to the sombre black of the Colonials.
>
> Amidst a silence that could almost be felt, the Colonials stood in the centre of the field and sang . . . their weird war-cry.

They stood and chanted the words that had been the prelude to so many other afternoons —

> It is Death! It is Death!
> It is Life! It is Life!
> This is the strong one!
> He has caused the sun to shine!

Though engulfed in cheers once more the fifteen visitors now had to feel, in their turn, the full effect of the crowd's pent-up fervour as the frail melody of 'Hen Wlad Fy Nhadau' rose up, for the first time, from the players themselves until it was picked up by the multitude and returned from what to those on the field seemed a 'great wall in mosaic, composed chiefly of flesh-coloured tiles set in sombre-hued cement, splashed with vivid spots of colour'. Gallaher said afterwards that he had never been more impressed in his life than when he stood there and listened to the chorus. New Zealanders on 26 January 1906 read a full, thoughtful account of the five-week-old game in the *Lyttelton Times*, the paper with the largest circulation in New Zealand, written a week after it had occurred:

> The scene at the ground was unique in the New Zealanders experience . . . What a contrast between this frenzied throng at Cardiff and that other great gathering at the Crystal Palace a fortnight previously! The English crowd was quiet, orderly and undemonstrative, only mildly partisan . . . The Welsh . . . were there to sing and to cheer their champions to victory . . . Imagine some forty thousand people singing their National Anthem with all the fervour of which the Celtic heart is capable . . . It was the most impressive incident I have ever witnessed on a football field. It gave a semi-religious solemnity to this memorable contest . . . was intensely thrilling, even awe-inspiring . . . It was a wonderful revelation of the serious spirit in which the Welsh take their football.
>
> The game that followed was an Homeric contest of skill, endurance, pace and sheer brute strength — the hardest, keenest struggle I can ever remember. But long after the incidents of play have grown dim and blurred in one's memory, the impression that will linger still vividly will be that vast chorus sounding forth the death-knell . . . of the All Blacks . . .

Hodges kicked off for Wales. For ten minutes it was thrust and counter-thrust. The All Blacks' forwards were checked when they tried to move the ball away, Winfield behind the Welsh team began to field the ball and put it into touch with unerring accuracy that would have such an effect on the game. The pace was a hot one from the start. Wales, it became clear, was intent on taking the initiative. Their placing of the third front row man at the loose head was impeding a quick heel whilst Owen darted around his own scrum to whip the ball away or, typically, leaving the ball in his four-man back row, accepted the burly New Zealander's tackle in return for the penalty. When the All Blacks did break in a body to the open field it was Owen who fell on the ball. He was knocked out but soon up and, turning the psychological screw, was noticeably grinning at Gallaher. Shortly after this the Welsh pack broke through so that only hurried play by Mynott and Deans cleared the ball. After fifteen minutes the All Blacks, though tackling ferociously, had not managed a single sweeping attack movement. Their forwards were being beaten in the set pieces and finding it hard to hold the Welsh 7 in the loose. When Gillett kicked away possession, Winfield caught it and, nursing the pack, sent them back to their encampment in the New Zealand 25 where the All Blacks were reeling under the incessant Welsh onslaught. Owen gave rapidly to Bush who feinted to go blind, wrong-footed the converging tacklers and dropped for goal. It was on target but fell short. Within a minute Wales almost scored

159

again when J. F. Williams did well to field a cross-kick to the right wing and even better to swerve around Wallace. Deans and Gillett were not in position. Williams gave Llewellyn the ball as he went at top speed. It was an awkward low pass that he took almost around his back and, with no-one to beat, he dropped the ball after half a dozen strides (in 1926 Llewellyn would recall that he was 'afterwards told by Mr Percy Bush that no player should attempt to pick up a ball with his shoulder blades'.). Each time Wales had run the ball the New Zealanders had moved in on their men, rightly fearful of the individual genius of the Welsh backs. Percy Bush in particular had already done enough in his role of elusive pimpernel, able to stop dead in his tracks allowing opponents to flounder past, beaten by their own momentum, to indicate they were right so to do. There, were, however, other cards available to Wales. Owen now chose to play the Welsh joker.

Gwyn Nicholls had taken the ball as the New Zealanders tried to break out and sent it back. A few more robust exchanges led to a scrum, 15 yards in front of the right touch-line and about mid-way between the half-way line and the New Zealand 25. This was the place, now was the time. Nicholls confirmed with his line that the maneouvre was definitely on. There would be no second chance. So far Cliff Pritchard had been deliberately shunned in any Welsh attacks, all of which had been orthodox four three-quarter movements. The idea was to use him when chance arose to widen the attack unexpectedly. Owen was famed for his reverse pass from a standing position so that it has been accepted that it was this which let him switch the points of the attack after a blind-side feint. On the contrary it was the scrum-half's change of direction like a revolving door that brought the famous score. Owen wrote over twenty-years later:

> . . . I can claim some credit for the move that tricked a deadly keen defence — Placing Willie Llewellyn, our right wing three-quarter, on the short side of the scrummage, and Percy Bush, my partner, about two yards inside Llewellyn, and also to the right of the scrummage, there remained about two-thirds of the width of the field on my left. Our forwards made the effort expected of them and gave me possession of the ball by a quick heel . . . I . . . decided that the moment had indeed come, and varied the attack by running a few yards to the right touch-line, knowing how the blind side of a Welsh scrummage would attract an anxious defence. In a flash I realized that the gap on the right had been filled at the expense of the rest of the field . . . I pulled up sharp and, seeing Teddy Morgan unmarked, I changed my direction and made for the left . . . try to imagine all this happening very quickly . . .

160

Gwyn Nicholls, our great right centre, according to plan had followed me in my run to the right so as further to deceive the defence. Having turned, I ran to the left for a few yards before passing the ball on to Cliff Pritchard, our rover, who played up well by taking the ball on the run. My pass to Pritchard had been long enough to do the trick, and I remember standing still for a moment to size up the situation and then realizing that, barring accidents, a try was almost certain.

A Welsh team had often passed irresistibly in combination; this one had feinted in concert. Even so Owen had only provided the key. The door had still to be opened. Pritchard had picked the ball up off his toes as it went to ground, then swerved to the left, losing one man, and giving to Gabe who went as if to run inside, straightened and handed on to Morgan 20 yards out. He outpaced the flailing McGregor and sped between Gillett, caught in two minds by a barely perceptible change of pace, and the line in a last lung-bursting surge of acceleration. There had been almost twenty-five minutes played. Morgan had scored far out on the left at the Westgate Street end. Up in the air went hats, handkerchiefs, leeks and cheers that sounded more like the screams and roars of those who could not suppress their emotion, or delight, anymore. The pandemonium was so loud and prolonged, well after Winfield had missed the difficult conversion, that a cart-horse bolted down Westgate Street. Inside the ground Arthur Gould, forgetting the dignity of a selector, had forsaken the confines of his seat and was dancing all over the press tables, his hat gyrating wildly in his hand, as he shouted to any who still disbelieved — 'The fastest Rugby sprinter in the world! Teddy Morgan has scored!'

It was to be the only score. Wales would have other chances: later Bush scurried around the blind side to put Morgan away only for that hero to drop the ball; Bush himself narrowly missed another drop goal, and late in the second half Nicholls made a searing run (the greatest of the day some thought) only to see Harding fumble the ball with the posts in front of him. The game's outcome was settled by that solitary, masterly-worked and supremely executed try but its shape until the defeat was finally, ruefully, conceded was dramatically altered as it became Wales's turn to defend desperately and counter-attack sporadically. In part this was a Welsh error, born of the understandable belief that they had better concentrate on keeping their noses in front (Rhys Gabe and Nicholls himself regretted the decision in later years). Mostly it was the recoil of a New Zealand team, unsteadied by the crowd and the force of early play, who bit on the bullet that Owen had manufactured. They stopped lofting the ball up in favour of low trajectory kicks. Winfield still gobbled them up and pushed them back as he would all afternoon in an incredible demonstration of line-kicking. When the first half petered out it was Wales who were pressed back and the All Blacks forwards who were winning more and more ball only to see their backs squander it. During the interval the crowd sang to keep their team on the slippery peak they had ascended. The second half saw some of the toughest exchanges ever meted out on a rugby field. It was dauntingly hard play. In the first session the Welsh forwards had given their backs the chances they needed and so won the game — those same forwards now ensured, by play as intelligent as it was resolute, that the prize would not be lost for, beaten in the tight, they broke up quickly to act as auxiliary units in defence, harrying, tackling and covering like men possessed. The *Daily Mail* called the 'greatest game of the century' a victory for forwards whose part in the first Welsh Golden Era they rightly pinpointed at its most significant moment:

> It has long been the contention of competent Welsh critics that the supremacy gained by the Principality at Rugby Football has been as much due to the fine work of their forwards as to the combination and cleverness of their backs. This theory received ample proof on Saturday, as it was her forwards whom Wales had mainly to thank for her victory. For the first time since their arrival in this country the New Zealand pack found themselves beaten for cleverness in the scrum . . . (Welsh) forwards . . . play very much the same style of game as the New Zealanders in that they regard the scrum as an integral piece of the machinery.

The Welsh pack swarmed onto the ball 'like terriers after a rat'. Joseph and Travers, both tireless pursuers, would join Harding, Williams and Hodges in foot rushes or back up Dai Jones in the line-out and scrums where his strength was sorely needed. The star of the pack was undoubtedly Charlie Pritchard of Newport, 'always in the thick of the fight', throwing himself at the man in possession as did all the Welsh tacklers in their efforts to disrupt New Zealand's rhythm. 'He knocked 'em down like nine pins', said George Travers. And behind him, Owen, Nicholls and Gabe were waiting if the extra back should miss, but Cliff Pritchard, the Pontypool undertaker, was measuring his victims — 'To have played only 7 backs', concluded the *Western Mail*, '. . . would have been disastrous in view of the tremendous amount of stopping work put in by the Pontypool man . . . His deadly tackling was chiefly the means of preventing the attack of the Colonial backs being fully developed on a single occasion. As the half wore on, despite some mispassing and fumbles from the increasingly anxious All Blacks, it became clear that only straight running and individual brilliance would break this deadly keen defence'.

There were less than ten minutes left when that effort was made. Although, on the balance of the day's play, no-one in the press expressed any doubt about Wales deserving victory, perhaps, with some luck, by two more clear tries if the ball had gone to hand, what happened now has reverberated throughout the rugby history of both nations. Terry McLean, the distinguished New Zealand rugby writer, has affirmed that it was a moment 'which . . . was to be the greatest event in the history of New Zealand rugby because it provided a basis, a starting point, a seed of nationalism upon which all aspects of the game were to depend in succeeding years'. There was never to be a non-score like it again. There could never be a game like this one again, for it was the sum total of a constellation of factors in rugby and in these two societies which would never be repeated. The Bob Deans incident was, paradoxically, vital for rugby history, because of the way in which it could not be resolved. It symbolized the continuing struggle for supremacy. Deans, whose own form all afternoon had been disappointing — the *Western Mail* noted, 'He was very slow and always easily tackled by the Welsh backs despite his great weight' — in his thrust for the line, and in his actions thereafter, resurrected the All Blacks from their defeat. The Deans 'try' was the grit in the oyster that produced a black pearl for future generations. It was a seed that would survive his own death by peritonitis a mere three years later, before he was twenty-four; it has survived the deaths of Dave Gallaher in France in 1917 and of his great rival that day, Charlie Pritchard, who died, in 1915, from his wounds in that same war that reduced Dai 'Tarw' Jones to a crippled shadow. The Deans 'try' was in all probability, and so far as can be reconstructed from contradictory evidence seventy-five years later, *not* a try, but it remains a very important event.

It began when from a line-out just inside the New Zealand half the ball, having been won by Wales, was kicked over Roberts' head and Wallace, lurking on the left wing, swooped on it to set off on one of those runs across the face of his opponents for which, long-striding and deceptively fast, he was famed. 'Carbine' Wallace crossed half-way, cut left across Nicholls and sped away upfield as Gabe converged on him — 'The great Colonial went through the Welsh back division like a mackerel through a shoal of herrings, and it looked as if nothing would stop him'. Outside the Welsh 25 he was confronted by Winfield who made this wonderful three-quarter hesitate a fraction. In that instant Wallace, throwing a pass left to Deans was tackled by Llewellyn who had raced infield from the right wing. Deans was 30 yards out and running in a line mid-way between goal-posts

163

and corner flag with no Welsh player in front of him. To make sure of 5 points he made the fatal error of turning in towards the post which put him, as he could see out of the corner of his eye, into the path of the fastest man on both sides, little Teddy Morgan who had hared back to cover from his left wing position. Deans straightened up about 10 yards from the goal-line. So much is not in dispute. What occurred now, is.

That a newspaper should have a central role in the affair is significant. The press had, from the 1880s, begun to report rugby more and more fully in the accurate surmise that the game's popularity sold copies. Indeed the life of the South Wales daily and evening papers was, from their first steps in the early 1870s paralleled by the growth of the society and its sport. It is, however, quite appropriate that the newspaper which fanned the flames of Deans' grievance was the London *Daily Mail*. Founded by Alfred Harmsworth in 1896, the half-penny *Mail* was skilfully designed to appeal to a new mass audience who wanted a paper that looked like the 'quality' penny papers but, in fact, purveyed sensationalism. Northcliffe insisted that his paper carry 'talking-points' on every page; he gave saturation cover to sport, especially both types of football, inaugurating the 'gossip' sports writer as well as straightforward reports; above all he was the master of the 'stunt' story which he depicted to his editors as 'something which astounds' or 'any act which is surprising, theatrically effective'. The invincible All Blacks were , through their unstoppable progress, exactly such a stunt in motion. *Mail* reporters followed them everywhere. The nature of their winning was used as credence for the proprietor's views on the growing superiority of 'colonial' stock to those left in over-populated, unadventurous Britain. When the tour was over it was the *Daily Mail* who published the booklet *Why the All Blacks Triumphed* with a lead piece by Gallaher but, mostly, a collection of their match reports. And in that book appeared a facsimile of the telegram Deans had sent to the newspaper at 10.26 a.m. on the Sunday after the match, in a response, as a New Zealand paper revealed in February 1906, 'to a query by the *Daily Mail* as to his try, which was disallowed in the match against Wales'. Deans was a part, albeit unwittingly, of a *Daily Mail* stunt when he sent his famous telegram. It read:

> Grounded Ball 6 inches over line some of Welsh players admit try. Hunter and Glasgow can confirm was pulled back by Welshmen before Referee arrived. Deans.

Hardly surprising then that the *Daily Mail* in its match report used the words — 'Those in a best position to judge state that Deans grounded the ball six inches over the line and some of the Welsh players admit . . . that Deans, after crossing the line, was pulled back'. The only Welshman who believed Deans had scored was Teddy Morgan whose own testimony in the 1920s revivified the matter. George Dixon confided to his diary that Deans had gone over 'the chalk mark' but his understandable belief in Deans' assertion is not really backed up by the facts that he saw it happen from the touch-line and, more importantly, thought Wallace 'made a brilliant run and right on the line passed to Deans who dived over' (the pass was made just before the Welsh 25 line); he went on to assert that Gabe 'who tackled Deans as he was falling' could be counted amongst those who thought it an 'absolutely fair try'. Rhys Gabe's own views were very different. At the time the slightly incredulous press, given the unreliable nature of the newspaper source, tended to dismiss the issue. Unfortunately their own reports do not clarify things since they were, including the *Mail* man, at ground level half a field's length and more than half its breadth away, peering through a late-afternoon December mist. The *Western Mail* has Wallace passing to Hunter (not Deans) who was 'held up a yard outside'; the *South Wales Daily News* writer admitted that his view was 'obstructed' for the early part of Wallace's run but that he saw Morgan come over to help Winfield tackle Deans before the centre could touch down. Deans' attempts to struggle over were then prevented by reinforcements. Hunter, of course, was not the recipient of Wallace's pass any more than it was Winfield who helped tackle Deans. The incident, in other words, was too far away for any reporter to know what had really happened. Further, the sequence of events was too rapid for all the players near to be sure of their outcome. If we begin by assuming complete probity on the part of all the players who recollected events a likely outcome does nonetheless emerge in which the much-maligned Mr Dallas retrieves some credit.

In 1934 Billy Wallace wrote in New Zealand that Deans had scored and that Dickie Owen had re-placed the ball to confound the referee: in Wales Willie Llewellyn effectively countered this by pointing out that he had brought Wallace down so that both were on the floor — 'and neither he nor I could form an opinion on a matter in which only a few inches were involved and that some yards away from us'. Similarly we can place the words of George Nicholson, a New Zealand forward who was running the line, — 'I saw the dive and the tackle . . . It was a try, true enough', alongside Cliff Pritchard's view in 1935 — 'I was near enough to be able to say that it was not a try'. Deans apart, the crucial piece of evidence, for a score comes from Teddy Morgan whose statements certainly bedevilled the issue. For E. H. D. Sewell's book *Rugby Football* in 1921, Dr Morgan ended his contribution by saying that Ack Llewellyn (the Welsh touch judge of the day) thought Deans had scored ' . . . it was I who tackled him to prevent him running behind. As I tackled him (a few yards outside) I distinctly saw the white goal line underneath me, and yet, when I got up off Deans' legs, he was holding on to the ball (with two others of our side) which was grounded about a foot outside the line. Dallas, the referee, came running up and had not seen what had happened after the tackle'. When the 1924 All Blacks came it was Morgan's personal assertion that Deans had scored which confirmed New Zealand opinion, though a book, *The Triumphant Tour,* about the 1924 visitors, which was published in Wellington in 1925, has Morgan saying that Wallace 'scored' and that Gabe believed this too. Both assertions are entirely groundless and made more intriguing by the assembly of Morgan, Gabe and Nicholls in a broadcasting studio in 1935 where, although the winger still held his view, he did not question Gabe's own tackle:

> *Teddy Morgan:* . . . I was close by at the time. When I got to the actual spot Deans was over the line with the ball, but by the time the referee reached there he had been pushed back.

> *Rhys Gabe:* . . . It was I who tackled Deans . . . in 1905 a player who grounded the ball outside was not allowed to continue his efforts to the line. A scrummage had to be ordered outside . . . I brought Deans down outside the line. That is definite . . . In the pavilion later Deans claimed he had scored . . . he said 'Why did you pull me back?' I replied 'Why did you struggle to go forward after you had been tackled outside? If you had been on the line you needn't have struggled to go further. If you hadn't reached the line why didn't you leave the ball there?' To that there was no reply.

> *Gwyn Nicholls:* . . . Yes, I was standing over you at the time. Deans did wriggle his way after you had brought him down outside and he ought to have been penalised for doing it.

Gabe's is the complete counter-assertion to Bob Deans. In the 1960s he spelled out his case succinctly — 'The legend that Deans scored has been built up over the years on a misconception. Dr Teddy Morgan . . . after the Wales - All Blacks dinner in 1924 . . . wrote his views on the menu for New Zealand captain Cliff Porter (who said) . . . "If the man who collared Deans says he scored that's the end of the argument." But it was me, not Morgan, made that tackle. I confess that, just for a moment, I thought Deans had made it. Then he started to try to wriggle forward. I knew the truth. He had grounded short of the line. I hung on'.

There is obviously no way of fully reconciling these accounts but they may, perhaps, fit as jigsaw pieces of a puzzle almost no-one saw whole. The pivotal issue is the double-tackle of Morgan and Gabe (later assisted by Harding); Morgan was running diagonally leftwards towards Deans. The big centre had straightened up for the line when Morgan dived laterally (hence perhaps the white line beneath Morgan though since he also says this was 'a few yards outside' it is difficult to credit both pieces of evidence) and brought Deans to earth slightly sideways given the direction of the tackle. At which moment Gabe pounced on the New Zealander whose forward movement had been slowed but not entirely stopped by the first tackle. Deans now jerked over the line and, for a moment or two, with others in attendance, the tug-of-war went on. It was Percy Bush, himself no sluggard, not Owen, who removed the ball — 'I was on the spot and immediately picked up the ball and replaced it in the exact position in which it had been originally grounded by Deans'. Bush thought this was to assist the referee; naturally this act can be interpreted as over-zealous if, as New Zealanders asserted, John Dallas was adrift in his street clothes and 'ordinary walking boots'. It is the nature of the referee's evidence, however, which finally clinches the matter.

There was nothing unusual in 1905 for referees to wear street clothes nor is there any evidence other than Dixon's angry assertions in private that this ex-International was far from the game at any other point through lack of speed about the field; the press in general commented on his strict control of a strenuous game. Most referees would have struggled in the wake of Wallace's powerful run so that it would be perfectly in order to disallow a try if he had any doubts. Mr Dallas had no doubts. He thought he saw what had happened. His judgement may have been faulty but it cannot be said to be blind. When Wallace, after slight pause, gave the ball to Deans who cut in on a longer route to the posts the referee was running to the centre's right and, as Deans moved away from the posts Dallas, in the perfect style for observation, maintained his own shorter path to the line parallel with the action. If he had been so far behind play he would surely have run straight to the mêlée around Deans. Coming up after, as he did, some players who had, of course, followed the path of the ball itself, assumed this is what he had done. On the contrary Dallas had already given his judgement, and blown his whistle before he ran over to order a scrum. Bob Deans might still consider his thrust had legitimately taken him over but the referee ruled otherwise because he had not seen it that way at all. In a letter he wrote:

On Monday morning I was astonished to read in the papers on my return to Edinburgh, that Deans had 'scored' a try that I had disallowed.

When the ball went back on its way out to Deans I kept going hard and when Deans was tackled he grounded the ball 6 to 12 inches short of the goal-line. At that moment he could neither pass nor play the ball, and as I passed between the Welsh goal posts my whistle went shrill and loud.

It is true that when I got to the spot to order a scrum, the ball was over the goal-line, but without hesitation I ordered a scrum at the place where Deans was grounded. I never blew my whistle at the spot. It had gone before. No try was scored by Deans.

The ironic feature was that early rejection of other referees had caused the appointment of John Dallas who, because he was a Scot, was, even before the game, suspect in New Zealand eyes. The *Manchester Guardian* reported five days after the game that an official member of the All Black party said that what had 'hurt his sense of rightness was the selection of a Scots referee' since he was 'certain that any native of Scotland would necessarily, by previous events, be forced into prejudice against New Zealand interests'. The 'previous events' mentioned was not the Scotland defeat but an acrimonious dispute over the division of the gate money for that international. In Wales this was one area where amicability reigned for the New Zealand share of the record £2,650 gate receipts was much more than the £500 they had been guaranteed. Perhaps that was no consolation to Dave Gallaher as he hurried over to Gwyn Nicholls to shake his hand and exchange jerseys before the Welsh captain was chaired off by the crowd, but he and his team had more than played their part in what remains because of all that serves, then and now, as background to that afternoon, in Terry McLean's words 'the greatest match of all'. And Gwyn Nicholls would remember with some gratitude the black cat who had wandered into the laundry business that he and Bert Winfield, his partner, were operating as usual that morning.

The night of 16 December was given over to junketings that surpassed even those that had followed on the relief of Mafeking. Editors waxed eloquent that night about the vigour still left in non-colonial 'stay at homes' who 'had come to the rescue of the Empire' and 'enhanced tremendously' Welsh prestige 'as a nation'. The natives went on the town. Bars, hotels and restaurants were full and closed within fifteen minutes after the end. The trains that chugged the revellers home were met at each station by songs and cheers. The telegraph and telephone services were used to twice any previous capacity as reporters filed their stories: in

Cowbridge people waited on street corners for cyclists to bring the news; at Pontypridd an elated newsagent gave away free the *Evening Express* football paper; men who had been on strike in Monmouthshire walked back from Cardiff as they had walked the 15 miles there to the game; the Welsh team and guests were taken in two four-in-hand carriages to dinner at the Esplanade, Penarth, and Cliff Pritchard arriving wearily back, in Pontypool, on the last train found several hundred people waiting after midnight to hoist him up and to carry him home.

Home was still a long trek for the New Zealand side who had to hold back their disappointment to move rapidly into further Welsh frays. Their remaining games in Wales left them with only that one defeat on their record. The mauling they received, however, by a rampant Welsh dragon meant that it was only a large measure of luck that saved them. It was luck they could not be begrudged after the international. On 21 December they beat the hastily-assembled Glamorgan side (a number of first-choice Internationals had withdrawn) at Swansea by 9 points to nil; two days later Newport, playing Cliff Pritchard as a guest, revived in the second half under the goading of scrum-half Tommy Vile, himself a master on the day, to lose narrowly 6 points to 3. Worse was to come for Welsh clubs seeking a famous victory. First, in Cardiff on Boxing Day, before a crowd of 40,000, Cardiff, unbeaten that season, went down 10 points to 8 after being 5 - 5 at half-time. The New Zealand victory swivelled on the cheeky-chappie antics of Cardiff's captain, Percy Bush who allowed a loose ball over his line to bobble whilst Nicholson set out on a futile run towards it. The futility became Bush's despair when it turned on its end away from him, he miskicked in panic and the New Zealand forward touched down. Finally, again at St. Helen's, on 30 December 1905, Fred Scrines, operating effectively as a 'rover' crashed over for an unconverted try in the first half only to see it overtaken by a huge drop-goal from Wallace that the unpredictable, high wind assisted through the posts for a 4 - 3 triumph.

Then they were gone, leaving a rugby memory that contributed enormously to the future of the sport in Wales. In the thirty-two games they had played through the length and breadth of the British Isles, they had conceded only seven tries, and four of these had been scored in Wales. To the end some of them would be haunted by the Welsh days of their amazing tour. It was not easy to forget. When the party boarded the liner *New York* at Southampton they paused on the gangway as Welsh melodies drifted up to them — 'for a moment several . . . thought they must have got into the wrong train and were at Cardiff. There could be no mistaking

'Hen Wlad fy Nhadau' and 'Sospan Fach' — What could it mean?' The singers were thirty red-capped Welsh students from the Hartley University School come to send the All Blacks away. They delivered a final catechism on the jetty.

What's the matter with the New Zealanders? — They're *all right!*

Who has the best footballers? — WALES!

Who has the next best? — New Zealand!

Who has the worst? — England!

Who carried the leek? — Gwyn Nicholls!

Who ate the leek? — Gallaher!

The amused New Zealanders smiled and waved. They would be back.

'A GAME DEMOCRATIC AND AMATEUR'

A DECEMBER afternoon in 1905 finally established that rugby had indeed become the national sport of Wales. Just as the political and social concerns of rural Wales (disestablishment of the Church; temperance; nonconformity) had continued to have an appeal, and much support, in the industrial South, thereby investing a distinct region with national undertones, so this distinctively regional game now presented a national appeal to the rest of Wales. The key was success. David Lloyd George's elevation to cabinet office in the climacteric month of December 1905, the first Welshman to hold such a high government post since the seventeenth century, was hailed by contemporaries as the achievement in politics that Welsh attainments in the world of commerce, music *and* rugby had long promised. Within a few years his son would be turning out for London Welsh and, in March 1911 when Wales defeated Ireland 16 - 0, Ellis Jones Griffith, M.P. for Anglesey and leader of the Welsh group in Parliament, lamented his relative ignorance of a game that would have delighted him, because of Welsh superiority, even more if 'North Wales had been represented in so great a side.' Earlier prejudices had, it seemed, been discarded almost totally for now the crowds themselves, it was noted, contained a fair sprinkling of clergy. Concern by 1914 was no longer over the deleterious effects of rugby football on the life of Wales. Now it was the apparent decline in rugby fortunes that was worrying staunch supporters of Welsh nonconformity and nationalist sentiment, like the journalist and M.P., J. Hugh Edwards, who would write in his magazine *Wales*, in February 1914 after the third successive defeat by England, that the result 'cannot but be disappointing to all devotees of the Principality who are as anxious to see the prestige of our little land as triumphantly upheld in the

171

domain of play as it is in the more strenuous spheres of administrative work and of commercial enterprise.'

Rugby had become a central focus for debate within wider Welsh society just before the First World War for two reasons only loosely related. The first was that, despite continued expansion of population and of exports, especially in coal, the crises from loss of overseas markets that had earlier afflicted slate in the North and tinplate in the West, began to be felt in a coal trade (already experiencing geological difficulties because of deeper seams) notably under-mechanized and over-manned. After 1906, conflicts over 'abnormal' working places underground and the idea of a guaranteed minimum wage led on to harsh local, regional and even national disputes that dented the conciliatory patterns of labour relations which relative prosperity had allowed room to manoeuvre. To an extent, the decline of some rugby clubs in the coastal hinterland, as well as standards of play, was a foretaste of what was to come in the inter-war years. Secondly, there was a crisis within rugby itself. This was, partly, an exaggerated despondency over the national side, more seriously an awareness that a falling rate of popular interest was connected to a decline in the type and standards of Welsh play. In fact, the widespread sense of a coming crisis within Wales led some social commentators to overplay the degree of community stability that had been experienced in the past, and some rugby writers to stress a loss of greatness at the expense of remembering how suddenly the 'golden era' had dawned. Either way, rugby was now stitched into the pattern of Welsh life forever. Thomas Jones, one of the most influential Welshmen of the twentieth century, a man who would serve as secretary to four prime ministers, the Liberal Lloyd George, the Tories Bonar Law and Stanley Baldwin and even the first Labour P.M., Ramsay MacDonald, launched a new magazine in January 1914, *The Welsh Outlook*, to examine the nature of modern Wales. Rugby was immediately praised for its role within the changed social structure of Wales:

> Why . . . should the challenge of Association to Rugby . . . be a thing that demands serious thought . . .? In the first instance, Rugby is, and can remain, the game of the Welshman. The international records of the past twenty years show that the Principality can hold an equal if not superior hand in the game. The names of the giants are on the lips of the people: there are traditions in Rugby that will rouse a crusading fire: there is a merit of past achievement that sustains, as nations are upheld by victories. The Association code in Wales is new and alien and comes in on the back of its popularity elsewhere: it is the game of the alien of the valleys whose immigration and de-nationalizing tendency is one of the major problems of

our countury. It is best reported in alien newspapers . . . The centres of interest . . . will be in Newcastle, Manchester, London, and the eyes of its followers will be outward and not inward. The intimate value of internal rivalry will be absent and the social context of the game will be cosmopolitan.

Rugby, on the contrary, will remain, as in the past — our inter-Welsh club game . . . the proportion of game [that is] entirely Welsh enormously outweights the others . . . Wales possesses in Rugby Football a game . . . which is immeasurably more valuable than the popular code of the other countries . . . It has established an unassailable tradition upon the basis of the game as a game, apart from its spectacular draw: it has made a democracy not only familiar with an amateur sport of distinguished rank but is in reality a discovery of democracy which acts as participant and patron. On the other hand, Rugby in Scotland is aristocratic in the sense that artisan players can be found in few clubs other than the Border fifteens . . . English Rugby is precisely similar except in those outposts of the game which have developed under the direct stimulus and encouragement of the Welsh game — Leicester, Gloucester and Devonshire . . .

This then is the centre of the position. A game democratic and amateur is a rare thing — a unique thing to be cherished, and therefore the concern of thinking men who value the complex influences making for higher levels of citizenship. Other countries are handicapped . . . Wales begins many evolutionary turns forward.

Inaccurate in a number of particulars (the F.A.W. was founded five years before the W.F.U., and so can hardly be said to be 'alien') this perspective from 1914 is, nonetheless, acute in its emphasis on the attraction of the game itself and, albeit a little idealistic, to the point in assessing the game as a cultural artefact, as a facet of society. It rather skips over, however, two vital matters: the automatic assumption of rugby both as an expression of Welshness and the guarantor of amateur sport for all social classes. Betweeen 1906 and 1914, the latter was to become one of the sore points of Welsh rugby, whilst it was only in the wake of 1905 that playing success became firmly associated in popular thinking with racial characteristics culled, mostly, from a Celtic past as mythical as they were imaginary. Myths, though, can be important shapers of subsequent reality. This one fitted well into a contemporary Wales intent on showing how its 'Welsh' society was the unique motor of its amazing progress, in so many diverse areas, within the British Empire. The most important newspaper in Wales at the time voiced this position in a lengthy, eloquent editorial on 18 December 1905 that trumpeted the shift of rugby from pastime to popular institution onto a national standard bearer whose conduct, therefore, would come under increasing scrutiny on and off the fields:

Football is the historic national game of England. It is, in its primitive forms, the essence of nearly every form of modern sport . . . Today there is no game to equal it, both in the popular and the scientific phases. The game demands not only the trained and sound physique, but the well-balanced mind, sane judgement, tact and resource. Its finest exponents may well represent a nation mentally active and physically strong. So far we have not been on debatable ground, but we must come to less firm ground. The New Zealanders came to this country with a great reputation and it has been more than justified . . . leading London organs of public opinion had no hesitation in saying that as a body of athletes these visitors were unequalled, and to be overcome by Wales, the smallest of all nationalities was an 'unthinkable contingency' . . . Nothing had interfered with the triumphal march of the Colonials. Before them England, Scotland and Ireland went down . . . Wales was the last of the nations to be met, and the coming contest was regarded as the greatest of the century . . . Public enthusiasm was as fervent as on the morning of some great Waterloo when the destinies of Empires hung in the balance. Cardiff for the day was centre of interest in the Old and the New World. Never before in the history of the greatest of all games was there such a situation . . . Wales broke the spell; she accomplished what the sister nations had found impossible, she achieved the highest record in the annals of modern sport . . . When you consider for a moment what Wales had to do, and when you think of how she did it, there arises in every man the feeling of highest admiration for qualities that find the most popular expression. The men — these heroes of many victories — that represented Wales embodied the best manhood of the race. And here we are met with some of the greatest problems in the development of distinct nationalities. We all know the racial qualities that made Wales supreme on Saturday: but how have they been obtained? Wales has a more restricted choice of champions than the other nations. She has had fewer opportunities in the exercise of some of the mental and physical powers than the nations with ancient Universities and wider fields of training. It is admitted she is the most poetic of the nations. It is amazing that in the greatest of all popular pastimes she should be equally distinguished . . . the great quality of defence and attack in the Welsh race is to be traced to the training of the early period when powerful enemies drove them to their mountain fortresses. There was developed, then, those traits of character that find fruition today. 'Gallant little Wales' has produced sons of strong determination, invincible stamina, resolute, mentally keen, physically sound. It needs no imaginative power to perceive that the qualities that conquered on Saturday have found another expression in the history of Welsh education: that long struggle against odds that has given the Principality her great schools and her progressive colleges. The national traits are equally apparent in both contexts.

174

A National University with its constituent colleges had been followed in the early twentieth century by a National Library and a National Museum. From its own apex of attainment the W.F.U. turned to consider again the provision of a suitable arena, a National Ground. Throughout 1905, under the impetus of Ack Llewellyn of Pontypridd, the Committee had considered hard whether to invest funds in such a project. The Scots had already purchased their ground at Inverleith and, in 1906, the offer of the G.W.R. to lease land, with a railway siding, in Roath, caused the Secretary to investigate. With an annual credit balance hovering around, and often well over, £3,000 in each year down to 1914, the investment would seem to have been a wise one. Twickenham opened as the English international ground in 1910. However, the W.F.U., not quite prepared to settle for a sole international venue and bemused by falling attendances, preferred to continue payment for stand and turf renewal (£2,000 in 1904 and £2,500 in 1912) especially at the Arms Park whose tenure in 1911 was assured to the Cardiff Club and the W.F.U. by the Bute family. In retrospect this was a poor half-way house that the Union would come to regret, but it is symptomatic of the surprising uncertainty that still dogged rugby in Wales.

There was a ready willingness to rebut what were regarded as the jealous jibes of 'such men as Mr E. H. D. Sewell and others of his kidney' when they extolled the 'public school virtues' of other countries. In Wales, it was alleged, 'ill deeds began.' These remarks, made in 1906 and 1909 respectively, caused 'Forward' of the *Western Mail* to assert, yet again, that 'Football in Wales is a democratic game, and the dock labourer or collier has an equal chance of playing for his country as the man from either of the great varsities . . . It is no use burking the fact that the supremacy of Wales is not accepted with a good grace by the other countries.' A. F. Harding of London Welsh captained an Anglo-Welsh touring team to New Zealand and Australia in 1908, but the Welshmen in the party were drawn exclusively from the ranks of a well-educated, professional class, some of whom were wealthy in their own right. Clearly this did not square with the accepted practice within Wales, so that when a British side was mooted to tour South Africa in 1910, the W.F.U. resolved: 'That the team be selected irrespective of the social position of the players. That this Union make a selection from the list of Welsh players applying to participate . . . and . . . in the event of any player being rejected on the ground of Social Position that the Union withdraw their co-operation in the tour.'

Not all of the XV recommended (including Dickie Owen and Dick Jones) went on tour, under the joint managership of Walter Rees, but the

175

Welsh contingent, heavily drawn from Newport for whom the captain, the Irish International Dr. Tom Smyth was playing, did contain a carpenter and a brace of miners, so the point may be considered made. On the other hand, the W.F.U. within its own domestic confines, tried to leaven the unpalatable dough of 'objectionable play' by writing, in 1912, to the Headmasters of Llandovery, Brecon and Monmouth Schools to request 'the names and home addresses of prominent school players when leaving with the view of securing their services for Welsh Union clubs.' The schools were to receive touch-flags for use along with stand tickets for Head and Games Masters for home internationals. University Colleges, it was hoped, would provide suitable players as their own teams matured, and the W.F.U., despite an initial penny-pinching attitude that the Welsh Schools' Union combatted indignantly, stepped up their interest in, and doubled their monetary contribution to, the spread of rugby football in the Intermediate Schools. Such boosting, by funds and favours, of the 'amateur' was partly impelled by an alteration in the 'democratic' features of the game which no longer compelled automatic allegiance.

The correspondent who, in mid-season 1906, asserted that football was waxing not waning, with ticket-holders brandishing their entry cards 'as if they were going to an opera or any other entertainment' did add the caveat that 'to a large extent the fortunes of the game are wrapped up in the success of the national team.' This might explain why only 15,000 saw England lose at home to Wales in January, and why a paltry 9,000 turned out in Belfast to watch Ireland beat a lacklustre Welsh side, but the reason why the smallest crowd in years (albeit 25,000) had assembled in February to watch Wales narrowly defeat Scotland was more puzzling. Contemporaries began to wonder if Welsh crowds were so glutted with success as to be indifferent. Certainly the spectators and the Welsh XV in 1906 seemed to be suffering a hangover from the giddy days of 1905, but records, in crowds and in play itself, were soon broken again. What is incontestable is that rugby could not remain on one plane — the contradictions of these years were symptomatic of a transitional stage in Welsh rugby which, though still tinged by the glow of a harvest of success reaped from previous sowing, gradually lost its earlier innovatory thrust. The W.F.U. had to react now to opposition outside its purview, and to an enemy within, both of whom threatened to undercut the club rivalry upon which international leadership was based.

To begin with, soccer, so long ousted in the populous areas by the grip of rugby, began to mount a serious challenge. The foundation of the F.A.W.

at Ruabon in 1876 can hardly be said to have had the same repercussions that the establishment of the W.F.U. would cause from its inception in 1881. The principal cause of this was the virtual isolation of the 'dribbling code' in the North, so the formation, in 1893, of a South Wales and Monmouthshire Association for the sport was a shrewd move. Rugby, however, had so grapple-hooked the Welsh psyche that, in 1894, when the first soccer international, Wales v. Ireland, was held in South Wales the only suitable ground was that of the municipally-owned St. Helen's in Swansea. There were no South Walians in the side. Indeed, the *Western Mail* had to print a plan of a soccer field and rules to explain proceedings. Nonetheless around 8,000 people saw Wales win by four goals to one and 'Old Stager' was moved to remark that 'the votaries of "Socker" in the Principality, and particularly its southern portion, may congratulate themselves.' The first international at Cardiff, in 1896, was a disastrous 9 - 1 defeat but, slowly, Wales made its mark at soccer even if, on their second appearance in Cardiff, in 1900, with the wonderful Billy Meredith on the wing, they had to borrow the Arms Park and play on a Monday because Cardiff R.F.C. met Newport on the Saturday. It would be 1912 before any club from South Wales won the Welsh F.A. Cup, but the first Welsh soccer championship in 1907 confirmed the rise in popularity that was sending excursion trains out of South Wales to watch Bristol, just as North Wales journeyed to see the Merseyside teams. This explosion of interest in soccer, greatly stimulated by the F.A. Challenge Cup, was readily apparent after 1906. In that year there were 74 affiliated clubs in the South; by 1910 there were 262, and a plethora of local leagues. Even more significant of the extent of support was the launching of Cardiff Riverside F.C. as a professional club in 1910; in 1912 Newport County, Swansea Town and Llanelli had joined them, whilst the Southern League was bursting with South Welsh clubs who now, at least, had a prominent role within Welsh soccer. Rising gates were the by-product of this local rivalry, as they had been in rugby. The open play pursued by soccer clubs at this time proved attractive to those disenchanted by the defensive tactics so assiduously perfected by leading Welsh rugby clubs.

There were professional incursions within the handling code, too. The Northern Union (not called the Rugby League formally until 1922) judged it time to move bodily into Wales. In the course of 1907 a Northern Union football side was established at Aberdare (where the soccer team was a strong draw anyway), to join the teams formed in Ebbw Vale and Merthyr. At the start of the 1907-08 season Walter Rees, whilst admitting the reasonable gates being attracted, promised that premier clubs would visit 'the Hills' where, 'when that novelty has worn off, there will be a revulsion of feeling against the mongrel game that the professionals have introduced.' One of the problems was the relative decline of the Glamorgan and Monmouthsire Leagues whose ranks some leading, or rising, clubs were deserting (Pontypridd, Aberavon and Pontypool absented themselves in these years). Nor were Northern Union officials slow to repeat the success of overseas visitors. A New Zealand professional side were in Wales in late 1907. They played an international against Wales at Aberdare in January 1908. A crowd of around 10,000 saw Wales win a lively game by 9 points to 8. By April 1908 there were Welsh professional rugby teams at Aberdare, Barry, Ebbw Vale, Merthyr, Mid Rhondda and Treherbert. Their incision into the heartland of Welsh rugby was given depth by unity with soccer, as when after Wales beat Ireland 1 - 0, at a soccer international in Aberdare, in April 1908, Wigan immediately played Merthyr at rugby. Nonetheless, Welsh professional clubs had to be subsidized for their expensive journeys to the North of England, and the H.Q. of the Welsh Northern Union was, significantly enough, situated at Wrexham. The following season Wales was visited by Australia (the 'Wallabies') and a professional side (the 'Kangaroos') who would lose their international with Wales, by 14 points to 13, at Merthyr in January 1909. This rivalry, at international and club level, continued in Wales for a few more years, but its impetus (Ebbw Vale apart, where there was no major rival to the sport) fell away in the areas where it had began because those who did not watch amateur rugby turned, more and more, to soccer. It was in these sports that Merthyr and Aberdare would now excel for the next couple of decades, whereas the Northern Union reverted to poaching amateur talents for its own native clubs. George Hayward, the Swansea forward capped five times in 1908 and 1909, went to Wigan in December 1913 for £155 and 'good emoluments', as the northern scouts 'with bags of gold in quest of the cream of Cymric footballers' swooped down. Hayward's occupation in 1908 was given as 'learning to be a diver' — an arduous occupation that a New Zealand forward brought to a different kind of perfection in 1978 — and there was full understanding in Wales of the acceptance of money that, as the press put it, 'a poor workingman cannot honestly refuse when he has a family to consider'. There could be no truck, however, with the insidious growth of monetary payments made inside the code of Welsh rugby. On this development, and the W.F.U.'s stern response, had Northern Union based itself.

This was especially the case in the towns of Aberdare and Merthyr, the latter as recently as the 1860s still the largest urban settlement in Wales, where distance from the top clubs, an ebullient middle class willing to foster its own local initiatives, and a large working-class population, itself the oldest industrial workforce in Wales, worked as an unholy trinity of differentiation from the uniform pattern of amateurism that had been laid as a grid over South Wales. It was the variegated social structure of that coalfield which had grown at a varied pace and contained a number of separate traditions, including leisure pursuits, that now surfaced. Intense interest in cycling (producing professional world champions) and foot-racing (later professional Powderhall running), the playing of 'fives' (a pre-industrial hangover, a sort of hand-ball version of squash), whippet-training and, of course, the marathon mountain fighting that moved, via fair-ground booths, to the production of a clutch of world champions; all paralleled the avid taste for rugby football. It became difficult to resist the pressures towards equalization of rewards that payment would bring. Besides, to compete with these other magnets, and especially the mushrooming interest in soccer, success had, so far as possible, to be guaranteed. Expenses, and even patronage, could break the spirit yet stay inside the letter of the stern laws imposed by the I.B., but there was no gainsaying the illegality of inducements to play and bribes to lose. When the lid was blown on these scandals in 1907, those who had slandered the W.F.U. smiled with satisfaction; what is astonishing is how limited, given the possibilities, the abuses really were and how firmly the Union, convinced utterly of the value of amateur sport for their mixed society, acted.

Both Merthyr and Aberdare enjoyed a lively rugby life for a few seasons down to 1905. Aberdare won the Glamorgan League in the 1904-05 season by beating Treorchy in the last match. The press covered games fully in the town's local newspapers. W. J. Edwards of Aberaman, a future County Councillor for Glamorgan, recalled in his autobiography *From the Valley I Came* (1956) how, after returning from Ruskin College, Oxford, he was without employment or wages until the postman called: 'The first three letters were invitations to address meetings in the neighbourhood and to each invitation was attached a fee . . . Liza said, "You had better read the other letter" . . . It contained another invitation — to play rugby football; and there was a fee attached to this invitation, too, even a better one . . . By playing football every Saturday and addressing a few meetings in between, I was able to earn a better wage than I could possibly have earned by working in the pit'. More distinguished players received even better treatment. Dai 'Tarw' Jones, working as a collier in Aberaman, had come to play for Aberdare, whom he captained for two years from 1905, for 10s. a week in addition to train fares and meals. When the club reduced 'the wages' of all players to 5s. a week to pay off mounting debts, the great Welsh forward (capped against South Africa in December 1906) moved back to his old club Treherbert, although he still lived in Aberdare. This was the most notorious individual case caused by the practice of '. . . when we found that home players were not smart enough, we drew men from wherever we could get them at a wage we could scrape together.' Those were the words of E. M. Rees, ex-secretary of the Aberdare Club in 1907, whose reiterated allegations in the press from January 1907 led to a full-scale investigation by the Union. Rees had claimed that, apart from wages, leading players from other clubs had brought teams to play in Aberdare for exorbitant expenses and, worse, that in 1905 several of the Treorchy team had 'thrown' the crucial League match for 'a consideration of £15.' Rees, who had gone on to help form a Northern Union side in the locality and whose motives were, therefore, rather suspect, claimed that his sole interest was to inform the central authority of abuses beyond their knowledge. The repercussions of the lengthy investigation undertaken were considerable.

The sub-committee's final report of September 1907, asserted that the allegations that professionalism was 'rampant in Welsh clubs' were not proven, although some clubs and players were 'in the habit of paying and receiving hotel or travelling expenses in excess of the sum actually disbursed.' However, the documented revelations of the affairs of Aberdare rugby club were enough to ensure temporary suspensions for six players (including Fred Scrines of Swansea), a warning for less than scrupulous observance of the rules by Merthyr, and the permanent suspension of the entire committees of Aberdare and Treorchy, as well as of eight players, including Dai Jones. The W.F.U. were of the opinion that nothing as unfortunate had ever occurred in Welsh rugby before. Despite the fact that the Northern Union was on the wane immediately preceding the 1914-18 War, the disaffection was enough to ensure that amateur rugby was absent from Ebbw Vale until the post-war years, and struggled to keep going in Aberdare and Merthyr.

The principle of amateurism had moved the W.F.U. to foster their game in the schools, but the principle of democracy, at the root of the Welsh success, also had to be preserved when popularity waned. Ardent discussion took place over the desirability of leagues and a new cup

180

competition. The weather added to the urgency of the debate, for 1907 had been the wettest year for two decades and rugby fixtures in early 1908 were disrupted by persistent, heavy frosts. A team like Llwynypia from the Rhondda had re-formed in 1907 to look for its old, transient glory, but the grass-roots were in need of a good watering. Already, in April 1907, the W.F.U. had agreed to the eleven Junior Rugby Leagues forming a Junior Rugby Union that was subsidized by the parent body in addition to grants to individual clubs (twenty-two received £327 in 1908), yet the consensus of opinion grew that the status-quo was no longer healthy. The W.F.U. drew up, in late 1908, a scheme for two divisions in Welsh rugby, consisting of eight and twelve clubs respectively (with Cardiff, Swansea, Newport and Llanelli guaranteed perpetuity in the former), as well as two district divisions (East and West of Bridgend). Two clubs were to go up and down each season, on a points basis. Only Llanelli, of the four named clubs, agreed unreservedly to the scheme which, apart from offers to play more junior clubs, was thus rendered inoperative, despite all protests by the junior sides. The matter was raised at subsequent A.G.M.s with the final result, in 1911, that leading clubs would give eight away fixtures to nominated clubs in Wales, but that the League remained in abeyance. The grants to clubs in difficulty grew as a second-best alternative.

The press in 1910 and 1911 were ready to berate the short-sighted view of more established clubs whose 'lack of enterprise . . . is more dangerous than the steady progress of soccer.' The cry was now for the re-introduction of the knock-out game since the fact that 'cup competitions in the old days were sometimes fighting contests without regard to any rules is no sound argument against cup competitions today, for laws of the game are more clearly defined, players as well as crowds are better educated, and the governing body are now in a position to exercise greater control.' Once more, however, the W.F.U. proved reluctant to act with any great resolution, so that it was only at the instigation of W. J. Trew, elected to the committee at the 1913 A.G.M., that a cup competition was proposed and accepted. The one rumbustious season it had before the War saw Llanelli disqualified in March, and Aberavon emerge from a tussle with Blaina as the eventual winners. That first, and until 1971-72, last season, did not fulfill the hopes of the revived competition's advocates who felt sure that its 'influence on the ambitious clubs in the colliery and tinplate districts' would be considerable. If anything, it confirmed the view that roughness in the game was becoming insupportable.

Seasoned observers tied this trend to the over-defensive play that was itself now isolated as the Welsh malaise. Hamish Stuart, watching Welsh club rugby over the 1910 Christmas period, was moved to comment harshly on the state of the Welsh game. Coming from a recognizably objective source, the words stung. It had 'degenerated into as gross a libel on real rugby as the purist ever visioned in a nightmare.' The evils were 'unfair and foul play', the weak toleration of referees and the immunity from punishment seemingly enjoyed by leading clubs and players. The Cardiff - Newport game that the former won by a point amidst 'scenes of great enthusiasm' was, he thought, a disgrace that revealed why 'Welsh football, for all its cleverness (had become) a hissing and a reproach'. The identifiable villain was detected as excessive rivalry that demoted playing in favour of mere results. Certainly, the W.F.U. were worried enough about rough play to convene a conference for referees in 1912. The day it met, a minor report of a friendly game between Neyland and the Welch Regiment declared there 'was no football in the game, only wrestling and fighting'. T. D. Schofield from Bridgend had been a prominent administrator from the second decade of Welsh international rugby, so his sour words in 1912, suggestive of many later complaints, were all the more unpalatable for being those of experience. Schofield told the conference that in 'almost every senior Welsh club match for some time past the engagements have been practically barren of skilled attacking play except by spasms, and many unpleasant incidents . . . violent and foul play have been common'. Players who were 'undesirable' because of their inability to prevent themselves crossing the border-line to 'sheer brutality' had to be eliminated before their 'ruffianism' and 'blackguardism' disfigured the game. The W.F.U. urged referees to be stricter on this, as well as obstructive and time-wasting tactics, before J.P.s themselves intervened directly.

The gloom was compounded in 1912 through the prolonged industrial stoppages caused by the successful minimum wage strike undertaken by the British miners, and on through the national rail strike. Rugby found itself, especially in the coalfield, faced with postponed or cancelled games, and a running deficit that 'has spelled financial ruin to some of the Welsh clubs'. There is, then, no disguising the fact that in these years there was a crisis brought on by a series of happenings which had seemed far removed in 1905. At the same time, the sudden relative decline from unprecedented heights was often taken as an absolute fall from grace that neither playing results nor welcome, new developments in club rugby could really support. The truth was, that the years 1906 and 1914 were not a further ascent but they were dotted with splendid achievements that the transitory, perhaps patchy, state of the game should not completely obscure. The complaint until 1908, for example, was not of too much rivalry, but of the almost irremovable grip of Cardiff and Swansea.

The same Hamish Stuart who wrung his hands over the nightmare of Welsh football in 1910, was, in 1908, lauding the concentration of talent in the top Welsh sides. Cardiff had in the previous three seasons lost a mere 8 out of the 90 games they played and Swansea, their chief rivals, only 14 out of 75. This conservatism was, however, inimical to the Welsh rugby wheel of fortune. At the end of the 1909-10 season, two clubs who had temporarily slipped from the highest consideration were re-asserting themselves as Neath, holding a four year ground record from 1907 to 1911, narrowly took the unofficial championship from Newport. The latter were very much the coming force in club games by 1914, but what attracted attention from 1910 on was the spectacular rise of hitherto unconsidered clubs. The 1910-11 season began with a heartening revival of rugby interest in Maesteg, and the dash into the front ranks of Pontypool, guided by good halves and the 'super-excellence' of their pack. When the 1911-12 season began, all the indications were that a sea-change was taking place especially in the eastern valleys of Monmouthshire whose upper extremities were now experiencing the flux of population and prosperity from coal and steel that had visited other districts earlier. In October 1911, 'Forward' of the *Western Mail* was delighted to observe that 'History is in the making with a vengeance. Some record or another is being broken every Saturday . . . We had . . . seen Pontypool defeating Newport, Aberavon beating Neath, Newport beating Cardiff and Cardiff beating Swansea, but who can truly say he was prepared for the defeat of Swansea on their own ground by Pontypool, or for a victory for Abertillery over Llanelli,' (this was the first time Pontypool, re-founded in 1901, and Abertillery, founded in 1885, had secured such wins).

It was still considered that the general standard of play had been weakened, but the progress of these clubs, to whom Penarth could be added, was taken as an encouraging seed-bed for the next stage of rugby growth. This resurrection of the game outside limited areas had long been seen as a priority; it could herald nothing but good, provided the essentials of Welsh football play were not forgotten. Ultimately, it was the wearing thin of these qualities that most disturbed knowledgeable contemporaries inside Wales. Welsh style, they considered, had degenerated into a 'dog-eat-dog' contest that spoiled the game for spectators and players alike. In short, it had become 'decadent'. The contention, sustained with some vigour well before the Golden Era decade can be considered ended, was at the root of the jaundiced view generally postulated before 1914. It is not Welsh defeats from 1910 that signalled the end of Welsh supremacy for this is a subsequent, somewhat dubious conclusion from the statistics. What was unnerving was the string of victories registered without the prerequisite of Welsh satisfaction — style.

Nothing illustrates better the irredeemable, intrinsic aesthetic purpose that the game, at its best, had come to signify in Wales. Winning, for those who understood the rhythms of this drama in sport, was a happy incidental. On 13 March 1909 Wales won her sixth Triple Crown by being the only country to have won two in succession. Ten games had been chalked up in a row since Scotland won in February 1907; and the full sequence would be an uninterrupted eleven wins until the next defeat, England's first victory over Wales since 1898, in 1910. Wales had taken the first Grand Slam, with France now in the arena, in 1908, and repeated it in 1909. At precisely this point, 'Old Stager' in the *South Wales Daily News* of November 1909 asked whether Welsh rugby was in decline. His reasoned answer was not, it has to be stressed, indicating *future* defeats. It was a cold-eyed look at a period of unprecedented power whose force was seen to lie in the similarities of Welsh club sides. The twist was that the perfected skills and ploys had exhausted originality, leaving only its traces in the smoothly-running mechanisms of teams that knew how to cancel each other out.

The art of combination, then, had been transferred to the less demanding work of defence. Scores, especially between Welsh clubs, became lower as familiarity bred respect. Only the occasional flash of brilliance from an individual would pierce the 'catenaccio' policy of alert defenders. Reckless daring in the tackle had replaced a willingness to chance something in attack. Forwards had increased in all-round general play, but the game played by the backs was not conducive to eliciting the service qualities of a quick heel. The burden of this misery was the amnesia that afflicted Welsh teams, especially at international level, causing them to put aside the attacking decisiveness which, in turn, was reliant on constant practice. The run of victories seems to have eased the pressing determination to polish moves to a finish. Clubs had trouble in making their sides cohere as units through organized training. The critic concluded by worrying at the breach between player and spectator that would be the downfall of the Welsh game:—

> We hear a lot about the game being for the player not for the spectator. That is only partly true. The game as played today [1909], so far as the bulk of its players are concerned, could only be played if popular interest is maintained, for the gates provide the funds . . . Many good points as there are about present-day Welsh club football, the tendency is to make the play less spectacular, and this is neither for the prosperity of the game nor the pleasure of player or spectator . . . there has seemed to be a fear to open up the play, and far too much defensive screw-kicking.

The seasons that followed did little to mock these prognostications. Once more it is not a dismal playing record at international level that accused Welsh rugby of lacklustre performance. Repeated failure to achieve consistency in the 1890s had not undercut faith in the 'Welsh game', whereas Wales was more consistent than has been generally recognized, even after 1911. The 1909-10 season saw only one defeat at the hands of England, and Wales won the next six games on the trot, taking, in 1910-11, another Triple Crown and the championship. There were three defeats the following season, by England, Ireland and the South Africans, but the final two seasons before the First World War only brought one defeat per season by a revitalized England. The doubts that assailed Welsh rugby circles were present before 1910, the victorious onward march did not stop until 1912 and, even then, Wales was hardly out of contention. However, defeat was not the issue. The reasons for an alteration in standards which is what bewildered onlookers are, perhaps, complex — the retirement or ageing of outstanding players, the spread of talent more thinly amongst Welsh clubs, the preference for other sports by sections of the public, the sheer weight of a tradition to be emulated by each fresh generation, the cramping fear of losing a game and, hence, Welsh pre-eminence. There is no ready-made explanation for the crumble into imitation that overtakes all forms of artistic endeavour, especially those that rely on athleticism, but the understanding that this was what had happened is the real source of pre-1914 Welsh gloom. Of course, English success hardly made matters more palatable, though, yet again, the manner in which that was analyzed in 1913, and particularly the contribution made by Adrian Stoop via the Harlequins, shows the constant preoccupation with expressive play — 'What the 'Quins did is what any club in Wales can do — they dared to attack, not on new lines, but on a variety of orthodox ones that had been shelved because of decadence in our exponents. Not a move has originated with the 'Quins, such as the reverse pass . . . the quick line-out work, the high punt, the cross kick, and the appreciation that a pass should always be risked to a colleague, no matter what his relative position, provided only that he was better placed to carry on the attack . . . (too many matches) in which both parties set themselves to ignore the great object of the game which is the scoring of tries . . . (are) seldom, if ever, interesting to spectators or pleasing to the players. The open game it was that attracted the big crowds of the past, and it is the open style which alone will regain for rugby its popularity . . . in Wales'. This was, at least, the reiterated view of 'Old Stager'.

However, there might be still the outstanding personality who could capture his audience's imagination. That man in 1906 was Arthur Marsberg, the 'Lion of the Plains', full-back to the first Springboks. The South African tourists were led by the moustachioed, religiose Paul Roos, who took every opportunity to speak from Welsh pulpits. Following so soon in the wake of the Revival, he had more success on the field where a well-drilled unit quickly picked up the finer points of the game to deliver an unexpected but well-merited 11 - 0 drubbing to Wales. Their hero, though, was the fearless Marsberg, who took the breath away as he charged to take the ball on the run or dived to retrieve it at the foot of inconsiderate forwards. He smiled as he brought opponents down, and he smiled at Swansea when the crowd carried him off in his victory, and at Cardiff, where they bore him away in theirs.

Spectacle, whether founded on individual genius or collective rhythm, had long been a key part of Welsh rugby; now, as the advent of soccer in South Wales would show, entertainment could become the name of the game. The crowds from 1906 seem more intent on this than anything else. Perhaps because victory was almost assumed, at least at home. The music-hall had sung parodies of Welsh rugby personalities like Arthur Gould during the 1890s. Now the audience took up the trick in the rugby ground itself. When the Springboks scraped home 6 - 3 against a star-studded Glamorgan team in October, the crowd bellowed the familiar hymns but also warbled ditties in honour of the Welsh rugby players, particularly the tiny favourite Teddy Morgan, to the tune of 'Clementine'. Male voice choirs scattered amongst the onlookers might still cut through the indiscriminate buzz of noise with songs of martyrs and comrades in arms, but, in general, the evidence of a changing world was plain. Ribbon emblems of leeks were displacing the pungent vegetable; 'Men of Harlech' continued to jostle with 'Hen Wlad' for favour, and the chorus of the latter, though printed in English and Welsh on the cover of some programmes, was not always taken up. The Scottish game at Cardiff in

1910, was, despite the Welsh romping home by 14 points to nil, noticeable for its 'lack of fervour' until 'At fifteen minutes to three the first real burst of Cymric enthusiasm came with the singing of a Welsh hymn' but 'it was short-lived. Long before its conclusion a popular music-hall song replaced it'. Nor was this to be seen as only a further distressing example of Cardiff's 'cosmopolitanism', for at Swansea in January 1911, where almost 40,000 gathered to see Wales take the Triple Crown trail again (her last for thirty-nine years) with an exciting win over England, a similar atmosphere, compounded of lassitude and restless expectation for any amusement, prevailed, as the *Western Mail* noted:

> In the preliminaries to the match there was a striking absence of those interesting little incidents and episodes which have made international football in Wales famous. There was no singing, no shouting and 'no nothing' . . . One wondered whether we were in Swansea — the most typical of all the big Welsh towns — or whether we were in the land of the stoics . . . (but) within half an hour (of the kick off) an unprecedented and exciting incident occurred through an acrobatic performer, who is well known on Welsh football grounds, entering the arena with a bicycle and a couple of chairs. He was about to begin his performance when Mr Walter Rees crossed the ground. The acrobat disregarded the order from Mr Rees to leave, then proceeded to go through his evolutions. Mr. Rees promptly called upon the police, but even then the acrobat refused to leave. After one policeman had taken away the chairs, and another had wheeled off the bicycle, it required the combined forces of seven constables to carry the entertainer off the ground, amidst the vigorous booing of the crowd. The spectators became quite angry, and the police who were stationed at different points along the touch-line, were pelted with oranges and subjected to all manner of derision.

Supporters at Stradey Park continued, from their western outpost, to reserve their ire, and their snowballs, for the Durham referee who disallowed a try against the Springboks, who won 16 points to 3, on 29 December 1906, but, in general, Welsh crowds now oscillated erratically between a blasé indifference and their old, wilful enthusiasm. The former greeted the first Wallabies in 1908, for the Australian tourists, though popular enough, were treading a path well-beaten by other 'colonials' and, said the *South Wales Daily News* rather bluntly, 'the hands-across-the-sea sentiment' had worn a little thin. The Australians defeated Glamorgan, Penygraig and Neath/Aberavon with a degree of comfort before succumbing in turn to Llanelli (whose beating of the Wallabies added another immortal verse to 'Sospan Fach'), Wales, Swansea and Cardiff. Only the latter, however, had pierced the armour of Roos' Springboks who had entered a Wales confident of mauling the Africans. That tour, coming so soon after the savageries of the Boer War, was a public relations exercise that brought some unexpected rugby fruits. Marsberg aside, the fruits were plucked not by the power of the South African pack, in the manner that came to be so repeated and feared, but by a swift, raiding back-line, (Loubser, Krige, de Villiers and Stegmann — all from Stellenbosch University), who were launched by the skilled and wily Carolin and Dobbin at half-back. Indeed, once the trickery used by Welsh forwards to gain the loose-head, which so baffled them at Newport although they won the game, had been explained to them by the kindly C. M. Pritchard, the 'Boks proved themselves teachers more than pupils. Against Wales they packed a fourth man at the last moment into the front row, thereby ensuring the loose head on either side of the scrum. The Springboks' first game against Wales was vital, so far as the home side was concerned, for three reasons — it exposed the ageing of the Welsh pack who were out-scrummaged and outpaced so badly that four of them wore the jersey for the last time; it confirmed the oil-and-water non-mix of Owen and Bush who never played together for Wales again; and it ended the international career of the greatest player of his generation, E. Gwyn Nicholls.

Nicholls had been urged, and after Glamorgan's narrow defeat, cajoled, to lead Wales one more time although he had withdrawn from active playing. To his credit, and to his own later dismay, he responded to the siren call. In the international, Gwyn Nicholls was sadly out of touch. He fumbled the ball, missed a crucial tackle and, strangest of all for this prince of centres, ran for the line, only to fail, with Morgan free outside him. The Welsh team lacked cohesion in all departments. According to Gabe, who played these South Africans four times (for country, county and two clubs — Llanelli and Cardiff), the forwards had quarrelled beforehand over the alleged disposition of the three London Welshmen (Harding, Jenkins and J. F. Williams) to shine in the loose at the expense of tight play. Whatever the truth of the matter, this dissension spread from the harassed Owen right through the side. Only the new full back, J. C. M. Dyke of Christ College, Brecon, and Penarth, emerged with an enhanced reputation and, ironically enough, he, too, never put on a scarlet jersey afterwards. Gwyn Nicholls, however, cashed in the sporting credit he had accumulated to end his playing career not with the first Welsh downfall in Wales for nine years but with the giant-killing act which had once been the occasional hope of the Wales of his youth, and would now be the yearned for glory of Welsh club sides. On New Year's Day 1907 Gwyn Nicholls played for a Cardiff side who, under Bush's captaincy, played an extra back (Bush himself, with Reggie Gibbs at outside half) to accommodate him.

The pitch was a quagmire following weeks of rain. Players sank into a foot of mud. The wind whipped a stinging rain across the field. Cecil Biggs, the Cardiff wing, was reduced to a limping passenger after a few minutes so the omens for a memorable match were poor. And yet, Biggs won his 20 to 1 bet with Tom Williams, the Welsh selector irate with Bush after the Swansea débâcle, for Cardiff scored four tries in a devasting 17 -0 exhibition of running rugby. The first try was the best. The Cardiff backs had pressed early in classic, quick-transfer fashion, only to go amiss at the last on a couple of occasions. A scrum about fifteen yards inside the Springboks' half saw the ball swing away out to Nicholls in mid-field. The thirty-two-year-old centre did not hesitate. Over the mud he skated up to the opposing three-quarters. He bewildered them, in his old style, by that swerve at speed for which he had become renowned; a body movement, feinted by the hips, one way, and a final defiant dance through the morass to score. He had no peer as defender or attacker that day. Honour, which Nicholls personified above all other players, had been regained from the only possible donor for whom the centre would have willingly played recipient — himself.

When the South Africans returned for their second visit in 1912, Welsh rugby was not so likely to lose heavily, but neither was it equipped by personnel or overall ability to carry off unexpected glory. The second Springboks were not the men behind the pack that their predecessors had been, but they brought forwards whose physique was, in itself, a revelation; they had an accurate, sound full-back in Gerhard Morkel who impressed by his marvellous, anticipatory covering; and, in Douglas Morkel, one of their jumbo pack, a phenomenal goal-kicker of match-winning powers. Indeed, it was Morkel's twenty-five-yard penalty goal after a quarter of an hour that proved the solitary score in the international game. Wales, under the captaincy of Tommy Vile at scrum-half, had done well, with nine new caps and little confidence felt in the team, to come so close in another mud-bespattered game. Roos' side had lost to Scotland 6 - 0 but Billy Millar's 'Boks were the first touring side to win all four international games. They lost their game against London and this time stumbled twice in Wales. Llanelli had taken them so close, by rushing them aggressively and defending fearlessly, that they lost by a single point, 8 to 7. Five days later Newport, with five Welsh caps and the English international, Bob Dibble, in the pack, won a pulsating game by 9 points to 3.

Fred Birt, who had spent a boyhood acting as ball-boy to Gould when the centre practised kicking from all positions, was the hero himself now. Birt dropped a goal, snapped up a try and converted it to make him Newport's sole scorer. Birt won his sixth, and penultimate cap against South Africa, in an international career that lasted from 1911 to 1913. He was that season infallible as a goal-kicker; except for Wales, that is, because the unfortunate Birt missed an equalizing penalty easier than the one Morkel had kicked. Greatness had deserted Welsh international rugby but Birt had secured an inestimable prize for Newport; Cardiff would fail, like Llanelli, by the smallest possible margin whilst Swansea, led by the every-green Trew, remained unbeaten when a 3 - 0 victory on Boxing Day put the 'Boks down again on a water-logged pitch.

Less formidable foes also came within Welsh sights for the first time in these years. Their exhuberant emotionalism and junior status won them more patronizing sympathy than praise initially, but a shrewd observer noted how similar had been the response to Wales's early international career. 'France', Old Stager declared, 'can take heart . . . Welsh pre-eminence on the rugby field was not built in a few years and six matches had been played before Wales had even drawn with England'. That was in 1908. Fifteen French sides, including this first one at Cardiff, would lose to Wales until the first Gallic victory in Paris in 1928. Rugby in France, like soccer, had been introduced by British businessmen and officials. It was rooted at first in the ports and in the towns of the north and the west. Not until a predominantly peasant society shifted, as Britain had done from the 1850s, to an urban industrial future would team sports grow in stature, though there were iron Pyrenean forwards in French teams just as the 'Rhondda forward' had been discovered in Wales. The modernization of France would only occur after 1930 so until then the French were generally outclassed. Their first game against Wales was lost by 36 points to 4 but the circumstances surrounding it, and future contests, had hints of the carnival gaiety that relieved the excessive burden 'serious' rugby sometimes carried.

To begin with, the game was played on a Monday afternoon and preceded by a round of social activities for the French team who were transported in 'two pair-horsed charabancs'. At both the City Hall and the French Consulate the players and officials were plied with glasses of wine. They visited the shipping-crammed docks and climbed the monstrous coal-tipping cranes before venturing onto the ornate balustraded balcony of the Coal Exchange in Mount Stuart Square. At one end of the hall a clock held firmly by two money-conscious Dragons had their blunt purpose dignified by a Latin tag — *Tempus Fugit*. And down below, the traders, seeing the visitors, cheered heartily, though not quite in forgetfulness of the urgency of time's flight, for France was one of the chief importers of Welsh coal and Welsh coal-owners, with extensive interests in French shipping lines and ports, were well aware of the importance of the French market:

> The floor of the Exchange was crowded with businessmen . . . Mr J. A. Jones . . . introduced the visitors, and said Cardiff dockmen were brought closely into touch with commercial France, and there were so many steamers trading between the two countries that one might almost walk across the Channel on their decks. There was no place in the country where the spirit of *entente cordiale* existed so strongly as in Cardiff, and perhaps that was because Cardiff knew Frenchmen so well.

> M. Braennus, the president of the French Rugby Union, replied in French . . . they knew Cardiff by repute as a great trading port . . . the spectacle before them was a remarkable one . . . a wonderful sight.

A crowd of around 20,000 saw the game. Welsh long-passing nonplussed the visitors, who, it would seem, had to suffer the final blow of a Welsh dinner, printed in French on the menu, which included shelled *petits pois à l'anglaise*, tossed *Salade à la Française* and a doubtless formidable *Pouding à la Galloise*. It was the same again the following year when France were battered 47 to 5 in a Paris given over to a Shrove Tuesday Mardi Gras that the Welsh clearly associated with pancakes. Not all of the early games led to these cricket scores, however, for in 1913, before 20,000 Frenchmen, Wales scraped home 11 - 8 and Trew limped off, permanently, from the international scene. The year previously, at the first international in Newport since 1894, France had given firmer intentions of her future policy. A 10,000 crowd saw a fast, skilful French pack last the pace only to lose, by 14 points to 8, a game they could have won. There was pride for the Welsh, too, in the nature of French rugby: 'The progress has been amazing . . . athletics over the Channel is more than a passing craze . . . what one liked most about the play of the Frenchmen . . . was that they have followed Welsh methods in regarding attack as the best defence'.

The irony there, of course, was that Welsh teams were criticized for having forgotten how to attack. On either side of the 1912 French game were defeats by South Africa in December and by Ireland in March, where seven new Welsh caps and another five players with only one a-piece went down 12 - 5 as the backs failed lamentably. On the whole, Welsh capabilities were sustained by the new men among the forwards — men

191

like Jim Webb the iron-hard scrummager who won his first cap from Abertillery in 1907 and his twentieth in 1912, or his Abertillery colleague J. Bedwellty Jones, whose four caps in 1914 would surely have increased in number.

Indeed, a number of Welshmen in the pack had artificially short careers because of the intervention of the War — Glyn Stephens of Neath who won ten caps between 1912 and 1919 and, bearing another family name that would later recover some of the four lost years with the help of younger relatives, Harry Uzzell of Newport, who picked up fifteen caps from 1912 to 1920. Behind them were the seventeen times capped J. L. Williams (1906 to 1911) on the wing and the dashing Jack P. Jones of Pontypool whose career stretched from 1908 to 1921 and brought him thirteen caps, exactly twelve more than his brother 'Tuan' who played in 1913. T. H. 'Tommy' Vile, an astute scrum-half, especially in harness with his club partner, the gifted but rather erratic, Walter Martin (3 caps, 1912-19), won eight caps in the course of a prolonged rugby career which did not end with his playing days. He first played for Newport in 1902-3 and toured Australia with Bedell-Sivright's team in 1904 before winning his first cap in 1908, and his last in 1921. He went on to become a referee of distinction (13 internationals 1923-31), a respected administrator, and President of the W.R.U. in 1955-6. In his pre-war playing days, he was one of those scrum-halves, excellent in their own right, who are condemned to play in the shadow of the truly great.

In more than one sense, Dickie Owen continued to dominate Welsh international rugby. There was his own unwillingness to stop being Peter Pan, of course, but, more than this, the effectiveness of his play affected the fortunes of that 'star artiste', P. F. Bush. And whilst the arguments raged over what had become the glamour position in any Welsh team, the wonderful invincibility of Wales in 1908 and 1909 continued to rest firmly on the shoulders of those who had already carried the day before. An ease almost bordering on arrogance saw six different Welsh captains in successive games from 1907-1908 as the honour was literally passed around. Only when Rhys Gabe, Billy Trew, Dick Jones, Bert Winfield, George Travers and the incompatible pair, Owen and Bush, joined Gwyn Nicholls in retirement did the constantly-raised alarms about rugby in Wales really ring true.

Until that day there were some scintillating moments to cherish. Quite often they would be either Bush or Owen moments. The Swansea scrum-half had played with Trew in the first two games of 1907 and, despite

Scotland's brushing aside of Wales's seven-forward plan, would have gone on to figure in the Irish game that season. That he did not was a mixture of bad luck, petulance and independence of spirit on the part of others, and of selfless sportsmanship on his. Scrines, picked as the 'extra back' or rover, had been suspended by the W.F.U., whereupon Trew, Swansea and current Welsh captain who had urged the playing of Harry Toft, Swansea's outside-half in his place, stepped down. Dickie Owen, knowing the selectors' preference for a club pair, informed Walter Rees that he was prepared to withdraw. The selectors took him at his word, and the Swansea trio were replaced by the Cardiff trinity of Reggie Gibbs as 'rover', Bush at outside-half and Dicky David, the Cardiff window-cleaner, his partner, who gained this one cap. Gabe captained the team and Bush, on his home ground, without a Swansea man in the side for the first time, celebrated by turning in his greatest performance. Wales had scored two tries by half-time, but, even with eight men in the pack, had not really conquered the fiery Irish who had themselves beaten England shortly before. But Bush, whose teasing runs and quickness in counter-attack had already been stamped on the game, now came into his own as Wales romped home 29 - 0 with four more tries. Bush sparked them all off, dropped a goal and then scored himself. Harry Bowen, the Welsh selector said, 'Percy Bush's single-handed try made Gabe laugh aloud, the others smiling broadly . . . it was the sheer impudence of one man beating the whole of the Irish backs by a run which had speed with so many perky and polka-like interludes mixed up in it'.

This was the beginning of Bush's most satisfying time for Wales. He played in the first two games of the 1908 Triple Crown year with Vile as partner. The 28 - 18 victory over England was registered on Bristol City football ground in a mist so dense that Ack Llewellyn declared 'it must have been a great game', and the impish Bush (who congratulated Harding on his captaincy by adding 'I have never seen a team better led except when I captained Cardiff last year') told the Press beforehand, when asked which way Wales would be playing, 'We will play with the fog'. Bush played with everything, for, apart from a brilliant dropped goal, he made a try for Gabe by transferring the ball at speed before whooping off in the opposite direction pursued by an English back division more reliant on ear than eyes, while Gabe calmly dotted the ball down between the posts. At half-time Bush was discovered in the crowd chatting away like a jaybird. For those who delighted in his antics there could be only agreement with 'Bobby' Brice, the old International, who caught the fleeting unrepeatability of Bush at his best with the phrase 'the little man was a daisy'.

All daisies are cut down, but their brief time is a bright one. Bush played for Wales twice more, in 1910, with Teddy Morgan's brother, W. L. Morgan to feed him, and then, Vile again. That was at a time when Owen's parallel career seemed over. That was not to be, either. For Bush, the ex-schoolteacher working as Vice-Consul at Nantes from early 1910, there was the consolation of genius expressed at home and abroad, of a role in developing a French challenge that would eventually be as exciting as his own wayward, thrilling play. But first he had to show them how to do it — against Le Havre for Nantes in 1910 he scored 54 points himself (ten tries, eight converted goals and two dropped goals). There must still be some Havrais who walk today down Cardiff's Boulevard de Nantes thinking it is not the sister-town but the twinkling outside-half that is there honoured.

Where Bush, no sterling defender or user of a three-quarter line, required a selfless scrum-worker with a long slung pass to give him time, Owen needed an outside-half attuned to his own distinctive style. When one or the other fell short, in themselves or through their partners, then it was 'all change'. Owen, given a chance again through injuries to Vile and Bush, made the two places secure for himself and Jones for nine successive games between March 1908 and January 1910. Wales had lost in Ireland in 1904 and 1906. The final game of the 1907-08 season brought home the fifth Triple Crown from Belfast. Wales held on 5 - 5 at the half after a torrid series of attacks by the Irish pack who pounded Owen remorselessly. The scrum-half fell at their feet or whipped the ball away, reverse-passed or ran in darting combination with 'his fellow Dick' to prove the 'outstanding player'. Trew and Gabe in the centre put Williams and Gibbs, the Cardiff wings, in for two tries. Winfield had converted Williams' first-half effort and Wales won 11 - 5. All of this came in the last ten minutes as the Welsh back-line surged ahead in their old fashion. The Irish critics were 'impressed above everything else with the genius of Owen and the bewildering variety of the attacking tactics . . . and said they had still a great deal to learn from Wales'.

After a poor, snatched victory against England in the first game of the next season, Bush and Vile were re-called in an overhauled side. This was the first time since 1901 that Owen, when fully fit, was to be omitted. However, injuries in club games to Vile and, then, Bush saw the Swansea men restored. Scotland, on whose territory Wales had only won twice before, had recently raised the issue of 'amateurism' once more. They had resented the 3s. a day allowance paid to members of the Anglo-Welsh Tour. The referee for this game, R. W. Jeffares (of Ireland), awarded fourteen penalties to four in favour of the Scots. It was a remarkable display of Gaelic mistrust, for he informed the Press that he had watched Owen to see if the London critics were right about his 'fairness' and at one point actually took the ball himself, feinted to put it into the scrum, and then penalized Wales 'because a leg was put up'. These actions were not based on judgements of what was happening but on preconceptions: 'And once again, Wales', railed 'Old Stager', 'because of her great successes and the presence of so many working men in her side, suffered acutely, and difference in social status once more appeared to affect the arbiter in a contest which should know no grades of society and in which representatives of democracy should be judged entirely on their merits as players and their honesty should be no more questioned than that of the better circumstanced players'.

That working-class men should be known as 'the democracy' was perfectly natural. Until 1906 every British cabinet had had a majority of peers as its members. Even the House of Commons cannot be said to have been elected in anything approaching a universal male suffrage until the 1918 Representation of the People Act; and that only enfranchised women over the age of thirty. British society was, then, very steeply graded. By 1914 different social strata were not mixing on the field of play. Rugby was becoming more exclusively a game for 'gentlemen' and their well-educated sons. Except in Wales, that is. Wales, too, had her social divisions, but the pace and nature of her growth had not required or permitted any rigid demarcation within rugby football. Four thousand Welsh excursionists had journeyed the 400 miles to Scotland in 1909. There were red-capped ex-County Schoolboys from Ystalyfera and Rhondda colliers on a trip arranged 'by the committee who had made such a success of the champion prize-winning band which has brought Ferndale to the front'. Committees became synonymous with Welsh democratic deliberations. Later they ossified on occasion into a joke; at the time they were the vehicles of representation.

The representatives of the Match Committee saw Wales weather a 3 - 0 deficit from a penalty goal in the second half to score a brilliant try from Trew that Jack Bancroft, the incomparable W. J.'s brother, converted to bring a 5 - 3 victory. The game had been won by patient forbearance allied to a steadfast determination 'to adhere to essentially Welsh methods and

195

the spectators were treated to one of the best possible illustrations of the attractiveness of the combined game'. The season ended at St. Helen's with the sixth Triple Crown and an 18 - 5 defeat of Ireland. Owen, beating two men close to the scrum, got Jones away to put the diminutive Phil Hopkins in for a try, but it was the Grand Slam captain, Trew, who, having been hailed that season as the best defensive centre in Britain, now showed his attacking gifts. Waller of Newport came away from a line-out and gave to Trew three yards inside the Welsh half. Cutting inside, swerving away, feinting and jerking with all the guile of experience, Trew saved his crushing burst of speed for the last. He had run through the entire Irish team to score under the posts. Both teams congratulated the virtuoso.

Nothing was more fitting for the 1910-11 Triple Crown season than that Owen and Trew should bring it home for the seventh time. Both now veterans, they contributed, as always, not only their experience but their match-winning genius. At Swansea a very fine English side, itself in the throes of a purple period, lost 15 - 11 in a match that was anyone's right to the end. Owen played the finest game of his career after losing his place the previous season. In the first minute of the second half, with Wales clutching a 3-point lead, the ball went to Trew from a line-out on the English 25. The outside-half put in a delicate kick to touch two yards from the English line. Now the 'pretty little plot' hatched and practised beforehand was put into operation. Owen lifted the ball from the scrum and darted away on the blind side before passing to Trew racing up alongside him. The captain committed Stanley Williams, the English full-back from Newport, to the tackle that knocked Trew out before giving to Swansea wing-forward Ivor Morgan to score. Gwyn Nicholls commented, 'each of the three participants seemed to jump into their places as if the little plot had been pre-arranged.' Owen conquered the subsequent attentions of Pillman the marauding English destroyer by cutting back inside time and again to dodge through the grasping ranks of the English pack. 'Old Ebor' of the *Yorkshire Post* reported ruefully, 'Owen had as usual as much to do with the victory as anyone, and he does last extraordinary well'.

Against Scotland in the following game it was Owen and Trew, opening out the game 'in masterly style', that led a 32 - 10 rout of a youthful Scottish side in Edinburgh. Trew glided away to lay on eight tries, drawing all ferocious attention to himself 'before he parted with the ball (at) the very acme of strategical judgement'. Thoughts of lean years were banished. 'Sospan Fach' was sung again having 'almost passed into oblivion' and 'as it was in the beginning, so it was on Saturday'. Wales now drew level with Scotland in number of games won. Praise from outsiders was sweetest of all. The Edinburgh critics wrote — 'In rugby football Wales is pre-eminent. They possess a polish, a finish, a system, a training and a perfection in method which other nations quite lack. You may hit lean years but you have studied the game, and followed the study by tireless practice. Physical force may triumph at times, but there is always nowadays the cleverness and the deftness of the rapier about Welsh football'.

The democracy certainly flocked back, in a crowd larger than that of 1905, breaking through the police and the barriers to watch two sides, Ireland and Wales, bid for the Crown. This time, in a 16 - 0 victory, the Welsh pack, obeying Trew's instructions, held and carried the ball themselves. The cartoonist depicted Wales as the surviving gladiator proferring the Triple Crown to the spectators. That was a shrewd image with which to depict a relationship that would not flourish again, at that level, for another thirty-nine years. The lean years were coming after all. They had been signalled, perhaps, over a year before, in January 1910, when Wales played England in the first Twickenham international.

Adrian Stoop was the architect of English resurgence. In Birkett and Poulton, also of Harlequins, he had dashing three-quarters of genuine pace. English sides had West Country grit behind the pack too, in Johnson, Chapman and Solomon and Dai Gent, the former Welsh trialist to nurse it. Wales's bugbear, though, was the deadly C. H. 'Cherry' Pillman, the swarthy rover from Blackheath who heralded the era of the crushing wing-forward with his pouncing lunges at the opposition. Soon there would be 'the Pembrokeshire Welshman', W. J. A. Davies (United Services) to add his magnificent swaying play at outside-half, and English rugby was re-equipped for over a decade of triumph. Just before Wales went down for the second time at Twickenham in 1912 a prescient Welshman observed — 'There is an indefinable something in the atmosphere and the surroundings at Twickenham which is not congenial to the Celtic temperament.' That remained the case until 1933.

Only 18,000 saw the first game at Twickenham and the first English victory over Wales (11 - 6) since 1898. England, in fact, led 11 - 3 at half-time following a sensational first minute try when Stoop, fielding the kick-off from Ben Gronow, the Bridgend forward, unexpectedly ran diagonally to start the move that saw Chapman, the right-wing, hand-off Trew to score. Pillman harried Dick Jones, who never played for Wales again, into uncharacteristic errors and Dai Gent gave Owen, the man whose monopoly of the Welsh scrum-half berth had caused him to abandon Wales, a very difficult first half. The Welsh side, who, unlike their opponents, had stayed on the pitch at half-time for consultation, had a far better second period. Owen schemed a try by kicking the ball to Trew when expected to pass to Dick Jones and Trew had Gibbs away for a clever try. Jack P. Jones, however, had a nightmare game in the centre and Pillman 'was as a cat amongst the pigeons, time after time preventing the Welsh backs from getting into smooth working'. Trew had played in all of the previous eleven Welsh international victories; he would, of course, be there again in the 1910-11 season, but he was not there, in 1912, when Wales, under Owen's captaincy, lost 8 - 0. The value of the trials which the English selectors, leaving aside traditional North-South fixtures, had adopted in 1910, allied to a renaissance of English club rugby, was now undeniable. The crowd of some 20,000 was an English record whilst their captain, Dibble, was a Newport forward, and, like Owen, a former 'artisan . . . turned licensed victualler'. The only bright spot for a thoroughly outplayed Wales in this 8 - 0 defeat was the courageous, inspired performance of the cool Swansea 'custodian'. Jack Bancroft was winning his twelfth cap (the first was a replacement for the injured Winfield in 1909; the last, his eighteenth in 1914) and Owen his thirty-fourth, one more than Billy Bancroft's record number. The afternoon was still the Bancrofts' however, for Jack caught, tackled and kicked, in the face of overwhelming English superiority, 'as if he had as many arms and legs as a Hindu deity'. A. A. Thomson, the writer, later told a Welsh friend that as a boy he had 'seen and admired the great Bancroft' in 1912. The reply was 'Maybe the man you saw was wonderful . . . but he was not the great Bancroft. He was merely the great Bancroft's little brother'. Thomson concluded that 'if W. J. was all that better than J., he must have had wings as well'.

The angels had all temporarily flown. Wales had not been beaten at home by any of the home countries since 1899 when Ireland won. Scotland had last conquered there in 1892 and England in 1895. Few expected England to stop the trend at Cardiff in 1913. That she did so by 12 points to nil was interpreted as a crack of doom by Welsh critics. In fact England did not score until the second half whilst Wales wasted a great deal of the ball they did win, but Hamish Stuart was at last able to underline the message that 'the spell is broken and with it the absurd idea that Wales is invincible in Wales'. What was also clear was the fickleness of the crowd. The poor weather had kept the number who came to the South African game around 17,000; only 3,000 more saw this one. Owen and Trew had withdrawn against Ireland (which Wales lost 12 - 5) in 1912, and against France, at Newport, when Vile and Martin again deputized. Age and an easier life at club level were too beguiling. Owen did not add to his thirty-five caps. Trew, however, following the 1912 English game, unselfishly came back to shepherd a transitional Welsh side to two more victories; 8 - 0 against Scotland in Edinburgh (where only he had played before) and in Paris, where his ruptured groin ended his twenty-nine-cap career.

The last season before the War gave England her fourth Triple Crown when she equalled Wales's record in taking it in two successive seasons. The pendulum had assuredly swung. Yet not so far as all that. Wales had been beaten by England by a single point (10 - 9) in a game which her forwards did enough to win. Right at the end 'having trounced the Saxon octette' they were 9 - 5 in the lead when Willie Watts, a first and only cap at centre from Llanelli, overawed on the day, dropped the ball to let the predatory Pillman grab a winning try. The emphasis had moved from the backs to a magnificent pack of forwards led with inspiration by the Revd Alban Davies who, if not quite an angel, was as holy as this Welsh side could be. The 'Terrible Eight' stormed Wales to victory in Ireland (11 - 3) on a muddy battleground that saw what many, including Townsend Collins, thought 'the roughest ever'. Before that Scotland had felt the new Welsh power up front as they lost 24 - 5 at St. Helen's. The 1913-14 season cannot, then, be taken as any clear pointer to the miseries that would afflict Welsh rugby in the 1920s. Indeed, so much of the gloom that is seen as a pall over those pre-war years was retrospective in origin. Where it has point is in its memory of the internal domestic scene and the alteration in style brought on by the vanishing of superlative players who had had their 'squad substitutes' in rivals from other clubs but none who were being trained to take their place. 1914 was celebrated in Wales. It was a season, after all, with victories which would 'do much to restore enthusiasm' and bring, as concomitants, 'more attractive play in club matches and greater patronage'. Forty thousand had again gathered to see Wales play Scotland at rugby in a Swansea whose soccer side had reached the first full round of the F.A. Cup in the previous season — 'Pessimists who have preached in and out of season that rugby was fast dying in popular interest in Wales were confounded on Saturday'.

The diplomatic machinations and the power rivalry that would shortly plunge 'the democracy' into a war that did not end all wars would soon usher in sourer bouts of pessimism. Rugby, after all, was no panacea for human evils of that magnitude, nor even the lesser, mundane ones of society. Nor was it any opiate. The quickening pace of industrial and political conflict in Wales after 1909 contradicts that supposition. Rugby mixed social classes in Wales, at club and international level, more thoroughly and readily than elsewhere in Britain. It did not do any more than that for, after all, it too was a reflection of the structure of an Edwardian world. What it did, in its own terms, was perhaps more significant. Before this blood-letting war was fought, often to the mindless echoes of a sporting rhetoric, it showed, on the field, characteristics whose innate qualities, for players and spectators, would always remain unsullied. Hence its regular resurrection at club level, where the devotees nurtured the grass-roots of the national game. Rugby did not take people out of themselves by making them forgetful of more pressing realities. On the contrary, it indicated to them the possibilities for endeavour and delight that lay within themselves. Welsh rugby did not rely, by 1914, on newspaper editorialists or politicians or folklorists intent on delineating 'Celtic traits' that would serve *their* purpose. It had come to this point because it had become an ineradicable part, in victory and defeat, of the social culture of a Wales that had fostered, and in turn been influenced by, 'a game democratic and amateur'. That is why the stress by those concerned about rugby in Wales was not on the spontaneity of a happy instance (the glib 'flair') but on the flow of true articulation that can only be expressed when all the incidental elements are controlled. Only then does a style emerge. And it is the culture which produces the style, as T. H. Thomas, the Herald Bard of Wales, realized in 1909 after W. J. Trew's second Grand Slam season. The Herald, dismissing the facile generalizations about Celts so ardently worked-up inside and outside Wales, wrote:

> Wales is a very small country. The success which has attended her efforts in athletics is therefore a sort of miracle. It has been attained by the exercise of those qualities in which critics of the Welsh declare us to be deficient — hard work, self-control, discipline. The game has been intellectualized by our players . . . our teams 'play with brains'. Whatever may happen in future Wales is signalized . . . (by) . . . the merits of a band of her sons.

His suggested tribute was three endowed hospital beds in three South Welsh towns. Many more hospital beds than these were to be needed after August 1914.

THE LEAN YEARS

O N 5 March 1914 the W.F.U. considered a letter from the German
Rugby Union requesting a Welsh International XV's presence at
Hamburg on 3 May of that year. Whether the Committee were
prescient or not, they decided that 'the application be not entertained this
season', for Britain declared war on Germany on 4 August 1914, and the
next four seasons contained nothing that was entertaining and a great deal
that should never have been entertained. Most people expected an early
end to the war. Many flocked to join the colours buoyed up on a wave of
patriotic excitement that would finally die away on the plains of Northern
France, leaving only a grim resolve and a cynical acceptance. The W.F.U.,
in the early days of the war, treated it almost like another international
foray. Following the lead of the R.F.U., they called upon Welsh football
players to enlist in greater numbers and circulated all the clubs to this
effect:

> Considering that our players comprise . . . the very pick of men eligible
> for service in the Army, and considering that Welshmen have the reputation
> for not being wanting either in patriotism or pluck, we feel we shall not
> appeal in vain . . .
> If only every man in every First XV in Wales were to enlist, what a
> magnificent body there would be at the service of our country, and even then
> there would still be plenty of players left to enable the game to be played as
> usual . . .
> We therefore appeal with confidence to all Welsh Rugby Football players,
> untrammelled by imperative domestic ties, not to allow any selfish reason to
> prevent them from answering the urgent call of their King and Country.

By the autumn the fond hopes of continuing football for the war's
duration had gone. Clubs were advised to cease playing and international

fixtures were discontinued. A Wales XV did play a Barbarians XV, at Cardiff in April 1915, but this was to recruit for the Welsh Guards. Walter Rees, early in 1916, was appointed recruiting officer for the Neath district, and the War Office conferred on him the rank of Captain; as principal registration and tribunal officer he was responsible for more than a third of the county of Glamorgan. By 1916 the war crisis, and the blood-letting tactics of generals whose military expertise was limited to endless up-and-unders, required more than rhetoric from platforms. For the first time a British Army was to be conscripted. Some of the volunteers had already been up and, sadly, gone under. Others nurtured the familiar in very foreign fields. In May 1915 Private George Noyes of the Welch Regiment sent a letter to the *South Wales Daily News* from Altdamm in Germany where he was a prisoner of war. He wanted readers to know that the Welch had beaten the Yorkshire Light Infantry 6 - 0, and the Rest of the Camp 9 - 0. 'There are sixteen Cardiff men here', he wrote, 'and we would very much like a rugby ball sent out, or anything else to banish the monotony. The troops here are all in good health, except longing for the dear old home again. Hoping you will grant us our desires. P.S. It may interest Cardiffians to know that Wales still leads in sport'.

Among the horrific total of eight and a half million who did go under were several who had contributed towards lifting Wales to that position of sporting leadership to which Private Noyes referred. The Welsh rugby Internationals roll of honour reads:

Engineer-Captain C. G. Taylor, R.N., 9 caps 1884-7, killed at sea, Dogger Bank, 24 January 1915, aged 51; 2nd Lieutenant W. P. Geen, 9th Battalion, King's Royal Rifle Corps, 3 caps 1912-13, killed in action, Hooge, Belgium, 31 July 1915, aged 25; Lieut. Col. R. D. Garnons Williams, 12th Battalion, Royal Fusiliers, 1 cap 1881, killed in action, Loos, 27 September 1915, aged 59; Sergeant L. A. Phillips, Royal Fusiliers, 4 caps 1900-1, killed in action, Cambrai, 14 March 1916, aged 36; Sergeant E. J. R. Thomas, 16th Battalion, Welsh Regiment, 4 caps 1906-9, killed in action, Mametz Wood, 7 July 1916, aged 35; Capt. J. L. Williams, 16th Battalion, Welch Regiment, 17 caps 1906-11, died No. 5 Casualty Clearing Station, France, 12 July 1916, aged 34; Capt. C. M. Pritchard, 12th Battalion, South Wales Borderers, 14 caps 1904-10, died No. 1 Casualty Clearing Station, France, 14 August 1916, aged 33; 2nd Lieutenant H. W. Thomas, Rifle Brigade, 2 caps 1912-13, killed in action, the Somme, 3 September 1916, aged 25; Major B. R. Lewis, Royal Field Artillery, 2 caps 1912-13, killed in action, Ypres, 2 April 1917, aged 26;

Pte. D. Westacott, 16th Platoon D Company, Gloucester Regiment, 1 cap 1906, killed in action, 28 August 1917, aged 35; 2nd Lieutenant P. D. Waller, 71st Siege Battery, S. A. Heavy Artillery, 6 caps 1908-10, killed in action, Arras, 14 December 1917, aged 28.

The hideous carnage of the War was not easily forgotten, and for most of the twenties the W.F.U. party of officials and players visited the Cenotaph on the Sunday morning after the international at Twickenham. On the occasion of the first post-war visit to France in February 1920, the Union sent over a huge wreath to commemorate the players who had lost their lives, and presented it by laying it on the ground in front of the grandstand at Colombes while players and supporters gathered around to sing hymns and the National Anthem. Afterwards several visited the battlefields, on the tours that Thomas Cook & Son arranged, to see the graves of friends and relatives and where they themselves had fought. Before the 1926 game in Paris, the sizeable Welsh contingent in the crowd sang songs in turn with the French, and the singing of 'Tipperary' was a moving experience.

Rugby stuttered back to life in the 1918-19 season with an inter-Services tournament for the King George V Trophy, in which official British and Dominion sides participated, but there were also a number of unofficial military teams formed, involving amateurs and professionals. In January 1919 the W.F.U., taking its cue from the other unions, barred those Northern Union players who had been playing with Welsh amateur clubs during the war period, and refused to permit any game against the New Zealand Army team without a guarantee that they were amateurs — 'just as though it matters a damn whether they are amateurs or professionals when they have come all this way to fight and die for us', protested an officer in *Truth* magazine (to which was added the editorial gloss, 'the regenerating and purifying influence of the Great War is working in a mysterious way'). The Union also decided it had better prohibit fixtures by teams describing themselves as 'Wales' or 'a Welsh XV', but this was not in accord with its own, more tempered feelings. Horace Lyne revealed to a special meeting of club delegates and Press in February 1919 that the W.F.U. was in favour of reinstatement of 'professionals' who had served in the war but that the English Union would not support them before the I.B., whilst Ireland and Scotland had 'no working men players'. So in April it blithely disregarded its own commandments by sanctioning an official international between Wales and the New Zealand Army team when two days previously all the selected Welsh players had been involved, twelve on one side, three on the other, in a game between a Welsh XV and the 38th

Division. During the next decade, inconsistency, not always of this idealistic kind, would be a consistent policy of the W.F.U., or the W.R.U. as it was now commonly called.

That decade would be the least distinguished in the hundred-year history of Welsh rugby. To ponder the statistical record of international rugby in the twenties is a gloomy task. Between 1920 and 1929 only seventeen of the forty-two games played were won; twenty-two were lost. From 1923 to 1930 England won every game against Wales except for a draw at Cardiff in 1926. From 1920 to 1927 Scotland won every game against Wales except for a draw at Inverleith in 1922. In 1923 Scotland won at Cardiff for the first time since 1890; in 1924 England won at Swansea for the first time since 1895; in 1925 Ireland won her first match in Wales since 1899, and for the first time ever beat Wales in three successive seasons, 1923-4-5. In 1924 Scotland crossed the Welsh line eight times to inflict on Wales her heaviest defeat (35 - 10) since 1881. The French match was the annual consolation prize but in 1928 Wales was beaten by France, too, for the first time ever. It was the middle years of the decade that were the most excruciating, when Wales was conceding on average four tries a match, and the desperation was compounded by the incoherent policies of the selectors. In 1924 they tried thirty-five different players, including fourteen three-quarters, and Charlie Pugh of Maesteg was the only forward to play in all four games that year. Wales had a different fly-half in every match with England from 1920 to 1934. Captaincy was arbitrarily awarded: in 1924 and 1925 there were four different captains for each of the four championship games in both seasons. In the meantime, England, under two captains, won the Triple Crown four times between 1921 and 1928.

Yet the decade opened in sprightly enough fashion when some of the *élan* of the pre-war years was recaptured, often by survivors of that period like Jack P. Jones, Harry Uzzell, Clem Lewis, and, most remarkably of all, Tommy Vile, who was given the captaincy against Scotland in 1921 at thirty-seven years of age. Wales shared in a triple tie of the championship in 1920, and won it outright in 1922, the last time until 1931. For the three years 1920-1-2 Welsh results were reasonably good, though closer inspection reveals the reality behind them to be less substantial. They stemmed more from good fortune than design, from erratic individual brilliance, and from steam-roller packs whose want of mobility and technique was camouflaged by heavy conditions that bogged down their opponents and allowed their own elephantine tactics a deceptive freedom.

Two of the most notable victories of the decade were achieved against Ireland in 1920 and England in 1922. In March 1920, on a waterlogged Arms Park that resembled less a rugby ground than a tributary of the Taff, a pack of what were then considered mastodon proportions — like Edgar Morgan (Llanelli) 6foot 1inch, 14stone 6lb., Steve Morris (Cross Keys) 6foot, 14stone 3lb., Tom Parker (Swansea) 5foot 11inches, 13stone 8lb., Jack Whitfield (Newport) 5foot 11inches, 13stone 8lb. — led by the thirty-seven-year-old Newport veteran Harry Uzzell, pulverized Ireland 28 - 4. Ireland's only reply to six tries, three conversions and a dropped goal, was a dropped goal in return and the rueful remark of Dr. J.R. Finlay (one of the eleven doctors in the Irish side) that 'the lack of foresight on the part of the Welsh Union in not providing lifebelts was damnable'. Two years later, in similar conditions, the Welsh dreadnoughts smashed into the English grand fleet to score the greatest number of tries — eight in a 28 - 6 victory — recorded against England by anyone, anywhere, in a hundred years. The man who blew the English cruisers out of the water was the 5foot 8inches pocket-battleship, D. D. (Dai) Hiddlestone, who scudded over the muddy pools as only a fitness fanatic could. Dai was tirelessly fit: he took his dog on nightly training runs around the fields of his native Hendy, until the dog crept exhausted back to its kennel and Dai kept on lapping in the moonlight.

That was the second Welsh victory over England in three years. Wales's first post-war international had been played against England at St. Helen's in January 1920, when there had been an unprecedented demand for tickets. Even though accommodation had been increased for the game by erecting stands behind the posts and quadrupling seating inside the ropes, so that there was accommodation for nearly 40,000 (who paid record Swansea takings of £3,588, beating the £2,867 of the 1906 Springboks match), Walter Rees still had to return £700 worth of unsuccessful applications. The game itself was won by the score of 19 - 5, and the individual brilliance of the lurching, side-stepping Jerry Shea who scored 16 points. Had Shea not made another attempt, against Scotland, to win the match on his own, Wales could have won the Triple Crown that year.

The Welsh side of 1920 contained four Newport players — Shea, Uzzell, Whitfield and Jack Wetter — and this was a reflection of the gathering strength of Newport club rugby. It was a strength gathered from the fragments of the invincible Pill Harriers side of 1918-19, many of whose players had stayed together during the war years in reserved occupations on the Newport docks, but who were not penalized by the

W.R.U.'s anti-professional ban. As Pill declined, its eligible players gravitated across town to the Newport club, making it the most powerful in Wales in the early twenties. They were unbeaten in 1922-23. Like previous Newport invincible sides, this one, too, contributed to the technical development of the game: it was Jack Wetter who first suggested that the wing should throw into the line-out, rather than the inside-half. Overall, their play was effective rather than entertaining, consisting of the remorseless downfield progress of their formidable pack steered from half-back by Wetter — bald as a badger but brainier — who had mystified Wavell Wakefield on the Englishman's first appearance against Wales in 1920 'by the curious bird-like cry which he [Wetter] continually uttered all over the field'. Opportunistic, essentially dull, Newport's successful blueprint was widely imitated in a defensively-minded South Wales whose rugby became as introverted and cramped as its society. In their invincible season Newport won thirty-nine of their forty-five matches, four of the six draws being with Cardiff; when their unbeaten run, which had started on 1 May 1922, came to an end on 20 October 1923 at Leicester, they were greeted on their return by 10,000. It was, briefly, like the old days.

As in the old days, Newport owed much of its success to its cosmopolitan composition. In 1921 it had fielded a full fifteen of Internationals, including Hammett, Dibble and Edwards of England, McPherson of Scotland and Roche of Ireland. This caused problems, for Newport and the W.R.U., with regard to international qualifications. There had been pre-war instances of the difficulties that could arise from Newport's position as an Uskside League of Nations. In 1911 Stanley Williams was capped at full-back for England, after being a Welsh trialist and reserve to Jack Bancroft. The issue was revived when England called centre Ernie Hammett for a trial in 1921. The Welsh Match Committee fuelled the controversy by selecting him for their own trial a week later in order to partner him with Shea, his wing since their Pill days. Though Hammett, born at Radstock but a Welsh amateur soccer cap, admitted to a preference for Wales, he accepted the prior English invitation and went on to win eight caps. When Wales were trounced 18 - 3 at Twickenham a few weeks later, the debate escalated, and the Welsh press was deluged by dyspeptic protests that England was poaching her best players from Wales, for the English XV contained Hammett, Reg Edwards (born near Pontypool), Woods (also from Pontypool) and Gardner (from Cogan). But the unkindest cut of all was the white-shirted presence of the poised and polished W. J. A. Davies in the outside-half position, where Wales desperately needed a replacement for the ageing Clem Lewis. Born in Pembroke Dock, but by his own admission ignorant of rugby till he moved to England, Davies's cuts against Wales had indeed been unkind. His first appearance in the English jersey had been at Cardiff in 1913, and the match programme celebrated it with mixed feelings:

> Hurrah for the Leek, the succulent Leek
> That hall-marks our lads as true metal!
> Hurrah for the Rose, the real English Rose
> — Except for the Pembrokeshire petal.

> Today not 'Old Moore' could forecast the score
> In spite of his skill as an actor
> But no one's surprised; the rose is disguised
> That petal is quite a new factor.

England won then, and never lost when Davies was in the side. The further pillaging of Welshmen to play for England led the W.R.U. in 1921 to take the matter up with the R.F.U. as to whether birth, parentage or residence should prevail. The R.F.U.'s attitude was that since Newport had joined them (in the late 1870s) before affiliating to the Welsh Union (in 1881) it should sever its connection with the latter. The W.R.U. and Newport protested that this would make a mockery of the positions of Welsh Union men like Lyne, Packer and Rocyn Jones, and that England wanted it both ways in claiming Davies (born in Wales, playing in England) *and* Hammett (born in Somerset, playing in Wales). A calculated suggestion made to the *Western Mail* was that the parentage of the father should be the determinant, 'rather than the place of birth or where he plays his football'. By this criterion, as the proposer well knew, England could have Hammett and Edwards, 'but not Davies, whatever his inclinations may be to play against his own countrymen'. But the W.R.U. wanted it both ways, too, for they had given Reg Edwards trials on and off since 1908, and rejected him. Now that, at thirty-four, he had been given his opportunity by England, the first of eleven caps which established him as one of the best forwards in the kingdom, it was too late to cavil. Wales unsuccessfully sought a clear ruling from the I.B. on this contentious topic, but its 'sporting decision' that 'a player who takes part in a trial match of any country should be considered as having elected to play for that country' was not confirmed till 1960.

It was Newport who also got the W.R.U. embroiled with the Scottish Union. In the summer of 1923, several prominent Newport citizens, with the sanction of the Newport club and the W.R.U., raised nearly £500 by public subscription (the Prince of Wales himself gave a shilling) to mark Newport's invincible season. The club, who had given £120, decided the money should go to presenting the players with a gold watch each, as had been done with Tom Graham's 1892 side. The Scottish Union, who had been vigilantly watching for veiled professionalism in Welsh rugby since the Gould affair, ordered Newport's Scottish international Neil McPherson to hand back his watch under threat of suspension, and brought the matter before the I.B. in October 1923. The I.B. ruled ('a feeble decision', according to the Welsh press) that it disapproved of the W.R.U.'s granting of permission to the Newport club, on account of the high intrinsic value of the presentation, and recommended that £2 should be the limit in value of mementos to players. The presentation of the watches was allowed to stand, and the Scottish Union, its *amour propre* soothed, backed down; but Scottish highmindedness was viewed with some coldness of feeling in Wales. In 1925 the S.R.U. again protested to the I.B. about Welsh 'professionalism', over expenses allegedly paid to players and reserves when the Welsh team retreated to Porthcawl before the New Zealand game of 1924. The W.R.U.'s representatives, Lyne and Schofield, attended an I.B. meeting well-briefed and armed with a detailed statement prepared by Walter Rees, which silenced all criticism. The *Western Mail*, however, found it 'irritating to know that our every action in rugby is zealously watched by the Scottish Union'. Yet the W.R.U. could be deferential as well as prickly: on their visits to Scotland in the 1920s they did not number their players out of respect to the wishes of their hosts. The Scottish Union had, alone of the home countries, ignored the I.B.'s recommendation of 1921 that international sides number their jerseys as an aid to identification. It was not until 1933 that Scotland decided to number their jerseys; by then, Wales, obscurely, had switched to lettering them. Even English observers thought that Scottish attitudes to Welsh rugby were somewhat extreme. When the S.R.U. threatened to cancel their match with Wales in 1920 because Jerry Shea was a professional boxer, the *Daily Telegraph*'s frequently blimpish Col. Philip Trevor on this occasion expostulated 'Do it! Do it! And I'll make you the laughing-stock of two continents!' They did not do it, but until the social composition of Welsh sides changed, from the late twenties, with the influx of professional and university-educated men behind the scrum, relations with the Scottish Union were strained.

The Welsh Union found the Scots alone particularly unsympathetic to the losses suffered in Wales by the depredations of the Northern Union;

the Scots felt that the W.R.U. connived at covert professionalism to staunch the constant flow of players to the north of England. In this respect again, Wales's international success up to 1922 flattered to deceive, for the inducements of the professional game were already sapping the energies of Welsh rugby. By the end of 1921 nine post-war capped players had joined the Northern Union. Pontypool began the 1921-22 season with only seven players available because virtually the whole pack had gone north during the summer; by 1922-23 there were forty to fifty Welshmen appearing regularly in northern sides. Rochdale Hornets had captured ten by July 1923. The premier 'Welsh' side was Wigan, captained by Jerry Shea who had joined them in December 1921 for £700, and then strengthened by the acquisition in August 1922 of the dapper, speedy Johnny Ring. He had scored seventy-six tries from the wing for Aberavon in 1921-22 and was awarded one cap only to be needlessly dropped. Welsh back play was direly impoverished by the loss within three post-war seasons of international players like Shea, Ring, Ike Fowler, Frank Evans and Bryn Williams of Llanelli, Ben Beynon of Swansea, W. J. Powell of Cardiff, not to mention forwards like Edgar Morgan, George Oliver and Wilf Hodder of Pontypool, Archie Brown of Newport. But the selectors, in their unfathomable neglect of the talent that remained — they consistently overlooked Albert Jenkins and Dai John from 1923 to 1928 — made their own obtuse contribution to the sterility of Welsh back play during the twenties.

Its limitations were cruelly exposed at St. Helen's in 1924. England's 17 - 9 victory was her first win of the century at Swansea; it was based on a skilful and intelligent pack, and three-quarters whose strong running and swift passing revealed the Welshmen's imperfect grasp of what was once 'the Welsh game'. In the unavoidable absence of an injured Rowe Harding, and the entirely avoidable absence of Albert Jenkins, the Welsh back division looked and was an inferior outfit. Its ponderous predictability, lack of creativity in attack and of conviction in defence, confirmed that Welsh play behind the scrum was at a low ebb. England scored five tries against a three-quarter line which, although picked more for its defensive than its offensive qualities, resorted to shoulder-tackles which were as effective as tickles in restraining the aggressively straight-running Catcheside, Locke and Jacob. Beforehand, the 35,000 crowd had gone through a varied repertoire of opera and oratorio, with pride of place going to 'Yes, we have no bananas'. As they streamed away afterwards, 'bananas' was replaced by 'three-quarters'. Six of the side's nine new caps were in the pack, but while the steam-roller theory had been abandoned for dash and youth, it was enthusiasm at the expense of experience, and it was too much to expect the genial Cross Keys collier, Steve Morris, to knit them together. What was more dismaying was the aimlessness and technical inadequacy of the Welsh forward play. The English eight, in contrast, were not merely runners and handlers, though that in itself was surprising enough. Faced with a loose ball on the ground, the first instinct of a Welsh forward was to kick it; the first instinct of an English forward was to form a loose scrum and heel it back. One or two of them, especially in the back-row, combined the strength of a lock with the mobility of a heavy winger, and would often break away on their own.

None of them broke away more often, or with such effect, than Wavell Wakefield. As long as W. J. A. Davies captained the side, Wakefield led the pack, but from 1924 Wakefield took over the captaincy and tactical direction of the English team. He was now able to elaborate his innovative concept of the back-row as a striking force and specialist unit, within an entire pack where each forward had a specialized task. On this platform England built her triumphs of the 1920s, whilst those of Mullen's Ireland and Gwilliam's Wales in the post-1945 period were achieved by refining Wakefield's use of the back-row to spoil in midfield to a high technical perfection. The gain-line had materialized in Wakefield's scrum-capped head long before it was enshrined in coaching manuals. His back-row plugged any breach in the defence around the scrum, and would force the opposing back-division into an undignified back-pedal across field. But that back-row — Wakefield (6foot, 14stone), Tom Voyce (6foot 1 inch, 13stone 10lb.) and A. F. Blakiston (5foot 11inches, 13stone 4lb.) —was not only a defensive weapon. In anticipation of his own methods being adopted by opponents — though he had nothing to fear from Wales in that respect — Wakefield revived one of the favourite Harlequins moves of the pre-war era of Stoop and Birkett: the long pass to the deep stand-off, the ball moved swiftly and accurately to the wings, the cross-kick back inside for the forwards galloping up in support. English critics like D. R. Gent and O. L. Owen fully recognized that 'the Harlequins game' was only an English translation of the best Welsh back play of the Golden Era, but rapid switching of the point of attack by such means was as baffling to Welsh teams of the twenties as French 'peeling' ploys to Welsh sides of the sixties. Another English tactic was to work for the overlap by wheeling the scrum in the opposition twenty-five to pull in defenders. Wakefield's whole doctrine of forward play was, in Owen's words, 'constructively dynamic', and the only way to neutralize it, given the apparent Welsh dearth of fast, elusive backs, was to find a tightly-knit pack of scrummaging forwards that would slow the English heel and restrict the back-row by requiring them to shove. This solution the Welsh selectors failed to find.

Welsh packs of the twenties were strong but not skilled in their strength, for they were unable to control the decisive ball-winning areas of the contemporary game, the tightly-bound scrum and the loose heel. There was an abundance of powerful individual forwards, like Steve Morris, Whitfield, Sid Lawrence of Bridgend, and a clutch of faster 'winging' forwards like Hiddlestone, Tom Jones of Newport and Ivor Jones of Llanelli, but to expect the Welsh Match Committee to find the appropriate blend between them was like asking them to contemplate the mysteries of Einstein's physics. The selectors resumed their activities after the War with the aim of fielding a heavy pack of pushers. This unimaginative scheme came unstuck in the 18 - 3 defeat at Twickenham in 1921, so it was partially jettisoned in the belief that younger, faster men would supply the required vim and dash. This compounded the weakness, for the real deficiency was the refusal to recognize the significance of specialist skills. As late as 1935 Horace Lyne would be telling his members that 'specialist forwards distressed him for they were spoiling football in all the countries'. No particular importance was attached to the role of hooker: the best hooker in Wales in the 1920s was Llanelli's Idris Jones, but the selectors either ignored him or put him in the second row, as they did against Scotland in 1925. It was not entirely true that the obsolete axiom of 'first up, first down' still prevailed, for most Welsh clubs had two acknowledged 'front rankers', but bizarre national selection often forced bigger second-rank men into the front row, front rankers to the back-row, and left recognized hookers in limbo. This perversity sometimes took quite grotesque forms, such as against Ireland in 1929, when Cecil Pritchard was flanked in the front row by the tallest man in the pack, Tom Arthur, on the one side, and by Arthur Bowdler, who was the shortest, on the other. After Watcyn Thomas dared take his role as captain seriously by rectifying one particular selectorial lunacy in the team selected to meet Ireland in 1933, he never again appeared in the scarlet jersey. It was not until the end of the twenties that Wales once more began picking a specialist hooker like Pritchard; until then the captaincy, which went around like an unpacked parcel, theoretically on seniority but in practice virtually out of a hat, decided the disposition of the selected forwards. When Rowe Harding met the team he was to captain the following day against Ireland in 1926, he had to call them together and allocate them their positions in the scrum. But line-out play was changing too. Before the War, when the scrum-half threw the ball in, quick line-outs prevailed. In the twenties, play in this quarter became more specialized, but until the arrival of expert maulers like Tom Arthur and E. M. Jenkins, and the two-handed technician Watcyn Thomas, Welsh line-out play was haphazard, marking was untidy, covering was unco-ordinated, and any chance of a quick heel from a loose maul was sacrificed on the altar of the eternal foot-rush.

While the search for 'blend' went on among the forwards, the men behind were neglected. Only two backs of the nondescript team beaten by England at Swansea in January 1924 travelled to Scotland in February. Half-back was a problem, and for many years the selectors had a pious horror of playing club partners. This, again, is a trifle puzzling. It almost suggests that the dislocated economic world in which South Wales was now struggling to stay afloat had induced collective, or at least selectorial, rugby amnesia, since much of this policy was in contradiction of the lessons already learned before the War. Against England, the half-backs had been Albert Owen of Swansea and the diminutive Neath terrier, Eddie Watkins. Owen, hounded by the English back-row, had had an uncomfortable time; few were given a second chance in those days. The selectors, like many others, had been impressed by the many original touches in the play of Vincent Griffiths of Newport. The natural combination would have been Griffiths with his club partner, the evergreen Jack Wetter, or the coupling of Neath fly-half, Eddie Williams, with his club link, Eddie Watkins. Unhelpfully, the selectors paired Griffiths and Watkins. Three new caps were chosen at three-quarter, to face the famous all-Oxford University back line of Smith, McPherson, Aitken and Wallace. Few supporters were tempted north to Inverleith by the rail excursion fare of £1 3s. 0d., and those who did were outnumbered by the committee. The Scots thought they might win by a large margin, and they did. By half-time they were 22 - 0 up, and eventually ran in a total of eight tries, four from the wings. This highlighted another weakness: Wales had no answer to three-quarters who ran straight, drawing their men and passing swiftly, and in these years, apart from the exceptional heroic performance like Rowe Harding's in Belfast in 1926, the defence on the wings was lamentable, with no flanking coverers in support. Ian Smith, the Scottish patrician with the speed and leg strength of an ostrich, capitalized on a timetable service from Phil McPherson at centre, to score seven tries against Wales in 1924 and 1925. In 1924 he made life so miserable for his opposite number, the hapless Harold Davies of Newport, that later in the evening Davies gamely asked to be introduced to him since he had not seen him on the field. He was able to deepen the acquaintance later that year as Davies was one of the four Welshmen — Smith was one of the ten Scots — who toured South Africa with a British Lions party managed by Harry Packer, the Welsh Union member and former International. On the Sunday following the 35 - 10 rout, the Welsh team went on the traditional ride to see the Forth Bridge. 'Take a good look at it, boys', urged T. D. Schofield of Bridgend, 'it's the last time any of you will see it at the expense of the Welsh Union'.

This defeat accelerated demands for reforms in the administration of the W.R.U., and of its selection methods in particular. As early as 1921, *The Field* had condemned the Welsh Match Committee as 'an obsolete selecting force', and proposed replacing it by five former Internationals, as in England: Nicholls, Gabe, Hodges, Boots and Trew. Of these, Nicholls alone would become a selector. In March 1923, after Wales had lost to the other three home countries for the first time in over thirty years, 'Old Stager', who had been writing in the *South Wales Daily News* since the 1890s and, unique among pressmen of the time, used binoculars 'to distinguish pushers from non-pushers', began a campaign to change the nature of the selection committee. 'We would suggest', he editorialized, 'that the W.R.U. should seriously consider whether the present method of selecting players cannot be improved by reducing the number of persons on the match committee . . . the Union cannot be unaware that there is a considerable body of opinion which fears that some of the selectors are too much influenced by the members of clubs to which they owe their position'. For the next twelve months, as further defeats followed, 'Old Stager' never missed an opportunity to argue the case for a selection committee of five, irrespective of club or area interests, as Ireland had since 1894 and England since 1920. When the proposal that five members only of the Match Committee should act as selectors was put to the 1923 A.G.M., however, it was defeated overwhelmingly.

The ignominy of Inverleith in 1924 was the last straw to Lewis Jones, vice-president of the Swansea club. The following Monday he delivered forceful views, laced with dark hints. The Union, he said, 'must take warning that there is a movement on foot of an unofficial character which has for its aim the intention to get the W.R.U. to change its method of administration: and sooner or later it will bring to the notice of the supporters of the game matters of the utmost importance'. He urged that if the Union did not appoint a small selection committee of four or five, 'each first-class rugby club should immediately appoint three or four representatives to attend a conference at which the whole position of Welsh rugby should be thrashed out'. Loyalty compelled him, for the present, not to air these grievances in public, but he felt that 'there are numerous questions affecting the W.R.U., its control of the game and its expenditure, which are seriously troubling a large number of rugby enthusiasts'. This was a warning shot across the bows, with the implication that the next one would be a torpedo.

What sank the old régime was its tactless handling of the Male affair. Ossie Male had been first capped from Cross Keys against France in 1921, but Swansea's Joe Rees and Fred Samuel of Mountain Ash had prevented him regaining his place till 1924. He was now teaching in, and playing for, Cardiff. He survived the 13 - 10 defeat by Ireland in Cardiff in March 1924 to be selected for the final game of the season in Paris. The game was to be played on a Thursday, and the W.R.U. decided — in accordance with its Bye-law 14, which prohibited selected players from playing within six days of an international, without prior permission of the committee — that none of the players selected should play on the previous Saturday. Male did, helping out a weakened Cardiff at Birkenhead Park. The following Tuesday, as the Welsh party were *en route* to London, the committee emerged from a private session in the saloon to announce Male's suspension and that he would be leaving the train at Paddington: he was being sent home. The decision could be faulted on numerous grounds: that Male could have been spared embarrassment and indignity by being informed in advance; that there was no reserve full-back available among the travelling reserves (the Penarth centre Melville Rosser moved to full-back, and reserve centre Joe Jones of Swansea came into the three-quarters); that the W.R.U. had itself recently violated its own bye-law by playing the final trial only five days before the England game in January. On the other hand, it was not clear that the Union had much choice in the matter. Male and Cardiff had acted with their eyes open, since Newport and Neath had applied for permission to play their international players, were refused, and had abided by the decision. The size of the committee made it impossible to meet in the intervening period, and even Walter Rees could not make an individual decision in this situation. In any case, he was in London on the Monday collecting passports. A further complication was that Ivor Jones of Neath was the selected, but non-travelling reserve, and it would have been very awkward for Walter Rees, as president of Neath, to invite him to join the party. As for the treatment meted out to Male, the Union, constantly aware of the other unions' suspicions concerning the professionalism with which Welsh rugby was believed to be tainted, knew by heart the professional and transfer laws it had adopted in 1900, and specifically the ruling that it was 'an act of professionalism' to 'keep players on tour for longer than a reasonable time'. Having made its decision over Male, the Union had no option but to send him home.

These complexities, fair-mindedly pointed out to his readers by 'Old Stager', cut no ice with a scandalized Welsh public. Criticisms of the Union welled into a crescendo and incensed correspondents to the newspapers laid about them with gusto. 'What we want is not to defend the activities of the W.R.U., but shift them all', barked one to the *South Wales Daily News*, 'Let Walter Rees and the other old fogeys go into retirement and shake the cobwebs off themselves . . . [Another prominent member] is a joke to everybody who knows him. I can never understand how he came on the W.R.U.; it wasn't his knowledge of football'.

Personal abuse apart, there was a strong case for root and branch reform, but the Union decided to leave the roots, and prune one of the branches — the Match Committee. Since 1920, when it had been further enlarged to accommodate a representative from the Amman Valley, it stood at thirteen, and the selectors were expected to find places in the trial and, ideally, the national XV for players from the districts they represented. Strength of personality could be a decisive factor. Mountain Ash was one of the leading sides in Wales in the early 1920s. Between 1920 and 1925 it defeated every first-class club in Wales except Newport. In 1922-3, eight Mountain Ash players won trial places and Fred Samuel and Tom Collins went on to win full caps, with Sid Congdon and 'Buller' Loveluck as reserves. These were deserving selections, but they owed a great deal to the forceful advocacy of E. R. McGregor, of Mountain Ash, on the Match Committee. McGregor emigrated to Canada in 1924, and though Mountain Ash continued to be a powerful combination for at least another two years, its representation at international level ceased abruptly. Similarly, the influence of T. D. Schofield won promotion for a number of Bridgend players: Ben Gronow, Clem Lewis, assorted Thomases, Charles Jones, Dan Pascoe, Sid Lawrence, Bobby Delahay and Cyril Evans. Again, these were generally justified selections. No blame could be attached to them, or their advocates on the Committee. Ted McGregor, maybe, was not the sort of committee-man who would have commended himself to the high command of the other unions — with the aid of a giant leek draped in the national colours, he had conducted a spirited rendering of 'Hen Wlad fy Nhadau' by a large crowd on Cardiff station as the Welsh team left for Twickenham in 1923 — but T. D. Schofield without question was a figure highly respected in international rugby. A member of the Union since 1897, a representative on the I.B. from 1912 to 1927, an international referee, Chairman of Bridgend U.D.C. in 1923, Tom Schofield, head of a bill-posting business, was greatly missed when he died in January 1928 at sixty-one years of age. But while the selection of players from 'the Old Firm' and Bridgend was generally merited, there were certainly others less deserving of international honours. Some claims, urged out of parochialism and self-interest, were unaided by the informed eye which a T. D. Schofield brought to his task. There was a nice subtlety in match programme pen-portraits of internationals in the early twenties, when a player was described as having 'won his way into the team by sheer merit'. It was the system that needed overhaul, and the W.R.U. at last recognized a fact that threatened to leap up and bite it when, in March 1924, on the recommendation of Ernest Davies of Swansea, it set up a sub-committee 'to consider whether the present method of selecting international players can be improved, and if so, to prepare a scheme . . . with a view to its adoption at the annual meeting of the Union'.

A sub-committee of seven was appointed. Before May was out they had won the General Committee's agreement to propose five selectors (for international sides) to the A.G.M. So, in June 1924, the concept of the 'Big Five' was finally delivered and approved.

The first Big Five (the phrase was 'Old Stager's') was chosen on Monday, 1 September 1924, and was composed of T. D. Schofield, Bridgend (who had been on the committee for twenty-seven years), James Jarrett, Cwmbran (twenty-four years), R. P. Thomas, Llanelli (fifteen years), D. B. Jones, Swansea (seven years) and Ifor D. Thomas, Cardiff (two years). The announcement was not received with rapture. Dr Teddy Morgan strongly regretted there were no former players among the five, and hinted heavily that all but four of the 1905 team were 'still around'. In fact, apart from Harry Packer and Wyndham Jones of Mountain Ash, there was not a former player on the whole committee. In England, by contrast, in the same month that saw the appointment of the Welsh Big Five, Adrian Stoop had been succeeded as selector by the recently retired W. J. A. Davies. After a year, Gwyn Nicholls and Wyndham Jones would come on to the Big Five. The omission of Lions' manager Harry Packer remained surprising, but he replaced Wyndham Jones in 1926. The fact remained that apart from these three, and Lyne as President, the W.R.U. was made up, even in its selection procedures, not of former players, but administrators, or more exactly, committee-men. 'The Welsh Union is composed of many who have no qualification to be there', snapped Teddy Morgan.

The 'Big Five' began its career not with a roar, but a squeak. The second All Blacks were due to play Wales at St. Helen's in November 1924, and the selectors went into conclave. The mountain sweated, and brought forth a mouse. New Zealand won 19 - 0, one point for every year since 1905. But these were no ordinary mortals, they were Cliff Porter's 'Invincibles', who won every one of their twenty-eight games, and had at full-back the peerless Maori George Nepia, the only player to become the greatest in his position in the world at the age of nineteen. Before going out on to St. Helen's, Nepia could not stop his knees from knocking. They stopped knocking when he got out there, and his courage, anticipation and speed in plucking the ball from the feet of onrushing forwards endeared him to Welsh rugby followers. Said one admirer:

> There were times when it appeared that nothing would stay the fierce rushes of the Welsh pack. By sheer strength they barged their way through and there stood Nepia alone betweeen them and the desired objective. Then suddenly the rush, so typical of the forwards of this country, has broken up in a remarkable manner. Nepia creeps forward and unexpectedly dives at the ball. His judgement is uncanny and his pluck magnificent. He has snatched the ball from the very toes of the men, and his bullet-like rush carries him through the mass. By a miracle he has kept his feet and with the kick which comes in his stride he has cleared. There is a gasp from the crowd, which has been in a frenzy because a score seemed so certain . . . Occasionally a Welsh three-quarter eluded the vigilant outside men, but always there was the waiting Nepia. The embrace of man and ball was like that of an octopus.

Llanelli did not repeat the mistake of the national selectors, who had picked a seven-man pack and a roving back in the New Zealand fashion. The following Tuesday the All Blacks scraped home 8 - 3 against an inspired Scarlet eight and a back division containing five current or future internationals. Llanelli's points came from a try by speedy Ernie Finch. Finch, a schoolteacher from Pembroke Dock, won seven caps on the wing for Wales between 1924 and 1928, though he was entitled to several more. He had faced the All Blacks at Swansea three days earlier. Now, as he took a quick return from a line-out and raced for the corner, he was faced by Nepia. Finch knew all he needed to know about Nepia. He nonplussed

217

him by stopping dead, then stepping past him and over for a try. It looked and was, marvellous. Finch did indeed know all about Nepia. He had stopped dead not out of tactics but from trepidation born of knowledge.

The year 1925 brought no relief to Wales. For the third year running Wales was beaten by the other home countries. For the second year running nobody got near the 'Flying Scotsman', Ian Smith, who scored in the first minute at St. Helen's and kept on scoring at irregular intervals throughout the afternoon as Wales conceded six tries. The Welsh forwards, however, infused with new energy by the overdue recognition of P. C. Lawrence of Bridgend and the grafting Ron Herrera of Cross Keys, staggered their opponents with a fighting rally in the last fifteen minutes, that produced 14 points, so that the Scots were glad to jump on the 5.30 p.m. express to London. It was a tribute to the rousing captaincy of Steve Morris, whose reward was to be relieved of it for the next match, and dropped altogether for the Irish game which was lost 19 - 3 in Belfast.

There was no shortage of proposals as to how Wales's languishing fortunes might be revived. J. C. Morgan, a waggish columnist in the *Western Mail*, recognized the element of death-wish in national selection by advocating that teams be picked by national ballot, 'all entries to receive careful consideration by a specially selected staff of judges consisting of a member of the Welsh Whippet Association, a member of the Boilermakers Society, and a well-known undertaker'. Members of the W.R.U. viewed matters more seriously. T. D. Schofield, mindful of the newly-opened Murrayfield and Ravenhill grounds, returned to the theme of 'a Welsh Twickenham' holding 100,000. Walter Rees thought that Wales was falling behind through lack of speed, the result of a lack of facilities, and the week following the Scottish defeat he launched a campaign to raise £2,000 for a new pavilion and clubhouse for his own club of Neath. Fund raising was no easy matter in the inter-war years but the W.R.U. are not entirely blameless for their lack of acumen over the issue of a ground. At a time of considerable hardship their own assets rose annually whilst deflation kept the value of money steady. Besides, from the early 1930s British society began to rise from the trough of the Depression on the basis of a building boom. A credit balance of around £6,000 in 1921 had been transformed into £22,000 by 1932 but, heavy calls in grant aid notwithstanding, the Union were singularly unimaginative in their deployment of money. T. R. Griffiths, the Treasurer since 1903, had been succeeded, after ill health, by another bank manager, Sam West, in 1930, yet until the 1950s the Treasurer was permitted to do little more than cast an eye over the accounts prepared meticulously by the long-serving Wilson Bartlett of Newport. It was not that the W.R.U. was ungenerous — Walter Rees was made permanent secretary in 1921 at the very handsome salary of £400 p.a. — nor uncaring — they sanctioned a charity game by Brynamman in late 1921 to aid the Russian Famine Fund and contributed, as before, to pit disaster funds and relief agencies like the 1930s Rhondda Boot Fund —but they were, undeniably, pre-war men in a post-war world.

They were confronted by the problem of ground accommodation directly in 1922 when they had come to review their expenditure on ground and stand improvements at Cardiff alone since 1900. Not counting running costs and repairs this was a figure in excess of £11,000. The Union concentrated their minds because the Arms Park was to be taken over by the specially formed Cardiff Arms Park Company who intended to lease the ground to the Cardiff Athletic Club after purchase from the Marquess of Bute. The W.R.U., in 1923, refused to pay rent for internationals, but did take out £4,000 in debentures in the Company in return for the continuance of their agreed use of the ground. Further requests for money impelled Schofield to press, in 1925, for a ground of their own but, in 1926, extensions to the stands were, again, paid for by the W.R.U. The interest on the debentures was to be paid by the Cardiff club but their own revenue was proving inadequate to the purpose. In 1927 greyhound racing began at the Arms Park to the horror of some Union members who appeared to think that wings who had been overlooked by Rugby League might replace either the dogs or the electric hare. Others hoped the current crop of wing three-quarters might pick up a tip or two from the dogs. Either way, the Cardiff finances continued to plummet. Pre-war takings (gross revenue) had been as high as £10,000 p.a. and, even in 1920, had amounted to £7,000, but in the late 1920s they were taking under half that amount. In 1929 the club approached the Union to take on a bigger financial burden to prevent the club's closure and the sale of the Arms Park. Purchase of the Brewery Field, near Bridgend, for £2,000 in 1929, gave them pause, and, in 1931, after several reports on capital expenditure and lease agreements, so far as Cardiff and Swansea were concerned, the W.R.U. resolved 'that in the interests of this Union it is desirable that we should have an international ground of our own'. From this statement of principle no firm intention or bold initiative flowed. Indeed in 1932, shortly before the expiry of the 1923 Agreement, the W.R.U. once again agreed to an arrangement which committed it to continue the playing of international matches at Cardiff.

By a complicated financial manoeuvre, but at considerable financial cost, the Union acquired an effective majority control of the Company. New leases were negotiated with the Cardiff Athletic Club and the Greyhound Company. The Union were given the right to use the ground on six occasions annually and to carry out improvements, but the lessees were left in effective possession — the Club until 2032 and the Greyhound Company until 1983. In return for taking the majority of shares, the Union was entitled to lease the ground to the Club and the Greyhound Company. They would reserve use for W.R.U. games and be allowed to alter the ground as they required. The delegates to the 1932 A.G.M. agreed by 90 to 58, though 'a considerable number' refrained from voting. Certainly this gave the W.R.U. far greater freedom of manoeuvre than before, but they had acquired neither exclusive use of the pitch, nor a single international venue. Worse, as was only too apparent in the 1960s, they had limited powers of disposition in the affairs of the Company. Only endless legal enquiry and intricate negotiation saw an unravelling of this *ad hoc* hotch potch with the final removal in July 1977, before agreement had expired, of the dog track. Henceforth, the pitch of the new National Ground was to be for one species of runner only.

Even in strict playing terms, neither tinkering nor tailoring seemed an effective antidote to the poverty of Welsh rugby, as Captain Rees frankly admitted. By April 1925 he conceded that the 'Big Five' idea was not a success, and that a new procedure was required. At the Union's annual meeting that year, Horace Lyne wanted to increase them to seven. 'Old Stager' sought to divert attention to the low standard of refereeing in Wales. At Easter that year, the Cardiff v. Barbarians match had ended in uproar, with enraged spectators trying to get on to the field, and police called to escort the W.R.U.'s Morgan Moses off it. After the referee had lost control of a Cardiff v. Newport game in April, 'Old Stager' urged the Union to adopt a new system for testing aspiring referees under playing conditions, and grading them according to merit — an overdue reform since 'there are many on the Welsh Union's list of referees who would not carry confidence in controlling a game of marbles'. The Union needed, too, to abandon its practice of handing out the position of touch-judge at internationals as a 'perk'. The committee-man appointed for the England match at Swansea in 1924 had to be dropped at the last moment because he knew nothing of the game or his duties. 'Old Stager' advocated linesmen who could offer a word of tactical advice at half-time. But having campaigned so energetically to establish the principle of the 'Big Five', he

220

would not easily abandon it. 'All that is necessary to secure the success of the experiment', he argued, 'is that the practice shall be as sound as the principle'. Noting the high success rate of English clubs against Welsh sides, he urged that greater attention be paid to Anglo-Welshmen and Welshmen playing in England, and underscored his argument by advocating the claims of 'Guardsman Powell' of London Welsh. W. C. Powell, born in Aberbeeg, formerly of the Welsh Guards, now articled to an architect, would be the greatest scrum-half between Owen and Tanner, and it was not 'Old Stager's' fault that, having drawn Powell to the selectors' attention, they chose him on the wing for his first cap in 1926.

So long as the Match Committee's conception of its task was to present to the 'Big Five' all the talent available — the thirteen selected the teams for the three trials, the five only the national XV — anomalies were bound to persist. It was a system that seriously precluded any long-term considerations of strategy and team-building, and its illogicality led Dr David Rocyn Jones, a senior vice-president of the Union, to declare at Neath in February 1926 that the 'Big Five' should be allowed to choose at least the Probables for the final trial, but this did not come about till 1930-1. An example of the anomalous situation that could arise from these circumstances was that the Probables backs for the third trial of 1925-6, selected by the full Match Committee, were: Lewis Williams (Crumlin), Bruce Barter (Swansea), Tom Loveland (Llanelli), Harold Davies, Ernie Finch, Bobby Delahay (Bridgend) at fly-half, and W. C. Powell. The backs that the 'Big Five' selected for the ensuing international with England were: D. B. Evans (Swansea), George Andrews and Albert Stock (Newport), Arthur Cornish (Cardiff), Rowe Harding (Swansea), Bobby Jones (Northampton), a discarded English trialist, and Delahay at scrum-half. In picking Jones, the selectors had cast their net wider than even 'Old Stager' could have anticipated; it was a choice so mystifying as to be positively oriental. Jones, in fact, was born in Shanghai, but his grandfather was Welsh, which commended him to the selectors and the Welsh rugby public, who promptly dubbed him 'Japanee Jones'. The pack was constructed in the familiar, unscientific manner. The nearest approach to a wing-forward among them, Tom Hopkins (Swansea), was chosen in the front row; the selection for wing-forward was Bryn Phillips (Aberavon), whose weight might have been put to better advantage in the scrum. It was typically confusing that this turned out to be the best eight that Wales had fielded since 1922. It had England groggy by the end, but seemed unable to deliver the knock-out blow. Its main idea was to subject the opposition to shivering but unimaginative assaults. Wales lived on the

English line for the last quarter, but hampered by slow heeling and untidy hooking, as well as their own predictability, the backs were quite unable to penetrate the English defence. Their only ploy was the short punt ahead with half the team tearing after it. The apostolic succession of 'short-sighted Irish referees' had its origins in the early twenties. In 1922 referee R. A. Lloyd had accidentally blown his whistle when Swansea's Bill Bowen, in a three-to-one situation against Scotland, had Hiddlestone and Islwyn Evans unmarked each side of him (Mr Lloyd apologized to Bowen afterwards). Now, at Swansea in 1926, referee W. A. Acton of Dublin disallowed a try by Delahay, though Welsh touch-judge Wyndham Jones who was on the spot indicated that he thought it valid by leaping in the air waving his arms. 'I do not know why unknown referees of other countries should be tried out in Wales', demanded one Welsh critic, hotly; he would want to know why again in 1929, 1931, and if he was still alive, in 1974; it was always against England. Less subjective observers might have attributed the Welsh defeat of 1926 less to Irish myopia than Welsh want of skill and science, as well as to the English back-row, which had plenty of both commodities. Wakefield claimed he could not begin to play until someone punched him on the nose. That day someone must have punched him early — *The Times* noted that the game 'was never of the parlour type' — for he played his greatest game against Wales; and wherever Wakefield was, there was Tom Voyce, a grinning, hand-grenade of a flanker, sleeves rolled, arms flailing, arousing the wrath of the crowd by some less than gentlemanly activities. The Welsh pack was hardly composed of gentlemen either, but there was little it could teach an English eight that had mixed it to some effect with New Zealand's Brownlie brothers in 1925, and had been booed off the ground after the Calcutta Cup match of that year in Murrayfield. O. L. Owen, the historian of the Rugby Football Union, admitted that England's opponents in the 1920s 'had to take the rough with the smooth', while Rowe Harding, well-versed in Varsity rugby and captain of Wales that day, noted in 1929 that 'the difference between rough rugby in England and rough rugby in Wales is largely a matter of accent'.

The Welsh forwards that day were not lambs. Neither were they, as they have been so often portrayed, colliers. Apart from Tom Hopkins, who *was*, they were all policemen. There had, of course, been policemen in the packs of the Golden Era, like Dai Evans and Bobby Brice, and men like Gwyn Evans, Tamplin, Bob Evans, Dai Davies and Allen Forward, brought skill and intelligence to post-1945 sides. But the number of policemen capped for Wales in the inter-war period was striking. In the 1920s, members of the Glamorgan Constabulary who played for Wales included Sid Lawrence, Bryn Phillips, Charlie Pugh, Jack John, Tom Lewis, Sid Hinam, Gus Broughton, and W. J. Ould. Tom Arthur, Ned Jenkins and Archie Skym played into the thirties, where the tradition was maintained by Bob Barrell, Dai Thomas, Arthur Rees, Russell Taylor, Iorrie Isaacs, Harry Rees and Eddie Watkins. This is not to mention Monmouthshire policemen like Tom Roberts, Ron Herrera and Cliff Williams, or backs like Bill Everson and the hefty Penarth full-back Jack Bassett. Cardiff had an average of ten policemen in its first XV every year between 1923 and 1939; in 1925-6 it had twelve. Police teams were a familiar aspect of South Wales in these years, and they raised over £7,000 in charities between 1921 and 1930.

While these policemen were immensely popular as individuals, the institution they represented was viewed less cordially in some parts of South Wales. There was plenty for policemen to do in that part of the country in the 1920s, and there were plenty of policemen to do it. The Chief Constable of Glamorgan, Lionel Lindsay, saw to that. In 1922 he was advised by the Home Office to reduce the number of his policemen, as he kept more than he needed. Lindsay ensured that his force always contained a good proportion of rugby forwards, and his motives were not wholly disinterested. It was a tense time in the coalfield, and the tension spilled over on to the rugby field. One referee took the field in Glyncorrwg in these years with a revolver strapped to his waist. P.C. Bryn Phillips, who was winning his fifth cap in 1926 against England, had been a bloody casualty of the anthracite disturbances in the Dulais Valley in the summer of 1925, after which strikers and strike-breakers partly settled their scores on the rugby field. In March 1928 a Glamorgan Police XV was stoned at Redruth by clay miners with bitter memories of the role the Glamorgan Constabulary had played in breaking their strike in 1913.

But even in the strife-torn industrial valleys, the situation was too varied and complex to be reduced to a crude polarity. Thus, when the Pontypridd Club, faced by liabilities of £230 and a rival Northern Union team, appealed for aid and better fixtures in August 1926, the W.R.U.'s investigators were anxious to establish the social prominence in the town of leading members; and three or four policemen were in the team, they reported. But the major part of their report centred on support for the secretary, who had been denounced by a policeman in the team for his 'extreme' views. The W.R.U. were told that Mr Berriman had been instrumental in rescuing the club from an even worse financial mess and that while he 'certainly holds Labour views . . . he is a most respected person in Pontypridd . . . a member of the Pontypridd section of the Miners' Federation'. Money and games were duly allotted. In the Cynon Valley, too, there were seven policemen in the Aberaman team of 1927-8; in the Rhondda, in 1928, Treorchy elected as their captain the popular Gus Broughton. There were no more hugely liked members of the community, or the Welsh side, than the amiable and strictly teetotal amateur boxers, Tom Arthur and Ned Jenkins; none laughed more uproariously than Ned on discovering in the programme of his first international in 1927 that he was 'the fourth member of the Glamorgan Constabulary on duty today, and not the least clever by any means'. Those two, and P.C. Archie Skym, became the bed-rock of a pack that by the early thirties was winning sufficient ball for a new generation of backs to revive traditional Welsh three-quarter play.

But that time was not yet, for throughout the twenties the dour nature of much club play, and the not unconnected dull spectacle presented by the constantly unenterprising and unsuccessful Welsh international sides contrasted unfavourably with the attractive handling skills of professional rugby, the great success of Welsh soccer teams, and the economic inducements of both, which threatened to eclipse rugby union in appeal and challenged its primacy as the one great pastime of the people of South Wales.

Indeed, it is no exaggeration to say that the very existence of South Wales as a society was under threat. Perhaps the dire nature of the problem only became fully apparent after 1927, but it was inescapable thereafter. The coal trade on whose basic prosperity the whole culture had rested enjoyed an artificial boost in war-time conditions. After 1918, with navies switching to oil, the fuller use of other forms of power, the chaotic superstructure of the coal industry, and above all, the loss of export markets, the economy of South Wales fell in like a collapsed lung. An initial post-war boomlet expired by 1920 and, from then on, the pattern was one of deepening misery. The politics of South Wales switched dramatically to Labour representation, even if more erratically in the big towns, at local and parliamentary level. Neither the rise of Labour to power on the councils nor the return of the first Labour governments, in 1924 and 1929, stemmed the tide. Running in tandem was the alternative of direct action through strikes — in 1921 a three-month coalfield lock-out, and in 1926 a strike that went on for eight months. All of the institutions of pre-war South Wales, from the Miners' Federation to the Liberal Party and on to the W.R.U., were damaged badly, in terms of personnel and self-confidence, by this savaging of their once bouncy world. Recovery, from the mid-1930s, was slow and painful. The legacy was a harsh one.

The human cost, in contemporary terms, was almost unbearable. The quarter million coalminers employed in 1920 had dwindled to half that number within a decade. By the end of the 1930s they were only around 100,000 in number and great ports like Cardiff, with no separate industries built up in her heyday, lay inert like beached galleons. Unemployment drilled into the populous valleys like a virulent woodworm. It was longterm, high-percentage, and numbing. A thousand people a year left Merthyr in the 1920s. The total loss for Wales, in bodily removal and consequent decline of natural increase, was approaching half a million. The social fabric and cultural vitality of South Wales began to crumble. Money coming in dwindled to a tiny proportion of pre-war capital and earnings. People going out put a new gloss on Cecil B. de Mille's silent film version of *Exodus*, 'The Ten Commandments'.

In terms of Welsh rugby, these were developments beyond even the control of Walter Rees. The losses to the professional code in particular, can only be inadequately quantified. Forty-eight capped players — the equivalent of more than three full national fifteens — 'went north' between 1919 and 1939, but this only indicates the vast size of the submerged part of the iceberg, the unknown and unknowable number of trialists and ordinary club players who felt the pull of the magnetic north, where their rugby potential was ultimately realized. When Ossie Male deputized for the injured Joe Rees against France in 1921, there was in Cardiff a player already greater than either. Though his mature 5foot 11inches and 11stone 9lb. belied it, he was only seventeen-years-old, but he would not be playing in Cardiff much longer. In July 1921 Jim Sullivan signed for Wigan, destined to become, in the course of a playing career extending to 1946, one of the greatest full-backs ever produced by the Principality, though he would not tread the Arms Park turf again until a charity match in 1945, in the company of Haydn Tanner and Bleddyn Williams. Similarly, when the uncapped William Absalom, captain of Abercarn, signed for Wakefield Trinity in November 1926, Wales lost one of her brainiest forwards, just as the loss of Emlyn Jenkins of Treorchy to Salford in November 1930 deprived her of a fly-half of quite exceptional ability. Many Union players prejudiced their future by going to the North of England, playing a game under an alias, and returning home when not

225

offered terms. Billo Rees, of Amman United and then Swinton, brother of Welsh full-back Joe Rees, was caught trying to turn the process on its head. In a game between Morriston and Cwmllynfell in November 1923, the referee stopped play after five minutes when he was told that Billo Rees, home on holiday, was playing for Cwmllynfell, and both clubs were temporarily suspended by the W.R.U. in consequence.

The losses sustained in the years 1919-22 were a trickle compared with the haemorrhage that was to follow as the economic indicators plummeted. In 1924, Internationals Ambrose Baker, Melville Rosser, A. C. (Candy) Evans and Eddie Watkins turned professional. Aberavon lost half its high scoring international back division to Leeds in September and October 1925. Mountain Ash lost both its Internationals to Hull in June 1923; Swinton paid £450 and £300 on the same day in November 1925 to Neath's full-back Ivor Jones and wing Ivor Davies. The down-payment of £350, alluringly laid out on the kitchen table by a persuasive agent, plus a job, with £4 for a win and £3 draw or lose, was, to an unemployed miner like Emlyn Watkins, who had already won three caps from Blaina in 1926, an offer not to be refused, and he joined Leeds in September. The unemployed Dai Jones of Newport, capped five times in 1926 and 1927, found the prospect of £300 down irresistible, and went to Wigan in January 1927; a month later his club-mate and unsuccessful trialist, Ernie Dowdall, joined him for £500; in April, Newport also lost international winger George Andrews, still only twenty-three-years-old. Leeds paid him £600, and Bridgend's twice-capped Dan Pascoe, now of Neath, a strapping but unemployed miner, another £600 the same season. And so the trek North went on.

Wales had been playing professional rugby internationals with England, in England, since 1910. Now, in the fateful year of 1926, the Northern Union came south to consolidate a toehold into a bridgehead. In December 1921, a crowd of 18,000 had watched a Welsh professional side play Australasia at Pontypridd. In April 1926, again at Pontypridd, Wales's Rugby League side lost 22 - 30 to England. That Welsh XIII comprised: Jim Sullivan (Wigan, formerly of Cardiff), Frank Evans (Batley, Llanelli and Wales), Melville Rosser (Leeds, Penarth and Wales), Joe Jones (Leeds, Swansea and Wales), J. A. Bacon (Leeds, Cross Keys), Ike Fowler (Batley, Llanelli and Wales), Eddie Williams (Huddersfield, Neath and Wales), Wilf Hodder (Wigan, Pontypool and Wales), Edgar Morgan (Hull, Llanelli and Wales), F. L. Roffey (St. Helens, Ebbw Vale), Joe Thompson (Leeds, Cross Keys and Wales), D. Rees (Halifax, Llanelli) and Bryn

Phillips (Huddersfield, Aberavon and Wales). The 22,000 spectators at Taff Vale Park were enthralled by the fast, open play. While Pontypridd R.F.C. played at Ynysangharad Park in front of a crowd of 200, the Rugby League bought the Taff Vale ground from Pontypridd A.F.C., and a Rugby League Commission for Wales was set up, with J. L. Leake of Bassaleg as its secretary. The intention was to attract Union clubs to join the League, but many were unable to do so, had they wished, because of their indebtedness to the W.R.U., who were the guarantors of their fields and stands. Pontypridd were elected to the Rugby League in June 1926. In December 1927 rugby league was established at the new Sloper Road greyhound stadium in Cardiff, and 12,000 saw England beat Wales 39 - 15 at 'the Welsh White City' the following year. That year, too, Glamorgan and Monmouthshire played in the R.L. County Championship. The distance involved in fulfilling fixtures forced Pontypridd to resign from the League in 1927, but the thirteen-a-side game had by now come to exercise such a hold on the local population that an amateur Pontypridd and District R.L. was set up, with sides from Tonyrefail, Trebanog, Graigwen, Abertridwr, Rhydyfelin, Treforest, and Norton Rangers. It collapsed in 1929, and its players received absolution from the W.R.U., which helped Pontypridd R.F.C. to re-establish itself fully the following year.

The Union's response to the threat posed by the counter-attraction of the professional game in South Wales was not always so constructive. In 1927 a rugby league game was staged on the Welfare Ground used by Ebbw Vale R.F.C., and the W.R.U. threatened it with expulsion. It was an ill-considered and pointless response, for the club did not own the ground and could not be held answerable for the use to which it was put. What was needed by clubs like Ebbw Vale, at the end of their tether through falling gates and the rival attractions of soccer and rugby league, was not threats but assistance, and there was grumbling that the Union was unsympathetic to the plight of the valley clubs. The Union, for its part, could point out that it often assigned schoolboy trials and internationals to places like Pontypridd and Aberdare. It could also, and did, claim that it was offering generous financial help to clubs: the W.R.U. paid out £28,000 towards clubs and junior leagues between 1920 and 1933, and proceeded to argue that 'the working-class nature of the game in Wales' meant that it was because the Union was making grants on a scale unknown in the other countries where the game was confined to the professional classes and where unions were little troubled by impecunious clubs, that it could not afford a national ground.

The 'working-class nature of the game in Wales' raised social as well as economic problems. The relative lack of sophistication of Welsh rugby in the 1920s, at the administrative and playing levels, drew critical comment from outsiders. The spontaneity of Welsh crowds could look like uncouthness when even ticket-holders showed the same deficiency in the social graces as the devotees of the popular bank. Col. Trevor of the *Daily Telegraph* was constantly irked by the booing of unpopular decisions by the referee, 'especially when it comes from the grandstand'. The tone of the Wales v. New Zealand game of 1924 apparently 'was not the tone of the matches played, say, at London and at Oxford', which was self-evidently true, but ignored the fact that the spectators at London and Oxford did not carry victorious opposing captains off the field, as the Cardiff crowd did with Scotland's Leslie Gracie in 1923 after he had scored the winning try in the dying minutes (in marked contrast to the 'stunned silence' which had greeted Islwyn Evans's last-minute equalizing drop-goal at Inverleith the previous year); and carried off French full-back Magnol shoulder-high after he had single-handedly repulsed the Welsh back-line in 1929. Wavell Wakefield freely acknowledged that at Swansea in 1924, 'the extremely sporting crowd gave the [victorious] English side a wonderful ovation'. Other aspects of Welsh crowd behaviour — crowding on to the field of play, surrounding players at half-time, and 'the insensate autograph mania' — were viewed censoriously by E. H. D. Sewell. 'To crowd round the players in an international match is one of those things which simply is not done', he protested. 'There was a time when the public understood the limits surrounding where it is "not wanted", but the war has changed all that, and with this absurd spread of Communism and "what's yourn's mine" everywhere rampant, the uninitiated portions of the public obey no such unwritten laws of decent usage and civilized gentlefolk'.

The crude equation between 'indiscipline' and political subversion was a recurrent theme of the Conservative *Western Mail*, which became so paranoid about the Red menace stalking post-war Britain that it headlined its fears that the traditional melody, 'Dafydd y Garreg Wen', might have Russian origins, via the colony of Welsh migrant iron-workers at Hughesovska in the Volga basin. In 1921 it saw Reds on the terraces. The Scottish visit to St. Helen's that February provoked great anticipation in the Swansea area. The W.R.U. had made arrangements for the accommodation of around 35,000. Walter Rees prayed for rain; otherwise, he thought, there might be crowd trouble. He got crowd trouble. Over 60,000 spectators passed through the turnstiles, and with the crowd surging around the touch-line from the start, it was only a matter of time before they bulged on to the field of play itself. Halfway through the second half, play was suspended and the teams retired to the pavilion. It cost Wales the game, for the Scots were desperately hanging on to a narrow lead before the twelve-minute respite allowed them to get their wind. Tommy Vile was about to take a penalty in front of the posts when the teams went off; when they returned, Albert Jenkins took it, and missed (though in other respects he played the Scottish team virtually on his own and scored all Wales's points). The *South Wales Daily News* did not commend the afternoon's activities, for there were several 'discreditable features . . . One was the language which was so lurid that ladies had to leave the ground. Another was the action of large numbers in taking flagons and bottles of beer with them, consuming the contents and throwing the bottles all over the place. A lady in the stand heard a bottle whizz past her ear, and on looking round was advised to turn quickly back again or it might be her face that would be struck by the next bottle. Simultaneously a cork banged out of a bottle, and part of its contents ran down the back of her neck. She sought safety by leaving'. It was the tumultuous crowd scenes elsewhere in the ground that provoked most comment. The *Western Mail* was not content to attribute crowd disorder simply to a disorderly crowd: it had to be 'the outcome of an organized movement' led by Labour leaders, a 'gang of irresponsible hooligans posing as followers of Lenin and Trotsky', who had distributed unauthorized tickets to the unemployed, allowing admission at half-price. Some plain cards stamped 'Ministry of Labour, Labour Exchange, Swansea' had been distributed in Manselton, and some people thought that if these were presented at the turnstiles with a shilling, this would gain admission. Walter Rees turned sleuth, tracked the story to its source, and discovered that a 'prominent Labour leader', whose name he would not release, had been misrepresented. The unauthorized tickets were dismissed as a red-herring by the *South Wales Daily News*, but the *Western Mail* saw it as 'another and very serious symptom of the spirit of unrest which is abroad in these troublous times . . . a new and unwelcome feature in amateur sport which must be put down with an iron hand'.

The bogey of indiscipline was frequently invoked during the 1920s to explain Welsh lack of success at international level. Surveying the 1926-7 season, the *Rugby Football Annual* purported to be baffled by the failure of a Welsh pack that contained the nucleus of the previous season's eight: 'Based on such a pack, Wales should have had the best team in the championship, but somehow they fizzled out as a striking force. It was a strange relapse, though not untypical of the modern South Wales, where discipline and belief in anything is at a discount'. Speaking to the Glamorgan County R.F.C. in September 1926, towards the end of the agonizing miners' lock-out of that year, the W.R.U.'s T. D. Schofield saw rugby as the panacea to cure the ills of a troubled and divided society. 'Men who play football are sportsmen, and sportsmen are good citizens. If we could make every one in this country play football, we would not have this trouble we are passing through now'.

Rugby's role as a social healer at a time of industrial strife and overt class conflict was a theme constantly harped upon by leaders of public opinion who regretted the breakdown of the progressive consensus of the pre-war years. One way was to make a virtue of that feature of Welsh rugby which, at bottom, most vexed the other home unions; that it was the game of the masses and the classes. 'Old Stager', who since the takeover of the Liberal *South Wales Daily News*, itself a graphic comment on the demise of Edwardian Wales and all its glories, by its rival in August 1928, was now writing for the *Western Mail*, spoke in October 1929 to the Crynant Lit. and Deb. Society on 'Rugby and its meaning', and made it plain that rugby was the handmaiden of a responsible citizenship: 'The working men of Wales — among the best sportsmen in the world — should be jealous of the privilege accorded them on participating in Rugby, especially as that privilege was largely withheld from working men in the other rugby countries'. This perspective on the game was evidently not that of 'the other rugby countries'. The same month, at the unveiling of the Rowland Hill memorial gates at Twickenham, the President of the R.F.U., W. T. Pearce, spoke of 'the Rugby atmosphere — which could only circulate freely among the public school element of the community'. There could be no greater contrast than the terms in which the President of the W.R.U., Horace Lyne, spoke a week later at a jubilee match celebrating the historic first encounter between Newport and Blackheath: 'just about that time [1879], some significant changes took place in the Newport team —men who worked with their hands mingled with players who worked with their heads. Some of the wiseacres of the day . . . told us we were making a mistake . . . their prognostications were all wrong. Newport played better football after that than previously'.

The idea that rugby, and rugby tours in particular, was as good a means as any in furthering harmonious social relationships — considered necessary, at a time of bitter class antagonism, 'if we are to maintain a

230

balanced and healthy society' — lay behind the formation of Crawshay's Welsh XV in 1922. The Crawshays of Cyfarthfa, ever since their halcyon days as Merthyr's iron masters, had been anxious to foster social harmony. Like the Gilbertsons of Pontardawe, and the Mansel Lewises, the squires of Stradey, they had patronized rugby as well as the arts. Geoffrey Crawshay (1892-1954) was a Herald Bard, eisteddfodwr, and parliamentary Liberal candidate in 1929 and 1930. In 1934 he was appointed Special Areas Commissioner for South Wales; his interests ramified into industry, politics, finance, the arts, and things Welsh. A romantic, even chivalric, Arthurian figure in a green cloak, he founded the Welsh Guards Choir, Welsh Guards XV, and his own Crawshay's XV. It was founded on the belief that rugby was a game for gentlemen of all classes, and in the first of many subsequent West Country tours in 1922 a few colliers joined a fairly martial group of Welsh Guards and Glamorgan Policemen. Thereafter it widened its ranks 'to enable men from all walks of life to take part in a rugby tour'. Crawshay's West Country tour became an established feature of the rugby calendar for over fifty years until in 1979 they chose to switch to North Wales. With its initiations, ceremonial, and Celtic rituals, it grew into a rugby freemasonry which provided some individual compensation for many Welsh players whose economic circumstances prevented them from accepting invitations to join the Lions' tours of the inter-war period. It reflected, too, the rather hopeful consensus viewpoint, that the divisiveness that was such a marked characteristic of contemporary social, political and industrial life might be transcended by a sport that was democratic, amateur and expressive of Welsh nationality. In 1929 Urdd Gobaith Cymru, the Welsh young people's movement founded in the same year as Crawshay's, though based mostly in soccer-playing Mid and North Wales, adopted rugby as its premier winter game, and began negotiating with the Welsh Schools R.U. Geoffrey Crawshay and Ifan ab Owen Edwards, founder of the Urdd, would, from their different vantage points, have commended 'Old Stager's' sentiments on the morning of the Wales v. England match of 1930, 'A Rugby international penetrates and permeates Welsh life to an extent that nothing else is capable of doing . . . Welsh life in all its many facets is never so truly represented at any national event as at a Rugby international match in Wales. Creeds, political opinions and social distinctions are all forgotten'. The point was elaborated in a leading article: 'Rugby football is more democratic in Wales than elsewhere in respect both of players and followers. The game of the high schools in England is the game of the masses in Wales, or to be more correct, the game of all

231

classes. There is no vexed problem of social opportunity or preference on this side of Offa's Dyke, for the humblest exponent of the game in the social order claims the kindred of sportsmanship with the select and elect and has his claims allowed. So with the spectators: the Welsh rugby crowd is like the English association crowd in its broad representation of all classes'. It was the amateur character of the game that made it the repository of democratic values. In 1927 Captain Crawshay attempted to launch a Glamorgan amateur rugby league 'to play in a competitive spirit where only true sportsmanship was allowed'. The thirteen-a-side game was not instrinically malignant; it was its mercenary professionalism that made it so.

If professional rugby was to be condemned, then even more so was association football, which, it was argued, apart from being professional, was neither Welsh, nor as socially inclusive as rugby. Yet the strident success of Welsh soccer in the 1920s was undeniable. It was, at international level, just as successful in the thirties, but by then rugby too was recapturing some of the glories of former years. In contrast to the consecutive defeats suffered by the Welsh rugby XV in the twenties, Wales's soccer team won the championship three times; Cardiff City were promoted to Division One in 1921, reached the Cup Final in 1925, and won it in 1927, when Arsenal's Welsh goalkeeper, Dan Lewis, fumbled an innocuous-looking shot and allowed the ball to trickle into the net. The previous year Swansea Town had reached the semi-final. In 1924, when Wales held the rugby wooden spoon, the Welsh XI won the soccer triple crown and the championship, and Cardiff came within .024 of a goal of winning the Football League championship. Merthyr Town joined the Third Division (South) in 1920, and Aberdare Athletic in 1921, to make five South Wales teams in the Football League, though both were relegated by 1930, for valley soccer was no more immune to the business-cycle than valley rugby.

Cardiff City's winning of the F.A. Cup in 1927 was universally acclaimed throughout Wales, but purists were quick to notice that there were only three Welshmen in the side. This was the unacceptable face of soccer: it was the game of the English (though also the North Welsh) immigrant, whose club took precedence over his country. The week-end of Cardiff's historic Cup victory, a correspondent from Cymmer in the Rhondda felt compelled to inform the *Western Mail*, 'Although Cardiff is the capital city of my country and the chief town of my country, the Cardiff City team does not represent either in the sense that a Rugby

Football team represents Cardiff or Wales . . . Long may Rugby Football flourish, where we can take a personal interest in and enjoy a reflected glory of the prowess of our townsmen and fellow nationals'.

In the immediate aftermath of the War, an attempt was made to elevate the status of rugby at the expense of soccer by branding the latter not merely as a mercenary importation, but as unpatriotic. When a rumpus broke out late in 1920 as to which game should be taught in Cardiff schools, the arguments first assumed a familiar pattern: professionalism debased the human character, amateurism was morally uplifting, 'it is better to encourage the playing of rugby as an amateur game in our schools than to create an ambition in the minds of the lads to become professional hirelings'. But when W. A. Brown, founder, treasurer and secretary of the Welsh Schools R.U., 1905-1949, joined the fray by pointing out that 'schools rugger' was abandoned during the War ('the school-teachers in charge of our principal nursery having forsaken it for a greater game') thus allowing the association code to be established or re-established in the schools of Swansea and elsewhere, a war-wound was re-opened. It was recalled how soccer had continued to be played until the end of 1915, to the moral outrage of many, though, of course, this was scarcely unique since conscription was not introduced until 1916; how amateurs had flocked to the colours, while professionals 'simply had to be shamed and taunted into doing their duty to their country', and when they did join up they tried to get into 'cushy and safe jobs'. Professional sportsmen had, it was rather sanctimoniously felt, been found wanting in 1914, and rugby men played the patriotic card well into the twenties to stem the rising soccer tide.

'Observer' and 'Forward' of the *Western Mail* made quite flagrant attempts to exaggerate attendance figures at rugby matches to conceal the fact that soccer was drawing bigger crowds. 'Forward' was the paper's Swansea correspondent, and seeing crowds thronging to the Vetch, professed himself 'completely at a loss to explain this sudden conversion of so many thousands of people'. But this would prove to be 'only a passing phase, a new toy whose attractions will diminish . . . before long, he who surveys the shifting scene will be able to look out through his window and see the Mumbles Road crammed, jammed with people as in the days of yore. They will not be going to see men playing football who are paid for it, but men of their own town and neighbourhood, racy of the soil, who play the game for the love of the game, and for the honour of the town which gave them birth. It is bound to come'. It was not. The crowds returned briefly to the 20,000 mark at Cardiff and Swansea's club games in 1920-21, but as the economy began to falter, as club games became dour and opportunistic, and international rugby unimaginative and defeatist, the crowds fell away. The nadir was reached in 1927 when barely 15,000 watched an international at St. Helen's.

Throughout the twenties, however, there was one rugby stronghold that withstood the twin assaults of rugby league and soccer. At the end of 1918, Llanelli R.F.C. was £1,000 in debt; by the following May the arrears had been wiped out; by Christmas the club had renewed its lease on Stradey Park for another ten years. In that period when so many other clubs trembled on the verge of extinction, Llanelli became one of the wealthiest in Wales, not least because after playing with the 36th Division in France, Albert Jenkins had returned home to lift Llanelli from post-war despondency to consistent success. In 1925-6 Llanelli was unbeaten at home, in 1926-7 they won 33 out of 44 matches, scoring 555 points in the process, and beating Cardiff four times, the only side ever to do so in one season. The club's high-scoring feats condemned professional rugby in the area to a short life. The Stebonheath ground was let to a rugby league syndicate in September 1926, to exploit the coal stoppage, but it collapsed within five months. Llanelli A.F.C. had enjoyed a hey-day just before the War, reaching the final of the Welsh Cup. By 1925 it had been reduced to such financial straits that it failed to be re-admitted to the Welsh League. There was no more emphatic example of rugby as *the* Welsh game, or of soccer as the importation of immigrants, than Llanelli. On Saturday, 12 January 1924, Llanelli's association XI was: Abbott, Marshall, Haug, Stanton, Reilly, Kettleborough, Goldie, McLaughlan, Power, Lindsay and Cartwright. None was Welsh. Llanelli's rugby XV the same day was: D. H. Davies, Elwyn Evans, Mortimer Evans, Albert Jenkins, Ernie Finch, Dai John, Arthur John, Bobby Evans, W. J. Jones, Ivor Jones, Gwyn Francis, Evan Phillips, Will Lewis, Fred Harris, Jack Owen. All were Welsh, all, but two, Welsh-speaking.

Llanelli rugby had a colourful following, with unique characters. Most clubs had them — like Swansea's Mr Derricott, who followed the All-Whites for half a century in white moleskin trousers and with a voice that could be heard the other side of Swansea Bay — but Llanelli seemed to have more. In his autobiography, Watcyn Thomas remembers the Llanelli crowd of that time as 'fanatical, knowledgeable and witty'. There on the popular bank were Tom Sports, Dai Salvation, Tom Betsy (with a domineering wife), Will Up and Down (with one leg shorter than the

234

other) and Billy Tidy (whose mother said what a tidy boy he was, always took toilet paper to work). There was Jimmy Daicco, who invariably turned up for the game with an appropriate symbol for the visiting team — two dead crows for all-black Neath, a bunch of keys for Cross Keys, a dead white duck for Swansea. There was also Tosh Evans, a one-man circus who provided pre-match entertainment by dancing, juggling and whistling. Llanelli supporters seemed to follow their team in greater numbers too. Half of the 15,000 crowd at St. Helen's in October 1919 came from Llanelli. A Swansea fan removed a scarlet-ribboned saucepan which Tosh Evans had tied to the cross-bar and free fights broke out. 'One Llanelli supporter, who could be distinguished by his pink shirt', recalled Watcyn, 'was "Jamesie" Davies, who did some slamming and five Swansea-ites fell like logs . . . thirty to forty fights were soon in progress but luckily the two teams took the field and order was restored'. When Dai and Arthur John were not picked for the 1926 game against Ireland, the W.R.U. received 200 angry and abusive letters, 199 bearing the Llanelli postmark. (The censorious posturing of critics in and beyond Wales who professed concern at the 'indiscipline' of football crowds overlooked the extent to which those crowds had their own notions of legality and fair play. In October 1925, when Penygraig, with Roy Gabe Jones at fly-half enjoying a highly successful period, were at home to Llanelli — and beat them 11 - 0 — a thousand unemployed miners, unable to pay the few coppers admission, rushed the gates to settle on the cheap bank and allowed the game to proceed without hindrance).

Llanelli, as ever, had a marvellously partisan press. After the Twickenham defeat in 1923, the *Llanelly Mercury* adjudicated '. . . it is very pleasing to find that the Swansea critics have in this instance written in a manner which commends itself to Llanellyites. Anyone who was at Twickenham must have been staggered to read in certain reports that Albert Jenkins was selfish and did not feed his wing. The Swansea critics hit the nail on the head when they justly pointed out that the ball had a nasty habit of gravitating towards Cornish and Johnson, the Cardiff pair of backs, and that this gravitation started at the Cardiff outside-half, Clem Lewis. For the sake not merely of Albert Jenkins (the finest centre in the country) but of the Welsh team, it is to be hoped that in the Scottish match the Welsh outside-half will sink his fondness for his clubmates in his love for sportsmanship and give Jenkins a fair opportunity'. It added, 'It is a pity that some of the critics could not discard their parochial viewpoint when dealing with a national XV'. There was total, and justified, incredulity in Llanelli at the neglect of their team by the Welsh selectors during the middle years of the decade. When eventually five Scarlets were selected for the side to meet England in 1928, the Llanelli press could not understand how, having chosen the Llanelli back-row and the Llanelli half-backs, the selectors had failed to pick Albert, Ned Samuel and Ernie Finch, too. After Wales lost 10-8, the *Llanelly Post* was compelled to point out that 'If Albert Jenkins had been playing [he] would have dropped at least two goals and got a try as well'. The *Mercury* rubbed it in: 'If the Big Five have the courage of their convictions, they will give Llanelli at least seven caps for the next match'. They almost did; there were six in the 'saucepan side' that achieved the first Welsh victory over Scotland since the War, and there *were* seven against Ireland, when Albert Jenkins appeared in the Welsh jersey for the last time.

Llanelli produced many great players in the 1920s; by the end of the decade Ivor and Iorwerth Jones, Archie Skym and Watcyn Thomas had emerged as among the finest forwards of the post-war era. Behind, too, there was a bagful of talent, like the elusive Finch on one wing and Frank Evans on the other, master of the dummy kick with which he lulled his opposite number into thinking he was about to kick before shooting past him. Llanelli lost several of her star backs to the Northern Union in the early twenties, but the relative prosperity of West Wales, and the absolute prosperity of the Llanelli club, was sufficient for her greatest to remain and make the decade one of the club's greatest, too. There was D. E. (Dai) John, steelworker, screw-kicker and master tactician, who turned down £500 to join Salford in 1926, and whose high forehead, receding hairline and 5foot 6inches, 10stone 10lb. stamped him indelibly as the archetypal Welsh fly-half. And there was Albert.

Albert Jenkins was corporate property. He belonged to the community, where he was known as 'Albert' from the highest to the humblest. Like so many sons of Stradey, he was often a Samson shorn when he crossed the Llwchwr river. On the Llanelli side of it, he was dynamite. Born in 1895 in Llanelli and bred there, he had played his Army football at full-back, where his kicking and tackling powers were further tested and developed. On his return to civilian rugby in 1919, he was offered £500 to join Hull; he refused then, and resisted even higher sums later. The Llanelli scoring records of that era owed much to drop- and place-kickers like Dai John, Ivor Jones and Iorwerth Jones, the last of whom signed professional forms for Swansea Town in 1930. They all accumulated points at a logarithmic rate, but none with such phenomenal success as Albert. He could take a game into his own hands. Against Ireland in 1920 he dropped a goal, kicked two conversions, scored a try and made another three for his club partner Bryn Williams. Against Scotland in 1921 he broke the defence time and again only to see his efforts squandered by his outsides. With Scotland 11 - 0 up, he began to bombard the Scottish posts with a ferocious barrage of pot-shots and kicks. He dropped two goals to bring Wales within three points, but then had to go off (the stories of Albert the mighty drinker who downed eight pints before a game, to retire briefly during the course of it with a strategic injury, were myths such as only legendary figures generate). After he went off, Scotland scored again to put the game beyond Wales's reach. He had certain specialities for which he was unrivalled. He could punt or drop-kick half the length of the field with either foot; he was adept at taking the ball one-handed at speed; he evoked admiring shouts as with miraculous agility he rolled over and bounded up when knocked down. Only once was he knocked out, when tackled in scoring a try against Cardiff. The tackler was Jim Sullivan, and he was knocked out too, for trying to stop one of Albert's thirty-yard bursts was to invite concussion. At 5foot 8inches and 12½stone, his barrel chest and squat, stocky frame made him look shorter than he was, but those muscle-packed proportions tapered down to a sprinter's calves, narrow ankles and small, balletic feet. No ballet dancer, though, could have tackled like Albert. Blood coursed at the sight of him forcing a whole opposing three-quarter line across field, until the luckless winger received both the ball and Albert simultaneously, and was deposited half way up the bank. He was often criticized for erratic and mistimed passing, but Rowe Harding never forgot the first time he played on the left wing outside him. 'The game was against Penarth', he recalled, 'and in ten minutes Albert gave me three scoring passes with no-one to beat; but the ball came at a speed I had never experienced before. I dropped them all'. Albert's grace of movement and fastidious attention to technique was reflected in a punctilious concern for his outward appearance. Immaculately groomed on the field of play, his brilliantined hair swept back flat on his head, the gleaming polish of his boots and crisp cleanliness of his carefully ironed outfit illumined many a dark afternoon; off the field, his spotless white muffler made him easily recognizable about town, though he often complained of the endless attention.

There were two Alberts. Shy and withdrawn away from it, as soon as he entered the changing room he shed his reserve like a skin, to become charged with the energies of the atmosphere which was the one constant certainty of his uncertainly shifting occupations as coal-trimmer, docker and tinplater. On Saturday afternoons, long queues formed outside the gates of Stradey, to have the opportunity merely to carry the great man's bag. If it were rumoured that Albert was not playing, hundreds retraced their steps away from the ground. On his death at fifty-eight years in October 1953, this hero of his community was honoured with a civic burial, with the Mayor, the Deputy Mayor and a whole battery of local dignitaries at the graveside; it was the full and emotional tribute of a town whose name he had made synonymous with his own prowess. He had been an idol at Llanelli, but Stradey's gods were not included in the mythology of the W.R.U. It was one of the great rugby idiocies of the decade that Albert Jenkins won only fourteen caps. For most of the 1920s, Welsh rugby paid a dear price for the perversity of its national selectors. But by the end of the decade, not even the selectors could ignore the new talents that were coming to the fore.

A TOUCH OF CLASS

IN his lively yet mordant survey of Welsh rugby in the twenties, *Rugby Reminiscences and Opinions,* published in 1929, Rowe Harding had no doubt where the responsibility for past errors lay, nor where the hope for future improvement could be discerned. Ridiculing 'portly elderly gentlemen wearing Rugby blazers and tasteless red ties with life-size ostrich feathers', excoriating parochial selection committees who were 'representatives of an outworn but not discarded tradition, encumbered by pre-war principles', lamenting the inability of the Union to attract men of business ability and social standing 'to guide the destiny of Welsh rugby . . . a task for which some of the sitting members are not fitted either by education or experience', Harding, who had gone up from Gowerton County School to win four blues and captain Cambridge in 1927, was convinced that 'it is to the public schools and secondary schools that Welshmen must look for the revival of Welsh rugby.'

As he wrote that revival was already under way. In January 1926, 'Observer' of the *Western Mail* had given notice: 'Each boys' game I witness makes me more optimistic regarding the future of Welsh rugby . . . [and] more than ever convinced that the Rugby of a couple of years hence will be as good as it was in the halcyon days'. A month later R. T. Gabe saw Christ College, Brecon, beat Cardiff H.S. by 23 points to 3. 'I have great hopes about the future of Welsh back play after seeing games of this standard', he reported, impressed by the combined three-quarter movements and hard, straight running he remembered as the prime feature of Welsh back play in his time, but now little in evidence at senior level.

Contemporary politicians and economists also looked wistfully to the certainties of pre-war days and grabbed at symbolic straws of reassurance. Britain's restoration of the Gold Standard in 1925 was economic imbecility given the state of world trade and was, finally, abandoned irrevocably in 1931 but, at the time, was a psychological comforter, a simple solution for a country desperate for confident answers. Welsh rugby was handicapped badly by the desperate decline of the working-class scope of its game. There was little it could do directly about that. The other aspect of its 'social inclusiveness' had been its professional and academic exponents. The former were also less to the fore in deprived South Wales and so it was towards the latter, symbol of England's revived power in the game from 1910, that Welsh administrators now cast envious glances. Horace Lyne had taken up the theme in 1919 when, urging greater encouragement of rugby, he lamented 'of course it was one of the drawbacks in Wales that they had no public school football'. It was to remedy this deficiency that the Welsh Secondary Schools Rugby Union was established in 1923. It was no accident that it was founded at the end of the season in which Wales had become the reluctant recipients of the wooden spoon for the first time this century. The guiding spirit of the W.S.S.R.U., and chairman at its founding meeting in Cardiff on 9 June 1923, was Dr R. D. Chalke, the headmaster of Porth Secondary School; Horace Lyne was its president, and Eric Evans of Cardiff H.S. its honorary secretary. Its stated aims were threefold: 'to bring about a return of the glorious days of Gwyn Nicholls, Willie Llewellyn and Dr E. T. Morgan; to remedy the lack of that public school spirit which emanated from the playing fields; and to make the youths Athenean and Spartan'. Dr Chalke made no bones of the fact that society at large would benefit. After the Welsh Secondary Schools (with W. Guy Morgan, H. M. Bowcott and J. D. Bartlett among their backs) had beaten Yorkshire Schools 18 - 13 at Pontypridd in April 1926, Dr Chalke had remarked, to loud applause, that 'judging from that day's display, the future of amateur rugby was safe in the North of England and in South Wales. It was dignified Welsh Rugby that paved the way to the victory, and he was bound to say that the members of the W.S.S.R.U. were determined to cultivate the right type of manhood in sport. If a boy played the game on the field, he would play the game in every affair of life'.

The boys who were the lifeblood of the new union were for the moment quite content just to play the game of rugby, and they were doing it very well. In April 1923, on the Arms Park, Wales played her first secondary schools fixture, beating France 15 - 0. The team included John Roberts

(Cardiff H.S.), Noel Morgan (Brecon), nephew of Dr Teddy, W. D. B. Hopkins (Llandovery) and Windsor Lewis (also of Brecon). Captaining the side was Watcyn Thomas (Llanelli C.S.) 'a sterling forward of whom much should be heard in the future'. In 1924-5-6, a glittering Christ College Brecon XV, spear-headed by Windsor Lewis at fly-half and Guy Morgan at centre, was winning its matches by astronomical margins. Lewis and Morgan then joined Gowerton's Rowe Harding at Pembroke College, Cambridge, and the three of them were chiefly responsible for the swamping of Oxford 30 - 5 in the 1926 Varsity match. Cardiff H.S. introduced rugby in 1923; there were three boys of the school in the 1928 Varsity match. When the Welsh S.S. beat France at Aberdare in 1927, there were seven future caps on view: Morley of Newport S.S., Davey of Ystalyfera C.S., Tarr of Amman Valley C.S., Hickman of Neath C.S., D. E. A. Roberts and A. H. Jones, both of Llandovery, and W. Roberts of Cardiff H.S. There was not a Varsity match played between 1924 and 1934 without a sprinkling of Welshmen on both sides: there were five in 1925 and 1931, and in 1933, six. Rowe Harding and Windsor Lewis were elected captain and secretary, respectively, of Cambridge University for 1927; Guy Morgan was captain in 1929. The Welsh teams against Scotland in 1927 and England in 1928, had three-quarter lines consisting entirely of Cambridge backs. In September 1926 a Welsh University R.F.C. was formed, with Watcyn Thomas as its first captain. During the Christmas vacation, 1927, the seed that grew to be the Welsh Academicals R.F.C. was planted at Mountain Ash, in order that grammar and secondary school products might not be lost to Welsh rugby while away from home at college and university. In 1928 Swansea University College, with Idwal Rees at fly-half, reached the finals of the U.A.U. competition. There could be no greater vindication of the setting up of the W.S.S.R.U. than the heroic Welsh victory over New Zealand in 1935, when every player behind the scrum was a product of secondary school and university rugby. The organization of schools rugby in Wales impressed educationalists beyond its borders to the extent that in 1937, the *Western Mail's* chief rugby writer W. J. Hoare ('Old Stager'), its consistent advocate, was invited to deliver a lecture on 'Schoolboy Rugby Football' to the N.U.T. annual conference at Margate.

Arguably, it was not the scholastic credentials that provided the basis for the Welsh rugby renaissance, but organization and the opportunity for regular coaching. The best organized, most regularly coached, most attractive and consistently successful side of the 1920s was not strictly a school side at all: it was a team of ex-schoolboys, gathered together and trained under the watchful and authoritarian eye of Albert Freethy of Cwrt Sart School, Neath. Freethy's own playing career as a full-back had been cut short by injury, but he went on to make more than a name for himself as one of Wales's finest referees. The first W.R.U. referee invited to control a club match in England (Blackheath v. Cardiff, 6 November, 1920) he officiated at six Varsity matches, the Paris Olympic Rugby final of 1924, and sixteen internationals between 1924 and 1931. He immortalized himself by sending off Cyril Brownlie, of the 1924-5 All Blacks, in the eighth minute of their international at Twickenham, in front of the Prince of Wales. It was an action for which he was roundly condemned, although having warned both sides three times already, he was entirely within his rights in sending the next offender off. Whether Brownlie was the real culprit is debatable; he was certainly the offender Freethy saw, but many of those present thought Reg Edwards was very lucky not to be accompanying him. Despite the obloquy heaped on him by uninformed critics (including Welshmen: Teddy Morgan grimaced at 'this nasty decision'), and contrary to popular belief, the incident did not blight Freethy's career as an international referee, for he went on to officiate at another thirteen matches, five of them at Twickenham. He was elected to the W.R.U. in 1926 and subsequently became a selector, but in Wales at least, his fame stemmed mostly from the feats achieved by his ex-schoolboys team. It was a side composed mostly of Neath boys who had played in a local schools league and been invincible in the Dewar Shield schools rugby competition in 1922 and 1923. Freethy kept the side together, and they became renowned throughout South Wales. A noted disciplinarian, the autocratic Freethy instructed his boys in technique on the field, and in tactics on the blackboard. They played exciting, attacking, running rugby. In their first full season, 1922-23, they played on the Gnoll and made £100 for Neath and £700 for charities. They went undefeated for four years, and their backs — Trevor Walters, hailed as another Percy Bush at fly-half, Sam Bates and Griff Bevan at centre, Howie Jones and Arthur Hickman on the wings — were easily the peer of the best in senior football. In February 1925 they met a star-studded Christ College, Brecon, side at the Gnoll, and beat them 6 - 3 in front of a crowd of 5,000. In February 1926, they beat Llandovery 18 - 4 and Christ College 18 - 5 within a week. Such was the success, and the attractiveness, of Freethy's brilliant youngsters that friction developed with the Neath club. Neath, understandably, wanted to include some of them in its own side, but Freethy felt that 'the spirit of Welsh rugby was not what it should be', and asked to be allowed to keep his side together for a couple more seasons; were he to release a few now, the whole side would disintegrate. Smarting at Freethy's refusal, Neath refused him the use of the Gnoll, but playing at Cwrt Herbert, the 'Invincibles' still drew larger crowds than the town team. They lost their invincibility at Cardiff Arms Park on 30 April 1927, to a Cardiff ex-schoolboys team including Norman Fender and Tommy Stone. It marked the end of an era of ex-schoolboy rugby, and the concept of youth rugby would not be revived until the 1940s, but several of Freethy's stars orbited into senior football. Neath, certainly, owed its great season of 1928-29, when only four matches in forty-nine were lost and 930 points scored, to the influx of ex-schoolboys like Howie Jones, Arthur Hickman and Tom Day, all of whom went on to win full international caps in the early thirties.

By then a generation of schoolmaster coaches had arisen to sustain the momentum generated by the founding of the W.S.S.R.U. Eric Evans (1894-1955) had gone from Neath to Cambridge just before the War. After serving in Gallipoli he had returned to the University, where he narrowly missed a blue and played for Neath during vacations. After graduating in 1922, he became English master and rugby coach at Cardiff H.S. As founder secretary of the W.S.S.R.U. from 1923 to his appointment as successor to Walter Rees as Secretary of the W.R.U. in 1948, he saw the number of schools in the union rise from 13 to 91. At Cardiff he constructed and set in motion a conveyor belt of schoolboy internationals of whom the brothers John and Bill Roberts and the Bowcott brothers were the first to emerge. Another stream of schoolboy talent was to flow from Llandovery College, where sports master D. R. Williams was in 1927 joined by his brother T. P. At Brecon was W. A. G. Howell; at Gowerton, W. E. Bowen was about to transform the rugby initiative of the school which had recently produced Rowe Harding into a notable tradition.

What the schools of the twenties had grasped were the advantages that could accrue from teaching technique and training players when they are maturing together, in schools and colleges. They also realized that the success of the other countries stemmed from their high proportion of ex-grammar and public schoolboys, former pupils and students. The democratic nature of the Welsh game, so much extolled, could be a weakness when working-class boys were leaving school in their early 'teens insufficiently seasoned for senior rugby, their promise destined to remain raw without appropriate technical guidance as they developed physically. This attentively-nurtured athleticism had brought England and

Scotland their successes in the twenties, for their teams were composed of boys who had remained in school until the age of eighteen or over, so that their rugby development had matched their physical maturing. But for even the most gifted footballing products of the schools, it still required resilience and toughness to make the transition from schoolboy to senior football.

It was a lesson painfully learned by two of the most glittering backs of the decade. The exploits of Windsor Lewis and Guy Morgan of Christ College, Brecon, revived memories of the great Breconian backs who had brought lustre and style to the Welsh sides of the Golden Era — Willie Llewellyn, Teddy Morgan, the Dykes and Jack P. Jones. The hip-swivelling, Maesteg-born Windsor Lewis cut a swathe through schools and Varsity rugby in the mid-twenties. At 5 foot 9 inches and 11½ stone, he had all the attributes: he had the necessary devastating speed over thirty yards, his positioning was often uncanny, and he could give and take a pass with the easy grace of a man caressing the ball as well as catching it. He received the first of his six senior caps in 1926 while a freshman at Cambridge. He had not yet got further than a trial at the university. His selection for the Irish match at Swansea was acclaimed with almost messianic expectancy.

The performance a month before at Murrayfield had shown that nothing short of a Second Coming would lift the sagging morale of Welsh rugby. The four thousand supporters who had travelled up to see for themselves the new Murrayfield ground, opened the year before at a cost of £140,000, and been welcomed by menus offering 'Delahay pudding', 'Herrera soup' and 'Hinam sauce', saw a brave forward effort nullified by the studied ineptness of the backs. 'It was tragic', one critic had written, 'that so great a vanguard should have such futile men to support them'. If the aim of Windsor Lewis's selection against Ireland was to hone the back-line into an attacking edge, it worked. Ireland, bidding for the Triple Crown, was beaten 11 - 8, as Wales registered her first victory over one of the other home countries for four years. The devastating performance of the nineteen-year-old Lewis was a feature of the match. Wales scored three tries and Lewis had a hand in them all. The first came from a scrum on the Irish 25. Powell, though sandwiched by two tacklers, shook them off and found Lewis in support to put Tom Hopkins over for a try which Guardsman Tommy Rees, of Pontyclun and London Welsh, converted. Ireland replied with a try from loose marking at a line-out, but soon afterwards Lewis intercepted, knifed clean through, and with cool judgement chipped it past Crawford. Only a desperate fly-kick by Cussen racing across from the other wing, prevented a certain score. Lewis then accelerated away from broken play to give Herrera a scoring pass, and rounded the afternoon off by initiating an orthodox three-quarter movement — a luxury rarely permitted Welsh supporters in the previous three seasons — which culminated in Rowe Harding crossing half-way out. The three London Welshmen, Rees, Lewis and Powell, were carried shoulder high from the ground. 'Cymric Rugby Glory at Swansea: the Revival', yelled the *South Wales Daily News*. 'A New Wales' intoned *The Times*. 'A turning-point in Welsh rugby history' agreed the *Western Mail*.

It was not be. Lewis was unable to make the crossing to Paris in April, Bobby Jones returned to fly-half, with a temperature of 103°, and the dull nature of play in a 9 - 7 win made it appear as if the Irish game had never been. The 'turning-point' became a cul-de-sac as the grim events of the spring and summer of 1926 cast their baleful shadow over Welsh life, including its rugby. The Godfrey Jones Cup had been put up for competition in 1924-5 among Monmouthshire clubs 'to improve Welsh rugby via the running game'. But 'an ugly spirit ran very high throughout' the final of April 1926 as the referee sent six players off when Blaenavon beat Cross Keys 6 - 5. In presenting the trophy, Mr Arthur James said 'the object of the trophy was to produce good clean rugby. Rugby was under a cloud at present, and this game would not help it'. Agents of the Northern Union, and their Welsh scouts, found congenial conditions for an intensified campaign in a strike-bound South Wales. Symbolically, Emlyn Watkins of Blaina, scorer of the last Welsh try of the season, went to Leeds for £350 and a job; Sid Hinam left the international pack for Rochdale Hornets. The League dug in at Pontypridd.

Anxious to confront the argument that professional rugby was more attractive, the W.R.U. at its June meeting sought to divert attention from demands for a return to the old selection methods, and from searching questions about its heavy expenditure on away fixtures, by announcing a new ruling intended to restore adventure and enterprise to the game. To this end the W.R.U. had already proposed to the I.B. in 1925 that a dropped goal be reduced to 3 points, but this would not be accepted till 1947. In 1926 it tried to legislate against obstruction by penalizing any interference with a player off the ball, and proposed to introduce it at club level in Wales before apprising the I.B. of their intention. It was Harry Packer's suggestion, in imitation of the Rugby League practice, that 'no player shall advance beyond the centre of the scrum until the ball has been heeled'. While the problem it was intended to resolve indicated the tight and competitive nature of Welsh rugby, it also reflected the muddled thinking of the Union that it seemed to have given little thought to the implications of the new law as it affected outside teams playing in Wales. Since the arbitration of 1890, international matches could only be played under the rules of the R.F.U., sanctioned by the I.B.; therefore, the new Welsh rule could be played up to trial level, but not beyond. This could only be confusing to the new crop of backs, especially the London Welsh partners Lewis and Powell, who played their rugby in England but would have to adapt to the Welsh rule for the trials. In October, the W.R.U. were rebuffed by the I.B. when the Board announced that R.F.U. rules must prevail in matches between different unions, to take effect from November that year. Some English clubs, like Bristol and Gloucester, played Welsh rules in Wales and liked them; Harlequins 'of course' (as the Welsh press noted) refused to play Welsh rules in Wales; the visiting Maoris of 1926-7 initially objected to the Welsh rule then professed themselves happy with it. To cut the Gordian knot, in March 1927 Horace Lyne successfully proposed to the I.B. 'that it be recommended to each union that in future no matches shall be played in any country except under I.B. laws'. Wales would raise a version of the Packer proposal again in 1934 and 1954, and again be rejected. Only in 1964 was it ruled that no player should advance either foot in front of the ball whilst it remained in the scrum. The return to the running game would not wait upon legislators. The spur came from the schools. The high hopes that Gabe and other observers of schoolboy rugby had expressed earlier in the year were revived in November 1926 when the Llandovery v. Brecon game exhibited all the skills of 'scientific football'. The skills were in evidence before a much larger audience a month later as Windsor Lewis and Guy Morgan aroused the Twickenham crowd to something approaching excitement in a dazzling display of attacking football in the Varsity match. The rapier-like thrusts of Windsor Lewis led him to be hailed as 'a genius', while 'a brilliant Rugby future' was prophesied for the 5 foot 6 inch baby-faced Guy Morgan, 'this apparently frail youth'.

The Welsh selectors refused to be bowled over by the eloquent ravings of the English press, and out of a wily amalgam of realism and cussedness decided to reverse Cambridge's choice for the Welsh team to meet England in 1927. Lewis and Harding were included, but they plumped for the nineteen-year-old John Roberts of Cardiff H.S. instead of Guy Morgan, where Cambridge had done the opposite. Captaining the side from the other centre position was B. R. 'Lou' Turnbull, a Cambridge Blue of 1924 and 1925, educated at Downside College. With the exception of Male at full-back (back in favour now that Tommy Rees had celebrated Christmas by breaking his leg), Newport's George Andrews on the wing, and Powell at scrum-half, the Welsh backs were all varsity men. There was a varsity man in the pack, too, for Watcyn Thomas of Swansea University was making his début.

For the first time since the War, Wales was going to Twickenham with a superior back division; for the first time since 1908 Wales, away from home, outscored England in the matter of tries by two to one. But ill-luck dogged them. The unfathomable decisions of the referee; the loss of Dai Jones (Newport) after fifteen minutes with a fractured shoulder, sustained in the movement leading to Rowe Harding's try; the quirk of misfortune that caused Harding to slip and unintentionally touch down while he was turning in for the posts in scoring that try; the concussive injury to Wick Powell. These did not conceal the Welsh weakness: the lack of penetration at centre, the want of devil and drive at forward (which underlined the folly of omitting Ivor Jones), the perennial inability to heel from the loose. There were positive aspects to the Welsh performance too: the sinuous Harding racing across to tackle Corbett a few yards out, the exhilarating try scored by the stocky speedster, George Andrews, who flashed outside Windsor Lewis on the opposite wing from his own; Watcyn Thomas's two-handed catching in the line-out; the immense physical presence of Powell, endlessly pounded at the base of the scrum, but despite his concussion, dribbling through with skilful control when he was not throwing out breathtaking reverse passes which were often longer and (sometimes) more accurate than his orthodox services. Powell was far more than the ninth forward of which he was the prototype: from a scrum at the corner flag he could fling a reverse pass to a centre at the far post. In this game he became a law to himself, spraying out passes like a maniac with a machine-gun. The sure-handed Lewis took them at angles undreamed of by Euclid, but at some cost — estimated by one critic at ten yards — to his own game in attack. Powell would repay that debt tenfold in their other appearances together, to the extent that some argued that, at international level, it was Powell who made Windsor Lewis.

The selectors opted for Lewis and Powell for the next match of 1927, against Scotland, but when Lewis cried off with flu, the selectors, with characteristic incoherence, now dropped his partner to choose Richards and Delahay of Cardiff. It was ill-advised. Herbert Waddell took more than a fatherly interest in the newcomer Gwyn Richards, and Bobby Delahay, on his last appearance for Wales, had to struggle manfully to elude the clannish attentions of the Scottish loose forwards. The pocket-sized Delahay, a mere 5 foot 4 inches and 10 stone, was a carpenter used to making the best out of unpromising material. Since his first cap against England in 1922, he had served Wales eighteen times at scrum-half, fly-half and centre — just like Jack Wetter, with Wetter's guile, but not his frame — and his attempts to impart some life to his wooden midfielders all but exhausted him. Thrown back on his innate wits, which were considerable, he devised a weapon of his own, 'the Delahay kick', a tapped penalty instead of a kick through the mark to touch, goal or infield. By now, at twenty-seven, his best years were behind him. He battled heroically in the mud and rain of Cardiff with a muster of Highland chiefs led by Bannerman, but was physically spent after the first quarter. Once again, the selectors had shown how arbitrarily they chopped and changed their minds. They dropped Herrera on the sole grounds, apparently, of a missed place-kick against England, and they recalled Ivor Jones, who had last been capped three years before. There was an explanation of sorts: he had moved to Birmingham in the meantime. The selectors, it seemed, had in their minds transported him to Brazil. The Match Committee could find Anglo-Welshmen in London and shanghai fly-halves out of Northampton, but when the best loose forward of the decade went from Llanelli to the Midlands they lost interest. Watcyn Thomas would pay the same price. When Dudley Bartlett of Llandovery came in to complete an all-Cambridge three-quarter line, it looked as if the policy was to be one of attack through the backs, but rain fell all morning and for most of the match. After ten minutes the Scots gave up playing to their backs, and let their forwards wheel the scrums, break away and generally dominate the play. Wales stuck monotonously to her pre-match policy, and it was left to Ivor Jones to show some tactical appreciation by keeping the ball close and rushing it through like the Scots. He played a lone hand, for while Watcyn Thomas was again prominent in the line-out, the other forwards for the most part played a traditional shoving game. The idea, damagingly confirmed by the wet-weather victories of 1920 and 1922, that heavy-going suited Welsh forwards, was proved wrong: even steamrollers cannot operate in a swamp. Scotland scored a converted try; Wales did not score at all. An English critic tersely commented, 'The difference between the two teams was one of class. And class will always tell, apparently, even in a bog'.

The Scottish try had come just before half-time, when Rowe Harding was caught in possession near his own line. For this and another error against England in 1928 when he slipped trying to tackle Taylor as the winger accelerated away to score, he was mercilessly hounded by the Llanelli press, who had never forgiven him for moving to Swansea. They pilloried him as 'the holder of the world's record for the number of times he has crossed the line on the wrong side of the corner flag', mocked his 'fictitious ability' and alleged that 'he has had a pampered existence in club and international football and has had fame thrust upon him'. Such abuse was grossly misplaced. Harding, 5 foot 10 inches and 11 stone at the peak of his international career which brought him seventeen caps between 1923 and 1928, was one of the most stylish and effective wings of the twenties. Sleek and lithe in attack, as he showed in the try he made for Clem Lewis against Scotland in 1923 and, swooping and swerving, the ones he scored himself against France that year and against Ireland in 1926, he could also be alert in defence. His chief persecutor, 'Nomad' of the *Llanelly Mercury*, could not have been at Belfast in 1925 when Harding was the man of the match, once sprinting across field to grass Stephenson on the opposite wing, and saving certain tries on two other occasions. Another saving tackle on Corbett, after tearing across field in similar fashion was the highlight of the Twickenham game of 1927. His Llanelli critics would have done better to reflect how many tries he would have scored had he been given Albert Jenkins as his partner more often.

Harding was at Cambridge between 1924 and 1928, the first of the grammar school Blues of the inter-war years. The book he wrote on his retirement reflected the predicament that faced the selectors at the end of the twenties, and his own personal divided loyalties: how to reconcile the competing claims of the 'Cambridge backs', of whom he had been an adornment, and the Llanelli backs, and Albert Jenkins in particular, whom Harding frankly recognized as the greatest centre of the era. It was in essence a conflict of styles, of Llanelli craft and grit against Cambridge sophistication; it was a contrast of life-styles, too, of the rolling-mills as against more privileged enclaves of learning. It was a social and psychological contrast that in rugby terms presented itself as a selectorial headache. Llanelli scored points through kicking, Cambridge through running. Dai John, short and dark, made progress with his boot, manoeuvred his armoured divisions to within range of the line, and then released the mobile field artillery outside him to execute the *coup de grâce*. Windsor Lewis, medium height, fair-haired, made progress with the ball in his hands and could tear a defence to ribbons from half-way. The West Walians, who complained that, 'There is evidently something wrong with Welsh rugby' when Albert, Dai and Arthur John were continually passed over in favour of the more conventional Cardiff Varsity backs, had many sympathizers. But there was no denying the sheer class of some of the Cambridge backs, either, and there was no inherent reason why the cultural clash could not have been harmoniously resolved by shrewder selection, as it had been in pre-war days and would be, again, in the 1930s. Possibly the appalling social discrepancies of the classes, both in living standards and life expectancy, that underlay the political divisiveness of the 1920s mocked the ideal of harmony, for rugby and society, that the middle-aged selectors had grown old nurturing. Their disjointed teams were the sickly brain-children of men out of joint with the times.

Perhaps the greatest missed opportunity of the decade was the selectors' failure to form a centre partnership between the mature judgement and tactical sagacity of Albert Jenkins, and the incisive but immature genius of Guy Morgan. Morgan, a nephew of Dr Teddy, won four blues between 1926 and 1929, and was awarded his first cap against France at Swansea in 1927, with John Roberts as his co-centre. It was a comment on the despondency of that time that barely 15,000, the smallest Welsh international crowd of the century, turned up to see Wales, as it happened, run riot with seven tries. Handling securely on a sodden pitch — whose sandy soil never churned up as badly as the Arms Park, as Swansea partisans fell over themselves to point out — the Cambridge backs scored five of the tries with Guy Morgan prominent in them all. The apocalyptic fervour that had surrounded Windsor Lewis was transferred to the neat, nimble Morgan: 'in the history of Welsh Rugby Football, it will be recorded that on 7 February, year of grace 1927, it was Guy Morgan who re-established Welsh three-quarter play'. But again, talk of the Welsh Renaissance was premature, as the new order came apart at the seams a fortnight later in Dublin, torn to shreds by an Irish forward machine driven by remote control by Ernie Crawford at full-back and constantly lubricated by the incomparable Eugene Davey and Mark Sugden at half-back. It showed the extent to which the Cambridge backs were indebted, in The Times's description, to 'the ruthless and weighty Powell' at scrum-half. Against an apprentice France two weeks previously, he had been able effortlessly to draw a naïve defence before unleashing the Grange Road greyhounds outside him; here, himself hounded relentlessly by Sugden, Powell needed all his wits to look after himself, while the Cambridge backs were thrown back on their own fragile defensive resources, and resorted to hurried and inaccurate kicking. Only Rowe Harding's shrewd anticipation extricated them from several awkward tangles. 'Quite clearly, the return of the days of the supremacy of Welsh rugby is not yet', concluded the *Western Mail* resignedly, as Wales took the wooden spoon for the fourth time in five seasons. It was also the last Welsh appearance in Dublin till 1952, for although 3,000 Welsh supporters had gone over for the match, the I.R.F.U. reckoned they did not go in for buying stand tickets, and since there was more standing room at Ravenhill, the Welsh game was for the next quarter of a century allotted to Belfast, while the more commodious seating arrangements of Lansdowne Road were deemed more appropriate for the visits of England and Scotland.

The selectors had, at least, in 1926-7 stuck to a consistent policy in their attempts at team-building on the ruins of the previous disastrous four years. They had gone for combination as opposed to individualism, and found it at Cambridge. In picking the team to play New South Wales (the Waratahs, popularly known in Old South Wales as the 'Wara-têgs'), their policy was to have no policy. Only John Roberts and Windsor Lewis remained of the Cambridge backs and an oddly-assorted back division gave the appearance that the main object was to placate West Wales. Thanks to the efforts of R. P. Thomas of Llanelli, who had filled the vacancy on the 'Big Five' caused by the death of T. D. Schofield, nine players from Aberavon and points west found their way into the Welsh XV. Yet it was Roberts and Lewis who scored the Welsh tries in an 18 - 8 defeat by the young and enthusiastic tourists. If Windsor Lewis was to be the mainspring of the attack, he needed a fast and lengthy service from his inside-half, such as he got from his Cambridge partner, W. H. Sobey, or Powell at London Welsh: he was not best served by being given a scrum-half who tended to wind-up passes which were in any case short in length. Tommy Rees at full-back and John Roberts in the centre were the only backs retained to meet England two months later. The all-Cambridge three-quarter line was revived (though hardly the Cambridge line of the December Varsity match, whose centres were Guy Morgan and Harry Bowcott, whereas it was Roberts and Turnbull, Cambridge's full-back, whom Wales played in the centre), served at half-back by Llanelli's Dai and Arthur John, themselves in combination with their own back row of Iorwerth and Ivor Jones. The genial policeman Archie Skym, winning his first cap, was the fifth Scarlet in the side that met England in January 1928. A well-balanced Monmouthshire front row of Bowdler, Cecil Pritchard and Harry Phillips cemented a rousing forward effort that imprisoned England in its own 25 for the last half-hour, but the backs again failed to translate this pressure into points. The critics found an explanation readily to hand. It was summed up in the *Morning Post*'s remark that 'Cambridge and Llanelli don't make a good cocktail'. The fact was that the stolid Turnbull and Roberts were dogged, unimaginative centres whose forte was finishing the adventurous initiatives of others. Dai and Arthur John were not adventurers — they were tactical controllers. They needed a centre outside them with intimate knowledge of their crafty ploys and deft touches. The critics accused Dai John of lobbing his passes, whereas what he needed was a centre who could take that sort of pass, on the burst. It was plain who that centre was. The selector's dilemma was plain too; they could drop the Llanelli half-backs or give them the centre they needed. To the audible guffaws of the English press, and howls of delight from Llanelli, the selectors retained their half-backs and, at last, brought Albert Jenkins back into the centre.

There were 5,000 Welshmen at Murrayfield in February 1928, and most of them were from Llanelli. They saw one of the great upsets — and memorable Welsh victories — of the decade. Never was Albert's ability to inspire others by his mere presence greater in evidence: Dai John had his finest game for Wales. His judges reversed their critical gears and said he now passed properly. In fact, he passed no differently than he had against England but he was passing, this time, to Albert. It took five minutes for Albert Jenkins, now thirty-three, to impose psychological control on the game. He took Dai John's pass on the burst, sold McPherson an outsize dummy and sliced through the Scottish defence. The final pass went to ground, but six minutes later Dai John was through and under the posts. Within a quarter of an hour Wales were 10 points up in the period when the ball could still be handled. From now on in gusty, rainy conditions, the Llanelli halves harnessed the elements and dictated the tempo with the assurance that was the legacy of their long apprenticeship on the anvils of Stradey, the Gnoll and the Talbot Athletic Ground. Dai John and Albert each scored and also set up John Roberts for a third. Llanelli's joy knew no bounds. Albert was kissed six times by a gentleman on the train back. On arriving at Llanelli, the town's Murrayfield magnificos found the whole population out to welcome them, and, at a civic reception, Councillor Roland P. Thomas was congratulated on his re-election to the Big Five 'and having justified his selection'. The *Mercury* was reduced to breathless headlines: 'Wales' Glorious Win', followed by 'Triumph for Llanelli contemptibles . . . Albert Jenkins and Co. the heroes . . . Sospan Fach . . . Llanelli's Great Day . . . Scarlets Glorious Vindication . . . How the critics ate humble pie . . . Llanelli turns out to welcome her heroes'.

The addition of Ernie Finch made it a magnificent scarlet seven against Ireland in March but Albert, alas, fell from grace. The miracle of Murrayfield would not be repeated. Like Nicholls before him, and Bassett after him, he ended his career with the worst performance of his life. For every pass he held he dropped three, and finally lost the match in the last few minutes when he muffed Dai John's pass with Roberts and Powell unmarked outside him. The mud and the porous Scottish defence had played into the hands of the Llanelli contingent at Murrayfield; on a dry pitch, only John Roberts of the Cambridge backs was on view. Cambridge men in themselves were not the answer, however. In April, Wales lost to France for the first time ever. What Wales needed was backs with pace and penetration who were also tactically mature and physically strong enough to withstand the intensive marking of international football.

Throughout 1929 and 1930 Wales waited for such backs to emerge. She lost to England in both years, but beat Scotland twice, to suggest that the tide was turning. There were encouraging signs for the future. In the Llandovery v. Brecon match of November 1928, a hefty sixteen-year-old from Coity, near Bridgend, V. G. J. Jenkins, kicked 8 points in Llandovery's 11 - 6 victory, in a display of natural footballing skills and revealing a rare ability to retrieve awkward situations with the minimum fuss and maximum aplomb. That virtue would never be more keenly tested than in the first minute of the Wales v. New Zealand match in seven years time.

More immediately, the evidence of the 1928 Varsity match was that Guy Morgan was still lacerating opposing defences, but that his own rattled under pressure. At fly-half for Oxford was John Roberts's brother Bill, but the man who caught the eye was in the Cambridge centre, yet another product of Eric Evans's coaching at Cardiff H.S., Harry Bowcott, whose slide-rule kicking and astute positional play marked him out as a young player already matured. Bill Roberts, summoned to the Welsh final trial of 1929 literally from the railway station as he was about to leave for an away fixture with Cardiff, managed to play himself into the team to meet England and turned out to be, in 'Old Stager's' words, 'the most fortunate player of his generation'. Though sated with passes from Powell he proved an unimaginative link with a back division that moved ponderously and predictably. The three-quarter line needed lubricating and the stiffer components removed. John Roberts was put out on the wing, Bowcott brought into the centre, and a new product of Christ College, Brecon, tried at outside-half. Frank Williams, nineteen-years-old a week before the Scottish game, was now a sports master at Wakefield. He brought to the pivot position many of the natural gifts of his fellow Breconian, Windsor Lewis, plus a durable physique and resolute defence. Against Scotland at St. Helen's, Powell was once again pummelled at scrum-half, but still managed to fire off cannon-ball passes that Frank Williams took and exploited to bring out the best of his line. In that line, the twenty-two-year-old Bowcott, at 5 foot 11 inches and 11 stone 9lbs., was both oilcan and additive. In his measured kicking and swing pass he epitomised the contribution secondary school rugby was making to Welsh back play: the obvious advantages accruing from regular play and practice, carefully modulated from school through college to senior rugby. Things were done 'correctly' and coaches like Eric Evans identified and rectified imperfections of technique as they would correct a Latin prose or point out a faulty declension. Bowcott, even as a schoolboy, had impressed Townsend Collins with 'his classic perfection of technique. The "correctness" of it was something to wonder at. In fact, it seemed unnatural in a boy . . . The boy Bowcott played "copy-book" football and seemed pre-destined for a place in the Welsh team'. The educated left boot and text-book pass of the boy Bowcott would be much in evidence at Twickenham in 1933. Also making his first appearance in 1929 at nineteen years of age was another secondary school cap, Jack Morley of Newport S.S. During the course of his fourteen senior international appearances, Morley at 5 foot 7 inches, 11 stone 8lb., showed obvious football intelligence and a flair for the unorthodox that many would be reminded of twenty years later in the play of Lewis Jones: sudden switches of direction and a subtle variation of pace as he set off on elusive swerving runs. These skills were deployed in one magnificent piece of opportunism a quarter of an hour into the second half at Twickenham in 1929, when he received the ball forty yards out, broke infield then cut back again to cross wide out for Wales's only score in an 8 - 3 defeat.

The years 1928-31 were a transitional period. They were the waiting years, as the new crop of secondary school products played themselves in to fulfil the rich promise of their early years. In that time the flickering brilliance of Windsor Lewis and Guy Morgan burnt low and was eventually snuffed by the rigours of senior football. But while the rest of Wales waited, Llanelli fretted and grew downright impatient. Irritated to desperation by the preference of the selectors for Oxford and Cambridge men, 'Nomad' of the *Llanelly Mercury*, after the England match of 1929, fumed at 'the hopelessly futile, inglorious orthodoxy' of the college boys, although two years before it was their very unorthodoxy that he had found suspect: they were 'pretty pretty players of the superficially brilliant order which is not backed up by sterling merit . . . who flattered only to deceive and whose genius, whilst occasionally exhibited in minor matches and at trial games, was sadly conspicuous by its absence at the very time it was most needed'. The horror felt in Llanelli that not one Scarlet was selected to meet England in 1931 was almost tangible. 'It would be grotesque if it were not so tragic. I can only attribute it to deep-rooted prejudice and blind partisanship', proclaimed the manager of Buckley's Brewery. 'It is just as well that we in Llanelli have become so accustomed to extraordinary treatment at the hands of selectors of the Welsh team in the past that their whims and vagaries no longer give us heart palpitations. We now await the announcement of a Welsh team with philosophical calm. And it is just as well, for Llanelli continues to be subjected to treatment which is positively ghastly in its harsh injustice and indefensible in its utter lack of logic . . . Dai John might as well be a Frenchman for all the notice the selectors take of him . . . I have no hesitation in stating that the treatment accorded to Llanelli has been scandalous. The club has been slighted and insulted by a handful of men who are not fit for their job'. When no Scarlets were chosen for the following game, either, this 'Second Snub for the Scarlets' (headline) confirmed that 'The Big Five have treated the Scarlets with their usual shabbiness. It only shows they are not fit for their office'. When not one of the selectors was present to watch Llanelli beat Pontypool 28 - 0, they were criticised for choosing teams from their armchairs. The selection of Frank Williams as centre (against France in 1931) after his allegedly repeated failures at fly-half, was branded as 'the greatest tragi-comedy since "City Lights" '. The emerging Claude Davey was not thought to be of international class either (Davey had emerged principally as a result of a superb display in Swansea's 29 - 0 defeat of Llanelli in March 1930, in which he compounded the damage done by his bone-crunching tackles with a magnificent dummying, swerving, side-stepping seventy-five yard try) — as far as the *Mercury* was concerned, 'he can do nothing except emulate a battering ram, and too often he forgets to take the ball with him'.

This was good knockabout stuff, but there was one selectorial decision that even struck many outside boiling Sospanville as bordering on lunacy.

'The Big(-oted) Five — inexcusable insult to great Llanelli forward', blared the Mercurial trumpet. After establishing himself as the greatest wing forward ever seen in New Zealand, after his visit with the 1930 Lions, Ivor Jones was never selected again for Wales. The All Blacks would never have understood why. They never forgot him. 'He had a long, dreamy sort of face tapering down', recalled one admiring Kiwi, 'and a whacking great hunk of curly hair drooping over his forehead. Bit of a redhead but not really ginger. Very religious chap, so they said, quiet, wouldn't say boo to a goose. What a footballer! A ruddy Scarlet Pimpernel, to the life. He didn't run about the field, he just materialized.'

Ivor Jones's playing career spanned the years 1922 to 1938, during which he captained Llanelli for nine seasons and led them against four touring sides: the 1926 Maoris, 1927 Waratahs, 1931 Springboks and 1935 All Blacks. As a forward dribbler Ivor had no equal. He and his Loughor elementary school class-mate, Dai John, were foot-ball exponents, and Ivor became a prolific scorer for Llanelli, Wales and the Lions with his boot. But it was to the position of specialist wing-forward — a position to which the Welsh selectors of this era, not surprisingly, took an erratic attitude, although the other countries never took the field without one from the early 1920s — that he brought his skill and intuitive intelligence, welded together by a zest as fiery as the Bynea furnaces where his 6 foot 1 inch, 14 stone 3lb. had been tempered and tested. Rowe Harding, another pupil in that same Loughor infants' schoolroom, later vividly described Ivor on the field, 'lurking around the base of the scrum like a lurcher dog, anticipating and smothering his opponent's tactics, living on the limit of the offside rule himself, pointing out to the referee any infringement by his rival wing-forwards, profiting to the full from any penalty exacted thereby, never exerting himself unduly, but on the spot when danger threatened and feeding his own backs with a stream of shrewd passes'.

His international career had begun in inauspicious circumstances, for he won his first cap, at twenty-one years of age, at Inverleith in 1924, when Ian Smith had made attempts on the world land-speed record in the direction of the Welsh line; but it was not the last time that Ivor would see the Forth Bridge at the expense of the W.R.U. Merely by moving to Birmingham, however, he had disappeared beyond the selectors' horizons for three years, and though when recalled in 1927 he went on to win sixteen consecutive caps, the comparable tally of his contemporaries — Scotland's Bannerman (37 consecutive caps, 1921-9) and England's Wakefield (31 caps, 1920-27) — is sufficient comment on Welsh selection. It was in evidence again in the pack they gave Ivor to lead against England in 1930. This was the game in which Bristol hooker Sam Tucker descended from the skies, to which he had taken in an airplane, to inspire a young English team with nine new caps to an 11 - 3 victory at Cardiff. Tucker raised a mare's-nest by hooking throughout with the near foot, an action declared illegal by the R.F.U. but not yet by the I.B. Not that Arthur Bowdler, the Cross Keys hooker, who often played for Wales in the afternoon and then returned home immediately for the night shift underground, was helped by being squeezed in the front row between the mountainous Tom Arthur and Skym, despite the fact that Dai Parker and Tom Hollingdale, who *were* familiar with front-row play were in the second and third rows behind. This laughably unbalanced eight was outscrummaged from the start. Understandably, it was Ivor Jones's least distinguished game for Wales. His characteristic reward for this atypical display was to be given the captaincy for the next match against Scotland. He duly produced one of his greatest ever performances. His reward was to be dropped, the third captain in succession. Ivor Jones was given an all-Cardiff three-quarter line for the visit to Murrayfield, scene of the great triumph of the Scarlet Six two years before, but Bowcott was not among them, and their lame orthodoxy resulted in the wings receiving only three passes all afternoon. One of those wings, however, would not be so easily disheartened: making his first of twelve appearances was the ex-Barry County schoolboy, R. W. Boon, a fast, highly finished fly-half turned flyer, whose speed and kick would make him England's bogeyman in 1932 and 1933. In 1930 against Scotland it was his tackling that caught the eye, as he ruthlessly marked down a Flying Scotsman now running out of steam. It certainly caught 'Old Stager's' eye, and he reported that Ian Smith 'frequently found himself in difficulty when trying to make headway through Boon's extraordinary facility for retaining a grasp on whatever part of his anatomy he could lay his hands'.

Ivor Jones regretted his omission from the team whose 12 - 7 win at St. Helen's in March again prevented Ireland from winning their first Triple Crown of the century; but he could not have been sorry to have missed the ferocious final match in Paris, which even tough Archie Skym described as 'a bullfight'. Though Ivor Jones had played his last game for Wales, his career was hardly over. In 1947 he was elected on to the W.R.U. and almost immediately became a selector; he served for nineteen years. He helped form the Youth Union in 1949; between 1962 and 1965 he acted as a Welsh representative on the I.B., and in 1969 became President of the

W.R.U. In that year he accompanied the Welsh team to New Zealand, and was lionized, for as a player he had achieved his greatest fame as one of the seven Welshmen to tour Australia and New Zealand with the 1930 Lions. There he scored 22 points out of 29 against Australia, and immortalized himself in the First Test against the All Blacks. Terry McLean was there:

We were down in their 25, I remember. Practically on the goal-line as a matter of fact. There wasn't more than a minute left for play. Porter put the ball in and we got it. I think Jimmy Mill was a bit off balance when he picked it up. It looked as if he might might been going for one of those blindside tries of his. I suppose the way was blocked. That's when he turned and threw a pass at Herbie Lilburne.

It wasn't the best pass, but it looked good enough. It would have been good enough too, if it hadn't been for this bloody Welsh terror, Jones. He must have taken off from the side of the scrum like a shot, because he collected that pass at full speed. In a stride or two, he was clear of everybody. Amazing. I can still see him legging it up the field. Out towards the left touch-line going up the Workshops end.

Of course, as you might expect, Cookie and Freddie Lucas started tearing back and George Nepia stood there like the Rock of Gibraltar, too. So things weren't as bad as they might have looked. Then this crafty Jones gives a bit of a dummy — no one but a Welshman would think of doing a thing like that — and our boys sat back on their hunkers for a moment.

And then Jones was at Nepia at halfway. You get the picture? Jones was here and Nepia was there. Out on the right was Cookie, going like a rocket. And on the left was this little bloke, Morley, close to touch and scampering. No one else mattered two hoots in hell. Except us. We were making enough noise to sink a ship.

Jones was practically in George's arms when he passed, so that cancelled George out. That left just two, Morley and Cooke. They had 50 yards to go. I'm telling you, they don't play football like it, these days. Fifty yards. Have you ever screamed so much you can't even hear yourself think? Have you ever picked your hat off and just let 'er go and be damned to all the colds that ever infested the earth? Have you ever just gone mad? With 27,000 others all doing the same thing?

If you haven't, you haven't lived. There they went. Fifty mortal yards. What a race! I'd die happy if I could see it again. The goal-line coming up and Cookie inching nearer and nearer. Almost ready to dive. And Morley zipping along. Immortal.

Morley won by a yard.

And Britain won, by 6 - 3.

Cheering? I can hear it yet.

They almost heard it at home, but the Antipodean exploits of the 1930 Lions and the prematurely-dropped Ivor Jones were of little comfort to a W.R.U. whose international selections was only one of a dossier of grievances being prepared for hot-blast airing at that year's annual meeting. It was felt that the best talent in Wales was not being properly utilized. The enigmatic selection of a full-back from Torquay for the French match (the Torquay Corporation found employment for a number of Monmouthshire players in the late twenties; in 1929 Aberavon had complained to the Union about a notice in the local Labour Exchange, 'inviting prominent footballers, more particularly centre three-quarters and forwards to get in touch with Weston R.F.C. where, provided they fulfilled all requirements, they would be given permanent employment by the Weston U.D.C.' whose Surveyor and Engineer was also chairman of the club known in the 1930s, because of its strong Cymric complexion, as 'Weston Welsh'), the choice of a different reserve scrum-half for every game in 1929-30, and the fact that the Lions had taken as a scrum-half a Welsh player not yet capped by his country (Howard Poole of Cardiff) — this catalogue of complaint suggested that the Union was rapidly forfeiting the confidence of clubs, players and public. The Union met the proposal that the 'Big Five' choose the trial teams as well as the national XV by agreeing that they select the Probables for the final trial; otherwise the Match Committee picked all the other trials' teams. Predictably, the suggestion that the 'Big Five' need not necessarily be selected from among the Match Committee was shot down.

It was not only the clubs' patience that was stretched; the finances of many were at breaking-point as the economy of South Wales ground to a halt. The committee-men of Loughor R.F.C., the club which had produced five Internationals that decade in Rowe Harding, Dai John, Ivor Jones, Jack John and Iorwerth Jones, were by 1929 reduced to begging from house to house in the locality for old kit to keep rugby going. Penarth just survived thanks to the ingenuity of its secretary J. Lot Thorn, who organized countless fêtes and bazaars. As work at the dockyards of Pembrokeshire ceased, rugby at Haverfordwest collapsed from 1926 to 1929; Pembroke Dock Quins were reduced to five members by 1927. In the distressed industrial valleys, the cold hand of closure was tightening its grip. Treherbert, which had been in finanicial trouble since 1924, staggered on till its collapse in 1929. Nantyffyllon disbanded at the end of the decade. In Monmouthshire the scene was one of unrelieved gloom. Cross Keys' reputation as one of the leading clubs of the decade — its powerful pack inadequately represented at international level, but giving the Forward Movement in Gwent a new twist — was acquired in spite of often having to field teams in which only four players were employed. Machen was forced to withdraw from the W.R.U. in 1926, and no rugby was played there for the next two years. Pontypool, despite its historic double over the Waratahs and Maoris in 1927, had an overdraft of £2,000, was on the verge of bankruptcy by 1930, and understandably bitter at the Union's refusal to give them a fixture against the 1931 Springboks, while the selectors' continued neglect of Ben Butler, eighteen times a reserve, did nothing to alleviate 'Pooler's' anger. Pontnewynydd had been forced to close in 1927; Tredegar was driven into closure in 1929 because of ground difficulties. Ebbw Vale had been helped to its feet after the War under the umbrella of the welfare scheme inaugurated by Sir Frederick Mills of the local steel company. Launched in 1918 'to afford employees and the inhabitants of the district in general an opportunity for indulging in all healthy games, social intercourse, mutual helpfulness and general recreation', by 1921 it was providing facilities for rugby, cricket, athletics, tennis, choral societies, brass bands, an orchestra and ambulance classes. There was no welfare scheme more impressive in South Wales. But it did not survive the icy blasts of the chill economic climate. The scheme folded in 1924, the works themselves closed in 1928. Disaster looked the rugby club in the face. Even with the admission reduced to fourpence, a gate of £5 was handsome.

Despite the fact that West Wales, too, was blasted by the cold winds blowing across the Atlantic from Wall Street, her rugby followers were able to consider initiatives, in 1929, that were absolutely out of the question in the devastated east and mid sections of the coalfield. This was, in part, because of the relative security of employment and of wages in the diminished tinplate industry and the special nature of her coal. This was the anthracite (hard) coal region, not the steam (soft) coal which had fuelled the earlier boom. The latter's production progressively declined but the peak year for anthracite mining was not reached until 1934. Welsh-speaking West Wales now received migrants from older areas of the coalfield while they themselves, whilst remaining much closer to an indigenous Welsh culture than had their counterparts in the east, became more thoroughly an industrial, less and less, a semi-rural population. Welsh XVs caught the trend. These were the circumstances which surrounded the formation of the West Wales League in April 1929, with F. G. Phillips of Pontarddulais (W.R.U. President 1958-9) as its secretary.

Rugby was at a low ebb in the area, several clubs were in heavy financial trouble, and 'something had to be done to stimulate Rugby in the West'. Although it received the blessing of the W.R.U., that disenchantment with the parent body was the impulse behind the formation of the new union became clear at a meeting in March 1930. The delegates of more than fifty of the seventy-five clubs in the W.R.U. accused the Union of doing nothing to prevent the demotion of second-class clubs 'like Pontardawe, Skewen and Amman United' to the status of mere feeders to the bigger clubs. There was a time when Skewen drew gates of £150, or an average of £70, 'but today they were lucky if they took 15 shillings'. It also became clear that the concept of a 'Big Five' was seen as the death-knell to district representation at international level, and that again second-class clubs were being squeezed out. 'With loyalty and solidarity in the West Wales League they could get their players into the national side from the second-class teams as well as from the first-class sides'. Though it would develop into a nursery of international talent, the W.W.R.U. was founded as a defensive measure couched in aggressive terms. Speaker after speaker attacked the W.R.U. and all its works. It was accused of being stagnant: it had been formed to govern and promote rugby: it might govern but it did not promote. Councillor Jenkins of Skewen said he was 'out to fight the Union'. He did not object to their spending money to keep Welsh rugby alive, 'but he did object to keeping the secretary of the W.R.U. at a fairly good salary'. Mr Will Owen (Gowerton) said they must not talk of fighting. He did not like it. But the mood of the delegates was militant: another spokesman thought that 'by united action they could turn all the present members out and once they got a new organization they would revive'.

Mindful of the tides of criticism lapping about them, the selectors showed a more purposeful attitude to finding a team to meet England in 1931. For the first time, they asked for certain specified players, twelve in all, to be included in a Glamorgan County XV. Watcyn Thomas was one of them, and he went on to be selected in a pack which was developing a settled look and conveying a sense of corporate identity. Tom Day was the only new cap in an eight which had showed vigour and intelligence in the Irish and French games of 1930; he was the only newcomer in the whole team. Behind the scrum, every player between inside-half and full-back was a product of grammar school rugby, with Morley and Boon on the wings, the thrustful Claude Davey partnering London Welshman Jones-Davies (St. George's School, Harpenden and Cambridge) at centre;

Bowcott's defensive qualities won him preference at outside-half with Powell. Leading from behind was the Glamorgan policeman and Penarth custodian Jack Bassett. The exploits of Bancroft and Winfield had conferred glamour on the full-back position. Bassett was as glamorous as the beer-truck that he was built like, but in each of the fifteen appearances, except the last, that he made between 1929 and 1932, his defence was impregnable. He was not a stylist like his predecessors, but his punts, if not polished, were usually accurate, and he was a fearless rush-stopper and mighty tackler. The presence of two bone-crushers like Bassett and Davey among the backs was enough to dissuade any opponents trying anything too fancy.

If any Welsh XV of the inter-war period deserved to win the Triple Crown it was this side of 1931. Its eleven-all draw at Twickenham merely showed that a side unused to winning will find it difficult to win. After the match, both English captain Sam Tucker and the President of the R.F.U. said Wales deserved to have won. So did referee J. R. Wheeler of Ireland, though he was chiefly responsible that they had not. Throughout, both sides were disconcerted by frequent blowing-up for scrum offences, though Wales were disconcerted more because eighteen of the twenty-six penalties went against them. Powell opened the scoring with a goal from a mark, and Jones-Davies repeated his feat of scoring against England the previous year. The England second-row Brian Black kicked a touch-line penalty to make it 6 - 3 and then Wales conceded a simple score when England found touch near the Welsh corner flag. Powell threw in, but mishearing pack leader Watcyn Thomas's instruction to throw short, threw long into the hands of the grateful Burland who charged over under the posts. Both touch-judges indicated that the conversion had failed, but the referee dramatically indicated eight fingers at the score-board which was duly amended from six-all to 8 - 6. A flash of unorthodoxy from Morley rounded off a pulverizing burst by Claude Davey, when he cut infield for a try which Bassett converted. 11 - 8. Wales was about to record her first victory at Twickenham when, with five minutes left, a Welsh forward was penalized inside his own half and Brian Black kicked the cup of victory from Welsh lips by equalizing.

The selectors retained the same team — for the first time since the War — to meet Scotland, but despite a full house and a referee who let the game flow, it did not flow along the Welsh back division. The gates at the Arms Park were closed early to avoid trouble, and Morley scored before even the advertised time of kick-off. Boon scored too, though both wingmen had to make something out of nothing, for Davey had one of those days that confirmed the *Llanelly Mercury*'s description of him; and the 13 - 8 victory was remembered mostly for Watcyn Thomas's homeric try after fracturing his collar-bone nine minutes into the match, a feat to equal the tries of Owen Badger and Dick Hellings in 1896 and 1900. The selectors began showing unsuspected analytical powers, even if they took unexpected forms. Recognizing Davey had been below his best, and attributing this to the square pass he received from Bowcott, they dropped Bowcott in favour of Newport's Raymond Ralph, whose longer pass, it was calculated, would better suit the cyclonic Claude. They based this reasoning on the fact that Frank Williams had brought the best out of Davey by this style in Paris the previous year. In which case, it was odd that they should have left Frank Williams himself in the reserves. Ralph, on the other hand, had played with Powell at London Welsh, and would show during his six caps many subtle skills as link-man, swerving runner and nifty drop-kicker. When Jones-Davies withdrew, the straight-running Frank Williams came into the side, at centre, after all.

Having disposed of France, 35 - 3, the team crossed the Irish Sea to face a confident Hibernian fifteen. Captained by the scheming Sugden, spearheaded by a Wanderers pairing at half-back and all-Lansdowne three-quarter line, fired by a pack that included Jack Siggins, Noel Murphy, George Beamish and the boisterous 'Jammie' Clinch (who anxiously sought out the like-minded Arthur Lemon of Neath 'to make an orange out of him') this brothful brotherhood was once again set up for the Triple Crown. Wales, for the first time since 1922, was going for the championship. It was probably not a coincidence that, for the first time since 1922, she had been led by the same captain for the whole season.

Five thousand Welshmen crossed overnight from Heysham in three boatloads, and Belfast hotels echoed to the strains of 'Sospan Fach' at seven in the morning. Wales nearly scored from the first scrummage when Powell went blind, fed Ralph moving at speed, and Boon was swept into touch at the corner-flag. The Irish forwards then began to assert themselves, Sugden stole away from a scrum with Beamish in support to crash into Bassett and flip an overhead pass to the unmarked Siggins, who scored. Gradually, shrewd kicking by Powell, concerted forward play, and darting runs by Morley brought Wales back into contention. Bassett missed a penalty, but Murray missed three. The Irish backs fell into the habit of watching Davey and Bassett instead of the ball, which they kept dropping, and Wales moved into a half-time lead with an adroit left-footed long-range drop goal from Ralph. The second half was hardly a minute gone when Wales scored again. Ralph probed and fed Davey. The defence waited for the expected battering ram to arrive, but Claude made a crisp transfer to Morley who flat-footed two defenders in as many yards and sped for the line. For the next twenty minutes the Irish pack, undaunted by the loss of Murphy who had joined the three-quarter line in place of the concussed Crowe, rocked the Welsh forwards with a series of furious assaults. They pushed them in the scrums and pinned them down in the loose. The crowd shrieked as Arrigho cut clean through the centre and travelled half the length of the field. Once he did it; twice. The second time he was ten yards out, with only Bassett and Davey to beat, and Murphy outside him. But against the concentration and composure which was now revitalizing Welsh rugby, he got no further. With a gesture to Arrigho, and a hurried word of command to Davey, Bassett nudged the Irishman into two minds. As Arrigho momentarily chose between them, Bassett hit him like a tramcar, knocking him unconscious. In falling, Arrigho somehow got the ball out to Murphy, who took it in full stride and immediately regretted it, for with the ball came Davey, at terminal velocity; Murphy too was laid out.

It was the turning point, in the short run of the game, in the long run of Welsh international rugby. Until that moment, Ireland had as good a chance of winning as Wales. After that moment there would be no more chances. A fly-kick by Boon raised the seige and for a brief time Wales became animated with nervous electricity. Morley dropped a scoring pass; Davey charged; Bassett bombarded the posts with drop-shots. Then the composure returned. Ten minutes from the end, Boon threw a long pass out from a mêlée with the Irish defence dishevelled. The ball went through three or four pairs of hands before it reached Davey, with Morley outside him. Both were covered, but Claude clenched his shoulders, accelerated into the burst, and scored. Then in the final minute, Tom Arthur fielded a loose kick in the centre of the field and punted it back at Irish full-back Morris, who claimed a mark, had it disallowed, and desperately kicked the ball away. He kicked to the vigilant Morley, hovering like a hawk. He might have marked it, but instead engaged top gear and raced fifty yards to the corner for Bassett to convert. The 15 - 3 victory gave Wales her first championship for nine years, but it was the manner in which she had won it that augured so well: the concerted intelligence at forward, the confident vitality behind, the resistance, the recovery, the cohesion, the will to win; most of all, the skills to win.

Victory over Bennie Osler's Third Springboks later that year would have proved beyond all doubt that the corner had indeed been turned. The 1931 South Africans had no players to singe the imagination like Marsberg, Krige and Stegmann of 1906, and the Morkels of 1912, but they achieved what neither of their predecessors had managed to do: they won all their seven games in Wales. One or two encounters would become embedded in local folk-lore, like the 10 - 9 close-run affair at Abertillery Park, when Trevor Thomas for the Combined Cross Keys-Abertillery side placed two colossal goals from such a distance (fifty and sixty yards respectively) that he seemed to be kicking them from the next valley. Another combined side ran them close at the Gnoll, where an Osler penalty goal was the only difference between two teams that scored a converted try apiece, and where Danie Craven, the fourteen stone dive-passing Stellenbosch scrum-half, found himself harried as much by referee Megins of Pontyclun as by the steel-hard Arthur Lemon at wing-forward. Wales would see more of Craven, assistant manager to the Fourth Springboks in 1951-2; more immediately, Lemon, along with Tom Arthur and Ned Jenkins of that Combined Neath-Aberavon side, would see more of Craven, albeit through a rain-curtain, a week later at Swansea. They would see a repeat of the score, too. On an unusually soggy St. Helen's in December, tactical misjudgement accounted for a disappointing defeat by 8 points to 3. It was a genuine case of Wales not being beaten, but conceding more points. Danie Craven later recalled, 'I rate our 1931 Springbok pack as one of the best scrummaging machines ever to have been produced by us . . . against Wales this pack met its equal. When the ball was put into the scrummage by either Wick Powell or myself, the first shove was given simultaneously by both packs. Whereas we pushed all other packs away we made no impression on the Welsh pack. All one could see of the tremendous pushing efforts of these two packs was the lifting of the front ranks. After the match our locks had no skin on their shoulders and the props suffered the same fate where the locks pushed against them'. Maybe Bassett and Powell could be faulted in clinging to dry-ball tactics in monsoon conditions, while the South Africans more realistically chose to drive it through by foot; Wales's policy, though, reflected not merely exaggerated confidence in the sandy absorbent St. Helen's soil, but a justified confidence in the match-winning capabilities of the Welsh backs, and of the wings in particular. Boon and Morley had emerged as the best pair of wings since Willie Llewellyn and E. T. Morgan. Ronnie Boon, now twenty-two and Welsh amateur sprint champion, was quite convinced of his own ability to beat his opponents through speed, skill and brains. His name should really have been Miller, for he had the personality of the entertainer Max, and the pace of the greyhound Mick. His abrasive cheeky-chappiness was often mistaken for conceit, when it was in reality a facet of his confidence. He never went on to the field expecting to lose, and never expected the ball to come looking for him: his impatience and opportunism brought Boon, and Wales, several scores in the early thirties. That he was the master of the zippy Zimmerman was demonstrated early on in the game against South Africa, when he broke away on the blind side of a scrum, eluded his opposite number, and just failed to round Brand on the touch-line. The Welsh try had come when Boon caught Zimmerman in possession, robbed him and steered it on for Will 'Sgili' Davies to dribble it over. Boon went on to score a try and drop a goal against England on the same ground a month later, and replicate the same feat at Twickenham the following year. On the other wing, Morley's speedy opportunism — 'he was only knee-high to a grasshopper but when he got the ball it was goodnight, nurse' wrote Terry McLean after seeing him in New Zealand in 1930 — resulted in three (disallowed) tries in three successive matches in 1931-2. Davey, in commanding form throughout the season, was also pulled up when clear against Scotland; Irish referee Tom Bell, having recalled Morley and Davey, erroneously in the view of the Welsh press, collapsed with strain, exhaustion and perhaps remorse, at the end of the match. The backs were playing for and with each other, not as a machine but as an organism. Ralph, who had outplayed Osler as an attacking fly-half, carved out several openings, and against Ireland gave Davey a scoring pass that had itself prised apart the defence like a can-opener. Powell was simply himself, alternately delighting and terrifying the crowd with his spectacular long reverse passes into midfield. Having beaten England 12 - 5 and Scotland 6 - 0, Wales, who had prevented Ireland from lifting the Triple Crown in 1930 and 1931, were by March 1932 going for it themselves, for the first time since 1911. Bassett squarely took the blame that she failed, giving away two of the four tries which Ireland scored in a 12 - 10 victory, and failing to convert Ralph's last-minute try which would have secured at least a draw, and the championship. Like Albert Jenkins four years before, Gwyn Nicholls in 1906, even C. P. Lewis, one of Wales's earliest full-backs, in 1884, Jack Bassett bowed out of the international arena to cat-calls. He would feature in the next season's trials, but his representative career was over. Gone, but not forgotten. When the *Western Mail* asked entrants for its 1933 St. David's Day Essay Competition to nominate the greatest Welshman of the century, the three most popular choices were Lloyd George, Jack Petersen and Jack Bassett.

266

As one young scholar put it, 'Bassett, although fairly old, still has a kick in him'.

The revival in Welsh fortunes — Ireland's 1932 win was Wales's first defeat by any of the home countries since March 1930 — had owed plenty to Bassett, who had retained the selectors' confidence in his captaincy for precisely that length of time. It owed something, too, to the settled complexion of the team: nineteen players had been capped in 1930-1, a mere sixteen in 1931-2. The knowledge that the men behind the scrum could put the ball to maximum benefit seemed to inspire the forwards to greater efforts to provide them with it. There was a more cohesive and purposeful look about the Welsh pack such as it had not possessed for many a year. With Tom Arthur, Ned Jenkins and Tom Day it would not lack for weight, but that weight was now being synchronized. The admixture of Skym and Lemon had ensured a vigorous mobility. Line-out play was improved beyond recognition. Tom Arthur was encouraged by intelligent support work to indulge in a variety of fancy flips; Watcyn Thomas, increasingly playing a South African No. 8 role, was equally at home in the engine-room or locking the back-row, and had become among the greatest of all Welsh line-out ball-winners. What Wales needed above all now was a forward captain, a pack-leader in whom was also vested the overall tactical direction of the team. There was a man in the side ready to assume that dual responsibility, and in January 1933, with another crusade to Twickenham impending, the selectors finally matched him with their allotted hour.

THE NEW OLYMPIANS

T HE early thirties were not a good time in Europe. They were not much better in Britain. In Wales, people thought it impossible for conditions to become worse. It was possible. They did. Government surveys of 1932 and 1934 noted that the prevalence of rickets in South Walian children was thought to be connected to dietary deficiencies in the womb. David Rocyn Jones, and other medical officers of health, spent the thirties in despair. There was more calcium in blackboard chalk than in Welsh bones. The first real wage increase since 1915, and that did not restore the enormous lost differentials, was in 1937.

The economic outlook for rugby, too, remained sombre. The list of clubs whose own financial predicament was approaching a terminal condition lengthened. Abertillery was on the verge of extinction by 1931 because it could not afford its £3 10s. 0d. ground rent. By 1932 the gate at Ebbw Vale, despite a catchment area of 40,000, seldom reached twenty shillings, and the club was forced to resort to public subscriptions. In January 1933, the gates were rushed at Neath by a crowd protesting against the shilling admission charge, which was thereby reduced to sevenpence.

In February 1931, the executive of the W.W.R.U. appealed to the W.R.U. to intercede with colliery owners to allow an earlier finish on Saturday, or many clubs in the league — Ammanford, Amman United, Brynamman and Llandybie, which had 80 per cent miners in their ranks — would have to disband. They received short shrift instead of short, or even altered, shifts. Earlier and later approaches by the W.R.U., in 1928 and in June 1931, were supported by the miners' officials but rejected, high-handedly, by the Coalowners' Association who claimed, rather ingenuously, that they had no control over local collieries. A meagre 30,000 assembled at St. Helen's to watch even England in 1932, despite the added attraction of the presence of the Prince of Wales. The *Western Mail*, attributing the low attendance 'to the persistence of bad trade and a consequent diminution in the spending power of the people', added its by now familiar refrain that 'whatever may be the case in the other three countries, the fame and prosperity of the Rugby game in Wales have a truly democratic base'. That was what made it continuously vulnerable to the depredations of the Rugby League. In 1929 Welsh hooker D. R. Jenkins had left Swansea for Leeds, and rising scrum-half Billy Werrett, Pontypool for Halifax. In 1930 Emlyn Jenkins left for Salford and Trevor Thomas, capped from Abertillery, joined Oldham. In 1931 Norman Fender went to York, and in November 1932 Jack Morley to Wigan. In 1933 Raymond Ralph joined Leeds, Arthur Lemon went to St. Helens, and Swansea lost Roy Bateman, Glyn Jones and Billy Trew, junior, in the space of one August week. Club football became restrictive, plagued by aimless kicking at half-back, partly in reaction to the increasing role of specialist wing-forwards, partly in poor imitation of the matchless, and match-winning, short-punting of Bennie Osler.

But the new dawn could be discerned. Attracted by the social values of the amateur game, encouraged by the efforts of the W.S.S.R.U., inspired by the impact of schools like Cardiff H.S. and Christ College, Brecon on the game at Varsity and international levels, an increasing number of schools in South and North Wales, either deliberately switched from soccer to rugby, like Rydal in 1923 and Cowbridge in 1930, or set about encouraging rugby as an activity as scholastically valid as more academic pursuits. The fact that the depressed economic environment offered little apart from an inducement to stay longer in school was a further fillip to secondary school rugby. In 1930-1 T. P. Williams succeeded his brother Ritchie as coach to the senior side at Llandovery. 'Pope' Williams, himself an old Llandoverian, had been at Oxford when the Scottish quartet of Smith, McPherson, Aitken and Wallace had been the University's back division. He noticed that Ian Smith had been made to look twice as fast by the head-start he received from the swift transfer of the ball along the line to him. At Llandovery, 'Pope's' insistent encyclical was that the ball be moved to the wings 'like lightning'. But he also recognized that solid scrummaging was the essential platform on which to build any fluent back-play, and the clean heel not merely from the tight, but from the loose, too. He began applying and refining Wakefield's twenties tactics, teaching flankers to move across in support of the wing to be ready to redirect the attack away from converging defenders. The Llandovery doctrine of 'lightning' transfers and quick target-switching would still have a gospel freshness when preached in New Zealand forty years later by Carwyn James, an acolyte of Llandovery and its 'Pope'. Thanks to T. P. Williams, Llandovery College in the 1930s would supply the Welsh team with a player for every position behind the scrum and a couple in it as well. To one promising youngster, the son of a Rhondda fruit-merchant, who had come under his care at thirteen years of age, Williams insisted endlessly that a back should be able to cover nine yards in a second, and that a second wasted meant nine yards lost. Between 1931 and 1933 the exploits of this schoolboy set the Welsh press by the ears. In April 1932, when the Welsh S.S. beat the Yorkshire Schools 21 - 0 at Pontypridd, eyes were riveted on C. W. Jones at fly-half, 'who has the cleverness and audacity associated with Percy Bush'. He was never far from the headlines, 'darting through at will', as captain of Llandovery in 1932-33. Meanwhile, at Gowerton School, W. E. Bowen, who had joined the staff in 1931, was carefully nursing what would become a legendary partnership. In January 1933 the Welsh S.S. beat the West of England S.S. 22 - 9 at Bristol, where 'the halves, the Gowerton couple, W. T. H. Davies and H. Tanner, cut out many openings'. When Gowerton Old Boys played the traditional Easter fixture with the School XV in 1936, both teams were captained by full Welsh Internationals, the same Davies and Tanner, who had already toppled the might of New Zealand playing for Swansea the previous year.

Evidence that the wind of change was sweeping vigorously through the corridors of Welsh rugby came with a gust from an unlikely quarter. The crown of the National Eisteddfod of Wales when it was held at Bangor in August 1931, had been won by the Rev Albert Evans-Jones, popularly known as Cynan, and later to become the personification of the Eisteddfod itself. Cynan had written a *pryddest*, a long poem in free metre, on the set subject of *Y Dyrfa* ('The Crowd'), though not all the adjudicators were happy at the way in which he had interpreted his theme and mixed the secular with the sacred. What Cynan had done was convey the thoughts of a former Welsh rugby international, 'John', as he gazes over the rail at the phosphorescent wake of the ship which is taking him to the Christian mission-field in China, and reflects nostalgically on the greatest moment of his sporting life, which he is now renouncing. His consolation is that he has exchanged 'The Crowd' of the packed terraces for the Cloud of Witnesses who will bear testimony to the greater work that lies ahead of him. The subject-matter called to mind the life story of Eric Liddell, the Scottish Olympic runner and international wing who had played twice against Wales in the early twenties and, at the height of his sporting career, had given it up to become a missionary in China. But Cynan had a specific 'John' in mind. John Roberts, capped thirteen times for Wales in 1927-29, son of the minister of Pembroke Terrace Welsh Presbyterian Church in Cardiff, had for some time made known his intention of becoming a missionary in China, and in January 1932 he was given a rousing send-off by the Cardiff club before leaving for Amoy, where he spent the next six years. It was an interesting coincidence that John Roberts's grandfather, Iolo Caernarfon, had won the crown when the Eisteddfod had last visited Bangor, in 1890. It was even more fitting that Cynan's poem should have won at Bangor in 1931. That year, in January, at Wrexham, the North Wales Rugby Union had been formed with nine clubs, to seek affiliation to the W.R.U. In June, that affiliation was granted after W.F.U. delegates had met with North Walian representatives at approximately neutral Shrewsbury. Richard Davies, of Wrexham, pointed out 'the coming into existence of a recognized and authoritative body in North Wales' would not only be a gain for the northern clubs, for 'the W.R.U. as then constituted would become truly national', allowing the W.R.U. to 'reap the benefits . . . of the time and money which had been spent in cultivating secondary schools rugby in North Wales'.

The nucleus of the North Wales R.U. were the clubs of Llandudno, Colwyn Bay, Ruthin and Wrexham, which had been formed in the early 1920s, and the University College of North Wales, where rugby had been played, sporadically, since the turn of the century. Bangor R.F.C. was formed in 1929; by 1934-5 the nine founder clubs of the North Wales R.U. had been increased to twelve. Almost immediately, however, survival became a problem for several of them. By 1938, Holyhead, Llanidloes, Machynlleth and Porthmadog had all collapsed, and with the departure of founder-secretary Ieuan Williams of Wrexham to Leicester that year, the momentum generated in the early thirties was lost. The further expansion of North Wales rugby would have to wait until the 1970s but the dramatic developments of that decade — symbolized by the elevation to the Presidency of the W.R.U. of Gwyn Roblin of Bangor in 1979-80 — were built on the foundations laid in 1930-1, and celebrated in Cynan's crowned and widely-read *Y Dyrfa*.

There was something more. As Cynan told it, the greatest moment in the career of his imaginary China-bound international had been at

Twickenham, when, with Wales pressing and 'The Crowd' at fever-pitch, he had scored the winning try — 'the blinding moment when human clay becomes immortal like God' — which secured Wales her first win at the English capital. Cynan had not only encapsulated the immediate past; he foretold the immediate future. On Wales's next visit, the Twickenham bogey would be laid; and two North Walians would be in the team that would lay it.

The W.R.U. itself seemed infected by an awareness of impending drama as the date of that visit neared. In October 1932 Horace Lyne, its President, was presented with the South Wales Challenge Cup, and an illuminated address and album. In presenting it, Dr David Rocyn Jones remarked how Mr Lyne had 'in season and out of season . . . stood by Wales, sheltering her from the storms and courageously leading her out of the wilderness of doubt and scorn into her promised land of international friendship and equality'. Jim Jarrett added that 'in international Rugby affairs no-one carried greater weight than Mr Lyne, and his steady thoughtfulness and capacity for thinking Rugby imperially had been the Principality's greatest asset in the Councils of the nations'.

It needed a victory at imperial Twickenham to clinch that equality spoken of. As the trials unfolded in late 1932, the North Wales presence could not be missed. N. D. Guest of Llandudno appeared in the first trial, the first North Walian of the century to do so. In December, Raymond Bark-Jones, Uppingham-educated, of Liverpool-Welsh parentage, had an impressive Varsity match (refereed by Albert Freethy for the sixth consecutive year) and Vivian Jenkins of Llandovery shone at centre. 'It would not surprise me to see Jenkins and R. B. Jones playing for Wales in the near future', wrote H. Lascelles Carr in the *Western Mail* he edited. The future was approaching fast. The final trial teams were chock-full of surprises. The choice of R. B. Jones at forward was not by now one of them; that of Jenkins at full-back, was. His only experience in that position was that of the previous Tuesday, for Bridgend against Newport. Jenkins, now twenty years of age, 5foot 11inches and 13stone 9lb. had not lost any of the nonchalance he had displayed as a schoolboy, but his cricketers' hands were magnetically safe, and he had perfected a spiralling torpedo-kick which, frequently displayed in the course of the fourteen caps he would win between 1933 and 1939, reminded older followers of Bert Winfield.

Claude Davey was not originally chosen for the trial at all, but when Frank Williams went to fly-half after Ralph had dropped out, Davey filled the centre vacancy. He should have been there in the first place, one reason being that his jolting tackles would be needed against the likely English pair of Burland and Gerrard, the other that he would be partnering a prodigious North Wales schoolboy whose selection stunned the South Wales public but not Davey, who had played with him at Sale and, with 'Old Stager' as intermediary, brought him to the attention of the Welsh selectors.

Wilfred Wooller had just turned twenty and was still at Rydal School, on the North Wales coast, when summoned to the final trial at Swansea. Rydal's headmaster, the Rev A. J. Costain, who had introduced rugby into the curriculum ten years before, had taken a keen interest in the sporting prowess of the lean but heavy-boned Wooller, who was already 6foot 2inches and approaching his peak athletic weight of 13stone 10lb. In the winter of 1932 Wooller had begun to play for Sale where he rapidly graduated from the Third XV to play in the First, alongside Davey and future English international wing, Hal Sever. If Davey, whose father was English, had not been pre-empted by Wales to win his first cap against France in 1930, he would have been snapped up by England; Davey was now determined that England should not acquire the services of Wooller, born of English parentage in Colwyn Bay, and he drew the attention of the Welsh selectors to this leggy colossus who, like himself, had been physically hardened by playing most of his schoolboy rugby in the back-row. Wooller had an outstanding Welsh trial. Surrounded by generally shorter Welshmen, he looked to be ten foot tall and to take steps ten yards long. He wasted no time taking them either. 'Old Stager' could barely disguise the almost physical excitement he experienced at watching him: 'If what Wooller did at Swansea is representative of his ordinary form, Wales has discovered a centre who has greater possibilities than any centre Wales has had for over a quarter of a century. He has everything a centre could wish for, and he may become a second Gwyn Nicholls — or a greater player still'.

Every one of the backs selected for the England match of 1933 was a product of schools' rugby. Jenkins of Llandovery College at full-back; Boon of Barry C.S. and A. H. Jones of Llandovery on the wings; Davey of Ystalyfera C.S. and Wooller of Rydal at centre; Bowcott of Cardiff H.S. at outside-half, and partnering him, the Cardiff all-rounder, Maurice Turnbull, educated at Downside School, orthodox rather than brilliant but a fine passer and fearless faller. The democratic ideal was preserved by the composition of the pack which had a less scholastic appearance, but was virile and intelligent. The front row was 'sospan' scarlet, even if Archie

Skym had transferred from the Carmarthenshire to Glamorgan Constabulary. With him were Bryn Evans, a tin-worker, winning his first cap, and Edgar Jones, a steelworker, recalled after his début as a raw nineteen-year-old in the rough match at Colombes in 1930. Behind them were R. B. Jones, winning his first cap as forecast, and Dai Thomas, a burly Swansea policeman (6foot 1inch, 15stone, with a 52-inch chest) now twenty-three and winning his sixth cap. At blind-side wing-forward was fellow-policeman Tom Arthur, who had won his seventeen previous caps in the second row, but who was indispensable to the selectors' intentions of fielding a seven-man scrummaging pack. On the open side was the Cilfynydd policeman-turned-teacher, Iorrie Isaacs. Locking the back-row and at last awarded the captaincy, was the imperious figure of Watcyn Thomas.

Watcyn was now twenty-seven-years-old, and at 6foot 3inches, 15stone, physically at his zenith. He was sufficiently imposing in stature to make it entirely plausible that he did indeed, as he claimed, have as a great-uncle a mountain fighter known as Dai'r Dychrynllyd (Dai the Dreaded). His qualifications for the captaincy were beyond doubt: having played at full-back, wing, centre and scrum-half before moving into the pack, he had a comprehensive knowledge of all aspects of play. Captaincy was, to him, hardly an unfamiliar experience, either: he had captained Llanelli County School, the Welsh Secondary Schools, Swansea University College, the University of Wales, Waterloo, and Lancashire. As a pack-leader for Wales he had already acquired a reputation as a disciplinarian, and had won the personal gratitude of the referee for curbing the pugilistic tendencies of one Welsh forward against Scotland in 1932. A keen tactical student, he had the perception and flexibility to modify or change a plan according to the requirements of the game in hand: at half-time against Scotland in 1931, he switched Tom Day from prop to hooker to salvage a beaten scrum, and turned the course of the game. In his individual play, he knew that a forward was most effective not in charging around like a tormented heifer but in channelling his energies into their concentrated application at specific times and in specific places; his own technical skills, especially in the line-out, were unrivalled between the wars.

It was his fourth consecutive visit to Twickenham, where Wales had never won since the opening of the ground in 1910. None knew better than he that the bogey was no myth. In 1921 the match was not half-way through before Jack Whitfield had twisted a knee, Tom Johnson broken a finger and Jack P. Jones fractured a collar bone. In 1923 England had won as a result of a freak first-minute try when a muffed drop at goal swirled back into the hands of the kicker who ran on to score, and an even freakier score when Corbett passed back between his legs to Smallwood who then did drop a goal. In 1927 Dai Jones broke a collar bone after twenty minutes, Powell was a cripple by half-time, and still Wales scored two tries to one, only to lose 11 - 9. In 1931, a last-minute fifty-five-yard Black beauty had been a horse-kick to the Welsh heart. None knew better, either, the unsettling effect of the Twickenham ground — in Ivor Brown's memorable phrase, 'the last fortress of the Forsytes' — with its eerie, high-pitched wailing that re-echoed endlessly around the roofs of the towering stands, and what Watcyn himself described as its 'atmospheric eddies and whirlpools which make passing and kicking go fortuitously astray'. Cynan's words had peculiar significance to the Welsh captain of 1933:

> Roedd Cymru'n pwyso, pwyso'n drwm
> Ac eto — O! paham
> Na allem dorri ei hanlwc hir
> Wrth chwarae'n Twickenham?

(Wales pressed, and pressed again, and yet why, why, could we not break her long chain of misfortune at Twickenham?)

Watcyn Thomas communicated to his front row in Welsh throughout the match; six of the team were Welsh-speaking and another two had enough to 'get by', or at least understand their captain. (So too did one player on the opposite side, Lieutenant Vaughan Jones of Pontarddulais and the Army, his presence in the English back-row symbolic of South Wales's greatest export in the inter-war years: her people). Its two North Walians gave this Welsh XV its most representative appearance since 1881; in fact geographically, socially, occupationally, linguistically, this was the most truly representative *national* side ever to pull on the scarlet jersey.

The bogey was in no danger for the first quarter, when Wales were frequently in disarray. It became obvious that the English policy was to apply early pressure and disturb the composure of the seven inexperienced new caps. Burland did most of the disturbing, at the expense of the novice Wooller, whose excitable prancing and attempted frontal tackles made little impression on the strong England centre as time and again he burst through the Welsh midfield. Only wild passes to his wing, and a flying tackle by the 'flu-stricken Jenkins, saved certain scores. Half-way through the first half Burland again shook off Wooller and sent Booth away for the right-hand corner. The sight of Jenkins looming into his field of vision curbed his anxiety to get there, and he looked inside for support. He found Elliott, the English fly-half, who took the ball outside the Welsh line but appeared to have it jerked out of his grasp as he dived to score. The Welshmen in the crowd, and in the press box, were convinced that he had not grounded the ball properly, but Irish referee Tom Bell came up to award a try. The bogey was alive and well. Watcyn Thomas, for one, had come to bury it. He took Wooller to one side, as he later recalled, 'for a quiet fatherly talk', and suggested that he take Burland low, and sideways. Wooller responded immediately. Within a few minutes he beat Burland on the outside and punted ahead. Wooller's punts could be of stupendous length; on a later occasion, in another place, they would wreak havoc; this time he was beaten to the touchdown by the English full-back. When Burland came at him next, Wooller went for him at an angle, and brought him down.

At half-time Watcyn issued a new tactical directive. With its prodigal frittering of early opportunities, he knew the English attack could now be contained. He had seen that Wales were losing the scrums, but winning the line-outs; he noticed, too, that Bowcott had kicked faultlessly in defending his line. He was now instructed to harness the Twickenham cross-wind and just as faultlessly kick his forwards up the touch-line. Even before the new strategy could be deployed, Welsh confidence received a boost from the most confident man in the ground. Ronnie Boon could kick as well as any fly-half; he was also a supreme opportunist. Within a minute of the change-over, he fielded a fly-kick ahead by Aarvold, later renowned for better judgement. Boon was standing twenty yards out, immediately in front of the posts. Whether aware or not that Wooller was outside him, he turned neither hair nor head, dropped the ball in front of his left foot and put 4 points on the board. The pack now set about getting the ball back to Bowcott. There was not much combined play from the backs, but plenty from the forwards. The two Thomases, Tom Arthur and R. B. Jones dominated the line-outs; there the game was won. Yet although England won the scrums 31 - 27, she was never able to turn them to advantage, for Key at inside-half was continually spoilt by Turnbull, Arthur and Isaacs. From the line-outs, meanwhile, Turnbull fed Bowcott, who selected a point on the touch-line and detailed his academic left foot to place the ball within an inch of it. Once he briefly raised his sights and planed the wrong side of an upright with a drop at goal. Suddenly, England left-wing Booth fastened on to a ball that had been too vigorously knocked back from a Welsh line-out, and fed Elliott who streaked towards the open line forty yards away. Wooller, who in the course of an hour had matured from colt to charger, went after him with lengthening strides. The line beckoned, Elliott strained, Wooller closed, and nailed him ten yards out. With Gerrard off the field after Claude Davey had nearly pushed his eye through his head in a hand-off, Wales applied intense pressure on the left. Isaacs harrassed the English half-backs, and from the ensuing loose maul the advantage of the quick heel that Watcyn Thomas had particularly insisted on beforehand was demonstrated, when the ball came back for Wooller and Davey to handle before Boon raced over and round behind the posts. For the second successive year he had scored 7 points, a drop goal and a try, against England. This year, with the ease of a Hollywood crooner relaxing into a familiar song, he had scored all Wales's points. It was difficult to believe that Vivian Jenkins, after a stupendous afternoon's work, could miss the conversion. W. J. Llewelyn, the Welsh touch-judge, and international referee from Jenkins's home town of Bridgend, refused to believe it and raised his flag, although the ball had sailed a foot wide. No matter. At 7 - 3 it was Wales's first win in England since 1908, and her first ever win at Twickenham, as Cynan had foretold. The hoodoo had haunted Welshmen since the opening match at the famous ground in 1910, when Adrian Stoop had masterminded the Welsh defeat. It was nicely appropriate that the bogey was laid in the year of Stoop's presidency of the R.F.U. That night, a group of raucous and inebriated Welsh supporters found themselves watching the circus at Olympia. Throughout the evening one of them kept shouting, 'Come on Wales! Good old Wales!' until someone sitting behind told him to be quiet and look at the lions. The Welshman turned to focus glassily on the intruder. 'Lions?' he roared, 'Lions? Watcyn Thomas would eat the bloody lot, mun!'

The rest of 1933, for Welsh rugby at least, was an anti-climax as Wales went on to lose both her other matches. Injuries, and the selectors, combined to prevent the bogey-laying team from appearing together again. Bowcott rounded off a polished international career with a fine last-second try against Ireland; in later years he would continue to serve the game by administering the London Welsh club through a golden period, and acting as a national selector for ten years from 1963-74, culminating with his Presidency of the W.R.U. in 1974-75. The year 1933, too, saw the last appearances of the nucleus of forwards who had brought Welsh forward play from the shadows into the light: Tom Arthur, Arthur

Bowdler, Arthur Lemon, and, quite unnecessarily, Watcyn Thomas. Watcyn had won fourteen caps, but he could legitimately have expected several more. Though he never himself referred to it in his colourful autobiography, *Rugby Playing Man*, published a year before his death in 1978, the reason had already been disclosed by J. B. G. Thomas twenty years earlier. It was that Watcyn had mortally offended the selectors by refusing to play the Cardiff policeman Bob Barrell at open-side wing forward and Arthur Lemon at prop, against Ireland in 1933, when their proper positions were the reverse. Watcyn did reverse them, against selectorial diktat, and was subsequently relieved both of his captaincy and his place while at the height of his career. The 1935 All Blacks, after meeting him at his most formidable for Lancashire, could never understand why he was omitted from the Welsh team of that year.

It was a sign of the times that in the final trial of the 1933-34 season, sixteen of the thirty players on view played most of their rugby outside Wales. A further sign was that nine of them were Blues. The selectors now gave a reminder that they had lost none of their genius for bizarre and inscrutable choices. The pack that was fielded against England in 1934 was one of the most ill-assorted ever. Six of them were newcomers, most of them were locks or wing-forwards, not one had played alongside another before. It was summed up by the selection of a lock-forward as hooker, who was given the captaincy on his first appearance. Glyn Prosser of Neath and A. M. Rees of London Welsh would go on to higher things, but this 'intelligent eight' — strictly the 'intelligent three', since the designation was inspired by the presence of J. R. Evans of Newport H.S., Kenyon Jones of Monmouth and Oxford, and Arthur Rees of Llandovery and Cambridge — was swiftly dismantled and sent to the back of the class. The task of the backs was complicated by the inappropriate choice of a pint-sized new scrum-half. Even the rugged Wick Powell, behind a solid pack, would have been hard-pressed in coping with the robust Bernard Gadney at inside-half for England; behind a retreating pack and a non-existent back-row, the 5foot 3inch Dan Evans was doomed from the outset. The team contained thirteen new caps. Claude Davey was the only previously-capped player in a young back division that might have been shattered beyond repair; but some were there to stay, like Geoffrey Rees-Jones of Ipswich and Oxford University on the right-wing, the lean and dexterous Idwal Rees of Swansea G.S. and Cambridge University in the centre, and the nineteen-year-old fly-half Clifford W. Jones, who

278

barely nine months before had captained Llandovery and the Welsh Secondary Schools.

Cliff Jones was in his freshman year at Clare College, Cambridge, where he had already won the first of his three blues. Physically he would not develop beyond his 5foot 8inches and 10stone 12lb., but his game would. It was alleged he did not always know when to pass. As a schoolboy international he had been criticized for hanging on too long, and, at the same time, for not drawing his man before passing. But in his balance, his handling, his eye for an opening, his shattering speed off the mark, his killer instinct, his game blazed with the authentic light of genius. At Porth County School he had refused to play rugby because the shape of the ball upset him, so he played soccer, and like so many of the great fly-halves, before and after him, never regretted his apprenticeship with the round ball once he had switched codes. He had no option but to switch when he went to Llandovery, where he arrived in 1928 on the heels of T. P. Williams. Jones moved through the school under 'Pope's' wing. For four years, six days a week, Williams worked on the youngster's raw ability, cultivating it, refining it, improving it, like a diamond cutter with an amethyst. One thing he forbade him to do, and that was to drop goals. Jones never made up the lee-way, but his other skills more than compensated: the fly-paper hands, the mastery of the teasing, short punt, the electrifying sidestep. To copy-book moves he brought an audacity, an inspired impudence that transformed mechanical efficiency into match-winning unorthodoxy. He wedded the irrepressibility of Bush to the precision of Bowcott, and the off-spring of Rhondda ebullience and Llandovery meticulousness was pure gold, the magical product of inborn talent and a rugby alchemist. In a relatively short international career of thirteen caps, won between 1934 and 1938, he established himself as one of the greatest outside-halves of all time. Fittingly, after being elected on to the W.R.U. in 1956, and serving for twenty-one years as a national selector (1957-78), his seniority of unbroken service to the Union brought him the Presidency in Centenary Year. His views on rugby football he adjusted to the continuing evolution of the game, but his fundamental philosophy was what he had been taught at Llandovery: a second wasted is nine yards lost. Neither his speed nor his agility saved him from frequent damage: during his brief playing career he broke his wrist, his elbow, his collar bone and both ankles. During one enforced lay-off he wrote a trenchant study of the game, *Rugby Football*, that first appeared in 1937 and went through several subsequent editions. In it, he was prepared to challenge orthodox positions, advocating for instance the incorporation of certain aspects of the professional game into amateur rugby, and greater player representation on the W.R.U. Throughout, the Llandovery refrain could constantly be heard: 'one quick heel from the loose is worth five from the tight'. His injuries were mostly the result of the attentions of back-row hit-men, but he argued that the way to neutralize the problem of fast-breaking defences was not to amend the laws but to improve the endemic slow-heeling — 'possibly the result of slackness, possibly the result of cussedness, but more probably the result of poor leadership' — and rely on the inventiveness of the fly-half. 'The wing-forward does not live who can close the game against a fly-half with speed off the mark, who is benefiting from a quick heel, preferably from the loose'.

During his first year at international level, Jones played himself in. He survived the 9 - 0 defeat of January 1934 by England, and helped Wales score 13 points in each of the next two games. At Murrayfield his stabs and starts tormented a dour Scottish defence until Cowey and Idwal Rees breached it for three tries; against Ireland he lit the fuse of a six-minute scoring burst that brought tries for Albert Fear, Cowey and, remarkably, Vivian Jenkins. Jenkins had had little luck with his line-kicking in this match and when on one occasion he fielded the ball deep inside his own half, instead of trying to put it into touch and have it charged down by three or four onrushing Irishmen, he decided to run around them. Jenkins was, after all, a former centre-threequarter. Having run round them he kept on running for a quarter of the length of the field, linked with Idwal Rees, and was on hand to receive the final pass from Arthur Bassett to score the first ever international try by a Welsh full-back.

By the end of that year, Wooller was back in action for Cambridge. Since Easter 1933 he had been prescribed the wrong treatment for a knee injury and the muscle had atrophied. He had had time to fill out, and think about his game. He would never be quite as exceptionally fit as he was in 1932-33, and there would be times when he preferred another option to the final confident surge which must bring a score. But that self-knowledge was in itself beneficial. Recovering his zest for the game at university, he began to cultivate the art of making the ball do the work, of picking defensive locks rather than simply forcing them; guile rather than gelignite. At Cambridge he had with him the Llandovery firefly, Cliff Jones, and the 1934 Varsity match was the greatest exposition of Welsh attacking skills since that of 1926. The architects of a smashing Cambridge 29 - 4 win were Jones and Wooller. Jones set up the Scottish winger Fyfe for three tries and Wooller dropped a stupendous goal from five yards inside his own half. Wooller, in Townsend Collins's view, 'lacked the crowning quality of judgement', but Collins, ever since the four three-quarter system had come into being, measured every centre against the yardstick of the selfless Gwyn Nicholls's subordination of himself to his wing. It was true that Wooller was not the greatest feeder of wingers, but he himself was faster than most of the wingers he played with; between the departure of Boon and Morley, and the advent of Arthur Bassett and W. H. Clement, Wales was not too well-off in that position. One general result of this was that the cutting edge of the Welsh attack once more moved back to midfield, and to Jones, Wooller and Davey especially. A more particular consequence was the emphasis and encouragement this gave to Wooller's natural individualism. He had come to the game unencumbered by tradition, uninitiated into Welsh rugby lore and legend. He had never heard of Gwyn Nicholls. He had been educated at soccer schools in London before going to Rydal. He was not dark, compact, or particularly Welsh. Deception or sleight of hand were not his trade-marks. Neither was he a cog in a machine; he was the machine, the most prolific points scorer since Gould, and with his pounding knee action the most difficult centre to tackle since Gabe. In any case, most who criticized him for not being a combination player were looking in the wrong direction for their evidence: Wooller combined not with his wing, but with his outside-half — when that outside-half was Cliff Jones. Jones himself was hardly 'Dromio's' ideal pivot either — he was too much of a virtuoso to be that. But when Wooller was there accompanying him, to round off his flamboyant arpeggios and florid cadenzas, Jones would play solo and orchestrate, and conduct the entire back division. In harmony, Jones and Wooller could make sweet music indeed. Their party piece, practised to a fine art at Cambridge and frequently performed for Wales and Cardiff, was the quick burst by Jones into the gap between his opposite number and centre before he practically put it in the hands of Wooller striding through with an inside break. 'Wooller coming up at full speed to take a quick pass from Cliff Jones is one of the most thrilling sights in modern Rugby Football' wrote J. M. Kilburn, 'unless the viewpoint be the immediate path'. The final trial of 1935 drew an unprecedented 30,000 to see that combination in action; a fortnight later they made their first appearance together for Wales at Twickenham, where another record crowd of 72,000 came to see them perform. Jones needed a long, deep pass that he could run onto, stretching for it, and for nearly all his career he was fortunate in his inside halves. Bert Jones of Llanelli had provided him with a dependable and fluent service in

281

1934; in 1935 his partner was Powell, whose pass was longer, if more erratic. This was Powell's last season, after twenty-seven caps and nine years of momentous sacrifice at the base of the scrum; the resurgence of Welsh back play since the late twenties owed a remarkable debt to the fearless saving and lengthy service — in both senses — of the powerful ex-Guardsman. Against England, in 1935, Wooller had one try disallowed; then, early in the second half after Jenkins had arranged the position with a sixty-yard touch finder to the left-hand corner, the Welsh forwards heeled cleanly, Powell feinted to the narrow side then whipped out one of his reverse special deliveries to Jones in the open, who drew Candler and the English centre, Heaton, to feed Wooller a short, scoring pass. Once more, misfortune dogged the Welshmen at English headquarters: Edgar Jones fractured two ribs in the first ten minutes, Cowey wrenched his knee, and Skym, or somebody, was caught fatally offside in front of his posts ten minutes from the end. Once again, Wales could claim only a moral victory; the hoodoo had only hiccupped in 1933.

Against Scotland at Cardiff in 1935, Jones repeated his brilliance of the previous year at Murrayfield. In each, it was his constant probing and creating of attacking positions which eventually left the defence uncertain and demoralized, to give Wales her ascendancy. After six minutes at Cardiff, he was fed by Powell twenty yards out and set off on a diagonal side-stepping forty-yard run which left Scottish defenders, and his own wings, panting in his slipstream. After ten minutes, Jim Lang threw back to Powell, a magnetic Jones drew both centres before snapping the ball to Davey, who put Wooller over. On half-time, Jones paid the price of his own cleverness. Scampering around in front of his own posts, he was mauled in a tackle and had to leave with torn shoulder ligaments, but the reliable Idwal Rees, the comprehensive insurance policy of the Welsh back division of the thirties, came to fly-half, and Fear went out from the pack to the wing. The seven forwards held on until Vivian Jenkins slammed the door shut in the closing minutes when he swung on his heel and let fly from forty yards to make it 10 - 6 to Wales. A year later, sparkling running by Jones illuminated a murky Marrayfield afternoon as Wales romped to a 13 - 3 victory after a no-scoring stalemate with England. Jones fizzed like uncorked champagne till, exhausted by his own effervescence and shaken up by numerous tackles, he changed places with Idwal Rees to recover his breath. The dazzling back play concealed the fact that the strongest packs in Wales — those of Cross Keys and Abertillery, principally — were inadequately represented in the sides of these years; but the young Tanner,

282

in his third match for Wales, was well-protected by the experienced back row of Arthur Rees, Jim Lang and Eddie Long, to provide the fast, accurate service that was so essential to Cliff Jones. While he sometimes had to chop his stride to catch a suddenly wild pass from Powell, he could now accelerate into the long swinging passes that Tanner was serving up. As soon as he latched on to them, he was off like a scooter. Right from the start he began to bamboozle the Scotsmen with his electric-eel running. He manufactured Wales's first try after fifteen minutes when, tackled on the break by Wilson Shaw, he knew Wooller would be at his shoulder for the expected short pass. He was, and it came. Just before the interval, with Wales attacking, one of the Scottish centres threw the ball to no-one in particular and left his winger the thankless task of going for it. Davey went into him like a train, knocked the ball loose and picked it up to crash through Marshall's tackle to score. In the second half, Jones was propelled by the trajectory of another flowing pass from Tanner to sweep from right to left across a hypnotized defence to score himself.

Brought home to an ever-increasing audience through the advent of broadcasting (the Scottish match at Cardiff in 1927 was the first live international commentary from Wales, with Capt. Teddy Wakelam perched in the greyhound judges' box half-way along the roof of the old south stand, guiding his listeners through the maze of 'square four' and 'square five'), the cinema newsreel, and the extensive press coverage which the 1905 tour had first stimulated, the brilliant Welsh back play brought the crowds thronging back to international rugby. The breaking of fixtures with France in 1931 had meant that there was only one home, or one away game, per season, and each was awaited with eager expectancy. Thirteen thousand Welshmen trekked to Murrayfield in 1932; two years later, 15,000, the biggest Welsh invasion ever, travelled by twenty-seven special trains at the excursion rate of £1 4s. 0d. When advance bookings indicated to the L.M.S. that forty-three excursions would be conveying up to 20,000 Welshmen to Edinburgh in 1938, the company thoughtfully, but a trifle excessively, went to extreme lengths to ensure the success of the operation by drafting in Welsh-speaking railwaymen 'who will help through microphones and loudspeakers to guide and direct passengers at Princes Street Station and also be at barriers to act as interpreters when necessary.' Not that rail was the only mode of transport. In 1934 eight colliers from Tylorstown in the Rhondda Fach chartered a special plane, adorned its front with the Prince of Wales feathers, a leek and a daffodil, and took off to see Wales at Murrayfield. Confused by the compass, they ended up watching a soccer match in Portsmouth. Undeterred, the intrepid octet — 'the flying miners' as they became known — headed for Belfast and this time joined 10,000 other Welshmen at Ravenhill.

Home games, after the falling gates of the twenties, once again became sell-outs. The new double-decker stand was opened at Cardiff Arms Park in the 1933-34 season. Costing £20,000, 82 feet high and 120 yards long, it could accommodate 5,242 ticket-holders seated in 23 rows, and provided a total capacity on it, under it and in front of it, for 23,000: a net increase in the capacity of the ground of 10,742 to a total of 56,000. The new stand was 'a wonderfully solid structure built on a bed of reinforced concrete,' the match-programme assured wide-eyed arrivals, mightily impressed by this impressive monument to modern technology and W.R.U. wealth, as contrasted with the stark asbestos-roofed sheds of their own clubs, thrown up in the early years of the century with as little regard for aesthetics and comfort as the works and collieries for whose employees they were built. This new shrine of working-class communion could boast luxurious adornments, for 'provision is made on the ground floor of the stand for the service of refreshments, two counters, each 76 feet long, running the full length of the stand, so that spectators can get refreshment on the ground, *as is done at Twickenham*': that was important. The top-heavy new stand was officially opened before the kick-off of the England game in January 1934. Could those present have foreseen the indignity the cockleshell Welsh pack selected for the occasion was to suffer, they would have left straight afterwards. If the 59,000 who paid record receipts of over £9,000 to squeeze in found that occasion a squash, they were nearly crushed out of existence trying to watch Ireland at the same ground in 1936. Some were; as the Welsh team ran out, a dead man was brought in out of the crowd. But that was scant relief to the 69,999 still breathing, occasionally. Wales was poised to win the championship, Ireland the Triple Crown, and more Irishmen than ever before had crossed to see their side denied it, in the event, by a sole Vivian Jenkins penalty. The gates were due to open at 11.30 a.m., four hours before the advertised time of kick-off, but there were queues outside the entrances from 8 o'clock in the morning. At 1.00 p.m. the Angel Hotel entrance to the ground was closed, since the west terrace seemed full. Supporters then converged on the Quay Street and Westgate Street entrances, where police barriers broke and the crowd surged through. Several people were knocked down, others began climbing an unfinished building in Park Street. The City Fire Brigade, whose station was on the other side of Westgate Street, helped dampen the ardour of the crowd, though according to the *Report on Crowd Invasion* jointly prepared by Walter Rees and the Chief Constable, what really happened was that 'A fireman carrying fire extinguishers was passing and sensing the danger turned an extinguisher on the crowd . . . [which] had the desired effect. The statement that the Fire Brigade turned the hose upon the crowd is utterly untrue'. Whatever the accuracy of that statement — and there were several hundred sodden spectators to challenge it — the report's attendance figure of 49,059 was ludicrously wide of the mark. Far more plausible was the unofficial estimate of 70,000 that included many who, protesting what they considered the lack of cheap accommodation, had rushed the gates and got inside the ground to spill over the railings until they were fifteen deep around the touch-line. Joseph Parry's 'Aberystwyth', with its line 'While the nearer waters roll', was sung with particular feeling that afternoon, especially by those who had been on the receiving end of the fire extinguisher.

Observers in the mid-thirties were struck how 'the old optimism and confidence has returned to Welsh football', an impression they formed not only from the quality of the rugby, but the magnificence of the pre-match singing. The Welsh crowd had sung since the 1890s, when international rugby had first become a mass spectator sport in South Wales, but it was informal and spontaneous, only coincidentally related to what the musicians were playing on the field. The crowd's preference was for popular songs. At St. Helen's in 1921 wartime and music-hall favourites were drowned out by the band playing hymns, but when the crowd took up the minor triplets of 'Tôn-y-botel', the words of the hymn 'Dyma gariad fel y moroedd' swelled to a thrilling crescendo. It was at Cardiff in 1924 that the conductor of the band of the Welsh Guards left his musicians to lead the crowd in 'Cwm Rhondda' and 'Aberystwyth'. It was the first visit by royalty to a rugby international in Wales, and the occasion was embellished by two future monarchs for the price of one, for the Prince of Wales (later Edward VIII) was accompanied by his brother (later George VI) as well as Ramsay MacDonald, the first Labour prime minister and former M.P. for Aberavon, and J. H. Thomas, part-time Welshman and full-time Colonial Secretary. Much was made of 'distinguished visitors giving their patronage at difficult times', and 'the sporting Prince' visited the Arms Park again in 1927 where he 'received a wonderful welcome from his people'. Witnessing the pedestrian performance of the Welsh team on both occasions, as well as encountering some of the rum characters adorning the W.R.U. in those days, the Prince left Wales thinking that something must be done. But he could not fail to have been moved, in 1924 especially, by the sound of the ascending bass line of 'Cwm Rhondda', composed by John Hughes, a colliery clerk from Llantwit Fardre, in the climactic year of 1905, rising majestically from thousands of Welsh throats to hold wayfarers spellbound in the streets and eddy outwards to the suburbs of the city. The ritual of pre-match community hymn-singing was sealed for the next fifty years. 'If their men could play football as well as their supporters sing, the international tourney would be a farce', wrote 'Astral' of the *Daily News* in 1926. At Swansea, eisteddfodic champions like the Cwmavon, Ystalyfera and Gwaun-cae-Gurwen silver bands supplied the music. In Cardiff, the Welsh Guards alternated with the St. Alban's Band, which had become a feature of club games at the Arms Park since 1919, and become 'an organization which has a great reputation locally' by the time it made its first international appearance against France in 1929. It was a reputation that grew both with the years and the accumulated experience of blending the residual religiosity of the 50,000 non-aligned nonconformists it sought to synchronize into a wall of sound, so that in 1958 the W.R.U. officially appointed the St. Alban's musicians to play at international matches. 'Those unhappy people who have never heard the Welsh mass of anything from 30 to 50,000 singing "Land of My Fathers" and "God Save the King" have heard very little music', wrote E. H. D. Sewell in 1931. 'There is no community singing elsewhere to equal it. Other sounds at our chief temples of music are by comparison just cheeps. To hear "Land of My Fathers" resound in one mighty diapason from thousands of throats is an unforgettable experience'. Some Welshmen wished it were less so, on the grounds that the singing of hymns at football matches was blasphemous. To the quarryman-collier-poet Huw Menai in 1934, 'Boxing and football . . . are but large scale commercial impositions from without. Is not the singing of Welsh hymns at international football matches anything other than a sop to conscience; not grace before meat but a kind of penance before leather?' It was the voice of a lost cause, as the Revival had been a lost battle. The chapels, built in sufficient numbers to accommodate a multiplying population but now shoved towards bankruptcy as only a poorer, smaller and increasingly secular people remained, were emptying. For a while yet, however, their language and imagery retained a hold on their errant flocks. As 'Cwm Rhondda', 'Aberystwyth', 'Crimond', 'Penlan', 'Calon Lân' and 'Diadem' reverberated around the cavernous roof of the towering new two-deck stand, the largest massed male choir in the history of sport, or music, now found perfect acoustic conditions for lofting its spontaneous and instinctive harmonies.

That choir never sang with greater fervour, nor were those acoustics more strenuously tested, than on the sunny, cold afternoon of 21 December 1935. No match had aroused such interest for exactly thirty years. Everywhere else matches were abandoned because of the severe overnight frost. It had even penetrated the seven tons of straw laid on the Arms Park beforehand as a precaution, but now lying deep and crisp and uneven around the touch-line. Frozen spots still remained in some places on the field. One was in the in-goal area at the river end, and Vivian Jenkins's feet slid from under him as he was in the act of fielding Gilbert's long kick-off into the breeze, the sun, and history.

Jenkins's coolness did not desert him; he recovered and touched-down under the very noses of the descending horde of black shirts. For the composure he showed, he might have been playing Neath in a club game; but these black shirts were not from the Gnoll. They belonged to Jack Manchester's Third All Blacks. Since Gallaher's men had first disembarked thirty years before, the New Zealand national team had played eighty-five games throughout the length and breadth of the British Isles, and lost only two of them. One had been in December 1905; the other was in the fifth match of this present tour in September 1935, when Swansea had beaten them 11 - 3. The All Whites were no ordinary side that day. Inspired by the volcanic force of Claude Davey at centre and a pack of furious, foraging forwards led by Eddie Long, Tanner, the Gowerton schoolboy, and W.T.H. Davies, his nineteen-year-old-cousin, tormented and tantalized the All Black bulls to devastating effect. Now, at Cardiff, in the scarlet jersey of their country were two of that All White front row, Harry Payne at prop and the former secondary school cap, Don Tarr, hooker. The third new cap at forward was Eddie Watkins, a police cadet fresh from Caerphilly County School and a mere nineteen years of age. The presence of Glyn Prosser, a Resolven blacksmith, Newport's Tom Rees and Trevor Williams of Cross Keys, upholding the name of the tough Monmouthshire valley forwards of the thirties, ensured that the pack would not lack for hardness. Since the selectors preferred to ignore the existence of Watcyn Thomas, a Napoleon on his Lancashire Elba, they looked to the rangy twenty-six-year-old tinplate worker Jim Lang (6foot 3inches, 14stone 6lb.), winning the eighth of 12 caps 1931-37, to win the line-out ball, aided by the twenty-two-year-old Llandovery Light Blue, Arthur Rees

287

(6foot 2inches, 13stone 7lb.) as pack-leader and vice-captain. The captaincy was naturally Claude Davey's. His demoniac display for Swansea against the New Zealanders, when he had scored two tries, was proof that the occasionally wayward Davey was, for the moment, catching everything that was thrown at him. The centre *would* hold. Claude's tornado tackling of his opposite number Caughey at St. Helen's had provided further confirmation that this Garnant electrical engineer was fully acquainted with the formula that force equals mass times velocity squared. The 'c' in $E = mc^2$ stood for Claude. This was the eighteenth of the twenty-three caps he would win in an international career extending from 1930 to 1938. He was now twenty-seven, and could concentrate every cubic centimetre of his 5foot 10inches and 12stone 8lb. into the surging acceleration with which he smashed into the man he was tackling. Davey's presence was particularly reassuring to the schoolboy selected at scrum-half. Haydn Tanner, a month short of his nineteenth birthday, was already the master of the art of scooping the ball from the base of the scrum and swinging it out in one flowing action. 'The pass is not a good one', Tanner would write in his own coaching manual, *Rugby Football* (1949), 'if it is aimed at the outside half . . . I very often don't see the outside half until the ball has actually been thrown . . . I simply catch a glimpse of him moving into position'. Moving into position this December day, stretching for that fast and fluent service was Cliff Jones. There had been much pre-match discussion as to who should partner the inevitable Tanner at half-back. In Swansea there was little doubt that it should be his cousin, W. T. H. Davies, who had earlier outplayed Jones for Swansea against Cambridge University. It was argued in other quarters that Jones would have to be included, but at second five-eighths, or even on the wing. But there was no room for Jones in the centre, for the Welsh tactic would be to use her midfield men to tackle offensively for the first half-hour, perhaps to jolt the ball free, certainly to force the New Zealanders into hurried transfers and dissuade them from their noted reverse passes. Yet Jones's scorching speed, international experience, familiarity with Davey's play, and proven match-winning skills were quite indispensable. He would have to go in, at outside-half; Davies would have to wait.

The component parts of the new half-back mechanism met at Swansea a week before the match, where under the colonnade of the St. Helen's stand, their mutual respect took a tangible, even edible form. From Penclawdd, Tanner brought a bag of cockles; from behind his back, but actually from Porth, Jones produced a hand of bananas. Then, and in subsequent practice sessions, they worked on familiarizing themselves with each other's play. As Jones glided into Tanner's pass he could only wonder at the purring, apparently effortless grace of it; it was like sitting in his father's Rolls-Royce. What he did with that service would be his affair; and Wooller's. The rangy Rydal racehorse was selected on the left wing, with Rees-Jones on the other. Where a few seasons back the shunting of Wooller to the flank would have looked like the result of a random revolution of the selectors' roulette, this time it was a more rational decision. The selectors, in consultation with Davey, had grounded their attacking strategy on a constructive tactical basis. Wooller had a role to play in that strategy, but for the first half-hour he chafed impatiently on the wing, often forgetting, until he was reminded, that it was his task to throw in.

An unreal silence had momentarily fallen on the ground when referee Gadney whistled for the kick-off, but as Gilbert thumped the ball down to the Welsh line, a full-throated roar went up. Early on Wales played it tight, seeking not possession but psychological superiority through hard tackling from Davey and Idwal Rees. 'We were mortally afraid of a snap try', wrote Wooller later of the early stages, 'everything about our visitors had emphasized their unusual ability to seize on every little mistake and turn it into points'. The methodical pre-match planning paid off early. Contingencies, as they arose, were met. Davey subjected his opposite number, Oliver, to a series of tigerish tackles; only once did Oliver slip him, and then a defensive ploy perfected by Wales in her championship-winning games of 1935 plugged the gap. The ploy assumed that Jenkins at full-back would always go for the outside man, so that if an attacking player cut in, there would be corner-flagging backs there to stop him. When Oliver did once evade the unrequited affections of Davey's Roland, he had Hart outside him with only Jenkins to beat. But Rees was rapidly overhauling Oliver, who was forced to feed Hart. Jenkins now had an extra yard of distance in which to build up speed before he launched himself in a hurtling, horizontal tackle: a few yards short of the corner-flag, Hart was engulfed by a flying landslide. The All Blacks maintained their territorial pressure. Pack-leader Arthur Rees strove to settle an eight drawn from seven clubs. This untried vanguard would hold its own in the line-out, though outplayed in the set scrums. It managed to heel the ball only eight times during the game; of these, four were quick and clean; from those Wales would score three tries. Although the New Zealanders were winning the scrums, their backs preferred to kick rather than encounter

Rees and Davey, who once knocked Mitchell cold in one fearsome tackle. Davey then interrupted a passing bout and steered the ball into the 25 before being stopped; immediately afterwards the Welsh forwards dribbled up to the line and Glyn Prosser fell on it to claim a try. The referee ordered a scrum; Tarr hooked, Tanner sent Jones sidestepping away, beating man after man till pulled down a yard short. Then Sadler sliced through and Mahoney was buried by an avalanche of Welshmen near the line. The thrust and counter-thrust continued, except that by half-time New Zealand had gone three points up from a fine blind-side break by Griffiths who sent Nelson Ball racing in for an unconverted try.

By half-time, too, Claude Davey was satisfied that the containment policy of the first half-hour had worked. A. M. Rees's amazing telescopic reach and Jim Lang's Himalayan height were beginning to tell in the line-out, even if the scrums were lost: three points was a cheap lesson in welding the forwards from eight units into one. The backs now wanted the ball themselves. Ten minutes before the half, Wooller had been brought into the centre. Within six minutes of the resumption Wales had scored 10 points. After sixty seconds Jones jerked and jinked through four or five defenders before short-punting ahead. Davey came thundering through like an enraged bison to gather on the 25 and charge in at the posts. Jenkins converted. 5 - 3. A minute later, Tanner fed Jones from a scrum ten yards inside the Welsh half. Jones went for his favourite gap between the opposing fly-half and centre, and as he inserted himself into it, slipped a fast transfer to Wooller, striding like a stag down the centre. This was the Wooller that Howard Marshall had seen at Cambridge, 'pounding his way through the opposition like the sacrificial car of Juggernaut'. He had a long way to go, but few legs were longer than Wooller's. To speed the transit of the ball, he hoisted a mighty sky-scraping kick, and the backs streamed after it. Wooller, faster than them all, beat a slow-turning Gilbert, but was in turn beaten by the ball's capricious bounce, only for it to pitch easily into Rees-Jones's grateful embrace, as he came chasing up to veer in to the posts. Jenkins made his second conversion. 10 - 3. The crowd excited themselves into near-delirium; they were now on their feet roaring with ecstacy every time the Welsh backs got the ball. Tanner, abetted by Rees and Prosser, spoiled Sadler continually; Jones probed and twisted; Wooller strode; Rees-Jones was brought down just short of the line. The New Zealanders came back down the left. Again Jones wriggled and punted for touch. But Gilbert got to it, moved infield and from fully forty yards dropped a low, gulping goal. 10 - 7. This inspired the All Blacks to an all-out onslaught. Gilbert missed a penalty; Jenkins minored just ahead of Hart; Gilbert fired off another mortar of a drop-kick. This time the mechanism misfired, and the ball skidded off his boot to bounce on the Welsh 25. Davey and Rees-Jones were at hand; there was no danger if either took it. Neither did; until it was too late. Davey shovelled a hurried pass to Rees-Jones who dropped it, Ball hacked it on, regathered and raced over close in. Gilbert kicked the goal. Score: 10 - 12 to New Zealand. But just as the Welsh pack set about responding to Arthur Rees's galvanizing calls to wrest back the initiative, a loose scrum broke up to reveal Don Tarr, the Welsh hooker, prostrate. Referee Gadney called for a stretcher, and gingerly Tarr was lifted face-downwards onto it. This action saved his life, for he had broken his neck, and any attempt to sit him up would have killed him. The sombre procession withdrew, and a dank mist descended on the ground, chilling the bones and numbing the minds of the hushed and despondent multitude. Sullenly they cursed the gods for their malevolence.

The last four minutes defied even Greek mythology; no Homer, no Aeschylus could have scripted them. The seven-man Welsh pack, vilified throughout the twenties for their inadequacies, heeled from the scrum. Tanner scooped and swung that immaculate pass. Jones, going right, spurted into it and towards that crevice between the two five-eighths. He moved away outside his opposite number just sufficiently to draw the inside-centre into his gravitational field. At precisely the splittest of atomic seconds, Jones gave to Wooller. The centre moved into gear, then momentarily checked as he saw Davey coming towards him at a tangent. It was a favourite ploy from their days at Sale. Wooller sold, and as Davey thundered past, pulling Oliver with him, he swung out into the open paddock and lengthened his stride. The crowd roared. Like Prometheus bursting his bonds, Wooller surged out of the Welsh half, ahead of the field, and alone. On he galloped as Gilbert waited for him; again he kicked, though this time he chipped it, barely twenty feet over the full-back's head; again its treacherous bounce eluded him, and once more there was the faithful Rees-Jones to gather and score. The kick failed. 13 - 12. Idwal Rees now seemed to be playing New Zealand on his own. In the last three minutes Gilbert shelled the Welsh line with an awesome aerial bombardment, but each time there was Rees, all sinew and skill to the end, coolly making his angle and intersecting the line of touch with scholarly precision, even as Mr Gadney ended the game. 'There were astounding scenes as the final whistle sounded', cabled the *Press Association* to New

Zealand. 'The crowd rose and cheered tumultuously for many minutes and then sang the Welsh anthem 'Land of My Fathers'. Thousands rushed the field and surrounded and congratulated the Welsh players, who were mobbed and kissed by women. Davey was carried off shoulder high . . . Cardiff is celebrating the victory, crowds roaming the streets and singing'.

Arguments soon raged. Some Welshmen claimed that Wooller had been pushed off the ball by Gilbert when chasing his first punt ahead. Some New Zealanders thought there was an element of luck in all the Welsh tries, that Davey was the fortunate beneficiary of a rebound from the post when he scored the first Welsh try, that he had obstructed Oliver in the build-up to the third. So they said. E. N. Greatorex, covering the tour for the Christchurch *Press*, thought such points irrelevant:

> Even had Wales not got those tries and been beaten, they would still have been the better players. In attack and defence, the All Blacks were outclassed by Tanner, Cliff Jones, Davey, Wooller, Idwal Rees and Rees-Jones . . . Individually and collectively, the Welsh backs did cleverer things than the New Zealanders and had they won as much of the ball as did the tourists, they might have scored two or three more tries. In the second half, the Welsh backs were operating so smoothly and with such understanding of each other's methods that they brought the thousands of spectators to their feet practically every time they got moving. The New Zealand backs did not break down, nor were they really disorganized; it simply amounted to this — they were not good enough . . . Welsh Rugby owes the All Blacks a debt of gratitude in proving the knowledge that there is nothing wrong with the game in this country. It was a privilege to be present and the memory of it will last while life remains.

'Old Stager's' comments showed once again how rugby could be invested with a significance beyond the game itself. 'Wales is proud of this victory: she is particularly proud of the fact that Welsh peers and Welsh labourers — with all the intervening stratas of society — were united in acclaiming and cheering the Welsh team. It was . . . a victory for Wales in a sense that probably is impossible in any other sphere'.

SHADOW ACROSS THE SUN

T HE year 1935 marked the mid-point of the Hungry Thirties whose cramping pains were to be felt awhile yet, but it also caught echoes of a happier era for Welsh rugby and its society. The end of the year had seen the beginning of the end of the travails that had affected the South Wales miners since 1926. Their organization was still the dominant social and political body in Wales. The start of the year had seen an unprecedented series of peaceful marches, weekend after weekend, by all sections of stricken South Wales in protest against the government's over-rigid Means Test plans. Faced with a communal appeal of this order and magnitude, the government withdrew. What was left to salvage from the wreckage was being saved and re-fashioned to suit new circumstances. Groping in the dark was now, at last, replaced by more purposeful action. Appropriately enough, the still officially-titled Welsh Football Union had seen the new year in by formally altering its by-laws to accord with popular usage, so that 'the name of the Union shall be "The Welsh Rugby Union".' Horace Lyne, who had been there all the time the W.F.U. was changing into the W.R.U., had been Life President, to general acclaim, since 1927. He was to stay at the helm of the newly christened body as it organized rugby in Wales out of the thirties, through the Second World War, and into the austere forties.

While the W.R.U. rediscovered its purpose, mere existence continued to be a problem of many of its constituent clubs. In 1936 a clutch of Welshmen, bewilderingly adrift in Didcot, requested W.R.U. aid for their all-Welsh rugby team. The Union was finding it difficult to sustain those clubs left in Wales, many of which were closing as abruptly as the pits and steelworks which had once spawned them. Abercynon disbanded in 1934;

in the mid-thirties, rugby ceased at Abercarn in the east and Cwmtwrch in the west; Taibach was forced to close in 1937. That year forced closure, too, upon the Nelson club, in the wake of the Taff Merthyr and Nine-Mile Point collieries disputes which saw the imprisonment of several club stalwarts. Rugby League re-activated its campaign in South Wales, and a number of professional internationals were played in Pontypridd and Llanelli in the late thirties. In November 1936, the Welsh XIII which beat England 3 - 2 at Taff Vale Park included talents as rare as those of Jim Sullivan, Gus Risman and Alan Edwards, as well as recent international acquisitions from the union game like Emlyn Watkins, D. R. Prosser and Norman Fender. In April 1938, a crowd of 22,000 watched a Wales XIII beat France 18 - 2 at Stebonheath. The number and quality of Welsh players in the Rugby League ensured that Wales won the R.L. Championship for three successive seasons, 1936-7-8: in the 1939 R.L. Cup Final between Salford and Halifax, half the players on the field were Welsh.

All the same, there still remained a cornucopia of talent in amateur rugby in Wales. Wilfred Wooller and Cliff Jones were in themselves sizeable drawing-cards. They came up trumps at Rodney Parade, as the historian of Newport R.F.C., Jack Davis, has recorded: 'Newport's rugby had become dull and support was dwindling, but the box-office allure of Jones and Wooller boosted Newport's finances just when this was necessary. Their visit to Newport [in 1936] drew a crowd of 13,000, the biggest for many years, and right up to the war Newport had reason to be thankful for the visits of these two personalities'. Exchanging the blue and black for the scarlet jersey of Wales, they drew the biggest crowd since 1921 to St. Helen's in 1936, as well as the massive influx for the championship match with Ireland at Cardiff. It was the last year Wales would win it outright till 1950. Vivian Jenkins's title-clinching penalty goal was Wales's only score in the two home internationals of that season: for the rest of the decade the close scores which would be such a feature of the post-war period (the 14 - 8 victory of England in 1938 interrupted a catalogue of subsistence scoring against the old enemy from 1933 of 7 - 3, 0 - 9, 3 - 3, 0 - 0, 3 - 4, 0 - 3, and it was the only time Wales scored more than 13 points against anybody since 1931) reflected the increasing sophistication of defensive play and the prevalence of tight marking.

One man whose game could confound the tightest marking was Cliff Jones's rival for the fly-half position, W. T. H. Davies. Willie Davies carved his openings with a body-swerve and gliding motion, rather than the stabbing side-step. The key to his deception was change of pace, so that his legs seemed to be going in a different direction from his body. He was also very fast: he once chased and overhauled Obolensky in a match for Swansea against the Barbarians. He played with Haydn Tanner for Gowerton County School, Swansea, and Swansea University, but then went to Carnegie College in Yorkshire where he saw the professional game at its best, and became the focus of northern interest. When, by the summer of 1939, the Swansea Corporation had failed to find him a teaching post in the area, he accepted a position at Bradford G.S., and in August, at twenty-three years of age, joined Bradford Northern R.L. club for a record sum approaching £1,000. He won the first of his six caps for Wales in the centre, with Jones at fly-half, against Ireland in 1936. After a nervous start, when he was glad of the protection offered by his co-centre, Wooller, he made it plain that he was too good to be left out of the national XV: the highlight of the afternoon came in the last few minutes when Davies broke out of his own 25 to link up with Jones and they both came down the field inter-passing at speed, splitting the defence wide open. When Jones broke his collar-bone in a club game at Swansea in November 1936, Davies was able to make the fly-half berth his own for the ensuing international season. But he was not able to redeem a glum season of three defeats.

Momentarily it seemed as if the selectors were slipping back into old habits: there were new caps at forward, a different full-back and a different captain for each game. Against Scotland, 'Bunner' Travers , who inherited the hooking skills of his famous father, won the first of a dozen caps which would span the next twelve years, but for the first time since the twenties, the forwards were let down by the men behind. Davies and Tanner combined like sausage and mash, but several of the other backs were below par that year, and only Idwal Rees, playing with customary aplomb, lived up to his reputation. One was being made on the wing, though, where the elusive running and staunch tackling of Llanelli's W. H. Clement caught the eye. At 11stone and 5foot 10inches, Clement had speed and a side-step; an unselfish wing, he could score tries himself and make them for others, as he showed at Twickenham in 1937 when Tanner and Davey worked him clear to go tearing down the touch-line before drawing the defence and passing inside for Wooller to score; and as he showed the following year against England, when he delicately chipped through to make a try for Idwal Rees. His sixth consecutive cap against Ireland in 1938, which he celebrated with a clever individual try, would prove to be his last, for a knee injury prematurely terminated his international career, though not before his consistent performances in 1938 — that established him as the best defensive wing of the decade — clinched his selection with eight other Welshmen for the Lions tour to South Africa. That was the culmination of his career in international rugby in a playing sense only, for in 1956 he would succeed Eric Evans to become, after Walter Rees, the longest-serving Secretary of the W.R.U.

It was the misfortune of Clement, and the entire Lions party of 1938, that some of Britain's best players were unable to make the tour: Wilson Shaw and Dick of Scotland, England's Bert Toft, Wooller and Cliff Jones of Wales. Jones was concentrating on his legal studies but he had — in intention at least — only temporarily retired from rugby at the end of the 1937-38 season. As it turned out, in 1938 he had played his last game for Wales, captaining his country in all three matches. The aggressive forward spoiling which was becoming the dominant feature of play anticipated post-war developments: it was reflected in the physical battering that forced the wiry and durable Cliff Jones to consider the prospect, and ultimately the reality, of retirement at the age of twenty-four: reflected, too, in the fact that four of Wales's six tries in 1938 were scored by wing-forwards, three of them by the bustling Alan McCarley of Neath. He scored on his début, in Wales's 14 - 8 defeat of England, when Jones shot around the field like a meteorite; he scored twice in the next game, against Scotland. In circumstances reminiscent of the match at Inverleith in 1909, when Jack Bancroft was penalized for lying on the ball, concussed from a kick on the head, at Murrayfield in 1938 Wales were penalized near their own posts, and even nearer the end of the match. With a pack depleted by the departure of Swansea's Eddie Morgan after fifteen minutes, Wales was tenaciously hanging on to a 6 - 5 lead when a loose scrum was blown up to reveal the ball sandwiched betweeen an unconscious Tanner on the ground, and a Welsh forward on top, shouting dazedly at his colleagues to look at the aeroplanes. Wales were harshly penalized for not releasing the ball, and whereas Scotland had failed to profit from the situation in 1909, in 1938 they did. The 8 - 6 defeat cost Wales the Triple Crown, and referee Gadney, the hero of December 1935, was not spoken to by any of the Welsh players afterwards, nor did he ever officiate at another Welsh game.

With the European situation deteriorating, Wales, in 1939 under Wooller's captaincy, again came within an ace of her first Triple Crown since 1911. Vivian Jenkins declared his retirement after the England game, at twenty-seven years of age and after fourteen caps, and W. T. H. Davies had his finest game for Wales in Belfast, scoring all the points in a 7 - 0 victory which foiled yet again an Irish bid for the Triple Crown. The thirties ended, as the twenties had begun, with Wales sharing a triple tie of the championship; with an exodus of players to the Rugby League; and in a cloud of controversy over international qualifications. The star of the Scottish match of 1939 was Mickey Davies, a Welsh South African who had never been to Wales until he assembled with the team on the eve of the match. Law of Newport had had an Irish trial and, rejected, was chosen by Wales against Ireland. Les Manfield, born in Mountain Ash and a former captain of the Welsh S.S., raised a hornet's nest when he played in an English trial in December 1938, then accepted an invitation to the second Welsh trial, and was rewarded by caps for Wales against Scotland and Ireland in 1939. Such controversies as these selections sparked off seemed academic by September 1939, but Manfield, a fast and intelligent forward constantly to be found in support of his backs, as well as Travers, Tanner and full-back Howard Davies, were the only players of the 1930s who would reappear in post-war international rugby. There is no doubt that Willie Davies would have done, too, but his defection to Bradford in August, in the steps of Idwal Davies to Leeds, Arthur Bassett to Halifax, Eddie Watkins to Wigan and Sid Williams to Salford, all capped players who had gone earlier in 1939, brought the inter-war period almost full circle. They would not all have such golden careers in the League as Willie Davies, who went on to win the Lance Todd Trophy in 1947 and become the first modern 'star' to enjoy as much fame in the professional code as he had as an amateur International, but the continued seepage of players to the North of England was a reminder that the economic condition of South Wales had little improved during the decade.

Rugby Union hardly exercised an exclusive influence on the sporting public of South Wales in the late thirties, for this was a great era in the history of Welsh soccer. The signing of Merthyr's Bryn Jones by Arsenal in 1938 for a record fee of £14,000 was emblematic of the hold that association, more than rugby, held on the eastern valleys of Glamorgan at this time. Apart from the crowd-pulling allure of certain 'star' players, rugby lost the momentum which the revitalized back play of 1931-36 had generated. International occasions attracted a full house, but club rugby languished. The 18,000 Welshmen who went to Murrayfield in 1938 were more than double the aggregate of spectators who watched first-class rugby on an average Saturday. On 13 December 1937, the soccer and rugby clubs of Newport, Cardiff and Swansea all played at home. The rugby games attracted 7,000; the soccer, 44,000. Entertainment-starved crowds would throng back after 1945 to rugby, as they would to soccer, but the quality of football provided by super-fit servicemen was of a higher order than the drab and frequently over-vigorous matches that predominated in club rugby in the second half of the pre-war decade. The breaking off of fixtures, and sending off of players, became increasingly the order of the day, and in a club match at Abertillery in April 1937 the referee was compelled to send even the linesman off. With club games becoming unimaginative and unattractive, and with rival professional codes attracting the crowds away from rugby union, fitful attempts were made to restore creativity to the game. Indeed, at Eric Evans's instigation, a sub-committee was established in May 1938, 'to discover and consider fully the true causes of the decline in the interest taken in Welsh rugby and . . . the serious financial state of the Welsh clubs'. Smaller clubs, it was considered, should have the benefit of keeping their better players through the agency of tighter transfer rules; referees were urged to make better application of the laws, whilst in 1938-9, some Welsh clubs made 'gentlemen's agreements' to keep the wing-forwards down in the scrum until the ball was clear. Another response was the W.R.U.'s decision finally to lift its ban on seven-a-side football. Though the Middlesex 'Sevens' had become an established part of the English programme since their inception in 1926, throughout the thirties the Welsh Union had refused clubs like Swansea and Cardiff permission to organize their own tournaments or accept invitations to participate at Twickenham. When the Union eventually allowed Glamorgan Wanderers R.F.C. to hold a seven-a-side competition in April 1939 (the profits to be donated to stipulated charities) and Cardiff to accept a third invitation to play in the Middlesex Sevens (which they promptly won), it appeared to be giving its blessing to a game new to Wales. In fact, though played in the Scottish Border country since the early 1880s, it had been pioneered in West Wales in the first decade of the century by the members of one family, the seven Williams brothers of Haverfordwest. In 1904 they had issued a challenge which was taken up by the seven Randall brothers of Llanelli, and their match was played at Carmarthen in front of a large crowd with a sidestake of £100. It remains an open question whether, had the Union known of this, its acceptance of the game would have been any less delayed or grudging.

If senior rugby was too often colourless, its schoolboy counterpart was far from anaemic. Its red corpuscles promised well for the future. The fly-half for North Wales in the North v. South schools' final trial late in 1938 was a Taff's Well fifteen-year-old, B. L. Williams of Rydal. The captain of the Welsh S.S. in January 1939 was J. Matthews of Bridgend C.S., and J. R. G. Stephens (Llandovery) was in the pack. Matthews so impressed that he was required to be in attendance as a reserve for the final Welsh trial, where he was given the chance to play against, and keep a firm grip, on Wooller. 'No harm will be done by seeing more of Matthews', wrote 'Old Stager' afterwards. No harm indeed, except to opposing centres who would in due course encounter Dr Jack's thirteen and a half stone at close quarters, and mistake them for a runaway brick wall.

The 1939-40 season began on Friday, 1 September. Cliff Jones revised his previous decision to retire, but in Cardiff's first game of the season that day, the traditional match against a District XV, he dislocated his elbow. The whole of Europe was about to be dislocated. The season ended on 3 September with the declaration of war, and football felt the immediate impact of the Emergency Act prohibiting the gathering of crowds in public places for entertainment or sport. On 5 September the W.R.U. decided 'That this Union, together with its subsidiary organizations and affiliated clubs, suspend their activities during the period of war or until further notice'.

There were several contrasts between the First and Second World Wars. One was in the human losses suffered. In the First, Britain lost perhaps three-quarters of a million people; less than a quarter of a million in the Second. There had been eleven Welsh rugby Internationals among the dead of the First War; of the Second, two: Major John R. Evans of the Welsh Guards, 1 cap 1934, killed in the Middle East in February 1943, aged twenty-nine, and Captain Maurice Turnbull of the South Wales Borderers, 2 caps 1933, killed in Normandy in August 1944, aged thirty-eight. There was a contrast in attitudes at home, too. In 1914-18 the continuation of organized leisure had been condemned as contradictory to the war effort, and, where possible, resisted. In 1939-45 a new generation recognized the value of providing facilities for entertainment, to encourage morale and complement the nation's military and industrial performance. The change in attitude was no more clearly seen than in sport. Now, government and local authorities made greater efforts to encourage football. It would later be shown statistically that in wartime the British people spent an increasing proportion of their income on leisure, notably beer, the cinema, and sport. As the war advanced, and the danger of aerial attack receded, the limits on the size of crowds became more flexible. Football soon adapted itself to the peculiar conditions, and rugby and soccer matches proved useful means of raising money for wartime charities like the Red Cross and St. John's, for which £3,000,000 had been raised by 1945.

For six years the W.R.U. ceased to exercise any real control over the game. The war not only brought a cessation of income from international football, it also added to the Union's debts when, in 1941, a German land-mine destroyed the Arms Park's north stand and west terrace. Nevertheless Wales, as a neutral zone under the evacuation scheme, became one of the most important centres for wartime football, and rugby, like soccer, continued on a friendly basis. In some places it was impossible. Aberavon's Talbot Athletic Ground, which in tune with the committee's injunction to all players 'to rally to Lord Kitchener's Call', had in the First World War been used as allotments, was in 1939-40 converted into a barrage balloon site. In other areas, some clubs were kept reasonably intact because their nucleus was engaged in reserved occupations. Newport was one such club, where the efforts of men like Alf Panting and W. A. Everson kept rugby going for much of the period. Newbridge was another. Because most of the team were miners in the North Celynen colliery, Newbridge were able to field a strong side during the war years. From this platform the club would advance confidently into the post-war period, attain recognized first-class status, become runners-up to a great Cardiff side in the unofficial Welsh championship in 1947-8, and provide a notable line of international forwards for the next two decades, including a quarter of the Triple Crown pack of 1950. Cardiff's own post-war greatness similarly stemmed from the fact that its foundations had been laid during the war period, by players occupied in mining and medicine.

Since the W.R.U. had effectively ceased to function, it could not maintain its ban on rugby league professionals playing with amateurs, or prevent bodies or individuals organizing any games they wished. As a club, Swansea went out of existence in 1940 when it surrendered its lease to the Swansea Corporation, but a group headed by C. B. Jones, T. C. Prosser (President of the W.R.U. 1966-67) and Reg. Bancroft (son of W.J.), aided by other hardworking individuals, organized the Swansea and West Wales Rugby War Charities Effort and arranged a series of wartime internationals between 1941-2 and 1944-5. These raised nearly £15,000, and games such as South Wales v. R.A.F., v. A.A. Command, v. British Army, v. N.Z.R.A.F., and Welsh Services v. English Services, offered a unique opportunity for amateurs and professionals to play alongside each other. The programme for one such match noted, 'It must stagger our enemies to think that while Britain is engaged in the most momentous struggle of its existence, in the sterner game of war, the sporting community in its midst find time and facilities for participation in its favourite games and pastimes . . . The constitution of the British Army XV that met the French Army [in February 1940] revealed the fact that leading rugby "stars" have joined that great International side which is determined to administer utter defeat to the "Barbarians of Central Europe", and perhaps this very fact in itself may induce many rugby patrons on the field today to follow their rugby idols into khaki, in which outfit more undying glory can be won than in an International jersey'. Those rugby patrons could not fail to marvel at the combined skills of Lieut. H. Tanner, Lieut. A. J. H. Risman, F/O Bleddyn Williams, Sgt. Alan Edwards, Sgt. W. T. H. Davies, F/O Idwal Davies, Guardsman R. F. Trott, and Gunner E. Coleman, and 5,000 Welshmen travelled to Gloucester in April 1945 to see the last of the Services internationals when Wales beat England 24 - 9, and the 25,000 crowd was treated to a sumptuous feast of sizzling interplay, intricate scissors movements and quick-fire reverse passes, all executed at top speed. A bitter-sweet reminder of the talent drained from Wales in the thirties, it also raised high hopes that the union game was moving away from the dreary stalemates of the immediate pre-war years into a new age of attacking, running rugby.

Club games were resumed in September 1945. There was a fair amount of criticism of the W.R.U., whose leading figures were now in the veteran stage, that it had gone into mothballs for the war and was slow coming out of it. But it readily welcomed the ideas of a series of 'Victory' internationals in 1945-6, which would recapture the flavour of the international tourney and, more importantly, by cramming in as many fixtures as possible make up for revenue lost to the home unions by the war. No caps were awarded, but the games between the home countries, France, and the Second N.Z. Expeditionary Force, the 'Kiwis', indicated that the new age was coming up fast. Retrospectively, it would be seen how these unofficial 'Victory' matches contained several pointers to the future: the drop-kicking of 'Nim'.Hall of England against Wales in January 1946, and the emergence of Rees Stephens as the outstanding forward in the same game; the neat combination of Tanner and Newport's Bob Evans at Twickenham in February, when there were eight Cardiff players in the side; the balanced running of Glyn Davies and the stiletto side-step of Bleddyn Williams; the growing challenge of France, who beat Wales 12 - 0 at Colombes. But it was the Kiwis who drew the crowds, and the superlatives. Captained by the compact, pocket-sized Charles Saxton, whose dictum it was that 'the object of rugby is for fourteen men to give the fifteenth a start of half a yard', the Kiwis played zestful, quick-moving rugby, which they were well-equipped to do with a wealth of attacking talent behind the scrum — Johnny Smith, Wally Argus and Jim Sherratt — who were used to best advantage through fast passing, even faster backing up, and a determination to retain possession rather than kick it to the opposition. They beat Wales 11 - 3 at Cardiff in January 1946, and in only one of their thirty-three games in Britain and France did they fail to score, against a Monmouthshire side, led by Bob Evans, who beat them 15 - 0 at Pontypool. They were long remembered as the most attractive of touring sides to visit Wales, and it was no accident that their reputation was matched only by the 1967 All Blacks, who were managed by Saxton and coached by Fred Allen, a member of Saxton's 1946 Kiwis.

The Welsh defeat in Paris was significant not merely for the 12 -0 margin, but also because France was now welcomed back to the international field after a break of fifteen years. The International Board had broken off games with the French in 1931: the Swansea match of February that year was France's last game with Wales in the five nations tourney till 1946-7. Since the 1920s, she had begun closing the leeway which the other countries had over her through the earlier development of organized sports in British society. In 1920 France beat Ireland in Dublin, in 1921 Scotland at Inverleith; in 1927 England, and the following year Wales, 8 - 3, in Paris. By then, however, the game in France was sinking into anarchy, riven by dispute and tainted with professionalism. These internal dissensions manifested themselves on the field of play in a lack of discipline and an excess of violence. For the previous twenty years, Scotland and Ireland had regularly complained about French rough play, and by 1930 Wales too began to feel uneasy. Her match at Colombes that year was one of the roughest ever, in front of the largest crowd to watch a rugby game in France. Boon needed all his speed to avoid the clutches of his opposite number who went on to strangle an opponent the following Christmas; Hubert Day, the pre-stressed Newport front-row forward had his lip practically severed from his mouth; and, as time ran out, referee Hellewell waited for play to reach the exit tunnel before blowing his whistle and swiftly disappearing. Hostilities continued into the evening, and the F.F.R. felt compelled to suspend flank-forward Bioussa of Toulouse. This had an apparently anaesthetic effect on the French the following year when they tamely submitted to their heaviest defeat by Wales since 1910. The illness of nearly every member of the French team had not helped, but the real cause was the divided state of their domestic game, where two rival unions were in conflict. Two days after the Swansea match, the I.B. announced that the home countries were breaking off relations with France 'owing to the unsatisfactory conditions of the game of Rugby Football in France . . . until . . . the control and conduct of the game has been placed on a satisfactory basis in all essentials'. The I.B. sought assurances that the rival factions would unite, that professionalism be outlawed and that the French club championship, which was believed to be an incitement to violence, be abandoned. The F.F.R. accepted the allegations concerning professionalism but were unwilling to abandon the championship as it was a lucrative source of profit. There matters remained for the rest of the decade. From the outset however, opinion in Wales was sympathetic to France, who were seen to be whipping boys for the prejudices of the other unions in a way that the W.F.U. had itself suffered before the War. While the I.B. was entitled to express its disapproval of the way the French were managing their rugby affairs, it was felt, by 'Old Stager' for one, that the Board was acting inconsistently with its own policy of letting individual unions handle their own domestic business. France, of course, was not a member of the Board, and it was not through lack of frequent advocacy on the part of Wales's I.B. representatives that it was 1978 before France was finally, and rightfully, admitted. As it was, the abandonment of fixtures deprived Welshmen of the opportunity of seeing many French stars of the thirties, several of whom, like the great Max Rousié, eventually switched to the thirteen-a-side game. Coincidentally, 1931, the year of 'la rupture' was also the year in which the economic indices showed that France had now attained the level of development that Britain had been the first in the world to reach in 1851: a country half rural but also, now, half urban. From this stage, all aspects of French life, including its sport, would feel the impact of that transformation: as its social and educational facilities developed, a physiological change, helped by improved nutritional standards, ensued. The French became bigger in physique, and British rugby would notice the difference once France was readmitted to the international championship in 1947. Efforts were already being made to rebuild the bridges in the late thirties, for as the international political situation deteriorated, the probability of a united military effort made the reforging of sporting bonds a useful preliminary. The *entente cordiale* was restored in a Forces international at the Parc des Princes in February 1940, when the British Army, including Cadet V. G. J. Jenkins, Corporal W. H. Travers, Gunner W. E. N. Davies and 2nd Lieut. W. Wooller (who scored two tries) won 36 - 3. 1940 was not a good year

303

for the French Army. Once the war was over, France, who had already beaten Ireland as well as Wales in the 'Victory' internationals, announced that she had emphatically arrived by holding Wales to a penalty goal to nil at Colombes in 1947, and then beating her in 1948 and 1949. She beat all the home countries at least once in the first three post-war seasons, and shared with Wales the distinction of beating the 1948 Wallabies. It was the shape of things to come.

The immediate post-war period was not a vintage one in terms of results for Wales (1947-9, played 13, won 6) but for the Cardiff club it was. Every team that Wales fielded from the first post-war championship game against England in 1947 to the Irish match of 1949 contained at least five Cardiff players. There were nine against the Wallabies, and an unprecedented ten for three games in 1948. Cynics might point out that in 1948 Wales lost three of her four matches, and perhaps there were too many players from a club whose average playing age was around thirty, but the selectors did not help by choosing men out of position, like Jack Matthews on the wing. Yet Cardiff's playing record for these years, in quality even more than in quantity, remains a magnificent achievement. The greatness of the team, as with the Pill Harriers side of 1918-19, revolved around the nucleus of wartime occupational reservists: mining engineers like Billy Cleaver and Maldwyn James, doctors like Jack Matthews and Glyn Jones. The war over, these were reinforced by returning servicemen like Bleddyn Williams, Ewart Tamplin and Les Manfield, who lifted the club to new heights. In its first four post-war seasons, it won 140 out of 166 games, scoring over 2,600 points and averaging nearly four tries a match. In Jack Matthews's first year as captain 1945-6, 661 points were scored, Bleddyn Williams scored 30 tries, Glyn Jones 28, and all matches were won except the 3 - 0 defeat by the Kiwis on Boxing Day. The greatest season of all in play and results was 1947-8, when 803 points were scored, 39 out of 41 matches won, Bleddyn Williams set a club record of 41 tries, the Wallabies were beaten 11 - 3, and 30,000 regularly attended the Arms Park. It took a Cambridge University side including Glyn Davies, John Gwilliam and Clem Thomas to deprive Cardiff of its eighteen-month ground record in December 1948. The crowds who thronged to see 'the greatest club in the world' in action showed that the enthusiasm for organized entertainment had survived the war into peace-time. Whether because of, or in spite of austerity, there was a massive upsurge in the nation's pursuit of leisure. Welsh international rugby resumed with high hopes that would be deflated by the end of 1949. They were difficult enough to maintain in 1947, the coldest winter of the century, when snow-bound Britain shivered through insufficient fuel — itself a sad comment on the lack of forethought of the thirties. The Ministry of Transport ruled out a special W.R.U. dining car for the Edinburgh trip in February through lack of coal, and the Ministry of Food confirmed that the five compartments allowed would have no guarantee of food supplies. Only the consequent rugby lightened the burden.

Despite the first appearance of Bleddyn Williams (at fly-half), Cleaver, Les Williams and Ken Jones, the opening match of the revived championship was lost 9 - 6. It was the victory over Scotland by 22 - 8, the biggest Welsh win ever at Murrayfield, that revealed rich new promise and confirmed the stature of the old. Haydn Tanner was now at his peak. Since moving to Bristol, he had transferred from Swansea to play for Cardiff and switched from teaching to industrial chemistry. If there were still alchemists around searching for the philosopher's stone, they could stop looking: Tanner had it. His unobtrusive but complete mastery of his craft, the felinity of movement he brought to his service, his break, his covering defence, these made possible much of the scintillating back play of these years. His superlative service was already legendary, and a succession of outside-halves from Cliff Jones to Glyn Davies was indebted to that swift, raking pass from the base of the scrum. It was not only fast, but unerringly accurate. By 1947, Tanner was thirty. His 5foot 10inches had filled out to a hefty 12½ stone, and while he knew that the essence of scrum-half play was to link, he had brought an extra dimension to his game by his readiness to vary the attack by running with the ball himself. 'What is very important', he argued '[is that] once the scrum-half has started to run with the ball . . . he must carry on running'. Tanner's break from the scrum was lethal. Its deadliness lay in its timing, its infrequency, its economy, and its total success. Like many of the things that made life worth living in those days, it was severely rationed. He never attempted more than three breaks a match, but 'it should be the aim of the scrum-half that every time he makes a successful break the result shall be a try'. All his majestic skills were on display in 1947. In Paris he was so completely the master of Bergougnan that the tall Frenchman was reduced to tears. In the first half against Ireland at St. Helen's he fed Glyn Davies a constant stream of flawless but orthodox passes, as a cat, biding its time before pouncing, lulls its victim into a deceptive sense of security. At a scrum in the twenty-fourth minute, the cat pounced. Wales hooked and began wheeling the opposing back row marginally out of tackling range. As the ball emerged, Tanner stooped for it and with that characteristic leaning, loping style, broke straight upfield, swept past his opposite number, dummied the back-row, fed Cleaver, and Bob Evans finished it off with a twenty-yard unopposed run to the line. At Murrayfield that year, he combined his attacking and spoiling abilities in one breath-taking movement when, after a Scottish heel, he ran round the scrum, robbed the opposing scrum-half, gained possession himself and then threw Glyn Davies a rocketing reverse pass, so that the Scottish forwards rose from the scrum they had just won to see the Welsh three-quarters streaming away to their goal-line.

The twenty-six caps Tanner won between 1935 and 1949, which the war prevented from being doubled, would have been consecutive had it not been for an injury which stopped him from playing against the 1947 Wallabies. For that one occasion, Llanelli's nuggety Handel Greville came into the side to give an international-class performance, but like 'Chico' Hopkins at Twickenham in 1970, he had to snatch at glory as it passed him by: Haydn Tanner, like Gareth Edwards, was an immortal. Tanner found some compensation for missing that game by leading the Barbarians against the tourists in January 1948. Though the Barbarians had been in existence since 1890, they had never played a touring side, and when the Australians expressed a wish to travel home via North America, officials of the home unions agreed to invite the Barbarians to select a strong XV to meet the Wallabies at Cardiff to raise the money. Since 1901, the spiritual home of the Barbarians had been at Penarth — more accurately, the Esplanade Hotel and the local golf course — and the Arms Park was the one ground where a sell-out would be guaranteed. It was, and the success of the venture, in front of 40,000, set a precedent for future tourist curtain-calls. The performance of the Barbarians' captain that day won the unqualified admiration of friend and foe. After a game of thrustful, exuberant rugby, in which Tanner rounded off a swinging combined movement that he himself had initiated half the field's length away, Wallaby manager Arnold Tancred, who had fuelled controversial flames earlier in the tour, for once spoke for everybody when he declared, 'We are all agreed that Haydn Tanner stands alone. He is one of the greatest scrum-halves of all time'.

Tanner was accused of tactical inflexibility after the 6 - 5 Welsh defeat at Murrayfield in 1949, when Glyn Davies was ensnared by the defensive web spun by the Scottish back-row of Keller, Kininmonth and Elliot. With the Welsh three-quarters standing too far apart from each other, and from their outside-half, the Scots gratefully poured into the gaps, intercepting passes and increasingly isolating Glyn Davies. As against South Africa in 1951, tactics were adjusted when it was too late to salvage the match, but even then Tanner's sober genius engineered a beautiful try when, from a scrum on the left outside the Scottish 25, he feinted to the blind side in concert with Glyn Davies, and then whipped a reverse pass across the scrum for Bleddyn Williams to jink one, two, three defenders and cross over beneath the bar, crowning extravagance with exquisite economy. Economy was not generally so exciting in post-war Britain. While that try is too often overlooked by Welsh masochists stalking the spoor of the Murrayfield bogey — they could well look to 1938 — it must be admitted that in general terms, Wales was not, in 1949, championship material, for she went on to lose against Ireland and France.

For those games, and into 1950, W. B. Cleaver was brought back as a tactical general instead of Glyn Davies. To reduce the differences between them to a simple antithesis is to do less than justice to two superb players. Like Cliff Jones, Emlyn Jenkins and Bush before them, and Cliff Morgan after them, they were Rhondda pivots, though Glyn Davies came from Cilfynydd, which strictly is only on the threshold of the great central wound of South Wales. Davies was a member of a highly talented Pontypridd G.S. XV that contained several future internationals and Welsh trialists, like Maldwyn James, Hubert Jones, Glyn Jones, Alan Goodfield, and Davies's namesake, Wynford, with whom he played a 'Victory' international against England in January 1946. What Tanner and Davies, the Gowerton halves, had done before the war, the Pontypridd pair threatened to do after it, but Wynford, like Handel Greville, would have to languish in the shadow of the nonpareil Tanner. Like innumerable players from within a jink and punt of Cilfynydd, Glyn Davies, broad of shoulder and narrow of hip, a shock of dark wavy hair bouncing on top of his 5foot 9inches and 11stone, could side-step on a sixpence. It was a natural ability, but it acquired extra venom from the endless sessions he and his partner spent at Taff Vale Park under the tuition of the groundsman, Dick Coates. Coates was a rugby fanatic, but he was also an old-time dancing master, and from him Davies's footwork acquired the polish of patent leather. When he went up to Cambridge in 1948, to win three blues and captain the University in 1950, he was already dancing to the insistent, shuffling rhythms of his own attacking impulses, and already an International, an elegant mover who was now developing his defensive game. He won the first of his eleven caps against Scotland in 1947, and the fact that every member of the three-quarter line scored in the 22 - 8 victory testified to the deft distribution of the Pontypridd fly-half. He played a major role in the 1948 game against Scotland, too, when early in the second half he received from the loose and with blistering change of pace and direction switched the attack from right to left for Bleddyn to spreadeagle a stunned Scottish defence. It was against England in 1949 that Glyn Davies produced his finest display, his crisp, sparkling running the perfect celebrant of the new white shorts that Wales first wore that year. Impelled by Tanner's long, pulsating passes, he lanced through the England defence with ease, swinging his body away from the pass in the classical manner to provide Les Williams on the left wing with some copy-book tries.

Davies, poised and rapier-like, was the perfect foil to the human cannon-ball Jack Matthews. In the course of seventeen caps won between 1947 and 1951, Dr Jack acquired Claude Davey's reputation of being the most aggressive tackler in Welsh rugby. 'Once Jackie Matthews committed himself to the tackle', wrote Fred Allen, 'the next person to arrive on the scene should have been the rag-and-bone collector'. At 5foot 8inches, Matthews was more squat and barrel-chested than Davey, and where the Swansea man demolished his opposite number with his chest, Matthews — who eventually became Honorary Physician to the W.R.U. — applied full frontal shock-treatment with his shoulders, directed with surgical precision to the stomach or short ribs. Matthews's handling, like Davey's, could be erratic: the former never lived down dropping an (atrocious) pass against England in 1948 with the line yawning in front of him. While his tackling was in itself a considerable offensive weapon, particularly as a demoralizing and ball-loosening tactic, Matthews in possession was an attacking player of speed and substance. A Welsh schools' sprint champion, his anticipation and acceleration into the burst secured several tries for Wales, most notably when he finished off a forty-yard break by Tanner against Scotland in 1948, and the two unstoppable tries he scored in the 23 - 5 defeat of England in 1951. The first of them came after a Welsh forward rush was checked on the England 25, and a Willis pass was neatly transferred by Glyn Davies to the exploding Matthews who shot off to the right like a piece of shrapnel before swinging in under the posts. The second was scored after he had stuck like a limpet to Lewis Jones as that unpredictable genius wove through for Dr Jack to bring the house down with a typical thirty-yard burst to the line.

Matthews struck an effective harmony with Glyn Davies, but he was very much at home, too, with Billy Cleaver. In terms of physique, the

Treorchy-born Cleaver was not unlike Matthews, a sturdy, stubby 13 stone and 5foot 9inches. With his jabbing runs and shrewd change of pace, his attacking talents were not always given their due. Certainly Cardiff had not scored ninety-eight tries in 1947-8 by ignoring their outside-half, though in West Wales, after one dour game in Swansea when the heavy conditions allowed him little option, he would forever be labelled 'Billy Kick'. His positional judgement, two-footed dexterity and strong tackling suggested that his natural position was full-back, where he was only once able to distinguish himself for Wales, against the 1947 Wallabies, a game notable also for the first appearance of the wily hooker Maldwyn James, and John Gwilliam, an iron chancellor in the making; notable too for the lusty captaincy, in Tanner's absence, of the burly policeman Ewart Tamplin, and for the baldest brigade of back-row brigands (Manfield, Gwyn Evans and Keller) ever seen on one rugby field.

While the arrival of clever and technically expert forwards like Bob Evans, Maldwyn James, and, winning their first caps in Glyn Davies's match against England in 1949, Don Hayward and Ray Cale of Newbridge, augured well for the immediate future, the long-term too looked good. Members of the Welsh S.S. who attracted attention in 1947 were R. C. C. Thomas of Blundell's School, 'a hardworking, fast and intelligent wing-forward', T. J. Brewer of Newport H.S., and C. James of Gwendraeth G.S., acclaimed as 'a typical product of Welsh S.S. football, being elusive, neat, good at handling, and blessed with an eye for the half-opening'. The same C. James captained the Welsh S.S. in 1948, with B. Lewis Jones of Gowerton G.S. at full-back; in 1949 the Welsh S.S. that beat the English Schools 30 - 3 included Glyn John (Garw G.S.) at centre, C. I. Morgan (Tonyrefail G.S.) at fly-half, and B. V. Meredith (West Mon. G.S.) and R. Robins (Pontypridd G.S.) at forward. There were ten secondary school caps in each of the Triple Crown sides of 1950 and 1952.

As Welsh rugby insured itself for the future, the life policies of the two men who had guided its fortunes since its infancy, ran out. Within six weeks of each other in 1949, the deaths occurred of Walter Rees and Horace Lyne. In July 1947 Horace Lyne had retired from the Presidency of the W.R.U., a position he had occupied with distinction since succeeding Sir John Llewellyn in 1906. Born at Newport in 1860, the son of Charles Lyne, twice Mayor of the town, he had been educated at Plymouth and the Royal Naval College, and played full-back for Newport at eighteen years of age. He captained the club in 1883, the year he became a solicitor, and switched to forward, where he won six Welsh caps between

1883 and 1885, and then retired from the game. But only from playing it. Apart from his career in the administration of Welsh rugby, he also served as a representative on the I.B. from 1887 to 1938, which made him, with R. G. Warren of Ireland who served for exactly the same period, the longest serving member in its history. His close involvement with the civic life of his home town brought him the freedom of the borough in 1934, on his retirement from half a century's service as Chief Fire Officer of Newport. A life-long Anglican, a Chancellor of the diocese of Monmouth and member of the governing body of the Church in Wales, his fire-fighting expertise stood him in good stead in dousing the flames of controversy which sporadically threatened to engulf the Union from the 1890s onwards. In a gesture which was entirely typical of the man, he left to the W.R.U., in his will, the silver Welsh Challenge Cup which had been presented to him on the occasion of his Life Presidency. Thus Horace Lyne's memory would be perpetuated in the resurrection of the Cup Competition in the 1970s.

He was succeeded as President by Dr David Rocyn Jones, who had joined the Union as a vice-president in 1907-8. Born in 1872 in Rhymney, Rocyn Jones had gone from Lewis School, Pengam, to Cardiff University College, and on to London and Edinburgh Universities. He came from a family of manipulative surgeons, running to five generations, and after serving as chief surgeon at the Powell collieries in Abertillery 1899-1908, he was appointed Monmouthshire's first M.O.H. a post he held until 1946 when he was succeeded by his son Gwyn. The conferring of a knighthood on him in 1948 recognized the wide range of his interests, for he was second only to Thomas Jones, another son of Rhymney, as one of Wales's best-known men of affairs. He would serve as President of the W.R.U. from 1947 until his death in April 1953, after which the office was settled at one year's duration, and under the new dispensation Sir David Rocyn Jones's son, Nathan, capped against Scotland in 1921, and upholder of the family's medical tradition, became President in the Triple Crown season 1964-65.

The death of Horace Lyne, on 1 May 1949, was followed on 6 June by the death of the man who had, less than a year before, relinquished the Secretaryship of the Union, and who had been his constant companion in guiding the affairs of the W.R.U. since 1889, Walter Rees. In March 1948 Captain Rees, by then eighty-six-years-old, announced that from 30 June he would cease to be Secretary of the W.R.U., a position he had held for fifty-two years. In that time he had seen momentous changes. When he became Secretary in 1896, there were 37 clubs in the Union, when he

310

retired, 104. The receipts of the first international of his Secretaryship, in 1897, were £1,100; those of his last, in 1948, £9,000. He was a well-known figure in local government as well. Elected to the Neath Town Council in 1900, he became Mayor in the best possible year, 1905. A Freemason, a Conservative and an Anglican, he was untypical of the vast majority of the players whose football destinies he supervised, though certainly not untypical of the men who steered the Union in its formative years. Unquestionably, he was synonymous with Welsh rugby throughout the first half of the twentieth century. Where the telegraphic address of the R.F.U. was 'Scrummage, Twickenham', and that of the Scottish R.U. 'Scrum, Edinburgh', that of the Welsh Union was simply 'Walter Rees, Neath'. The poker-face he offered to photographers was a façade which concealed the labyrinths of rules, bye-laws and administrative minutiae by which the Union controlled rugby in Wales and which sometimes had little formal existence outside Walter Rees's head, or at least his home in Victoria Gardens, Neath. His traditional pre-match perambulation of the touch-line with the Chief Constable on international days at Cardiff and St. Helen's was as much a part of the afternoon's ritual as the singing and the game itself. The notorious black pocket-book containing the names of those to whom he allocated match tickets was the best-guarded, most fabulous volume since the twelfth-century Black Book of Carmarthen. During the years between 1896 and 1947 when he served as its Secretary, the Union's motto, *Ich Dien*, was best translated by the immortal phrase, 'Ask Walter; he knows'.

In July 1948 Walter Rees was formally succeeded by Eric Evans, who had acted as honorary assistant secretary for two years prior to his appointment. Eric Evans was by now fifty-five years old, and like his predecessor, a native of Neath. A member of the Union for twenty-one years, his appointment was well-received, for his achievements in organizing and propagating secondary school rugby had been long recognized. He had been the honorary secretary of the W.S.S.R.U. since its inception, and he was now followed in that post by H. S. Warrington of Merthyr. To his position as Secretary of the W.R.U. he brought administrative experience, a meticulous concern for detail, and knowledge of the game at all levels. His untimely death in 1955 deprived him of the opportunity to steer the Union into the modern age, and, in one sense, continuity of practice was maintained. Whereas for the previous fifty-odd years the affairs of the Union had been managed from 'Norwood', Neath, for the next seven they would be run from 'Craig Wen', Rumney Hill,

311

Cardiff: the W.R.U. still lacked an office, let alone a proper secretariat. In another sense though, there was no doubt that an era had ended. The first Christmas that Eric Evans served in office, he politely but firmly returned nearly a hundred gifts to donors who had hoped for some consideration when it came to the distribution of international tickets. He would not live to see the administrative and institutional developments that occurred during the quarter-century tenure of his successor, W. H. Clement, but he did see Wales win two Triple Crowns, the formation of the Welsh Youth Union in 1949, the ultimately crucial appointment of K. M. Harris as the Union's Honorary Treasurer in 1952, and steps taken towards the democratization of the W.R.U.: the basis of ticket allocation reorganized and the Presidency made an annual office.

One challenge which confronted him soon after he took up his position, he had successfully overcome by the early 1950s. That problem was the third and final attempt to establish professional rugby league in South Wales. In February 1949 the Rugby League, judging that Welsh club rugby was dull, announced a new campaign in Wales, with Neath and Abertillery as the springboards for attack. The language of challengers and challenged rang with military symbolism. Harold Stacey of Neath, the Rugby League organizer for South Wales, was quoted as saying in March 1949 that nothing would be spared to establish the League code in the Principality. 'From Neath . . . cohorts are to go out into every town and village in Wales preaching the League game . . . in an honest endeavour to raise the standard of Rugby football in South Wales and regain some of the past glories of the game . . . Nothing will prevent us . . . even if it takes up to fifteen years, we are coming into Wales'. Eric Evans took up the gauntlet. 'My Union intend to fight the challenge of the Rugby League, and support those clubs wherever they may be in Wales who are threatened with opposition'. Stacey's rejoinder was to obtain a playing field in front of Neath Abbey, by buying a plot from the self-styled Red Abbot, Alun Thomas, a Communist member of the Glamorgan C.C. who had bought it on the break-up of the Dynevor Estate three years previously. Stacey then circulated all South Wales clubs with the Pauline injunction to 'come over and join us'. The *Western Mail* caught the flavour of the jousting by wondering whether, 'like the monks of Neath Abbey, the W.R.U. will pull their cowls over their heads and ignore this latest challenge, or emulate the Crusader monks and attack to defend their citadel'.

The League's campaign unfolded. In March, application was made to the local miners' welfare committee at Ystradgynlais for use of the land on which Ystradgynlais R.F.C. played. Tom James, a former captain of Neath, was despatched to form an Ystradgynlais R.L. team. In May the Welsh R.L. Commission bought Jenner Park in Barry, thus crossing swords with the soccer authorities, for although Barry Town A.F.C. had had a poor financial year, it was unlikely that the local population would want to see the demise of Welsh and Southern League soccer in the town. Llanelli A.F.C. were successfully approached for a share of Stebonheath Park; Bridgend R.F.C. lost the Brewery Field to the League in May 1949, and did not recover it till 1957; Ebbw Vale also welcomed rugby league football. It seemed that all grounds owned by welfare committees and municipal authorities were in danger. In May, Huddersfield, St. Helens, Wigan and Warrington played exhibition matches at Pontarddulais, Bridgend and Llanelli. At Abertillery, the teams and officials were given a civic reception. In June an Amman Valley R.L. was formed, and the League set about establishing a Welsh League of eight teams for the 1949-50 season. It came into operation, too, though the crowds it attracted were far fewer than those hoped for. In September 1949, crowds of 900 watched rugby league games between Neath and Cardiff, 1,000 Cardiff v. Amman Valley, 1,500 Ystradgynlais v. Amman Valley. The first R.L. international to be held in Monmouthshire was staged at Abertillery in October between Wales and Other Nationalities, but only 2,500 watched it. The League lost some of its early crusading fervour. Harold Stacey resigned in November, to be succeeded as R.L. organizer in South Wales by pre-war Welsh centre, Idwal Davies. League clubs in Wales protested against the signing of their best players by northern clubs. By the end of 1949 only Ystradgynlais could claim to be at all successful; it was drawing spectators and players from neighbouring clubs, so that gates at Abercrave R.F.C. were down to £3 a match by the New Year. When Featherstone Rovers visited Ystradgynlais in April 1950 they were greeted by a brass band. The local R.F.C. was reduced to a supporters club of a dozen, but tenaciously they fought the professional challenge and presented their club with a cheque for £50 at Christmas 1950. Their dogged determination to survive was symbolic. During 1950 the rugby league bubble burst. An international between Wales and Italy at Bridgend in September lost £40, and the factors that eventually forced Cardiff R.L. club, playing on a ground in Penarth Road, to withdraw from the Northern Rugby League in 1951-2 (poor playing record, winning five out of thirty-six games; worse attendance figures, often fewer than 100 spectators paying receipts that were insufficient to cover the expenses of referee and linesmen), summarized the problems attendant upon the foundation of the professional game in South Wales. Increasing economic prosperity as the post-war recovery got under way, the diversification of Welsh industry and its concomitant effect on the occupational composition of Welsh rugby, the improvement in the social amenities that clubs could offer, and the luring of the ablest players so minded to the North of England — together these developments condemned the professional game in Wales to death. The continued trickle of players north only served to indicate how the promoters of the Rugby League in South Wales were being undermined by the parent body in England, who drew north 'Victory' and post-war internationals like W. E. Williams (Newport to Swinton, 1946), George Reeves (Abertillery and Newport to St. Helens, 1948), Les Williams, W. G. Jones and Terry Cook from Cardiff to Hunslet, Hull and Halifax, respectively, in January 1949, as well as, in 1950, Ray Cale and unsuccessful trialists Russell Burns of Cardiff and Haydn Thomas of Newport.

Northern Rugby League clubs would continue to make the occasional sensational signing into the 1970s, but the offensive it mounted in 1949 was the last attempt to strike root in Wales itself. The challenge, though short, was also sharp, and it concentrated the mind of the W.R.U. wonderfully. While it did not abandon the trusty expedient of missionary matches — and the crowd of 6,000 that saw international-studded Cardiff play a Combined Amman Valley XV at Cwmamman in September 1949 confirmed that these still had a role to play — there was also recognition that this was a palliative rather than a cure. The threat of the Rugby League in West Wales posed particular problems for the union game in that area. In December 1949 the thirty-five clubs of the West Wales R.U. threatened to break away from the W.R.U. if they were not given direct affiliation. This was promptly granted them. There was no doubt either that the professional presence in West Wales postponed the transfer of international matches from St. Helen's, which the Abercarn club had formally proposed, only to be defeated by a large majority, at the 1947 A.G.M. This was pursued at the A.G.M. of 1949, when Merthyr and Treorchy continued the campaign which would not be abandoned until its success in the 1953 meeting, to make Cardiff Arms Park the venue for all home internationals. At the 1950 A.G.M. Rowe Harding reminded delegates that the battle against the League in West Wales was far from won. 'The Rugby League is only an infant, but it wants strangling', he declared. Other West Wales delegates claimed that St. Helen's itself was under threat. In fact, the Swansea Corporation had not been approached by the Rugby League, but the argument that if international matches went from Swansea, so in two years would the Swansea club and the Union game itself, carried some weight with the assembled delegates, who voted 138 to 120 to retain internationals at Swansea; for the time being.

Against the background of the Rugby League threat in West Wales, and its expressed intention of attracting youngsters to amateur rugby league as a preliminary step, occurred a fresh, exciting initiative from inside the amateur code. This development was the provision of rugby facilities for that age group in limbo — Welsh youth. Their plight had been, from the 1920s, as much social as pubescent for those, the great majority, who, unable to continue at school, found the alternative of employment denied them. By the end of the 1930s the unemployed young adults justified a book-length study — by Archie Lush for the Carnegie Trust — in themselves. The demand for coal and labour once more during the war scarcely eased matters for this underpaid, underprivileged and, for so long, underutilized part of the population. The war saw a number of 'Boys' Strikes' in South Wales and a stream of contemporary observation about their bored dissatisfaction with their lives. The schools' bodies had continued to function, but the Junior Leagues, along with their senior counterpart, had gone in to abeyance, leaving rugby for youth to be organized, haphazardly and alongside other sports, by the various youth bodies encouraged by government since 1939. There were, then, City and County Youth movements, Y.M.C.A. groups, and even a Welsh National Council of Youth Clubs. The W.R.U., as early as 1943, contacted the 'rugby enthusiast' Chairman of the National Council, James Griffiths, M.P. for Llanelli since 1936 and a long-time resident of the Amman Valley, to see if he could 'assist in our efforts to co-ordinate Youth Rugby'.

The immediate post-war years were hardly conducive to launching a new venture. Youth teams, generally associated with the Junior leagues, found great difficulty in obtaining soap (the Ministry advised on 'a substitute') and clothing coupons to obtain their kits. Nonetheless the Union of Junior Leagues, supported by their secretary F. D. Day, insisted to the W.R.U. in 1948 that the boys in youth sides were, unlike the 1920s when the ex-schoolboy movement had foundered after six years, properly organized and controlled. The dispute had arisen because of the pressing needs of youth in the Amman Valley where, powered by the energetic drive of Gorseinon's secretary, Will Lang, a Youth competition was under way. The Amman Valley men, upheld by their W.R.U. representatives, Ivor Jones and D. Ewart Davies, believed that the needs of boys aged fourteen and over were not properly catered for and that a Youth League under the auspices of the Union of Junior Leagues, was no proper solution. The anthracite valleys of West Wales had been progressive in their social thinking for a number of decades by the 1940s and they did not prove unwilling now to risk the ire of senior clubs and the stand-offish élitism of the secondary schools in their quest for a rugby outlet for what would, within a few short years, be the 1950s 'teenage problem'.

On 1 December 1948, D. Ewart Davies raised before the W.R.U. General Committee the question of the formation of a Youth Rugby Union. Discussion was fierce but the matter was not dropped. In March 1949 a conference of all those connected with recreation for youth was called and resolved to form a Youth Rugby Union to be integrated into the W.R.U. The task of beginning to draw up a planned constitution at a re-convened meeting was entrusted to the man appointed to be the acting Assistant Secretary, Hermas Evans. He was then teaching in further education in Cardiff but was himself an ex-Gowerton County School and Swansea University player with strong family ties in the Amman Valley. When 11 May 1949 came around, he had channelled the necessity he, and others similarly associated with youth, knew to exist into the formal foundation of the Youth Union at that Castle Hotel, Neath, where the parent body had been established sixty-eight years previously. Hermas Evans was to act as the first secretary until 1956, with W. B. Cleaver as chairman.

Any infant body requires sustenance to survive. The Youth Union, despite some goodwill from the W.R.U., had to struggle to ensure its supply of players from clubs unwilling to abide by the notion that boys under eighteen were not their prime meat. The Youth Union, in 1951, managed to see to it that the W.R.U. finally passed a resolution to this effect. By the end of that year there were over eighty clubs in the Youth Union who catered, in the Secretary's words, 'for a boy's football and for his welfare, both physically and mentally'. Slowly prejudices were overcome and youth football began a remarkable unearthing of talent in addition to its grass-roots function. The value of the work was recognized by the resolution, from the platform, at the June 1952 A.G.M. that a nominee of the Youth Union should become a vice-president of the W.R.U. Hermas Evans served in that capacity until he retired in 1956 because of the pressures incumbent on him after becoming Principal of Gorseinon Technical College in 1954. His successor as Youth Secretary was another old Gowertonian and Swansea University captain, Jim Dark, whilst the advocacy of the man who had laid the early foundations could be heard in the Union's inner councils again from 1963 when Hermas Evans was elected as a district representative in succession to D. Ewart Davies.

It had been symptomatic that the Youth Union in its early months received less than active encouragement from the senior clubs of the W.R.U. There had been an unwarranted element of suspicion at the appearance of what appeared to be a potential rival that was consonant with the dog-in-the-manger attitude that some of the better-off major clubs had adopted since the war. Partly because their wartime survival, and subsequent success, had owed little or nothing to the W.R.U., some leading clubs had become increasingly self-sufficient. From the point of view of internal cohesion within the W.R.U., the Rugby League challenge of the late forties had the salutary effect of bringing the Union and its now 112 clubs into a more harmonious relationship. On 28 May 1949 the Union held an unprecedented conference of clubs at Porthcawl to discuss the state of the game — not only at grass-roots level, for in the international tourney Wales had taken the wooden spoon — and how to improve it. A series of ten-minute talks were given on topics like training, coaching and refereeing and the Union unveiled an eleven-point plan for revitalizing the game in Wales.

This would be followed up by participation in the Central Council for Physical Recreation Course at Swansea in 1949 in line witht the W.R.U.'s resolution in the previous April to take 'advantage of the coaching scheme' of the C.C.P.R. The growing role of the latter, governmental body (founded in the less ambitious 1930s) would help the W.R.U. eventually to fulfil a directive it gave to its clubs in the spring of 1949 'to adhere to the true spirit of the open game . . . to abolish the win-at-all-costs spirit'. The rhetoric did not always match the reality or available resources, but the W.R.U. was already concerned with improving standards of play through 'instruction and training'. The need would come to appear more and more urgent in the next decade.

It was ironic, in view of the W.R.U.'s 1949 directive to its clubs to brighten their play and curb the spoiling activities of wing-forwards, that the next season would see Wales recapture the Triple Crown for the first time since 1911 in defiance of those sentiments: it was won through aggressive, marauding forward play, speed to the loose ball by the back-row, and a quick-thinking opportunism behind that was almost neo-classical in its stark yet oddly imaginative efficiency. Overall, these had not been the characteristics of the Services, 'Victory' and post-war internationals, where the legacy of the wartime experiment of integrating amateur and profesional players had been carried over into peace-time. The success of Ireland's Triple Crown sides of 1948 and 1949, however, based as they were on Karl Mullen's astute forward captaincy, a fast and predatory specialist back-row of McCarthy, McKay and O'Brien, and the urbane Jack Kyle at fly-half, tipped the balance away from free-running back-play to forward domination, the elimination of mistakes, the policing of the midfield and single-minded playing for position and possession. The way in which the Irish and, at Murrayfield, the Scottish back-rows, had nullified the attacking potential of the Welsh sides of 1948 and 1949, warned Wales that she needed to adjust to the defensive sophistication of the new era. The retirement of Haydn Tanner, aged thirty-two, in August 1949, made that adjustment all the more urgent, but also much more practicable, for there was no doubt that post-war Welsh XVs had danced very much to Tanner's tune. Whether Wales would, in the early fifties, have made the required transition under the captaincy of the man the selectors originally earmarked for the post and whose attacking genius had sparkled throughout the forties — Bleddyn Williams — remains forever a tantalizing riddle. On the eve of the first game of the new decade at Twickenham in January 1950, Bleddyn had to withdraw from the team, and the leadership of the side was entrusted, fatefully, to John Arthur Gwilliam.

Gwilliam would lead that side not only to victory at Twickenham, for only the second Welsh win there ever, but go on to dispose of Scotland in Cardiff and break Ireland's monopoly of the Triple Crown in Belfast. Under Gwilliam's captaincy, Wales won the Crown and Grand Slam in 1950, and again in 1952. In terms of previous Welsh captains, Gwilliam was something else. Because he played most of his rugby outside Wales, was a schoolmaster, a forward leader, a noted disciplinarian, and won at Twickenham, he invited comparison with Watcyn Thomas. Wholly dissimilar in personality, as players they did share some similarities. At 6foot 3inches and 15stone 2lb., the Pontypridd-born, Monmouth and Cambridge-educated Gwilliam could operate with equal facility in the second row or in the middle of the third, like Watcyn Thomas. He was as much a line-out expert as Watcyn, too; as a one-armed jumper his stretch was almost as stratospheric as Roy John's. But Watcyn was a roistering, rollicking figure. Gwilliam did not roister or rollick. The nearest in that sense to Watcyn was Ewart Tamplin, another second-row forward who led by uproarious example. Gwilliam led by directing. Though that long-boned, ascetic face disguised a wry and self-effacing humour, his wintry air of headmasterly detachment generated the myth that he was a Quaker. He was no more a Quaker than Watcyn Thomas was a Jesuit, but it is not without interest that even his Welsh team colleagues thought he was. He was merely inscrutable. Watcyn Thomas was a gargantuan figure straight out of Rabelais; Gwilliam was the blank page between the Old Testament and the New. Watcyn was an extrovert, he appealed to the gut; Gwilliam was the opposite, not visceral but cerebral. He got results by getting under players' skins, for he inspired them by irritating them. The Cardiff backs of that era were as loath to be dictated to by an outsider as their club was by the W.R.U. Gwilliam knew it, but feigned otherwise. In the final trial of 1951 he took Jack Matthews and Bleddyn Williams aside to show them how to pass the ball. He goaded players to do well not because of him but in spite of him.

Gwilliam was a history graduate, and though it was not an inevitable consequence, in his case this heightened his sense of the interpenetration of the present and the past. He was as well versed in the game's evolution as he was a student of its tactics. 'This does not mean the gossip of the game', he wrote, 'but acquaintance with its history and keen interest in the ways of some of the great players of the past, their techniques and ideas. He must know of all the major battles in former internationals and the way in which the game has grown. This may seem of academic interest only, but an appreciation of the way it has grown in the past is of great value in forecasting how the game will develop'. The book which Dave Gallaher and W. J. Stead wrote in 1906 after returning to New Zealand from Britain, was almost unobtainable even by 1914. Gwilliam, born in 1923, had a copy and knew what was in it. By 1950 his study of the contemporary game, and of Irish Triple Crown methods in particular, told him that a tactical redirection was needed if Wales's uncritical devotion to a free-running game was not to be ruthlessly exploited by her opponents. It told him too that the Irish game lacked a dimension beyond the venomous combination of Mullen, the back-row, and Kyle. Wales had the backs that could provide that dimension, though of late Wales's patent three-quarter supremacy had been squandered through aimless spoiling at forward instead of hard scrummaging. The Irish tactic was to subdue forward, and carry on subduing for eighty minutes, essentially the style of Wetter's Newport team of the early 1920s. The Welsh tactic under Gwilliam would be to subdue forward and then employ the backs as a strike weapon: essentially

319

the style of the Llanelli team of the late twenties. Exchange Cleaver's cherubic babyface and blond curls for a furrowed brow and black combed-back hair, and you were watching Dai John. The scoring statistics of Gwilliam's two Triple Crown teams tell their own story. In 1911, when the last Triple Crown of the first Golden Era was won, Wales scored fifteen tries in the three matches; in 1969, when the first Crown of the second Golden Era was won, twelve tries. In 1950 and 1952, the Triple Crown was won by six tries in each year. In the age of austerity, John Gwilliam was Welsh rugby's Stafford Cripps, and his men played coupon-book football. But Cripps is not numbered among the country's greatest chancellors, whereas Gwilliam remains perhaps Wales's greatest captain in a hundred years.

'The first requirement of captaincy', declared Gwilliam, 'is a team to captain'. In the early 1950s he had that team. The pack he led throughout the four matches of 1950 was one of the finest packs Wales ever fielded, though three of them were newcomers that year. One of them was E. R. John of Neath, a twenty-three-year-old quantity surveyor who would win nineteen consecutive caps. By an odd twist, Crynant-born Roy John, a product of Sam Evans's coaching at Neath G.S. — where he had played on the wing, at centre, and at fly-half before moving into the back-row — and a graduate of the West Wales League before entering first-class rugby in 1947, was making his first appearance for Wales because his club partner Rees Stephens, who had been chosen as vice-captain, had withdrawn. In style and temperament there could be no greater contrast than that between Neath's 'terrible twins', but theirs would be an indomitable partnership on the ten occasions they formed the Welsh second row. There would be taller forwards than Roy John, but none ever got higher off the ground. His elevation was a revelation. He could hoist his 6foot 3inches to such a height that the white portions of the scrum-cap which made him immediately recognizable even at ground level might have been snow. During the five years of his international career he lorded it over every line-out he contested, as, arm outstretched, he leapt with the split-second timing of a ballet dancer to secure the catch — two-handed, not a deflection —with a grace and agility that mocked both gravity and his granitic fourteen stone. This Nureyev of the Gnoll was not just a ball-winner, he was a ball-user, too. As Roy John came galloping away, defenders could be baffled by a swerve and dummy worthy of a half-back. The French and New Zealanders found that out to their cost in 1950, and so did the Irish at Dublin in 1952, when he side-stepped and dummied from a line-out before giving Clem Thomas a neat under-arm scoring pass. Bunched around like lions at the feet of Nelson's column, providing the jumper with essential support and protection (which were illegalized by amendments to the laws in 1954, to the detriment of line-out play ever since) were Don Hayward, and props Cliff Davies and John Robins. Tubby, cheery, thirty-year-old Davies was the Porthos of the front-row musketeers. He was a miner from Kenfig Hill, which, as he announced to a stunned audience in New Zealand in 1950, was the most historic site in the world, after Jerusalem. Only Davies could get away with singing songs *penillion*-style about Walter Rees, in his presence, as happened when the Welsh party were returning from Paris in 1947. Only Cliff Davies, too, would have stood on a chair at a Scottish R.U. dinner, minus collar and tie, to conduct Welsh hymns. It was as much in appreciation of Cliff's rich baritone as it was a psychological move that John Gwilliam appointed him choirmaster of the team throughout 1950. Before every international, the doors of the Welsh changing room were thrown wide open and the opposition was subjected to a full-throatal rendition of 'Calon Lân'. Cliff Davies knew all the various harmonic shifts that created and resolved discord in the front row of the scrum, too. Immensely strong around his shoulders and nineteen-inch neck, he was exceptionally fast for a man of 5foot 9inches and 13stone 8lb., a precursor of the running, handling prop forwards of Lucien Mias's French sides of the late 1950s.

The Welsh counterpart to Dumas's studious Aramis was John Robins. A Cardiff-born schoolteacher playing for Birkenhead Park, Robins, at 14stone and 5foot 9inches, had the build of a bulldog and the mind of a mathematician. He thought about the game as intently as he played it, and after winning eleven caps between 1950 and 1953, went on to achieve fame as coach at Loughborough Colleges, from where many of his ideas and innovations would be widely diffused. It reflected the changing face of South Wales that three of the Triple Crown side of 1950 — Gwilliam, Robins and Gerwyn Williams — were schoolteachers and rugby coaches, outside Wales. Completing the front row, also winning his first cap with John Robins at Twickenham in 1950, was the quick-striking, Penygraig-born hooker, D. M. (Dai) Davies. Something of the inflexibility of Athos could be detected in the unbending scrummaging of Dai Davies, but when it came to hooking, the 5foot 11inch, 13stone Somerset Policeman could be elastic itself, a quality required in a science which, until amended laws imposed a common interpretation in 1954, was, in J. B. G. Thomas's words, 'a world of witchcraft and fantasy, where legs struck not in rhythm but at varying angles, speeds and directions'. Davies's post-war predecessors, Billy Gore, Maldwyn James and W. H. Travers had been adept at this arcane craft, but they lacked the concerted support at prop and behind that would enable Dai Davies to get the best of most hookers he encountered in the course of the seventeen caps he won between 1950 and 1954.

The second policeman in the side in 1950 was the twenty-nine-year-old Newport C.I.D. officer, Bob Evans. Trained to keep an open eye for stealth in all its forms, the 6foot 1inch, 13stone Evans had been an ideal support player for Haydn Tanner when the inside-half indulged his fondness for the steal-away from the scrum. At Twickenham in 1950, where he was winning the third of ten caps, Evans's early and consuming tackle on English fly-half and captain Ivor Preece proved as decisive as Steve Fenwick's 1979 Triple Crown tackle on English centre Dodge in delivering the game psychologically to Wales. It also endeared him to Gwilliam, who regarded a missed tackle by any of his team as a personal bereavement, and let the offender know it. The burly, good-looking Don Hayward, a Newbridge railwayman, who had won two caps in 1949, was in 1950 resuming an international sequence of fourteen consecutive caps. His jumbo-proportions of 6foot 1inch and 16stone 4lb. conjured up memories of the elephantine eights of the 1920s, but Hayward was twice as clever and three times as mobile. In 1951 he switched to prop to enable Rees Stephens to play Gog to Roy John's Magog, helped Wales to another Crown in 1952, and signed for Wigan in 1954. He was one of the six of the Welsh pack of 1950 who toured with the Lions later that year. Gwilliam was not one of them, but had his teaching commitments at Glenalmond not prevented him from travelling, there is no doubt that he would have become the first Welshman to captain the Lions; or, at least, he should have been, for the Lions' selectors could make peculiar decisions. None more so than their omission of Wales's blind-side wing-forward throughout 1950, W. R. Cale. A greengrocer in Pontypool, the 5foot 11inch, 13½stone, Usk-born Ray Cale was the most vigorous spoiler since Arthur Lemon, but his vigour was constructive and the argument that he was too 'robust' for New Zealand was ludicrous. He could still taste the bitter fruits of disappointment when he signed for St. Helens R.L. club in May 1950.

This Welsh pack was a well-constructed amalgam of weight, height, strength and skill. It also contained some firebrands that required all Gwilliam's headmasterly authority to keep in check, but inspired by his favourite axiom, 'Be quicker on the ball than the other side', under his leadership they developed stamina, spirit and a readiness to support each other. It was Cliff Davies and Cale who scored both Wales's tries in the 11 - 5 win at Twickenham. Behind those forwards, Gwilliam had the perfect complement in the Cardiff triangle of Willis, Cleaver and Matthews. The international appearance of cinema supervisor Rex Willis was the most startling since Rudolf Valentino had appeared as 'The Sheik' thirty years before. With his olive complexion and well-oiled black hair, Willis might have doubled for him, except that he came not from the Yemen, but from Ystrad, in the Rhondda. The twenty-four-year-old 5foot 9inch, 12stone 4lb. Willis, having studied patiently at the feet of the caliph himself, Tanner, that Ali Baba of thieving scrum-halves, had developed a rhythmic chest-high dive-pass — even on the run Rex dive-passed — which the master himself would not have disowned, though he might have aimed it lower. But it would be just right for the emerging Cliff Morgan, who liked it at exactly that height and held it there as if he could never believe his luck. What was surprising was that Willis had not figured in any of the trials: Swansea's Roy Sutton, Llanelli's Greville and Newport's Haydn Thomas were regarded as the front-runners. The unexpected choice of Willis was equalled only by the first appearance at full-back of an eighteen-year-old, though the cause of this surprise was positional rather than personal. It was generally recognized that, sooner or later, room would have to be found for the Gorseinon-born Devonport Serviceman who threatened to be the greatest natural footballer since Arthur Gould. Lewis Jones was a product of the Gowerton G.S. rugby nursery, where Bill Bowen, like all great coaches, corrected imperfect technique but did not interfere with style and outlook. Bowen knew that in Lewis Jones he had something special. At 5foot 11inches and 12stone 6lb., Jones possessed phenomenal kicking skills (at which he worked assiduously), scorching speed, a mesmerizing variation of pace and stride, hips that oscillated as if on ball-bearings, and shoulders that shrugged and twisted through thickets of tacklers. The allegation that he was no tackler was a hollow one, for he had won his cap after a crucial tackle on the Maesteg winger Windsor Major in the final trial. Though he would break every record as a kicker in the professional game with Leeds, to whom he transferred in October 1952, it was as an attacking runner that he made his mark in the Union code. His speciality was an Ali-like double shuffle, a scissoring movement of the legs which signalled, too late for his opponent, that he was about to move into a fifth gear. Convinced that he was of more value to his team on his feet than on the floor, never afraid to concede three yards if it meant gaining five, attack to Lewis Jones was an attitude of mind, not least from defensive positions when the opposition were least prepared for it. He would demonstrate that attribute most sensationally for the Lions in the Fourth Test at Auckland in July 1950, but he first revealed it at international level at Twickenham earlier in the year when, eight minutes before the interval, he fielded a kick inside his own half, engaged that fifth gear and embarked on an elusive cross-field run towards the left-hand touch-line before switching direction for Cliff Davies to take an eventual scoring pass near the right-hand corner-flag. Lewis Jones was at full-back against England and Scotland, but the selectors were not prepared to let the Triple Crown slip Wales's grasp through over-investment in unorthodoxy, and so they brought in the resolute rush-stopper Gerwyn Williams for the first of his thirteen caps, against Ireland. Lewis Jones was accommodated in the centre, while his fellow Devonport utility back, the twenty-year-old Malcolm Thomas moved out to the wing. A skilful footballer equally at home in the centre, where he played against England and Scotland in 1950, or on the flank where, with epic consequence, he found himself in Belfast for the Triple Crown decider, Thomas's versatility and resilience brought him twenty-seven caps in a decade of international rugby. With him, Lewis Jones and Jack Matthews, there was at three-quarter an effective blend of muscle and mystery, enriched by the Olympic presence on the right wing of Newport's Ken Jones, who had not missed a cap since the resumption of the international tourney in 1947.

The Twickenham hurdle cleared, the Welsh forwards inspired by Gwilliam's personal leadership and infuriated by his scant praise and stern reprimands, tore into the Scottish side at St. Helen's to win 12 - 0. Again the disciplined aggression of the back-row was the key to the victory. Cale and Bob Evans swarmed after every ball shaken loose by the hard tackling Welsh centres, and plundered Scottish possession as the Scots themselves had done the previous year. Cleaver nursed his forwards with rare solicitude, time and again kicking them into attacking positions with long, rolling touch-finders and cheeky short punts. When the opportunity presented itself, he set his back-line moving. The first try against Scotland — when Roy John rose like a salmon to feed Willis from the line-out, to Cleaver, to Matthews careering through the centre, to Malcolm Thomas with twenty yards to go — was as aesthetically satisfying as it was lethal.

A titanic struggle was in prospect at Belfast. Ireland had just pulverized Scotland 21 - 0, and while they had narrowly lost 3 - 0 at Twickenham and so were out of the reckoning for the Triple Crown, the Irish pack had not been checked since 1947 when Wales yet again prevented them from securing the mythical trophy. Since then the boot had been on the other foot. The red scare was no problem to Mullen's men, for McCarthy was in a green jersey. This McCarthy was not the feisty senator from Minnesota, but the auburn flanker from Dolphin. Even Irishmen recognized that beyond the back-row and half-back, where Jack Kyle burned like hot ice, there was not too much menace. Barney Mullen, on the wing, was so slow they said he used to talk his way over. He talked to some effect in Belfast in 1948, when his try against Wales helped Ireland to her first Crown since 1899. The following year, Kyle broke on the blind-side at St. Helen's to punt across for the ubiquitous McCarthy to leap, score and record Ireland's first win at Swansea since 1889 — her second successive triple triumph. Ireland's victories had been slight in terms of points, but substantial in terms of pressure. Wales had lost by playing a spoiling game for which she was not properly equipped. By 1950, Gwilliam, who had played on both those previous occasions, was himself in charge. Controlling affairs from the middle of the back-row, he would ensure that the weight and mobility of the Welsh pack would keep the Irish eight under incessant pressure. Ireland's piratical back-row trio would be committed to a tighter game than they relished.

By half-time there was no score. Some thought Wales had lost her chance, for she had been playing with the wind and missed several shots at goal. Six minutes after the interval, Irish passing broke down in their own half, Jackie Matthews picked up and shot through a gap for an unmarked Ken Jones to score. A wide-angle short-range Norton penalty goal neutralized it, and fanned the flames of Irish fervour. In front of the baying Ravenhill banshees, the Welsh forwards might have wilted had it not been for the cool generalship of Gwilliam. Cleaver kicked the ball dead from underneath McCarthy's diving figure and saved the match, for with three minutes remaining, Ireland heeled on her 25, Cale harried both scrum-half Carroll and Kyle, Cleaver snapped up the loose ball and found Lewis Jones on his left, who half-drew Lane and threw Malcolm Thomas an overhead but accurate pass at top speed, giving the wing fifteen yards to go before crashing over in the corner. It was Wales's first Triple Crown for thirty-nine years, and the 21 - 0 demolition of France two weeks later, with Roy John and Dai Davies gambolling like gazelles with disturbed hormones, Cliff Davies making one try for Jack Matthews and another for Ken Jones, Lewis Jones audaciously passing behind his back for Bob Evans and

Matthews to send in Roy John, brought Wales her first Grand Slam since 1911. It had been a long wait.

Not surprisingly, the 1950 Welsh XV attracted many thousands of supporters, home and away. An estimated third of the crowd at Twickenham, officially numbered at 75,532, the largest-ever known at the ground, was Welsh, and the gates were closed some time before the kick-off. A hint at a changing life-style was contained in O. L. Owen's remark that the headquarters of English rugby that day was 'subject to a pincer movement . . . by a highly mechanized army of Welsh rugby enthusiasts'. The roads for miles around were choked by endless columns of coaches and disappointed, mostly Welsh, supporters. The singing of 'Hen Wlad fy Nhadau' was remarkable for its volume, and an English observer remarked afterwards that unless the R.F.U. were careful, Twickenham would end up as one of the more famous Welsh grounds. The R.F.U. was careful, and henceforth decided to make its internationals all-ticket occasions, just as a mammoth invasion of Welsh supporters on Murrayfield in 1975 would swell the crowd to a world record 104,000 and force the S.R.U. to adopt the same measure.

Another 8,000 Welshmen crossed to Ireland in March. Two weeks later, most, but not all of them, were among the 53,000 at the Arms Park for the game with France, to stand moved and silent as the Last Post was sounded in memory of the victims of the worst disaster in aviation history. At 2.10 p.m., the Sunday following the triumph in Belfast, an Avro Tudor V with five crew and seventy-eight Welsh supporters who had paid £10 5s. for the trip, took off from Dublin for the return flight to Llandow in the Vale of Glamorgan. Its estimated time of arrival was 3.03 p.m.

That estimate would never be confirmed. At 3 p.m. it came in over Siginston, at fifty feet, and within a quarter of a mile of its destination. Eye-witnesses who saw the huge aircraft approaching ('the plane was coming in so low we thought it was going to hit us') would later describe how it rose sharply to 150 feet, its engines screaming and starboard wing slightly down. At the top of the climb the engines stalled and everything went still as it went into a nose-dive and ploughed into a field. On impact, the passenger seats came away and shot forward with horrific force. The plane broke up, but did not catch fire. There was just an absolute, deathly silence.

By 3.47 p.m. forty ambulances from all over South Wales were on the scene, to find all sorts of gifts from nylons to packets of meat bought in non-rationed Dublin, strewn over the field. Ten people were brought out alive, but they died almost immediately. The total death-roll was eighty. One of the three survivors was a thirty-three-year-old ship's chandler, Handel Rogers, who went back to Dublin to see Wales win the Triple Crown in 1976, the year of his Presidency of the W.R.U. During an eight-day tribunal, which concluded that the crash had occurred through 'causes unknown', some interesting facts came to light and several rumours were scotched. There had been *no* singing and dancing in the aisle as the plane came in: everyone was sitting, tired and quiet. The survivors were *not* the last aboard: another twenty got in after them. It *was* true that while bookings had been made for 72, originally, part of the aircraft had been stripped to accommodate another six, and that 83 was an exceptional number; but it was one still within the capacity of a Tudor V on such a short flight: it was *not* overloaded, with people or luggage. All the same, the Tudors had an unhappy design history. The first three had been involved in accidents, two in mysterious circumstances over the Atlantic, which investigators had failed to discover. After that, the Ministry of Aviation had ordered that the Tudor IV be grounded, and not restored to passenger service.

The Tudor V was grounded now; for good. But too late for those towns and villages in Monmouthshire from which half its victims came. Too late for Abercarn whose club lost its captain, its coach and its star three-quarter; for Newbridge, where a seventy-five-year-old widow lost her three sons; for Llantarnam, where a house lost three menfolk; for Pontypridd, where four children were abruptly orphaned; for Alltwen, where two brothers and their next-door neighbour never came home; for Glynneath, Risca, Nelson, and the Amman Valley, where fathers, sons and daughters were mourned by communities that lived in ever-present dread of disaster beneath the ground, but not above it. 'There is shadow across the sun in South Wales', said the *Belfast Telegraph* the next day, and the £40,000 which soon poured into the disaster fund showed how the magnitude of the event, enlarged by the irony of the accompanying circumstances, had stirred the whole country. Methodically planned and superbly won, the Triple Crown came back to Wales shrouded in the pall of tragedy.

CHAPTER

13 SINGING IN THE RAIN

THE dislocation in Welsh society caused by the First World War had been obvious and dramatic. By contrast the Second World War, following upon two shabby decades of lost opportunities for a whole generation, did not seem so violent a wrench from pre-war days. The politics of Wales in the late 1940s, though more collectivist and more firmly centred on the British state than ever before, were not in essence different from the patterns established in the 1920s. The economy was still based on the primary extractive industry, coal, and the heavy manufacturing industries in metal, whilst in terms of transport, housing and leisure South Wales, rugby's cradle in Wales, continued to bear the imprint of its origins. It was not the Liberal Lloyd George who now graced a British cabinet but the ex-miners' leaders Aneurin Bevan and James Griffiths whose briefs, of Health and Industrial Insurance, reflected the immediate preoccupations with a secure individual and social future that gripped their world. 1945 marked a year of considerable hope whose promise elicited further sacrifices through the tough years of post-war re-adjustment. When a degree of disillusion and considerable fatigue began to set in, the bright dreams faded a little, but more to the point for South Wales, these years can be seen in retrospect as the final bloom of that unique culture which had begun flowering in the late nineteenth century.

Of course, the after-effects of the culture would linger on for a while yet, but in reality the war had brought a profound alteration in economic and social perspectives. It had seen the removal to Wales of various light engineering and manufacturing industries which did more than any of the industrial estate schemes of the 1930s to ensure, after 1945, the diversification of industry in Wales. Government ordnance factories had moved in to employ women who traditionally had been confined to domestic work at home or in service. The new industries were complemented by a rationalization and re-furbishing of the steel industry; at Ebbw Vale in 1939 the first integrated steel and tin-plate plant started its production, and the late 1940s saw the kind of re-grouping and capital investment in steel that would underlay the prosperity of the steel towns in the fifties. In a nutshell, the indices of an older society — religion, language, type of industry — were flagging, despite the temporary respite of the war years. The fifties were a stagnant decade in many ways. Innovation was in short supply as governments and people savoured the long-awaited, rather sickly, fruits of post-war prosperity. However, beneath the surface a whole way of life was being shifted and the adjustment was often slow and bewildered. Perhaps the relative immobility of Welsh rugby thinking in the 1950s had its roots here, although, as in the society at large, other voices, those of newer men, would soon be urging a change of gear, especially in the administration of the game. Their eventual success, like that of the re-structured economy, would be first detected in the new Welsh world of the 1960s.

Until then, however, rugby seemed curiously uncertain of its future developments. Safe and cherished in its clubs and towns, it shivered in the wider world. At international level, while there was no dearth of forwards of the highest quality, the retirement of a generation of outstanding backs left a vacuum behind the scrum which no dominating personality had yet emerged to fill. Between 1950 and 1956 Wales won the championship outright three times and shared it twice, but it would be eight years before she could again claim even a share of it, and thirteen years would separate the 1952 Triple Crown from the next. In 1949 the Union had resolved to appoint a 'Committee of Instruction to advise clubs . . . with a view to bringing about a better standard of play throughout Wales' and they supplied representatives to advise on the C.C.P.R.'s Courses for Coaches which, in turn, produced a W.R.U. coaching certificate. Much dedicated work from a few enthusiasts was done, yet Cliff Jones, elected a vice-president in 1956, could still plead in 1957 for more interest to be shown in this 'very necessary requirement' of the game in Wales. The W.R.U. Coaching Supervisory Sub-Committee kept firing away on the power supplied by determined members like J. Weslake-Hill of Penarth and its unpaid C.C.P.R. secretaries Ted Prater and then, from 1958 to 1964, Ray Humphreys. So when Cliff Jones, the Sub-Committee's enthusiastic chairman, was also made a selector he would urge his support on others actively involved in the playing side of the game and T. H. Vile, in the twilight of his own service, insisted that the Union must take control of these developments itself. The number of courses, the use of aids and new examining techniques were, indeed, increased and refined from this date on, but given other in-built features in the tradition and nature of the Welsh game, the initiatives of the 1950s would require a major push, even from the unwelcome spectre of playing bankruptcy, before they would finally take off. The decade really ran into the ground in 1962, when Wales failed to score a try in the whole season and aggregated a total of 9 points in four matches. At the same time, the game at grass-roots level was continuously vital, though again there was a contradiction between the healthy social and financial situation of club rugby, and its weakening hold, relative to the booming attendance figures of the immediate post-war era, as a spectator sport. The W.R.U. had emerged from the War with 104 member clubs in 1946-7; ten years later there were 130, and the number was increasing annually without any relaxation of the Union's probationary regulations.

Welsh rugby in the fifties was both beneficiary and victim of the upward swing of the economic pendulum. It was a decade that saw an upsurge in consumer power which, by comparison with the 1930s and the rigours of post-war austerity, made it seem a promised land. This increase in material wealth diverted many away from traditional pursuits — football, cinema, even the churches. As entertainment moved away from public arenas to the home, television claimed the nation's attention. Falling gates caused by the live televising of rugby internationals were a major concern to clubs from the mid-fifties. When the 1955 Scotland v. Wales match was broadcast live from Murrayfield, the game between Aberavon and Abertillery, which would normally have produced a crowd of 4,000 and receipts of £150, attracted less than 400 and a gate of £9. This highlighted a further paradox, for although millions more people were watching sport — and international rugby drew an ever-increasing television audience — attendances at club matches declined. Yet the fifties saw Welsh club rugby acquire a modern face-lift as dedicated officials and members set about attaining improved status, financial independence, and increased accommodation for their players and followers. The post-war years had been bleak for many clubs: Carmarthen R.F.C. moved into peace-time with 15s. 8d. in the bank, Cefneithin with 5s. 6d. Machen faced the future with a membership of eight and shorts made out of black-out material; but all saw renewed expansion in the 1950s. Blaina resorted to a device simultaneously adopted by many struggling post-war clubs: they set up a 'coupon fund' to which committee-men and players contributed clothing coupons to acquire kit. From there, Blaina went on to build a new stand in 1954 and a clubhouse eight years later. By then, one of Blaina's most famous products, David Watkins, was playing for Newport and on the verge of international fame which brought further renown to the valley club with whom he had begun his senior career in 1959. Not all clubs could claim a David Watkins nor, either, an administrator like David Jones — the legendary 'Dai Blaina' right up to his death in 1970 devoted a lifetime of service to rugby in Blaina and Wales, serving the W.R.U. from 1930 in innumerable capacities as selector, I.B. representative, trustee, and finally President of the Union in 1965-66 — but Blaina's experience was otherwise typical of many Welsh clubs, large and small, in the fifties, as grounds were bought or leased from generally co-operative local authorities. Glamorgan Wanderers purchased the Memorial Ground at Ely in 1951, Llanelli bought the rugby portion of Stradey Park in 1952: both clubs immediately set about developing their new acquisitions. The social activities of clubs were extended, the formation of ladies' committees became an integral part of club administration — in 1975, it was one of its women members who would write Blaina's centenary history.

Nor was it only South Wales rugby that saw this strengthening of its physical and social fabric. In rural Cardiganshire, clubs like Lampeter and Aberystwyth entered on a period of striking expansion. The post-war history of rugby at both university towns is a notable illustration of the interaction of general and local factors making for growth. With its rail network linking it to the soccer-playing woollen towns of the Severn Valley and North Wales, Aberystwyth was never a rugby stronghold, but the general post-war enthusiasm for sport, the growth of secondary school rugby, the influx of South Walians, improved motor transport, a change in the composition of the town council that led to the provision of playing fields, the influence and high quality of College rugby — future internationals like Peter Stone, Alun Thomas, Carwyn James and John Dawes turned out for the town as well as the university — these resulted in the climb of Aberystwyth R.F.C. from its foundation in 1947 by a nucleus of southern émigrés, to probationary membership of the W.R.U. in 1954, and two years later, after a visitation by representatives of the Union, the status of full membership. Then, thanks to strenuous effort and the help of an interest-free ten-year loan from the W.R.U., a clubhouse was opened in 1960. The cup of joy of this 'small club' — by its own definition —

'peripheral to the hotbed of South Wales rugby but separated by a million miles gulf from the Dovey divide', overflowed when a local boy, W. J. (Bill) Morris, by then playing for Pontypool, won two caps for Wales in 1963. It typified the experience of countless small clubs extending in a broad arc from Ceredigion to Gwent.

North of 'the Dovey divide', though, the situation was less promising. There, the bridgehead established in the 1930s was in danger of collapse by the early fifties, and it was in answer to repeated pleas for help that the W.R.U. eventually consented to send a fact-finding party to North Wales to assess the situation. Matters had not been entirely satisfactory in the thirties themselves for, though the number of clubs in the North Wales R.U. had risen from four in 1930 to eleven in 1938, their financial state was parlous enough for the W.R.U. to increase their grant to £120 per annum. The war cancelled any hopes of resurrection and it was not until 1947 that the North Wales Union held its first post-war meeting. Woefully they sent a deputation south, yet again, in 1948 to report the existence of seven small clubs, no gate money, sparse equipment and few recruits — 'although', the W.R.U. were informed, 'they are members of the W.R.U., they get to know very little about it. They would like to know more for the sake of rugby in North Wales'. Beset by their own post-war difficulties, the Union felt unable to do more than increase the grant once more, to £150, and it was not until the 1950s that closer, more lasting, links were forged. The W.R.U. had been reminded in 1950 by complaints from London Welsh that the Union had, in 1898, taken a decision, never rescinded, to favour for international honours those Welshmen in the English metropolis who turned out for London Welsh. Encouragement for rugby in the north was clearly, as dedicated men encouraged it in the schools and towns, no less a priority (North Walian London Welshmen would make the point, in the best possible way, from the late 1960s). Rowe Harding, who had been elected a vice-president in 1953, investigated the N.W.R.U. later that year and reported favourably on the hard work being done to overcome the difficulty of distances between clubs, and the rooted popularity of soccer. Down south the advice was that, Wrexham and Bangor apart, the clubs of the N.W.R.U., with no prejudice to that body's authority, should join the Welsh Junior Union. Sympathy would not be lacking again and those who fostered rugby in North Wales would end by repaying the interest shown in a rich dividend of administrators and players. The meteoric rise to fame of Dewi Bebb in 1959 would be a salutary, early reminder of the potential of North Wales rugby.

In the south, meanwhile, clubs were making their own initiatives. In the 1956-7 season, Glamorgan R.F.C. launched the Silver Ball competition, to be contested by the county's second-class clubs. It was first won by Taibach, prospering in the shadow of the Port Talbot steel works. Swansea, in 1954, became the first team to lift a corner of the Iron Curtain by visiting Romania, and Cardiff went there three years later; in 1957, too, Llanelli became the first rugby side from Britain to play in Moscow. As the fifties opened, economic prosperity once again propelled valley clubs to the fore of Welsh rugby: Newbridge, Ebbw Vale and Maesteg. In 1949-50 Maesteg enjoyed an invincible season and headed the unofficial Welsh club championship for the first time ever. Its inspiration was scrum-half captain Trevor Lloyd, who won two caps in 1953, following on from Windsor Major's two caps of three years before, and who later carried the reputation of the Old Parish to the South African veldt, as a 1955 Lion. Maesteg's unbeaten run of fifty-two games had ended in September 1950 when they lost 3 - 0 to their homeless rivals, Bridgend. The fifties were a turning-point for Bridgend, too; in 1957 they regained possession of the Brewery Field, and immediately resumed supplying the Welsh team with men like W. R. (Roddy) Evans and the long-legged Ken Richards. That mid-Glamorgan rugby was now of international class was confirmed when in 1962 Richards was succeeded as Wales's fly-half by Alan Rees of Maesteg.

The inter-club rivalry which was still the life-blood of Welsh rugby was at its peak in the exhilarating though keenly fought early fifties' clashes of the 'sister ports' of Cardiff and Newport. The Blue-and-Blacks were a major attraction wherever they played: in 1952, a crowd of 23,000 saw them at Pontypool Park, 20,000 at the Talbot Athletic Ground, 40,000 at St. Helen's. The turnstiles revolved like tops at Rodney Parade, too, where the Black-and-Ambers were themselves one of the most polished and efficient of club sides; with Roy Burnett, Ken Jones and John Lane behind the scrum, they won 37 of their 40 games in 1950-1, and scored an average of 14 points a match in 1951-2. In 1955-6 Newport v. Cardiff clashes could still draw 30,000 to Rodney Parade, and 35,000 to the Arms Park. It was at the Arms Park, in February 1951, that a club world record attendance of 48,500 — paying receipts of £2,587, a far cry from the £72 taken at the 1879 Cup Final between the two clubs — saw Newport beat Cardiff 8 - 3. With every stand ticket snapped up a week in advance, and the Cardiff club deluged by requests for tickets from coach parties all over the south of England, let alone Wales, the drama of the occasion was heightened mid-way through the second half, when the sky went theatrically dark and a violent storm broke over the ground. Bombarded by hailstones as big as rugby balls, the players threw themselves to the ground in the approved 'blitz' style. Although the tempest eased, the thrills had not, for with Newport ahead, Cardiff's elegant left-winger Haydn Morris was worked clear by his centres and went flat-out for the corner. A try seemed certain until Newport's Ken Jones, equally graceful and just as fast, hurled himself at Morris and flung him into touch at the corner flag.

The high-speed clashes of Morris and Jones, constantly renewed in club and trial matches throughout the early fifties, epitomized the spirit and much of the style of Welsh club and international rugby in that period. Mountain Ash-born Haydn Morris, 5foot 9inches, 11stone 12lb., was a sinewy, silky greyhound whose flowing speed won him a handful of caps between 1951 and 1955, as well as a Lions tour. A Barry sports-master, he recovered from an injury that had threatened to terminate his career in 1953 to play his best rugby in 1954-55. In the 21 - 3 defeat of Ireland that season he spiced his pace with a neat opportunism by kicking on a pass placed three yards in front of him and outstripping everyone to the touch-down in a style on which J. J. Williams might have modelled his play in the 1970s. Two weeks later in Paris, when Maurice Prat was tackled in midfield, a quick heel by the Welsh forwards saw the ball reach Alun Thomas on the right-wing who kicked across into the centre for Morris to race up and jump high for it on the line with a leap that practically took him back to Barry without bothering about the boat.

K. J. Jones had an equal appetite for try-getting, but could claim even more attributes — a resistance to injury and a gritty defence — that brought him forty-four caps. He established himself as one of the outstanding personalities of the decade, a fact which Newport Borough Council duly recognized in April 1956 when they held a civic reception in his honour and gave him an illuminated scroll. With his jet-black hair, his head slightly forward from his angular, bony frame, and his stamina and streamlined grace of movement, Ken Jones in flight resembled nothing as much as a jaguar. Welsh wings, and there were many great ones in the three post-war decades, moved in different ways. Haydn Morris flowed, Gwyn Rowlands pounded, John Collins scorched, Lynn 'Cowboy' Davies high-tailed, Dewi Bebb scampered, Stuart Watkins powered, Keri Jones sprinted, Maurice Richards shimmied, John Bevan bulldozed, Gerald Davies sizzled, J. J. Williams flew: they all ran in the long shadow cast by Kenneth Jeffrey Jones, who did all those things at different times, and often simultaneously. Born in Blaenavon in 1921, Ken had been guided by

Gilbert Garnett at West Monmouth G.S. in Pontypool, and gone on to win his Welsh S.S. cap. From 1950 he taught at Newport H.S., whilst his fame as a rugby player caught up with his reputation as an athlete. Already Welsh and A.A.A. sprint champion, in 1948 he had reached the semi-final of the 100 metres at the London Olympic Games — an event itself symbolic of the post-war British enthusiasm for sport — and he ran again in the Empire Games at Vancouver in 1954. As much in recognition of his innate sportsmanship as his speed on the cinders, he was honoured with the captaincy of the British team at the European games in Berne in the same year. He had not missed an international since 1947, though his position on the right wing — three-quarter lines move naturally to the left: it was from there that Les Williams, Dewi Bebb and Maurice Richards scored their bagfuls of tries against England in 1949-59-69 — meant that he had few tries to show for it. The writer A. A. Thomson, concerned at Ken's constant isolation, suggested that he should have a notice stuck to his jersey announcing, 'Running in, please pass'. Still, he went some way to restoring the balance on tour with the Lions to Australia and New Zealand in 1950, when he scored 17 tries in 17 matches. Those who saw it would years later still be calling it 'the greatest try of all', that cardiac-arresting moment in the Fourth Test at Auckland when Lewis Jones, at full-back, with supreme effrontery intercepted a pass from Kyle to Bleddyn Williams in his own in-goal area, knifed through a hallucinated defence — as his namesake Ivor had done in 1930 — committed Bob Scott to the tackle and found Ken Jones outside him with fifty yards to widen the gap between himself and the formidably fast Peter Henderson to touch-down between the posts. It was not the last the All Blacks had seen of Ken's retreating form.

The sight of Ken Jones in full flight for the line induced even experienced commentators to abandon their code of professional ethics and just yell. J. B. G. Thomas confessed how he thumped the press box and shouted 'Go on Ken!' as Jones streaked for the line in Dublin in 1952. G. V. Wynne-Jones was another sort of commentator: thousands who never saw him were raised to frantic excitement by Geevers's throaty descriptions of Ken Jones racing to score. It was one of his countless admirers, Alun Richards, the novelist who scripted the B.B.C. Wales-W.R.U. Centenary film, *A Touch of Glory*, who referred to Geevers's 'port and cigars'-accented match commentaries. Those commentaries were as inextricably woven into the schoolboy (and upwards) culture of the post-war radio era in a pre-television Wales as *Dick Barton, P.C. 49, S.O.S. Galw Gari Tryfan*, and the Treorchy choir's aggressive 'Sospan Fach' introduction to *Welsh*

Sports Medley on Saturday nights at 6.30 p.m. with Jack Elwyn Watkins and Jack Salter. For two decades from 1947 'Geevers' was the broadcast voice of Welsh rugby, the eyes and ears of millions, as he was at Twickenham in January 1952 — 'and now Morgan is tearing away down the middle of the field there' (Geevers's 'there' was his trademark) — becoming agitated — 'with Ken Jones outside him' — suddenly shouting hoarsely — '. . . KEN JONES IS GOING TO SCORE . . . FROM FORTY YARDS OUT . . . THEY'LL NEVER CATCH HIM NOW . . . UNDER, BEHIND THE POSTS, A BEAUTIFUL TRY'.

The year 1952 was indeed a vintage year for Ken Jones. That season Wales returned in renewed quest of the Triple Crown. The Welsh XV was not substantially different from that which had won it in 1950. Gwilliam was still in command, though W. O. Williams was now at prop, Rees Stephens was reunited with his Gnoll parner Roy John, and Allen Forward filled the vacancy left by a chagrined, and now professional, Ray Cale. P.C. Allen Forward was the sort of well-built flanker who, had he not been weaned on Monmouthshire valley forward folklore, would anywhere else have played at centre, for he could have fitted with little difficulty into any back division. (The situation was reversed by the 1970s, when it would be claimed that natural flankers were playing in the Welsh centre). Behind the scrum the backs had changed little since 1950, except for the emergence of Cliff Morgan at fly-half. With greater flexibility at half-back, English rugby finding its bearings, Scotland in the process of losing theirs, and Ireland's perceptibly rusting, Wales was able to play a more expansive game in the Triple Crown campaign of 1952 than two years before, when the opposition was tougher. The one who most benefited from the new conditions was Ken Jones.

By 1952 Ken was as fit as Stephane Grappelli's fiddle, and even faster. At 5foot 11inches and 12½stone, as tapered as a propelling pencil, he had a lean and hungry look that made Shakespeare's Cassius look over-fed. He was hungry enough to score in all three Triple Crown matches. At Twickenham, his first effort had induced a paroxysm of excitement in the commentary box, as G. V. Wynne-Jones's listeners adjusted their volume control or risked perforation of the ear-drums. His second showed that he had skill as well as speed, though the build-up to it suggested that the team had learnt something from watching Nervo and Knox of the Crazy Gang the night before. With Wales 6 - 5 down, from a scrum ten minutes into the second half and thirty yards from the English line, a limping Lewis Jones hobbled in to make the extra man, even while standing still made a half-dummy that bemused the England defence, and moved the ball along the line to Ken Jones, now at full stretch, who first turned inside his opposite number then swung outside full-back Bill Hook to cross wide out. The Scottish match was less dramatic, though the 56,000 who paid record Arms Park receipts of £14,506 saw Rex Willis play with 'tremendous courage' (the words were those of Emlyn Lewis, head of the plastic surgery unit at St. Lawrence Hospital, Chepstow) after breaking his jaw in two places early in the second half. Ken Jones's try this time came from that thoughtful preparation beforehand, allied to speed and science, which hall-marked the Gwilliam era. It came from the variation of an idea that Gwilliam had adapted from Gallaher and Stead's priceless 1906 volume, involving the use of the blind-side wing coming into the three-quarters. Rex Willis threw the ball into a line-out, where Roy John at no. 3 deflected it back to the scrum-half racing infield, fast. Willis, naturally, could not resist dive-passing, but taking the ball on the run his pass acquired stupendous length. Cliff Morgan took it standing out in the middle of the field, Alun Thomas raced in from the blind-side wing to take the fly-half's in-pass, cut through, and sent a long pass out to Ken Jones who streaked away to score.

With the challenge of Lansdowne Road looming, the selectors recalled Clem Thomas, and he was the one chiefly responsible for ripping the holes in the Irish defence through which Wales poured to score three tries in a 14 - 3 win. Eight thousand followers went over, though only half that number of tickets had been allocated to Wales — such was the demand on both sides of the Celtic Sea that an Irish advert offering a Rolls-Royce in part payment for four stand tickets drew the anxious query 'What year Rolls-Royce?' — and a capacity crowd saw the Welsh pack wear down spirited Irish resistance. Clem Thomas bottled up the genie that was Kyle, Alun Thomas got among the Irish backs, Lewis Jones, still only twenty, was 'just himself, the Welsh wag', Allen Forward was so energetic he burst a blood vessel, and Cliff Morgan contrived one of the best tries in post-war international rugby. Naturally it was the ever-vigilant Ken Jones who finished it off. Cliff received from a line-out inside his own 25, cut across field, and on the ten-yard line slipped a short pass to Ken who had come in, as was his fashion, from the right, to execute a huge scissors and hare away for a fifty-yard Triple Crown try. There would be no more Welsh crowns during the fifties and only two more international tries, both in 1953, for Ken Jones, though no Welsh XV would take the field without him till 1957. His long career was safely in the hands of another unassuming son of

Monmouthshire, the quiet physiotherapist from Cross Keys who had been appointed the first permanent team attendant for Wales in the 1930s. This was Ray 'Mr Magic Hands' Lewis of whom Ken Jones would say — 'Without Ray Lewis I don't think Welsh rugby and I, personally, would have survived'. 1957 would see the end of the great wing's career but not of that Lewis loving care.

The year 1953, though, would be remembered for a number of reasons. In rugby terms it saw the coronation of Bleddyn Williams's international career, when he became captain for the visit to Murrayfield, scored two marvellous tries in a 12 - 0 revenge for the massacre of 1951, and then led Cardiff and Wales to a historic double against the Fourth All Blacks; Ken Jones scored his last and most famous international try in that thrombotic encounter, too. But 1953 was a particularly memorable year for his club-mate Roy Burnett, who climbed his own Everest by unseating Cliff Morgan, albeit briefly, from the Welsh fly-half position. Much of the greatness of the Newport side of the 1950s turned on the Cwmcarn-born, fair-haired Burnett, who had lost a brother in the Llandow disaster and played with the verve and commitment of a man determined to compress two careers into one. He served his club for thirteen years, during which he made a record number of 372 appearances, mostly at fly-half, but finally on the wing. He was the greatest single attraction at Rodney Parade since Gould, and on his retirement the affection in which he was held by his legion of admirers was shown when he was presented with his portrait in oils. Elusive, intricate, yet unselfish, he was the mainspring of the high-scoring Newport side of the early fifties. 'Followers of the game, many without any Newport allegiance, regularly travelled long distances just to see them play', wrote the club's historian, Jack Davis, of those years. 'They were the biggest money-spinners the game had ever known . . . it was just attack, attack, attack. Greybeards shook their heads as Burnett and his colleagues, quite as a matter of habit, began scoring tries from moves within their own 25, even from behind their own goal-line'. Paradoxically, it was precisely during these heady high-scoring years that Ken Jones learned to develop a stoical but cheery indifference to his neglect on the right wing, for the ball, moving insistently to the left where John Lane in two season 1951-2-3 scored 55 tries, seldom reached Ken Jones on the right, so that he scored only 27 tries in the five seasons 1948-52, and a meagre 6 of the 67 scored by Newport in 1950-1. Yet the real continuity man, the lynch-pin of the Newport, and often Welsh, three-quarter line throughout the entire decade was M. C. Thomas, the Idwal Rees of the

1950s. Named after the record-breaking racing driver Malcolm Campbell, the Machen-born Thomas, a sturdy 5foot 10inches and 13½stone, broke records of his own as an individual points scorer with the 1950 and 1959 Lions in New Zealand. Resilient, fast enough to play on the wing, an astute tactical punter and accurate place-kicker, strong in the tackle and equipped with a hand-off that could upend an elephant, Thomas played in every game from his first cap in 1949 to the England match of 1953, then fought his way back into the Welsh side in 1956 to win a total of 27 caps in a career that finally ended in 1959, at Colombes, where it had begun ten years before.

Best remembered as a centre, it was not until the French match of 1951 that he first appeared in that position. In that game Jack Matthews and Bob Evans wore the Welsh jersey for the last time, while making their first appearance were the twenty-two-year-old Haydn Morris and the Royal Navy and Swansea boilermaker W. O. (Billy) Williams who would put his 5foot 11inches and 14½stone to maximum advantage in the front-row for Wales for another twenty-one consecutive caps. The Cardiff pair of Rex Willis and Cliff Morgan played themselves into the Welsh side at the end of 1951, too, and would play together fifteen times in all until 1955, when Willis won the last of his twenty-one caps. Morgan had come into the side against Ireland in place of Glyn Davies who was paying the price, with others, of the notorious Murrayfield massacre. In February 1951 a Welsh team of all the talents, including eleven Lions, had gone to Scotland having just demolished England 23 - 5 at St. Helen's. The Scots had big forwards, but an extremely young and inexperienced back division, and against a Welsh XV that had not been subdued since first combining at Twickenham in 1950, their chances were generally thought to be microscopic. Moreover, Gwilliam, who was teaching at Glenalmond and playing for Edinburgh Wanderers, had a greater knowledge of Scottish rugby than Scotland's own captain, Peter Kininmonth, who played for Richmond. Whether the Welshmen were over-confident, or simply stale, this team of galactic brilliance was shredded 19 - 0, and their 25,000 supporters in the record 81,000 crowd returned shell-shocked through the snowbound Scottish lowlands like Napoleon's *grande armée* retreating from Moscow. As the stop presses flashed the result to the world, it was greeted with the same incredulity as the 53 - 4 score of the First All Blacks' opening match in 1905. Gwilliam's response to the disaster was characteristically clear-headed. There was 'no dark unrevealed secret' to explain it: the Scottish victory was purely 'a prime example of the tenet that the art of rugby football is to be better than the other side at any given moment . . . On the day the Scots were simply a livelier, more spirited side'. Before, and afterwards, the Welsh were certainly a superior side; they would hold the victorious Springboks to 6 - 3 later that year, and take the Grand Slam in 1952, whereas Scotland, afterwards, would be annihilated 44 - 0 by the Springboks and fail to win again for another sixteen games. That would be in February 1955, at Murrayfield, heralded by a drop goal, as Kininmonth's had announced impending nemesis for Gwilliam's team in 1951, and it would be against Wales, who did not beat England at home and Scotland away in the same season between 1932 and 1965. The selectors' response in 1951 was far less phlegmatic than Gwilliam's. In choosing the team to meet Ireland, they left an unprecedented five positions vacant. One of them was at fly-half. Eyes were on Roy Burnett, but in the final minutes of a game against Cardiff he broke his collarbone, and despite fears that he was being tried too early, into the Welsh side spun the Rhondda roundabout, Cliff Morgan.

The succession of William Benjamin Cleaver by Clifford Isaac Morgan as Triple Crown fly-half confirmed a long-held suspicion that, years ago, one of the lost tribes of Israel had somehow wandered into South Wales. Cliff always played with the passionate urgency of a man trying to get out again. With the ball held at arm's length in front of him, his tongue out almost as far, his bow legs pumping like pistons, eyes rolling, nostrils flaring, and a range of facial expressions seldom seen north of Milan — either at the opera house or the soccer stadium — the dark-haired, Celtically-constructed, perky Morgan was, at 5foot 7inches and 12 stone, the identikit Welsh outside-half. But no-one could have assembled Cliff; he was an amalgam of the social and cultural forces that had shaped modern Wales and of the currents that were defining Welshness anew in the second half of the twentieth century. Cliff came from Trebanog, a precipitous offshoot of the Rhondda, on whose windy ridge people clung together for warmth and safety lest the storms of the world blew them away; he would never lose a sense of this induced Welsh, almost cosy, togetherness. His was the Welshness of a nonconformist home where Mam ruled and Sunday was for chapel, which meant that Cliff was humming snatches of oratorio before he was out of the shawl. The rugby crowds of the 1950s —strong, now, on 'Blaenwern', 'I bob un', 'We'll keep a Welcome', and 'The Holy City' ('. . . lift up your gates, and sing') — were the last of the harmonious generations brought up on choir practice and the Band of Hope. If there had been room on the terraces to dance then the incessant rain of the fifties would have completed a mass Welsh imitation of the era's favourite Hollywood musical; and if that international crowd could have managed something from the 'Messiah' — as, in the fifties, sections of it still could — the chorus best calculated to inspire Cliff Morgan would have been, 'Let us break their bonds asunder'. It might have been written with him specifically in mind — South Wales is liberally endowed with Handels — for Cliff's india-rubber face typified the unbelievable springiness of his whole body: a favourite ruse of his for evading the clutches of opponents who had managed actually to lay hands on him was to go limp in their embrace; then, as the tackler momentarily relaxed his grip, Cliff jumped out of the tackle with an agility that made Harry Houdini look arthritic, and scurried away.

Born in 1930, Cliff had gone to Tonyrefail G.S. and came under the sensitive care of sportsmaster E. R. Gribble. It was 'Ned' Gribble who in 1956 would lead a W.S.S.R.U. party — with Alan Rees (Glanafan G.S.) and Clive Rowlands (Ystradgynlais G.S.) at half-back — to South Africa, where it won seven of its eight matches. His reputation as a rugby mentor was established by his nurturing of the effervescent genius of the boy Morgan, whom he guided to international schoolboy honours just after the war. It was not only the joys of rugby that Cliff discovered in school, but his own Welsh identity. Writing on the occasion of the Urdd Jubilee Match (*Gêm y Dathlu*), played, to celebrate the fiftieth anniversary of its founding, at the National Ground in April 1972, where both teams were selected by two other former Urdd members and international fly-halves, Carwyn James and Barry John — it was 'The King's' last appearance and he left as a lingering memory a ghostly fifty-yard solo try — Cliff Morgan recalled what Urdd Gobaith Cymru (the Welsh League of Youth) had done for him. 'It was around the age of 11 or 12 that I became a member [of the Urdd] at Tonyrefail Grammar School. D. J. Williams ran a flourishing branch with a variety of activities. Visits by Dr. Iorwerth Peate, the doyen of Folk Life Studies, Cliff Jones, the Welsh rugby international, a trio from University College, Cardiff, and a Folk Group from Pontlottyn. We had dances and discussions, Noson Lawen and Mabolgampau [sports]. But it wasn't until I went to the Urdd camp at Llangrannog about 1945 or 6 that I really felt a sense of Welshness and of belonging. It's easy to fall in love with Llangrannog with its beaches and the green-blue sea . . .' Cliff had fallen in love with a Welshness that was, culturally and geographically, distinct from the one he knew in his native Rhondda. His reinforced sense of identity reflected a muted national awareness of broken links that rumbled off-stage during the 1950s. Lacking the sharp edges, the readiness to defy authority and challenge power structures that became features of Welsh political and language movements in the sixties and seventies, the mini-nationalism of the fifties — the Parliament for Wales movement led by Lady Megan Lloyd George, ex-Liberal and Labour M.P. for Carmarthen from 1957 to 1966, and S. O. Davies, Labour and then Independent Labour M.P. for Merthyr from 1934 to 1972; the Welsh Schools movement that made inroads into anglicized Glamorgan (though, as late as 1951, most Welsh speakers still lived there); the campaign for the formal recognition of Cardiff as Wales's capital city — was most agreeably personified on the rugby field by Cliff Morgan.

His international career — he played his first home game for Cardiff at nineteen against Oxford University in October 1949 — extended from the drawn match with Ireland in 1951 to the historic 16 - 6 defeat by France at Cardiff in 1958. During the course of his twenty-nine-cap career he adjusted his play to the changing requirements of those years. By instinct an attacking player of unquenchable spirit, he played his finest running game for Wales in 1952 against Ireland. His most memorable Welsh try was also against Ireland in 1955 when a generally lifeless game was transformed in its last quarter when Wales suddenly ran up 18 points in as many minutes to turn a 3 - 3 stalemate into a 21 - 3 demolition job. The points avalanche included one furiously individualistic try by the Trebanog terrier as he tore into a thicket of defenders, got lost, and shot out the other side and over the line. But there was more to his game than just pyrotechnics. Though sometimes as unpredictable as a jackie-jumper, he generally jumped with a purpose. He spent his whole rugby career working endlessly for an extra half yard of space; when he failed to pierce the defence himself, his pass often did, and he gave a masterly exposition of his skill as distributor, as well as dodger, in partnership with England's Jeff Butterfield in South Africa in 1955, when his pass in itself often put that gifted centre into the gap. From that year on, he revealed extra qualities as tactical kicker and tireless coverer. In 1958, his creativity increasingly at the mercy of tighter back-row defences and ruthless midfield marking, he harnessed the notorious Twickenham swirl and dominated the match tactically to earn an injury-hit Wales a 3-all draw by kicking cleverly and insistently to the right-hand corner in the lee of the west stand. Beneath the lilting voice and warm personality there was a decisive streak that later took him to the Head of B.B.C. Outside Broadcasting. In the scarlet jersey, he learned decisiveness the hard way. Against Ireland, on his début, he faced

342

Jack Kyle. He was rightly apprehensive of the Irishman's reputation, but as the game progressed and Kyle seemed reluctant to do anything much, Morgan allowed his concentration to flicker. Kyle sensed it and was suddenly past him for a crucial, equalizing score. It was not the only lesson Morgan learned in 1951.

In December Wales met South Africa. Coming as they did betweeen Osler's 'incorrigibly dull' team of 1931 (in O. L. Owen's phrase) and Malan's dour and seemingly unsociable party of 1960-1, Basil Kenyon's Fourth Springboks won universal acclaim, and the years have not diminished their reputation as the most attractive of all South African tourists. It was a team well-equipped in all departments. Forwards like Chris Koch at prop, 'Salty' du Rand at lock, and the priceless back-row of Stephen Fry, 'Basie' van Wyk and Hennie Muller arrived with formidable reputations after their 4 - 0 victories in the Test Series against the 1949 All Blacks. The self-confident, sunken-eyed, round-shouldered but fast and predatory Muller set new standards for all aspiring No. 8 forwards to emulate. After Kenyon suffered an unfortunate eye injury in the third game of the tour at Pontypool Park, it was Muller, 'the greyhound of the veldt', who assumed the leadership and led his team through a clean sweep of the internationals and an unbeaten tour except for the 11 - 3 defeat by London Counties who, with Gerwyn Williams at full-back, relieved the team of its invincible tag and enabled it to play to its full, and attractive, potential. At fly-half was 'Hansie' Brewis, a Northern Transvaal police sergeant who modelled his play on that of Osler, his master, but who knew, too, how to utilize the men behind him — centres like M. T. Lategan and the crash-tackling Ryk van Schoor, and, on the left-wing, the square-faced, especial Welsh favourite, J. K. (Chum) Ochse. With his baggy shorts flapping like pillow cases, Ochse pronounced 'Oosh' — scored match-winning tries against Cardiff and Wales: nobody would have given anyone in the world a chance of scoring a try through a double tackle by Ken Jones and Gerwyn Williams, but 'Chum' did it. Behind them all was the twenty-one-year-old Baptist lay-preacher, Johnny Buchler, who at the age of seven was already dropping goals over the roof of his house. Coached by assistant manager Danie Craven, who had been initiated into the intensity of Welsh rugby with Osler's team of 1931, the 1951-2 Springboks specialized in close support work interpassing among the forwards, the snap shove perfected by a scientific use of an angled 3-4-1 scrum, and diagonal punts to the corner, placed generally with unnerving accuracy by Brewis. Like their 1931 predecessors, this Springbok pack met

343

its match in Wales: held in the scrums, where the Welsh selectors, embarrassed by their wealth of second-row talent, had converted Don Hayward and W. O. Williams to props, they were beaten out of sight in the line-outs. Where Wales lost was in a lack of tactical variation; the key-note of non-spontaneity had been struck before the kick-off by the unfamiliar and subsequently unrepeated sight of a man in a white coat leading the pre-match singing. For some reason, maybe the conviction that the only way to restrict the South African back-row was to put the ball behind them, it had been decided that the Springboks would be vulnerable to assorted stab-punts, grubbers and short kicks ahead. That was what the Welsh midfield backs did all afternoon, though a three-quarter line of Ken Jones, Malcolm Thomas, Bleddyn Williams and Lewis Jones constituted a far greater threat than their opponents; as it was, Buchler's superb anticipation made it look as if all the kicks were being directed specifically at him. On Craven's orders, no attempt was made to control the unequal line-out struggle with Roy John, who was supreme — Wales dominated this phase of play 38 - 21 — but Fry was detailed to look after Willis, while van Wyk and Muller moved on to Morgan. 'As I see it', wrote Muller, 'the job of the number eight in the line-out is to make the opposing fly-half part with the ball in a hurry', and he ensured that Morgan saw it that way, too, as Wales snatched defeat from the jaws of victory and lost 6 - 3.

It was a tribute to Morgan's character that he survived that ordeal, physically and psychologically. In 1955 a mature Morgan was avenged in the First Test in front of a world record 95,000 at Ellis Park, Johannesburg. By now his menace lay not so much in what he did as in what he made his opponents think he might do. In the split second his great rival 'Basie' van Wyk thought, Cliff did it. Receiving a long pass from Dick Jeeps, his sharp rugby intelligence detected a momentary second of indecision in the face of the Springbok flanker. In that moment, 'Basie' and South Africa were lost as Morgan, in Vivian Jenkins's description, 'his slightly bandy legs moving like the wheels of a clockwork engine lifted off the rails' broke past van Wyk on the outside and tore around the Springbok defence in a great arc to score in the Lions' 23 - 22 victory. In the Third Test Morgan captained them to a 9 - 6 win, controlling the game tactically and keeping the ball close to his forwards, as Brewis had done in 1951. For the first time this century, the Lions had shared a Test series, and there was little doubt that the inspirational genius was Cliff Morgan. His revenge was sweet indeed after having played all afternoon into Buchler's hands in 1951. Thanks to

344

that experience, when he had been made to look the best full-back in the world, Buchler later returned Wales's generosity by acclaiming all things Welsh. Cliff Morgan was a genius, Roy John the greatest forward, Ken Jones the greatest wing, Gwilliam the greatest captain. Cardiff was the best club, Welsh spectators the most intelligent, Morriston Orpheus the greatest choir. He said too that Bleddyn Williams was the 'classiest' centre.

Bleddyn scored a record 185 'classy' tries for Cardiff in the course of his ten seasons with the club, 7 for Wales during a twenty-two-cap international career between 1947 and 1955 and 13 for the Lions in 1950. By 1951 he was, like Ken Jones, already a legend, and none of those tries was finer than the one he scored for Wales against South Africa that year. In the dying minutes, Gwilliam fed Morgan underarm from a line-out: the pivot, learning fast but too late to alter the result, noticed the Springboks lying back in anticipation of the inevitable kick. Instead, Morgan moved it to Bleddyn Williams who scissored perfectly with Malcolm Thomas for the Newport centre to go racing up to Buchler and find Bleddyn once again on his right to take the final scoring pass. It was a try of limpid perfection, illustrating superbly the serene skills that earned B. L. Williams the accolade of being 'the Prince of centre three-quarters'. His football prowess merely confirmed the suitability of his Christian names, Bleddyn Llewellyn, which were themselves resonantly evocative of the princely rulers, and poets, of medieval Wales. He could never satiate his thirst for rugby —amateur rugby; he resisted constant professional inducements approaching £10,000, a three-year contract and a job. Returning almost immediately to the fray after the tiring Lions tour of 1950, he was plagued by a series of niggling injuries which kept him out of all but one game in the triumphant 1950 and 1952 seasons. He made only one international appearance at Twickenham, in 1948, though his reputation was as resplendent in England, and beyond, as it was in Wales. He also played wholeheartedly right up to the final whistle — against Scotland in 1947, Ireland in 1948 and South Africa in 1951, although the game was slipping conclusively from Wales's grasp, Bleddyn still produced scoring sparks of that genius which flared throughout the post-war years.

Bleddyn Williams, one of a remarkable family of eight rugby-playing sons of a Taff's Well coal-trimmer, was born in 1923. All eight boys played for Cardiff and two of them captained Wales. It was on the recommendation of Wilfred Wooller, who had glimpsed premonitions of his greatness for Cardiff Schoolboys, that Rydal School offered Bleddyn a scholarship at fourteen years of age. There, under the keen eye of A. J. Costain, he played at outside-half, though the presence of W. T. H. Davies in the R.A.F. side of the war years forced him into the centre. It was at fly-half that he was first capped in 1947, against England, when he pulled a muscle in the first minute and had an uncomfortable afternoon. Thereafter his position was always left-centre. He had played his first game for Cardiff Athletic in 1938 while still at Rydal, but already he knew he could do what he had first seen Cardiff's impish pre-war full-back Tommy Stone once do and decided to try it himself: jink. As with all great players, the self-knowledge acquired from discovering that he was naturally gifted enabled him confidently to build a variety of skills on that foundation. The excellence of his judgement, the selflessness of his centre play, the perfection with which he timed his passes to his wing who received the ball in a postion where he had only the full-back to beat, enabled others to play to their fullest potential. Haydn Morris never forgot that Bleddyn had once told him that he would never give him the ball unless he could score: the 101 tries that Morris scored on Cardiff's left-wing between 1950 and 1956 bore this out. A former fly-half, Bleddyn could kick equally well off either foot, his short punting, as he showed for Cardiff against the 1953 All Blacks, was masterful, while his tackling and covering carried the same impeccable hall-mark as his attacking craft. However, it was the jink that immortalized him. It must have been devised with Bleddyn — a hefty 13½ stone packed into 5foot 10inches, a face like a well-inflated football, a torso like a tree-trunk and the muscular thighs of a Renaissance sculpture — specifically in mind. He elevated it to such an art that it became a species separate from the sidestep. He could do that naturally too, off either foot, though he was at his deadliest going off his right. The sidestep is done at speed, performed as Gerald Davies would again breath-takingly demonstrate, without any perceptible lessening of pace. Its essence is timing. The jink, Bleddyn's jink, was a more static affair. It meant coming almost to a temporary halt. Its essence was positional and psychological, whereby one drew the opponent into knowing the jink was coming, though when it did come he was helpless to do anything about it. The thousands who thronged to see Cardiff play went to see Bleddyn's rippling jink. The best vantage point from which to appreciate it was behind the posts: as Bleddyn received the ball along the line and moved up on his man, checked, and transferred his weight from one foot to the other, tremors of expectation ran through the crowd. Knowing fathers nudged their sons: watch Bleddyn. And invariably Bleddyn justified the expectation, enhanced the legend and tore the defence wide open.

346

With Jack Matthews as his co-centre, Bleddyn had cut a swathe through New Zealand in 1950. At the end of 1952-3, Dr Jack, his Antipodean reputation as 'the iron man' firmly secure, retired, and Bleddyn went on to conquer new heights. He continued playing in new but no less illustrious company. Malcom Thomas and Ken Jones were still with him for Wales; now too, for club and country, was the versatile Alun Thomas, later to play a key role in the coaching debate of the 1960s. Alun Thomas was a deceptive runner and fine tactical and line-kicker, who, like his namesake Malcolm, played in a variety of positions behind the scrum for Wales and the 1955 Lions, returning to South Africa in 1974 as honorary manager of Willie John McBride's unbeaten side. There was also Gareth Griffiths from Treorchy, a richly gifted footballer of strong physique and natural attacking ability which brought him four tries in his first international year, a Lions tour, and a dozen caps. For them, but especially for Bleddyn, 1953 was the year of victories. After the 8 - 3 defeat by England, Gwilliam was relieved of the captaincy, and for the visit to Edinburgh it was given to Bleddyn Williams. Even with six changes including new caps for Neath's Courtenay Meredith at prop and Russell Robins of Pontypridd at No. 8, and even with Rex Willis off the field so that Cliff Morgan went to scrum-half, inspiring pack leadership from Rees Stephens provided the platform for Bleddyn to return to his best form. With two knifing tries from twenty-five and thirty yards out, it was the Williams jink that beat the Murrayfield jinx. Later that year he overcame the might of New Zealand in one of the great club matches of the century. Cliff Morgan was at his mercurial best, bobbing, weaving, darting and sniping in a manner reminiscent of Cliff Jones, sometimes impudently chipping the ball over the heads of opponents and racing round them to gather it himself. A plan devised by Bleddyn Williams's fertile football brain to engage the buccaneering All Black back-row by long throws at the line-out, tries by Gwyn Rowlands and Sid Judd in the first eighteen minutes, and the continual roaring of 53,000 for the remaining sixty, saw Cardiff win 8 - 3. Bob Stuart's Fourth All Blacks were as well blessed as always with impressive forwards like Kevin Skinner and 'Tiny' White, but lacked any personality to punctuate their orthodoxy behind. Their backs looked very ordinary against Swansea in December, where a rousing pack, led by W. D. Johnson from a back-row that also contained Len Blyth and Clem Thomas, all but showed the tourists the way home, and twenty-year-old John Faull, who had just began his first-class career that October, playing at centre (though he would later win twelve caps and a Lions tour at forward), kicked two penalty goals from half-way to earn the All Whites a

6 - 6 draw. The All Blacks drew with Ulster as well, but otherwise they won all their other matches, except two, at Cardiff Arms Park against Cardiff and Wales. Under the captaincy of Bleddyn Williams, Wales entered the international as favourites but for most of the game defeat, unexpected but not uninvited, stared them in the face. Only in the last twenty minutes did a lethargic Welsh pack shake itself and mount a real offensive. That was when Gareth Griffiths returned to the field in defiance of medical advice after dislocating his shoulder. Clem Thomas went back into the pack, and Wales scored 8 points in five minutes to transform a situation that looked like being a re-run of 1935 without the pay-off. Gwyn Rowlands kicked a penalty to level the score at 8-all, and with five minutes remaining Clem Thomas made a dash down the left-hand touch-line towards the river end, found himself and his centres baulked, looked quickly across, and in an inspired moment cross-kicked ('I just hoofed it across', said Clem) for Ken Jones to take it on the bounce, round Jarden on the inside and race behind the posts. Gwyn Rowlands converted, and Wales had won a closer-run victory than the bald 13 - 8 scoreline suggested. The All Blacks had yet to beat Wales on the Arms Park. In the hope of meeting their historic rivals on their own ground, they invited Wales to make a tour of New Zealand in 1954, but the I.B. ruled against it in view of the major British tour to South Africa the following year. It would be 1969 before Wales finally got to New Zealand, and by then the New Zealanders were so unquestionably the world champions that the Welshmen occasionally wished they had stayed at home.

Time was running out in 1953-4 for a number of great players now in the autumn of their careers, like Gwilliam, Roy John and Dai Davies; Gerwyn Williams was forced to retire through injury, Rex Willis played his last game in 1955. It was suggested that neither Bleddyn nor Rees Stephens were the players they used to be, but both confounded their critics with some powerful performances in the mid-fifties. Rees Stephens, now thirty-two, was not merely the maestro of the maul but at 6foot 2inches and 15½stone the personification of Neath's awesome reputation for producing power-packs built of what 1912 Springbok Douglas Morkel had called 'cast-iron men'. After leading Wales to two notable victories over Ireland and championship-seeking France in 1955 — he repeated the performance in his final season, 1957, when his father Glyn, an earlier Neath 'cast-iron' international lock-forward whom Morkel met twice in 1912, was President of the W.R.U. — Rees Stephens was unlucky not to be given the captaincy of the 1955 Lions. Peculiarly, because of an obtuse ruling that no-one over thirty would be considered for the tour, he did not even make the party, nor did Bleddyn Williams or Ken Jones. The increasingly soggy Arms Park surface disadvantaged both these great three-quarters — it was at its most glutinous when Bleddyn played his last game for Wales in 1955 — but they would have relished the hard, fast grounds of South Africa. As it was, ten Welshmen were originally selected, Gareth Griffiths was flown out as a replacement, and with the appointment of Cardiff's 'Danny' Davies as honorary secretary, Wales still claimed the Lions' share.

The year 1954 saw another international departure, though not in the conventional sense. The first home international in the history of Welsh rugby had been played on 16 December 1882, against England, at St. Helen's. On 10 April 1954 St. Helen's hosted its last rugby union international. The decision to abandon it as an international venue was not unexpected in the light of post-war developments, or more accurately, non-development at the Swansea ground. As a sports-hungry generation swarmed to see post-war rugby, disorderly crowd scenes of the kind that had made the headlines in 1921 returned to international occasions at Swansea. For the French match of 1948, the 38,000-capacity ground was again overstretched by the sale of an alleged 7,000 forged tickets. As in 1921, it was Wales rather than the visitors who were the more affected by the frequent and chilly interruptions that held up proceedings. Tamplin threw one protesting spectator out of a line-out as France, thanks to the efforts of their 32-stone second row Robert Soro and Alban Moga (playing with the battling fury of a Welsh Alban of earlier vintage) and the undulating speed of the much-admired Michel Pomathios on the wing, achieved her first victory on Welsh soil by 11 points to 3. The events of that afternoon provided further ammunition for those in the east who regarded the Swansea ground as inconvenient because of the congestion along the A48 road leading there. The match with Ireland in 1947 had kicked off half an hour late because it had taken the Irish team two hours to get from their Porthcawl hotel to the ground. There was also the financial angle: by the mid-1930s, revenue from internationals at Swansea was £5,000 less than at Cardiff, for St. Helen's was as much a casualty of the W.R.U.'s inability to develop it in the inter-war period as it was of the notorious Port Talbot bottleneck. Between 1921 and 1939 the Union had made £100,000 from matches at Swansea, but had themselves contributed no more than £7,500 towards the cost of a £12,500 stand erected in the early twenties. The remaining £5,000 had been paid by the Swansea club who held the lease. In

1940 it had to surrender this to the corporation, and this effectively ended the W.R.U.'s interest in the ground. There was talk of raising the accommodation to 70,000, even 82,000, but it was admitted that only 17,000 of these would be seated. Understandably, the severe war-time bomb damage inflicted on Swansea had forced the corporation to revise its building priorities. The capacity was raised to 50,000 by 1951 as the corporation spent over £20,000 on the site, but future development seemed remote. Since the late 1940s East Walians had been chafing to bring all internationals to the Arms Park. It was at the Union's 1953 meeting — ironically the occasion on which Ernest Davies of Swansea, a staunch defender of St. Helen's, succeeded Sir David Rocyn Jones as W.R.U. President on the first annual rotation of the office — that D. C. Williams of Merthyr, supported by Abercynon, at last successfully carried by 136 votes to 110 a motion that 'until other grounds capable of adequately staging international matches become available, all future matches be held at Cardiff'. The matter was raised again at the 1954 A.G.M., but despite subsequent improvements made to the St. Helen's ground, and impassioned pleas on behalf of tradition, the resolution to abandon St. Helen's was confirmed 'once and for all'. The decision was bitterly received in West Wales, and Merthyr got it in the neck. They were accused of being 'stooges of Cardiff', since, as a member of Swansea corporation declared, 'the membership in Merthyr would not fill a double-decker bus. They are the stronghold of soccer'. Indignant letters to the Swansea press condemned the decision as 'one of the greatest sporting tragedies of our time', as 'base ingratitude', and urged a boycott of international tickets 'so that Merthyr and Abercynon can have all the tickets they want . . . There is no consistency in a body that turns its back upon a ground whose turf felt the tread of Bancroft, Dickie Owen, Billy Trew and a host of others whose names will never die'. The turf felt again the tread of Bancroft that April day in 1954 when the last international was played at St. Helen's and the great W.J., a dapper eighty-four-year-old, stepped on to the field whose traditions he had so richly embroidered, to congratulate Ken Jones, made captain that afternoon in celebration of his equalling Dickie Owen's thirty-five-cap record and breaking W.J.'s own number of thirty-three consecutive caps. Ken would go on to win his final and forty-fourth cap against Scotland in 1957, but he had already against New Zealand scored the last of his seventeen tries for Wales. The four tries scored in the 15 - 3 victory over Scotland at Swansea in 1954 were scored by Llanelli's Ray Williams, Cliff Morgan, and — announcing the forward-based direction that Welsh rugby would now take — R. H. Williams and Bryn Meredith.

350

One forward who might have taken it even further had his thirteen-cap international career not prematurely ended when he joined Leeds R.L. club in September 1958 was Pontypridd's Russell Robins. Twenty-two years old in 1954, Robins that season had exerted his powerful 14 stone, 6foot 1inch frame in the engine-room of the pack, but he throve as much in the fast and open as in the tight. As he showed in South Africa in 1955, he was ideally equipped for the back-row; his modern approach to No. 8 play, foregoing deep corner-flagging in favour of a forward-driving, ball-carrying role, anticipated combined aspects of the play of both Alun Pask and Mervyn Davies and marked him as a player ahead of his time. He had seen the future, and it worked.

For the moment, the present offered less assurance. Just as West Wales was left to warm itself at the hearth of nostalgia, Welsh supporters generally had to be content with memories of past glories — memories that Pontypridd-born J. B. G. Thomas, who had retired from playing and refereeing with the Royal Navy in 1946 to become chief rugby correspondent of the *Western Mail*, rekindled with the first of, eventually, nearly thirty books on the game — *On Tour* (1954), *Great Rugger Players* (1955) and *Great Rugger Matches* (1959) — as the second half of the decade led into the early sixties with low-scoring, closely fought but generally sterile encounters and an overall mentality at international level that seemed most concerned to see how few points the other side could score. Matters might have been different had the I.B. accepted the proposal made by Wales, jointly with New Zealand, in 1954 and again in 1956 — essentially that of Harry Packer's thirty years earlier — 'to keep players behind a line through the centre of the scrummage . . . until the ball has left'; it was a proposal designed to counter the incipient negativity that was shortly to stifle the running game. By 1964 rugby's legislators had become so convinced of the necessity for breaking defensive strongholds that they introduced an amendment concerning off-side at the scrummage considerably more drastic than that proposed in the mid-fifties. In the meantime, only twice, from 1956 to 1963, did Wales get into double figures, in 1957 in Paris and in 1960 in Dublin. It would be nine years, between the Irish match of 1955 and the Scotland game of 1964, before Wales scored more than single figures at home.

The 19 - 13 win achieved in Paris in 1957 was a masterpiece of misinformation, for it only deflected the increasing menace of France, who even on that occasion outscored Wales by three tries to two. The 5 - 3 Welsh defeat of France the previous year had been cavernously hollow, when C. D. Williams, chasing a punt ahead by Onllwyn Brace, was credited with a try that was grounded so far over the deadball line it was nearly in the Taff. The stirring 16 - 11 victory in Paris in 1955 was the last convincing win over France for sixteen years. An all-ticket match, a record French crowd of 62,500 paying 20,000,000 francs and odds of 15 to 1 against Wales, saw *'ce vieux renard de Rees Stephens'* foxily plot victory and furiously galvanize a Welsh eight that included the nucleus of the Lions Test pack later that year, to produce his personal best performance in an eleven-year thirty-two-cap international career, and bring Wales a share of the championship. Yet France's final flourish in that match, when Dufau ran diagonally for forty yards before throwing the ball with artful abandon over his head for Baulon to gather and score, warned Wales, and everyone else, that they were living on borrowed time. Since the war it had become increasingly obvious that France was reaping the harvest of the growth of sporting facilities. Basket-ball had become especially popular for its spectacular ball-handling skills, soon to be introduced in her rugby. The Lourdes club led by Jean Prat dominated the post-war French championship and gave club hardness to international teams. Having won in Wales for the first time in 1948, France achieved their first victory at Twickenham in 1951, when they beat Scotland and Wales as well. In 1954 they won a share of the championship for the first time ever in a triple-tie with Wales and England; in 1955 they shared it with Wales. If the near-arithmetic record of French progress against Wales was anything to go by — 1908, 1928, 1948 had all been milestones — then 1958 was the year to look out for. It was, and by the same decennial logic, in 1968 France would achieve her first Grand Slam over the four home countries. By 1958 Lucien Mias had returned to the French team after a four-year absence in which he had turned his doctoral mind to exploring the technical possibilities of the game. Mias controlled the high-speed execution of acrobatic flips, lobbed throws, delicately snatched passes, and the balletic flamboyance with which the French were already dressing the salad of their game, with a variety of sophisticated ploys. These were guaranteed to baffle opponents by bringing flexibility to phases of play that had traditionally been more static and in Britain seemed inevitably to end in fruitless mauls. Positional reshuffling, peel-offs from the line-out and churning moves from the back of the scrum, sucked in as many defenders as possible into a small area and opened new perspectives on back-row play. The key was an overall forward mobility. Against the *élan* of forwards like Roques, Domenech, Mommejat, Domec, Barthe, Crauste and Celaya, who could handle and run like seasoned three-quarters, and the pacey panache of backs like Bouquet, the Boniface brothers, Dupuy, Rancoule, Albaladejo and Vannier, trying to contain the French sides of the late fifties was like trying to box an octopus. Wales found this out annually from 1958, the year when France first won at Cardiff by a score, 16 - 6, as sensational in rugby terms as the 6 - 3 defeat of England's soccer team by the 1953 Hungarians. France went on winning. In the summer of 1958 they won a Test series in South Africa, came back to win the five-nations' championship outright for the first time in 1959, shared it with England in 1960, and won it again in 1961 and 1962: only a Kelvin Coslett penalty goal at Cardiff in 1962 secured Wales her first victory against France for five years, and it would be 1971 before Wales won again in Paris.

The victory of 1958 announced the arrival of France as, currently, the leading rugby nation in the northern hemisphere, though it only confirmed what had threatened for the previous few seasons. The fortunate Welsh win of 1956 looked even flukier in retrospect. 1956 was a transitional year in many ways, on the field and off it, in Welsh rugby. It was the last year in which enterprise could be discerned behind the Welsh scrum before it sank into a morass of mud. It was the last year for nearly a decade that Wales scented the Triple Crown, and Cliff Morgan's hopes of captaining the side to victory in Dublin were dashed 11 - 3, the defeat prefigured, as so many times for Wales in the fifties and sixties, by a vital dropped goal — by Kininmonth, Docherty and Dorward at Murrayfield in 1951, 1955 and 1957, Kyle, Gibson and McGann at Lansdowne Road in 1956, 1966 and 1970. What enterprise there was flickered from Onllwyn Brace, making the first of his nine appearances for Wales at Twickenham in 1956. He was then twenty-three, a willowy 5foot 6inches, 9stone 10lb., and another unorthodox protégé of Bill Bowen's at Gowerton. He went on to the field to make the other team apprehensive, since he was a past master at running blind and then throwing reverse passes. Those apprehensions were sensible; they were also self-destructive. At Oxford, Brace elaborated a repertoire of bewildering switch movements with the England cricketer, M. J. K. Smith; elected captain, after a cracking Varsity match in 1955 as a freshman, he led the Dark Blues in 1956 from stand-off. Equally at home at inside or outside-half, the resourceful Brace was in physique and outlook the heir of the James brothers. Playing with the similarly elfin Cliff Ashton as his partner at Aberavon, they often interchanged positions to keep the opposition guessing. Suggestions that he and Cliff Morgan were too contrary in style — like Bush and Owen — were undercut against

Scotland in 1956, when from a scrum at the Westgate Street left-hand corner, Brace ran flat to the open for ten yards, then flicked a reverse pass for Morgan on the narrow side to scuttle over the line with hardly an eye or hand laid on him.

Also from Gowerton, even smaller in frame than the spindle-legged Brace, but greater in world-wide stature — and, by virtue of his lonely and thankless position, more immediately recognizable — was D. Gwynne Walters. Welsh rugby's very first decade had seen Richard Mullock and Horace Lyne inaugurate a tradition of firm but fair-minded international referees that officials like Meirion Joseph (19 games, 1966-77), Ron Lewis, Clive Norling and Cenydd Thomas were upholding in its tenth. Inevitably there had been some quite outstanding names in this succession. Tommy Vile and Albert Freethy had dominated the inter-war period. Refereeing his first match as a W.R.U. referee at Skewen's oil refinery ground in 1932, and his first international at Twickenham in 1938 when Scotland lifted the Calcutta Cup and their last Triple Crown in modern memory, had been Ivor David of Neath, who went on to control another thirteen internationals up to 1956, including five in 1954. Gwynne Walters had qualified as a W.R.U. referee at eighteen, but had few games until he came of age, and his first important match was a secondary schools international between Wales and France at the Arms Park in April 1950. In the early fifties he found he was much in demand as a referee in the English Midlands and West Country, and he enjoyed it, but his pleasure was not shared by the W.R.U. who in 1954 removed him from their list of referees because he had not refereed enough games in Wales. Reinstated in 1955, he won a place on the international panel in 1956-7 with Ivor David and Gwilym Treharne. Coincident as this was with the growth of televised rugby, the pint-sized Walters first captured the public eye as referee of the 1957 Varsity match, and for the next nine years the appearance of the diminutive Gowertonian, resplendent in his distinctive striped blazer, became as eagerly awaited as the entry of the thirty players. He refereed the first of the record twenty-one internationals he controlled between 1959 and 1966 in Paris, when Scotland played there, but the game which catapulted his reputation to the clouds was that between France and South Africa in February 1961, also in Paris. The French physically attacked the tough Afrikaner front row at the very first scrum, and Walters prised them apart, wagged his finger at their navels, and conveyed in his high Welsh tenor voice (in counterpoint to the operatic tenor of his uncle, Walter Glynne) that he was prepared to send both sides off, individually, until he was the only man left on the field. As with Orpheus and the wild beasts, he was heeded, and the game was played for a full, torrid and scoreless eighty minutes. Gladiatorial forward contests were not the sort of situations relished by Onllwyn Brace, and of the two, the sturdy Cliff Morgan was physically better equipped to adapt to them. Yet it was with Brace, in the Scotland match of 1956, that he had demonstrated his attacking capabilities for the last time in the Welsh jersey, though his international career had another two years and ten appearances to run: the traditional Welsh game that he and a cluster of excitingly-gifted players had enhanced in the first half of the fifties would not, with a few solitary exceptions, be revived until 1969.

The second Golden Era which that year heralded was grounded on a revolution in the organization and administration of the game in Wales wrought in the 1960s. Two men who would be closely involved with that revolution assumed office in the 1950s, K. M. Harris as Treasurer of the W.R.U., and W. H. Clement as its Secretary. The Scotland game of 1956 was Bill Clement's first home international, and it was truly a baptism by fire, for the scorch-marks that were still visible on the field of play while the match took place testified to the dramatic precautions that had to be taken — similar to the famous brazier match of 1893 — to thaw out the field after a severe frost. W. H. Clement had been appointed successor to Eric Evans, who died after a period of ill-health in June 1955 at sixty-one years of age, in November, though he did not formally take up his position till 1 February 1956. While the search for a successor went on, the Union's affairs were managed by Brice Jenkins, a Cardiff civil servant and secretary of Cardiff R.F.C. since 1948. Llanelli-born W. H. Clement, selected from eighty-three applicants, was at forty years of age returning to international rugby where he had made his name as a wing-threequarter for Wales and the Lions in the late 1930s. Having served with the Welch Regiment, risen to the rank of Major and won the Military Cross, at the time of his appointment by the W.R.U. he was chief internal auditor with Brecon County Council. He had taken an active part in the post-war sporting life of that town whose rugby-minded citizens had in the 1870s played a formative role in the early years of Welsh rugby: what H. W. Davies, the first secretary of the South Wales Football Club had been in the pre-history of the W.R.U., W. H. Clement would be in the last quarter of its first century. Bill Clement's geniality was combined with the professional expertise that his training in administration had given him. He built on the scrupulous fair-mindedness of Eric Evans to establish a more anonymous, though not less effective style for the chief officer of the growing Union. Slowly the multifarious activities of the Union were harnessed by a central control whose power lay not in its sudden diktat but in its thoughtful knowledgeability. During his time of office, the development of procedure to match the complexity of any given task would be his considerable contribution, but the strength of the W.R.U. administration — from 1956 to 1960 at Imperial Buildings and then at Royal London House, both in St. Mary Street, from 1960 to 1977, and finally at the new National Ground itself — was its constant desire to devolve power. The Secretary, along with some others, believed that more issues could, and should, be dealt with at district level. In 1957 the partially-revised constitution saw the re-designation of districts by letters of the alphabet and, in the re-drawn areas, meetings to discuss district rugby as well as the election of delegates. The drawing-board intentions would not, then or later, leap from the page into immediate reality but it was, already, a clear indication of more ordered thinking, and in the twenty-five years he served the internal structure and public face of the Union would be transformed.

One indicator of those changes is that whereas in 1956 the gate receipts of an international at Cardiff were £16,000, by 1980 they were over £175,000 with a further £35,000 from television fees. The financial revolution — even taking inflation into account — which had made that possible was very much the work of one man. One of the Union's dominant figures in Centenary Year — spiritually, if not in a titular sense, the heir of Horace Lyne — was K. M. Harris, who became Honorary Treasurer of the Union in 1952. He succeeded P. O. Evans, who had been the third manager of Barclay's Cardiff Docks Branch to hold the position, but his original post links him, geographically anyway, to T. R. Griffiths, the first bank manager/Treasurer in 1903, whose Capital and Counties Bank had been in Pontypridd, the town to which Kenneth Harris first went in his professional capacity at the age of seventeen. Born into a business family in Whitchurch, K. M. Harris grew up and worked in those Welsh inter-war years which were short of confidence as a commodity. It gave him, perhaps, a distaste for other people's lack of understanding that made him convinced that Wales, in all aspects of her life, had to spurn the second-best whenever the chance came to strike out for the top. His own career had blossomed in less than favourable circumstances and, through the 1950s, his holdings of various responsibilities in the banking world, allied to Honorary Treasurerships of the University College of South Wales and of the Welsh National School of Medicine in Cardiff, testified to his

356

individual standing. But the W.R.U. had become his first love and in its service he set his face firmly against further half-cock measures. This was not always easy. Traditionally the auditor, Wilson Bartlett, had presented the accounts but Kenneth Harris now did this himself, advising the Union of its financial duties and opportunities in a characteristically trenchant manner. Within a year of his election as Treasurer, already, 'in view of his services to the Union', the bye-laws were altered to allow him to act, with voting powers, 'as a full and proper member of the General Committee'. Almost three decades later he would, still as Treasurer, be acting as Chairman of the W.R.U.'s Centenary Committee.

Kenneth Morgan Harris brought considerable financial acumen and a tough-minded realism to the councils of the W.R.U., and his greatest contribution would be in the development of the Cardiff Arms Park as a truly national ground, the apex of a pyramid whose club base was in the fifties becoming increasingly secure. At the A.G.M. of 1956 Kenneth Harris launched a new loan fund scheme for clubs to purchase their grounds and improve their accommodation. A key factor in financial salvation was the long-running, eventually successful, battle with the Inland Revenue to have ticket income classed as mutual income on which, since tickets are disbursed to member clubs, no tax is payable. This alone amounted to an enormous saving. The W.R.U. was in a position to do this since Kenneth Harris's accession to the Treasurership had coincided with the emergence of the Union from post-war debt. By 1956 its net profit was £14,775. Ken Harris had been from the first determined to raise the prestige of Welsh rugby by providing a physical theatre worthy of the players. His main determination, and he devised the means by which this would be realized, was to oversee the building of a National Ground for Wales. In bringing this scheme to fruition, he would emerge as one of the most decisive administrators in the hundred-year history of the Union. Initially, his main priority was to increase its income by adding further seating at the Arms Park at the lowest practicable cost. In that respect 1956 was again a significant year, for before the Scotland match the Upper South Stand, a quarter of whose £60,000 cost was borne by the Cardiff R.F.C., was formally opened, increasing the seating accommodation of the ground to 12,800 and its overall capacity to 60,000.

Another scene in the drama of the ground was enacted in July 1958 when the event for which the new South Stand was geared, the Sixth British Empire and Commonwealth Games, was staged on the Cardiff Arms Park. The organizers of the Games had set a target of £150,000, and it was the

W.R.U. that made by far the greatest single contribution to it, £13,000 raised by the playing of a special match in April 1957 between a Welsh XV captained by Rees Stephens, and an International XV led by England's Eric Evans. With Cliff Morgan and Carwyn James switching positions at fly-half and centre, and backs like Tony O'Reilly, Jeff Butterfield, Phil Davies and Arthur Smith serving up a rich rugby repast in front of an exhilarated capacity crowd, the aggregate of points in the Welsh XV's 17 - 16 victory was the highest seen in a senior representative match in Cardiff since the 1922 win over England. The Games themselves were reminded that the Cardiff Arms Park was the home of Welsh international rugby when 'the mystery runner' who entered the Marathon Gate bearing the Queen's message on opening day, 18 July, proved to be Ken Jones, who had himself run at the previous Empire Games in Canada, and not lost any of his speed. As he handed the baton to the Duke, after over-shooting the dais by a few yards, a man in the crowd shouted, 'Forward pass, Ken'.

Highly successful though the Games were, staging them had added to the deterioration of the pitch. With the W.R.U. using its full allocation of six matches a year, and Cardiff playing its quota of home games in a club fixture list of over forty matches, not only was the notorious mud patch in front of the North Stand worsening, but there was now a slick between both 25 yard lines in front of the South Stand as well. From 1955 until the first stage of the ground development plan had been completed in 1969, the January game with England was played in a quagmire, with the exception of 1963 when arctic conditions converted it into a skating rink. If the abiding memory of Wales's away fixtures in the late fifties and early sixties is either of losing at Murrayfield or of scarlet-jerseyed players wilting like Saharan legionnaires in 75° temperatures at Colombes, the dominant impression that remains of home games is of muddied forwards locked together like prehistoric monsters, slithering up and down the North Enclosure touch-line. The English games would be best remembered for this because not until 1973-4 did the other home unions finally accede to pressing Welsh representations to rotate international fixtures. Four years earlier it was Wales who had also convinced them of the merits of introducing 'doubleton' internationals, with two games played the same day. Rotation had in fact been advocated by Wales since 1963, only to see the proposal scotched by the apparent immoveability of the Calcutta Cup and its associated golf matches in the third Saturday of March. With those proposals yet to be accepted, too many games of the late fifties were muddy encounters decided by a solitary penalty goal: again Wales, with Australia, proposed in 1961 that the penalty goal be reduced to 2 points, though it was 1971-2 before its corollary, increased value of the try to 4 points, was eventually introduced. Games like those with England in 1955 and 1959, Ireland in 1957, South Africa in 1960 and Scotland in 1962 were played in conditions detrimental to players, spectators, and the game itself: in December 1960, the River Taff on whose original bed the ground had been built revenged itself on the rugby men who had expropriated its domain, by bursting its banks in the early hours of the Sunday following the Wales v. South Africa match, and in an act of elemental reclamation flooded the ground to a depth of four feet.

Environmental factors, therefore, as well as the departure of outstanding backs, explain why, as the fifties tailed off into the sixties, it is the names of forwards that come most readily to mind, the bed-rock of Lions' as well as Welsh XVs: Ray Prosser and Bryn Meredith in the front row, R. H. Williams in the second, Clem Thomas and John Faull behind. All were in the Welsh pack that met England in January 1959. England was at this time in the middle of a highly successful period when she won two Triple Crowns and three outright championships between 1957 and 1963. She was still ahead of Wales by 30 victories to 25, and with a back-line of Thompson, Butterfield, Phillips and Peter Jackson possessed riches indeed, not to mention a brand new fly-half in Beverly Risman, the son of former Welsh R.L. international Gus Risman, who had declined a Welsh trial invitation that year to take his chance with England. On the day, the Cardiff mud would be a great leveller, but Wales too was not without attacking potential, even if four of her backs were new caps. They were not by now from Cardiff and Newport. One of them was from Pontypool, traditionally associated with hard forwards like Ray Prosser, who was in the team at prop. Pontypool, though, had not won the championship in 1958-9 through playing ten-man rugby, for of the four caps the club could boast in 1959 and 1960, three were behind the scrum. These years saw some of the best backs to wear the Pontypool colours since the pre-1914 days of Jack P. Jones and his brothers 'Tuan' and 'Ponty': Ray Cheney at full-back, the wily Benny Jones at fly-half, scrum-half Colin Evans and wing Fenton Coles who were both capped in 1960, and, finest of all in the centre, winning his first cap against England in 1959 at twenty-one years of age, the former Youth international Malcolm Price. His long-striding thrusts for the line brought him tries against Scotland and Ireland that season, another fourteen tries with the 1959 Lions, and nine caps. The late fifties and early sixties were for Aberavon also, as for Pontypool, a return

359

to former glories. With steely internationals like Len Cunningham and Phil Morgan at prop, a devastating back-row of Peter Jones, Rory O'Connor and Omri Jones, wizardry at half-back from Cliff Ashton in partnership with the two Dark Blues, Brace and Tony O'Connor, backs like John Collins, David Thomas and Cyril Jones, and century-clocking points-kickers at full-back in Ross Richards and Kel Coslett, it was not surprising that Aberavon supplied nine players to Welsh XVs between 1957 and 1962, and headed the championship table in 1960-1. In the twenties locals sang 'On the wing there's Johnny Ring'. In the fifties John Collins was less easy to rhyme, but at full throttle he was just as difficult to stop. Employed like so many of his fellow Wizards at the newly expanding Margam steelworks, Collins wore contact lenses, which gave him the glassy look of a bionic man in photos, but also had the effect of bringing the try-line more firmly into focus. Twenty-six-years-old in 1959, Collins had made his first appearance on Wales's right-wing against John Thornett's Third Wallabies in January 1958; he scored then, and twice more that season. By all accounts, his hilarious double-act with Cliff Ashton on the piano was much in demand at social functions. The only cabaret turn the Arms Park in January 1959 was likely to stage was wrestling in the mud, but it would not unduly bog down the pixie-like Cliff Ashton, chosen above the competing claims of Swansea's Bryan Richards, Ebbw Vale's Wilf Hunt and Pontypool's Benny Jones (the conveyor belt never slackened even in the late, frustrated fifties) to fill the aching void left by Cliff Morgan. The habitually head-banded 5foot 7inches 11stone 11lb. Ashton, winning the first of his seven caps, at twenty-five, would be glad of the protection provided him by the strongest inside-half in British rugby, and the biggest at the base of the Welsh scrum between Wick Powell and Terry Holmes, the twenty-five years-old 6foot, 13stone 7lb. Lloyd Williams. Lloyd was Bleddyn's brother, which was enough in itself, but endowed with the physique of a ninth forward and a lengthy pass, his intelligent reading of the game brought him thirteen caps and the captaincy, but not, as it should have done in the wet New Zealand winter of 1959, a Lions tour. The number one choice at full-back for that tour, and for Wales, making his seventeenth appearance in 1959 against England, was the Bynea timber-merchant Terry Davies. Fair-headed, indomitably gutsy — the catalogue of breakages he suffered, and overcame, in the course of his twenty-one-cap international career was an osteopath's and insurer's nightmare — was one of Wales's most accomplished ever custodians. A superbly balanced fielder and punter, a place-kicker of laser-beam accuracy, at 5foot 11inches and 13½ stone, he could bring down his man in the tackle like a lumberjack with an axe. He was provided with an unexpected addition to his timber pile when some over-zealous admirers presented him with a section of the Twickenham cross-bar whose intervention had prevented his fifty-yard penalty shot from securing victory for an injury-hit Welsh side that drew 3 - 3 in 1958.

At forward, Wales had in 1959, men who were likely to give Marques, Currie and company as good as they got, and more. Terry Davies's Llanelli club-mate, R. H. Williams, one of the outstanding lock-forwards in world rugby, was one of them. Born in Cwmllynfell in 1930, and a product of Ystalyfera G.S., Rhys Williams was the greatest Llanelli forward since Watcyn Thomas, whose style of play was recalled by the 6foot 3inch, 16 stone 'R.H.', later to be returned by a generation wiser than Watcyn's own to the councils of Welsh rugby in the late 1970s as a vice-president and selector. As one who relished work in the line-out and mauls, equally dangerous with the ball at his feet, 'R.H.' had been an automatic Test selection in South Africa in 1955, and would be again in 1959 in New Zealand, where the crustiest critics rated him the greatest they had ever seen in the lock position. New Zealanders knew all about John Faull, too, whose exploits with the Lions that year reminded them of the hefty young centre who had carried a V-2 in his boot for Swansea in 1953. John Faull, son of pre-war international referee Wilfred Faull (and subsequently W.R.U. President, 1962-3), was no longer a centre, no shorter than the 6foot 1inch he had been in 1953, but heavier at 15 stone, and withstanding the challenge for the No. 8 position from the ascending Alun Pask. Captaining the team alongside Faull at blind-side wing-forward was his club-mate, the Blundells-educated master butcher, R. C. C. Thomas. Like 'R.H.' at Cwmllynfell, Clem had been hardened in the rigorous school of West Wales rugby, with Brynamman. First capped against France in 1949, before winning his Cambridge Blue that year, he was now making the twenty-third of 26 appearances for Wales and captaining Wales for the sixth successive time. He drove himself and his team vigorously, inspired in 1959 by what was in effect an All White back-row, for as well as Faull and himself was John Leleu of London Welsh, a product of Swansea G.S. and Mumbles R.F.C. The front row was hardly a push-over either. By now twenty-seven-years-old, the Pontnewynydd-born Bryn Meredith was bidding fair to be recognized as one of the finest hookers in Welsh rugby history. Square-shouldered and bony-kneed, Meredith, like Ken Jones before him, was indebted to the early tuition he received from Gilbert Garnett at West Monmouth G.S., though his exceptional mobility and telepathic hooking were his own. After winning his secondary schools' cap he had gone on to St. Luke's, Exeter, a college that was in the 1950s training so many Welsh rugby players to become teachers — Gareth Griffiths, Glyn John, Gordon Wells, Billy Watkins, and Derek Main, who was propping Bryn Meredith in 1959 — that it had become known as St. Leek's. First capped against Ireland in 1954, Bryn had been a member of the all-Welsh Lions front row of 1955 with W. O. Williams and C. C. Meredith; in the Second Test, his quickness in the loose was demonstrated when he scored a corner try after hooking the ball in the scrum which had launched the movement. His ability with the ball in hand as well as on the ground made him an exceptional 'sevens' player, and he was vital to Newport's domination of the Snelling competition, launched in 1954 and won by the Usksiders seven times in its first ten years. The Snelling Sevens, with its free running and high scoring, attracted near-capacity end-of-season crowds to Newport, Swansea and (permanently from 1966) Cardiff, though its popularity declined in the seventies when Welsh rugby, especially at the highest level, was displaying those features which 'sevens' alone offered in the late fifties and sixties. Bryn Meredith once sprinted fully sixty yards to score in a Snellings final, with three-quarters chasing him all the way, but the prevailing defensive approach, and the Cardiff mud, ruled out such extravagant behaviour in the fifteen-a-side game. As an international hooker he continued to strike gold into the early sixties, winning thirty-four caps in all, making three Lions tours, and leading Wales to a close but deserved victory over France in 1962. Such was his mastery of his craft that in that game he achieved a miracle of the kind normally associated with the Lourdes contingent on the opposite side. A scrum went down with Bryn unprepared, so that he was standing upright in the centre of the fifteen scrummaging heavyweights like the stalk of an apple. Lacroix put the ball in for France, and Meredith, seeing nothing but sensing all, struck for it like a black but blind mamba and, incredibly, won it. Alongside him in the front row in 1959 was the pride of Pontypool, Ray Prosser. By his own cheerful admission, Ray was eighteen-months-old before his mother knew whether he was going to walk or fly; even at that age Ray knew he would hate flying, so he opted to walk. In January 1959 he was making his twelfth consecutive appearance. Rugged Ray was a solid scrummager who also put his 6foot and 15 stone to intelligent use in the line-out. A convert from the second row, he showed in the course of the twenty-two caps he won between 1956 and 1961 that his heart and effort were as big as the bulldozer he drove, and if he failed to do himself justice as a 1959 Lion, on account of his renowned homesickness, inherited by Terry

Cobner, as well as the legendary detestation of flying he would pass on to Bobby Windsor, he absorbed and applied the lessons he learned there to build the best club pack in Britain in the 1970s, and made the name of Pontypool synonymous with his own.

The match itself, won by Wales 5 - 0, was played on a pitch that resembled the Sargasso Sea. 'It was', wrote John Morgan and Geoffrey Nicholson in their perceptive *Report on Rugby* (1959) 'the kind of game which offers few lessons but is complete in itself, which might have taken place at any time in the last fifty years . . . The Welsh forwards . . . rushed and wheeled like characters out of the 1890s, carrying the ball and inside-half and anyone else before them; R. H. Williams a terrible sight to see; their captain, R. C. C. Thomas leading them in ˰rushes or frequent wheels . . . with tremendous enthusiasm. Clem Thomas is a great believer in allowing the other side to have the ball on a wet day: no day was wetter than this, and no side has been allowed to have more of the ball than England were. With the ball came Leleu, Thomas and Williams'. Entirely representative of Welsh international rugby as the fifties ran out, the game would always be best remembered for the fairy-tale début of twenty-year-old Dewi Bebb on the left-wing. The programme noted his arrival with prophetic understatement: 'gains his first cap in unusual circumstances but may prove Welsh match winner . . . is quick off the mark and elusive . . . should do well'. Bebb would do very well. Darkly smouldering with the accumulated injustices suffered over the centuries by the mountainous principality of Gwynedd, Bebb's background was not Aberavon steel, Bynea timber, or Brynamman meat, but Bangor books. He came from an eminent Welsh literary and academic family. His father, W. Ambrose Bebb, a lecturer at Bangor Normal College, had been closely involved with Plaid Cymru since its early days in the 1920s. He had edited its Welsh language newspaper *Y Ddraig Goch*, and written several books on Welsh history. Bebb, junior, had been educated at Friars School, Bangor, thus becoming, after Wilfred Wooller and Bleddyn Williams, the third North Wales Schools' player to attain senior honours. Having played for the Royal Navy in 1957-8, he entered Trinity College, Carmarthen, in 1958 and tried his hand with Swansea. On his first appearance for them he scored a sensational try against Llanelli. 'Bebb . . . has brains and pace — much more is going to be heard of him', wrote 'Scarlet' in the *Evening Post*. Two first class matches later, one of them the final trial, he was in the Welsh team. Thirty minutes into the first half against England, with the pitch already churned into an Amazonian swamp, Wales worked the ball out to Bebb who was collared fifteen yards out by Jackson. From the ensuing line-out, it was tapped back direct to Bebb who skimmed over the mire, inside Jackson, around full-back Hetherington and over, for Terry Davies to convert from wide-out. Bebb went on to win thirty-four caps and two Lions tours. His club, Swansea, though it bestowed upon him the captaincy, was going through a lean period, and the starvation diet he existed on at St. Helen's only sharpened his appetite to forage for his own opportunities. Given his family's nationalist convictions, it was only fitting that Bebb should play his best rugby against England. He scored his last try for Wales against them in 1967, as he had his first; in between, he scored twice against them in 'Bebb's corner' in 1961, and twice again at Twickenham in 1964. It was nicely symbolic, too, that as dusk descended in the final stages of the mud-bath in 1959, the rain still falling relentlessly, and Wales mounting a squelching forward assault in defence of that 5 point lead, the crowd packed under the North Stand, sensing the danger was over, broke into an emotional, hair-prickling rendering of 'Hen Wlad fy Nhadau'. Spontaneously, harmoniously, perfectly pitched, unpunctuated by cheering or applause, the majestic anthem rolled across the ground, enveloping and sustaining its exhausted heroes in an unforgettable expression of relief and gratitude. Something similar happened again against England in 1961, before the kick-off of the Barbarians v. New Zealand match of 1964 (after the band had been perversely instructed to file off after 'The Queen') and against France in 1962 and 1966. The disembowelling of the North Enclosure in favour of seats in the mid-seventies worked against future choral thrills of this kind, but the primeval elements of rain and mud were less in evidence then, and Wales was not often hanging on to narrow one-score margins. As Welsh rugby advanced, its musicality declined.

The dominant bass-note of late fifties' frustration was promptly struck again as Wales went optimistically to Murrayfield in 1959, and lost. The situation was repeated after the 6 - 3 win over England in 1961. It was difficult to apportion any particular blame to the selectors; remarkably, it was only in 1957 that the time-hallowed 'match committee' system was abolished, and the 'Big Five' alone entrusted with selecting all the trials' teams, as well as the National XV. The spotting and promotion of a Bebb spoke well for their ability to pick a winner. Picking winning teams was more of a problem, though there was no lack of winning clubs in Wales. In that respect, the 1959 Welsh team was *not* entirely representative, for there was no-one in it from the club that, in the wake of new investment in the steel industry, had enjoyed constant success throughout the decade: Ebbw Vale. Fourth to Maesteg in the championship in 1950, they were third to Newport and Cardiff in 1951, and won it in 1952; they were undisputed champions again in 1954, 1957 and 1960. Their considerable forward power was represented by the massive 17 stone and 6 foot 3inches of Eric Finney, a second-row and No. 8 constantly on the verge of the Welsh team, but destined to become no more than constant trialist and stoically patient reserve. Like their Monmouthshire valley rivals, Pontypool, the Vale had more than useful backs: in 1958 Graham Powell became the club's first direct cap, at centre, while the brains of the side as it entered the sixties lay at half-back where Wilf Hunt and Roy Evans were one of the best club pairs in Wales. In the early sixties, its traditions as a forward nursery were forcefully upheld by men like Len Dimmick and David Nash. The doughty Dimmick, with Mike Hurn of Abertillery, gave the neckless South African props S. P. Kuhn and 'Mof' Myburgh a gruelling eighty minutes as the combined Ebbw Vale-Abertillery XV held Malan's Fifth Springboks to a wafer-thin 3 - 0 margin in November 1960.

Those tourists were forced as much by the rainy British winter of 1960-1 as by their own temperamental and physical inclinations to play a tough, attrition style of football. Deservedly winners over Wales, for the fifth consecutive time, in farcical conditions at Cardiff, where the indestructible South African No. 8 Doug Hopwood took on the whole Welsh pack by himself in the second half to defend Keith Oxlee's penalty goal lead, they did not make too many friends and there was relief on both sides when they were deprived of their unbeaten record in the last game of the tour against the Barbarians at Cardiff. Their 6 - 0 defeat was registered on a seismograph after the pulverizing shoulder-tackle that Swansea's Haydn Mainwaring, at full-back, made on the rampaging young leader of the South African herd, Avril Malan, who was in full flight for the line. Indicative of the times was that the two Barbarian tries were scored by back-row forwards from Monmouthshire, since positionally and geographically that was where Welsh rugby's gravitational centre now lay. Derek Morgan of Newbridge won nine caps for England in the early sixties, while Haydn Morgan, Abertillery's ex-paratrooper turned piranha fish, preferred to wear the jersey that was the same colour as his hair — red. Abertillery was a valley side whose ground, instead of being surrounded by serrated rows of uniform terraced houses, chimney-stacks and slag-heaps, was verdantly situated in one of the most picturesque locations

365

anywhere. The club's origins and its traditions were in the Monmouthshire League, where it was blooded, often literally, in the first decade of the century. In 1908 it had attained first-class status when the W.F.U., recognizing it as champions of the League, gave it a fixture against the First Wallabies, who were held to a draw. Thereafter Abertillery, in combination with either Cross Keys or Ebbw Vale, always gave touring sides a strong dose of forward medicine. By 1960, two world-class forwards had emerged at Abertillery. Haydn Morgan was one, poisonously fast away from the open flank of the scrum. First capped at twenty-one-years-old at Twickenham in 1958, his marking of English fly-half Horrocks-Taylor complemented the wicked tactical kicking of his namesake, Cliff, that day. Equipped with the build and speed of a three-quarter, the Oakdale-born Haydn Morgan won twenty-seven caps in all, plus a Lions tour in 1959. His back-row colleague at Abertillery was the burgeoning Alun Pask, about to become one of the charismatic forwards of the decade. Both played together at Colombes in 1961, flanking David Nash. When Nash withdrew from the team at Twickenham the following year, the twenty-three-year old Pask came in at No. 8 to begin an unbroken sequence of 24 games. Morgan's relish for the fast and furious contrasted with Pask's majestic imperturbability, as the latter, sweat-banded and grasping the ball in one paw, transported his 6foot 3inches and 15 stone around the field like an overgrown fly-half. The French thought they had encountered their own mistral blowing back at them in Cardiff in 1962 when Nash and Keith Rowlands squeezed Mommejat out of the line-out and themselves into the Lions party to South Africa that summer, while Pask turned, chased, and overhauled right-wing Rancoule in a spectacular piece of self-advertisement that took him to South Africa too.

A change in the laws in 1958 removed the necessity to play the ball with the foot after a tackle, so that the speed of the back-row to the point of the breakdown made it now as important in attack as in its traditional marauding role. Athletic ball-users like Nash and Pask thrived in the new conditions, while at the confluence of the valleys of Gwent was an entire back-row unit tailor-made to be chosen for Wales, as it was when Newport's Cresswell, Davidge and Whitson were selected *en bloc* in 1960. With intelligent, pillaging breakaways like these and Cardiff's tireless Dai Hayward and Elwyn Williams increasingly calling the tune, it called for midfield backs of outstanding abilities and resilience to survive at the topmost level with their natural attacking instincts undiminished. The potentially exciting combination of two masters of resource, Ken Richards and Onllwyn Brace, was frustrated to impotence as both back lines lay up on each other flatter than last week's beer, on an untypically warm, firm Arms Park, against Ireland in 1961.

Llanelli remained, as always, the nursery of sweet Scarlet runners. Stradey supporters felt that penetrative backs like wingers Ray Williams and Geoff Howells, the dazzlingly gifted Cyril Davies at centre, and Carwyn James and Wynne Evans at half-back, had been underexposed at international level in the fifties. The six Scarlets who did appear against Australia in January 1958 recalled the 'sospan six' at Murrayfield in 1928: both sides won. As the sixties dawned, much was expected from the Llanelli and Gwendraeth schoolboy stars, D. Brian Davies, D. Robert Morgan and D. Ken Jones, whose attacking prowess was so outstanding as to be indeed 3-D. Eventimers and quick-silver side-steppers, the higher the rugby ladder they climbed, the more limited became the opportunities to fulfil their sumptuous schoolboy promise. In 1960 Wales lost to France at all three levels, senior, youth and schools, the Welsh S.S. losing 0 - 3 in Cardiff with Brian Davies at centre and Ken Jones captaining the side at fly-half gamely attempting to play in the classical Welsh style with small concern for the tactical realities of the contemporary situation. It would be 1966 before the stocky, fair-haired Ken Jones — whose jink conjured up memories of Bleddyn — could deploy for Wales those attacking attributes fleetingly glimpsed from him in the First Test at Johannesburg in 1962 when a sixty-yard dash, spectacular side-step past full-back Lionel Wilson and sensational dive for the line, parallel to the ground and four feet above it, earned the Lions a 3-all draw in a series lost 3 - 0. Ken was back in South Africa in 1964, on the first-ever tour made by Wales. It proved to be 'a trek to disaster'. As Wales suffered her heaviest defeat in forty years, it was realized that a nadir had been reached in Welsh rugby fortunes. Ironically, it was not in the rain gusting relentlessly in from the Taff end that the point was driven home, but in the blistering sun of the African sub-continent.

At home, the stage-managers behind the scenes renewed their efforts to ensure that Welsh rugby would not see out its first century singing only with relief. There would be joy in the singing again, and plenty to dance about, too. But there was a lot of ground-work to be done first.

CHAPTER

14

FROM THE GROUND UP

THE delegates who assembled at Porthcawl on 20 June 1964 for their A.G.M. came in apprehensive mood. The concern was different depending on what position one adopted within the spectrum of opinion. Undeniably the W.R.U. was at a cross-roads. The immediate occasion of the gloom was the disaster in Durban. The first overseas tour undertaken by Wales had ended in a 24 points to 3 defeat at the hands of South Africa. And the Welsh score was a penalty goal. No matter how intriguing domestic rugby at grass roots level remained, it was the interaction between the club and national sides that was the motor of development. If play was becalmed, sometimes permanently it seemed, in the doldrums then, perhaps, another re-tuning of the motor was futile. Voices had been raised, for a long time in some cases, urging changes that others had shied away from as revolutionary in their impact. In 1964 the W.R.U. delegates, spurred by a dissatisfaction with the game, began to shift their parent body away from a rather ossified conservatism that was at odds both with its own past history and the climate of the 1960s.

Nothing drastic occurred overnight. At the end of the 1969 season the second Welsh overseas tour came spiralling to earth, this time in New Zealand, and a major plan for the complete restructuring of the Union's distribution of power was rejected as too sweeping in its implications. The incoming President in 1964, Nathan Rocyn Jones, son of Sir David Rocyn Jones, had emphasized, in traditional manner, that the game was 'essentially played for enjoyment and that too much emphasis could be placed on technical and tactical skill.' During his year of office there would be a fierce clash between him and the Selection Committee (Alun Thomas, Glyn Morgan, Rees Stephens, Cliff Jones and Harry Bowcott) whose

368

success in capturing a Triple Crown under Clive Rowlands's captaincy was duly applauded by the outgoing President in 1965. He had added that however much coaching was required it should not extend to the stage where, to the detriment of intuitive play, a 'Rugby Robot' was produced. Division of opinion on such matters remained with Welsh rugby for a long time. Nonetheless the pendulum had begun to swing left rather than right; change was in the air and it is 1964 that marks the foundation of what would be the last, and greatest, decade in the first hundred years of the Welsh Rugby Union.

The retiring President in 1964 was D. Ewart Davies of Ammanford, a man ardent in his support of Youth rugby in 1948, and now determined to leave on a provoking note: 'It was evident from the experience of the South African Tour that a much more positive attitude to the game was required in Wales. Players must be prepared to learn, and indeed re-learn, to the point of absolute mastery, the basic principles of Rugby Union football. In this connection the importance of correct coaching at all levels cannot be over emphasized. The Schools Union and the Youth Union shoulder a special responsibility in this connection'.

The material was certainly to hand. The Welsh Schools Under-15 group had won their own Triple Crown in 1963-64 season. During the English game, with what had become typical Welsh profligacy, they lost possession in front over and over again only to run and pass their way to victory. There was an A. Martin in the pack from Aberavon, a J. Williams of Bridgend at full-back and, said J. B. G. Thomas, 'a brilliant runner at outside half' who also dropped a goal. That was P. Bennett of Llanelli. If this talent was not to run into the sand then the words of V. J. Parfitt of the Coaching Committee who complained of the lack of interest by clubs in the available coaching courses would have to be heeded. The W.R.U. had indeed already set up a working party of Union members, ex-players and coaches to examine future requirements but the Coaching Committee were to receive a significant boost, at this pivotal A.G.M., from the floor. Elvet Jones of Llanelli, a former International and British Lion of 1938, had risen to speak. The burden of his remarks was that clubs, and the W.R.U. itself, had shown insufficient attention to coaching whilst what was done 'concentrated too much on physical fitness and neglected . . . basic skills and tactics'. Rugby 'at international and club level had deteriorated and even International players lack the ability to handle the ball accurately . . . it may have been pleasing to read that the Welsh team were "great ambassadors" [in South Africa] but the intention [had been] to play rugby in the best of Welsh traditions, and to win matches'. The delegate from the West ended by urging a reconstituted Coaching Committee and, more, called on the W.R.U. 'to consider the appointment of an official Rugby Coach with several assistants, lest the A.G.M. of the W.R.U. degenerate into a meeting of social, instead of rugby, clubs'.

When he came, in the high summer of 1971, to bid farewell to his year's term of office as President, Kenneth Harris, the Treasurer of the W.R.U., was speaking to a meeting that was in a new world. But it was emphatically still a rugby world, for he described his year of office, itself an unprecedented position for the Treasurer to hold, as 'one of the most momentous and successful in the long history of Welsh rugby football'. Wales had won the Grand Slam after a wait of nineteen years and thirteen of the British Lions, including for the first time ever the captain, not to mention the coach, were from Wales. Cliff Jones, the chairman of the Coaching Committee, was able to bask in the warmth of all seventeen international matches, at every level, having been won but, more importantly still, because 'it is the quality of rugby . . . that made us at last realize that Wales had truly arrived'. The seven years that had passed between those two A.G.M.s were not all lean ones by any means yet the moments of success had never been assured. What imbued Welsh rugby with confidence from 1971 was the feeling that a sick patient had been nursed to lasting health. The recovery was most obvious on the field of play and yet there were structured institutional changes behind the spearpoint of the National XV whose own physical presence was now matched by the visual impact of the new National Ground, itself opened on 17 October 1970.

The achievements of the 1960s were inextricably connected. No one at the 1971 A.G.M. believed one swallow makes a summer but few now thought the Welsh bubble would burst either. The President's explanation of the course of events was an inclusive one:

> I am convinced that, fundamentally, some of the credit must go to the W.R.U. Coaching Organization and to Mr Ray Williams the man at its head . . . He has never promised miracles but it would be equally fair to suggest that the results of the work which he and his Organization have been doing are beginning to become apparent. That the original impetus for this scheme came from the floor of an A.G.M. and thus from the Clubs themselves is another healthy indication of . . . the democratic organization of Welsh rugby.

The stress was falling naturally on the lines of co-operation that had been tugged in unison. No single individual or group could be credited for it had been the work 'of the whole community of Rugby people in Wales'. This was the note that Kenneth Harris emphasized in his appeal 'for a continuation of that spirit of community between Clubs and the parent body, between players and administrators, and indeed between us all and the Rugby following public'. He, above all others, knew that the coaching which provided the success through pleasure and victory not only relied on the financial security of the Union but was the Union's own running investment, a potential credit balance for the future. Equipped with a modern stadium for spectators and a perfect turf on which players could exhibit their skills, the rugby community of Wales had emerged by 1971 from a long, uncertain period.

That emergence had not come about by chance. It had taken courage and imagination. Coaching was one side of the coin but, and the fiscal simile is apt, the National Ground was the other. The 1950s had seen a long haul back to financial solvency but the Development Committee, spurred on by the Treasurer, were not content with short-term solutions. The provision of their own ground was, in the long run, a move that would place the Union's finances on such a sound basis that the promotion of rugby in Wales would be assured. The undertaking would, however, saddle the Union with enormous debt. In fact the final push towards action came not because of the secondary consideration of money but the primary one of the requirements of Welsh rugby. Put simply, the constant use of the Arms Park pitch by club and country, allied to its position below the level of the river Taff, led to flooding, mud-baths and, often, the reduction of a game of skill to one of chance. Welsh rugby was not based on the precepts of a lottery.

There had been substantial improvements during the 1950s but it was quite apparent that the Union's income, as it stood, was not able to accumulate a Capital Fund to finance greater development. In turn only increased accommodation would bring about a substantial rise in revenue. On 6 March 1958, K. M. Harris concluded his survey to the Committee by 'hinting that perhaps the time was now opportune to give serious consideration to the financial future of the W.R.U., including the possibility of acquiring a new national ground'. At the A.G.M. in 1958 he urged the setting aside of a reserve fund for such purpose. The matter grew larger when the Cardiff R.F.C. at first proved unwilling to hold joint discussions on the state of the ground which they considered good enough.

The W.R.U. now wondered whether the ground could be considered, in any straightforward sense, as a national ground. Comparison with other countries proved embarrassing. Although minor differences between the Cardiff club and the Union were patched up, the W.R.U. began to move, in 1959, to consider an alternative site. It was an onerous task for the sub-committee involved and only the beginning of the saga, for when, in 1962, it was finally resolved to purchase land near Bridgend for this project, there was a considerable outcry, especially by the municipal and commercial interests of the city of Cardiff. In fact the W.R.U. had never really wished to move from the Welsh capital but were, at the same time, determined to have absolute authority over their own ground.

Fortunately the hitherto irreconcilable views of club and country were now resolved by an initiative from the Cardiff club who met with the Development Committee in October 1962. Negotiations were complicated by the ramshackle structure of leases and shareholding established under the umbrella of the Cardiff Arms Park Company. Whilst discussion continued between these interested parties, including the City Council and the Greyhound Company, there could be no complete relinquishing of the Bridgend scheme. Only in 1964 was the Committee able to recommend acceptance of the Cardiff club's scheme. The W.R.U. would hold the unencumbered freehold of the main stadium in return for which the W.R.U. (at the eventual cost of £250,000) would construct a new cricket ground at Sophia Gardens, a reconstructed tennis court at the Arms Park and transform the old cricket pitch into a brand new ground for the Cardiff club, backing onto the projected National Ground. In November 1967 delegates from the clubs attended a special general meeting described by the Chairman, Glyn Morgan, as 'the most important meeting in the long history of the W.R.U.' The architects (Osborne V. Webb & Partners, Cardiff), the consulting engineers (G. A. Williamson & Associates, Porthcawl) and the quantity surveyors (Patterson, Seaton & Co., Cardiff) had been in close consultations with the W.R.U. and it was their plans that Ken Harris now revealed. The costs, which inflation would soon push ever upwards, were staggering. The delegates listened in silence to the Treasurer who concluded by saying that 'for the first time in its history, the W.R.U. were making a positive approach towards the achievement of a National Rugby Ground of which Wales and its rugby followers could be justly proud. The scheme was imaginative and courageous and, looking ahead, would be an asset which would serve Rugby football in Wales indefinitely'. The money would come from the

Union's resources, bank loans and the issue of debentures to clubs, individuals and business concerns, enabling the holders, thereby members of the W.R.U., to purchase a stand ticket. The dream was finally about to become reality. There would be difficulties of course. Some would be obviated by the thoughtful intervention of A. S. John in 1969 (then Chairman of Pontypridd R.F.C.) who suggested that insurance companies' involvement in the debenture issue guaranteeing a stand ticket at home matches would allow wider participation by the public on an instalment plan in conjunction with life policies; others, in the construction undertaken by Andrew Scott & Co. of Port Talbot, involving the physical moving of the pitch, would be helped by the early buying out of the Greyhound Company's Lease in 1977. No one could have anticipated the spiralling inflationary process that overtook all major building works in the early 1970s but, as the girders and concrete came crashing down, and the huge canopy of the new North Stand spread its mushroom-ribbed fan in its place, in the first phase of complete redevelopment, it became clearer that this was what had long been missing from Welsh rugby. The National Ground was a proud tangible summation of the past of the game, and it was an earnest of its capacity for regeneration. Born in those years of Welsh economic dynamism that had seen so many other 'National' buildings and institutions, the W.R.U. had been by-passed in the meantime. The 1960s would bring another wave of Welsh development — a Secretary of State and a Welsh Office in 1964, followed by a clutch of government-sponsored agencies for Wales. This time the W.R.U. would not be found lagging behind. The celebration game between the President's XV and an Invitation XV, assembled by Sir William Ramsay of the R.F.U., that marked the official opening of the Ground in 1970, had ended that anomaly. The new ground was always more than a commercial proposition, it was a determined insistence on the important place Welsh rugby had come to occupy in the culture of Wales. From Quay Street the grey concrete beams stretched up and out like an open hand about to grasp a prize. Those who hurried through the black-painted Gwyn Nicholls gates to stride to their places alongside the wide concourses beneath the rumbling stands knew what the prize was, and never before had the scarlet jerseys enjoyed such a perfect setting on a pitch, of the richest green colour, permanently in top condition. The second century of Welsh rugby had been anticipated.

The 1960s were a decade of change for Wales in aspects of the national life other than rugby. The game would feel their impact too. The diversification of her basic industries had proceeded under successive governments since 1945 but it was only in the sixties that the implications were fully seen. South Wales became less and less dependent on traditional industries. The steel industry continued to enjoy the buoyancy brought in the wake of the few massive steel plants that had replaced the scattered smaller mills, once all over South Wales, but it was a dangerous single-industry prosperity that was being created. The recession of the 1970s would undercut the affluence of the steel towns just as coal, itself, had been undercut in earlier decades. Above all else it was the legacy of the past that marked the mis-named 'swinging sixties'. The total population of Wales had hardly risen by 1971 beyond its 1921 level. The drain of the inter-war years had been heavy. Affluence, in areas where many amenities were basically unchanged since before 1914, was a relative term. There were more coal-miners in Wales than steelworkers at the start of the sixties. By 1971 there were over 30,000 fewer as manpower in the mines slumped from 91,000 to 41,000, and would shrink below 30,000 by 1979. Fossil fuel, governments had decided, was outmoded so 137 pits in 1959 became 54 in 1970. Changing occupational patterns and rising expectations saw subtle shifts in the leisure habits of people, certainly a more demanding, or discerning, public taste. More and more rugby clubs began to function as social centres as well. Doors were opened more readily to women and children. The range of activities increased. The population, itself, had shifted its balance from the hinterland to the coastal plain where the steel plants were re-sited, where the growing service industries, engineering plants, chemical works and new factories were to be found. The suburbs enroached further at the edges of the conurbations of towns like Swansea and Cardiff, reducing further their old connection between inland population and the product of their work. Almost a third of the work force was now female. It tended to travel towards the coast. Educational opportunities had risen for Welshmen both inside and outside Wales. If coal was in decline, then decidedly Wales's second export commodity, teachers, were not. There were still miners and steelworkers and policemen in Welsh XVs but, increasingly, teachers, especially those with a specialist training in physical education, were swelling the ranks.

Most of these changes in social and economic life had been in the pipeline since the re-structuring of the Welsh economy after the Second World War. Only now, however, did a new generation come of age who were unscarred by the inhibiting lessons of the 1930s. New cars and new roads reduced distances and the feelings of parochial isolation that had been so prevalent. Foreign travel broadened horizons even further. The net result was that the cultural lag that had existed in the 1950s was ended. People, rugby players included, were more questing again, less introverted. The confidence, or the willingness, to move from immemorial attitudes, was however a brittle one. Nonetheless it *was* there. The waters of politics, for example, so long frozen into two camps were muddied by the sudden thaw of Nationalist aspirations that took Gwynfor Evans to Parliament for Carmarthen in July 1966. The following year saw Rhondda, and 1968, Caerphilly, shaken by this breeze. The latter year was one of widespread demonstrations, in America and in Europe, that gave rise to further queries and what was, for traditionalists, a disturbing tendency to refuse to compartmentalize society's separate activities, including sport. This was not, for all its gains in human comfort and freedom, a settled world. Wales did not live in a vacuum. The dangers of the future invaded her comparative security (the South African tour of 1969 ended the real ability of anyone to divorce politics and sport) and, with a reminder of the past unimaginably horrific, the Aberfan tragedy in 1966 underlined how miserably close the brave new world was to its dark past. There were no certainties left towards the end of a decade that had begun brightly enough.

Rugby football did not give a straightforward mirror image of all this but nor was it immune. Parts of its crowds became more overtly nationalistic, from T-shirts in praise of the 'Free Wales Army' to the concerted booing of 'The Queen'. International days were used, more consciously than ever by some, as vehicles of a more abrasive, more political nationalism. The majority, including thoughtful nationalists, deplored the trend. It would continue into the 1970s when there were arguments that the demolition of the North Enclosure had ruined the hymn-singing fervour of the crowds. The reasons were other than nationalistic or rugby ones, and reconstruction had little to do with it. Max Boyce songs, and the elongated teenage howl of 'Waaay-uls!', were sometimes amusing, occasionally disturbing symptoms of a world whose links with its own past were, in the sixties and seventies, either severed or emasculated into the mindless grin of nostalgia. The proper conservatism of rugby, within a society uncertain of its values, did not lie in the apopleptic response of a few rugby backwoodsmen to the intrusion of an unwelcome modernity but in the refurbishing of the ideals of the rugby game itself. What is impressive about the administration of the game by the W.R.U., over these years of rapid change, is the acknowledgement that the sport had to alter its institutional rigidity or lose what it professed to value above all else. The path of Welsh rugby down to 1970 was not always straight nor were its fortunes absolutely certain, either on or off the field. But the coincidence of a new National Ground and a new Grand Slam side in season 1970-71 was not merely fortuitous either. Both were the fruition, in a creative decade, of hopes so long dormant that they had looked to be dead.

It took the tour to South Africa in 1964 to concentrate the Union's thoughts on coaching until they were finally translated into action but, before that day came, the older substitute of leadership on the field had led to the appointment, as captain of the Probables XV in the final trial, of 1962-3, of D. C. T. Rowlands. His first cap in January 1963 was also as captain. His last, 14 consecutive appearances later, was still as captain. Clive Rowlands, captain (1963-65), coach (1968-74) and selector (1974-79), personifies the transition period and shows, by his career, the link between continuity, change and success that has been Welsh rugby's recent hallmark. His greatest achievement as a player was, despite ups and downs as precipitous as any undertaken by a ball he had kicked, to restore the grit of faith to the Welsh oyster. It was in sore need of it in the early 1960s.

The 1961-62 season had yielded one victory, a defeat and two draws. Wales had not scored a single try. Nor was Rowlands's first season a great deal better. The Welsh team scored two tries but they lost both championship games (to England and Ireland) at home and only recorded one win (over Scotland). They took the wooden spoon for the first time since 1949 and, in December, New Zealand beat Wales at Cardiff for the first time ever. Neither Rowlands nor the selectors changed course. The new captain had played well anyway in bitterly cold, icy weather that had influenced the English game in particular. This showed a resolution, in the eye of defeat and through a gale of criticism, that was exemplified by that solitary victory against Scotland. The circumstances were controversial enough to highlight the Welsh captain's two supreme gifts as a player, his judgement and his kicking, and, in time, to help change the laws of the game.

Clive Rowlands was born at Cwmtwrch in the upper Swansea valley. This was a village, like Gareth Edwards's Gwaun-cae-Gurwen, in the very heart of the Welsh-speaking western coalfield. The career of the young schoolteacher blossomed, however, at Pontypool in eastern Monmouthshire. Passionate and Welsh-speaking though he was, language, of the verbal kind, was never an issue for this scrum-half once on the field. He was one of the great mime artists of the game. Indeed the sheer weight of Rowlands's playing personality misled some into ignoring the special rugby skills he had honed to perfection. No one knew better when to time a run from the base of his pack or when to vary the speed of play. He was the master of placing the ball with his boot, thudding it to touch or deftly punting it over the heads of opponents. Within the rules of the day this mastery was a vital weapon in the Welsh armoury. Above all else, though, this was a maestro of the rugby stage. 'Dai Ding-Dong' he might have been to critics, or even less euphoniously, 'Clive the Kick', but to his players, and spectators who warmed to the cunning that this alchemist's mixture of Cleaver and Brace brought to rugby, he was 'Top Cat'. The nickname caught perfectly the restless energy of this Welsh Bilko, forever pacing up and down alongside his pack at a line-out, exhorting, threatening, pleading, thumping his fist into his open hand until, as a Pontypool forward remarked admiringly, it was the 'only cauliflower palm in the game'. Even the stance was cerebral — head thrust well away from the arched body whose physical attributes were willed into doing more than their natural ability allowed.

At Murrayfield in 1963 the captain played to record the first Welsh victory there for ten years. It was not a game for the purists. Rowlands would never win a Barbarians honour nor, more startlingly, given his special qualities, a Lions jersey. No matter, this was the taste Wales had long missed. Behind a dominant pack the captain danced the game up and down the touch-line in an endless *pas-de-deux* with the ball that brought a 6 - 0 victory (drop goal and penalty) and 111 line-outs. The following season the laws would change to prevent the opposition advancing within 10 yards until a line-out had ended. This certainly paved the way for the more open game. It also, of course, allowed a wily fox like Rowlands to play the other strings to his bow, and release more readily his constant partner, the mercurial David Watkins. The scurrying Newport fly-half had joined Rowlands to form the first enduring half-back partnership since Morgan and Willis. They played three full seasons — fourteen internationals — together. Even while he languished in the shadow of Rowlands's tactical demands, Watkins was not afraid to make the most of the few opportunities that came his way: in Dublin in 1964 he received from Rowlands at a line-out to slice through for a classic outside-half try that closely matched Barry John's in Paris in 1971. By November 1967 when he had won twenty-one caps and joined Salford for a record fee of £16,000 as the current Welsh captain, this unassuming product of Blaina had matured into one of the most prodigiously equipped of all Welsh outside-halves. Apart from his tireless covering, the acceleration off the mark that made him so dangerous as an attacking force had been allied to a judgement that saw greater concern for his centres, seen at its peak when he skimmed over the mud-pools against Scotland at Cardiff in 1966 to bring out the best in a mature D. K. Jones. Watkins was not fading in 1967, his final year, for he held off the challenge of Barry John and went on to become perhaps the most successful Welshman ever to play rugby league. That frailty, married to courage and the swarthy good looks of a sixties pop star, endeared him to the Welsh public warmed, in different manner, to a pack whose shape, and skill, hardened in the early 1960s.

To Pask and Brian Price were added, in 1963, the ferocious mauling of Brian Thomas of Neath and the combative propping of Denzil Williams of Ebbw Vale. Norman Gale, first capped in 1960, now returned to be an almost permanent fixture of the decade. The dark arts of the entombed hooker never had a better physical representative than in the saturnine visage of this bulky Llanelli stalwart. David Hayward of Cardiff brought his constructive speedy play and Gary Prothero, of Bridgend, his smothering strength and durability to the back-row, but Haydn Morgan did not finally leave Pask as Abertillery's sole representative in the back-row until 1966. Wales was blessed with formidable wing-forwards during the final years of open and blind-side play. Behind them were players of dash possessed of older Welsh virtues, like the jink of D. K. Jones, the razor-edged opportunism of Dewi Bebb, who won the last of his thirty-four caps in 1967, and from 1964, the pulsating runs of Newport's statuesque Stuart Watkins — none more pulsating than his 1966 match and championship-winning eighty-yard race down the right hand touch-line to the Taff end after intercepting a French three-quarter movement inside his own 25. The Neath full-back Grahame Hodgson was a cool, immaculate and resourceful footballer whose speed and handling were wonderful on a muddy February pitch at the Arms Park in 1966. At one point with the Scottish pack bearing down on him, he ran across-field without falter to scoop, one-handed, a rolling ball and despatch it to touch with all the aplomb that was his enduring mark. Hodgson's career as full-back was punctuated, though not ended, in 1965, with the rise of a new star, the teenaged Terry Price of Llanelli. Price, grandson of the Hendy hurricane of the 1920s, Dai Hiddlestone, was to have a brief but remarkable career before he became a professional in 1967. Eight games for Wales brought him 45 points. In the final trial he had given notice by notching up 16 points, including two tries, from full-back. He was, in reality, of the generation of Gerald Davies and Barry John, come too soon, perhaps, to the full international arena. A member of a famous Llanelli G.S. team that swept the board in the Roehampton and Oxfordshire seven-a-side tournaments for several successive years in the early 1960s, he had played for Llanelli against Whineray's All Blacks. His goal kicking was prodigious but it was the glamour with which he invested the no. 15 shirt that recalls W. J. Bancroft and points on to the imaginative play of his successors. Again it is the cameo action which reveals the man. When Scotland pounded the Welsh line at Murrayfield in 1965 Clive Rowlands moved Price up, in Watkins's place, to take a scrum ball Wales should win and kick down-field for a safe touch. Wales heeled. Rowlands sent it back, and his callow full-back, standing right behind him, a long-forgotten bravado beating irresistibly in his blood, audaciously accelerated up-field shaving the scrum and side-stepping inside the Scottish back-row to redirect the game by screwing the ball into touch near the half-way line.

Welsh spectators savoured this. Once winning ways were restored then the search of the *aficionado* was, again, for the disdain of the rugby matador, his contempt for self-imposed limitations. No fuller expression of the dominant sense of frustration that, none the less, lay heavy over Welsh rugby can be detected than the delight with which the Fijian touring side was greeted in 1964. The season, overall, had seen wooden spoonists Wales reclaim a share in the championship, with Scotland, but two draws and two wins did not disguise the stuttering performance of the engine, whilst the early summer had seen Wales fold against the heat and pace of the Springboks. Welsh tactics were still too mechanical. Individual brilliance, spluttering fitfully, could not compensate. There were, for all that, initiatives under way within Welsh rugby that would change this pattern. At the suggestion of Secretary W. H. Clement the door of a rather stale room was opened now to a South Seas country who, unexpectedly and wonderfully, blew in like a warming zephyr.

The decision to invite the Fijians to tour was taken in the bleak February of 1963. The expenses for this novel enterprise were to be met entirely by the W.R.U. but in June they were informed that the I.B., who did not approve of the tour, would not allow Wales to play a full international. Notwithstanding this, and thanks to the co-operation of the F.F.R. who agreed to arrange a French section of the tour, the W.R.U. pressed ahead hoping 'that the rugby public of Wales would appreciate the efforts of the Union to introduce a breath of fresh air into the Welsh rugby scene and would support the tour'. The five games they played in Wales attracted just under 100,000 people. The Fijians were bright, they were exuberant, and they were entertaining. Above all they ran. Players like Sela Toga, Sogosogo, Noucabalavu, Cavu their captain, and Walisoliso, the prop who scored three times against a Welsh XV, dispelled through their sunshine rugby any minor problems of pronunciation. They put a lot of joy back into the game. On their final spectacular day, and despite losing a man after ten minutes, they came back from a 21 point deficit to score 13 points in twelve minutes. Wales had scored seven tries, the Fijians six in the 28 points to 22 extravaganza. This was the bracing tonic Wales needed before a new international season that was to be the best for Wales since 1952.

It was also Clive Rowlands's last in a Welsh jersey. He had been mauled severely by press and public after the South African tour. That was, off the field, having its own repercussions. Already, on the field, there had been changes, with Terry Price coming in as full-back against Fiji and Allan Lewis, the Abertillery scrum-half with the lengthy service thought to be more helpful to Watkins, in place of the injured Welsh skipper. However that Welsh XV had a number of experimental places in it and when the season's earnest duel began, against England in rain and wind, it was the seasoned campaigner who was recalled. The Welsh pack, with the powerful veteran Waldron of Neath at last winning his cap at prop, showed why they would dominate all season with driving play and clever line-out operations to take advantage of the newly re-jigged laws. Welsh back-play did not reach the heights but the competence they had acquired through the vicissitudes of two uneven seasons saw them defeat England (14-3) and squeeze home at Murrayfield (14-12). There Gale battered his way over around the front of the line with a combination of brute force and a low centre of gravity that breached the Scottish defensive wall and left a gaping hole in the laws that was plugged later that season when it was decided to limit the line-out to a single parallel line of players, thus outlawing the double-banking ploy which Wales had used to such great effect at Murrayfield. By the time Ireland came to Cardiff on 13 March 1965 anticipatory excitement had reached a pitch that had not visited Wales for a few years. Ireland, too, were in contention for the Triple Crown, just as both sides had been in 1911 when Wales denied them to claim the seventh Welsh Crown. There had only been two more after that, both clinched away in 1950 and 1952. A small rain fell relentlessly on the ground, making conditions treacherous, but failing to deter over 58,000 spectators.

The Irish team was a strong one. They were captained by the studious Ray McLoughlin, from prop-forward, with a pack that included Willie

John McBride and Noel Murphy; the accomplished Tom Kiernan was at full-back, with Roger Young and Mike Gibson as the halves. Wales had been criticized throughout the season for lack of inspiration in the backs, especially at centre where Uzzell of Newport and Dawes of London Welsh were felt to lack the inspiration of D. K. Jones, who had joined Cardiff, and Maurice Richards, who had played against Fiji in his club position of centre. Uzzell would win his fifth and final cap in the last game of the season against France. John Dawes had won his first cap against Ireland in 1964 as a replacement for the crocked Ken Jones. Against France in 1965 he would win his eighth cap but, thereafter, his international career would be a stop-go one until it flowered late, and gloriously, in 1970-1. At the Arms Park in 1965 John Dawes was not the most acclaimed of Welsh players; his virtues were not, perhaps, appreciated by a crowd eager for old style centre play. No Welshman, equally desirous of the Triple Crown, can have done anything but groan, however, when a clash led to Dawes going off injured after only five minutes. With unconscious irony Clive Rowlands later told the press, 'The best thing that could have happened to us was to lose Dawes'. He meant that the centre's absence, for about half of the first half, caused the team to concentrate all the more. Rowlands's typical improvisatory flourish was to move Terry Price to centre and place Alun Pask, to the No. 8's considerable surprise, at full-back. The gamble paid off. Pask was one of the most accomplished all-round footballers in his position that Wales had seen, certainly the best since Pontypridd's Russell Robins who had been to the 1955 Lions in South Africa what Pask was to those of 1962. Now aged twenty-six, big at 6foot 3inches but mobile at 15 stone, he seemed to revel in the demands made on him by Irish kicking. He fielded, ran and kicked until Welsh anxiety and Irish hopefulness seemed quite misplaced, and then Dawes returned to the field.

Kiernan missed a straightforward penalty. The game which had seen some heated exchanges at forward was calmed by the referee, and then, with the first forty minutes almost gone David Watkins showed his pace, even on a slippery surface, to score far out at the river end. Terry Price did not miss. In the second period Bebb burst over after a Brian Price tap-down at the line-out. Kiernan's penalty goal took the score to 8 - 3 but the Welsh crowd burst into song as Price, now restored to full-back, fielded an Irish clearance ten yards in from touch, glanced at the posts, steadied himself and swung over a stupendous 45-yard drop goal. The song died in Welsh throats as Ireland scored a beautifully worked scissors that bamboozled the Welsh back-row and put Flynn, the centre, in near the

381

river-end posts. Kiernan made it 11 points to 8. There were five minutes to go in a match of dramatic shifts. Wales sent the Irish, now stoking their own special fires, back to their own half where a scrum was ordered near the 25. The Irish, with Murphy as ever in the van, came round a little too quickly and an empty-handed Rowlands, moving menacingly away, was hammered to the ground. Price kicked the penalty to the echoing cheers of a crowd applauding the wiliest scrum-half since Dickie Owen. Rowlands would, appropriately, play out his day in club football for Swansea. Held aloft in the drizzle by ecstatic supporters he could reflect that he had captained Wales to her tenth Triple Crown.

It was, as these things go in international rugby, all too short a reflection. In Paris a fortnight later Wales, already champions outright, were run ragged (22 – 0 at the half) by France. Pride was salvaged by a 13 point recovery in a second half that denied France a further score but the damage was done. Wales would go on to retain the championship the following season, and even beat France at Cardiff because of Stuart Watkins's thundering interception, but there would be no Triple Crown (Ireland took her customary revenge), no Clive Rowlands. He was replaced at scrum-half by Allan Lewis and as captain by Alun Pask. The latter began by becoming only the fourth Welshman to lead a team to victory at Twickenham but, oddly enough, his own predilection for daring, imaginative rugby now brought him the criticism that had been heaped on Rowlands. Eleven Welshmen, including Pask, went to New Zealand but Campbell-Lammerton, the Scottish lock, was, in Welsh eyes, an inexplicable choice as leader of a tour in which all four Tests were lost. Some Welsh reputations, and especially that of the lively David Watkins, were enhanced but even Watkins now saw the wheel of fortune spin him off when, for the first home game of the 1966-67 season, Barry John replaced him against Australia. Wales lost for the first time to an excellent Wallabies team superbly captained by a much-admired scrum-half, Ken Catchpole. Wales lost the next three games on the trot, whether John or Watkins played, whether Pask or Watkins was captain. Inexplicably Wales had climbed to the top of the greasy pole only to fall to earth again. The 1967-8 season produced three new captains (Norman Gale, Gareth Edwards and John Dawes) and one victory in five games. Once more the house had had foundations of sand. Once more the crumbling edifice had new features installed which gave cause for hope.

At first sight the game in April 1967, which was David Watkins's last for Wales, before he left for Salford, and a fellow Newportonian's first in a career that, like Terry Price, took him from teenage anonymity to national adulation as the new Welsh full-back before he, too, went North, to Barrow, was just a freak. Keith Jarrett, a 6 foot 13 stone eighteen-year-old, had left Monmouth School the previous Christmas. For Newport he had scored 109 points in 16 games, from the centre position. His goal kicking feats, allied to Terry Price's poor form in the previous game in Paris, led to his surprise selection for a Wales, without a win all season, against an English side able to take the Triple Crown. J. B. G. Thomas wrote beforehand: 'The periods of success enjoyed by countries nowadays are shorter, and it is unlikely that there will be another period of triumph as long as the "Golden Era" at the turn of the century'. Despite the miraculous début of Jarrett who converted all five tries, kicked two penalties and, seizing on a loose kick from McFadyean the English centre, ran hard from a deep position down the left touch-line to score himself, the *Western Mail's* correspondent would have had little cause to change his mind. True, in this 34 points to 21 victory Wales had beaten England as never before and done better, in a winning margin, than at any time since 1910; true, that never had England scored 21 points and lost; true, that only Vivian Jenkins had scored a try for Wales from full-back; true that Jarrett's 19 points equalled the Welsh record set up by Jack Bancroft against France in 1910; but then it was a day he might have walked on water with impunity. The following season, Jarrett never really happy at full-back, missed some games through injury and in the two he played was picked at centre. Wales did little better than before, and France, guided by the performing fleas of French rugby, the diminutive, ubiquitous Camberabero brothers, won at Cardiff to take the Grand Slam for the first time. The clouds, it seemed, had let the Welsh sun shine very briefly.

With hindsight the dawn had proved premature, but not false. Keith Jarrett would only win another ten caps and stay in the national game for two more seasons; but his was no mean contribution and in his final season he had begun to emerge as a powerful surging centre in the Wooller mould. Even more crucially, players now emerged or matured for Wales who would form the hard core of Welsh rugby for over a decade. They were, from the start, phenomenally gifted men. A few would be amongst the greatest the world had ever seen. Part of the second Golden Era must be put down to this simple fact. Barry John, twice capped already, did not play in the English game of 1967 but Gareth Owen Edwards, himself only nineteen, did. It was Edwards's second cap after a sound display against France. The official programme note commented — 'Edwards should have a long run in the Welsh side in view of his all-round ability'. Gerald Davies, at left-centre, had been first capped, with John, against Australia but, unlike the Llanelli fly-half, he had remained for five consecutive caps. Within a year John would have formed a club, then country, partnerhip with Edwards of enduring significance. John Lloyd, the mobile Bridgend prop, had replaced Waldron in 1966 against England. Now he won the ninth of his twenty-four caps. And into the back-row had come, against France when Pask had to withdraw after 26 consecutive appearances, Dai 'Shadow' Morris an unassuming replacement at No. 8 for the flamboyant Pask. The Neath forward, a colliery welder from the Tower Colliery, Hirwaun, would win most of his thirty-five caps at flanker and a place in the affection of his countrymen that was as unsurpassed as it will prove undying for all who saw his unrelenting, tireless covering and support. Alongside him, one fast, raiding flanker, a twenty-one-year-old, as yet clean-shaven, English-born, Welsh-mothered London Welshman was winning his fourth cap after, to the horror of many in Wales, having ended the illustrious career of Haydn Morgan. John Taylor had proved irresistible in the final trial. His speed to the break-down and constructive distribution of the ball would silence doubts about his size (both he and Dai Morris were just 6 foot and 13½ stone) in a magnificent run of twenty-six caps and two Lions tours. The team, however, was neither rounded out in personnel nor, with the exception of the experienced Gale, Denzil Williams and Brian Price, matured. Wales had produced others who had looked as impressive. But if 1964 was the hinge on which the door had moved, 1967 was the year the door finally swung open. Or rather, like the double doors of a western saloon, it swung wide to let in a man whose long-standing mission had, at last, found its spiritual home. There were quite a few willing to hear the message that would transform a National XV into a National Club.

Ray Williams had been appointed the Coaching Organizer for Wales in January 1967. It was the first post of its kind in the world and it had gone, in good rugby tradition, to the son of a miner. Except that this shrewd, hard-headed, voluble man now leaving, at some financial loss, his job as Senior Technical Representative for the C.C.P.R. in the West Midlands, was a North Walian whose rugby career had been, via Wrexham and Loughborough College, as outside half for London Welsh, Northampton and Moseley. A final Welsh trial in 1953 was, he knew, scarcely enough to overcome the scepticism, even hostility, that parts of the close-guarded Welsh rugby world felt about the man and his dreams. Ray Williams intended to translate dream, and potential, into reality, and achievement. The first A.G.M. he addressed, in 1967, was left in no doubt of the force they had unleashed. The new boy told them:

> I am not naïve enough to think that everyone in this gathering is 100 per cent in favour of coaching. There are those among you who are not certain what it involves and there are those who, quite rightly, regard any change with great caution. Part of my job will be to convince everyone that coaching is in the best interests of the game. I can assure you that I shall pursue the task with great vigour . . . Make no mistake, gentlemen, I intend to convince you . . . I start with a great advantage for, although some of you may not be 100 per cent for coaching, all of us are 100 per cent for rugby football and from this basis from which to work how could anyone fail? . . . I will get about, demonstrating, motivating, stimulating.

Ray Williams was keenly aware of how much there was to do. He also made a point of singling out the Working Party, set up in 1964, and particularly its three principal members, Cliff Jones, Alun Thomas and Cadfan Davies. They had been busy, deliberating and investigating, for three years under their allotted brief 'to examine the state of Rugby football within the Union and its constituent clubs and to recommend . . . what steps if any, should be taken to improve the standard of play.' This Working Party was made up of former players, administrators and officials, indeed of anyone considered close enough to the modern game to help with advice. Cadfan Davies had acted as the Honorary Secretary of the W.R.U. Coaching Sub-Committee whose W.R.U. membership, in the aftermath of the 1964 A.G.M., had been increased to five (V. J. Parfitt, Ken Gwilym, V. C. Phelps, Rees Stephens and Alun Thomas). By the time of the June 1965 A.G.M., V. J. Parfitt, as chairman of the Coaching Committee, was able to report that more club coaches had been appointed and that a Coaching Advisory Committee, under the chairmanship of Cliff Jones, had been established to examine technical aspects. Even so matters had not stopped there and, in December 1965, a recommendation was presented from the Coaching to the General Committee, by Vernon Parfitt, that a 'full time Coaching Administrator be appointed'. The choice was 'a comprehensive and continuous Coaching scheme' or its utter abandonment. The view was accepted 'by an overwhelming majority'. The enthusiasm that was being shown at grass roots could not be sustained any longer on a part-time, amateur basis. To this end Cliff Jones, as succeeding chairman of the Coaching Committee, was, despite the achievements in appointing club and advisory W.R.U. staff coaches, insistent that the co-ordinating work done by Cadfan Davies was now too onerous. His own 1966 advisory panel (consisting of Clive Rowlands, Alun Pask, Brian Price, Carwyn James, Roy Bish, Dai Hayward, Ieuan Evans and John Robins) was convinced of the extreme urgency and, finally, in the summer of 1966 the recommendation to appoint was implemented. The decision was expedited at this time because the newly-elected Labour government had not only appointed the first Minister of Sport but also, through the Sports Council of Great Britain (later devolved to Wales) made hefty grants available to develop the technical requirements of any given sport. Cliff Jones sat for the W.R.U. on this Council and was, now, not slow to press his Union's claims for a substantial contribution towards the salary of any Coaching Organizer the Union might appoint. The case was stated and won. The post was, at last, available. Ray Williams took up this new, and challenging role, in June 1967.

The long-term policy that the Organizer now laid down was not one to pay immediate dividends. It was, however, set about with pressing immediacy. Liaison with all existing bodies in Wales (from Sports Councils to educational bodies to clubs) was established on the basis of encouragement and advice. To the Coaching Committee, itself now upgraded to full status within the hierarchy of W.R.U. committees, he would act as adviser and secretary. Courses, conferences and teach-ins were established for players, coaches and referees. Out of this would come a register of coaches who had attained the Welsh Coaching Award, itself revamped in 1968. The Coaching Advisory Committee was an important adjunct to the Coaching Committee proper since the former, though chaired by two W.R.U. members, consisted of eight others whose links with and expertise about the game gave them special value. By the mid 1970s the register of coaches would have gone well over three hundred and, in senior and junior rugby, a basic pattern of coaching was being implemented. After a year in the job Ray Williams had laid the grid of his approach. He insisted that it would be five years before the fruits of his work were apparent — 'if the standard is not higher I will have failed . . . but I can assure you I do not intend to fail . . . if you want to know whether coaching works don't ask me, ask the players . . .' Within a year of that he was confident that 'the coaching bogey has been laid for good', and in 1973 J. Malcolm Lewis, in the clearest manner of approval possible, was made Assistant Coaching Organizer. Coaching in Wales had owed much not only to the dedication of its advocates but, even more perhaps, in good years and bad, to the philosophy preached so eloquently by Ray Williams that underlay it — 'to win by scoring the greatest number of points that prevailing circumstances will permit . . . Coaches [should be] men with boldness and imagination who respect the great tradition and spirit of Rugby football and, at the same time, strive to reach new and better standards in the eternal pursuits of excellence'.

This was the spirit that had been at work earlier in the Youth Union, which between 1960 and 1962 had organized its own coaching courses, squad system and even appointed an official coach to its international XV. This was Ammanford's Ieuan Evans, whose wide-ranging social awareness, inherited from a family background of intense and active commitment to the values of South Wales coalfield society, no less than his progressive rugby thinking and forceful personality, enabled him to establish an immediate and fruitful rapport with the Welsh Youth, and then with Swansea R.F.C. The philosophy already at work at Youth level was now applied to the one area of Union activity directly concerned with senior rugby, as the Selection Committee increased the separation of its specialist functions by allying itself with coaching development. Through the long years of propaganda for coaching within the Union, one man had managed to unite this dual function within himself. Cliff Jones had served from 1956 as chairman of the Coaching Supervisory (later Advisory) Committees, and from 1967 of the Coaching Committee itself; he had been a selector for the same period. By 1979, when he had retired as a selector at the end of the most sustained period of success ever enjoyed by the W.R.U., he had been five times chairman of the Selection Committee, its convenor for ten years and was still the chairman of the Coaching Committee itself. This unique record of service was vital in establishing a bridgehead between the traditionalism of selection procedure and the innovation of coaching. It was carried on by his successor in these posts, Alun Thomas, and by the automatic appointment of the National Coach as the first appointed selector. Cliff Jones had, in 1964, urged 'a modern and progressive outlook' in his Union and had striven to bring into the Union 'present-day players, and those closely concerned with the game as played today'. He knew how hard it would be, even for truly gifted players, to achieve anything without a dedicated organization behind them. However, he was, by 1970, convinced, and soon convincing, when he told a major coaching conference that 'Wales could beat the world'. From the outset, then, the work with youth and schools rugby was not allowed to obscure the belief that coaching had to be identified with the very highest levels because the national side was 'the shop-window of Welsh rugby and from it many young players find inspiration'. The further involvement, and training, of referees was placed high on the agenda. There followed, in conjunction with the active Welsh Society of Rugby Union Referees, a full programme that led later to a unique, computerized grading of referees whose vital role was an essential element in the health of the competitive Welsh game. New developments in the game, the world over, were to be tabulated and passed on too; in 1970 Ray Williams travelled the Southern hemisphere as a Churchill Fellow, advising emergent nations in addition to learning.

Not all was plain sailing. In early 1968, for example, the Coaching Organizer had to insist before the Coaching Committee that he be allowed to attend all away matches in order to be in touch with the highest echelons of the game. The General Committee debated the issue before agreeing that he was indeed 'a senior member of the W.R.U. staff' and that to deny him such facilities would be 'a retrograde step'. Matters were moving at a very fast pace indeed. The Selection Committee, in September 1967, had won the unanimous approval of the General Committee to appoint three honorary coaches, David Nash to coach the Welsh XV for the season, Carwyn James and David Hayward to coach, respectively, the West and East Wales XVs against the New Zealand tourists, whilst Monmouthshire appointed David Harries of Newbridge. Further they proposed to choose, assemble and co-ordinate their squads of players well in advance. Alun Thomas who had presented the report made clear the motivation behind their thinking was not dominated by the duty to select a winning team — 'they also had a duty . . . to influence the quality of play in the International and other sides'. The logical conclusion to all this pioneering activity was a further step away from the past when appointing officials to accompany Wales, in their second overseas tour, to the Argentine in 1968. Glyn Morgan was the Honorary Manager and Harry Bowcott his assistant, but no qualified coach had been selected. Unable to accept this block on the intricate relationship of coaching to playing, Alun Thomas, after failing to influence the General Committee, resigned; David Nash later followed suit. At which point, in April, all seemed cut and dried, until, once more, the club delegates at the June A.G.M. showed they were not prepared to see the executive drag its feet. After Ray Williams presented his report, delegates rose to accuse the General Committee of not practising what they preached. The motion 'to think again' was accepted. By the end of the month Clive Rowlands, elected a Vice-president at this same A.G.M., became the official coach to the Argentine. This was the end of the opposition to coaching in Wales. From 1969 onwards coaches were accorded a position of status, and often authority, in Welsh rugby clubs that ensured the revolution in attitude would permeate through the game. When the manager for the 1969 short tour of Australia was chosen in December 1968, there was no question but that a coach would accompany Handel Rogers. Cliff Jones told the executive that whoever was appointed would go on to coach the National Squad and the National XV for 1968-69. Once more Clive Rowlands received the job. What had begun in the 1960s would be taken into the forthcoming decade. Those who had seen the future knew that it worked. Those who had been through the 1960s did not want the kind of success through power-play that New Zealand rugby had imposed. This was true, so far as advanced Welsh thinking is concerned, even of the 1967 All Blacks side led by Lochore. Wales could not match that power on its own terms. The 1969 tour of the Antipodes hammered home the point. What coaching promised, but had not yet delivered, was that Wales might find her own way. Cliff Jones admitted to the 1969 A.G.M. that the two defeats in New Zealand were harsh 'moments of truth' but he was adamant that the aim of Wales was 'to emerge not as second class New Zealanders but as first class Welshmen'.

In the meantime it was undeniable that, notwithstanding a few moments to savour, the 1960s had been the decade of New Zealand triumph. Wales, however, learned more from her isolated moments of success when the rolling juggernaut was stopped in its tracks than she did in defeats that owed as much to misguided imitation as to All Black power. Wilson Whineray's 1963 team inspired awe and a respect that became affection for such well-endowed forwards as Meads, Stewart, Nathan, Tremain and Gray. From the platforms to attack established by their power, the more than competent, yet less than brilliant, backs did enough to keep winning. They were helped by a goal-kicking machine at full back called Don Clarke. In fact Clarke was more cumbersome than most sides seemed to appreciate until he had gone. After three minutes against Wales he strained his groin so badly that he could hardly kick with his right leg for the rest of the game, but no Welshman noticed. It was a grim, albeit deeply satisfying, 6 - 0 victory at the Arms Park with no try scored. New Zealand had come to win at last and Wales were in a bronze not golden era. They won almost everything — though Scotland held them to a 0 - 0 draw and Cardiff were pipped by kicks, 6 - 5 — with only the third match of the tour at Newport to mar their record and keep Welsh pride intact. Newport's three coaches, Bryn Meredith, Bryn Williams and Ian McJennett drilled their team to counter All Black strengths and, on a slippery turf in drizzling rain, a searing break by David Watkins, a cross kick by wing Stuart Watkins and well-won ball in front of the posts let John Uzzell slot a goal. Price and Ford in the line-out, Poole and Thomas's speed from the back-row, above all, the sacrifical, near-suicidal willingness of veteran Glyn Davidge to kill every loose ball, took Newport alongside Swansea and Cardiff as the only Welsh clubs to defeat the New Zealanders. Whineray's men ended a well-conducted, often dour, tour by letting their hair down against a weak Barbarians side, beaten 36 - 3 at Cardiff. The whitewash of the odd selection for the Lions Tour of 1966 gave little satisfaction to New Zealanders who proudly re-called the exploits of their past XVs. Terry McLean, not a shy beater of the New Zealand drum by any means, wrote a year later:

> Although New Zealand may now fairly claim to be the most successful of the world's rugby nations, it has, coincidentally, lost its old place and standing as an innovator of new and brilliant methods of attack . . . Before the radical alteration of the laws in 1964, marauding play by no. 8 forwards, chest-to-chest defensive stations by opposing backlines, constant use of the touchline by inside and outside halves and a general aim to promote mistakes by spoiling play were staples of the New Zealand style of play . . . with at least 50 per cent of scoring chances from penalty onwards . . . It was cruelly efficient, markedly successful, quite abominably dull.

Brian Lochore had been a raw twenty-three-year-old on Whineray's tour. The Sixth All Blacks, with whom he returned in 1967 for a shorter tour, were managed and coached by Messrs. Saxton and Allen, of 1946 Kiwis fame. Again they were formidable but this time they had come to use their power more constructively in line with Charles Saxton's conception of a team as a unit, with forwards and backs linking in attack and defence. Meads, Gray, Nathan and Tremain were all back and there were some outstanding new faces in Kirkpatrick on the flank, Laidlaw at scrum-half and McCormick at full-back to remind everyone of the importance of penalty goals. At outside-half they had Earle Kirton, crucified after the 1963 Newport game, now matured into the ideal, sound link the All Blacks required after their greatest strength had been exerted. And this was in the ruck. So devastating was their binding and driving in the loose that British teams became, again, obsessed with imitation of the technique and its concomitant stages of 'phase' possession. Lochore's team was undefeated. Wales went down again, 11 — 6, in another match that lacked either the passion or the dazzle of past encounters. Wales had picked Brian Thomas at prop, as well as the big Aberavon second-row forwards, Mainwaring and Wiltshire. Norman Gale's men battled hard, but neither side lifted the occasion on another Arms Park mud-heap.

What gives the 1967 tour its importance, however, are three inter-connected matters — first, that New Zealand, complacently, saw no need for further development, especially against opponents who generally lacked their physique as well as their forward skill; secondly, that by 1970 the insistence on tight scrummaging by specialist forwards, the alternative use of the newly-defined maul with its superior ball-using possibilities and the end of touch-kicking outside the '25s' presented imaginative, and indigenous, alternatives to All Black engrossing of the ball; thirdly, two matches in Wales had lifted Welsh expectations. Both were the product of squad-training and coaches.

On a bright sunny November day at St. Helen's, Carwyn James's West Wales team, a careful mixture of youthful vigour and tight-forward expertise, played scintillating rugby on a surface made for running. Over 40,000 people came to see Clive Rowlands, captain of Swansea and of West Wales, tilt once more at the All Blacks. The pack scrummed hard to prevent New Zealand taking tight play for granted and the hungry trio of Dai Morris (Neath), Morrie Evans (Swansea) and Bobby Wanbon (Aberavon) showed, by their plundering paces, what a fine Welsh back-row they would have made. The final score was 21 - 14 against West Wales but the lead had changed hands several times and the last New Zealand score was a trifle gratuitous. Above all Rowlands, whilst employing every kick in his encyclopaedic knowledge of boot-to-ball, varied play behind in a tactical display of virtuoso standards. The thoughtful coaching of Carwyn James was married here, for the first and last time, to Rowland's pounding rhetoric of play. Both would have further, and after this performance, justified chances against New Zealand's might.

After this anything else might have been an anti-climax. The weather almost guaranteed that it was a dying fall. On Wednesday 6 December 1967, at Rodney Parade, a Monmouthshire side intent on spoiling for possession, and backed by four penalties from Keith Jarrett, did well until, tiring, the All Blacks took the lead in the game's later stages, and ran out 23-12 winners. The big game on the Saturday was to be against Dai Hayward's East Wales squad but a heavy fall of snow prevented the game being played. To their credit the New Zealanders agreed to travel down on the following Wednesday. The eventual game gave Welsh rugby a fresh boost and introduced New Zealanders, on Welsh soil, to a man who, in conjunction with Carwyn James in 1971, and in his own right, in 1977, would become very familiar. S. J. Dawes, not currently in the Welsh XV, was at centre only because Billy Raybould, who had played for Wales, had withdrawn. Gerald Davies, who also had not played in the international, was co-centre, with John and Edwards at half-back. Apart from Dawes, it was an all Cardiff back-line, for the wings were the Commonwealth Games sprinter Keri Jones and Frank Wilson. The pack was, again, a judicious mix of hardness and mobility. New Zealand's side was not the full Test XV but it contained enough of their first side to make an East Wales triumph unlikely. Dai Hayward's plan, as he told his young captain, Gareth Edwards, was to pressure them at all times and attack by running at them on all available occasions. Simply put but, in a nutshell, the tactical plan that would be spelled out in detail thereafter by other coaches.

On the terraces that day the snow still lingered, collapsing, here and there, into a thin, shoe-soaking slush. The crowd was sparser because of this, the mid-week date, and the skid warnings that lined the treacherous A48 all the way from Swansea. Thirty thousand people managed to be there for all that. It was a mobile back-row (Hickey of Cardiff, Ron Jones of Coventry, and Tony Gray of London Welsh) who did the initial damage of harrassment that disrupted New Zealand's potentially awesome rhythm and then instant cover-tackling by the centres with John Dawes a rock on which most waves crashed. For the first time New Zealanders, and Welshmen, too, were then privileged to see what the talents of John and Edwards could do in unison. The latter was all probing, darting busyness, content to let his partner's sangfroid further chill the hearts of the men in black. Wilson grabbed a try mid-way through the first half. The score remained 3 — 0 until almost the end. The other foraging wing, Keri Jones, was twice obstructed, once when a try was imminent, by the burly, hustling McCormick, and Frank Wilson had a further try disallowed. Ten minutes from the end, after a second half of constant East Welsh pressure, Steel, the New Zealand wing, broke away for an undeserved, but well-taken, equalizing try. The final result of 3 - 3 flattered the All Blacks as their manager admitted. He added that he had seen brilliant Welsh back play for the first time that tour. None more so than that of Barry John who floated above the icy turf full of killing nonchalance. A final drop goal went wide by the smallest of margins. His turn, too, would come again.

Obviously, there was no denying the re-iterated words of J. B. G. Thomas, the man who had, by now, become the most prolific writer about rugby of all time, that 'the game goes on' even if, for Wales, these re-

392

captured hints of glory were not sustained during the following season despite having, in David Nash, a national coach for the first time. Welsh players did well enough, however, as individuals, to be the largest single group on the Lions tour to South Africa. Jarrett's late arrival as a replacement took their number to eleven. Injuries hampered their contribution. Most notably, Barry John broke a collar bone after fifteen minutes of the first Test and Edwards who, like his outside-half, was coming to his best form, missed the last two Tests. The Lions lost three and drew one of the Test games to continue, despite being a well-led and talented side, the dismal story of overseas tours by the British Isles. Nor were Wales to fare any better on their tour to the Argentine in September 1968. Admittedly the Welsh Lions were not available after the ardours of the veldt but the side chosen was well-balanced and under the coaching eye of Clive Rowlands. Apart from difficulties of refereeing interpretation and the Latin fervour of the crowd, who christened John Williams, the young full-back, 'Canasta' (basket) and threw beer bottles and other emptied missiles to help him prove it, there was a jolt to be had from the strength of Argentinian rugby. Three victories, two draws and a defeat was no disgrace but they failed to beat Argentina in either Test. The 1960s was drawing to an end with Welsh rugby poised to undertake more overseas missions. Before that could happen with any degree of equanimity the thought behind the game that was now positively simmering with zeal would need to find its appropriate channels.

One such was the Coaching Advisory Committee's response to Ray Williams's suggestion in early 1968 that the negative, defensive qualities of British back-row play were limiting the chances of winning the ball. The subsequent paper *Back-Row Forward Play*, in the opinion of Ray Williams, 'revolutionized Welsh International forward play'. The Selection Committee, as before, backed the Coaching Committee's views, chided clubs for not implementing them and pointed the way by insisting that they would no longer pick open and blind-side wing-forwards. The quest now was for left and right flankers, not especially big or heavy men in the New Zealand style. The laws had limited the role of the destructive, open-side wing-forward, anyway, so the new concept was to envisage the back-row as a *unit*, in defence or attack, whose role was, though specialist, integral to the whole eight forwards. The assumption was that of the virtue of positive play at all times. What followed on from this, in the course of time, was the fundamental precept of 'continuity'. This idea, which involved every player supporting every other player, when and where circumstances dictated or allowed, turned the Welsh XVs of the 1970s into the total footballing sides that found their soccer counterparts in the Dutch and West German XIs of the mid-1970s. Welsh centres now mauled as a matter of course, a Welsh full-back would end the 1970s as an international flanker, and prop-forwards would run, pass and score tries, if not quite like deer then at least no longer as donkeys.

Profundity of tactical thinking, with long-term aims and a developing institutional structure, plus a number of exceptional players were, clearly, the hopes of Welsh rugby from the late 1960s. There was one more, catalytic agent that was needed in the brew. It came from a domestic club scene that had itself moved from the limited horizons that had marked all but the biggest of clubs in the past. The stimulus to more flowing play for which the Sevens competitions (both the Snellings and the National competition) had been designed, was pushed further in the late 1960s through the two-leg Floodlight Alliance, initiated by Ebbw Vale, where the most tries counted, whilst the 1970s would resurrect pre-1914 arguments about the nature of domestic competition. However, the unofficial championship during the sixties was not unconnected to the desire of a few clubs to increase their patronage, their receipts and their standing by claiming the title. The first three were, as pre-1914 clubs knew, dependent not only on victory but on the way it had come. Clubs turned seriously, both junior and senior, to utilize the loans from government bodies and the traditionally interested breweries, that would give them better fields, facilities and the kind of club house that would prove attractive to a public weaned away from male-only public houses. The result was a sad loss of uniquely flavoured local beer in return for welcome money to be ploughed in to the sporting purposes of the club. Rugby followers who had grown old on real ale sighed, but drank up.

Seven different clubs took the unofficial championship in this decade (with newcomers to the title like Aberavon, Pontypridd and Newbridge jostling with Neath, Llanelli and Newport) but it was Bridgend, emerging from the cocoon of preparation, as Ebbw Vale had in the 1950s and Pontypridd would from the mid-1970s, who caught the eye with a young team, well coached by Cadfan Davies, who came out on top three times, and made it four by winning in the first year of the new decade. Theirs was essentially a team effort — though the high scoring feats of centres Ron Evans and Keith Bradshaw, nimble movers and computerized kickers, were deservedly recognized by the national selectors. They were blessed in many departments, from Prothero and Colin Standing in the back-row to the dashing, singing Glen Landeg at full-back, but they were transformed into a unit that acted as precursor for other running sides by the vision of Cadfan Davies, one of the first coaches appointed to a first class club in Britain. That was in 1964: 'Our aim was simple — to play continuous Rugby involving fifteen players and run the opposition off their feet. We determined to be at break-downs before rucks could be set up, to retain possession and attack the opposition at all times, particularly when they were at their most vulnerable — in our 25!' Simple it may have been but stereotyped it was not. Its attractive play pleased Welsh crowds used to a starvation diet so far as points were concerned.

If Bridgend was a thriving club of a town whose position was attracting investment and population so London was the world capital, at least the cultural mecca, of the 1960s. The enormous expansion in higher education across Britain as a whole made London, in particular, a magnet for Welsh students and teachers. They went at a time when the glum soul-searching in Welsh rugby was at its height. Many of them found the outward-looking world into which they had moved far less cramped than the battered society they left behind. Those who played rugby and who gravitated to Old Deer Park enjoyed the more casual approach of London club football. A few hidings at the hands of 'real' clubs back home was only to be expected. That is until the arrival in the early 1960s of the ex-Aberystwyth student, ex-Newbridge centre, S. J. Dawes.

John Dawes had been a Welsh reserve in the early 1960s and was first capped in 1964, at the age of twenty-four against Ireland. The years 1966 to 1969, however, when his international career was limited, were the crucial ones in what turned out to be a remarkable rugby career. Appointed vice-captain at the club for 1964-65, and then, with Roger Michaelson, the Cambridge Blue and one-cap Welsh International as vice-captain, he captained the club for four successive seasons in the 1960s. A tougher training regime was imposed but, more importantly, they concentrated on using a light, mobile pack to arrive first at the break-down of play rather than waste energy in the forward strengths on which Welsh clubs relied. A philosophy of hard tackling and counter-attacking play was elevated from a necessity to a priority. Gareth James at full-back smiled because he ran and ran because he smiled. The result, even before established players began to join them, was sensational. Each season became better than the last. By 1968-69 they were a force with whom to be reckoned on all occasions — only Llanelli won on their ground, whilst the current Welsh champions, Neath, fell 45 - 3. Next season saw no falling away;

Newport went down 31 - 5 and Aberavon 52 - 8. A visit from the 'Welsh' on their Christmas tour to Wales became an anticipated event in the rugby calendar. This was particularly so on Boxing Day at Stradey where Carwyn James was preaching the gospel of integrated, 'eighteen-man rugby' that made Llanelli the Welsh equivalent of the Old Deer Park metropolitans at the turn of the decade whilst, in Richmond, a £97,000 pavilion had been erected for the new season when the club could boast ten Internationals and nine Barbarians on their strength. Generally London Welsh only played once a week on a good playing surface, and, of course, freedom from the unremitting, grinding pressure of South Walian club rugby permitted experiment and, often, a relaxed approach. Under the combined coaching-captaincy of Dawes, however, the team was able to translate these attitudes into positive advantages when they needed to move up a gear. Tony Gray and John Taylor had already won caps as swift flankers from the club's ranks; now selectorial eyes turned their way again.

J. P. R. Williams had won schoolboy caps after being converted into a full-back and it was as a full-back that John Dawes drafted the young medical student into his side when Gareth James was injured. That same season a newly-arrived teacher, ex-Swansea Training College, started playing for the London club. He took his gangling form into the First XV and, after Dennis Hughes of Newbridge dropped out of a final trial, into the W.R.U. trials and on to the first of thirty-eight consecutive Welsh caps. The No. 8 was Mervyn Davies, covered for club and country by Taylor. That first cap, against Scotland, was the first full cap of the London Welsh full-back, too. Exceptional talent had been spotted but it had been detected and set to flourish initially in what was fast becoming a rugby hothouse. The man who nurtured these tender plants was not an automatic choice for Wales, whose preferred centres were Keith Jarrett and Gerald Davies. Nonetheless, in the absence of so many senior players for selection in the wake of the 1968 Lions tour, Dawes had gone to Argentina as captain, just as he had been called in, earlier in 1968, rather suddenly, to brandish the magic wand of leadership that he was using in London. Wales lost to Ireland and John Dawes, handed a wand but no real authority, gave back the captaincy. Despite his triumphs at club level it is likely that the role he was yet to play in Welsh and British rugby would have died here if it had not been for the grip that coaching, and hence the squad system, now exerted. Interchangeable, not discarded parts; a blend of skills, not one-off players; a team, not a hastily assembled bunch of strangers — these were the factors that allowed Wales to become European champions in 1969 and take her second Triple Crown of the 1960s.

The season began with the full installation of national squad training sessions at the Afan Lido. The storm of controversy they caused was stilled by acceptance of their amateur legality at the I.B. meeting in March 1969. By then Wales was well on the way to the best record she had attained since the early 1950s. At the July A.G.M. Ray Williams likened the coaching schemes he had inaugurated to an iceberg — 'only the tip shows, its greater mass and strength is hidden . . . the National side gets the publicity but far more work is done at a lower level . . . The National Squad met five times . . . but people outside Wales regarded the National Squad as some sort of secret society which was confined in the hills, practising all the time and which were only brought out to play International matches'. In fact only eighteen players appeared for Wales that season. (The lack of serious injuries, now and later, allied to prompt treatment was a great credit to the efficient medical system controlled by Gordon Rowley, the Honorary Surgeon to the Union). Dawes and Delme Thomas, both squad members, came in against England for the final game when Gerald Davies and the captain, the thirty-one-year-old Brian Price, had to withdraw: and Phil Bennett, the first ever Welsh substitute when he played out four minutes against France after Gerald Davies dislocated his elbow. The season was full of such rugby vignettes — Brian Price injudiciously felling Noel Murphy the Irish captain before the Prince of Wales; at the same game, where after early frustration, a great deal of running rugby produced one Irish and four Welsh tries, the crowd, reduced to 29,000 because the work of reconstruction had began, saw Denzil Williams, winning his twenty-third cap to become the most capped Welsh prop, instruct Jarrett to tap a penalty to him. He had called this move many times for his club when opponents retreated before the expected accuracy of full-back Barry Edwards' boot. Since the kick was only twenty yards out and the Irish now retreating in false expectation of a kick at goal, the Ebbw Vale electrician reckoned his 16 stone could make it. With a bull-elephant charge which seemed to go on forever, he did. And Jarrett added the extra two. For Ivor Jones, the great Llanelli wing-forward then gracing the Presidency of the Union, better than anything 'was the manner in which the games were played'. He meant fourteen tries in four games. Five came against England when Maurice Richards, his sinuous six feet leaving defenders helpless, equalled the pre-1914 four tries record of Willie Llewellyn and Reggie Gibbs. All of this, it was plain, had not just happened. Too many moves

397

were co-ordinated by backs and forwards, too many tries had come from a side anticipating the needs and intentions of others. They were now drilled to do so. One of the best, considered features had been the driving scrummaging on every ball of the Welsh eight. Brian Price, the Roy John of Rodney Parade, had been invaluable both for his own towering (6 foot 4 inches) expertise and the way he knuckled down to the captaincy.

It was natural, therefore, that he, and his team, would be sent to Australia in May, no longer the complete underdogs who had begun the European season. Once more, however, a Welsh overseas tour would crumble into disarray. Once more crumbs of comfort only would be picked up. The Jonahs returned to the belly of Wales. There was, in fact, very little wrong that the imminent retirement of some players and the maturity of others would not put right. That, and a selection policy for captain, would prove the firm foundations on which Wales was building. There was also the not insignificant mis-arrangement of the 1969 tour. The details of the projected tour had been confirmed and accepted in March 1968. They involved direct, non-stop travel to New Zealand followed by three Test matches from a total of seven games. Air travel had taken fifty-two hours. Now literally down-under, the tourists, still reeling from the heady days of the past season, were given an impossible task. The first game, against strong Taranaki, was scheduled for four days after touch down. The second game was a Test. New Zealand was now looking forward to the best Welsh XV (in terms of its immediate past results) of the 1960s but, even more, to the further opportunity to twist the rather bedraggled tail of the red devil. Most critics, too-much-too-soon apart, point to three principal factors in the Welsh disappointment of the tour. First and foremost, Wales met a superb All Blacks XV with a pack basically the same but if anything more skilled and resolute than in 1967. Mervyn Davies's recollection was that they 'outplayed our forwards at line-out, scrummage, ruck and maul, all aspects of the play in which we truly believed we had improved no end'. Secondly the Welsh XV, with some notable exceptions, did not play to its own true standard. Colin Meads, an old adversary of Wales, thought of the 19 - 0 defeat inflicted in the First Test — 'The poor play of the Welsh gave us an inflated idea of our own ability. The Welsh . . . played so unlike the Welsh, they didn't contest or combat'. And thirdly there was refereeing which, in Welsh eyes, travelled the spectrum from indifferent to improbable and on to impossible. Referee Pat Murphy's leap in the air when Fergie McCormick dropped a goal in the

Second Test had television viewers in Wales hurrying to adjust their control knobs; had the picture slipped?

Welsh pride would need to re-group itself into Lions before going to the mat with New Zealand again. There were compensations even in 1969. The tour was, off the field, a happy one for the Welsh party. Older heads saw New Zealand for the last time, younger men were chastened but fired in the battle. Although the Second Test was lost 33 — 12 they were only outscored in tries by three to two. The score this time certainly flattered New Zealand even if they still deserved to win. Wales went unbeaten in her three provincial games and an exciting 19 - 16 triumph over Australia in muddy Sydney saw another piece of the Welsh jigsaw fit. This was to prove even more significant after the tour when both Maurice Richards, whose try in the Second New Zealand Test was thought the best seen there for years, and Keith Jarrett, whose power play as a centre saw him establish himself in Welsh XVs irrespective of goal-kicking, turned professional. The event was the transfer of T. G. R. Davies to the wing. The idea had occurred to Clive Rowlands as his team, beset by injuries, approached the Second Test, in Auckland. In mid-flight he sold the idea to an uncertain Davies. John Dawes came into the centre and Gerald Davies went to left wing. Against Australia the dash and dazzle that had been bottled up in the centre fizzed to its proper vintage on the wing where he scored the first of his touch-line tries for Wales and set up John Taylor's try. Necessity, fertilized by a puckish Clive Rowlands, consented to be the mother of genius. Not all loss, by any means then, for the first Welsh visit to Australia. The last year of the decade ended, appropriately enough, by a happy eight-try match (six for Wales and two for Fiji) at Suva. Welsh players came home to a fond reception and little criticism, for 1969 did not feel like 1964 even if the results, on paper, looked as bad. Nor indeed was it. The 1969-70 season, the last of the fascinating whirligig of fortune for Welsh rugby that had revolved through this decade was, on the whole, a successful one. Admittedly the Irish baulked a Triple Crown attempt in Dublin (the fifth time in history they had done so) by exacting full revenge for the previous encounter. John and Edwards played well below form though enjoying a sixteenth, record-breaking appearance together. The Irish won 14 - 0 and Ken Goodall, their devastating No. 8 forward, was a relentless, unstoppable force. Acute eyes noticed mutual Welsh recrimination on the field and drew all sorts of unwarrantable conclusions. The simpler deduction was poor tactics, the inexperienced captaincy of Gareth Edwards and a distinct absence of grace under pressure when faced with a boisterous Irish XV. Welsh memories would run deep enough in future years for reserves of stamina and resolve to be drawn from the well. Setting this body-blow on one side the team still retained a half share of the championship by, in their turn, stopping a second French Grand Slam at Cardiff. Only one match, then, was lost that season.

The first international had been the last Wales would ever play on the misery of a sodden Arms Park turf. This game, a 6 - 6 draw, was the first occasion Wales had ever held a South African team. It took a last gasp try in the corner by the captain, Edwards, to hold Dawie de Villiers' Sixth Springboks. Both sides came out of a gruelling encounter that South Africa should have won, covered, indistinguishably, in an obliterating layer of mud. For South Africa, who had already lost to Scotland and England and drawn with Ireland, it was a new experience not to win a single international, whilst for Wales the gilt was tarnished by the recollection that the Springboks, though not as well-equipped as their predecessors at forward or back, had played under the constant handicap of organized public opposition to their controversial tour. Their playing record in Wales was exceptionally poor for such a traditional stronghold of the game — Newport, in their opening game, completed a unique double, recapturing the glory of 1912, in winning 11 - 6; Swansea, Aberavon/Neath and Cardiff succumbed to the 'Boks but Llanelli, playing with fire and intricate, inter-passing expertise, lost a wonderful game by a mere point. Gwent hammered home the Welsh message by registering a 14 - 8 victory laid down by the pinpoint goal kicking of the Cardiff student, Robin Williams.

What was encouraging on the field of play that season was the relative well-being of a side already re-building. Jarrett and Richards had departed irrevocably. Gerald Davies had made himself unavailable in order to concentrate on studies and rugby at Cambridge. Gale, Price and Thomas, a troika bristling with courage and years, did not play for Wales again. A shortage of first-class wings led the selectors to pick Llanelli outside-half Phil Bennett on one wing and Ian Hall, a centre for Aberavon, on the other. Against Scotland, Newport's Laurie Daniel, a goal-kicking trump card in Newport's superb championship season the previous year, was right-wing and Bennett became a centre upon W. H. Raybould's withdrawal. The changes were rung again when England confronted Wales at Twickenham. W. H. (Billy) Raybould, first capped in 1967, following a polished performance for Cambridge in the previous December's Varsity match, returned to the centre position he had held against South Africa.

For Newport, Raybould had been a shrewd outside-half against the South Africans and his last cap which came that year against France was won, late in the game, as a substitute for another utility player, J. L. Shanklin of London Welsh, winning a first cap on the right-wing. Billy Raybould's clever cover-tackle on Cantoni, his French opposite, in that game confirmed the impression that Wales had never seen the full flowering of this supremely-fit, yet injury-prone, utility-back. Selection amongst the backs was strictly experimental. Before Shanklin's appearance on the wing, Stuart Watkins, now transferred to Cardiff, had picked up two final caps and Roy Mathias, the carrot-haired flyer from Llanelli, came in on the left. New young stars did not shine too brightly amongst the backs that season in which the Welsh half-backs, especially John, seemed to have withdrawn, after New Zealand, into a protective shell — either doing too little or, more characteristically for Edwards, too much. A number of factors were, however, crystal clear by the end of the year.

The squad system underlined the ability of newcomers to fit in at a moment's notice. To Welsh horror at Twickenham Gareth Edwards had to limp off with Wales 13 - 6 adrift; to English amazement one of the many scrum halves whose career was eclipsed by Edwards's presence, Ray Hopkins from Maesteg, trotted on to alter the course of the game. 'Chico', low slung, quick and crafty, double-banked thighs bulging at the top of his short legs, looked the antithesis of the athletic Edwards. Perhaps the difference bewildered England who let him in for a cheekily stolen blind-side score and then let him begin an avalanche which would rumble in English ears for game upon game: he set up J. P. R. Williams for the third ever Welsh full-back try, and Williams's first, while Barry John dropped an insouciant lethal forty-yard goal in the last minute to lift Wales to an improbable, thrilling 17 - 13 victory. When Welsh ability to play neither Ray Hopkins nor Phil Bennett as their halves is taken into account the depth and maturity of the Welsh reserves already sustained the optimism now running through W.R.U. thinking. Barry John's withdrawal against France let Bennett appear in his own outside-half position for the first time in a Welsh jersey. And another innovation that season reminded selectors of the potential of men who had grown experienced in club rugby. This was the first 'B' international. Played and lost against France in Paris during March it forced the neglected claims of a man who would be picked to captain his country two years later. A. J. Lewis of Ebbw Vale was twenty-six. As a schoolboy for Abertillery and Blaina his game at outside-half was good enough to keep David Watkins in the scrum-half berth. John

401

Dawes had been ever-present all season. At last, albeit now aged thirty, his capability as a sound reader of the game allied to unobstrusive, yet masterly distribution of the ball was recognized. In Lewis, strong, tricky on the burst and as exceptional as Dawes in his timing of the ball's flight to the wings, Wales had found cooks in the line able to produce the recipe for three-quarter play that was now her constant aim. Once the wing three-quarter positions became settled in 1970-71, following the re-entry of Gerald Davies and the discovery of yet another student, the twenty-year-old John Bevan, the Welsh back division was even better balanced than that of 1969.

The lessons of forward domination had been pounded home again by New Zealand. The end of the season produced a rota of forwards capable of giving talented three-quarters the ball *and* their support. Denzil Williams gave way against France to John Lloyd of Bridgend but the Ebbw Vale man, already the most capped Welsh forward of all time, would return to make a point or two about 'mobility'. Barry Llewelyn (then with Newport, by 1971 with Llanelli) had developed tremendously on the New Zealand tour and was a new asset to Wales in the front row. The fading out of Brian Price had seen the complete arrival on the international scene of Delme Thomas, chosen for the British Lions in 1966 before winning the first of his twenty-six caps for Wales against Australia in Cardiff later that year. The Llanelli man's tireless jumping was soon to be as much a feature of Welsh play as had the Newport captain's through the 1960s. J. B. G. Thomas paid him the compliment of calling him 'a real "spring-heel jack"', though that could well have been misconstrued in Llanelli. Two new London Welsh caps, Geoff Evans and Mike Roberts, provided boilerhouse support for Thomas. Stuart Gallacher, another squad member, played second-row against France, to secure one cap and one winning try in a game sewn up by the Welsh forwards, before he, too, headed North. Five London Welshmen figured that day under the captaincy of John Dawes. His leadership of this impressive array of talented footballers was the hitherto missing final part of the puzzle Wales had pondered over.

The W.R.U. had had its own internal wrangles before the chosen policy was fully accepted. However, its ascertainable validity silenced all but the most vociferous critics. More courageous had been the Union's willingness to defend its rugby revolution before the dislike of more conservative nations. Its open-door philosophy towards emergent rugby nations would also sweep all before it. The 1970s would produce even newer, more exotic visitors. France would at long last, and after constant Welsh advocacy, be admitted to the International Board in 1978. 'Wales', the Rumanian national XV's manager would declare in 1979, 'show their love for the game by their willingness to play anybody'. It was that same willingness, cemented by long-lasting ties of personal friendship, that kept Wales in line with the other Home Unions in 1969 during the Springbok visit. The tour, the first after South Africa's expulsion from the Commonwealth in 1961, was the toughest problem that the minds and consciences of rugby players and administrators had ever had to face. Opinion was deeply divided. Feelings often ran beyond the bounds of control on both sides. The W.R.U. did not bury its head in the sand over the issue.

There was far less overt pressure over sporting contacts with the South African Republic when the 1964 tour took place but the reality of *apartheid* was being spelled out inside and outside the sub-continent so that by the mid-1960s, and particularly after the shooting down of defenceless blacks at Sharpeville in 1960, there was universal condemnation, in Britain, of the policy of separate development for races enshrined in South African law, government and daily life. Whether this should prohibit sporting links and, more importantly, whether boycott or contact would act as the better solvent of this deplorable situation, was the subject of fierce debate. At the 1967 A.G.M. Brynamman and Llangennech R.F.C.s moved a motion against further links with South Africa because that country's discriminatory segregation amounted to racialism. Their motion was lost by 120 to 192 votes on the urging of the W.R.U. executive. The argument mounted, to which in essence they have been consistent to date, was threefold. The W.R.U. took the line that their own firm rejection of *apartheid* would be more credible, so far as influence inside South Africa went, by maintenance of sporting relations; that they, as a Union, could not tell individual members or clubs what to do or think in such matters and, finally, that a unilateral declaration of severance by Wales would only isolate Wales in the international rugby community.

Opponents of sporting relationships countered that the planned tour was, by its very nature, symbolic of unacceptable white supremacy. The white South Africans who came were, therefore, to be decried not because they were rugby players or South African individuals but because they carried the flag of a nation the rest of the world, from the Olympic Committee to the United Nations, had labelled a pariah. Perhaps only those who fully appreciated the tortured history of South Africa, both black and white, could speak with true authority; perhaps only those who knew the central role of South African rugby, long before the system of *apartheid*, in world rugby history could understand the genuine anguish of rugby men that their sport was not, however much they wished it, untrammelled by other considerations. But for many others from all walks of life and often led by Christian denominations, none of whom would do anything but call for an end to the tour, this ambiguity, once understandable, had become, at best, a political naïveté, at worst, a moral blindness.

It was this polarity of opinion that ensured the 1969 Springboks tour would not be just another rugby tour. The W.R.U., in accord with their own admission of divided, sincere differences of opinion, had acknowledged John Taylor's letter asking not to be considered for selection against the visitors. Taylor had been to South Africa with the Lions in 1968 and felt he could not show any sign of sympathy for the régime. The W.R.U. assured him of their understanding of his own decision and that his future selection for Wales would not be jeopardized; nor was it. At the end of the season he displaced Dennis Hughes of Newbridge with whom he had been vying for a couple of seasons. This measured, passive expression of dissent was palatable. The level of dissent soon reached was beyond the calculation of rugby and civil authorities.

1969 was still a year of protest over human and civil rights in large parts of Europe. The previous year, especially in France but with strong echoes in Britain where American involvement in Vietnam drew rising opposition, had been the most disturbed peace-time year in western Europe for over a generation. The timing of the Springbok tour was, in this sense alone, unfortunate. Demonstrations were to be expected. Large-scale disruptions and continuous, well-organized hounding of the South African players was not. Wales had its full share of this eyeball-to-eyeball stuff. Many Welsh rugby fans just stayed away, many more went as usual but it could not be alleged, as a bewildered press corps did, that only 'militants' or only 'girls' or, even, only 'non-Welsh' demonstrators were involved. The point is that *no-one* was happy about a tour that became an ordeal. Mostly the protests were orderly and peaceful, but at Swansea on 15 November 1969 some of the most unpleasant scenes in Welsh rugby history occurred. There had been tension outside the ground; worse followed after demonstrators invaded the pitch during the game. This may have been an unwise, even counter-productive action in hardening the hearts and minds of rugby supporters whose sympathy went out, irrespective of their status as symbols, to fifteen lonely men in green, but it was compounded into a day of violence by the manner in which some

404

Swansea R.F.C. 'vigilantes' over-reacted. Lacking discipline and control, their heavy-handling of demonstrators, many of them young women, brought severe criticism. Two hundred demonstrators and ten policemen were injured; numbers were arrested. An unpublished police enquiry exonerated the police and those who assisted them but from then on the civil authorities alone took absolute control of peace-keeping operations.

Rugby could not gain from this. For the international at the Arms Park, despite a totally peaceful march of anti-apartheid demonstrators and full police security, it was felt necessary to ring the pitch with barbed wire. Argument could still rage over the rights and wrongs on both sides but there was no doubt now that rugby in South Africa would have to change radically before another Springboks team might arrive. When that case arose towards the end of the 1970s the W.R.U., along with other Home Unions, would indicate the changes that had been made and point to the anti-apartheid pronouncements of Danie Craven, the doyen of South African rugby. The South African Barbarians, a team of white, black and coloured players, would tour to a great deal of opposition but, unlike 1969, no disruption, in the 1979-80 season. The W.R.U., once more assailed for complicity in South Africa's racial policy, went so far as to issue a statement in reply to those who opposed the tour:

> The Welsh Rugby Union accepts all that has been said about the evils of *apartheid*. Equally we support the principle that there ought not to be any discrimination in sport on grounds of race, religion or political affiliation . . . We have considerable respect for the views of those who seek to influence the behaviour of the South African Government by severing all contact with that country and its people and yet we believe that view to be mistaken and that its implementation would result in suffering first and foremost by the non-white population.

However, no secure bridge between the two sides could be built since the issue, for other opponents of South African racial policy, had never been *apartheid* in rugby but *apartheid* in society. From this mixture of dream, illusion and reality, depending on where one stood, could come no unity of voice, even in Wales, except, oddly enough, in that both sides could insist on their own colour blindness.

Welsh Rugby had recoiled from its own lack of imagination and organization in 1964 until the memory of the veldt could be expunged from rugby history by fresh ideas, thrustful personnel and winning teams. At the end of this period it was South Africa, in a much more profound and sad sense, who were to do the soul searching. Wales was fortunate that rugby *in* Wales, despite the detractions of those keen to see their own

405

deficient influence in society as due to others' success in sport, was still 'only a game'. From October 1970 the welcoming stage of the National Ground was ready to frame the most splendid period ever in Welsh rugby history. It was the understanding of those who administered the game that to say 'only a game' was to say everything, and yet nothing, about this sport in Welsh society, which had brought Welsh rugby to this platform. It was that, too, which left the enormity of the debate about South Africa in 1969 ever-present in the minds of those who understood how the new vitality of Welsh rugby had brought an increased importance that threatened a laborious, necessary responsibility.

CYMRU AM BYTH

IN the distance a raucous cacophony of traffic noise grew insistently harsher as the city began to anticipate the end of the week. Already hundreds, draped in red and white scarves, their woollen bobble hats askew and thin protection against the late afternoon's cold, were trudging disconsolately back to the electric flicker of Edinburgh's warmth. Wales, whose pack had pulverized an English XV in their centenary year only three weeks before; Wales, whose half-backs, John and Edwards, were finding new dimensions to their play with every game; Wales, who had again overtaken England in victories recorded; Wales, whose wing discovery, the student John Bevan, now complemented with his strength the delicate skills of a tempered back division; this richly promising Welsh side who had pulled north in their wake a small army of the faithful had fallen away from the heights of their 22 - 6 dismissal of a raw English team. A Scottish side, with grim tenacity, had gripped Wales in the tight and harried them in the loose. Wales had nosed ahead by two points, to 14 - 12, only to dash the hopes of their followers yet again when Peter Brown, the Scottish captain, stepped up for another penalty shot. He had put three over already. It no longer helped Welsh sensibilities that he seemed uncertain whether to kick the ball or ostracise it. There was dispute, at this time, over kicking methods — the classical straight-on run and toe-ended follow-through or the round-the-corner smack that cut across the ball with the instep to curve it inwards to the posts. Wales used a battery of kickers — Barry John on the left, John Williams straight on, John Taylor on the right. The Scots gave them all to Brown, and Wales now knew why. The Scottish No. 8 cleared his nose, hitched his sleeves a little further up, turned his coat-hanger shoulders on the ball, lurched a few yards away with his head dropping on one side, then abruptly wheeled about, dipped his right hip a little further to complete his imitation of Bela Lugosi and ran sideways on, in broken rhythm, to belt the ball which cartwheeled and swung and hovered until it chose to wander between the sticks. Peter Brown was as seemingly casual with his kicking as Perry Como with a song, and just as dauntingly effective. When John Bevan, in only his second international, auditioned for Brown's part by swinging hurriedly to clear a loose ball, Scottish hands were in the way and Chris Rea, their bustling little centre, scrambled over the Welsh line. Mercifully, Brown, with the easiest kick of the afternoon, hit a post but Scotland were 18 to 14 in front so Wales needed two more scores and there were only five minutes left to play. That was why Welsh heads dropped and, the Triple Crown yet another lost Grail, the Welsh river of support started to trickle away from the graveyard of Murrayfield.

Now it was that John Dawes, captain for his third game in a row, told a white lie. His weary team, 4 points down though having outscored the Scots by three tries to two, had to be calmed again to play controlled rugby. Dawes let it be known that there was no need to panic for the game had plenty of time left to run. Wales moved downfield for a final assault. At a line-out just inside the Scottish 25, Delme Thomas once again did the Indian rope trick without the rope, and won the vital ball. Edwards grabbed the deflection and started his line. The ball missed out Ian Hall, moved along to J. P. R. Williams running forcefully to make the extra man and on to Gerald Davies on the right. The wing sprinted outwards in a parabola that evaded the cover. His try took the score to 18-17 but the touch-down was quite far out from the posts so that the kicker would have to bring the ball back considerably to widen the angle.

Delme Thomas could not watch. The Welsh fans leaving Murrayfield thought Scotland had scored again. To their great credit, the Scots fell silent as John Taylor placed the ball. Taylor had scored the first Welsh try under the posts almost eighty minutes previously. That would matter little if he could not land this difficult conversion. The flanker was taking it because his left-footed kicking was more assured of success from this side of the field. The programme note pointed out that when he had kicked two conversions against England at Cardiff he had been the first Welsh forward, apart from Norman Gale in 1967, to kick points for Wales in sixteen years. It is doubtful if the London Welshman had in mind Rees Stephens's successful conversion of the second of two tries scored by another London Welshman, Trevor Brewer, in 1955. Besides Wales had gone down 14 points to 8 that day at Murrayfield and Taylor was not one to let unfavourable omens cloud his mind. The eyes of those normally eager for all the sights of a rugby international closed, the lips of the customarily irreverent mouthed fervent prayer, and perennial irresponsibles offered up unlikely promises of a stainless future. At least that is what Welsh hearts and heads were about. No one, least of all the Scots, would blame the twenty-five-year-old schoolmaster if he failed. The straining tension that had invaded the terraces and the stands was almost tangible. Other games had had last defiant scores that delivered up a victory beyond reasonable hope but none had experienced this endless waiting in the couple of minutes that had followed Gerald Davies's try. The whole game was brought to this unfair, exquisite focus. Never had the word 'foot-ball' possessed more resonance. The crowd was held in the paralysis of fear that contemplation of great achievement or sickening failure brings. Surely he would take more time, not dare to risk the moment, put off flaunting hope before the impossible temptation.

Taylor stepped backwards from the ball. He took a few paces laterally. He looked up at those mocking uprights. He looked down at the inanimate ball, and then, almost contemptuously calm in the eye of this storm that fate and the crowd's yearning had created, he lifted the ball high and true towards the Scottish posts. After all, it was just another kick. But what a kick! The moment would assure the Triple Crown and, beyond that, the Grand Slam. It was as brave and as unforgettable in the history of Welsh rugby as Billy Bancroft's 1893 dropped penalty goal that won the first Crown. Bancroft's moment would not immediately usher in the golden days of playing success that the 1900s brought but it was their advance trumpet. Taylor's, too, was the brassy note that heralded the second Golden Era.

The Welsh side at Murrayfield on 6 February 1971 had had one change from the team originally chosen. Arthur Lewis had had to withdraw. Ian Hall, at centre, had played his part and became the sixteenth of the fifteen men who won all their games that season. Lewis returned against Ireland whose 14 - 0 trouncing of Wales the previous season was wiped out in a 23 - 9 rout. Wales scored four tries to none. Barry John, kept at a distance in Scotland by the wary Caledonians, resumed his drop goal habit and Ireland were to go through the rest of the decade without a win against Wales. Scotland would win two of her nine games with Wales between 1971 and 1979, and England, without a win at Cardiff since 1963, would collect one solitary win at Twickenham in 1974. In the Five Nations championship it was France alone who challenged Welsh supremacy with three victories — though none at Cardiff — in the nine games played.

Her side in 1971 was exceptionally strong. It, too, was undefeated, though draws with Ireland and England meant that Wales were champions outright when they crossed the Channel to meet France on 27 March. Wales had not won a Grand Slam since 1952 and, more to the point, had not won in Paris since 1957. Clive Rowlands, the Welsh coach, had lost his Grand Slam as a captain at Stade Colombes in the 1965 match, his fourteenth consecutive game, that ended his international career. He would rail and rant until any shred of complacency had vanished. John Dawes would need no reminder for he had been in the centre in 1965. There was one other survivor from the Welsh XV of that year and his would turn out to be a significant supporting role in the game which remains perhaps the best single international contest of the 1970s.

Denzil Williams, the loose-head prop on both occasions, was playing in his thirty-sixth international since a début, with Clive Rowlands, against England in 1963. At the end of Wales's previous game, against Ireland, he had passed Bryn Meredith's record to become the most-capped Welsh forward. He had been to New Zealand, with the 1966 Lions and with Wales in 1969, winning high praise from the All Blacks both times. He had won back his Welsh position and his old form after being dropped in the penultimate game of 1970. At thirty-one he was scarcely too old to tour again as a prop whilst his 16 stone 6 foot frame would be useful in the second row where he played for Ebbw Vale. After the Irish game in 1971 the Lions for that year were chosen. Eleven of the current Welsh XV were selected — all the backs and four forwards. Of these Llewelyn and Jeff Young had ruled themselves out. Dai Morris did not go and neither did Denzil Williams. There was talk of his relative immobility. In his last game this durable prop forward would make an unforgettable point, though only those who knew his determined intention would be able to interpret it.

France, captained by the rock-like Christian Carrère from the back-row, were a mix of passion and maturity blended into a team by superb individual skills. Pierre Villepreux was a full-back whose athletic grace so emphasized his elegance that his more mundane qualities of safety and courage tended to be overlooked. He was as admired in Wales as the redoubtable Benoit Dauga who now locked the French pack in the middle of the back-row. Bougarel, Lux, Bertranne and Cantoni made up a light, speedy set of three-quarters who could hope for some good service from

Berot and Barrau at half-back. The Spanghero brothers, Claude and Walter, faced Delme Thomas and Mike Roberts in the core of the pack, whilst Iraçabal, Benesis and Lasserre closed whatever horns front rows have left after so many close encounters of the ultimate kind with Denzil Williams, Jeff Young, most precipitate of strikers, and even deadlier since Ray Williams had convinced him of the advantages of hooking with the outside foot, and Barry Llewelyn, the converted No. 8 who had emerged in New Zealand as the kind of big, running prop the 1967 All Black philosophy so much admired. Ironically enough the absence of these Welsh props in New Zealand where both were so respected would contribute to the downfall of All Black thinking on tight forwards for, after Ray McLoughlin had taken the Lions through the more esoteric points of thermodynamics and the engineering of bodily stress, even the loss of the wonderful Irishman himself, and his Scottish colleague, Sandy Carmichael, in the infamous Canterbury brawl, would not significantly weaken the Lions pack. Denzil Williams and Barry Llewelyn were skilled international props in the way that Brian Thomas and Delme Thomas, both of whom had to play against All Black sides as props, were not, but, in the Darwinian process of prop-forward mutation that would end with the Pontypool front row, they were, in 1971, still evolving. The French pack would dominate the tight for most of this game but the Welsh eight worked in the loose to counteract French possession. Here the speedy Taylor and Morris were indispensable, with the indefatigable Mervyn Davies to dominate the end of the line. Ken Goodall, Ireland's remarkable No. 8 forward, had turned professional to leave Mervyn Davies a clear field this year to establish himself as the best No. 8 available to the Lions. Within five years many hailed him as the best in his position they had ever seen. Wales won the match primarily because the team had no collective fears. They had become the most complete Welsh XV since perhaps the early twentieth century, certainly since the early 1950s.

The first half was a torrid affair. The French probed, smashed and exploded over Wales like the whistles and firecrackers of their decidedly non-vocal but very loud supporters. Welsh cover tackling was first time and fierce. Dawes and Lewis in the centre, both only slightly smaller and lighter than Taylor and Morris, proved themselves no gentle fishers of men. Their disciples were as ardent. A ragged forty yard run by Arthur Lewis, bursting through the midfield defence, spearheaded an early Welsh incursion into the French 25. Nonetheless it could only be a matter of time before mounting French pressure became points on the board. Just over

411

half of the first period had gone when Dauga crashed over from close in and Villepreux gave France a precious 5 points lead. It might well have been more, and within minutes would have doubled, but for Barry John. The Welsh outside-half, now twenty-six-years-old and winning his twenty-first cap, was a well-proportioned 11stone 11lb. and 5foot 9inches; the French try-scorer, Dauga, was twenty-nine and the holder of forty-eight caps. That, perhaps, was no advantage, but a difference of eight inches in height and three and three-quarter stones in weight was another matter. Dauga, now on the rampage that would break the Welsh resistance, burst for the line again. He was held up near the corner flag but not stopped. He toppled forward over the line when John jumped up at him, knocking the leaning tower of Montois into touch. It was the only possible way to prevent a score ('I wish I knew who pushed me', John said later) and it was heart-stoppingly brave. Barry John's playing days were not to be punctuated by death-defying leaps of this sort but such an instinctive willingness to sacrifice himself was characteristic of the collective spirit that informed this team's play. Dauga did not score; John suffered a broken nose and went off. He played out the remainder of the half only vaguely aware of play. Nonetheless his commitment had kept his side alive and a moment of French hesitation would now give Wales fresh hope.

The game had been played at a pace which sucked air from the lungs of the fittest players. France had moved the ball at will. They trusted the quickness of their wingers, Cantoni on the left and Roger Bougarel on the right flank, to slit the Welsh defence. From a scrum inside the Welsh half the ball moved out to Bougarel speeding down the touch-line to confront the young, but dauntingly experienced J. P. R. Williams. The Welsh full-back had already given Bougarel one of his teeth-rattling embraces and the Frenchman, shying away from another, checked slightly to throw out a pass. Williams, knowing Taylor had moved to cover him, had sensed the intention and went, full-bloodedly as always, to risk the interception. And then, all alone, he was away. Or not quite alone, for Denzil Williams cutting back across field was rumbling along behind. The prop was to J. P. R.'s right and falling behind but, amazingly he was thereabouts and his presence, with French defenders converging on the Welsh full-back, ensured the possibility of a pass infield. It would be, then, a forlorn hope that the line could be reached but the full-back, who had done more than there was a right to expect now showed the constant alertness that playing for London Welsh had brought to a peak. Out of the corner of his eye he became aware of Gareth Edwards pounding up the left-hand touch-line, so he moved infield, drawing the defence still wary for the two Williamses, then swung his body and the ball back the other way for Edwards to take, race and score in the corner.

To be 2 points adrift when they turned round was more than Wales could have hoped for. During the second half the tackling was as unrelenting, the control more certain. John kicked a penalty goal to put them in front. It was not his last contribution for his was to be the final, and most satisfying, try of the game. It was a try that had 'John' lettered through it like rock from Barry. It was a try that was made by a team. Inside the French 25 Barrau moved to put the ball in, the Welsh pack closed like a steel trap, Jeff Young won the ball and a swift channel saw Edwards fling the ball to his partner — 'I saw that Berot . . . was slightly out of position and as I accelerated I saw the others bearing down on me. I ran straight at Bertranne, the inside-centre, but he started to move across . . . anticipating I would pass to John Dawes. Berot was within feet of me now, moving very fast, but I sensed that we already had the try . . . In an instant I changed the course of my sweeping run and beat Berot: I felt his outstretched fingers running down my back as I went over for the try . . . It was . . . a complete performance in terms of attacking and covering'.

The 9 - 5 victory captured the Grand Slam. Barry John's contribution of 6 points allowed him to equal Jarrett's record of 31 points in four matches in the 1968-69 season. Before the 1970s were over records would be made and broken almost at will. Statistics were after all the fodder of the Computer Age. Welsh teams were soon compared directly to computers in an updating of the old jibe about mechanical play. The criticism had been misplaced in the 1900s. It was a sour, inaccurate simile for the teams of the 1970s. That of 1971 and of 1972 escaped, in part, because the days of dominance were yet to come. Their own exceptional talents, and particularly those of Barry John, laid an emphasis on their individuality that allowed the critics to see them as a team fortunately endowed with the star quality that glittered, now and then, in Welsh play. The same reasoning would see advance unofficial team selection for the Lions in which only the 'stars' appeared and where Dawes, as player and captain, not at all. When the Lions conquered, for the first time this century, in 1971 with thirteen Welsh players selected (and a fourteenth flown out) from a total of thirty, with Carwyn James of Llanelli as assistant manager and coach, and John Dawes as the first Welshmen ever to captain a British Lions side, then understandable Welsh pride could be leavened by the equally justifiable reflection that the contribution to the sophistication of

413

forward play by McLoughlin and McBride and to the drive of the pack by MacLauchlan and Brown was priceless. Behind the pack, David Duckham demonstrated his rich array of running wares and Michael Gibson, at last, revelled in the opportunity provided by such high-class company to demonstrate that he was the most rounded footballer seen anywhere in living memory. The point the historian with hindsight can make, however, is that this Welsh contribution was not merely a passing phenomenon, not incidentally a lucky merger of skilled in-dividuals and national success. Above all it was a promise of things to come. Welsh XVs after 1971 would not invariably win nor were they, generally, more gifted but they were all prepared. The ideal had been set beforehand and the preparation, from 1964 onwards, was to find the means that would allow expression of the ideal. That is why when Wales beat England by 21 points to 9 at 'H.Q.' in 1976 to record the biggest margin of defeat by an English side there, John Dawes, then the Welsh Coach, could confess on television to a sense of frustration. Winning was not, and never had been, enough. Similarly when Ray Williams told the 1971 A.G.M. that 'the whole thinking behind this tour of New Zealand is totally Welsh' or when he wrote, in 1976, that the rugby he advocated was the kind that the national team played, accusations of arrogance, both about coaching and Welsh rugby itself, abounded. The finger has not ceased to point but it is the emotion of contemporary observers that wags it, not cold reason backed by facts.

Ray Williams told that same A.G.M. in 1971 that 'Welsh rugby has been transformed . . . radically changed'. The 1970s only underlined the observation. It was, in a different way, made by one of the most perceptive rugby writers of the modern period, Vivian Jenkins, who wrote of the 1971 French game — 'No Welsh team of comparatively modern times has surpassed this one in collective will-to-win and capacity to keep going to the end . . .' From that season onwards no Welsh side has failed to possess that collective spirit. Of course the will can be countered, even splintered, but it is now a malleable, national rugby asset. As the truly great players dropped from the Welsh side through the decade — Barry John, Mervyn Davies, Gareth Edwards, Gerald Davies, and J. P. R. Williams, followed, throughout, by those scarcely less magnificent, John Dawes, John Bevan (both of them), Dai Morris, Delme Thomas, Arthur Lewis, Terry Cobner and Phil Bennett, the critics waited for the fall that would come with so many invaluable men gone. Stubbornly Wales refused to fall. When no home country side beat Wales, home or away for four years (1976 to 1979), then it was the quality of the others' rugby that was berated, in ironic echo of John Dawes in 1976. When Wales succumbed to New Zealand or, in alternate years, to France, it was the superiority of others that counted and the alleged poverty of Welsh three-quarter play that was indicted.

Explanation is simpler, and more important. The fundamentals of organization and of principle that were laid down in the late sixties flourished when rugby brilliance arrived fortuitously, but brilliance does not become genius without nurture, nor did the successful, if less dazzling Welsh XVs, of the late 1970s rely exclusively on its magic properties. Not all of this was unique to Wales but the W.R.U. had moved, by the very fact of its being Welsh, to a different rugby plane from the other British rugby countries. Now the great players who might emerge and might come through to the National XV were doing so within an ambience deliberately created for them. Their genius would become that within the supportive context of overall Welsh play and their play would take its cue and its resonance from that of their team mates. The organization would ensure the pattern and the possibilities. Confidence, not fear of failure, or success, would impregnate Welsh players so that when J. P. R. Williams finally limped off in the last game of 1979 and English hearts sighed, with pleasure and gratitude, to see their constant destroyer go, his young substitute Clive Griffiths could, within minutes, pick up a ball from his toes and, with a burst of speed, a dummy and a delicate chip, turn a crumb into a Welsh try.

Self-confidence is not merely an individual attribute. Indeed it is a characteristic that the Welsh have often accused each other of lacking. The Welsh, so many 'histories' run, have been servile, without national pride, dominated. The taunt of arrogance would sound refreshing in many Welsh ears. The 1970s were, perhaps, the biggest crisis in the dominant culture of England herself since the Civil War of the 1640s had dug new channels for it. English rugby was, since the late nineteenth century, an integral part of the culture of imperial sway that had emerged. Welsh jabs at its underbelly, from a radically different society, were infrequent — hence the celebration of rugby victories. But the 1970s were, paradoxically, not a time of cultural dislocation for Wales since the social and economic shifts that threatened the 'break-up' of Britain did not, in themselves, undermine the majority or minority cultures of Wales. Their difficulties were other than this, indigenous to themselves. So, on the contrary, not since the early twentieth century had Wales been so self-conscious or so aware of her expression of identity. The self-confidence of her rugby sides, especially when they 'won well', was a reflection of that principle of play which, twinned with organization, stemmed, not from happy geographical circumstance or fortuitous individuality, but from the level at which the culture had arrived. There continued, within Wales herself, to be abrasive questioning over future political and social direction, over Welsh identity, real and desired; the issue of national independence was aired more seriously than it had been since the 1890s. However, no matter what the differences between Welshmen over what 'Wales' was, there was no doubt that most people firmly considered themselves 'Welsh'. In this light the 4 to 1 rejection of Devolution on St. David's Day in 1979, whatever its wisdom or foolishness as a vote, cannot justly be interpreted by a resurrection of the old, lame cry of 'servility'. To vote for retention of a bond with an ailing kingdom in such overwhelming numbers may be the purblind arrogance of the 1970s Welsh but it is scarcely a humbling act. Historians walk on eggs when they blithely interpret the future, but this particular immediate past, the 1970s, is, for Wales, so umbilically linked to the modern Wales that had been spawned, with all its attendant problems for the past culture and future prosperity of twentieth-century Wales, in the late Victorian age, that the connection between past and present for *all* the cultural modes of Wales stares those who will confront the history, direct, in the face.

Perception of change in the range of factors that determine our social being lags behind the alteration. The transformation of the Welsh economy on which, one way or the other, Welsh rugby, unlike rugby in the rest of Britain, has been directly dependent, was starkly apparent in the early 1970s. The shift from a heavy industrial base in extractive and manufacturing industry left only remnants of the production mode which had created the social relationships of urban, industrial Wales. Not all the changes were painless or necessarily encouraging for future years but, in turn, the relative paralysis of will that had overlaid, as a legacy from the disasters of the inter-war years, the initiatives that an earlier Wales had thrown up readily — in politics, in social welfare, in business entrepreneurship — was now ended. The burgeoning institutions of Wales were run by a fast-growing professional stratum that was, on this scale anyway, a new phenomenon for Wales. Their technocratic sway did not satisfy all the requirements of Welsh life, cultural or commercial, but the net result of their existence on government commissions, councils and committees was to stimulate rather than stifle debate. Enough generations had come and gone to make the risk of action and thought preferable again. Certainly this is what re-vitalized an organization like that of the South

Wales miners in the late 1960s and led to the establishment of a Wales T.U.C. in 1973. Similarly, the dimension of Wales was seen, again, in its whole aspects. Devolution became an issue for debate in the general arena, not a fringe interest; nationalist politics flowed and ebbed in successive waves of interest or dissatisfaction. Perhaps the best sign of all was the developing interest shown in unravelling the complexities of an involved, involving, Welsh culture and history. This desire, healthiest when it understood there was no single solution or skeleton key, can be traced in the scale and quality of work now undertaken in schools, colleges and universities; in the production of new magazines in both languages; in a concentration, often foiled, on the possibilities for style of life through better architecture and preservation of a neglected heritage; in a conviction that, despite disagreements and differences, there was a pattern of human interrelationships in Wales that could serve for a future society. The W.R.U., with all its necessary emphasis on future progress at every level of the game it administered, was a part of this cultural process of remembrance that marks the 1970s. The interaction between the two was the dialectic it favoured. Past had to be confronted by present before the latter could move on — it was only in June 1974 that the W.R.U. finally sanctioned club games on a Sunday. On 30 June 1973, Vernon Parfitt, President of the Union, told the A.G.M., which had just noted the death in March of Willie Llewellyn, the last survivor from 1905, that despite present popularity, 'We must avoid the dangers of complacency, and simply assume that we can achieve success . . . without hard and forward planning. Your Committee is conscious of the fact that they must continually take into account the many changes which have and are taking place in society'. Later that year, in September 1973, the Centenary Committee, set up the previous year, met to consider commissioning a book on the Union's history and it was stressed most strongly by Hermas Evans that it should be 'an account of the evolution of Rugby in Wales, and its involvement in the historical and sociological development of the Principality and not merely a statistical record of facts and figures . . . Members favoured this suggestion'. The translation of history, unwritten and unmade, into a mutually fructifying relationship is the pivot on which an institution, and a wider society, intent on meaningful change, turns.

Rugby players, in ever increasing numbers, ceased being the miners, steelworkers and policemen of yesterday to become the sons of those who had so worked. The gates of colleges and universities had swung open to let the potential teachers through. From the 1970s another path, trod only by

417

a few in the past, became now an avenue as teachers and, soon, players from almost any other previous occupation, became representatives of a commercial and industrial world for whom rugby faces and rugby reputations had become a·marketable commodity. Business executives, finance advisers, industrial consultants, sports shop owners, sales representatives and sundry other 'public' occupations for top rugby players reflected the widespread nature of the service economy in Wales. It was certainly easier, now, for international players to exchange blue-collar for white-collar employment. None of this was new in itself, though the accompanying sponsorship of rugby games, teams and competitions was. Nor was it considered a broaching of the concept of amateurism. What was novel about it was its scale and its rapidity. From it flowed rugby magazines, memorabilia, intensified coverage of Welsh rugby by the media, cartoons, songs and a sub-culture which, though it had existed all along, had never been packaged and presented hitherto. For some players about to retire the earlier, possible consideration of an autobiography, ghosted or otherwise, was hardened into a fixed certainty after which they would not, if personally rewarded, be able to participate in the game again. Life-stories, and then books of pictures and tactics and anecdotes, rolled off the presses, especially in Wales. What is perhaps more revealing than the constant account of hotel breakfasts ate, jerseys treasured and air-journeys loathed, even than the eye-witness description of particular games, is the connecting thread that shows each author acutely aware, if not of his personal removal from an older society, then, of the massive social transformation in relationship to which he is part witness and part symbol.

J. P. R. Williams detected it, in general, in the decline of London Welsh from the mid-1970s with an alteration in the intake of players available to the club. He ascribed this to a growing determination to achieve educational and personal goals within Wales. Gareth Edwards compared Gwaun-cae-Gurwen's asphalt and Millfield's turf with the wide-eyed disbelief of the boy ('I had been scoring tries against England since I was four') who would be Wales's youngest captain. Gerald Davies movingly saw the miner father who once adored Aneurin Bevan in the shining eyes of Gareth Edwards's miner father. And Barry John began the book that began the books not by talking of drop goals or sleight-of-body tries but, in the very first sentence, of his Uncle Lloyd who 'was a miner and had blue scars on his hands and dust in his lungs to show for it'. The freedom to be confident that many young Welshmen and women felt in the 1970s was the greatest gift from those whose lives had been far more determined, and restricted. The material rewards were not to be spurned but the awareness of a miner coiled up in the anthracite seam that is becoming, fatally, a part of his own body, was also not to be forgotten. William John worked for twenty-eight years in Great Mountain colliery, Tumble, so that Barry John could play the kind of rugby he did. And those who saw the son play knew, in Wales anyway, that this had been a recurring, essential, counterpoint for what had passed, but only pretended, to be the greater reality. Existence was not for work except inasmuch as the latter provided the basis for existence to find fulfilment. With Barry John the lines of force that direct individuals and their societies intersected. The history of Welsh rugby shows him not to be the first such lucky victim, and those of his contemporaries to whom the same transmission of energy would come prove he was no more alone as a dazzling exhibitor of his art than Shakespeare was the only Elizabethan dramatist; but it had not happened to anyone quite so enormously, or constantly or publicly as it did to the quiet man from Cefneithin. Not since Arthur Gould had a Welsh International played rugby football with such supercilious ease.

Barry John, like Cliff Morgan in 1955, displayed the incomparable range of his talents most fully on a Lions tour. He had been a natural ball player all his life. It was the ball that invigorated him for his interest in physical activity, especially training, for its own sake was minimal. The tranquil self-possession that had been ingrained in another Cefneithin fly-half, Carwyn James, had come down to John. Both Clive Rowlands, for Wales, and James, for the British Lions, respected the fragility of their star player who needed neither cajoling nor pressure. His game had always borne the same unhurried, unflappable characteristics that ended by serving him, in the heat of a match, as a cold protective shield but, since that first international appearance against Australia in 1966, the armoury of offensive weapons and the range of his tactics had not stopped their increase. Setbacks, like the injury he suffered in South Africa in 1968 or the morale-destroying 1969 tour by Wales, did not prevent the slow accretion of judgement though it did mean that his complete emergence, glimpsed in 1969, waited on the European season of 1971. Now he had it all. In New Zealand he was a match winner in his own right, ending with the highest aggregate of points scored (180) by any tourist there. The following season, for Wales, he passed his own points record of 31 (held with Jarrett) in a season by notching 35. Not one of those points came from a try, though in his total for Wales, in twenty-five appearances, of 90 points which topped Jack Bancroft's 88, he had scored five tries and (another record) eight dropped goals. His kicking for goal was often of prodigious length; more noticeably, it was almost casual in appearance for he scarcely seemed to waste a moment or even wait for confirmation of the kick's flight. The cool certainty was an acceptance on his part of this late bonus, for though his drop goals (two against England in January 1971, and a winning four against Llanelli, his old club, for Cardiff in November 1970) were produced for Wales like rabbits from a hat since his first against New Zealand in 1967, he did not convert a Welsh try or kick a penalty goal until he did both against Scotland in February 1971. The true joy in his boots was the unerring manner in which he could choose to place the teasing ball. It is given to very few team players to destroy an opponent's individual game but this is what John did in the First Test against the All Blacks in 1971 when that bustling McCormick who had saved his side, rather 'belatedly', against East Wales in 1967 and sunk Wales with his 24 kicked points in 1969, faced a matured John one more, final time. McCormick had played a prominent part in the Canterbury game which had become a brawl. John made the New Zealander's final confrontation with Welsh skill his last, for he taunted and turned McCormick from one corner of the field to the other with every variety of kick he had mastered.

However, the memory Barry John mostly evokes is of his wraith-like running. Against New Zealand Universities he scored a try beneath the posts that was composed as much from his opponents' self-deception as from his own trickery. Indeed, the clue to an understanding of his achieved style lies here, in what he could make others do to themselves. The kicking, whether spinning trajectories that rolled away or precise chips or scudding grubbers, was a long-range control but his running, deft, poised, a fragile illusion that one wrong instant could crack, yet rarely did, was the art of the fly-half at its most testing. He was the dragon-fly on the anvil of destruction. John ran in another dimension of time and space. His opponents ran into the glass walls which covered his escape routes from their bewildered clutches. He was never robust but deceptively sturdy from the waist down whilst his willowy trunk was held upright, the ball grasped two-handed in front, his head almost hypnotically staring, trance-like, away from the moment of confrontation to the pattern of its resolve. His angles of running were indefinable, possibilities opening up before him by the tiniest drop in pace or fractional pause before acceleration; add to this ability to play in a different sphere of interest the classic attributes of Welsh fly-half play — the outrageous dummy, the sidestep of the two-sided maestro, the seductive, rebuffing swerve from the hips, the nonchalant, inviting dip of the shoulders to send an assailant sprawling — and a Barry John was assembled who left mouths, and back-rows, agape.

Ten Welshmen appeared in the First Test (with 'Chico' Hopkins substituting for Edwards), eight in the next two, and seven in the final one where J. P. R. Williams took leave of his senses to drop a goal from half-way. It was a spectacular reply to those who had whispered over the years about the inability of the Welsh to tour happily, leave alone coach and captain a British Lions side. John Bevan, who only played in one Test, equalled Tony O'Reilly's seventeen-try record of 1959, and Gerald Davies underlined his pyrotechnical brilliance with four tries against Hawkes Bay and an unspoken frisson of anxiety for New Zealanders each time, anywhere, he was given the ball. Mervyn Davies, in Colin Meads's estimation the chief destroyer of the All Blacks by his end-of-the-line play, in attack or defence, was the spoke in the wheels of the All Black machine. John Dawes had gone as an undisputed captain-coach on the field, he had returned as one of the undisputed playing successes. It had been a long seven years from 1964, the nadir of Welsh fortunes to this triumphant zenith. As a player he had gone almost to the limit, though there was one plum left for him in 1973, and from international rugby he now retired.

The new Welsh captain would be another schoolteacher, Bridgend's John Lloyd whose remarkable mobility had first caught national attention in the famous Fijian match of 1964, and who was now captain of a club wedded for the last decade to the concept of total, integrated fifteen-man rugby. The Welsh side would, again, go undefeated for a season though, like Scotland, Wales reluctantly declined the Irish match in Dublin through fears for the safety of their players and supporters at a time of renewed outbreaks of violence. That was a hard decision, not taken lightly, in the face of considerable Irish persuasion and one that denied an unbeaten Irish side a tilt at a Wales who had not won in Ireland since 1964. Wales won, at a controlled pace, in Twickenham before turning on their now formidable power against Scots and French. Four points for a try was welcome news for Welsh intentions. The season was distinguished, though, by three factors. The first was that Wales selected the same XV for each international: in the centre Llanelli's Roy Bergiers, another Cardiff College of Education student, replaced the guile of Dawes with the powerful bursts of a twenty-year-old frame. He was helped into scoring position by the equally powerful presence of thirty-year-old Arthur Lewis whose contribution to the Lions tour was now seen in the way he took up

Dawes's mantle in the Welsh mid-field. Geoff Evans, coming back in for the injured Mike Roberts, completed the changes from the 1971 team in which the back-row began to look like a physical representation of the sea-changes in Welsh life — the slow-burning ferocity of Dai Morris's play was etched in his hewn-out face no less than John Taylor's fiercely artistic dummy and try against Scotland were promised in his bearded bohemianism, and between them Mervyn Davies made being nearly 6foot 5inches look naturally Welsh. Secondly, this team carried Barry John almost as an appendage to its power. This was just as well, for the languid outside-half had returned to discover himself, in the theatrical jargon of the day, a 'superstar', and he did not relish it. Adulation had been the lot of other Welsh players but the frenzy which now invaded his life was not confined to rugby addicts. Barry John had put the breath of a people's dream into his rugby and there was no quickness to that rugby life if it was divorced from their attainable aspirations. He had moved, through no fault of his own, too far from those sustaining roots — 'Living in a kind of goldfish bowl is not living at all', he would write, since '. . . adulation was alienating me from the human race' — and found, like that Northern Irish footballer, George Best, with whom he discovered so much in common, that his rugby had become other people's glamour. Barry John was the first Welsh player in modern conditions of press hounding and commercial publicity to go to this psychological abyss. He survived by retiring from the game. The third Welsh discovery that season was also not without precedent: all the great half-back pairings in Welsh rugby history (and John and Edwards now reached a record twenty-three times) had been complementary. Barry John thrived on the ever-lengthening spin-pass of his scrum-half and, in the fullness of his self-confidence, dictated the play from his position. The outside-half had the personality to still his partner's extravagances and to make the best personal use of Edwards's own battery of rugby skills. 'Now, when you're with me', Gareth had told him when they first met to practise before a trial in January 1967, 'you've got to concentrate all the time, because I can get passes out of certain situations that other scrum-halves wouldn't dream about'. In the last season of John's drifting, perfectionist appearances for Wales, with nothing left for him to prove to himself, Edwards began to chart the international career that would equally have, in its own right, no parallel in Welsh rugby.

Gareth Edwards, nursing the hamstring injury that plagued his early career, had been, by *his* standards, a trifle subdued in New Zealand. There was the indelicate hand-off of Bob Burgess in the Third Test that gave John a simple try to relish but Edwards, as the superlative Lion, would be the brilliant tactical controller who went through South Africa with McBride's undefeated team in 1974. By that time he was, in succession to Barry John, the most exciting player in world rugby and becoming ever more so, for on the scorched earth of the veldt he had added a lethal new weapon to his armoury. This was the long, rolling, punishing, low-trajectoried diagonal touchfinder which he would put to devastating use in transforming defensive situations into attacking platforms in the championship matches of 1976-7-8. His retirement at the end of 1978 saw him bow out, after eleven years, weighed down with honours — three Lions tours; the most caps ever won for his country, fifty-three of them; and a shared record of twenty tries for Wales. At the Cardigan Eisteddfod in 1976 he was made a Bard of the Gorsedd; in 1979, his key contribution to the fame of Welsh rugby was recognized by U.N.E.S.C.O. who gave him an award for the standard of fair play in sport that he had carried so long at the highest level. With that award from outside Wales Gareth Edwards, in the penultimate year of the Welsh rugby centenary, managed to be the individual summation of the ideal enshrined in the motto adopted in their centenary year by the W.R.U. — *Teg chwarae, chwarae teg.*

Gareth Owen Edwards, from a Welsh-speaking mining village perched in the bare north-west plateau of Glamorgan, was to carry the gregarious, chattering vivacity, bred and sheltered in Gwaun-cae-Gurwen, to fields of endeavour far removed from the scatter of streets whose backdrop was the Black Mountains. The talent that accompanied his intensely competitive personality channelled aggression into a rugby theatricality whose virtuosity was honed to perfection by the discipline and expertise of Bill Samuel, P.E. master at Pontardawe Technical School. Gareth Edwards the man was born in 1948, Gareth the rugby international was born in 1964 — 'I remember vividly the day at school . . . when Wales lost . . . 24 - 3 in Durban. It had been a typical sporting Saturday for me, with an hour's cricket and a lot of running. I was about to join everyone in the changing room when Samuel, who had told me the Durban score said: "Edwards, where do you think you're going, you haven't finished yet. I want you to do six 220 yards". He suggested some ridiculous time, like twenty-four seconds for each. When he took me home that night I was faint and swaying all over the road and cried when I saw my parents. "He's mad, he's mad", I said'.

'Bill Sam' stands in a long line of Welsh schoolteachers, sung and unsung, to whom Welsh rugby owes an unpayable debt. The bill is never presented, only extended. The young Edwards, almost more an athlete than a rugby player, under his guidance and with parental self-sacrifice takes a sporting scholarship to Millfield that is, given his potential, akin to a novitiate's removal from the world before re-entry. The boy who had starred in Welsh Secondary School games is not a mature player when he risks the hurly-burly of Welsh club rugby in 1966 but this college student, and soon Cardiff player, is already formed in attitude. At a trial game for Cardiff's third team even before this, Bill Samuel, his vigilant mentor, had told him when and where a try would materialize, and Edwards scored it. The fact that it was from the blind side of a scrum on the half-way line only delayed, could not prevent, its fashioning. Time would bring the experience for all the rest — seasons of encouraging club and Welsh and British XVs with rolling, devouring kicks that ate up opposition gains and opponents' hearts with their frequency as much as their accuracy; years of combination with the battering ram of Mervyn Davies acting as softener for his spearthrust; games on a wet, greasy November pitch in a Gwent valley or a sun-baked plain half-way round the world; nail-biting games whose outcome hung on Edwards's absorbing punishment at the line-out, as in the first half in each of the two Triple Crown clinching games in Dublin in 1976 and 1978, until his forwards sealed the gaps and his backs were inspired by his courage and composure to assert their own superiority in the second half. On several occasions, it was his sheer indestructibility alone that held Wales together when the storm was at its fiercest, to reveal — and as the Lions tour of 1977, of which he was not a part, confirmed — the hollowness of the convenient cliché that no one is indispensable. In terms of Welsh and British rugby between 1971 and 1978, Gareth Edwards, whose prodigious gifts amounted to nothing less than genius, was *wholly* indispensable. At the end he was master of everything, even of his weaknesses — the poor, shovelled pass of his early games had become, via spin and power, an extended arm that gave his outside-half a ball for all seasons and a fresh attacking momentum, but he still knew enough to counteract a less reliable left arm with a varied tactic. The last score he registered for Wales was in his last match, against France in 1978, his third drop goal for his country.

Having offered so much in so many facets of play Edwards can be regarded as the best-equipped rugby player of an era intent on a 'total' concept of team and individual play. That would be sufficient to guarantee his niche of fame; the tries he totted up emblazon his name in the game's history. Nothing stopped the conveyor belt of Edwards specials, neither a thickening girth nor an alerted defence, and even less a flicker of doubt that he might not, could not, cross the line. From short distances he became virtually unstoppable. The crowd at Cardiff came to sense when an Edwards charge for the line behind a scrum or round the line-out was 'on' and then, the score achieved, would relapse into a sated stupor that their wishes were at one with this man's capability. Incredibly, throughout his entire career, he never broke a bone, or suffered even a cut that required a stitch; all his injuries were muscular, from which he, like others was always able to make a remarkably rapid recovery thanks to the expert attentions of physiotherapist Gerry Lewis, like his father Ray before him, a magical masseur of national Welsh muscles.

In 1967 the nineteen-year-old tyro international was 5foot 8inches and 11stone 9lb; in 1978 the thirty-one-year-old veteran carried 13stone 4lb. He had not grown an inch but his stature was now immense. From 1973 the French, against whom he had made his debut in 1967, simply captioned their programme notes — *'un des grands du rugby mondial'*. That was exactly half-way through his international career. Edwards's first try against France had been in 1969, when he ricocheted down the right touch-line like a demented spinning top, breaking at least four tackles and proving in a gyrating, urgent quest for the line, that the determination that came scorching out of his eyes like a double-headed oxy-acytelene flame would burn through any human obstacle. Wales drew 8 - 8 that day but two years later an Edwards try on the left began their downfall. Where Barry John had moved like a self-regulating pendulum, Edwards brought to scrum-half play the pent-up explosive star-burst that Cliff Jones and Cliff Morgan gave to fly-half running, and since Gareth Edwards, knowing the power of his stocky physique, struck for his kingdom from closer in, the coiled inner spring he unwound whiplashed its way to triumph upon glorious triumph.

If he was, through training and education, a back amongst backs, he was, by temperament and shared work, a forward amongst forwards. Edwards often hunted with the foraging Morris whose origins and features echoed his own and the greatest individual try he scored, in a game won crushingly by 35 - 12 against Scotland, ended not in the elegant touch-down of a graceful three-quarter but in a lunge that covered his face in the anonymity of mud. The uncertainly raised hand to acknowledge the crowd's acclaim — because 'I felt the applause was different' — accepted the common bond and the lack of anonymity that will forever attend a man who scored a seventy-five yard try by breaking round the back of a scrum, handing off a restraining Scot, and running on. It was Cardiff on 5 February 1972 and he had already crashed over from short range, after seemingly being held, still festooned with four Scots; only minutes later, he was to do the impossible. There was no support, for he had broken too quickly and too far out for that; scarcely expecting to broach the first defence but now loose and alone, he raced with Renwick and Steele to dive at the crucially-timed second for the ball before it slithered away to the right-hand touch-in-goal. He lunged, into the mud and onto the red cinder path, beyond the ball that he had, in that final instance of will, touched down.

At the end of the final season of his telepathic partnership with Barry John, then, Gareth Edwards had given notice that his incomparable ability would not stagnate at this junction point. In fact it would be harder for whoever had to follow 'King' John than for the scrum-half to continue his own stately progress but, despite these difficulties, that successor would end by sharing a new Welsh and world record partnership at half-back. He would be only the second Welshman to captain the British Lions and would earn a place in the affection of his countrymen as much for his courageous perseverance as for his own special brand of rugby. Phil Bennett was the automatic choice to replace Barry John against Ian Kirkpatrick's Seventh All Blacks at Cardiff in the winter of 1972.

The 1970s saw the production of more books on rugby than ever before. The growing attractiveness of rugby football and the greater frequency of tours and visits had ensured this as much as a deepening awareness, on the part of sociologists and historians, of the implications for society of nationalism, professionalism, brutalism and amateurism in sport. The history of rugby certainly calls into question whether the unwelcome aspects of the game are, in any real sense, on the increase. More to the point is the structural shift in advanced societies that has, outside rugby, and, therefore, for rugby too, altered expectations. That is an administrative or institutional problem as such, not a moral issue. On the other hand, burgeoning interest in the intricacies of the game often magnified, sometimes trivialized, by the increased attentions of the TV cameras has been accompanied by less worthy intrusion into the private moments of players. Pressure rises on the terraces and on the fields. These 1972 All Blacks were judged where others had been discussed. The wrongs of their tour — the dismissal of Keith Murdoch for an after-match indiscretion; the sullenness of some of their pronouncements, in public and private; the petulance of a few leading players — did not endear them to a British public who had relished previous All Blacks. The rights of their tour — no home international lost, some sparkling wing play and effective interaction between Going, at scrum-half, and his back-row — received, perhaps, less credit than it should have done. After all, New Zealand had entered the 1970s with an urgent need to reassess its economy and its traditional trading relationship with a Britain now looking to Europe more than the Commonwealth. Rugby for New Zealanders had been intimately associated with that expectation of life, and so had winning. The 1972 All Blacks came to claw back some victories with the means available to them. The worse their press became, the more they withdrew. By the third match of the tour, in Cardiff, the die was cast. Cardiff played poorly, and roughly, their opponents played better, and roughly, but a forty-six thousand crowd sent many older rugby supporters away in disbelief at the moody, ill-temper of the ugliest Welsh crowd in history. Where exactly this degeneration of the former spirit had started is immaterial for there was no one point or explanation. Nor would this sourness evaporate despite the best efforts of many individuals and both unions during this decade. It was, perhaps, the saddest aspect of the 1970s, one that requires the catharsis of a centenary year to end and, hopefully, attention to the words of Colin Meads who in 1974 viewed with grave dismay the recent tours and the deterioration of 'one of the healthiest rivalries in international sport [which should cause] New Zealanders to study critically trends in their own crowd behaviour . . . an emerging petulance'. He stressed:

> If ever the Press had a mission in Welsh rugby it is now . . . they have contributed to the breaking down of a rugby relationship which I have always thought to be one of the most wonderful things in my playing experience . . . a massive self-analysis assisted by the Press could help to bring balance back to crowd attitudes. But may their playing philosophy never change. It is akin to our own for . . . When a New Zealander goes out there to play against a Welsh club side he knows he is playing against fifteen men bent on writing their names into Welsh history . . . it does mean a lot to me and I know it means as much to many other All Blacks. We want to keep — restore, if you like — the proud image of New Zealand rugby in Wales and the esteem in which All Blacks are held there.

Meads remembered, with a pang of regret for the tighter game it forced them to play as much as for the defeat, by Newport in 1963, the Fifth All Blacks' first Welsh game. Kirkpatrick's men had their traditional Welsh experience on 31 October 1972 at Stradey Park, Llanelli. It was their second game, their first in Wales and a return match with British Lions coach, Carwyn James, whose dossier on All Black strengths and weaknesses had become positively encyclopaedic. The All Blacks were a young side for whom the emotional electricity in Llanelli's damp air seemed to act as a short circuit to future enjoyment. After this, neither the Cardiff game nor the Welsh international would be thrills, rather games to be endured and won. But, for the moment, Stradey sucked almost twenty-four thousand into its orbit for a day of celebration of its own bravura Welshness. 'Llanelli', boasted the tiny black and white scoreboard, versus 'Seland Newydd' (in October 1976 the W.R.U. would follow suit as 'Cymru' met 'Ariannin'; Argentina narrowly succumbed to this linguistic challenge as, soon, did the white shirts of 'Lloegr', the green of 'Iwerddon', the dark blue of 'Yr Alban' and the light blue of 'Ffrainc') and New Zealand saw themselves metamorphosized into Welsh shape in the very bubble of James the Wizard's cauldron. The singing did not help, least of all at half-time with the band of the Welsh Guards in active conspiracy with the crowd. It rose from the ranks of the huddled onlookers to settle over the ground in swelling counter-harmony to the heavy tone of gloom presaged by the waiting rain in the air.

This was the day for which Llanelli had waited one hundred years. They were, in their centenary season, in the middle of one of their greatest periods. Under Carwyn James, and then Norman Gale, their sturdy pack and darting backs would move and switch with the ball, and off it, irresistibly. London Welsh had, under Tony Gray's captaincy, taken the unofficial championship in 1971-72 to crown the Exiles' achievements, but Llanelli had been registering their presence just as attractively. The Floodlit Alliance, begun in 1964-5 literally to brighten up Welsh rugby, ended incomplete because of government restrictions on power in 1973-74, and was then collapsed as a tournament in which only tries had counted from 1967-68. Llanelli won it six times in a row from that year. In 1972 they had reached the final of the resurrected W.R.U. Cup Competition to face Neath, the first major Welsh club to celebrate its centenary in a decade full of centurions. Neath's All Blacks through a magnificent forward drive quelled the Scarlet runners but the latter returned to the National Ground four consecutive years after that to win the Cup on each occasion despite sometimes missing their key players through overseas duty. The 1970s brought them two unofficial club championships, in 1974 and 1977, as they vied in the early 1970s with the forward might of Ray Prosser's Pontypool, who headed the table in 1973 and 1975, and in the late 1970s with the co-ordinated team work of Joe Smith's revitalized Pontypridd who won three championships, two consecutively, between 1976 and 1979. Even when their undoubted team brilliance faded after the mid-1970s Llanelli's influence within the Welsh domestic game was imprinted on the national side. The side that met New Zealand in 1972 contained six full Internationals and another three who would wear the Welsh colours within a few years. Three of these were already, and four more would be, British Lions. Of the remaining six, four would be Welsh 'B' Internationals. They had been significantly strengthened by three current 'B' Internationals who had transferred in the close season — the fleet J. J. Williams of Bridgend on the left wing; chunky Ray Hopkins, Welsh and British scrum-half, from Maesteg to relegate Llanelli's own fine Selwyn Williams to the substitute bench; and in the back-row, Thomas Patrick David, whose driving, try-scoring power would help Pontypridd to the championship in their own centenary year when he re-joined his local club in 1975-6. Llanelli had, on their right wing, Andy Hill, their record scorer whose long-range goal kicking demoralized opponents over these years and, at lock, Derek Quinnell, a fiery Lion from 1971. Above all this was to be the day of another long-serving Welsh forward, the uncomplaining line-out winner, W. Delme Thomas, whose cigar-store Indian impassivity would crack into a triumphant grin that day as first Bergiers charged down an early clearance to score for Bennett to convert and then Quinnell, David and the Jenkins boys (Hefin and Gareth) tamed their opposite numbers. Joe Karam's penalty goal kept New Zealand in the game but Andy Hill's monstrous, climbing second-half reply restored the differential to leave the final score of a tense, keenly disputed game 9 points to 3. The lasting memory it held was of Bennett, in his own in-goal area and under imminent danger of black immersion, coolly clearing his line from the acutest of angles and finding touch on half-way. It was a gesture irresistibly compounded of delicacy and defiance.

No other All Blacks team throughout the decade had the door slammed on it in Wales by a Welsh team. The saga that had once been heroic in its tradition and its execution was to lose its way in the wastelands made by a new generation of tourists who had not understood how a game must surmount the actuality of victory or defeat if it is to retain any meaning for human memory. Right at the end of the 1972-73 tour, Kirkpatrick's All Blacks showed they could understand this when they played a full part in the swan-song of John Dawes's playing career. Dawes led a Barbarians side that looked quite leonine through a game that crackled and flared with good intentions and even better football. The fact that the Barbarians won 23 to 11 and led 17 - 0 at half-time delighted a crowd who chanted 'Wales! Wales!' to make their intentions clear (and re-baptized David Duckham,

'Dai') but it was the joy of the tries scored by both sides that restored faith in the saga from the moment the diminutive Bennett began his side-stepping stammer into history by giving television, and Gareth Edwards, the most spectacular combined try on tape. Towards the end, Duckham, taking wings in this game, flirted and flashed his blonde way through black ranks until J. P. R. Williams sold a dummy as huge as Cardiff's University Hospital to put the issue beyond doubt.

Almost two months before, on the same ground, everything, bar the final score of 19 points to 16 in New Zealand's favour, was in doubt. J. P. R. Williams believed he had scored a try, in the second half, that was legitimate if Keith Murdoch's crawl over the line had been in the first half, and Bennett's final kick at goal sailed hauntingly wide. Yet none of this really mattered. Arthur Lewis, chosen to captain the team, had withdrawn so that Delme Thomas, too absorbed a player to be a forceful captain, had been given the honour. Many thought that the bulldozing Tommy David, a robust player who took the game to New Zealand for Llanelli and the Barbarians, should have played. Whatever the cause a gloomy, cloud-sopped day was reflected in a lacklustre first half for Wales when 13 points were conceded and only 3 taken. The second half saw New Zealand's Karam, faultless on the day, kick two more penalties but John Bevan, as he did for the Barbarians, ran wide and powerfully from forty yards to score and the Welsh pack showed their old form. What was unacceptable was not the 19 - 16 defeat, nor even the arguable decisions of referee Johnny Johnson, but three late and deliberate obstructions on Wales's flying wingers, Davies and Bevan, only one of which was penalized and all of which reduced the tempo of a game Wales was turning.

When Andy Leslie brought a New Zealand side to play a Welsh XV in 1974, on a short tour for the Irish centenary, an indifferent Welsh team was well beaten by 12 points to 3 by a superb New Zealand forward effort. Disappointment was not the same as disgruntlement. The wounds of injured sensibilities that had healed by 1974 were old, forgotten scars when Graham Mourie's Eighth All Blacks made the now familiar pilgrimage to Cardiff. They had a well-drilled side, an exceptional wing in Stuart Wilson and a rare centre pair, Osborne and Robertson, of combined penetrative and defensive capability. The forwards, invariably, at the very least held their own, and Mourie in the back-row was a tireless cover defender and attacking support. It was, in short, a very good team led and managed in a way that reminded older observers of New Zealand sides before 1972.

430

Wales were caught again at a time of rebuilding. From her 1978 Grand Slam side, Gareth Edwards, Gerald Davies, Bennett and Cobner were gone, respectively, into permanent and international retirement. Graham Mourie's side had offended no one on or off the field. Their captain set such an impeccable example that he was bidding fair to be the most admired (and feared) All Black captain since Whineray or even Gallaher, in whose advanced footsteps he often hastened to tread. Then whatever gremlin it was that has been appointed to sit on the shoulders of these encounters appeared again. Wales lost the November international by 12 points to 13, the score of 1935 was reversed, and while the spectacle of that encounter was absent, the two essential ingredients of Wales v. New Zealand matches were not: tension and controversy. New Zealand, though mostly, and surprisingly, outplayed at forward and half-back had withstood a rather blunted Welsh midfield, taken a neatly designed try and won the match with a last-minute penalty shot by substitute full-back, McKechnie. Whether England's Roger Quittenton was correct or not in penalizing Wales's Geoff Wheel, for levering himself up at the fatal line-out on New Zealander Frank Oliver's shoulder, was not the major talking-point for a Wales who *had* both undergone that self-analysis, in press and on television, that Colin Meads had requested, and had forgiven the past. Dying embers of resentment were poked back to life by the hopeful, unassisted dive from the line-out that Welsh spectators thought they had seen. Photography confirmed that neither Andy Haden who shot away, untouched, from the middle of the line nor Oliver, whose back was turned to Wheel, had made any effort to contest a crucial line-out. Why not? Whatever the whitewash, and little that stuck was offered, whatever the respectful silence of the W.R.U., the public effect of the act was numbing. The fracture was compounded not when, on 17 March 1979, John Ashworth, an All Black prop, allegedly raked his unfeeling boot across the face of a pinned Bridgend skipper, J. P. R. Williams, in his club's centenary year, but when that same forward appeared as a substitute three days later against Derek Quinnell's Barbarians at Cardiff. Even if the bounds of charity were stretched to accept total, albeit foolish innocence on the parts of Haden and Ashworth, the role of management, to rise above the excuses of players, was left unfulfilled in the eyes of a number of experienced observers.

The spice of rugby antagonism between these old rivals is rooted in their contrast of temperaments and cultures. Their styles clash. A victory used to be a triumph for means not just ends. Perhaps the statistical exercise, with New Zealand so far in front, may now be forgotten so that the Centenary game can wipe all slates clean in celebration. Gamesmanship is only an iota removed from brutality. Wales certainly did not claim to have a simon-pure record in either respect, but Clive Rowlands, tour manager to Australia on the ill-fated 1978 trip where Wales lost both Tests, had spoken unprecedentedly for the sentiments of the W.R.U. in an after-dinner response when he insisted that *all* involved in rugby must condemn *all* brands of thuggery anywhere it occurred. Australia had made its rugby power known that year in revenge for their 24 - 0 defeat in 1973 and their 28 - 3 demolition by Wales on the Wallabies' British tour of 1975, but reputation is not respect. J. B. G. Thomas, whose *Rugby in Focus* (1979) was one of his more comprehensive, and sadder, books, noted that it was the brilliant Australian schoolboys, who toured during 1977-78 and won all their games, including a 25 - 6 humbling of Wales, with flowing football and counter-attacking panache, who would keep alive Welsh respect for the Wallabies. The 1970s may be seen, in retrospect, as a lynch-pin decade in the expansion of world rugby that the W.R.U. have been so keen to foster. Coming and goings were, at times, helter-skelter. Wales met and defeated 56 - 10 a brave Canadian side at Cardiff in 1971 and then toured, enjoyably and successfully, in that country in 1973; the W.R.U., with France helping to defray costs, went for another first in 1973 when Japan brought their small-statured, enormously inventive and popular team to Wales, who overwhelmed them by 62 points to 14; Wales returned that compliment by a Far Eastern tour in 1975 when Japan again felt Welsh might in two defeats of 56 - 12 and 82 - 6; in between times Wales played in green jerseys to accommodate the red of an enterprising Tongan rugby side who, though they lost by 26 to 7, wafted in with the same Pacific breeziness that the Fijians, who played a Welsh Under-25 side in 1970, had brought with them; in 1976, the touring Japanese, under the observant Shiggy Kono, did not play a Wales side, only 'Welsh clubs' and once more succumbed heavily, unlike the impressive Argentinians who on their first visit to Wales beat East Wales, Cardiff and Aberavon before losing narrowly to the West, and, most unluckily, by a single point 20 - 19, to Wales at the National Ground. The return of the Pumas in 1978 saw a Welsh 'B' side go down at Stradey in October and a hardening of opinion that the Argentine's captain, Hugo Porta, was at the top of the league amongst world outside-halves; finally, as the penultimate year of a rugby century started, Wales welcomed Romania, a hard, scrupulously fair East European team who brought an undefeated side through tough club and representative games to meet a Welsh XV in October 1979 and, in

432

an absorbing contest, went down by the narrowest margin of a point, 13 to 12, by now Wales's favourite cliff-hanging score.

It had been the busiest decade of travel and tours — with three Lions tours in 1971, 1974 and 1977, and innumerable club jaunts overseas in the summer — that the W.R.U. and leading Welsh players had ever undergone. The world of rugby had shrunk globally only by expanding in all other ways. The role of International Board members was no longer that of an occasional wise casting of the runes; their involvement, through the scope and speed of developments was, year by year, assuming a greater importance. Welsh success as a rugby country, allied to her longevity in the game, made her voice an important one so that from the late sixties when Hermas Evans joined Kenneth Harris, the pronouncements, ideas and initiatives of her I.B. representatives were crucial in establishing Welsh standing at the expanding frontiers of rugby. The re-vamping of fixtures between the home countries was followed by constant efforts to have 'neutral' referees on overseas tours. Older problems, such as the definition of amateurism in the game, were thrashed out with the R.F.U. and later accepted for international purposes by the I.B. whilst newer issues, such as the metrication of the laws of the game, were readily propounded by Wales's legal specialists. However gratifying Welsh international playing victories were, the Welsh rugby world was, before the 1970s ended, no less proud that her representatives had come to be regarded by other nations as at the forefront of the international administration of the game. Wales had never attained this particular reputation in the past. The courage and expertise they provided was interconnected with their country's determined stance to use the past in order to progress to the future. The base of any international projection, in playing and in administration, remained that local Welsh world which, in rugby as in so much else, had striven for control over its often haphazard fortunes since the nineteenth century.

It is in this respect that the debate at committee level within the W.R.U., whether resolved or not, can be seen as a drive to establish an institutional framework within which further advances could be made. Possibly some clubs and representatives were lulled into a fixed desire to retain the status quo by virtue of their own holdings of power and status at a specific time; others may have felt, with those who opposed coaching in the 1960s, that the game was moving away from their idea of its better days; notwithstanding this, there was a sizeable minority within the W.R.U. who pressed hard for radical changes from 1969, and a willing majority who went a long way along the road with them. It is the representatives of the Union to the outside world who speak for the W.R.U. but they do this, of course, in a specified capacity so that it is necessary always to remember the work carried out, in the districts and at endless meetings, by all members of the Committee who generally, if not always, managed to act in concert.

The two most contentious, still unsettled, matters were examined by the Union before the 1970s had started. In 1968 there was a total of thirty-two members on the Union Committee, from the President and his immediate predecessor down through the Treasurer, Vice-Presidents, Life Members, nominees of affiliated bodies and District representatives. That year a report on structure and organization, prepared by Hermas Evans, proposed dividing the Union into six autonomous areas (plus North Wales), each having its own officers to deal with routine matters and each sending three representatives, serving three-year terms, to the central committee. The Junior Union would be dissolved to allow direct affiliation of all W.R.U. clubs (there would then be an addition of about 120 clubs to raise the total to 280) with attendance rights at the A.G.M. The Schools, Secondary Schools and Youth Unions would retain their autonomy and direct representation but the separate affiliation of London Welsh and the retention of Vice-Presidents would disappear along with the committee status of Life Members; instead there would be three co-opted members with specialist qualifications in such matters as coaching, finance, publicity or whatever was required. The overall intention was to de-centralize in the interests of greater efficiency and in order to reflect, more logically, a different society from the one the Union's structure had come to reflect by piecemeal accretion of functions and personnel. Instead, the Committee, all of whom would now be directly responsible to clubs, would elect a President, Senior and Junior Vice-President from their ranks on a rotation basis with each member so elected maintaining his district representation rather than his expertise being lost through unwillingness to stand or, through automatic removal, having stood. Numbers would, thereby, be reduced by six.

Discussion of this document, in principle the most profound alteration in the history of the W.R.U. since the South Wales Football Union became the W.F.U., was only brought to a head in December 1969 when, after various tinkering variations had been dismissed, the scheme fell by a small majority so that in 1979 there were still thirty-two members of the Committee, and 181 clubs. Perhaps the force of the institutional logic had outrun the organic growth that had been so characteristic of the W.R.U. in its relation to social change but, to prevent a fossilization, there had, anyway, to be some streamlining of bureaucratic procedure just as admission of junior clubs, if the Union's stretched finances were not to be weakened bit by bit, had, if not accomplished at a stroke, to be restricted. This happened in 1974, the year when the Committee structure was rationalized to allow Coaching and Laws to come under one head; a re-organized eight-man Coaching Advisory Committee, with chairman Clive Rowlands and vice-chairman John Dawes, was set up simultaneously. That reduced the major committees from six to five but the amount of administrative work that the spread and success of the game entailed was now leaping beyond the grasp of the existing staff. By the early 1970s there were eleven sub-committees in addition to the six main ones, not to mention representation by the Union on the I.B., the Welsh Games Council, the Welsh Advisory Sports Committee and so on. In late 1969 the W.R.U. appointed Brian Kempson of Llandaff North as Assistant Secretary to Bill Clement. The decision to keep a centralized control over matters guaranteed a further extension of ancillary staff so that by the time the new offices were ready in the summer of 1977 to allow removal from St. Mary Street to the National Ground, the W.R.U. had gathered together a staff of twelve whose combined expertise, from Len Matthews and Peter Williams on the tickets headache, to Avril Power's masterly handling of referees, on down through secretaries and telephonists, allowed safe manoeuvre within the rugby Star Trek module these rugby offices resembled. But, their command was not hovering in space, only over the turf of the National Ground kept green and expectant by the Ground Manager, Bill Hardiman, and his staff of five. This was not the root-and-branch reform envisaged in 1969 but it was, by the past history of the Union's homely administration, a palace revolution. The ripples of wider possibilities did not entirely die away — symbolically, if not substantially, the Welsh Junior Rugby Union became the Welsh Districts Rugby Union in 1976 with thirteen districts and 343 clubs under its aegis.

That year saw further suggestions on geographical re-organization of the Union with a phasing out of all affiliated or associate members and the introduction of direct club membership through regional unions on a ten-year probation. The impetus behind the move, namely removal of the existing anomalies within the Union, was once more halted by the brake of those same anomalies; and in 1976, too, the other major proposal from the late 1960s was laid on the table. This was the suggestion for League tables that would have altered to an extent the long established fixture lists of the Union's clubs. As before 1914, the aspiring clubs were for the scheme with 135 replying favourably to the Union's questionnaire by March 1976 and only 35 against. Re-submission failed to win over these whose ranks included all the principal gate-taking clubs and so made the suggestions unworkable. These had been mulled over, principally by sub-committees guided by Ray Williams, since 1968 and, in 1969, the half-way house of a knock-out competition began to receive consensus approval until passed by the clubs in 1970. This, too, finally launched in 1971-72, ran into endless teething troubles and some serious dissension over dates, seeding, the rights of the smaller clubs, and, eventually, the threatened withdrawal in 1977, of fourteen out of the sixteen major, so-called 'Snelling', clubs. This would have been a disaster, since each year the interest in the Cup had risen until the Final came to be seen as the culminating event in the W.R.U. calendar that reached far beyond the participation of the two clubs finally contesting for the trophy. Ken Gwilym and, later, George Morgan for the Competition sub-committee struggled with the arguments between the smaller clubs and their more famous opponents, over seeding, finance, and fixed dates, until by the end of the decade the competition which had been so vital a part of the spread of rugby in the 1870s became, to the surprise of many and the delight of thousands, an even grander example of the possibilities of club rugby's attraction in the 1970s.

The question of competitive rugby had, however, exercised the mind of Ray Williams in another sense. Foiled in 1969, he returned to the argument with renewed fervour after his visit to New Zealand in 1970. By 1973, on behalf of the Coaching Advisory Committee, he presented a paper on *A Rugby Structure for Wales* which began by acknowledging the rooted conditions of Welsh rugby but insisted there was no sensible, gradual progression from base to apex — 'The present structure of Welsh rugby is fragmented . . . so that Wales does not necessarily make the best of what it has got. The system . . . is an historical accident and like Topsy it has just growed . . . The game in Wales has been played for over one hundred years, but the organization of the game is based on a structure which was established many years ago and which is not now necessarily relevant in modern society'. The subsequent argument was two-fold in its uniting of apparently paradoxical points. First, the pressures on first-class players (the number of fixtures, representative and invitation games) was becoming intolerable and could threaten the amateur status of the game;

436

but the promotion of Welsh rugby relied on its image to the world, especially through its representative strength, so this needed strengthening, particularly when touring sides visited. Therefore the 'fixtures of convenience' (one-off club amalgamations) and the traditions of clubs should not ride roughshod over the needs and chances of players, nor over the future raising of standards which only a radical re-structure could supply. Ray Williams argued for a regional rugby championship on an annual basis which would also provide a permanent structure of representative teams, drawn more widely, against the frequent touring sides to be expected in a jet age. Four of the five sides, Gwent, East Glamorgan, West Glamorgan and West Wales — with North Wales ruled out — would play incoming visitors, who would also meet the Challenge Cup winners and a Wales 'B' team. That proposal, clearly linked to an administrative re-structure, remained on the drawing board. The Coaching Organiser's fertile mind re-introduced the 1968 idea of three National Leagues and nine District Leagues, each bunch in three divisions with home and away fixtures and a graded system of promotion and relegation, in 1975. The groundswell of opinion at that A.G.M., and thereafter in 1976, was strong but failed to persuade those clubs whose participation alone would give the scheme viability so, in 1977, it was once more deferred.

History does not stop when the historian does; final judgement on these matters will have to wait for the next century of Welsh rugby to unfold. What is clear already, however, it that the legitimate traditions and rooted strength of Welsh club rugby must be preserved if the Welsh game is not to be denatured, whilst at the same time the promotion and projection of the game, both at international and district level, requires a frank, accepting encouragement of the aspirations of those clubs and players whose desire to be local and amateur was the original well-spring of the game. The role of the W.R.U. in giving a lead between the rights of *all* its constituents is not, therefore, as straightforward as some commentators, perhaps unaware of the historical tensions within the Welsh game, suggested. Equally the W.R.U. was now better established for fruitful intervention on rugby's behalf within society than at any time in its past. Nowhere was this more obvious than in its long, painful and eventually successful clarification of the problems that arose over schools rugby.

From 1971 the W.R.U. established a working party under the chairmanship of Hermas Evans to examine the state of rugby for those under-19 in Wales. Ray Williams had launched during that year a scheme for mini-rugby (nine-a-side) for the very young to enjoy handling and running skills without the pressures of the full game being imposed, but the transition from schools to club rugby remained in need of re-vamping at a time of considerable re-organization in Welsh schools. Hermas Evans presented the Fourth Interim Report of the Under-19 working party to the W.R.U. in 1974. Its burden was that the circumstances which had spawned the Welsh Schools R.U. and the Welsh Secondary Schools R.U. had now been by-passed, leaving their control of schools rugby at a cross-roads. The immediate problem was that caused by the statutory raising of school leaving age to sixteen from late 1974 since, traditionally, the line of division between the two schools bodies was pre- and post-15 years, whilst before the 1944 Education Act the W.S.S.R.U. had been, in effect, a 'Union of Grammar Schools'. After 1944, the raising of leaving age from fourteen to fifteen with the advent of Secondary Modern Schools had not really separated out the functions, but the further raising to sixteen, allied to the full-scale introduction of Comprehensive Schools, had blurred the picture. The Schools Internationals that had been played since 1904 could only continue if the age-limit was made under-16, in line with the R.F.U., so Hermas Evans had striven for one Welsh Schools Union in which all schools rugby would be based on the schools, rather than on towns and districts as had tended to happen in Wales, apart from the grammar schools. Both Schools Unions were anxious about the future of their particular grades so a steering committee continued to meet until, in 1976, its place could be taken by representatives of the different levels of schools rugby and W.R.U. personnel, including the W.R.U. Coaching Organiser. Thus, in a major advance, one unitary Welsh Schools Union with three groups (Under-19, Under-15 and Under-11) had been established to give schools rugby a continuing basis for independence in association with the governing Welsh rugby authority. Appropriately enough the President of the W.S.R.U. since its inception in 1976 has been its chief architect, Hermas Evans.

The W.R.U. was, of course, profoundly conscious of the role that schools rugby had played in the development of Welsh rugby in the past. Although financial stringencies, because of ground development and inflation, hampered the Union through the 1970s, the W.R.U. had wisely established a Charitable Trust Fund in December 1972 which, topped up annually by £20,000, would allow them to make bigger grants to affiliated organizations like the Schools and Youth Unions. They were, in addition, determined that a change in the nature of schools need not preclude an

438

ample provision for rugby, albeit in a world where leisure-centres were providing many attractive alternatives. In effect the 'scare' over Comprehensives that suggested they could not fill the rugby role of the old grammar schools was social timidity masquerading as sporting concern. Grammar schools in Wales had only been one adjunct of Welsh rugby anyway. Nothing stands still. Fewer Schools XVs will mean greater involvement of the clubs themselves in fostering schools rugby. The W.R.U. had encountered similar social effects on teenage rugby in the aftermath of the Second World War with the birth of the Youth Rugby Union for boys between fifteen and eighteen. That body, under its successive Secretaries, Hermas Evans, Jim Dark and E. B. Davies turned an ugly duckling into a swan. The Youth Union celebrated its twenty-fifth anniversary in 1974 with its first full fixture against an England Youth XV. On that day Llanelli's David Nicholas was in the centre and Terry Holmes of Cardiff was a reserve choice. Such a glut of talent was no surprise to coach Ieuan Evans for, already, twenty-three full Welsh international caps had emerged from the ranks of the Youth, including three Welsh captains and nine British Lions. The harvest had been a rich one with no signs at all of overworked soil.

Senior Welsh XVs continued, from the mid-1970s, to reap the benefits of these connecting links. They were lubricated by a coaching system whose sophistication grew annually. The thinking behind Welsh coaching remained what it had been in the 1960s — the technical skills that could be acquired and the tactics that could be devised were opportunities for improved play not imperatives for all circumstances nor recipes for victory. Ray Williams would, toward the decade's close, express his concern about the need for coaches to instil correct attitudes even more than perfected techniques and some senior players would question the limits of coaching itself. Even so, the proof of the value that coaching had come to assume lay not only in the way it was integrated into all aspects of Welsh rugby but also in the manner it helped Wales through a transitional period. In 1975 a paper on line-out play sensibly explored means of exploiting possibilities for possession at this crucial area within the existing laws (changed since 1973) whether they were entirely satisfactory, in terms of legislation and interpretation, or not. The paper argued that to 'lose a line-out should be as bad as losing a tight-head. Superiority in the set piece will breed the confidence necessary to achieve team success. Quality line-out ball would give backs that extra space and time and consequently they would be under less pressure. These factors should produce a higher

439

standard of back play'. And since the law amendments suggested by the W.R.U. in 1970, over the mark and the knock-on, were designed to help produce continuous play since 'possession and movement is the key to successful rugby . . . with consequential spectator value', the merging of legislation and coaching into one committee made perfect sense.

Arguably, the intention to speed the game's flow was confounded by unforseen factors such as alterations in the tackle-law and the intrusion of a term as ugly as the motorways from whence it came — the 'pile-up'. More controversially, the space now given to backs was felt to have reduced the traditional elusive qualities inbred in pressured backs — the jinking half-back and the side-stepping centre. The new Welsh emphasis on efficiency was now accused of killing the centre three-quarter. This sharply-reasoned critique did not lack support inside Wales in the late 1970s but it appears to founder both on the desire of Welsh selectors to choose such a centre when they can find one (David Richards was converted to good effect in 1979) and on the evidence that the problem had been spotted, analysed and publicly discussed in Wales as early as 1976 when Ray Williams's *Skilful Rugby* appeared:

> Few people would argue that the game has not improved over the previous ten years, but still there is a feeling that back play is not what it was. This is a correct assessment, but that does not mean that it is worse, it merely means that it is different . . . The facts are that back play has changed; it has, like the rest of the game, become more organized . . . Good centres now are often referred to as the 'organization' men . . . the outstanding example of such a player in recent years is John Dawes. A superb passer of the ball, excellent tackler and a player who was the 'oil-can' of the team; ally these to his qualities as a captain and you have a player of rare quality. Even John Dawes, however, was not fully appreciated, he was a player's player . . . but . . . This is not to say that back play cannot be improved. There is a lot of evidence to suggest that coaches do not give enough attention to the coaching of backs. Perhaps this is why so often a team's ball-using ability does not match its ball-winning ability . . . The W.R.U. Coaching Advisory Committee is currently engaged in writing a paper on back play, . . . for . . . mid-field players . . . should re-think their options. Rarely now do we see the mid-field (i.e. outside-half and centres) taking on their opposite numbers unless it is the crash ball. Running skills need to be encouraged, not in any attempt to recapture something that was, but rather to add to the armoury of players so that when problems are posed they will have more than one answer.

In the years immediately before Ray Williams wrote that passage, Wales, in 1973 and 1974, had experienced her dreariest period of play at international level in the seventies. The glories of yesterday seemed to have disappeared abruptly. Arthur Lewis's team succumbed to Scotland at Murrayfield in 1973 and two years later so did Mervyn Davies's side, whilst England in 1974 recorded her only win against Wales since Clive Rowlands had first begun to stiffen the three feathers eleven years previously. By recent standards of expectation, seven victories in fourteen games over three seasons was not encouraging but, in fact, Wales had only been defeated five times (once by New Zealand and once by France) whilst the 1975 team not only took the championship but also gave notification of the future by turning up six new caps who would figure prominently through the next few years. 1974 had not been Wales's year at home yet nine Welshmen (six of whom played in the four tests) helped the British Lions to move undefeated through South Africa so that, on their return, John Dawes, coach in succession to Clive Rowlands from September 1974, had a rich blend of experience and youthfulness with which to fashion his new teams.

So the temporary setbacks of 1973 and 1974 were not demoralizing for Wales. Cliff Jones introduced his alliterative trinity, 'progress, position and perseverance', at the end of the 1974 season to demonstrate the sea-change that had occurred since 1964 (progress), the improvements that had resulted (position), and the continuing work that was required (perseverance). One of the smaller but most significant satisfactions of that year was the presence at the annual Coaches Course held in Aberystwyth of Nelie Smith who had scored a try for South Africa against Wales in 1964. The world had turned upside down since that day. Ray Williams had been down under to advise Australia over the establishment of a coaching scheme — 'Let us hope' said Cliff Jones 'that it will not rebound on us too heavily when we visit there in four years time'. That was to be one of the few Welsh wishes to be unfulfilled. A re-shuffle of the Welsh cards turned up trumps time after time.

Gareth Edwards had held the Welsh captaincy for the longest extended run of his career in 1974, but leadership, though the ebullient Edwards disclaimed the view, seemed to inhibit his own game. A new coach changed the tempo. Mervyn Davies was given the captaincy in a move that was greeted with general approval. At the same time the selectors brought to a head one of the customary disputes about outside-half play that has blessed and afflicted Welsh rugby history. The incumbent was the long-serving Phil Bennett whose progress from utility player (he had by 1975 appeared, at times briefly, in every postion for Wales behind the scrum) to Barry John's rightful heir had not always seen him play for Wales the kind of football he turned in so regularly for his club. The Llanelli pivot was a devastating broken-field runner, at his best when forced by the pressure of events to improvise his way through the opposition. In many ways he was the antithesis of John, not least in his physical style. His furrowed brow, hunched shoulders and staccato, darting movement as he ferreted hither and thither for an opening seemed to exude anxiety. Behind Edwards and a dominant pack in South Africa he had played soundly throughout and was often brilliant. His solo try in the Third Test was the mesmeric run of a prodigiously gifted runner who had to be encouraged to be prodigal. Nonetheless, after this triumphant summer, he was relegated to the Possibles team in the final trial on 4 January 1975 and then lost his place against France to the man who had already figured, in December, in Wales 'B's victory over France. This was the compact, astute Aberavon man, John Bevan who, his advocates, claimed would be better able through cool control to bring the Welsh backs into play. An injury to Bevan in the Scottish game saw Bennett come on, cold, to a game the Scots were intent on winning. He played poorly but, with Bevan still injured, he retained his place against Ireland to launch a Welsh scoring spree of five tries in a scintillating 32 - 4 victory that took the championship away from a centenary-celebrating Irish side skippered by Lions captain Willie John McBride, one of Bennett's great admirers. This setback continued the following season when, initially, Bevan and the ex-schoolboy star, David Richards, were picked in preference to the Llanelli captain but it ended by proving the low point of a chequered career that would go on to see Bennett captain Wales and the British Lions, with Bevan *his* experienced reserve as he had once been Barry John's. The depth of talent in half-backs was hard on the players but a happy embarrassment for Welsh selectors.

It was in 1975, against France, that Wales blooded two young centres, S. P. Fenwick and Raymond Gravell. The latter had served Llanelli, along with Roy Bergiers, only to find himself propelled forward when his club colleagues dropped from the limelight. He gave uncompromising and emotional commitment to Welsh midfield play for the next three seasons as he gobbled up 'soft centres' with swashbuckling bravado. Fenwick proved no less formidable in hurtling against the confident French midfield and his intelligent support play won him a try when French vigilance relaxed. The sight of this stockily built anticipator of colleagues' needs and opponents' errors was a familiar one from the mid-1970s. Where the play broke down or a subtle touch was required, there Fenwick's shock of blonde hair would be. Neither of these men won praise for the brilliance of their running but their contribution to the years of unparalleled triumphs to come was undeniable for they exemplified the solidarity of Welsh teams clinically able to contain, weaken and then surge away in a final flourish. Gravell's hot-blooded charges to the post were complemented by the equally ferocious, yet sanguine, Fenwick who gave the impression of having iced spinach in his veins. No one had had international nerves so cool and steady since Barry John whose Welsh points record first Bennett, then Steve Fenwick, took to giddier heights.

J. J. Williams had won his first full cap in 1973, the year Bobby 'Duke' Windsor took over the Welsh hooking berth. Their careers, through two Lions tours and six years of top-flight rugby, were still flourishing at the end of the decade. J. J. Williams, retiring from the international arena in 1979 with thirty caps, was adept at the finely judged kick-ahead that turned his opposite numbers long enough for his exceptional speed to send him whistling past them. In South Africa in 1974 the hard grounds were made for his elegant, gazelle-like acceleration yet, in a wet New Zealand in 1977 he won equal praise, for there this former schoolboy outside-half bewildered those who expected the master of the chipped kick-on to do precisely that by, instead, dummying, feinting and swerving over the mud to score. His three superb tries against the Sixth Wallabies in 1975 were the best by any Welsh player since Maurice Richards's four in 1969, yet hardly more satisfying than another Australian present to Bobby Windsor who scored a try on his début against them in 1973. That would set a notable precedent because the Cross Keys specialist who had moved to Pontypool would, a season later, be supported for Wales by the shoulders of one of the oldest and one of the youngest players in Wales, his Pontypool props, A. G. 'Charlie' Faulkner and Graham Price.

The Pontypool front row — celebrated by the popular troubadour of Welsh rugby in the seventies, Max Boyce — was the rock-like base from which the formidable Welsh pack that was being assembled would build. Price was, within two seasons, the acknowledged master of his craft that Ray Prosser, Pontypool's rugged coach, had predicted. He, too, scored a try on his début in Paris showing how expertise in the tight need not preclude quick-wittedness and pace in open play by his booting and chasing of a loose ball. That remarkable score recalled the schoolboy track-star that Price had once been and it also gave notice that Welsh prop-forwards would seek to do more than labour anonymously for the knowledgeable recognition of front-row initiates. Incredibly, by the season's end, Tony Faulkner had joined his front-row comrades by bulldozing himself and a hapless Mike Gibson over Ireland's line. By this time the incredible was expected from the forwards minted in Gwent with Wales in mind, for Terry Cobner had joined the Welsh back-row, at the age of twenty-eight, in 1974. He had already broken the record of D. P. ('Ponty') Jones (1903-07) by captaining his club for the fifth successive winter — by 1978-79 season he had doubled that run. Cobner came late to the Welsh side, in the twilight of the careers of Morris and Taylor, and only because Tommy David withdrew against Scotland through injury. Cobner, however, kept his place until he, too, retired after captaining Wales in Australia. As strong in the maul as he showed in the mud of Twickenham in 1978, as he was fast and intelligent, which he had demonstrated on his first appearance against Scotland in 1974 when he finished off a Gerald Davies burst, the balding schoolteacher, 'Cob', was an outstanding motivator of men both by personal example and storming rhetoric. And what he did for Wales he went on to do for the Lions in 1977 where his handling of the pack's initial difficulties transformed them into the best British forward unit ever seen in that country. Tom David was unlucky enough to lose a place to Cobner but the squad system still allowed the piratical Pontypridd star to move into the 1976 Welsh side that won the Grand Slam when Cobner had to stand down. It was another case of a plethora of back-row talent for, in addition, there was that evergreen, versatile marauder Derek Quinnell who, when Allan Martin of Aberavon and Geoff Wheel of Swansea emerged as natural and complementary second-row men, could play at his preferred position of flanker or No. 8 as the occasion demanded, whilst faster destroyers, like Trevor Evans, Clive Burgess and Paul Ringer, moved in and out of Welsh XVs of these years with ease and distinction. Against Scotland in 1979 the Welsh back-row delivered the finest exposition of a rolling maul that any home country side had ever produced. Another Pontypool forward, Jeff Squire, who had transferred from Newport, led it — as he would lead Wales twelve months later — with Quinnell and Ringer in attendance, to demonstrate one more aspect of what was, by then, a Welsh side equipped to ring the changes on its varied skills. Lack of reserve cover was most apparent in the paucity of second-row forwards but this weakness was only seldom exposed because Martin proved, from 1973 to the decade's end, so long-serving. From 1974 the ex-schoolboy giant and shot-putter was assisted in his reaching for the skies in the increasingly crucial phase of line-out play by the tight work and ripping skills of the former soccer player, Geoff Wheel, whose commitment masked, yet never hid, amiability. Together these two enabled a pack strong in other positions to move confidently from the uncertainties of 1973 and 1974.

If 1975 marked the rebuilding of the Welsh XV, a great deal of credit for its rapid discovery of its potential lay with Mervyn Davies. After the 1971 expedition with the British Lions no doubts remained that the supple frame (6foot 4½inches and under 15 stone in 1972) of 'Merv the Swerve' was not only invaluable for line-out possession but was tough and resilient in any closer exchange. From 1972-73 this impeccable contribution to the more refined aspects of forward play was put to work in his native Swansea whose All Whites he led to fresher pastures from the ones to which they had grown accustomed. This lanky, rather languorous mover often looked a trifle slow around the field. He was not a dashing runner with the ball in the mould of the one man who was thought able to challenge him for the Test spot with the 1974 Lions, Andy Ripley of England. Both views were deceptive, for Mervyn Davies understood acutely the needs of No. 8 play in the modern game and intelligently appreciated shrewd coaching. 'You don't defend back there!' — he never forgot Ray Williams's injunction to him as he broke up from a lost scrum and retreated in the time-honoured fashion to the opposite corner flag — 'You defend in front of you!'. In accordance with this precept, only after everything possible had been offered in set-pieces should the No. 8 (one of the 'tight six', as he wrote) figure elsewhere and when he did it was not lame corner-flagging but his covering in defence and support in attack that marked him out. Davies plugged holes before any were drilled. His tackling in the open field was conclusive and in the last two season of international rugby that he played, there was no doubt that he was amongst the greatest back-row forwards of all time. He graduated from the secondary role he first played for glamorous London Welsh, where Taylor and Gray scavenged like jackals for every loose ball, until he initiated attacks himself, in concert with his pack or, more often, with consummate skill and timing, for Gareth Edwards to plunge for the line. Wales never dropped him and, already, when he pitched forward unconscious on Sunday 28 March 1976 in a W.R.U. Cup semi-final he had become the most-capped Welsh forward ever, with thirty-eight consecutive international appearances and two marvellous overseas tours for Britain to his credit. The brain haemorrhage that ended his playing days, and almost his life, so dramatically, prevented his making a third tour, in all likelihood as captain of the 1977 British Lions. He had, in the spring of 1976, just taken Wales to her second successive championship and her first Grand Slam since 1971.

It was a remarkable season all round: Phil Bennett who had been third choice against England until injury ruled out his rivals played all season to score more points (117) than any other Welshman overall or, with thirty-eight, in one season; J. P. R. Williams passed Billy Bancroft's number of appearances at full-back; Mervyn Davies outstripped Denzil Williams; and Gareth Edwards went beyond Ken Jones's forty-four caps. On top of all that Wales scored more points than at any time since 1908-09 when another Swansea captain, Billy Trew, guided Wales to a Grand Slam. The Welsh side, having knitted together over the summer in Japan, and acquired the art of the killing second-half surge, took a while to click into their form but once underway they proved irresistible to England and Scotland before meeting Ireland in Dublin where the 1974 side had only scraped a draw. True to their traditions the Irish threw sand into the Welsh engine which spluttered and coughed and stalled until, with even defeat a distinct possibility, it suddenly, in an eight-minute purple patch that saw Wales score three tries, fired and zoomed away. The final score made defeat, once quite near, look absurd. It was 34 to 9. Bennett scored his first try for Wales and though his kicking was deadly (three penalties and three conversions) as, with head modestly down, his toes dragged the turf in apologetic manner, after he stroked the ball over, it was his running that caught the eye, for the Llanelli sorcerer now fizzed and sparkled in the way his supporters knew was his true self. At one point, though it did not lead to a try, the ball rippled through innumerable Welsh hands, including those of the front row, in a breathtaking display that had the Irish spectators standing to applaud. France, goaded on by their pocket Napoleon, Jacques Fouroux, narrowly failed at Cardiff though a Welsh side below its best that day, and with early injuries to Mervyn Davies and Graham Price, revealed its character ('. . . we have so much confidence in our ability. This Welsh team just refuse to think of defeat — and with that kind of confidence, who can beat us?' said the Welsh captain) by hanging on to win the game, 19 - 13.

Like a gambler whose luck must turn, Phil Bennett, on a winning streak for Wales after years of triumph for Llanelli, now hit the jackpot. The legacy of Swansea's captain was a handsome one. When Cobner's prolonged illness prevented his captaining Wales after his one game against Argentina, Bennett took over for Wales. The side was now finely balanced. If injuries occurred the squad system, operating smoothly and inexorably at the Afan Lido, before insatiable Sunday afternoon camp-followers, to maintain the national *club* side, had reserves to call upon, whether veterans or raw recruits, whose role in the team was never an uncertain one. Scores were not so high nor was the mountain of France, playing for and winning the Grand Slam behind her steamroller pack, surmounted, but Wales were never absolutely down in any game. Critics, both press and public, seemed at times to ignore the difficulty of every international game in its own right. Lesser teams, and the relative weakness of the other home country sides cannot be gainsaid, can rise above their immediate limitations. It became important for national pride, especially that of forlorn England, to lower Welsh colours. All the more credit, then, to Wales that they retained the Triple Crown for the first time since 1909 by holding their enemies at crucial periods, blunting their rage and then striking like a cobra whose somnolence was no lethargy but a subtle strength.

The moment of the season came in Murrayfield where the Scottish team, a harsh test on their own soil, ran and ran to disrupt Welsh rhythm. J. P. R. Williams fell to deal with a ball on the left-hand side of the Welsh 25. The full-back sank to the ball not to kill it but, as forwards gathered with him, to turn it into possession for the alert Fenwick who ran to the open field and, at the right instant, gave to Gerald Davies who slashed in and out like a rapier, and fended-off like a ramrod, to rip open the Scottish cover. Bennett carried it on until Burcher, the Newport centre, now approaching the Scottish 25 towards the right touch-line, showed the improvization Wales treasured as much as classical skills when he bowled an overhead pass to the ever-intelligent Fenwick supporting on the inside and the Bridgend maestro, in the very instant of receiving it, magically finger-flicked the ball on to his captain who went right, side-stepped left, and with Scottish defenders too breathless or bemused to continue the chase, cruised effortlessly between the posts. Bennett lay, his chin cushioned on the ball, surveying the carnage that the whirlwind Welsh attack had left in its wake. This was a try to savour in the same way that the 1973 Barbarians had etched their scores on the memory.

For over a decade the actual shape of such an intricate movement had been available not only to those who were there or merely through the distortions of print and word-of-mouth. On 2 July 1969 the W.R.U. had accepted the offer of B.B.C. Wales to show, on a Sunday afternoon as a Welsh equivalent of the Saturday night soccer 'Match of the Day', a recording of a selected Welsh rugby game. Irritation in Wales at lack of the national sport's coverage would gradually disappear in the face of increased rugby on television and a developing sophistication of transmission. Tele-recordings tended to wrench the try or the spectacular passage out of the context of the game but, within its limitations, the sport had found a useful ally not only for its financial assistance but also in its shop-window role.

Rugby itself had now assumed, through its own attractiveness and its chair-bound audiences, greater commercial possibility. The sponsoring of clubs, competitions and the display of advertisements in grounds were both finally approved by the relevant authorities in the early 1970s. This allowed a substantial increase in revenue. By 1977, when Schweppes added its name to the W.R.U. Challenge Cup and club players had new flashes or insignia added to their famous colours, this major change could be visually discerned but its underlying problems remained ones for the I.B. and other Unions to consider deeply as the 1980s opened. It was no longer the payment of money, to clubs or individuals, that was now regarded as against rugby union practice but the precise nature of that payment and its eventual direction. For some the consequent definition of professionalism became blurred, if not in legal definition then in subsequent case law. In effect this problem was an old one yet its scale and particular type was new, the products of an altered relationship to a changing society.

Nothing was more symbolic, both inside and out, of these social and sporting links than the National Ground itself on which, over twelve years, almost £3 million was spent. During 1978 the new West Stand was ready for international games and the reconstruction programme, whose eventual aim was a 65,000 capacity, proceeded with the demolition of the old East Terrace, the rebuilding of which would go on in the 1979 close season. The project was, even before the centenary season proper, magnificent testimony to the arduous work, over years and years, done by the members of the Development Sub-committee. The decisions of principle and of risk that the W.R.U., through this committee, took were, undoubtedly, the most visionary and far-seeing in its whole history. A pitch built on river silt had become a magic carpet for Welsh merlins and, for the spectators, an act of faith that was fully justified. Major matters apart, the pernickety details to be sifted had stretched from lifts to the new ground safety regulations enforced by government in the mid-1970s, and on to the re-positioning of the turf itself. The Treasurer had told the 1971 A.G.M. in his own Presidential year that he was 'satisfied that the acceptance of these very heavy financial liabilities' had been the right policy since, even if another twenty years went before all was finished the W.R.U. would then have built 'a ground which will not only be a great earning asset for the benefit of Welsh rugby, but will be one of the finest rugby grounds in the world'. Entry to the ground was itself, by the late 1970s, a dramatic experience for the crowds craning up at the dinosaur-boned fabric of the exterior structure before moving into the bowl of sound

448

and tension that stretched and buzzed, and still sang, around the greener than ever pitch. The wonderment, a pride tinged with awe, that this National Ground generated among all Welsh followers was celebrated fittingly enough at the 1978 Cardiff National Eisteddfod, by the Dyfed farmer-poet, Dic Jones of Blaenannerch:

Daear hud yw'r erw hon,	(This acre of earth is magic,
Cartre cewri'r tair coron . . .	the home of the triple Triple Crown
Meca'r gêm yw cyrrau gwyrdd	heroes . . .
Stadiwm y llawr gwastadwyrdd,	the green-carpeted stadium
Daear werdd wedi'i hirhau	is the Mecca of the game,
A gwlith buddugoliaethau . . .	its lush turf nourished
	by the dew of victories . . .).

The Welsh national sport had its finest monument to one hundred years of struggle and achievement in this National Theatre of the Welsh people. 'I love the theatre, the arena' Gareth Edwards would confess, and even if a national Welsh playhouse failed to join other Welsh national institutions in this decade, the existence of the National Ground was some compensation for a people who love performance. The drama is, of course, circumscribed in rugby by set patterns. Yet once the eighty minutes is begun, like the play whose lines the actors know so well, the stress and the rhythm are always different, just as the outcome, that special tingle, is always unpredictable. The stage and the play remain and only the performers graduate from stumbling repertory farce to chillingly executed classicism.

The unassuming Phil Bennett, so long the understudy that he had, for a while, even understudied himself had, through grit and chance, given up his role as rugby's Hamlet in 1977. When he was chosen to take a record number of Welshmen — replacements took the chosen number to eighteen — to New Zealand as Lions captain, it seemed that, for him, slings and arrows were, finally, out of date. Yet outrageous misfortune showed no signs of retirement. New Zealand's skies emptied with rain all winter long until the wet Lions began to have a bedraggled look. 'Benny' was his players' true captain to the end but he and the backs, without J. P. R. Williams, Gareth Edwards and Gerald Davies, proved incapable of capitalizing on their forward superiority or in eliminating unforced error. The Lions, in a sharp reversal of recent British experience, lost the series by three Tests to one. John Dawes, who had returned as coach to the scene of his 1971 triumphs as captain, had a less happy experience this time. He wryly observed, 'We were only beaten once but lost three times in the Test matches'. Dawes's realism jarred down-under in the way it had occasionally done at home, but he had never elevated winning to the grim aim of some sporting nationalists. This view, given to the incredulous New Zealand press, was dismissed by Keith Quinn the New Zealand rugby commentator as 'a sentiment of old-world charm that has no place in modern sporting theory, where victory is the only winner and the only winner is victory'. That cold-eyed dismissal would sound after November 1978 even hollower in practice than it was in theory.

Before then, Dawes and his Welsh team would have dismissed the old adage that returning Welsh Lions would enjoy a poor season. In fact this had not happened in 1968-9 or 1971-2 and, emphatically, it did not in 1977-8. Probably no Grand Slam side has received, in the course of the season, more criticism of its jaded play although it was able, consistently, and in the heat of battle, to raise its game, forward and behind. They were fully aware, even if a rather blasé public were not, of their coach's instructions to play to enjoy themselves with as much spontaneity as circumstances would allow. The pride of this team demanded that it play this way but not, never, only to entertain. This galaxy of Welsh stars burned brightly with its own incandescent will for one more season. It played tight, when it needed, it danced out of reach when it was required, and it had someone in its ranks with that answer to whichever question was posed. England was the first hurdle. The day was dull, the ball wet and slippery and the scores restricted to penalty goals. The satisfaction of a hard-won victory was given a special burnish by the fact that Gareth Edwards, winning his fiftieth cap, had kicked England back through the driving rain, on one occasion with a wholly incredible narrow-angled, sixty-five yard touch-finder which thrust Wales back onto an offensive they never then relinquished, in a knowledgeable wet-weather performance that promised the receding hairline would be an optical illusion for a while yet. Against Scotland the Welsh team once again revealed their great strength: their unshakeable confidence in each other and their collective will to win, more particularly their ability to absorb punishment and then exert immense pressure of their own in a decisive ten-minute onslaught. On a bitterly cold February afternoon they moved suddenly from 8 - 7 to 22 - 7 in a scoring blizzard which was matched later that evening by a snowstorm that marooned thousands of supporters in hospitable conditions in and around Cardiff for three days. Although the Scots then exploited Welsh relaxation to pull back a further 7 points, Wales had outscored them by four tries to two. The first had come from an express-train dash and dive for the line from a scrummage twelve yards out. It was predictable, and the crowd buzzed with expectation as the scrum had formed, but its power and energy was always unpredictable when it eventually came, and it was totally unstoppable. The lunging scarlet-jersyed figure cradled the ball reverentially with his top hand before planting it over the line. It was the last of Gareth Edwards's twenty tries for his country. His appetite for the line had grown sharper over the years; that compulsive hunger would never be properly assuaged. He warmed even a sub-arctic day which suggested that the Welsh winter preferred freezing Gareth Edwards in perpetuity to losing him.

The Irish on their way to a possible Triple Crown did not really mind how Edwards was embalmed so long as it was on that March day in Dublin. Their improving side had a fly-half who delighted Welsh eyes with his bubbling play, though the bruising tactics of the Irish forwards were not quite as pleasing. J. P. R. Williams so far forgot his hippocratic principles as to late-tackle his friend Mike Gibson when commitment outstripped his judgement. The true mortician, however, was the deadly Fenwick. The ice-warrior from Taffs Well, unperturbed by a frenzied Irish crowd, kicked four penalties and scored the first of Wales's two tries to take sixteen out of the winning number of twenty, and thus equal Ireland's total score himself. Cobner had exhorted Wales to renewed forward power in the way he had done in New Zealand the previous summer. The team was, undeniably, wilting psychologically under the strain of encroaching age and the sheer loss of that inner energy which can be summoned up for only so long. They sat, speechless and exhausted, still in full kit, waiting for a collective return to the normal pace of rugby life before they left the dressing room together after one of the most mentally and physically draining matches ever played by any Wales team. This XV had dredged their last resources of experience and skill to pull away from a 13 - 13 stalemate to a final score of 20 - 16. What they had accomplished was not normal. This Welsh side was the first in anyone's history to win the Triple Crown in three successive years, and the toughest battle had been the last. Not the last for the Championship, though. Phil Bennett's cup would run over if France could be taken to bring a third 1970s Grand Slam to Wales. The giant French No. 8 Bastiat brought with him the nucleus of the 1977 French Grand Slammers with new scrum half Jerome Gallion ready to dispute, with the help of the viking Rives and the vulpine Skrela in an accomplished French back-row, Gareth Edwards's crown. The Welshman

451

had not announced his retirement yet. A warm, almost Parisian, spring day saw Wales reach half-time with a 13 - 7 lead. French fervour never recovered thereafter as Wales, composed and dominant, sewed up a 16 - 7 victory. France had scored their try and drop goal first, and early on, for a 7 points lead, but then Windsor took a ball against the head and Bennett ripped his side-stepping way over. The Welsh side ignited by Edwards, inspired by Bennett, played combined football of the highest order for ten minutes before the interval. Graham Price was ready, once, for a bullocking charge but decided instead to wait, hold and give to Edwards who dropped a goal. The second try came on the right when four players handled before the Welsh captain put a seal on a superb individual performance by streaking, low-crouched and hard, over the line, after a pass thrown miraculously by J. J. Williams from behind his right ear.

The Grand Slam captain had no intention of relinquishing club football but there were no peaks left for this modest, distinguished man to climb. He retired having scored a record 166 points during his twenty-nine international appearances. He would not go to Australia. Nor would Gareth Edwards, who left rugby as the most-capped Welsh player with fifty-three consecutive appearances. Terry Cobner went as captain but missed the last Test because of injury. On his return he joined the ranks of the ex-Internationals. One more record was left that season for this team of record-breakers. Gerald Davies scored a try in the Second Test at Sydney which, since he had also scored in the First, allowed him to equal Edwards's total of twenty tries. Gerald Davies was thirty-three. His first game for Wales had also been against Australia, at Cardiff in 1966; his last, in a side which he captained, was his forty-sixth appearance. Wales lost both games but Gerald Davies, from first to last, was a winner. Thomas Gerald Reames Davies left international rugby with the same quiet suddenness that had stranded opponents on the field of play. Everything he did carried the stamp of inner conviction. He had been a centre eleven times and a wing thirty-five times for his country, to make him the most capped three-quarter. It was as the greatest of many great Welsh wings that he will be remembered, for it was there on the flanks where he found, especially in the early to mid-1970s, that inch of extra space he needed to deploy his incomparable skills. Born at Llansaint, near Cydweli in Carmarthenshire, he had, as a schoolboy, the ability to overcome his relatively small stature (5feet 8inches and 11stone 8lb.) but it was under John Robins, who went as Assistant Manager to the 1966 Lions in New Zealand, that he emerged as the scintillating star of a gifted Loughborough

Colleges team. From then on, via Cardiff, Cambridge University, London Welsh and Cardiff again, where he captained the club in its centenary year, he was, apart from his own decision, a permanent fixture in the Welsh XV. Decision characterized him. Twice a Lion (1968 and 1971) and twice, by choice, not (in 1974 and 1977). He was, perhaps more than any Welsh International since 1945, deeply contemplative about his reasons for playing rugby far beyond his thinking about the technicalities of his own game. His autobiography was his own sharply chiselled work that strove hard to speak to his own people about his, and their, dreams. Together, the generations of Welsh who had fashioned the many-coloured dream coat of rugby to clothe their hard lives had fostered a human community whose memories coursed in common assumption through the veins of a man like Gerald Davies. He knew the wonderful absurdity of their visions: 'The essence of Welsh rugby . . . allows for displays of imaginative daring which go further than logic or any method should allow . . . and . . . a further dimension of perception and imagination which encourages inventiveness instead of . . . patterns and drills which tend towards the mechanical'.

His own upbringing, that of an industrial working-class village, yet one firmly Welsh-speaking and set still amidst green hills and the sea of Carmarthen Bay, mirrored the process of space and time through which the majority of Welsh people had passed into the modern world. The young Gerald Davies looked into the camera to question it, not to please it. He was, early, with his pinched-in face, close-cropped hair and buttoned-down collar, a physical throwback to the first Golden Era; and, late, now moustachioed, his collar turned up against his neck, hands in pockets when he was not snuggling them under his armpits, teetering on the balls of his feet, he could have wandered onto the wing from Arthur Gould's day. There were tries in his repertoire that no one else could have scored. Four in a Cup game at Pontypool Park for Cardiff in his final season were grabbed and created in a mixture of the opportunism, panache and determination that were Davies's hallmarks. His waiting, resigned immobility was that of a domestic cat whose quick pounce reveals the unforgettable instincts of the wild. He knew the physical risks and why they had to be faced and be overcome in his way. John Ormond, Welsh poet, and schoolboy wing, from a similar place and time, wrote, in his poem 'Salmon', lines whose applicability were never meant to be merely piscatorial:

> The river sucks them home.
> The lost past claims them. . .

They reaffirm the world,
The stars by which they ran,
Now this precise place holds them
Again . . .

Though hammering water
    Beats them back
Still their desire will not break.
They flourish, whip and kick,
    Tensile for their truth's
Sake, give to the miracle
Of their treadmill leaping
The illusion of the natural.
The present in torrential flow
    Nurtures its own
    Long undertow:

They work it, strike and streak again,
Filaments in suspense.
    The lost past shoots them
Into flight, out of their element,
In bright transilient sickle-blades
    Of light; . . .

Gerald Davies was poised on the field, *his* element, until the moment to switch and dart like a fish came. He sidestepped, at a speed whose rapidity still never made him lose control, to left or right, squeezing fearlessly through eye-of-needle gaps that no defence could cover for no one else could have gone through them. When his markers knew his intentions they could not master the execution of his desire; when he was checked in that one-to-one confrontation which comes to wing-threequarters more than other players he was supremely brave, moving in close and quickly before, ingeniously and bewilderingly, pausing, absolutely and fractionally, only to shoot away. Like the flickering tongue of a fly-eating lizard he was nakedly on show, and then retracted to his own satisfaction, all in an instant. His thighs were strong, despite a frail upper-body, so that he could, if held, break through any half-grasping hands whilst his own understanding of physical limitations, that would have made head-on, bone-crushing tackles either foolishly inept or, worse, counter-productive, never made him an easy man to elude. His exceptional pace could overtake flying opposite numbers; his tackle on Sillières in 1972 at

454

Cardiff was a masterpiece of Davies's art for the Frenchman was bound to score in the Taff-end corner if Gerald Davies had not rolled him, like a turtle, onto his back as he pounced from behind. Not enough was seen of his finishing, scalpel cuts to the opposition's hearts in his last few home internationals but the lurking, feline presence of Gerald Davies could instil a wary trepidation that let others in through less guarded entrances.

There was reason to expect this denuded Wales to succumb, if not completely, then surely marginally, during 1979 after so much talent had finally gone. And yet those who were replacements had been used already in Australia and, fairly settled, had come through the fiery furnace of the New Zealand game. Once again Wales found herself daring to play a young scrum-half, Terry Holmes, in preference to two British Lions, Brynmor Williams, himself capped in Australia, and Alun Lewis; and the disputatious debate over outside-halves temporarily turned around Gareth Davies and David Richards. Gerald Davies's place was filled by a new International, but 1977 Lion, Elgan Rees and other faces came into the Squad photographs. Wales lost, deservedly on the day, to a buzzing French side, in Paris, but this was only by one point and, with glittering prize following glittering prize, the new-look Wales were, again, the overall champions and holders of the fourth Triple Crown in a row. It was a fantastic end to a decade whose like Welsh rugby had never seen before. Ireland's challenge at the National Ground was strong enough to take them to 21 points, their highest score ever against Wales, but still they lost by 3 points. England had held Wales to 7 - 3 into the last quarter of the game before the Welsh captain had to limp off. Derek Quinnell now assumed command, and 20 more points demoralized England as a new generation of Welsh players came of age and J. J. Williams, since 1973 the national whippet, signed off with a final try-scoring flourish.

On the field was a perfect representation of the Welsh duality — the dapper, self-possessed West Walian Gareth Davies and the hefty, baseball-loving Cardiffian Terry Holmes. In the engine-room of the pack, at 6foot 4½inches and 16½ stone, was the thirty-three-year-old ex-Oxford Blue and British Lion Mike Roberts, who had been recalled, in place of the injured Wheel, for his eighth cap. He would see out this incomparable decade that he had helped inaugurate for Wales in 1971 by hurtling over for a 'six-inch' try. The mighty Roberts, born in Rhyl, could not have symbolized better the final, permanent arrival in Welsh rugby of North Wales where the decade, in terms of the game's growth and popularity north of Aberystwyth, had been momentous. From 1975-6 the Mid Wales clubs had formed their own District Union (with twelve clubs) leaving, by 1979, thirty-two clubs in the North Wales District. The expansion had been helped by increased television coverage in Wales but was founded on the game's rootedness in the schools where national success found the ready echo of emulation. There is no danger whatsoever that rugby will suffer a northern blight as in the 1930s. Rugby has now, truly, embraced every corner of Wales. This development was fittingly consummated by the accession of Gwyn Roblin, a Welsh Secondary Schoolboy cap from Port Talbot in the 1920s and, since the 1930s, a pillar of the game in the north, to the Presidency of the W.R.U. in 1979-80. That was the year when another North Walian, A. J. (Tony) Gray of Bangor, mentor to North Walian representative sides, became a national selector. Up in the stand was a man who with Tony Gray and Mike Roberts had made their London Welsh XV one of the great sides of all time. J. P. R. Williams, doctor and captain, fifty-two caps to his credit, had finished his international career not at the whistle's blast but, appropriately, in the thicket of play. He was the sole survivor that season of the 1969 Welsh XV in which he had first appeared at barely twenty years of age. Even at the end he was no immaculate touch-finder; his goal-kicking, tried sporadically, remained erratic; he was not the fastest man in his position in Wales and his enthusiasm could lead him into trouble rather than away from it. He was, nonetheless, a Welsh full-back without peer. Indomitable before thundering forwards whose strength he could match with his own (6foot 1inch and 15stone 5lb.) he made crowds, all over the world, suck in their breath to see him leap to pluck a high ball from the air when opponents advanced on him. Against Scotland in 1972 his jaw was fractured as a result. His defence never flinched. Behind successive Welsh sides his certainty added immeasurably to theirs. J. P. R. was the J.C.B. of Welsh rugby for a full decade. Indeed this charismatic, combative figure, who was unrivalled on the Lions tours of 1971 and 1974, seemed, in his play, an unlikely medical practitioner. His hair, fashionably long in the early seventies and tied back with a head-band, would stream behind the full-back as he careered messianically upfield. Or, socks down and hands bunched into fists, he would bend forward at the waist waiting expectantly, to buffalo his way into the next exciting piece of action. He relished the hard, bodily contact that forwards suffered. For him this penance was no endurance. At times he was drawn in almost beyond the sense of the game as *his* crushing need to penetrate or be stopped became paramount. Against Australia he was chosen, because of a spate of injuries, to play in the back-row. The junior tennis champion who could have played professional tennis was in love with rugby. Nobody communicated this better to the Welsh spectator.

He scored six tries for Wales from full-back, timing his block-busting runs into the line from almost any position to smash his way through. Against England he made it a positive habit with his first appetizer in 1970, and another one in 1972, followed by a full meal in 1976 when he scored twice, with a final try for dessert in 1977. The second of those two in 1976 saw J. P. R. as the extra man, move inside and plough his way, with Englishmen swarming round him, to the foot of the posts. His value from counter-attack to set-piece move was priceless in game after game. When his critics accused him of slowing-up or losing touch, the old faultless catcher and user of the ball would confound them. For Wales the one single instant that stands in relief amongst such constant contributions was the tackle he made to ensure the 1976 Grand Slam in Cardiff. J. P. R. Williams was an expert tackler, able to shepherd those faster or more skilled than himself, into his reach or disrupt them with ferocious body hugs. On 6 March 1976, however, with only minutes left and Wales a mere 6 points in the lead, Williams was out of position as a sizzling French attack sent Jean-Pierre Gourdon down the touch-line for an almost certain try. Gourdon was a big, power-packed runner and about to dive inside the corner flag when J. P. R. appeared, knowing that a straightforward tackle was pointless. Gourdon must have thought he was going to touch down until the very moment that J. P. R. Williams forearmed him bodily into touch. As the wing went sprawling over, the full-back, his feet planted squarely on the ground, clenched his hands and shook them in defiant, self-congratulatory triumph.

Yet this was a team player before all else. He had returned to Wales, as had those exiles of his youth in London, to lead his own home-town club, Bridgend, where ten years before he had first acquired a taste for the running game even before going to London. No one, least of all the beaten finalists, Pontypridd, begrudged the glory of Bridgend's centenary year that ended in April 1979 with the W.R.U. Challenge Cup in J. P. R. Williams's hands before an international capacity crowd. The game had been televised live for the first time. The century of Welsh rugby was drawing to a close not by regretting the past but with more vigour, ideas and interest in the game than ever before. With this enthusiasm and goodwill the problems in the sport, at domestic level anyway, could be solved, whatever they were. Story-book endings were in order for a game whose life-blood was the shaping of reality instead of succumbing to it.

The slow-burning resurgence of Welsh rugby from the early 1960s was on view both in the National Ground and in the shape of integrated Welsh teams; it was the same spirit that permeated club rugby, and the often embattled Welsh society that supported it, in the late 1970s. Here the symbolic team was Pontypridd, superbly drilled into a sparkling unit by the ex-centre, Joe Smith, and, despite severe losses to Rugby League, champions for two years running under the rousing, finger-wagging leadership of Tom David. The Taff Valley club had lost their ground to trunk road development at the end of the 1971 season but, with the aid of the local council, the self-sacrifice and hard work of committee men, those neglected, essential men everywhere, had put the club onto the path to a new, modern ground and three championships. The interaction of tradition and progress, of sport and society, of players and administrators, of spectators and press is now acting as a yeast in club after club. It is the connection between international glory and domestic pride that gave Welsh rugby its beginning and will, through the fostering of amateur, local rugby guarantee its continuity.

EXTRA TIME

THERE is no summation. After an account of what has been there is only anticipation of the future. Even as the new decade opened, the statisticians were still revising their figures, for Wales's convincing win over France in January 1980 broke the record of twenty-two consecutive championship victories at home set during the first Golden Era. Past and present intertwined again in March when Steve Fenwick, in winning his twenty-sixth cap against Scotland, broke Arthur Gould's 83-year-old record by becoming the most capped centre in Welsh rugby history. While Fenwick's menacing tranquillity was now sharpened by the razor-like skills of David Richards, Gareth Davies and Terry Holmes, it was the equally gifted and even younger Peter Morgan who appeared at the end of the season to spearhead Welsh rugby's thrust into its new century. He was the second International to come from Haverfordwest; his predecessor was Richard Summers, a member of the historic side of 1881 that had launched the first hundred years. A century later, there were far firmer grounds —as compared with the fragile, though ultimately vindicated optimism of 1881 — for welcoming the second hundred years with confident expectation. Certainly the W.R.U. had ended the 1970s by looking forward. Ray Williams relinquished his position as Coaching Organizer to become Centenary Officer and Deputy Secretary to Bill Clement for the latter's twenty-fifth, and final year, as Secretary. The detailed organization of the Centenary celebrations was thus put into Ray Williams's hands, whilst Ken Harris, leaving the International Board in 1979 after fourteen years, to be succeeded by Gwilym Treharne, concentrated his attention on the Chairmanship of the Centenary Committee. Although the intention of the Centenary Year was celebratory, the W.R.U. attached more serious objectives to it and, primarily, to the launching of a public appeal through their Charitable Fund to help rugby players and others connected with the game who have suffered serious personal misfortune through no fault of their own. Some of the £500,000 it is hoped to raise will be channelled into the grass roots of the game at School and Youth level to ensure the future, whilst other money raised through regular sources will be put to the completion of the National Ground whose setting will, over the 1980-81 season, 'celebrate the occasion, not only for the Union, but for the member clubs in a manner worthy of the place that the game occupies in the life of Wales'.

The Welsh contribution to the international game could have no better emblem than the holding of an International Board meeting in Wales, to coincide with the centenary date of the W.R.U.'s foundation, in March 1981. And there could be no more appropriate mark of Welsh links with the wider world than the production at that meeting of the re-written *Laws of the Game* to which Hermas Evans, Welsh representative since 1969, had brought, in his role of overseeing Chairman, the crystalline logic of a trained scientist as well as the passion of a life-long rugby devotee. It was enthusiasm for the game, fuelled by a clear perception that the taken-for-granted rules, with their arcane minutiae, were the underlying basis of all things connected with rugby football that fired him to wrestle with the prose of legislation in the interests of the poetry of rugby. The Laws will set the patterns within which the future rhythms will flow but the I.B. will, at this meeting in Wales, address itself, too, to those fundamental policy issues which might well alter the shape of the game which has spread so far around the world from its domestic origins. The Centenary year will, then, be one of international celebration, and not least on the national field with the new Welsh Coaching Organizer, John Dawes and the newly appointed Welsh Coach, John Lloyd, eager for zest and joy to accompany competitive seriousness in the game. Off the field, a W.R.U. conference for coaches and referees will accommodate these key figures from all over the globe. In this way the W.R.U. Committee will fulfil its stated intention of making a major contribution to the game in a world context. And Cliff Jones, who lit up a dark decade with his flitting brilliance, will, as thirty-third President of the Union, spearhead on behalf of the W.R.U. the celebration of the one hundred years that have created a thousand memories.

Welsh rugby is a rainy night at the end of the Llynfi valley watching Maesteg drive forward on their table-top ground; it is a sparkling Easter Monday in Swansea watching the Barbarians on their traditional, carefree tour; it is a cold Boxing Day on Cardiff's new ground as Pontypridd's grizzled veteran Bob Penberthy remembers over 750 first class games for his club since 1962 and leaps for more; it is the yell for the 'Scar-lets' that rebounds around Stradey; it is the rising crescendo of 'Come on the Po-art', the bass intimidation of 'Neath! Neath!', the drumming affirmation, for a beaten W.R.U. Cup semi-finalist, of 'Ebbw, Ebbw, Ebbw'; it is the youth coach, the ex-referee, the man who runs the line for the Athletic XV, the unsung, dedicated enthusiasts who turn up to offer their skills and knowledge, in all weathers, so that the game is never neglected at any level. It is men who bridge generations like Rhys E. Williams, still serving Crynant as club secretary after more than fifty years. It is seeing for the first time the boy who will 'play for Wales'; it is applauding your better opponents or, better still, your superior selves; it is the much-fingered programme, the rugby annuals, the pink 'uns, the torn tickets, the heated arguments, the warm reconciliations, the legendary trips, the cursed and blessed selectors, and, above all, the game which is, first and last, for the players and those who go to watch them. John Dawes remembered for himself what can, and should, apply for all — ' . . . there is so much enjoyment you can get from that eighty minutes if you're prepared to work at it in training and . . . in organization and coaching, that there's no price you can put on it. You can't buy it. The enjoyment from that eighty minutes is, in sport, the most I've ever had and . . . the magnificences of the game were something to be envied. We played, and displayed so much enjoyment for ourselves [and] the spectators . . . that they used to come . . . to enjoy . . . it'.

After the first century, there is another.

PHOTOGRAPHIC SECTION

1. Newport's invincible XV of the late 1870s, with the South Wales Challenge Cup.
Back row (left to right): T. Ponsford, W. Ponsford, W. Phillips (capt.), A. J. T. Goss, Horace Lyne (later President of the W.R.U.). *Middle row:* E. Jenkins, G. F. Harding, F. A. Goss, Ll. Evans, F. Phillips, Richard Mullock (with bowler hat and cane). *Front row:* R. H. Loane, G. Rosser, T. Spittle, C. H. Newman, C. F. Thompson

2. The first Welsh XV, 1881 — Richard Mullock's men
Back row (left to right): W. D. Phillips, G. F. Harding, R. Mullock (manager), F. Purdon, G. Darbishire, E. Treharne, R. D. G. Williams. *Middle row:* T. A. Rees, E. Peake, J. A. Bevan (capt.), B. E. Girling, B. B. Mann. *Front row:* L. Watkins, C. H. Newman, E. J. Lewis, R. H. B. Summers

Western Mail

3. Official opening of the Cardiff Arms Park grandstand, Boxing Day 1885

4. A. J. Gould — 'the great crack of Newport'

5. Frank Hancock, pioneer of the four three-quarter system

6. W. J. Bancroft — 'the great W.J.' — in Welsh trial jersey

7. Evan and David James — 'the curly-headed marmosets'

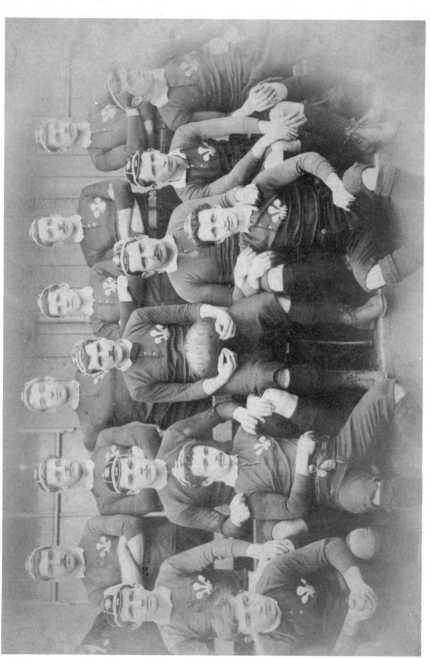

8.   Welsh XV v. Scotland, 1892

Back row (left to right): P. Bennett (Cardiff Harlequins), C. B. Nicholl (Llanelli), A. W. Boucher (Newport), T. C. Graham (Newport), W. H. Watts (Newport). *Middle row:* W. McCutcheon (Swansea), F. Mills (Swansea), A. J. Gould (Newport), J. Hannan (Newport), W. J. Bancroft (Swansea), T. W. Pearson (Cardiff). *Front row:* J. Conway Rees (Llanelli), D. James (Swansea), E. James

COMMITTEE
AND
OFFICERS

WELSH FOOTBALL
1901-1902.
UNION

MR. J. S. JONES.

MR. C. E. PARSONS.

MR. T. D. SCHOFIELD.

MR. W. WILKINS.

MR. G. HENRY.

MR. A. LLEWELLIN.

MR. J. GAMES.

MR. J. LIVINGSTONE.

MR. W. M. DOUGLAS.

MR. A. J. DAVIES.

SIR JOHN LLEWELYN.
BART.

MR. H. S. LYNE.

MR. A. J. GOULD.

MR. T. WILLIAMS.

MR. W. D. PHILLIPS.

MR. J. JARRETT.

MR. GEO. BOWEN.

MR. W. E. REES.

MR. D. H. BOWEN.

MR. H. J. SIMPSON.

10. Welsh XV v. New Zealand, 1905

Standing at rear: A. Llewellyn (touch-judge). *Back row (left to right):* Tom Williams (W.F.U.), J. F. Williams, George Travers, D. Jones, W. Joseph, R. T. Gabe, Sir J. T. D. Llewellyn, Bart. (President W.F.U.). *Middle row:* C. M. Pritchard, J. J. Hodges, W. M. Llewellyn, E. Gwyn Nicholls (capt.), H. B. Winfield, Cliff Pritchard, A. F. Harding. *Front row:* E. Morgan, R. M. Owen, P. F. Bush

11. New Zealand Touring Team, 1905

Back row (left to right): G. Gillett, S. Casey, D. McGregor, A. McDonald, F. Roberts. *Third row:* E. T. Harper, J. O'Sullivan, C. Seeling, R. G. Deans, W. Johnston, G. N. W. Nicholson, J. Corbett, W. Cunningham, F. Newton, J. Duncan (coach). *Second row:* H. L. Abbott, W. J. Wallace, G. A. Tyler, D. Gallaher (capt.), G. H. Dixon (manager), W. J. Stead (vice-capt.), W. Mackrell, F. Glasgow, W. S. Glenn. *Front row:* G. Hunter, H. G. Mynott, G. W. Smith, E. E. Booth, H. D. Thomson

ENGLAND v. WALES.

Mam Cymru : Lwc dda i ti, bachan.
Captain Nicholls : Wel, mi nawn yn gore, ta beth.
Dame Wales : Indeed to goodness—it's hoping you will go in and win I am.
Gwyn Nicholls (captain) : Well, all we can do, we will do, whatever.

12. Dame Wales, alias the *South Wales Daily News*, wishes the Welsh captain luck against England, 9 January 1904

THE MARCH OF THE MEN OF GWALIA.

DG John.

General Nicholls leads the warriors of Wales against the African invaders at the Battle of St. Helen's, A.D. 1906.

(With abject apologies to the Welsh Heroes whose beauty is herein thus brutally outraged.)

14. Welsh XV, 1907

Standing (left to right): Walter E. Rees (Sec. W.F.U.), J. Webb (Abertillery), W. Dowell (Newport), J. Brown (Cardiff), G. Travers (Pill Harriers), J. Evans (Llanelli), J. Watts (Llanelli), D. H. Bowen (W.F.U. linesman). *Middle row:* J. Evans (Pontypool), C. M. Pritchard (Newport), H. T. Maddocks (London Welsh), R. M. Owen (Swansea), R. T. Gabe (Cardiff), J. T. Williams (London Welsh), R. A. Gibbs (Cardiff). *In Front:* H. B. Winfield (Cardiff), W. J. Trew (Swansea)

Western Mail

15. Welsh XV v. France, 1911 — the last Triple Crown side for 39 years

Back row (left to right): A. J. Gould (touch-judge), Ivor Morgan, J. Webb, J. Pugsley, J. Birch, R. Thomas, Tom Evans, George Travers, D. J. Thomas. *Middle row:* Reggie Gibbs, Billy Spiller, J. L. Williams (capt.), Louis Dyke, Jack Bancroft. *In front:* R. M. Owen, W. J. Trew

16. 'The Terrible Eight', 1914

Standing (left to right): P. Jones, E. Morgan, H. Uzzell, T. C. Lloyd, D. Watts. *In front:* Tom Williams, Revd Alban Davies, W. E. Rees (Secretary W.F.U.), J. B. Jones

17.   Albert Jenkins — regarded by many, though not the Welsh selectors, as the greatest player of his era — in action against Scotland at Cardiff in 1923

Western Mail

THE "BIG FIVE" IN WELSH RUGBY FOOTBALL.

Mr. T. SCHOFIELD   Mr. J. JARRETT   Mr. I. D. THOMAS   Mr. R. P. THOMAS   Mr. D. B. JONES.
(Bridgend).   (Cwmbran).   (Cardiff).   (Llanelly).   (Swansea).

    Following a new rule passed at the last annual meeting of the Welsh Football Union a sub-committee of five will in future select the Welsh Rugby team for the international games. The above were on Monday evening appointed to act for this season.

18. The *Western Mail* highlights the appointment of the first 'Big Five', September 1924

19. Not Chicago mobsters, but members of the Welsh XV at the Forth Bridge, February 1926. *From left:* Tom Hopkins, Jack John, Sid Lawrence, Wick Powell, D. M. Jenkins. *In front:* Bobby Delahay and Bobby Jones

Western Mail

20.   The Llanelli Seven v. Ireland, 1928

Standing (left to right): Arthur John, Ernie Finch, Jack Auckland (club secretary), Albert Jenkins, Dai John. *In front:* Iorwerth Jones, Ivor Jones, Archie Skym

21.   J. D. Bartlett scores for Wales against England at St. Helen's, 1928

Central News London

22. The Prince of Wales is introduced to the 1933 Welsh side that is about to win at Twickenham for the first time. *Left to right:* Horace Lyne (President, W.R.U.), Watcyn Thomas (capt.), Vivian Jenkins, Wilfred Wooller, Archie Skym, Edgar Jones, Ronnie Boon, Claude Davey, Bryn Evans, Maurice Turnbull, Harry Bowcott

23. Cliff Jones scores for Wales in the 10 - 6 victory over Scotland at Cardiff, 1935

24. Welsh XV v. New Zealand, 1935

Standing (left to right): C. Gadney (referee), T. J. Rees, T. Williams, J. Lang, A. M. Rees, E. Watkins, D. J. Tarr, M. Moses (W.R.U.). *Middle Row:* V. G. J. Jenkins, H. Payne, G. Prosser, Claude Davey (capt.), Idwal Rees, W. Wooller, G. Rees-Jones. *In front:* Cliff Jones, H. Tanner

25. Welsh forwards in action during the memorable 1935 encounter with New Zealand. *Left to right:* Tom Rees, Trevor Williams, Jim Lang and Arthur Rees

26. Cardiff Arms Park on the occasion of the Wales v. Ireland match, 1932

27. 70,000 squeezed into the Arms Park to see Wales v. Ireland, 1936

28. Eleven players from the Cardiff club played for Wales during 1947-48 (including a record of 10 against England, Scotland and France. The 11th, Les Williams, played against Ireland). *Back row (left to right):* Les Williams, Cliff Davies, Gwyn Evans, Les Manfield, Frank Trott, Maldwyn James. *Front row:* Billy Cleaver, Haydn Tanner, Bleddyn Williams, Jack Matthews. *Inset:* Bill Tamplin

29. Glyn Davies sends Les Williams racing away for Wales's third try against England at Cardiff in 1949

30. Triple Crown XV, 1950

Standing (left to right): Ivor Jones (touch-judge); Rex Willis, Don Hayward, Roy John, Bob Evans, Malcolm Thomas, John Robins, Capt. M. J. Dowling (referee). *Middle row:* Ray Cale, Cliff Davies, Jack Matthews, John Gwilliam (capt.), Billy Cleaver, Ken Jones, Dai Davies. *In front:* Gerwyn Williams, Lewis Jones

© *Western Mail & Echo Ltd*

31. Malcolm Thomas, with Cliff Davies characteristically up in support, scores one of Wales's 5 tries against England at Swansea in 1951

32. Cliff Davies and John Gwilliam wonder what Roy John will do next against England in 1951

33. Roy John, lord of the line-out, against the 1951 Springboks, supported by John Gwilliam, Rees Stephens, Don Hayward and Dai Davies; van Wyk, far left, looks and marvels

34. The pace and the passion. Cliff Morgan spearheading Wales to victory and the Triple Crown at Dublin in 1952. Other Welsh players on view are: Roy John, John Gwilliam, Clem Thomas, W. A. Williams, and racing up in support, Alun Thomas

35. The record-breakers. Ken Jones, winning his 35th cap at St. Helen's in 1954, congratulated by W. J. Bancroft, himself the owner of 33 consecutive caps long before Ken was born

© *South Wales Evening Post*

36. Amazing grace. Alun Pask dramatically captured in mid-flight by the camera and Ian Laughland of Scotland in Wales's 11 – 3 victory at Cardiff in 1964

© *Sport and General Press Agency*

37.   St. Helen's, Swansea, venue of internationals from 1882 to 1954

38. Dewi Bebb plunges hungrily for the English line at Cardiff in 1961 as Dicky Jeeps (left) arrives too late, Cyril Davies (centre) supports, and Ken Richards (background) approves

39. The 1965 Triple Crown side

Standing (left to right): W. R. Gilliland (I.R.F.U.), N. R. Gale (Llanelli), A. E. I. Pask (Abertillery), J. R. Uzzell (Newport), S. J. Dawes (London Welsh), T. G. Price (Llanelli), K. A. Rowlands (Cardiff), D. Williams (Ebbw Vale), R. Waldron (Neath), B. Price (Newport), H. J. Morgan (Abertillery), R. Lewis (W.R.U. touch-judge). *Kneeling*: S. J. Watkins (Newport), G. J. Prothero (Bridgend), David Watkins (Newport), D. C. T. Rowlands (Pontypool, capt.), D. I. Bebb (Swansea)

40.   Perfectly fed by a prostrate David Watkins, D. K. Jones executes one of his favourite high dives in scoring against Scotland in 1966

41.   England's Budge Rogers and Bob Taylor reach for the sky as David Watkins clears at Twickenham in 1966

42. The first of twenty: Gareth Edwards's first international try, at Twickenham in 1968

43. Gareth Edwards, who possessed the the intuition of Owen, the strength of Powell, the technique of Tanner, the craft of Rowlands, the speed of Catchpole and the thrust of Going, dive-passed only when he had to. Against France in 1970 he had to. Wales won, 11 - 6.

44. King and Country — Barry John mesmerically on the move, with Gerald Davies and Keith Jarrett outside him, against Ireland at a partially demolished Arms Park in 1969

45. Grasping for the prize: the National Ground in the process of construction, 1969

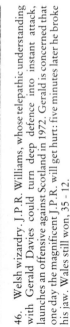

47. Terry Cobner's hairline and his Scottish opponents recede in tandem as 'Cob' brings especial joy to Pontypool by scoring on his début in 1974.

© *Western Mail & Echo Ltd.*

46. Welsh wizardry. J.P.R. Williams, whose telepathic understanding with Gerald Davies could turn deep defence into instant attack, launches an offensive against Scotland in 1972. Gerald is concerned that one day the magnificent J.P.R. will get hurt: five minutes later he broke his jaw. Wales still won, 35 - 12.

©*Western Mail & Echo Ltd.*

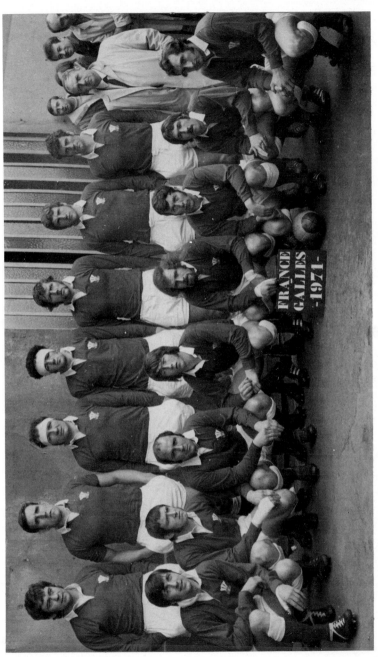

48. Grand Slam side v. France, 27 March 1971

Standing (left to right): A. J. Lewis (Ebbw Vale), W. D. Thomas (Llanelli), D. Williams (Ebbw Vale), T. M. Davies (London Welsh), M. G. Roberts (London Welsh), D. B. Llewelyn (Llanelli), W. D. Morris (Neath), Clive Rowlands (coach). *Kneeling*: B. John (Cardiff), J. C. Bevan (Cardiff College of Education & Cardiff), J. Young (Harrogate), J. P. R. Williams (London Welsh), J. Taylor (London Welsh), S. J. Dawes (London Welsh, capt.), T. G. R. Davies (London Welsh), G. O. Edwards (Cardiff), M. Bidder (touch-judge)

49.   Barry John holds court against England in 1969. Wales's margin of victory was majestic too — 30 - 9.

50.   'The No. 8 has to go forward. . . he is an attacking player. . . his job is to put pressure on the opposition by going at them. . . ball handling is very important.' Mervyn Davies practises what he preaches in the drawn game with France in 1974.

52. All the great Welsh half-backs could have achieved equal fame in the association game

51. Gareth

53. Gerald Davies has only five more yards to go!

54. Grand Slam and Triple Crown XV, 1978

Back row (left to right): J. D. Bevan (Aberavon), D. M. D. Rea (touch-judge — I.R.F.U.), M. Watkins (Cardiff), J. R. West (referee — I.R.F.U.), G. Price (Pontypool), J. Squire (Newport), D. L. Quinnell (Llanelli), A. J. Martin (Aberavon), G. A. D. Wheel (Swansea), A. G. Faulkner (Pontypool), T. J. Cobner (Pontypool), J. Richardson (Aberavon), A. W. Bevan (touch-judge — W.R.U.), T. P. Evans (Swansea). *Front row:* G. L. Evans (Newport), R. W. R. Gravell (Llanelli), T. G. R. Davies (Cardiff), J. P. R. Williams (Bridgend), P. Bennett (Llanelli, capt.), G. O. Edwards (Cardiff), R. W. Windsor (Pontypool), J. J. Williams (Llanelli), S. P. Fenwick (Bridgend), D. B. Williams (Newport)

55. W.R.U. Committee, 1980

Back row (*left to right*): Ray Williams (Deputy Secretary/Centenary Officer), E. D. Williams, H. C. Young, W. R. Pritchard, W. K. M. Jones, J. T. Richards, G. T. Bidder, W. G. Morgan, V. L. Price, M.B.E., B. K. Kempson (Assistant Secretary), G. Tregidon. *Middle row*: M. Jones, Alun Thomas, G. J. Treharne, Ieuan Evans, W. R. Morgan, M.B.E., A. J. Gray, Clive Rowlands, J. T. Rees, A. T. Vaux, J. M. Lewis (Assistant Coaching Organizer). *Front row*: K. W. Gwilym, Hermas Evans, Cliff Jones, O.B.E. (President 1980-81), Ivor Jones, C.B.E., K. M. Harris C.B.E. (Hon. Treasurer), Gwyn Roblin (President 1979-80), D. L. James, R. E. Williams, O. G. John, O.B.E., E. B. Davies, W. H. Clement, M.C., T.D. (Secretary). [*Absent*: J. W. Faull, R. H. Williams, K. A. Rowlands, D. Barnett, S. J. Dawes, O.B.E. (Coaching Organizer)]

APPENDIX I

WELSH INTERNATIONAL PLAYERS
1881-1980

Key: E — England, S — Scotland, I — Ireland, F — France, NZ — New Zealand, SA — South Africa, A — Australia, NSW — New South Wales, M — Maoris, R — Replacement

Alexander, E. P. *(Cambridge Univ. and Brecon)*, S. 85; E.S. 86; E.I. 87.

Alexander, W. H. *(Llwynypia)*, I.E. 98; E.S.I. 99; S.I. 1901.

Allen, C. P. *(Oxford Univ.)*, E.S. 84.

Andrews, F. G. *(Swansea)*, E.S. 84.

Andrews, F. *(Pontypool)*, SA. 1912, E.S.I. 1913.

Andrews, G. E. *(Newport)*, E.S. 1926; E.F.I. 1927.

Anthony, L. *(Neath)*, E.S.F. 1948.

Arnold, W. *(Swansea)*, S. 1903.

Arthur, C. S. *(Cardiff)*, I.M. 88; E. 91.

Arthur, T. *(Neath)*, S.I.F. 1927; E.S.I.F. 1929, 1930, 1931; SA. 1931; E.S. 1933.

Ashton, C. *(Aberavon)*, E.S.I. 1959, E.S.I. 1960; I. 1962.

Attewell, L. *(Newport)*, E.S.F. 1921.

Badger, O. *(Llanelli)*, E.S.I.95; E. 96.

Baker, A. *(Neath)*, I. 1921; E.S.I.F. 1923.

Baker, A. M. *(Newport)*, S.F. 1909; S. 1910.

Bancroft, J. *(Swansea)*, E.S.I.F. 1909, 1910; E.F.I. 1911; E.S.I. 1912; I. 1913; E.S.F. 1914.

Bancroft, W. J. *(Swansea)*, S.E.I. 90, 91, 92, 93, 94, 95, 96; E. 97; E.I. 98; E.S.I. 99, 1900, 1901

Bartlett, J. D. *(Llanelli and London Welsh)*, S. 1927; E.S. 1928.

Barlow, T. M. *(Cardiff)*, I. 84.

Barrell, R. *(Cardiff)*, S.I.F. 1929; I. 1933.

Bassett, A. *(Aberavon and Cardiff)*, I. 1934; E.S.I. 1935; E.S. 1938.

Bassett, J. *(Penarth)*, E.S.I.F. 1929; E.S.I. 1930; E.S.I.F.SA. 1931; E.S.I. 1932.

Bayliss, G. *(Pontypool)*, S. 1933.

Bebb, D. *(Carmarthen T.C. and Swansea)*, E.S.I.F. 1959; E.S.I.F.SA. 1960; E.S.I.F. 1961; I.E.S.F. 1962; E.F.NZ 1963; E.S.F.SA. 1964; E.I.S.F. 1965; F. 1966; E.S.I.F. 1967.

Beckingham, G. *(Cardiff)*, E.S. 1953; F. 1958.

Bennett, Ivor *(Aberavon)*, I. 1937.

Bennett, Phil *(Llanelli)*, F.(R) 1969; SA.S.F. 1970; S.(R) NZ. 1972; E.S.I.F.A. 1973; S.I.F.E. 1974; S.(R) I. 1975; E.S.I.F. 1976; I.F.E.S. 1977; E.S.I.F. 1978.

Bennett, P. *(Cardiff Harlequins)*, E.S. 91; S.I. 92.

Bergiers, R. T. E. *(Llanelli)*, E.S.F.NZ. 1972; E.S.I.F.A. 1973; E. 1974; I. 1975.

Bevan, Griff *(Llanelli)*, E. 1947.

Bevan, J. A. *(Cambridge Univ. and Newport)*, E. 81.

Bevan, J. C. *(Cardiff Coll. of Education and Cardiff)*, E.S.I.F. 1971; E.S.F.NZ. 1972; E.S. 1973.

Bevan, J. D. *(Aberavon)*, F.E.S.A 1975.

Bevan, Sid *(Swansea)*, I. 1904.

Beynon, Ben *(Swansea)*, E.S. 1920.

Beynon, E. *(Swansea)*, I.F. 1925.

Biggs, N. *(Cardiff Univ.)*, M. 88; I. 89; I. 92; E.S.I. 93; E.I. 94.

Biggs, S. *(Cardiff)*, E.S. 95; S. 96; E. 97; E.I. 98; S.I. 99; I. 1900.

Birch, J. *(Neath)*, S.F. 1911.

Birt, F. W. *(Newport)*, E.S. 1911, E.S.I.SA. 1912; E. 1913.

Bishop, E. H. *(Swansea)*, S. 89.

Blackmore, J. *(Abertillery)*, E. 1909.

Blake, J. *(Cardiff)*, E.S.I. 99, 1900, 1901.

Blakemore, R. E. *(Newport)*, E. 1947.

Bland, A. F. *(Cardiff)*, E.S.I. 87; M.S.I. 88; E.S.I. 90.

Blyth, L. *(Swansea)*, SA. 1951; E.S. 1952.

Blyth, W. R. *(Swansea)*, E. 1974; S. (R.) 1975; F.E.S.I. 1980.

Boon, R. W. *(Cardiff and Dunfermline)*, S.F. 1930; E.S.I.F.SA. 1931; E.S.I. 1932; E.I. 1933.

Booth, J. *(Pontymister)*, I. 98.

Boots, G. *(Newport)*, I.E. 98; I. 99; E.S.I. 1900, 1901, 1902, 1903; E. 1904.

Boucher, A. W. *(Newport)*, E.S.I. 92, 93; E. 94; E.S.I. 95; E.I. 96; E. 97.

Bowcott, H. M. *(Cardiff, Cambridge Univ. and London Welsh)*, S.I.F. 1929; E. 1930; E.S. 1931; E.I. 1933.

Bowdler, F. A. *(Cross Keys)*, NSW. 1927; E.S.I.F. 1928, 1929; E. 1930; SA. 1931; E.S.I. 1932; I. 1933.

Bowen, C. *(Llanelli)*, E.S.I. 96; E. 97.
Bowen, D. H. *(Llanelli)*, E. 83; E.S.86; E. 87.
Bowen, G. E. *(Swansea)*, S.I. 87, 88.
Bowen, W. *(Swansea)*, S.F. 1921; E.S.I.F. 1922.
Bowen, Wm. *(Swansea)*, E.S. 86; E.S.I. 87; M. 88; S.I. 89; E.S.I. 90; E.S. 91.
Brace, D. O. *(Newport, Oxford Univ. and Llanelli)*, E.S.I.F. 1956; E. 1957; S.I.F. 1960; I. 1961.
Braddock, K. J. *(Newbridge)*, A. 1966; S.I. 1967.
Bradshaw, K. *(Bridgend)*, E.S.I.F.SA. 1964; E.S.I.F. 1966.
Brewer, T. J. *(Newport, London Welsh and Oxford Univ.)*, E. 1950; E.S. 1955.
Brice, A. *(Aberavon and Cardiff)*, E.S.I. 99, 1900, 1901, 1902, 1903, 1904.
Bridie, R. *(Newport)*, I. 82.
Britton, G. R. *(Newport)*, S. 1961.
Broughton, A. *(Treorchy)*, NSW. 1927; S. 1929.
Brown, Archie *(Newport)*, I. 1921.
Brown, J. *(Cardiff)*, I. 1925.
Brown, Jack *(Cardiff)*, E.S.I. 1907; E.S.F. 1908; E. 1909.
Burcher, D. H. *(Newport and Cardiff)*, I.F.E.S. 1977.
Burgess, R. C. *(Ebbw Vale)*, I.F.E.S. 1977.
Burnett, R. *(Newport)*, E. 1953.
Burns, J. *(Cardiff)*, F.I. 1927.
Bush, P. F. *(Cardiff)*, NZ. 1905; E. 1906; SA. 1906; I. 1907; E.S. 1908; S.I. 1910.
Butler, E. T. *(Cambridge Univ. and Pontypool)*, F.E.S.I. 1980.

Cale, W. R. *(Newbridge and Pontypool)*, E.S.I. 1949; E.S.I.F. 1950.
Cattell, A. *(Llanelli)*, E. 82; S. 83.
Challinor, C. *(Neath)*, E. 1939.
Clapp, T. J. S. *(Nantyglo and Newport)*, I. 82; E.S. 83; E.S.I. 84; E.S. 85; S. 86; E.S.I. 87; S.I. 88.
Clare, J. *(Cardiff)*, E. 82.
Clarke, S. S. *(Neath)*, I. 82; I. 87.
Cleaver, W. B. *(Cardiff)*, E.S.F.I.A. 1947; E.S.F.I. 1948; I. 1949; E.S.I.F. 1950.
Clegg, B. *(Swansea)*, F. 1979.
Clement, W. H. *(Llanelli)*, E.S.I. 1937, 1938.
Cobner, T. J. *(Pontypool)*, S.I.F.E. 1974; F.E.S.I.A. 1975; E.S. 1976; F.E.S. 1977; E.S.I.F.A. *(1st Test)*, 1978.
Coldrick, A. P. *(Newport)*, E.S.I. 1911; E.S.F. 1912.
Coleman, E. *(Newport)*, E.S.I. 1949.
Coles, F. C. *(Pontypool)*, S.I.F. 1960.
Collins, J. *(Aberavon)*, A.E.S.F. 1958; E.S.I.F. 1959; E. 1960; F. 1961.
Collins, T. *(Mountain Ash)*, I. 1923.
Cook, T. *(Cardiff)*, S.I. 1949.
Cope, W. *(Cardiff, Blackheath and Cambridge Univ.)*, S. 96.

Cornish, F. H. *(Cardiff)*, E. 97; E.I. 98; I. 99.
Cornish, R. A. *(Cardiff)*, E.S. 1923; E. 1924; E.S.F. 1925; E.S.I.F. 1926.
Coslett, K. *(Aberavon)*, E.S.F. 1962.
Cowey, B. T. V. *(Newport)*, E.S.I. 1934; E. 1935.
Cresswell, B. *(Newport)*, E.S.I.F. 1960.
Cummins, W. *(Treorchy)*, E.S.I.F. 1922.
Cunningham, L. J. *(Aberavon)*, E.S.I.F. 1960; E.S.F.I. 1962; NZ. 1963; E.S.I.F.SA. 1964.

Daniel, D. J. *(Llanelli)*, S. 91; E.S.I. 94; E.I. 98; E.I. 99.
Daniel, L. *(Newport)*, S. 1970.
Darbishire, G. *(Bangor)*, E. 81.
Dauncey, F. H. *(Newport)*, E.S.I. 96.
Davey, Claude *(Swansea, Sale and London Welsh)*, F. 1930; E.S.I.F.SA. 1931; E.S.I. 1932; E.S. 1933; E.S.I. 1934, 1935; NZ. 1935; S. 1936; E.I. 1937, 1938.
David, R. *(Cardiff)*, I. 1907.
David, Tom *(Llanelli and Pontypridd)*, F.A. 1973; I.F. 1976.
Davidge, G. *(Newport)*, F. 1959; S.I.F.SA. 1960; E.S.I. 1961; F. 1962.
Davies, Rev. Alban *(Swansea and Llanelli)*, S.I.F. 1913; E.S.F.I. 1914.
Davies, A. C. *(London Welsh)*, I. 89.
Davies, B. *(Llanelli)*, E. 95, 96.
Davies, Bailey *(Oxford Univ. and Llanelli)*, E. 1907.
Davies, C. H. A. *(Cardiff and Llanelli)*, I. 1957; A.E.S.I. 1958; SA. 1960; E. 1961.
Davies, C. L. *(Cardiff)*, E.S.I. 1956.
Davies, C. R. *(Bedford and London Welsh)*, E. 1934.
Davies, Cliff *(Cardiff)*, S.F.I.A. 1947; E.S.F.I. 1948; F. 1949; E.S.I.F. 1950; E.S.I. 1951.
Davies, Daph. *(Bridgend)*, I. 1921, 1925.
Davies, D. Brian *(Llanelli)*, I. 1962; E.S. 1963.
Davies, D. G. *(Cardiff)*, E.S.1923.
Davies, D. H. *(Neath)*, S. 1904.
Davies, D. Hunt *(Aberavon)*, E. 1924.
Davies, D. Idwal *(Swansea)*, E. 1939.
Davies, D. J. *(Neath)*, I. 1962.
Davies, D. M. *(Somerset Police)*, E.S.I.F. 1950; E.S.I.F.SA. 1951; E.S.I.F. 1952; I.F.NZ. 1953; E. 1954.
Davies, E. *(Aberavon)*, A. 1947; I. 1948.
Davies, Evan *(Maesteg)*, NZ. 1919.
Davies, Ewan *(Cardiff)*, E.F. 1912.
Davies, George *(Swansea)*, E.S.I. 1900, 1901, 1905.
Davies, Glyn *(Pontypridd and Cambridge Univ.)*, S.A. 1947; E.S.F.I. 1948; E.S.F. 1949; E.S. 1951.
Davies, Graham *(Llanelli)*, F.I. 1921; F. 1925.
Davies, Gwyn *(Cardiff)*, F. 1928; E. 1929; S. 1930.
Davies, H. *(Swansea)*, I.E. 98; S.I. 1901.

Davies, H. J. *(Cambridge Univ. and Aberavon)*, E.S. 1959.
Davies, Harold *(Newport)*, S. 1924.
Davies, Howard *(Swansea and Llanelli)*, S.I. 1939; E.S.F.I. 1947.
Davies, Howell *(Neath)*, E.S. 1912.
Davies, J. H. *(Aberavon)*, I. 1923.
Davies, I. T. *(Llanelli)*, S.F.I. 1914.
Davies, Len *(Llanelli)*, F.S. 1954; I. 1955.
Davies, Leslie *(Swansea)*, S.I. 1939.
Davies, Lyn *(Bridgend)*, E.S.I. 1966.
Davies, M. J. *(Oxford Univ.)*, S.I. 1939.
Davies, N. Glyn *(London Welsh)*, E. 1955.
Davies, R. H. *(Oxford Univ. and London Welsh)*, S.I.F. 1957; A. 1958; E.S. 1962.
Davies, Stan. *(Treherbert)*, I. 1923.
Davies, Terry *(Swansea and Llanelli)*, E.S.I.F. 1953, 1957; A.E.S.F. 1958; E.S.I.F. 1959; E.SA. 1960; E.S.F. 1961.
Davies, T. G. R. *(Cardiff, Cambridge Univ. and London Welsh)*, A. 1966; E.S.I.F. 1967; E.S. 1968; S.I.F.NZ. *(1st and 2nd Tests)* A. 1969; E.S.I.F. 1971; E.S.F.NZ. 1972; E.S.I.F.A. 1973; S.F.E. 1974; F.E.S.I. 1975; E.S.I.F. 1976; I.F.E.S. 1977; E.S.I.A. *(1st and 2nd Tests)* 1978.
Davies, T. Mervyn *(London Welsh and Swansea)*, S.I.F.E.NZ. *(1st and 2nd Tests)* A. 1969; SA.S.E.I.F. 1970; E.S.I.F. 1971; E.S.F.NZ. 1972; E.S.I.F.A. 1973; S.I.F.E. 1974; F.E.S.I.A. 1975; E.S.I.F. 1976.
Davies, W. Gareth *(Cardiff)*, A. *(1st and 2nd Tests)* NZ. 1978; S.I.F.E. 1979; F.E.S. 1980.
Davies, W. *(Cardiff)*, S. 96.
Davies, Will *(Swansea)*, SA. 1931; E.S.I. 1932.
Davies, Willie *(Aberavon)*, S.I. 1912.
Davies, W. E. N. *(Cardiff)*, E.S.I. 1939.
Davies, W. T. H. *(Swansea and Headingley)*, I. 1936; E.I. 1937; E.S.I. 1939.
Davis, Clive *(Newbridge)*, A. *(2nd Test)* 1978.
Dawes, S. J. *(London Welsh)*, I.F.SA. 1964; E.S.I.F. 1965; A. 1966; I.F. 1968; E.NZ. *(2nd Test)* A. 1969; SA.S.E.I.F. 1970; E.S.I.F. 1971.
Day, H. T. *(Newport)*, I. 92; S.E. 93; S.I. 94.
Day, H. C. *(Newport)*, S.I.F. 1930; E.S. 1931.
Day, T. *(Swansea)*, E.S.I.F.SA. 1931; E.S.I. 1932; S.I. 1934; E.S.I. 1935.
Deacon, J. T. *(Swansea)*, I. 91; E.S.I. 92.
Delahay, W. J. *(Bridgend and Cardiff)*, E.S.I.F. 1922, 1923; NZ. 1924; E.S.I.F. 1925, 1926; S. 1927.
Devereux, D. *(Neath)*, A.E.S. 1958.
Dobson, G. *(Cardiff)*, S. 1900.
Dobson, T. *(Cardiff)*, E.I. 98; E.S. 99.
Donovan, A. *(Swansea)*, A. *(2nd Test)* 1978.
Douglas, W. M. *(Cardiff)*, E.S. 86, 87.
Dowell, W. *(Newport and Pontypool)*, E.S.I. 1907; E.S.I.F. 1908.
Dyke, J. C. M. *(Penarth)*, SA. 1906.

Dyke, L. M. *(Cardiff)*, I. 1910; S.I.F. 1911.

Edwards, A. B. *(London Welsh)*, E.S. 1955.
Edwards, Ben. *(Newport)*, I. 1951.
Edwards, D. *(Glynneath)*, E. 1921.
Edwards, Gareth *(Cardiff Coll. of Education and Cardiff)*, F.E.NZ. 1967; E.S.I.F. 1968; S.I.F.E.NZ. *(1st and 2nd Tests)* A. 1969; SA.S.E.I.F. 1970; E.S.I.F. 1971; E.S.F.NZ. 1972; E.S.I.F.A. 1973; S.I.F.E. 1974; F.E.S.I.A. 1975; E.S.I.F. 1976; I.F.E.S. 1977; E.S.I.F. 1978.
Elliott, J. E. *(Cardiff)*, I. 94; E.I. 98.
Elsey, W. J. *(Cardiff)*, E. 95.
Evans, A. C. *(Pontypool)*, E.I.F. 1924.
Evans, Bryn *(Swansea)*, S. 1933.
Evans, Bryn *(Llanelli)*, E.S. 1933; E.S.I. 1936; E. 1937.
Evans, Bryn E. *(Llanelli)*, E. 1920; E.S.I.F. 1922.
Evans, Colin *(Pontypool)*, E. 1960.
Evans, D. *(Penygraig)*, S.I. 96; E. 97; E. 98.
Evans, D. B. *(Swansea)*, E. 1926.
Evans, D. D. *(Barry and Old Caldeians)*, E. 1934.
Evans, D. P. *(Llanelli, Oxford Univ. and Ebbw Vale)*, SA. 1960.
Evans, D. W. *(Cardiff and Oxford Univ.)*, S.I. 89; E.I. 90; E. 91.
Evans, Emrys *(Llanelli)*, E. 1937; S.I. 1939.
Evans, Frank *(Llanelli)*, S. 1921.
Evans, Gareth *(Newport)*, F. (R) 1977; F.A. (R, 2nd Test) 1978.
Evans, G. *(Cardiff)*, E.S.F.I.A. 1947; E.S.F.I. 1948; E.S.I. 1949.
Evans, Iorwerth *(London Welsh)*, S.I. 1934.
Evans, Islwyn *(Swansea)*, E.S.I.F. 1922.
Evans, J. *(Llanelli)*, S.I. 96; E. 97.
Evans, J. *(Blaina)*, E. 1904.
Evans, J. *(Pontypool)*, E.S.I. 1907.
Evans, J. D. *(Cardiff)*, I.F. 1958.
Evans, J. Elwyn *(Llanelli)*, S. 1924.
Evans, John R. *(Newport)*, E. 1934.
Evans, O. J. *(Cardiff)*, E.S. 87; S.I. 88.
Evans, Peter *(Llanelli)*, E.F. 1951.
Evans, Rosser *(Cardiff)*, S. 89.
Evans, Ron. *(Bridgend)*, S.I.F. 1963.
Evans, R. T. *(Newport)*, F.I. 1947; E.S.I.F. 1950, 1951.
Evans, Tom *(Llanelli)*, I. 1906; E.S.I. 1907; I.A. 1908; E.S.I.F. 1909, 1910, 1911.
Evans, Tom *(Swansea)*, I. 1924.
Evans, T. G. *(London Welsh)*, SA.S.E.I. 1970; E.S.F. 1972.
Evans, T. P. *(Swansea)*, F.E.S.I.A. 1975; E.S.I.F. 1976; I. 1977.
Evans, Viv *(Neath)*, I.F.S. 1954.
Evans, Wynne *(Llanelli)*, A. 1958.
Evans, W. F. *(Rhymney and Cambridge Univ.)*, I. 82; S. 83.
Evans, W. G. *(Brynmawr)*, I. 1911.

Evans, W. H. *(Llwynypia)*, E.S.F.I. 1914.
Evans, W. J. *(Pontypool)*, S. 1947.
Evans, W. R. *(Bridgend, Cardiff and Cambridge Univ.)*, A.E.S.I.F. 1958; SA. 1960; E.S.I.F. 1961; E.S.I. 1962.
Evans, W. Rice *(Swansea)*, S. 90; E.S. 91.
Everson, W. A. *(Newport)*, S. 1926.

Faulkner, A. G. *(Pontypool)*, F.E.S.I.A. 1975; E.S.I.F. 1976; E.S.I.F.A. *(1st and 2nd Tests)* NZ. 1978; S.I.F. 1979.
Faull, J. *(Swansea)*, I.F. 1957; A.E.S.I.F. 1958; E.S.I. 1959; E.F. 1960.
Fear, A. *(Newport)*, S.I. 1934, 1935.
Fender, N. *(Cardiff)*, I.F. 1930; E.S.I.F. 1931.
Fenwick, S. P. *(Bridgend)*, F.E.S.A. 1975; E.S.I.F. 1976; I.F.E.S. 1977; E.S.I.F.A. *(1st and 2nd Tests)* NZ. 1978; S.I.F.E. 1979; F.E.S.I. 1980.
Finch, E. *(Llanelli)*, F.NZ. 1924; I.F. 1925; F. 1926; NSW. 1927; I. 1928.
Finlayson, A. A. J. *(Cardiff)*, I.F.E. 1974.
Fitzgerald, D. *(Cardiff)*, S.I. 94.
Ford, Ian *(Newport)*, E.S. 1959.
Ford, F. J. V. *(Welch Regt. and Newport)*, E. 1939.
Forward, A. *(Pontypool)*, S.SA. 1951; E.S.I.F. 1952.
Fowler, I. *(Llanelli)*, NZ. 1919.
Francis, G. *(Llanelli and Oxford Univ.)*, NZ. 1919; S. 1924.

Gabe, R. T. *(Llanelli and Cardiff)*, I. 1901; E.S.I. 1902, 1903, 1904, 1905; NZ. 1905; E.I.SA. 1906; E.S.I. 1907; E.S.I.F. 1908.
Gale, N. R. *(Swansea and Llanelli)*, I. 1960; E.S.I.NZ. 1963; E.S.I.F.SA. 1964; E.S.I.F. 1965, 1966, A. 1966; E.NZ. 1967; E. 1968; NZ. *(1st (R) and 2nd Tests)*; A. 1969.
Gallacher, Stuart *(Llanelli)*, F. 1970.
Garrett, R. M. *(Penarth)*, M. 88; S. 89; E.S.I. 90; S.I. 91; E. 92.
Geen, W. P. *(Oxford Univ. and Newport)*, SA. 1912; E.I. 1913.
George, E. *(Pontypridd and Cardiff)*, S.I. 95; E. 96.
Gething, Glyn *(Neath)*, F. 1913.
Gibbs, R. A. *(Cardiff)*, S.I. 1906; E.S. 1907; E.S.I.F. 1908, 1910, 1911.
Girling, B. E. *(Cardiff)*, E. 81.
Goldsworthy, S. *(Swansea)*, I. 84; E.S. 85.
Gore, J. *(Blaina)*, I.F.NZ. 1924; E. 1925.
Gore, W. *(Newbridge)*, S.F.I. 1947.
Gould, A. J. *(Newport, London Welsh and Richmond)*, E.S. 85, 86; E.S.I. 87; S. 88; I. 89; E.S.I. 90, 92, 93; E.S. 94; E.S.I. 95, 96; E. 97.
Gould, Bert *(Newport)*, I. 92; S.I. 93.
Gould, Bob *(Newport)*, E.I. 82; S. 83; E.S.I. 84; E.S. 85; E. 86; E.S. 87.
Graham, T. C. *(Newport)*, I. 90; S.I. 91; E.S. 92; E.S.I. 93; E.S. 94, 95.

Gravell, R. W. R. *(Llanelli)*, F.E.S.I.A. 1975; E.S.I.F. 1976; E.S.I.F.A. *(1st and 2nd Tests)* NZ. 1978; S.I. 1979.
Gray, A. J. *(London Welsh)*, E.S. 1968.
Greenslade, D. *(Newport)*, S. 1962.
Greville, H. *(Llanelli)*, A. 1947.
Griffin, Dr. A. *(Edinburgh Univ.)*, S. 83.
Griffiths, Clive *(Llanelli)*, E. (R) 1979.
Griffiths, D. *(Llanelli)*, M. 88; I. 89.
Griffiths, G. *(Llanelli)*, I. 89.
Griffiths, Gareth *(Cardiff)*, E.S.I.F.NZ. 1953; S.I.F. 1954; I.F. 1955; E.S. 1957.
Griffiths, V. M. *(Newport)*, S.I.F. 1924.
Gronow, B. *(Bridgend)*, F.E.S.I. 1910.
Gwilliam, J. A. *(Cambridge Univ., Newport, Edinburgh Wanderers and Gloucester)*, A. 1947; I. 1948; E.S.I.F. 1949, 1950; E.S.I.SA. 1951; E.S.I.F. 1952; E.I.F.NZ. 1953; E. 1954.
Gwynn, D. *(Swansea)*, E. 83; S. 87; E.I. 90; E.S. 91.
Gwynn, W. H. *(Swansea)*, E.S.I. 84; E.S. 85.

Hall, Ian *(Aberavon)*, NZ. 1967; SA.S.E. 1970; S. 1971; S.I.F. 1974.
Hancock, F. E. *(Cardiff)*, I. 84; E.S. 85; S. 86.
Hannan, J. *(Newport)*, M. 88; S.I. 89; E.S.I. 90; E. 91; E.S.I. 92, 93, 94, 95.
Harding, A. F. *(Cardiff and London Welsh)*, E.S.I. 1902, 1903, 1904, 1905; NZ. 1905; E.S.I.SA. 1906; I. 1907; E.S. 1908.
Harding, G. F. *(Newport)*, E. 81; I.E. 82; S. 83.
Harding, W. Rowe *(Swansea and Cambridge Univ.)*, E.S.I.F. 1923; I.F.NZ. 1924; I.F. 1925; E.I.F. 1926; E.S.I.F. 1927; E. 1928.
Harding, Theo. *(Newport)*, M. 88; S.I. 89.
Harris, D. J. E. *(Pontypridd and Cardiff)*, I.F. 1959; S.I.F.SA. 1960; E.S. 1961.
Harris, Tal. *(Aberavon)*, NSW. 1927.
Hathway, G. *(Newport)*, I.F. 1924.
Havard, Rev. W. T. *(Llanelli)*, NZ. 1919.
Hawkins, F. *(Pontypridd)*, I.F. 1912.
Hayward, Don *(Newbridge)*, E.F. 1949; E.S.I.F. 1950, 1951, 1952; SA. 1951.
Hayward, David *(Cardiff)*, E.NZ. 1963; S.I.F.SA. 1964.
Hayward, G. *(Swansea)*, S.I.F.A. 1908; E. 1909.
Hellings, R. *(Llwynypia)*, E. 97; E.I. 98; S.I. 99; E.I. 1900; E.S. 1901.
Herrera, R. C. *(Cross Keys)*, S.I.F. 1925; E.S.I.F. 1926; E. 1927.
Hiams, H. *(Swansea)*, I.F. 1912.
Hickman, Arthur *(Neath)*, E. 1930; S. 1933.
Hiddlestone, D. *(Neath)*, E.S.I.F. 1922; NZ. 1924.
Hill, A. F. *(Cardiff)*, S. 85; E.S. 86; M.S.I. 88; S. 89; S.I. 90; E.S.I. 93, 94.
Hinam, S. *(Cardiff)*, I. 1925; E.S.I.F. 1926.
Hinton, J. T. *(Cardiff)*, I. 84.
Hirst, G. L. *(Newport)*, S. 1912, 1913; E.S.F.I. 1914.

Hodder, W. *(Pontypool)*, E.S.F. 1921.
Hodges, J. J. *(Newport)*, E.S.I. 99, 1900; E.S. 1901; E.S.I. 1902, 1903; E.S. 1904; E.S.I.NZ. 1905; E.S.I. 1906.
Hodgson, G. T. R. *(Neath)*, I. 1962; E.S.I.F.NZ. 1963; E.S.I.F.SA. 1964; S.I.F. 1966; I. 1967.
Hollingdale, B. *(Swansea)*, SA. 1912; E. 1913.
Hollingdale, T. *(Neath)*, NSW. 1927; E.S.I.F. 1928; E. 1930.
Holmes, T. *(Cardiff)*, A. *(2nd Test)* NZ. 1978; S.I.F.E. 1979; F.E.S.I. 1980.
Hopkin, W. H. *(Newport)*, S. 1937.
Hopkins, Phil *(Swansea)*, A. 1908; E.I. 1909; E. 1910.
Hopkins, Ray *(Maesteg and Llanelli)*, E. (R) 1970.
Hopkins, T. *(Swansea)*, E.S.I.F. 1926.
Hopkins, W. J. *(Aberavon)*, E.S. 1925.
Howell, Bryn *(Llanelli)*, E. 1934.
Howells, Geoff *(Llanelli)*, E.S.I.F. 1957.
Howells, W. H. *(Swansea)*, S.I. 88.
Hughes, Dennis *(Newbridge)*, NZ. 1967; NZ. *(2nd Test)* 1969; SA.S.E.I. 1970.
Hughes, Gomer *(Penarth)*, E.S.I. 1934.
Hughes, H. *(Cardiff)*, S. 87, 89.
Hughes, Keith *(Camb. Univ. and London Welsh)*, I. 1970; A. 1973; S. 1974.
Hullin, W. *(Cardiff)*, S. 1967.
Hurrell, J. E. *(Newport)*, F. 1959.
Hutchinson, F. *(Neath)*, I. 94; S.I. 96.
Huxtable, R. *(Swansea)*, F.I. 1920.
Huzzey, H. V. P. *(Cardiff)*, E.I. 98; E.S.I. 99.
Hybart, A. J. *(Cardiff)*, E. 87.

Ingledew, H. M. *(Cardiff)*, I. 90; E.S. 91.
Isaacs, I. *(Cardiff)*, E.S. 1933.

Jackson, T. H. *(Swansea)*, E. 95.
James, Boyo *(Bridgend)*, E. 1968.
James, Carwyn *(Llanelli)*, A.F. 1958.
James, David *(Swansea)*, I. 91; S.I. 92; E. 99.
James, D. R. *(Treorchy)*, F.I. 1931.
James, Evan *(Swansea)*, S. 90; I. 91; S.I. 92; E. 99.
James, Maldwyn *(Cardiff)*, A. 1947; E.S.F.I. 1948.
James, T. O. *(Aberavon)*, I. 1935; S. 1937.
James, W. P. *(Aberavon)*, E.S. 1925.
Jarman, H. *(Newport)*, E.S.I. 1910; E. 1911.
Jarrett, K. S. *(Newport)*, E. 1967; E.S. 1968; S.I.F.E.NZ. *(1st and 2nd Tests)* A. 1969.
Jeffery J. J. *(Cardiff Coll. of Education and Newport)*, NZ. 1967.
Jenkins, Albert *(Llanelli)*, E.S.I.F. 1920; S.F. 1921; F. 1922; E.S.I.F. 1923; NZ. 1924; S.I. 1928.
Jenkins, A. M. *(Swansea)*, I. 95; E. 96.
Jenkins, D. *(Treorchy)*, E.S.I.F. 1926.
Jenkins, D. R. *(Swansea)*, NSW. 1927; E. 1929.

Jenkins, E. M. *(Aberavon)*, S.I.F.NSW. 1927; E.S.I.F. 1928; F. 1929; E.S.I.F. 1930, 1931; SA. 1931; E.S.I. 1932.
Jenkins, E. *(Newport)*, S.I. 1910.
Jenkins, J. C. *(London Welsh)*, SA. 1906.
Jenkins, L. *(Aberavon)*, S.F. 1923.
Jenkins, Leighton *(Caerleon T.C. and Newport)*, I. 1954; E.S.I.F. 1956.
Jenkins, V. G. J. *(Bridgend, Oxford Univ. and London Welsh)*, E.I. 1933; S.I. 1934; E.S.NZ. 1935; E.S.I. 1936; E. 1937; E.S. 1938; E. 1939.
Jenkins, W. *(Cardiff)*, I.F. 1912; S.I. 1913.
John, A. *(Llanelli)*, I. 1925; E.S.I. 1928.
John, B. *(Llanelli and Cardiff)*, A. 1966; S.NZ. 1967; E.S.I.F. 1968; S.I.F.E.NZ. *(1st and 2nd Tests)* A. 1969; SA.S.E.I. 1970; E.S.I.F. 1971; E.S.F. 1972.
John, D. E. *(Llanelli)*, F.I. 1923; E.S.I. 1928.
John, G. *(St. Luke's Coll., Exeter)*, E.F. 1954.
John, J. H. *(Swansea)*, E.S.I.F. 1926, 1927.
John, R. *(Neath)*, E.S.I.F. 1950, 1951; SA. 1951; E.S.I.F. 1952, 1953; NZ. 1953; E. 1954.
Johnson, T. *(Cardiff)*, E.F.I. 1921; E.S.F. 1923; E.S.NZ. 1924; E.S.F. 1925.
Johnson, W. D. *(Swansea)*, E. 1953.
Jones, A. H. *(Cardiff)*, E.S. 1933.
Jones, Bedwellty *(Abertillery)*, E.S.F.I. 1914.
Jones, Bert *(Llanelli)*, S.I. 1934.
Jones, Bob *(Llwynypia)*, I. 1901.
Jones, B. J. *(Newport)*, I.F. 1960.
Jones, Charles W. *(Bridgend)*, E.S.F. 1920.
Jones, Cliff W. *(Cambridge Univ. and Cardiff)*, E.S.I. 1934, 1935; NZ. 1935; E.S.I. 1936, 1938.
Jones, Dan *(Neath)*, NSW. 1927.
Jones, Dan *(Aberavon)*, E. 97.
Jones, David *(Swansea)*, E.F.I. 1947; E.S.I.F. 1949.
Jones, David *(Treherbert)*, E.S.I. 1902, 1903, 1905; NZ. 1905; E.S.SA. 1906.
Jones, David *(Newport)*, E.S.I.F. 1926; E. 1927.
Jones, Des *(Llanelli)*, E. 1948.
Jones, D. K. *(Llanelli, Oxford Univ. and Cardiff)*, E.S.F.I. 1962; E.F.NZ. 1963: E.S.SA. 1964; E.S.I.F. 1966.
Jones, David P. *(Pontypool)*, I. 1907.
Jones, D. N. Rocyn *(Newport, St. Mary's Hosp. and Cambridge Univ.)*, I. 1925.
Jones, Edgar *(Llanelli)*, F. 1930; E.S.I. 1933; E. 1935.
Jones, Elvet *(Llanelli)*, S. 1939.
Jones, Graham *(Cardiff)*, S. 1930; I. 1933.
Jones, Graham *(Ebbw Vale)*, S.I.F. 1963.
Jones, G. R. Rees- *(Oxford Univ. and London Welsh)*, E.S. 1934; I.NZ. 1935; E. 1936.
Jones, Harold *(Neath)*, E.S. 1929.
Jones, Harry *(Penygraig)*, S.I. 1902.
Jones, Howell *(Neath)*, I. 1904.
Jones, Howie *(Neath and Swansea)*, I.F. 1930.

Jones, Iorwerth *(Llanelli)*, NSW. 1927: E.S.I.F. 1928.

Jones, Ivor *(Llanelli)*, E.S. 1924; S.I.F.NSW. 1927; E.S.I.F. 1928, 1929; E.S. 1930.

Jones, I. C. *(Oxford Univ. and London Welsh)*, I. 1968.

Jones, J. *(Aberavon)*, E. 1901.

Jones, J. A. *(Cardiff)*, S. 83.

Jones, Jim *(Aberavon)*, NZ. 1919; E.S. 1920; S.F.I. 1921.

Jones, Joe *(Swansea)*, F. 1924.

Jones, J. P. *(Newport and Pontypool)*, A. 1908; E.S.I.F. 1909; E.F. 1910, 1912; I.F. 1913; I. 1920; E. 1921.

Jones, J. Strand *(Lampeter, Llanelli and Oxford Univ.)*, E.S.I. 1902; E.S. 1903.

Jones, Kenyon *(Monmouth and London Welsh)*, E. 1934.

Jones, Ken *(Newport)*, E.S.I.F.A. 1947; E.S.F.I. 1948, 1949, 1950, 1951; SA. 1951; E.S.I.F. 1952, 1953; NZ. 1953; E.S.I.F. 1954, 1955, 1956; S. 1957.

Jones, K. D. *(Cardiff)*, SA. 1960; E.S.I. 1961; E.F. 1962; E.S.I.NZ. 1963.

Jones, Lewis *(Devonport Services and Llanelli)*, E.S.I.F. 1950; E.S.SA. 1951; E.I.F. 1952.

Jones, Marsden *(Cardiff)*, E. 1921; NZ. 1924.

Jones, P. Baker *(Newport)*, S. 1921.

Jones, Percy *(Newport and Pontypool)*, SA. 1912; E.S.F. 1913; E.S.F.I. 1914.

Jones, R. *(Swansea)*, I. 1901; E. 1902; E.S.I. 1904; E. 1905; I.F.A. 1908; E.S.I.F. 1909; E.F. 1910.

Jones, Richard *(London Welsh)*, E. 1929.

Jones, R. B. *(Cambridge)*, E.S. 1933.

Jones, R. E. *(Coventry)*, F.E. 1967; S.I.F. 1968.

Jones, Robert *(Northampton)*, E.S.F. 1926.

Jones, Roy *(Swansea)*, NSW. 1927; F. 1928.

Jones, T. B. *(Newport)*, I.E. 82; S. 83, 84; E.S. 85.

Jones, Tom *(Newport)*, E.S.I.F. 1922; E.S. 1924.

Jones, J. 'Tuan' *(Pontypool)*, S. 1913.

Jones, W. *(Cardiff)*, E.I. 98.

Jones, W. Idris *(Llanelli and Cambridge Univ.)*, E.S.I.F. 1925.

Jones, W. J. *(Llanelli)*, I. 1924.

Jones, W. K. *(Cardiff)*, NZ. 1967; E.S.I.F. 1968.

Jones, Wyndham *(Mountain Ash)*, I. 1905.

Jones- Davies, T. E. *(London Welsh)*, E.I. 1930; E.S. 1931.

Jordan, H. M. *(Newport)*, E.S. 85; S. 89.

Joseph, W. *(Swansea)*, E.S.I. 1902, 1903; E.S. 1904; E.S.I.NZ. 1905; E.S.I.SA. 1906.

Jowett, F. *(Swansea)*, E. 1903.

Judd, S. *(Cardiff)*, E.S.I.F.NZ. 1953; E.S.F. 1954; E.S. 1955.

Judson, J. H. *(Llanelli)*, E. 82; S. 83.

Kedzlie, Q. D. *(Cardiff)*, S.I. 88.

Keen. L. *(Aberavon)*, F.E.S.I. 1980.

Knill, F. M. D. *(Cardiff)*, F. (R) 1976.

Lane, S. *(Cardiff)*, A. *(1st Test* (R) *and 2nd Test)* 1978; I. (R) 1979; S.I. 1980.

Lang, J. *(Llanelli)*, F.I. 1931; S.I. 1934; E.S.I.NZ. 1935; E.S.I. 1936; E. 1937.

Law, V. J. *(Newport)*, I. 1939.

Lawrence, S. *(Bridgend)*, S.I. 1925; S.I.F. 1926; E. 1927.

Legge, W. G. *(Newport)*, I. 1937, 1938.

Leleu, J. *(London Welsh and Swansea)*, E.S. 1959; F.SA. 1960.

Lemon, A. *(Neath)*, I. 1929; S.I.F. 1930; E.S.I.F.SA. 1931; E.S.I. 1932; I. 1933.

Lewis, Arthur *(Ebbw Vale)*, F. 1970; E.I.F. 1971; E.S.F. 1972; E.S.I.F. 1973.

Lewis, A. R. *(Abertillery)*, E.S.I.F.A. 1966; I. 1967.

Lewis, Bryn *(Swansea and Cambridge Univ.)*, I. 1912, 1913.

Lewis, J. M. C. *(Cardiff and Cambridge Univ.)*, E. 1912; S.I.F. 1913; E.S.F.I. 1914; I. 1921; E.S. 1923.

Lewis, C. P. *(Llandovery College)*, I.E. 82; S. 83; E.S. 84.

Lewis, D. H. *(Cardiff)*, E.S. 86.

Lewis, E. J. *(Llandovery Coll. and Cambridge Univ.)*, E. 81.

Lewis, Howell *(Swansea)*, S.I.F. 1913; E. 1914.

Lewis, J. *(Llanelli)*, I. 87.

Lewis, Mark *(Treorchy)*, F. 1913.

Lewis, Tom *(Cardiff)*, E. 1926; E.S. 1927.

Lewis, W. *(Llanelli)*, F. 1925.

Lewis, Geoffrey Windsor *(Cambridge Univ. and Richmond)*, E.S. 1960.

Lewis, Windsor H. *(Cambridge Univ. and London Welsh)*, I. 1926; E.I.F.NSW. 1927; F. 1928.

Llewelyn, Barry *(Newport and Llanelli)*, SA.S.E.I.F. 1970; E.S.I.F. 1971; E.S.F.NZ. 1972.

Llewellyn, P. D. *(Swansea)*, I.F.A. 1973; S.E. 1974.

Llewellyn, W. M. *(Llwynypia, London Welsh, Newport and Penygraig)*, E.S.I. 99, 1900, 1901, 1902; I. 1903; E.S.I. 1904, 1905; NZ. 1905.

Lloyd, D. J. *(Bridgend)*, E.S.I.F.A. 1966; S.I.F.E. 1967; S.I.F. 1968; S.I.F.E.NZ. *(1st Test)* A. 1969; F. 1970; E.S.F. 1972; E.S. 1973.

Lloyd, E. *(Llanelli)*, S. 95.

Lloyd, G. L. *(Newport)*, I. 96; S.I. 99; E.S. 1900; E.S. 1901; S.I. 1902; E.S.I. 1903.

Lloyd, Percy *(Llanelli)*, S.E. 90; E.I. 91.

Lloyd, R. *(Pontypool)*, S.I.F. 1913; E.S.F.I. 1914.

Lloyd, T. C. *(Neath)*, F. 1909; I.F. 1913; E.S.F.I. 1914.

Lloyd, T. *(Maesteg)*, I.F. 1953.

Lockwood, T. W. *(Newport)*, E.S.I. 87.

468

Long, Eddie *(Swansea)*, E.S.I. 1936; E.S. 1937; S.I. 1939.
Lyne, H. S. *(Newport)*, S. 83; E.S.I. 84; E. 85.

Maddocks, H. T. *(London Welsh)*, E.S.I. 1906; E.S. 1907; F. 1910.
Maddocks, K. *(Neath)*, E. 1957.
Main, D. R. *(London Welsh)*, E.S.I.F. 1959.
Mainwaring, H. J. *(Swansea)*, F. 1961.
Mainwaring, W. T. *(Aberavon)*, S.I.F.E.NZ. 1967; E. 1968.
Major, W. *(Maesteg)*, F. 1949; S. 1950.
Male, B. O. *(Cross Keys, Pontypool and Cardiff)*, F. 1921; S. 1923; S.I. 1924; E.S.I.F. 1927; S.I.F. 1928.
Manfield, L. *(Mountain Ash and Cardiff)*, S.I. 1939; A. 1947; E.S.F.I. 1948.
Mann, B. B. *(Cardiff)*, E. 81.
Mantle, J. *(Newport)*, E.SA. 1964.
Margrave, F. L. *(Llanelli)*, E.S. 84.
Martin, A. J. *(Aberavon)*, A. 1973; S.I. 1974; F.E.S.I.A. 1975; E.S.I.F. 1976; I.F.E.S. 1977; E.S.I.F.A. *(1st and 2nd Tests)* NZ. 1978; S.I.F.E. 1979; F.E.S.I. 1980.
Martin, W. J. *(Newport)*, I.F. 1912; NZ. 1919.
Mathias, R. *(Llanelli)*, F. 1970.
Matthews, Rev. A. A. *(Lampeter College)* S. 86.
Matthews, Chris *(Bridgend)*, I. 1939.
Matthews, Jack *(Cardiff)*, E.A. 1947; E.S.F. 1948; E.S.I.F. 1949, 1950, 1951.
McCall, B. E. W. *(Welch Regt. and Newport)*, E.S.I. 1936.
McCarley, A. *(Neath)*, E.S.I. 1938.
McCutcheon, W. *(Swansea and Oldham)*, S. 91; E.S. 92; E.S.I. 93; E. 94.
Meredith, A. *(Newport and Devonport Services)*, E.S.I. 1949.
Meredith, B. V. *(St. Luke's Coll., London Welsh and Newport)*, I.F.S. 1954; E.S.I.F. 1955, 1956, 1957; A.E.S.I. 1958; E.S.I.F. 1959; E.S.F. 1960; SA. 1960; E.S.I. 1961; E.S.F.I. 1962.
Meredith, C. C. *(Neath)*, S.NZ. 1953; E.I.F.S. 1954, 1955; E.I. 1956; E.S. 1957.
Meredith, J. *(Swansea)*, S.I. 88; E.S. 90.
Merry, G. E. *(Pill Harriers)*, I.F. 1912.
Michael, G. *(Swansea)*, E.S.F. 1923.
Michaelson, R. C. B. *(Cambridge Univ. and Aberavon)*, E. 1963.
Miller, F. *(Mountain Ash)*, I. 96; E.S.I. 1900, 1901.
Mills, F. *(Swansea and Cardiff)*, E.S.I. 92, 93, 94, 95; E. 96.
Moore, W. J. *(Bridgend)*, I. 1933.
Morgan, C. Henry *(Llanelli)*, I.F. 1957.
Morgan, C. I. *(Cardiff and Bective Rangers)*, I.F.SA. 1951; E.S.I.1952; S.I.F.NZ. 1953; E.S.I. 1954; E.S.I.F. 1955, 1956, 1957, 1958.
Morgan, D. *(Swansea)*, S. 85; E.S. 86; E.S.I. 87; I. 89.

Morgan, Dai *(Llanelli)*, I. 95; E. 96.
Morgan, D. R. *(Llanelli)*, E.S.F.I. 1962, 1963; NZ. 1963.
Morgan, E. *(Llanelli)*, I. 1920; E.S.F. 1921.
Morgan, E. *(London Welsh)*, E.S.I. 1902; I. 1903; E.S.I. 1904, 1905; NZ. 1905; E.S.I.SA. 1906; F. 1908.
Morgan, Eddie *(Swansea)*, E.S.I. 1938; E. 1939.
Morgan, Edgar *(Swansea)*, E.S.F.I. 1914.
Morgan, F. L. *(Llanelli)*, E.S.I. 1938; E. 1939.
Morgan, H. J. *(Abertillery)*, E.S.I.F. 1958; I.F. 1959; E. 1960; E.S.I.F. 1961, 1962; S.I.F. 1963; E.S.I.F. 1965, 1966; A. 1966.
Morgan, H. P. *(Cambridge Univ., Newport and Cardiff)*, E.S.I.F. 1956.
Morgan, Ivor *(Swansea)*, A. 1908; E.S.I.F. 1909. 1910; E.I.F. 1911; S. 1912.
Morgan, Jack *(Llanelli)*, SA. 1912; E. 1913.
Morgan, N. *(Newport)*, S.I.F. 1960.
Morgan, P. E. J. *(Aberavon)*, E.S.F. 1961.
Morgan, P. *(Llanelli)*, S. (R) I. 1980.
Morgan, T. *(Llanelli)*, I. 89.
Morgan, W. Guy *(Cambridge Univ., Guy's Hospital and Swansea)*, I.F. 1927; E.S.I.F. 1929; I.F. 1930.
Morgan, W. L. *(Cardiff)*, S. 1910.
Morley, J. C. *(Newport)*, E.S.I.F. 1929; E.I. 1930; E.S.F.I.SA. 1931; E.S.I. 1932.
Morris, G. L. *(Swansea)*, I.E. 82; S. 83; E.S. 84.
Morris, H. *(Cardiff)*, F. 1951; I.F. 1955.
Morris, Ivor *(Swansea)*, E.S. 1924.
Morris, R. R. *(Swansea and Bristol)*, S. 1933, 1937.
Morris, S. *(Cross Keys)*, E.S.I.F. 1920, 1922, 1923; E.S.F.NZ. 1924; E.S.F. 1925.
Morris, W. *(Abertillery)*, NZ. 1919; F. 1920, I. 1921.
Morris, William *(Llanelli)*, S.I. 96; E. 97.
Morris, W. D. *(Neath)*, F.E. 1967; E.S.I.F. 1968; S.I.F.E.NZ. *(1st and 2nd Tests)* A. 1969; SA.S.E.I.F. 1970; E.S.I.F. 1971; E.S.F.NZ. 1972; E.S.I.A. 1973; S.I.F.E. 1974.
Morris, W. J. *(Newport)*, S. 1965; F. 1966.
Morris, W. J. *(Pontypool)*, S.I. 1963.
Murphy, C. *(Cross Keys)*, E.S.I. 1935.

Nash, D. *(Ebbw Vale)*, SA. 1960; E.S.I.F. 1961; F. 1962.
Neill, W. *(Cardiff)*, S.I. 1904; E.S.I. 1905; E.I. 1907; E.S.I.F. 1908.
Newman, C. H. *(Newport and Durham)*, E. 81; I.E. 82; S. 83; E.S. 84, 85; E. 86, 87.
Nicholas, T. J. *(Cardiff)*, NZ. 1919.
Nicholl, C. B. *(Cambridge Univ. and Llanelli)*, I. 91; E.S.I. 92, 93; E.S. 94; E.S.I. 95, 96.
Nicholls, D. W. *(Llanelli)*, I. 94.
Nicholls, E. Gwyn *(Cardiff and Newport)*, S.I. 96; E. 97; E.I. 98; E.S.I. 99; S.I. 1900; E.S.I. 1901, 1902; I. 1903; E. 1904; I.NZ. 1905; E.S.I.SA. 1906.

469

Nicholls, F. E. *(Cardiff Harlequins)*, I. 92.
Nicholls, Howard *(Cardiff)*, I. 1958.
Nicholls, S. H. *(Cardiff)*, M. 88; S.I. 89, S. 91.
Norris, C. H. *(Cardiff)*, F. 1963; F. 1966.
Norton, W. B. *(Cardiff)*, I.E. 82; S. 83; E.S.I. 84.

O'Connor, A. *(Oxford Univ. and Aberavon)*, SA. 1960; E.S. 1961; F.I. 1962.
O'Connor, R. *(Aberavon)*, E. 1957.
O'Shea, J. P. *(Cardiff)*, S.I. 1967; S.I.F. 1968.
Oliver, G. *(Pontypool)*, E.S.I.F. 1920.
Osborne, W. T. *(Mountain Ash)*, E.S.I. 1902, 1903.
Ould, W. J. *(Cardiff)*, E.S. 1924.
Owen, Albert *(Swansea)*, E. 1924.
Owen, G. *(Newport)*, I.F. 1955; E.S.I.F. 1956.
Owen, R. M. *(Swansea)*, I. 1901; E.S.I. 1902, 1903, 1904, 1905, NZ. 1905; E.S.I.SA. 1906; E.S. 1907; I.F.A. 1908; E.S.I.F. 1909; E.F. 1910; E.S.I.F. 1911; E.S. 1912.

Packer, H. *(Newport)*, E. 91; S.I. 95; E.S.I. 96; E. 97.
Palmer, Frank *(Swansea)*, E.S.I. 1922.
Parfitt, F. C. *(Newport)*, E.S.I.93, 94; S. 95; S.I. 96.
Parker, D. *(Swansea)*, I.F.NZ. 1924; E.S.I.F. 1925; I.F. 1929; E. 1930.
Parker, T. *(Swansea)*, NZ. 1919; E.S.I. 1920; E.S.F.I. 1921, 1922; E.S.F. 1923.
Parker, W. *(Swansea)*, E.S. 99.
Parsons, G. *(Newport)*, E. 1947.
Pascoe, D. *(Bridgend)*, F.I. 1923.
Pask, A. E. I. *(Abertillery)*, F. 1961; E.S.F.I. 1962, 1963; NZ. 1963; E.S.I.F.SA. 1964; E.S.I.F. 1965, 1966; A. 1966; S.I. 1967.
Payne, G. W. *(Pontypridd)*, E.S.I. 1960.
Payne, H. *(Swansea)*, NZ. 1935.
Peacock, H. *(Newport)*, S.I.F. 1929, 1930.
Peake, E. *(Chepstow and Newport)*, E. 81.
Pearson, T. W. *(Cardiff and Newport)*, E.I. 91; E.S. 92; S.I. 94; E.S.I. 95; E. 97; E.I. 98; E. 1903.
Pegge, E. V. *(Neath)*, E. 91.
Perrett, F. *(Neath)*, SA. 1912; E.S.I.F. 1913.
Perrins, Vic *(Newport)*, SA.S. 1970.
Perry, W. *(Neath)*, 1911.
Phillips, Alan *(Cardiff)*, E. 1979; F.E.S.I. 1980.
Phillips, Bryn *(Aberavon)*, E.S.I.F. 1925; E. 1926.
Phillips, Harry *(Newport)*, E.S.I.F.NSW. 1927; E.S.I.F. 1928.
Phillips, H. *(Swansea)*, F. 1952.
Phillips, L. A. *(Newport)*, E.S.I. 1900; S. 1901.
Phillips, Percy *(Newport)*, E. 92; E.S.I. 93; E.S. 94.
Phillips, W. D. *(Cardiff)*, E. 81; I. 82; E.S.I. 84.
Plummer, R. C. S. *(Newport)*, S.I.F.SA. 1912; E. 1913.

Pook, T. *(Newport)*, S. 95.
Powell, Graham *(Ebbw Vale)*, I.F. 1957.
Powell, J. *(Cardiff)*, I. 1906.
Powell, J. *(Cardiff)*, I. 1923.
Powell, W. J. *(Cardiff)*, E.S.I.F. 1920.
Powell, R. W. *(Newport)*, S.I. 88.
Powell, W. C. *(London Welsh)*, S.I.F. 1926; E.I.F. 1927; S.I.F. 1928; E.S.I.F. 1929; S.I.F. 1930; E.S.I.F.SA. 1931; E.S.I. 1932, 1935.
Price, B. *(Newport)*, I.F. 1961; E.S. 1962; E.S.F.NZ. 1963; E.S.I.F. 1964; E.S.I.F. 1965, 1966; A. 1966; E.S.I.F. 1967, S.I.F.NZ. *(1st and 2nd Tests)* A. 1969.
Price, G. *(Pontypool)*, F.E.S.I.A. 1975; E.S.I.F. 1976; I.F.E.S. 1977; E.S.I.F.A. *(1st and 2nd Tests)* NZ. 1978; S.I.F.E. 1979; F.E.S.I. 1980.
Price, M. *(Pontypool)*, E.S.I.F. 1959, 1960; E. 1962.
Price, R. E. *(Weston)*, S.I. 1939.
Price, T. G. *(Llanelli)*, E.S.I.F. 1965; E.A. 1966; S.F. 1967.
Priday, A. J. *(Cardiff)*, I. 1958; I. 1961.
Pritchard, Cliff *(Newport and Pontypool)*, S.I. 1904; NZ. 1905; E.S. 1906.
Pritchard, C. M. *(Newport)*, I. 1904; E.S.NZ. 1905; E.S.I.SA. 1906; E.S.I.1907; E. 1908; E.F. 1910.
Pritchard, Cecil *(Pontypool)*, E.S.I.F. 1928, 1929.
Prosser, D. R. *(Neath)*, S.I. 1934.
Prosser, Glyn *(Neath)*, E.S.I.1934; NZ. 1935.
Prosser, J. *(Cardiff)*, I. 1921.
Prosser, R. *(Pontypool)*, S.F. 1956; E.S.I.F. 1957; A.E.S.I.F. 1958; E.S.I.F. 1959, 1960; SA. 1960; I.F. 1961.
Prothero, G. J. *(Bridgend)*, S.I.F. 1964; E.S.I.F. 1965, 1966.
Pryce-Jenkins, T. J. *(London Welsh)*, S.I. 88.
Pugh, C. *(Maesteg)*, E.S.I.F.NZ. 1924; E.S. 1925.
Pugsley, J. *(Cardiff)*, E.S.I. 1910; E.S.I.F. 1911.
Pullman, J. *(Neath)*, F. 1910.
Purdon, F. J. *(Newport)*, E. 81; I.E. 82; S. 83.

Quinnell, D. L. *(Llanelli)*, F. (R) NZ. 1972; E.S.A. 1973; S.F. 1974; E. (R) 1975; I. (R) F.E.S. 1977; E.S.I.F.A. *(1st Test)* NZ. 1978; S.I.F.E. 1979.

Radford, W. *(Newport)*, I. 1923.
Ralph, A. R. *(Newport)*, F.I.S.A. 1931; E.S.I. 1932.
Ramsey, S. H. *(Treorchy)*, E. 96; E. 1904.
Randell, R. *(Aberavon)*, I.F. 1924.
Raybould, W. H. *(Cambridge Univ., London Welsh and Newport)*, S.I.F.E.NZ. 1967; I.F. 1968; SA.E.I.F. (R) 1970.
Rees, Aeron *(Maesteg)*, NZ. 1919.
Rees, Alan *(Maesteg)*, E.S.F. 1962.

Rees, A. M. *(Cambridge Univ. and London Welsh)*, E. 1934; E.S.I. NZ. 1935; E.S.I. 1936, 1937; E.S. 1938.
Rees, B. I. *(Cambridge Univ. and London Welsh)*, S.I.F. 1967.
Rees, Clive *(London Welsh)*, I. 1974; A. 1975; NZ. 1978.
Rees, Doug *(Swansea)*, S.I.F. 1968.
Rees, Dan *(Swansea)*, E. 1900; E.S. 1903, 1905.
Rees, E. B. *(Swansea)*, NZ. 1919.
Rees, H. *(Cardiff)*, S.I. 1937; E.S.I. 1938.
Rees, H. Elgan *(Neath)*, S.I.F.E. 1979; F.E.S.I. 1980.
Rees, J. Conway *(Llanelli and Oxford Univ.)*, S. 92; E. 93, 94.
Rees, J. Idwal *(Cambridge Univ., Swansea and Edinburgh Wanderers)*, E.S.I. 1934; S.NZ. 1935; E.S.I. 1936, 1937, 1938.
Rees, Joe *(Swansea)*, E.S.I.F. 1920; E.S.I. 1921; E. 1922; E.I.F. 1923; E. 1924.
Rees, L. *(Cardiff)*, I. 1933.
Rees, Peter *(Llanelli)*, F.I. 1947.
Rees, P. M. *(Newport)*, E.S.I. 1961; I. 1964.
Rees, Tom *(Newport)*, S.I.NZ. 1935; E.S.I. 1936; E.S. 1937.
Rees, T. Aneurin *(Llandovery Coll. and Oxford Univ.)*, E. 81.
Rees, T. E. *(London Welsh)*, I.F. 1926; NSW. 1927; E. 1928.
Reeves, F. *(Cross Keys)*, F.I. 1920; E. 1921.
Rhapps, J. *(Penygraig)*, E. 97.
Richards, Bryan *(Swansea)*, F. 1960.
Richards, Cliff *(Pontypool)*, E.S.I.F. 1922; I. 1924.
Richards, D. S. *(Swansea)*, F.E. 1979; F.E.S.I. 1980.
Richards, E. S. *(Swansea)*, E. 85; S. 87.
Richards, Gwyn *(Cardiff)*, S. 1927.
Richards, Idris *(Cardiff)*, E.S.F. 1925.
Richards, Ken *(Bridgend and Cardiff)*, SA. 1960; E.S.I.F. 1961.
Richards, M. C. R. *(Cardiff)*, I.F. 1968, S.I.F.E.NZ. *(1st and 2nd Tests)* A. 1969.
Richards, Rees *(Aberavon)*, S.I.F. 1913.
Richards, Rex *(Cross Keys)*, F. 1956.
Richards, T. L. *(Maesteg)*,I. 1923.
Richardson, J. *(Aberavon)*, A. (R 2nd Test) 1978; E. 1979.
Rickard, A. *(Cardiff)*, F. 1924.
Ring, J. *(Aberavon)*, E. 1921.
Ringer, P. *(Ebbw Vale and Llanelli)*, NZ. 1978; S.I.F.E. 1979; F.E. 1980.
Roberts, Cyril *(Neath)*, I.F. 1958.
Roberts, D. E. A. *(London Welsh)*, E. 1930.
Roberts, E. *(Llanelli)*, E. 86; I. 87.
Roberts, E. J. *(Llanelli)*, S.I. 88; I. 89.
Roberts, H. M. *(Cardiff)*, SA. 1960; E.S.I.F. 1961; S.F. 1962; I. 1963.
Roberts, John *(Cambridge Univ. and Cardiff)*, E.S.I.F.NSW. 1927; E.S.I.F. 1928, 1929.

Roberts, M. G. *(Oxford Univ. and London Welsh)*, E.S.I.F. 1971; I.F. 1973; S. 1975; E. 1979.
Roberts, T. *(Risca and Newport)*, S.F.I. 1921; E.S.I.F. 1922; E.S. 1923.
Roberts, W. *(Oxford Univ. and Cardiff)*, E. 1929.
Robins, J. D. *(Birkenhead Park)*, E.S.I.F. 1950, 1951, E.I.F. 1953.
Robins, R. *(Pontypridd)*, S. 1953; S.F. 1954: E.S.I.F. 1955; E.F. 1956; E.S.I.F. 1957.
Robinson, I. R. *(Cardiff)*, F.E. 1974.
Roderick, W. B. *(Llanelli)*, I. 84.
Rosser, M. *(Penarth)*, S.F. 1924.
Rowlands, C. F. *(Aberavon)*, I. 1926.
Rowlands, D. C. T. *(Pontypool and Swansea)*, E.S.I.F.NZ. 1963; E.S.I.F.SA. 1964; E.S.I.F. 1965.
Rowlands, E. M. *(Lampeter College)*, E. 85.
Rowlands, Gwyn *(Cardiff)*, NZ. 1953; E.F. 1954; F. 1956.
Rowlands, K. A. *(Llanelli and Cardiff)*, F.I. 1962; I. 1963; I.F. 1965.
Rowles, G. R. *(Penarth)*, E. 92.

Samuel, D. *(Swansea)*, I. 91, 93.
Samuel, F. *(Mountain Ash)*, S.I.F. 1922.
Samuel, J. *(Swansea)*, I. 91.
Scourfield, T. *(Torquay)*, F. 1930.
Scrines, F. *(Swansea)*, E.S. 99; I. 1901.
Shanklin, J. L. *(London Welsh)*, F. 1970; NZ. 1972; I.F. 1973.
Shaw, G. *(Neath)*, NZ. 1972; E.S.I.F.A. 1973; S.I.F.E. 1974; I.F. 1977.
Shea, Jerry *(Pill Harriers and Newport)*, NZ. 1919; E.S. 1920; E. 1921.
Shell, R. C. *(Aberavon)*, A. (R) 1973.
Simpson, H. J. *(Cardiff)*, E.S.I. 84.
Skrimshire, R. T. *(Newport)*, E.S.I. 99.
Skym, A. *(Llanelli and Cardiff)*, E.S.I.F. 1928, 1930, 1931; SA. 1931; E.S.I. 1932, 1933; E. 1935.
Smith, J. S. *(Cardiff)*, E.I. 84; E. 85.
Sparks, B. *(Neath)*, I. 1954; E.F. 1955; E.S.I. 1956; S. 1957.
Spiller, W. *(Cardiff)*, S.I. 1910; E.S.I.F. 1911; E.F.SA. 1912; E. 1913.
Squire, J. *(Newport and Pontypool)*, I.F. 1977; E.S.I.F.A. *(1st Test)* NZ. 1978; S.I.F.E. 1979; F.E.S.I. 1980.
Stadden, W. H. *(Cardiff and Dewsbury)*, I. 84; E.S. 86; I. 87; M.S. 88; E.S. 90.
Stephens, G. *(Neath)*, E.S.I.F.SA. 1912; E.S.I.F. 1913; NZ. 1919.
Stephens, Rev. J. G. *(Llanelli)*, E.S.I.F. 1922.
Stephens, J. R. G. *(Neath)*, E.S.F.I. 1947; I. 1948; S.I.F. 1949; F.SA. 1951; E.S.I.F. 1952, 1953; NZ. 1953; E.I. 1954; E.S.I.F. 1955; S.I.F. 1956; E.S.I.F. 1957.
Stock, A. *(Newport)*, F.NZ. 1924; E.S. 1926.
Stone, P. *(Llanelli)*, F. 1949.

Summers, R. H. B. *(Haverfordwest)*, E. 81.
Sweet-Escott, R. B. *(Cardiff)*, S. 91; I. 94, 95.

Tamplin, W. E. *(Cardiff)*, S.I.F.A. 1947; E.S.F. 1948.
Tanner, Haydn *(Gowerton G.S., Swansea and Cardiff)*, NZ. 1935; E.S.I. 1936, 1937, 1938, 1939; E.S.F.I. 1947, 1948, 1949.
Tarr, D. J. *(Swansea)*, NZ. 1935.
Taylor, A. R. *(Cross Keys)*, I. 1937, 1938; E. 1939.
Taylor, C. G. *(Blackheath)*, E.S.I. 84; E.S. 85, 86; E.I. 87.
Taylor, J. *(London Welsh)*, S.I.F.E.NZ. 1967; I.F. 1968; S.I.F.E.NZ. *(1st Test)* A. 1969; F. 1970; E.S.I.F. 1971; E.S.F.NZ. 1972; E.S.I.F. 1973.
Thomas, Alun *(Cardiff and Llanelli)*, E.S.I.F. 1952; S.I.F. 1953; E.I.F. 1954; S.I.F. 1955.
Thomas, Alan *(Newport)*, NZ. 1963; E. 1964.
Thomas, B. *(Cambridge Univ. and Neath)*, E.S.I.F.NZ. 1963; E.S.I.F.SA. 1964; E. 1965; E.S.I. 1966; NZ. 1967; S.I.F.E.NZ. *(1st and 2nd Tests)* 1969.
Thomas, Bob *(Swansea)*, E.S.I. 1900; E. 1901.
Thomas, C. J. *(Newport)*, M.I. 88; S.I. 89; E.S.I. 90; E.I. 91.
Thomas, C. *(Bridgend)*, E.S. 1925.
Thomas, David *(Aberavon)*, I. 1961.
Thomas, D. *(Swansea)*, S.I. 1930; E.S.I. 1932; E.S. 1933; E. 1934; E.S.I. 1935.
Thomas, Denzil *(Llanelli)*, I. 1954.
Thomas, Dick *(Mountain Ash)*, SA. 1906; I.F. 1908; S. 1909.
Thomas, D. J. *(Swansea)*, E. 1904; A. 1908; E.S.I. 1910; E.S.I.F. 1911; E. 1912.
Thomas, D. L. *(Neath)*, E. 1937.
Thomas, E. *(Newport)*, S.I. 1904; S.I.F. 1909; F. 1910.
Thomas, Gethin *(Llanelli)*, E.S.I.F. 1923.
Thomas, George *(Newport)*, M. 88; I. 90; S. 91.
Thomas, Harold *(Llanelli)*, F. 1912.
Thomas, Harold *(Neath)*, E.S.I. 1936, 1937.
Thomas, H. W. *(Cambridge Univ. and Swansea)*, SA. 1912; E. 1913.
Thomas, Ifor *(Bryncethin)*, E. 1924.
Thomas, L. C. *(Cardiff)*, E.S. 85.
Thomas, M. C. *(Devonport Services and Newport)*, F. 1949; E.S.I.F. 1950, 1951; SA. 1951; E.S.I.F. 1952; E. 1953; E.S.I.F. 1956; E.S. 1957; E.S.I.F. 1958; I.F. 1959.
Thomas, Melbourne *(Bridgend and St. Bart's Hospital)*, NZ. 1919; S.F.I. 1921; F. 1923; E. 1924.
Thomas, R. C. C. *(Cambridge Univ. and Swansea)*, F. 1949; I.F. 1952; S.I.F.NZ. 1953; E.S.I.F. 1954; S.I. 1955; E.S.I. 1956; E. 1957; A.E.S.I.F. 1958; E.S.I.F. 1959.
Thomas, Rees *(Pontypool)*, F.I. 1909; S.F. 1911; E.S.SA. 1912; E. 1913.

Thomas, R. L. *(London Welsh)*, S.I. 89; I. 90; E.S.I. 91; E. 92.
Thomas, S. *(Llanelli)*, E.S. 90; I. 91.
Thomas, Watcyn *(Llanelli, Swansea and Waterloo)*, E.S.I.F. 1927; E. 1929; E.S.SA. 1931; E.S.I. 1932, 1933.
Thomas, W. D. *(Llanelli)*, A. 1966; S.I.F. 1968; E.NZ. *(2nd Test)* A. 1969; SA.S.E.I.F. 1970; E.S.I.F. 1971; E.S.F.NZ. 1972; E.S.I.F. 1973; E. 1974.
Thomas, W. J. *(Cardiff)*, F. 1961; F. 1963.
Thomas, W. H. *(Cambridge Univ., London Welsh and Llanelli)*, S. 85; E.S. 86, 87; S.I. 88; E.I. 90; S.I. 91.
Thomas, W. Ll. *(Newport)*, S. 94; E.I. 95.
Thomas, W. T. *(Abertillery)*, E. 1930.
Thompson, J. *(Cross Keys)*, E. 1923.
Towers, W. H. *(Swansea)*, I. 87; M. 88.
Travers, G. *(Pill Harriers and Newport)*, E.S.I. 1903, 1905; NZ. 1905; E.S.I.SA. 1906; E.S.I. 1907; E.S.I.F.A. 1908; E.S.I. 1909; S.I.F. 1911.
Travers, W. *(Newport)*, S.I. 1937; E.S.I. 1938, 1939; E.S.I.F. 1949.
Treharne, E. J. *(Cowbridge G.S. and Pontypridd)*, E. 81, 82.
Trew, W. J. *(Swansea)*, E.S.I. 1900; E.S. 1901; S. 1903, 1905, 1906; E.S. 1907; E.S.I.F.A. 1908; E.S.I.F. 1909; E.S.F. 1910; E.S.I.F. 1911; S. 1912; S.F. 1913.
Trott, R. F. *(Cardiff)*, E.S.F.I. 1948, 1949.
Truman, H. *(Llanelli)*, E. 1934, 1935.
Trump, L. *(Newport)*, E.S.I.F. 1912.
Turnbull, B. R. *(Cambridge Univ. and Cardiff)*, I. 1925; E.S. 1927; E.F. 1928; S. 1930.
Turnbull, M. J. *(Cardiff)*, E.I. 1933.

Uzzell, H. *(Newport)*, E.S.I.F. 1912; S.I.F. 1913; E.S.F.I. 1914, 1920.
Uzzell, R. J. *(Newport)*, NZ. 1963; E.S.I.F. 1965.

Vickery, W. *(Aberavon)*, E.S.I. 1938; E. 1939.
Vile, T. H. *(Newport)*, E.S. 1908; I. 1910; I.F.SA. 1912; E. 1913; S. 1921.
Vincent, H. C. *(Bangor)*, I. 82.

Waldron, R. *(Neath)*, E.S.I.F. 1965.
Waller, P. D. *(Newport)*, A. 1908; E.S.I.F. 1909; F. 1910.
Walters, Nathaniel 'Danny' *(Llanelli)*, E. 1902.
Wanbon, R. *(Aberavon)*, E. 1968.
Ward, W. *(Cross Keys)*, S.I. 1934.
Warlow, J. *(Llanelli)*, I. 1962.
Watkins, D. *(Newport)*, E.S.I.F.NZ. 1963; E.S.I.F.SA. 1964; E.S.I.F. 1965; 1966; E.I.F. 1967.
Watkins, Eddie *(Neath)*, E.S.I.F. 1924.
Watkins, E. *(Blaina)*, S.I.F. 1926.
Watkins, E. *(Cardiff)*, NZ. 1935; S.I. 1937; E.S.I. 1938; E.S. 1939.

Watkins, H. *(Llanelli)*, S.I. 1904; E.S.I. 1905; E. 1906.
Watkins, L. *(Oxford Univ., Llandaff and Cardiff)*, E. 81.
Watkins, S. J. *(Newport)*, S.I.F. 1964; E.S.I.F. 1965, 1966; A. 1966; E.S.I.F.NZ. 1967; E.S. 1968; S.I.F.E.NZ. *(1st Test)* 1969; E.I. 1970.
Watkins, W. *(Newport)*, F. 1959.
Watt, W. J. *(Llanelli)*, E. 1914.
Watts, D. *(Maesteg)*, E.S.F.I. 1914.
Watts, J. *(Llanelli)*, E.S.I. 1907; E.S.I.F.A. 1908; S.I.F. 1909.
Watts, Wallace *(Newport)*, E.S.I. 92, 93, 94; E.I. 95; E. 96.
Weaver, D. *(Swansea)*, E. 1964.
Webb, J. *(Abertillery)*, S. 1907; E.S.I.F.A. 1908; E.S.I.F. 1909, 1910, 1911; E.S. 1912.
Webb, J. E. *(Newport)*, M. 88; S. 89.
Wells, G. *(Cardiff)*, E.S. 1955; I.F. 1957; A.E.S. 1958.
Westacott, D. *(Cardiff)*, I. 1906.
Wetter, H. *(Newport)*, SA. 1912; E. 1913.
Wetter, J. *(Newport)*, S.F.I. 1914; E.S.F.I. 1920; E. 1921; I.NZ. 1924.
Wheel, G. *(Swansea)*, I.E. (R) 1974; F.E.I.A. 1975; E.S.I.F. 1976; I.E.S. 1977; E.S.I.F.A. *(1st and 2nd Tests)* NZ. 1978; S.I. 1979; F.E.S.I. 1980.
Wheeler, P. J. *(Aberavon)*, NZ. 1967; E. 1968.
Whitfield, J. *(Pill Harriers and Newport)*, NZ. 1919; E.S.I.F. 1920; E. 1921; E.S.I.F. 1922; S.I. 1924.
Whitson, G. *(Newport)*, F. 1956; S.I. 1960.
Williams, Bleddyn *(Cardiff)*, E.S.F.I.A. 1947; E.S.F.I. 1948; E.S.I. 1949; I.SA. 1951; S. 1952; E.S.I.F.NZ. 1953; S. 1954; E. 1955.
Williams, Bryn *(Llanelli)*, S.I.F. 1920.
Williams, C. *(Llanelli)*, NZ. 1924; E. 1925.
Williams, C. D. *(Oxford Univ., Cardiff and Neath)*, F. 1955; F. 1956.
Williams, Clive *(Aberavon and Swansea)*, E.S. 1977; F.E.S.I. 1980.
Williams, D. Brynmor *(Cardiff, Newport and Swansea)*, A. *(1st Test)* 1978.
Williams, D. *(Ebbw Vale)*, E.S.I.F. 1963, 1964; SA. 1964; E.S.I.F. 1965; E.S.I.A. 1966; E.F.NZ. 1967; E. 1968; S.I.F.E.NZ. *(1st and 2nd Tests)* A. 1969; SA.S.E.I. 1970; E.S.I.F. 1971.
Williams, Eddie *(Neath)*, NZ. 1924; F. 1952.
Williams, Evan *(Aberavon)*, E.S. 1925.
Williams, Frank L. *(Cardiff and Headingley)*, S.I.F. 1929; E.S.I.F. 1930; I.F.SA. 1931; E.S.I. 1932; I. 1933.
Williams, Gerwyn *(London Welsh)*, I.F. 1950; E.S.I.F.SA. 1951; E.S.I.F. 1952; NZ. 1953; E. 1954.
Williams, Griff *(Aberavon)*, E.S.I. 1936.
Williams, Jack *(Blaina)*, E.S.I.F. 1920; S.F.I. 1921.

Williams, J. F. *(London Welsh)*, I.NZ. 1905, S.SA. 1906.
Williams, J. J. *(Bridgend and Llanelli)*, F. (R) A. 1973; S.I.F.E. 1974; F.E.S.I.A. 1975; E.S.I.F. 1976; I.F.E.S. 1977; E.S.I.F.A. *(1st and 2nd Tests)* NZ. 1978; S.I.F.E. 1979.
Williams, J. L. *(Cardiff)*, SA. 1906; E.S.I. 1907, 1908; A. 1908; E.S.I.F. 1909; I. 1910; E.S.I.F. 1911.
Williams, J. P. R. *(St. Mary's Hospital, London Welsh and Bridgend)*, S.I.F.E.NZ. *(1st and 2nd Tests)* A. 1969; SA.S.E.I.F. 1970; E.S.I.F. 1971; E.S.F.NZ. 1972; E.S.I.F.A. 1973; S.I.F. 1974; F.E.S.I.A. 1975; E.S.I.F. 1976; I.F.E.S. 1977; E.S.I.F.A. *(1st and 2nd Tests)* NZ. 1978; S.I.F.E. 1979.
Williams, Lloyd *(Cardiff)*, S.I.F. 1957; E.S.I.F. 1958; E.S.I. 1959; F. 1961; E.S. 1962.
Williams, Les *(Llanelli and (Cardiff)*, E.S.F.I.A. 1947; I. 1948; E. 1949.
Williams, M. *(Newport)*, F. 1923.
Williams, Ossie *(Llanelli)*, E.S.A. 1947; E.S.F.I. 1948.
Williams, Ray *(Llanelli)*, S. 1954; F. 1957; A. 1958.
Williams, R. D. G. *(Cambridge Univ.)*, E. 81.
Williams, R. F. *(Cardiff)*, SA. 1912; E.S. 1913; I. 1914.
Williams, R. H. *(Llanelli)*, S.I.F. 1954; S.I.F. 1955; E.S.I. 1956; E.S.I.F. 1957; A.E.S.I.F. 1958; E.S.I.F. 1959; E. 1960.
Williams, Sid *(Aberavon)*, E.S.I. 1939.
Williams, Stan *(Llanelli)*, E.S.F.I. 1947; S.F. 1948.
Williams, Tom *(Pontypridd)*, I. 82.
Williams, T. *(Swansea)*, S.I. 88
Williams, Tom *(Swansea)*, I. 1912; F. 1913, E.S.F.I. 1914.
Williams, Trevor *(Cross Keys)*, S.I.NZ. 1935; E.S.I. 1936; S.I. 1937.
Williams, Tudor *(Swansea)*, F. 1921.
Williams, W. *(Crumlin)*, E.S.I.F. 1927.
Williams, W. A. *(Newport)*, I.F. 1952; E. 1953.
Williams, W.E.O. *(Cardiff)*, S.I. 87; S. 89; E.S. 90.
Williams, W. H. *(Pontymister)*, E.S.I. 1900; E. 1901.
Williams, W. O. *(Swansea)*, F.SA. 1951; E.S.I.F. 1952, 1953; NZ. 1953; E.S.I.F. 1954, 1955; E.S.I. 1956.
Williams, W. P. J. *(Neath)*, I.F. 1974.
Willis, W. R. *(Cardiff)*, E.S.I.F. 1950, 1951; SA. 1951; E.S. 1952; S.NZ. 1953; E.S.I.F. 1954, 1955.
Wiltshire, M. L. *(Aberavon)*, NZ. 1967; E.S.F. 1968.
Windsor, R. W. *(Pontypool)*, A. 1973; S.I.F.E. 1974; F.E.S.I.A. 1975; E.S.I.F. 1976; I.F.E.S. 1977; E.S.I.F.A. *(1st and 2nd Tests)* NZ. 1978; S.I.F. 1979.

473

Winfield, H. B. *(Cardiff)*, I. 1903; E.S.I. 1904; NZ. 1905; E.S.I.1906; S.I. 1907; E.S.I.F.A. 1908.
Winmill, S. *(Cross Keys)*, E.S.F.I. 1921.
Wooller, W. *(Rydal S., Sale, Cambridge Univ. and Cardiff)*, E.S.I. 1933, 1935; NZ. 1935: E.S.I. 1936, 1937; S.I. 1938; E.S.I. 1939.

Young, G. A. *(Cardiff)*, E.S. 86.
Young, J. *(Bridgend, Harrogate and London Welsh)*, S.I.F. 1968; S.I.F.E.N.Z. *(1st Test)* 1969; E.I.F. 1907; E.S.I.F. 1971; E.S.F.NZ. 1972; E.S.I.F. 1973.

APPENDIX II

WELSH INTERNATIONAL RESULTS
1881-1980

Note on scoring values:

In 1889 the I.B. ruled that 'a match shall be decided by a majority of points', with a try worth 2 points. The W.F.U. had already decided upon this in November 1888. England, however, who since 1886 had valued the try at 1 point, refused to recognize the I.B. until 1890, when the Arbitration Ruling of that year (discussed in Chapter 3) resolved the deadlock between the R.F.U. and I.B. by recommending that the I.B. adopt the rules and scoring methods of the R.F.U. For the 1890-1 season, therefore, the I.B., now representing the four Home Countries, accepted the reduction of the try to 1 point, but for the internationals played in 1892 and 1893 restored it to 2 points, and from 1894 reckoned it to be worth 3 points. Here its value remained until 1971-2 when it was upgraded to 4 points. The penalty goal has remained at 3 points since 1891-2; the dropped goal was reduced from 4 to 3 points in 1948-9.

AGAINST ENGLAND
Matches played 85   **Wales 40 wins, England 34, 11 drawn**

1880-81 ENGLAND 7G, 1DG, 6T to 0 *(Blackheath)*	1896-97 WALES 1G, 2T (11) to 0 *(Newport)*.
1881-82 No match.	1897-98 ENGLAND 1G, 3T (14) to 1DG, 1T (7) *(Blackheath)*.
1882-83 ENGLAND 2G, 4T to 0 *(Swansea)*.	
1883-84 ENGLAND 1G, 2T to 1G *(Leeds)*.	1898-99 WALES 4G, 2T (26) to 1T (3) *(Swansea)*.
1884-85 ENGLAND 1G, 4T to 1G, 1T *(Swansea)*.	1899-1900 WALES 2G, 1PG (13) to 1T (3) *(Gloucester)*.
1885-86 ENGLAND 1GM, 2T to 1G*(Blackheath)*.	1900-01 WALES 2G, 1T (13) to 0 *(Cardiff)*.
1886-87 DRAWN no score *(Llanelli)*.	1901-02 WALES 1PG, 2T (9) to 1G, 1T (8) *(Blackheath)*.
1887-88 and 1888-89 No matches.	
1889-90 WALES 1T (2) to 0 *(Dewsbury)*.	1902-03 WALES 3G, 2T (21) to 1G (5) *(Swansea)*.
1890-91 ENGLAND 2G, 1T (7) to 1G (3) *(Newport)*.	1903-04 DRAWN. ENGLAND 1G, 1PG, 2T (14) to WALES 2G, 1GM (14) *(Leicester)*.
1891-92 ENGLAND 3G, 1T (17) to 0 *(Blackheath)*.	
	1904-05 WALES 2G, 5T (25) to 0 *(Cardiff)*.
1892-93 WALES 1G, 1PG, 2T (12) to 1G, 3T (11) *(Cardiff)*.	1905-06 WALES 2G, 2T (16) to 1T (3) *(Richmond)*.
1893-94 ENGLAND 4G, 1GM (24) to 1T (3) *(Birkenhead)*.	1906-07 WALES 2G, 4T (22) to 0 *(Swansea)*.
	1907-08 WALES 3G, 1DG, 1PG, 2T (28) to 3G, 1T (18) *(Bristol)*.
1894-95 ENGLAND 1G, 3T (14) to 2T (6) *(Swansea)*.	
	1908-09 WALES 1G, 1T (8) to 0 *(Cardiff)*.
1895-96 ENGLAND 2G, 5T (25) to 0 *(Blackheath)*.	1909-10 ENGLAND 1G, 1PG, 1T (11) to 2T (6) *(Twickenham)*.

1910-11	**WALES** 1PG, 4T (15) to 1G, 2T (11) *(Swansea)*.
1911-12	**ENGLAND** 1G, 1T (8) to 0 *(Twickenham)*.
1912-13	**ENGLAND** 1G, 1DG, 1T (12) to 0 *(Cardiff)*.
1913-14	**ENGLAND** 2G (10) to 1G, 1DG (9) *(Twickenham)*.
1919-20	**WALES** 1G, 2DG, 1PG, 1T (19) to 1G (5) *(Swansea)*.
1920-21	**ENGLAND** 1G, 1DG, 3T (18) to 1T (3) *(Twickenham)*.
1921-22	**WALES** 2G, 6T (28) to 2T (6) *(Cardiff)*.
1922-23	**ENGLAND** 1DG, 1T (7) to 1T (3) *(Twickenham)*.
1923-24	**ENGLAND** 1G, 4T (17) to 3T (9) *(Swansea)*.
1924-25	**ENGLAND** 1PG, 3T (12) to 2T (6) *(Twickenham)*.
1925-26	**DRAWN** 1T (3) each *(Cardiff)*.
1926-27	**ENGLAND** 1G, 1PG, 1GM (11) to 1PG, 2T (9) *(Twickenham)*.
1927-28	**ENGLAND** 2G, (10) to 1G, 1T (8) *(Swansea)*.
1928-29	**ENGLAND** 1G, 1T (8) to 1T (3) *(Twickenham)*.
1929-30	**ENGLAND** 1G, 1PG, 1T (11) to 1T (3) *(Cardiff)*.
1930-31	**DRAWN.** ENGLAND 1G, 2PG (11) WALES 1G, 1GM, 1T (11) *(Twickenham)*.
1931-32	**WALES** 1G, 1DG, 1PG (12) to 1G (5) *(Swansea)*.
1932-33	**WALES** 1DG, 1T (7) to 1T (3) *(Twickenham)*.
1933-34	**ENGLAND** 3T (9) to 0 *(Cardiff)*.
1934-35	**DRAWN.** ENGLAND 1PG (3) WALES 1T (3) *(Twickenham)*.
1935-36	**DRAWN** no score *(Swansea)*.
1936-37	**ENGLAND** 1DG (4) to 1T (3) *(Twickenham)*.
1937-38	**WALES** 1G, 2PG, 1T (14) to 1G, 1T (8) *(Cardiff)*.
1938-39	**ENGLAND** 1T (3) to 0 *(Twickenham)*.
1946-47	**ENGLAND** 1G, 1DG (9) to 2T (6) *(Cardiff)*.
1947-48	**DRAWN.** ENGLAND 1PG (3), WALES 1T (3) *(Twickenham)*.
(DROPPED GOAL REVALUED TO 3 Pts.)	
1948-49	**WALES** 3T (9) to 1DG (3) *(Cardiff)*.
1949-50	**WALES** 1G, 1PG, 1T (11) to 1G (5) *(Twickenham)*.
1950-51	**WALES** 4G, 1T (23) to 1G (5) *(Swansea)*.

1951-52	**WALES** 1G, 1T (8) to 2T (6) *(Twickenham)*.
1952-53	**ENGLAND** 1G, 1PG (8) to 1PG (3) *(Cardiff)*.
1953-54	**ENGLAND** 3T (9) to 1PG, 1T (6) *(Twickenham)*.
1954-55	**WALES** 1PG (3) to 0 *(Cardiff)*.
1955-56	**WALES** 1G, 1T (8) to 1PG (3) *(Twickenham)*.
1956-57	**ENGLAND** 1PG (3) to 0 *(Cardiff)*.
1957-58	**DRAWN.** ENGLAND 1T (3), WALES 1PG (3) *(Twickenham)*.
1958-59	**WALES** 1G (5) to 0 *(Cardiff)*.
1959-60	**ENGLAND** 1G, 2PG, 1T (14) to 2PG (6) *(Twickenham)*.
1960-61	**WALES** 2T (6) to 1T (3) *(Cardiff)*.
1961-62	**DRAWN** no score *(Twickenham)*.
1962-63	**ENGLAND** 2G, 1DG (13) to 1PG, 1T (6) *(Cardiff)*.
1963-64	**DRAWN** 2T each *(Twickenham)*.
1964-65	**WALES** 1G, 1DG, 2T (14) to 1PG (3) *(Cardiff)*.
1965-66	**WALES** 1G, 2PG (11) to 1PG, 1T (6) *(Twickenham)*.
1966-67	**WALES** 5G, 2PG, 1DG (34) to 4PG 3T (21) *(Cardiff)*.
1967-68	**DRAWN.** ENGLAND 1G, 1PG, 1T (11), WALES 1G, 1DG, 1T (11) *(Twickenham)*.
1968-69	**WALES** 3G, 2PG, 1DG, 2T (30) to 3PG (9) *(Cardiff)*.
1969-70	**WALES** 1G, 1DG, 3T (17) to 2G, 1PG (13) *(Twickenham)*.
1970-71	**WALES** 2G, 2DG, 1PG, 1T (22) to 1PG, 1T (6) *(Cardiff)*.
(TRY UPGRADED TO 4 Pts.)	
1971-72	**WALES** 1G, 2PG (12) to 1PG (3) *(Twickenham)*.
1972-73	**WALES** 1G, 1PG, 4T (25) to 2PG, 1DG (9) *(Cardiff)*.
1973-74	**ENGLAND** 1G, 2PG, 1T (16) to 1G, 2PG (12) *(Twickenham)*.
1974-75	**WALES** 1G, 2PG, 2T (20) to 1T (4) *(Cardiff)*.
1975-76	**WALES** 2G, 1PG (21) to 3PG (9) *(Twickenham)*.
1976-77	**WALES** 2PG, 2T (14) to 3PG (9) *(Cardiff)*.
1977-78	**WALES** 3PG (9) to 2PG (6) *(Twickenham)*.
1978-79	**WALES** 2G, 1DG, 3T (27) to 1PG (3) *(Cardiff)*.
1979-80	**ENGLAND** 3PG (9) to 2T (8) *(Twickenham)*.

1882-83 **SCOTLAND** 3G to 1G *(Edinburgh)*.
1883-84 **SCOTLAND** 1DG, 1T to 0 *(Newport)*.
1884-85 **DRAWN** no score *(Glasgow)*.
1885-86 **SCOTLAND** 2G, 1T to 0 *(Cardiff)*.
1886-87 **SCOTLAND** 4G, 8T to 0 *(Edinburgh)*.
1887-88 **WALES** 1T to 0 *(Newport)*.
1888-89 **SCOTLAND** 2T to 0 *(Edinburgh)*.
1889-90 **SCOTLAND** 1G, 2T (8) to 1T (2) *(Cardiff)*.
1890-91 **SCOTLAND** 1G, 2DG, 5T (14) to 0 *(Edinburgh)*.
1891-92 **SCOTLAND** 1G, 1T (7) to 1T (2) *(Swansea)*.
1892-93 **WALES** 1PG, 3T (9) to 0 *(Edinburgh)*.
1893-94 **WALES** 1DG, 1T (7) to 0 *(Newport)*.
1894-95 **SCOTLAND** 1G (5) to 1GM (4) *(Edinburgh)*.
1895-96 **WALES** 2T (6) to 0 *(Cardiff)*.
1896-97 and 1897-98   No matches.
1898-99 **SCOTLAND** 1GM, 2DG 3T (21) to 2G (10) *(Edinburgh)*.
1899-1900 **WALES** 4T (12) to 1T (3) *(Swansea)*.
1900-01 **SCOTLAND** 3G, 1T (18) to 1G, 1T (8) *(Inverleith)*.
1901-02 **WALES** 1G, 3T (14) to 1G (5) *(Cardiff)*.
1902-03 **SCOTLAND** 1PG, 1T (6) to 0 *(Inverleith)*.
1903-04 **WALES** 3G, 1PG, 1T (21) to 1T (3) *(Swansea)*.
1904-05 **WALES** 2T (6) to 1T (3) *(Inverleith)*.
1905-06 **WALES** 3T (9) to 1PG (3) *(Cardiff)*.
1906-07 **SCOTLAND** 2T (6) to 1PG (3) *(Inverleith)*.
1907-08 **WALES** 2T (6) to 1G (5) *(Swansea)*.
1908-09 **WALES** 1G (5) to 1PG (3) *(Inverleith)*.
1909-10 **WALES** 1G, 3T (14) to 0 *(Cardiff)*.
1910-11 **WALES** 2G, 1DG, 6T (32) to 1DG, 2T (10) *(Inverleith)*.
1911-12 **WALES** 2G, 2DG, 1T (21) to 2T (6) *(Swansea)*.
1912-13 **WALES** 1G, 1T (8) to 0 *(Inverleith)*.
1913-14 **WALES** 2G, 2DG, 1PG, 1T (24) to 1G (5) *(Cardiff)*.
1919-20 **SCOTLAND** 2PG, 1T (9) to 1G (5) *(Inverleith)*.
1920-21 **SCOTLAND** 1G, 1PG, 2T (14) to 2DG (8) *(Swansea)*.
1921-22 **DRAWN.** SCOTLAND 1PG, 2T (9) WALES 1G, 1DG (9) *(Inverleith)*.
1922-23 **SCOTLAND** 1G, 2T (11) to 1G, 1PG (8) *(Cardiff)*.
1923-24 **SCOTLAND** 4G, 1PG, 4T (35) to 2G (10) *(Inverleith)*.

1924-25 **SCOTLAND** 1G, 1DG, 5T (24) to 1G, 1PG, 2T (14) *(Swansea)*.
1925-26 **SCOTLAND** 1G, 1PG, (8) to 1G (5) *(Murrayfield)*.
1926-27 **SCOTLAND** 1G (5) to 0 *(Cardiff)*.
1927-28 **WALES** 2G, 1T (13) to 0 *(Murrayfield.*
1928-29 **WALES** 1G, 3T (14) to 1DG, 1PG (7) *(Swansea)*.
1929-30 **SCOTLAND** 1G, 1DG, 1T (12) to 1G, 1DG (9) *(Murrayfield)*.
1930-31 **WALES** 2G, 1T (13) to 1G, 1T (8) *(Cardiff)*.
1931-32 **WALES** 1PG, 1T (6) to 0 *(Murrayfield)*.
1932-33 **SCOTLAND** 1G, 1PG, 1T (11) to 1T (3) *(Swansea)*.
1933-34 **WALES** 2G, 1T (13) to 1PG, 1T (6) *(Murrayfield)*.
1934-35 **WALES** 1DG, 2T (10) to 2T (6) *(Cardiff)*.
1935-36 **WALES** 2G, 1T (13) to 1T (3) *(Murrayfield)*.
1936-37 **SCOTLAND** 2G, 1T (13) to 2T (6) *(Swansea)*.
1937-38 **SCOTLAND** 1G, 1PG (8) to 2T (6) *(Murrayfield)*.
1938-39 **WALES** 1G, 1PG, 1T (11) to 1PG (3) *(Cardiff)*.
1946-47 **WALES** 2G, 1PG, 3T (22) to 1G, 1PG (8) *(Murrayfield)*.
1947-48 **WALES** 1G, 1PG, 2T (14) to 0 *(Cardiff)*.

(DROPPED GOAL REVALUED TO 3 Pts.)

1948-49 **SCOTLAND** 2T (6) to 1G (5) *(Murrayfield)*.
1949-50 **WALES** 1DG, 1PG, 2T (12) to 0 *(Swansea)*.
1950-51 **SCOTLAND** 2G, 1DG, 1PG, 1T (19) to 0 *(Murrayfield)*.
1951-52 **WALES** 1G, 2PG (11) to 0 *(Cardiff)*.
1952-53 **WALES** 1PG, 3T (12) to 0 *(Murrayfield)*.
1953-54 **WALES** 1PG, 4T (15) to 1T (3) *(Swansea)*.
1954-55 **SCOTLAND** 1G, 1DG, 1PG, 1T (14) to 1G, 1T (8) *(Murrayfield)*.
1955-56 **WALES** 3T (9) to 1PG (3) *(Cardiff)*.
1956-57 **SCOTLAND** 1DG, 1PG, 1T (9) to 1PG, 1T (6) *(Murrayfield)*.
1957-58 **WALES** 1G, 1T (8) to 1PG (3) *(Cardiff)*.
1958-59 **SCOTLAND** 1PG, 1T, (6) to 1G (5) *(Murrayfield)*.
1959-60 **WALES** 1G, 1PG (8) to 0 *(Cardiff)*.

1960-61	**SCOTLAND** 1T (3) to 0 *(Murray-field)*.	1971-72	**WALES** 2G, 3PG, 2T (35) to 1G, 2PG (12) *(Cardiff)*.
1961-62	**SCOTLAND** 1G, 1T (8) to 1DG (3) *(Cardiff)*.	1972-73	**SCOTLAND** 1G, 1T (10) to 3PG (9) *(Murrayfield)*.
1962-63	**WALES** 1DG, 1PG (6) to 0 *(Murray-field)*.	1973-74	**WALES** 1G (6) to 0 *(Cardiff)*.
		1974-75	**SCOTLAND** 3PG, 1DG (12) to 2PG 1T (10) *(Murrayfield)*.
1963-64	**WALES** 1G, 1PG, 1T (11) to 1T (3) *(Cardiff)*.	1975-76	**WALES** 2G, 3PG, 1DG, 1T (28) to 1G (6) *(Cardiff)*.
1964-65	**WALES** 1G, 2PG, 1T, (14) to 2DG, 2PG (12) *(Murrayfield)*.	1976-77	**WALES** 2G, 2PG (18) to 1G, 1DG (9) *(Murrayfield)*.
1965-66	**WALES** 1G, 1T (8) to 1PG (3) *(Cardiff)*.	1977-78	**WALES** 1DG, 1PG, 4T (22) to 2PG, 2T (14) *(Cardiff)*.
1966-67	**SCOTLAND** 1G, 1DG, 1T (11) to 1G (5) *(Murrayfield)*.	1978-79	**WALES** 1G, 3PG, 1T (19) to 3PG, 1T (13) *(Murrayfield)*.
1967-68	**WALES** 1G (5) to 0 *(Cardiff)*.	1979-80	**WALES** 1G, 1PG, 2T (17) to 1G (6) *(Cardiff)*.
1968-69	**WALES** 1G, 2PG, 2T (17) to 1PG (3) *(Murrayfield)*.		
1969-70	**WALES** 3G, 1T (18) to 1DG, 1PG, 1T (9) *(Cardiff)*.		
1970-71	**WALES** 2G, 1PG, 2T (19) to 4PG, 2T (18) *(Murrayfield)*.		
	(TRY UPGRADED TO 4 Pts.)		

AGAINST IRELAND

Matches played 82 **Wales 50 wins, Ireland 27, 5 drawn**

1881-82	**WALES** 2G, 2T to 0 *(Dublin)*.	1906-07	**WALES** 2G, 1DG, 1PG, 4T (29) to 0 *(Cardiff)*.
1882-83	No match.		
1883-84	**WALES** 1DG, 2T to 0 *(Cardiff)*.	1907-08	**WALES** 1G, 2T (11) to 1G (5) *(Belfast)*.
1884-85 and 1885-86 No matches.			
1886-87	**WALES** 1DG, 1T to 3T *(Birkenhead)*.	1908-09	**WALES** 3G, 1T (18) to 1G (5) *(Swansea)*.
1887-88	**IRELAND** 1G, 1DG, 1T to 0 *(Dublin)*.	1909-10	**WALES** 1DG, 5T (19) to 1T (3) *(Dublin)*.
1888-89	**IRELAND** 2T to 0 *(Swansea)*.	1910-11	**WALES** 2G, 1PG, 1T (16) to 0 *(Cardiff)*.
1889-90	**DRAWN** 1G each (4) *(Dublin)*.		
1890-91	**WALES** 1G, 1DG (6) to 1DG, 1T (4) *(Llanelli)*.	1911-12	**IRELAND** 1G, 1DG, 1T (12) to 1G (5) *(Belfast)*.
1891-92	**IRELAND** 1G, 2T (9) to 0 *(Dublin)*.	1912-13	**WALES** 2G, 1PG, 1T (16) to 2G, 1PG (13) *(Swansea)*.
1892-93	**WALES** 1T (2) to 0 *(Llanelli)*.	1913-14	**WALES** 1G, 2T (11) to 1T (3) *(Belfast)*.
1893-94	**IRELAND** 1PG (3) to 0 *(Belfast)*.		
1894-95	**WALES** 1G (5) to 1T (3) *(Cardiff)*.	1919-20	**WALES** 3G, 1DG, 3T (28) to 1DG (4) *(Cardiff)*.
1895-96	**IRELAND** 1G, 1T (8) to 1DG (4) *(Dublin)*.	1920-21	**WALES** 1PG, 1T (6) to 0 *(Belfast)*.
1896-97	No match.	1921-22	**WALES** 1G, 2T (11) to 1G (5) *(Swansea)*.
1897-98	**WALES** 1G, 1PG, 1T (11) to 1PG (3) *(Limerick)*.	1922-23	**IRELAND** 1G (5) to 1DG (4) *(Dublin)*.
1898-99	**IRELAND** 1T (3) to 0 *(Cardiff)*.	1923-24	**IRELAND** 2G, 1T (13) to 1DG, 2T (10) *(Cardiff)*.
1899-1900	**WALES** 1T (3) to 0 *(Belfast)*.		
1900-01	**WALES** 2G (10) to 3T (9) *(Swansea)*.	1924-25	**IRELAND** 2G, 1PG, 2T (19) to 1T (3) *(Belfast)*.
1901-02	**WALES** 1G, 1DG, 2T (15) to 0 *(Dublin)*.	1925-26	**WALES** 1G, 2T (11) to 1G, 1PG (8) *(Swansea)*.
1902-03	**WALES** 6T (18) to 0 *(Cardiff)*.	1926-27	**IRELAND** 2G, 1PG, 2T (19) to 1G, 1DG (9) *(Dublin)*.
1903-04	**IRELAND** 1G, 3T (14) to 4T (12) *(Belfast)*.		
1904-05	**WALES** 2G (10) to 1T (3) *(Swansea)*.		
1905-06	**IRELAND** 1G, 2T (11) to 2T (6) *(Belfast)*.		

1927-28	**IRELAND** 2G, 1T (13) to 2G (10) *(Cardiff)*.	1959-60	**WALES** 2G (10) to 2PG, 1T (9) *(Dublin)*.
1928-29	**DRAWN** 1G, (5) each *(Belfast)*.	1960-61	**WALES** 2PG, 1T (9) to 0 *(Cardiff)*.
1929-30	**WALES** 1PG, 3T (12) to 1DG, 1PG 7 *(Swansea)*.	1961-62	**DRAWN.** IRELAND 1DG (3), WALES 1PG (3) *(Dublin)*.
1930-31	**WALES** 1G, 1DG, 2T (15) to 1T (3) *(Belfast)*.	1962-63	**IRELAND** 1G, 1DG, 2PG (14) to 1DG, 1T (6) *(Cardiff)*.
1931-32	**IRELAND** 4T (12) to 1DG, 2T (10) *(Cardiff)*.	1963-64	**WALES** 3G (15) to 2PG (6) *(Dublin)*.
1932-33	**IRELAND** 1DG, 1PG, 1T (10) to 1G (5) *(Belfast)*.	1964-65	**WALES** 1G, 1DG, 1PG, 1T (14) to 1G, 1PG (8) *(Cardiff)*.
1933-34	**WALES** 2G, 1T (13) to 0 *(Swansea)*.	1965-66	**IRELAND** 1DG, 1PG, 1T (9) to 1PG, 1T (6) *(Dublin)*.
1934-35	**IRELAND** 2PG, 1T (9) to 1PG (3) *(Belfast)*.	1966-67	**IRELAND** 1T (3) to 0 *(Cardiff)*.
1935-36	**WALES** 1PG (3) to 0 *(Cardiff)*.	1967-68	**IRELAND** 1PG, 1DG, 1T (9) to 1PG, 1DG (6) *(Dublin)*.
1936-37	**IRELAND** 1G (5) to 1PG (3) *(Belfast)*.	1968-69	**WALES** 3G, 1PG, 1DG, 1T (24) to 1G, 2PG (11) *(Cardiff)*.
1937-38	**WALES** 1G, 1PG, 1T (11) to 1G (5) *(Swansea)*.	1969-70	**IRELAND** 1G, 1DG, 1PG, 1T (14) to 0 *(Dublin)*.
1938-39	**WALES** 1DG, 1T (7) to 0 *(Belfast)*.	1970-71	**WALES** 1G, 1DG, 2PG, 3T (23) to 3PG (9) *(Cardiff)*.
1946-47	**WALES** 1PG, 1T (6) to 0 *(Swansea)*.	**(TRY UPGRADED TO 4 Pts.)**	
1947-48	**IRELAND** 2T (6) to 1T (3) *(Belfast)*.	1971-72	No match.
(DROPPED GOAL REVALUED TO 3 Pts.)		1972-73	**WALES** 1G, 2PG, 1T (16) to 1G, 2PG (12) *(Cardiff)*.
1948-49	**IRELAND** 1G (5) to 0 *(Swansea)*.	1973-74	**DRAWN.** IRELAND 3PG (9), WALES 1G, 1PG (9) *(Dublin)*.
1949-50	**WALES** 2T (6) to 1PG (3) *(Belfast)*.	1974-75	**WALES** 3G, 2PG, 2T (32) to 1T (4) *(Cardiff)*.
1950-51	**DRAWN.** WALES 1PG (3), IRELAND 1T (3) *(Cardiff)*.	1975-76	**WALES** 3G, 4PG, 1T (34) to 3PG (9) *(Dublin)*.
1951-52	**WALES** 1G, 1PG, 2T (14) to 1PG (3) *(Dublin)*.	1976-77	**WALES** 2G, 3PG, 1DG, 1T (25) to 3PG (9) *(Cardiff)*.
1952-53	**WALES** 1G (5) to 1T (3) *(Swansea)*.	1977-78	**WALES** 4PG, 2T (20) to 3PG, 1DG, 1T (16) *(Dublin)*.
1953-54	**WALES** 1DG, 3PG (12) to 2PG, 1T (9) *(Dublin)*.	1978-79	**WALES** 2G, 4PG (24) to 2G, 3PG (21) *(Cardiff)*.
1954-55	**WALES** 3G, 1PG, 1T (21) to 1PG (3) *(Cardiff)*.	1979-80	**IRELAND** 3G, 1PG (21) to 1PG, 1T (7) *(Dublin)*.
1955-56	**IRELAND** 1G, 1DG, 1PG (11) to 1PG (3) *(Dublin)*.		
1956-57	**WALES** 2PG (6) to 1G (5) *(Cardiff)*.		
1957-58	**WALES** 3T (9) to 1PG, 1T (6) *(Dublin)*.		
1958-59	**WALES** 1G, 1T (8) to 1PG, 1T (6) *(Cardiff)*.		

AGAINST FRANCE

Matches played 53   Wales 35 wins, France 15, 3 drawn

1907-08	**WALES** 3G, 1PG, 6T (36) to 1DG (4) *(Cardiff)*.	1920-21	**WALES** 2PG, 2T (12) to 1DG (4) *(Cardiff)*.
1908-09	**WALES** 7G, 4T (47) to 1G (5) *(Paris)*.	1921-22	**WALES** 1G, 2T (11) to 1T (3) *(Paris)*.
1909-10	**WALES** 8G, 1PG, 2T (49) to 1G, 2PG, 1T (14) *(Swansea)*.	1922-23	**WALES** 2G, 1PG (16) to 1G, 1T (8) *(Swansea)*.
1910-11	**WALES** 3G, (15) to 0 *(Paris)*.	1923-24	**WALES** 1DG, 2T (10) to 2T (6) *(Paris)*.
1911-12	**WALES** 1G, 3T (14) to 1G, 1T (8) *(Newport)*.	1924-25	**WALES** 1G, 2T (11) to 1G (5) *(Cardiff)*.
1912-13	**WALES** 1G, 2T (11) to 1G, 1T (8) *(Paris)*.	1925-26	**WALES** 1DG, 1T (7) to 1G (5) *(Paris)*.
1913-14	**WALES** 5G, 2T (31) to 0 *(Swansea)*.	1926-27	**WALES** 2G, 5T (25) to 1DG, 1T (7) *(Swansea)*.
1919-20	**WALES** 2T (6) to 1G (5) *(Paris)*.		

478

1927-28	FRANCE 1G, 1T (8) to 1T (3) *(Paris)*.
1928-29	WALES 1G, 1T (8) to 1T (3) *(Cardiff)*.
1929-30	WALES 2DG, 1T (11) to 0 *(Paris)*.
1930-31	· WALES 5G, 1DG, 2T (35) to 1T (3) *(Swansea)*.
1946-47	WALES 1PG (3) to 0 *(Paris)*.
1947-48	FRANCE 1G, 2T (11) to 1PG (3) *(Swansea)*.

(DROPPED GOAL REVALUED TO 3 Pts.)

1948-49	FRANCE 1G (5) to 1T (3) *(Paris)*.
1949-50	WALES 3G, 1PG, 1T (21) to 0 *(Cardiff)*.
1950-51	FRANCE 1G, 1PG (8) to 1T (3) *(Paris)*.
1951-52	WALES 1DG, 2PG (9) to 1G (5) *(Swansea)*.
1952-53	WALES 2T (6) to 1PG (3) *(Paris)*.
1953-54	WALES 2G, 3PG, (19) to 2G, 1PG (13) *(Cardiff)*.
1954-55	WALES 2G, 2PG (16) to 1G, 1DG, 1PG (11) *(Paris)*.
1955-56	WALES 1G (5) to 1T (3) *(Cardiff)*.
1956-57	WALES 2G, 1PG, 2T (19) to 2G, 1T (13) *(Paris)*.
1957-58	FRANCE 2G, 2DG, (16) to 1PG, 1T (6) *(Cardiff)*.
1958-59	FRANCE 1G, 1PG, 1T (11) to 1PG (3) *(Paris)*.
1959-60	FRANCE 2G, 2T (16) to 1G, 1PG (8) *(Cardiff)*.
1960-61	FRANCE 1G, 1T (8) to 2T (6) *(Paris)*.
1961-62	WALES 1PG (3) to 0 *(Cardiff)*.
1962-63	FRANCE 1G (5) to 1PG (3) *(Paris)*.
1963-64	DRAWN 1G, 2PG (11) each *(Cardiff)*.

1964-65	FRANCE 2G, 1PG, 1DG, 2T (22) to 2G, 1T (13) *(Paris)*.
1956-66	WALES 2PG, 1T (9) to 1G, 1T (8) *(Cardiff)*.
1966-67	FRANCE 1G, 2DG, 1PG, 2T (20) to 1G, 2PG, 1DG (14) *(Paris)*.
1967-68	FRANCE 1G, 1PG, 1DG, 1T (14) to 2PG, 1T (9) *(Cardiff)*.
1968-69	DRAWN. FRANCE 1G, 1PG (8), WALES 1G, 1T (8) *(Paris)*.
1969-70	WALES 1G, 2PG (11) to 2T (6) *(Cardiff)*.
1970-71	WALES 1PG, 2T (9) to 1G (5) *(Paris)*.

(TRY UPGRADED TO 4 Pts.)

1971-72	WALES 4PG, 2T (20) to 2PG (6) *(Cardiff)*.
1972-73	FRANCE 3PG, 1DG (12) to 1DG (3) *(Paris)*.
1973-74	DRAWN. WALES 3PG, 1DG, 1T (16), FRANCE 3PG, 1DG, 1T (16) *(Cardiff)*.
1974-75	WALES 1G, 1PG, 4T (25) to 2P 1T (10) *(Paris)*.
1975-76	WALES 5PG, 1T (19) to 1G, 1PG 1T (13) *(Cardiff)*.
1976-77	FRANCE 1G, 2PG, 1T (16) to 3PG (9) *(Paris)*.
1977-78	WALES 1G, 2DG, 1T (16) to 1DG, 1T (7) *(Cardiff)*.
1978-79	FRANCE 2PG, 2T (14) to 3 PG, 1T (13) *(Paris)*.
1979-80	WALES 1G, 3T (18) to 1G, 1DG (9) *(Cardiff)*.

AGAINST NEW ZEALAND

Matches played 10

Wales 3 wins, New Zealand 7

1905	WALES 1T (3) to 0 *(Cardiff)*.
1924	N.Z. 2G, 1PG, 2T (19) to 0 *(Swansea)*.
1935	WALES 2G, 1T (13) to 1G, 1DG, 1T, (12) *(Cardiff)*.
1953	WALES 2G, 1PG (13) to 1G, 1PG (8) *(Cardiff)*.
1963	N.Z. 1PG, 1DG (6) to 0 *(Cardiff)*.
1967	N.Z. 2G, 1PG (13) to 1PG, 1DG (6) *(Cardiff)*.
1969	N.Z. 2G, 1PG, 2T (19) to 0 *(Christchurch)*.

1969	N.Z. 3G, 5PG, 1DG (33) to 2PG, 2T (12) *(Auckland)*.
1972	N.Z. 5PG, 1T (19) to 4PG, 1T (16) *(Cardiff)*.
1974	*N.Z. 1G, 2PG (12) to 1PG (3) *(Cardiff)*.
1978	N.Z. 3PG, 1T (13) to 4PG (12) *(Cardiff)*.

*Unofficial Match

479

AGAINST SOUTH AFRICA

Matches played 7   **South Africa 6 wins, 1 drawn**

1906 S.A. 1G, 2T (11) to 0 *(Swansea)*.	1960 S.A. 1PG (3) to 0 *(Cardiff)*.
1912 S.A. 1PG (3) to 0 *(Cardiff)*.	1964 S.A. 3G, 2PG, 1DG (24) to 1PG (3)
1931 S.A. 1G, 1T (8) to 1T (3) *(Swansea)*.	*(Durban)*.
1951 S.A. 1DG, 1T (6) to 1T (3) *(Cardiff)*.	1970 **DRAWN** 1PG, 1T (6) each *(Cardiff)*.

AGAINST AUSTRALIA

Matches played 9   **Wales 6 wins, Australia 3**

1908 **WALES** 1PG, 2T (9) to 2T (6) *(Cardiff)*.	1973 **WALES** 2G, 2PG, 3T (24) to 0 *(Cardiff)*.
1947 **WALES** 2PG (60 to 0 *(Cardiff)*.	1975 **WALES** 3G, 1PG, 1DG, 1T (28) to 1PG (3) *(Cardiff)*.
1958 **WALES** 1PG, 1DG, 1T (9) to 1T (3) *(Cardiff)*.	1978 **AUSTRALIA** 1G, 4PG (18) to 2T (8) *(Brisbane)*.
1966 **AUSTRALIA** 1G, 1PG, 1DG, 1T (14) to 1G, 1PG, 1T (11) *(Cardiff)*.	1978 **AUSTRALIA** 3PG, 2DG, 1T (19) to 2PG, 1DG, 2T (17) *(Sydney)*.
1969 **WALES** 2G, 2PG, 1T (19) to 2G, 2PG (16) *(Sydney)*.	

AGAINST NEW SOUTH WALES

1927   N.S.W. 3G, 1T (18) to 1G, 1T (8) *(Cardiff)*.

AGAINST MAORIS

1888   **WALES** 1G, 2T to 0 *(Swansea)*.

AGAINST N.Z. ARMY TEAMS

1919 **N.Z. ARMY** 2PG (6) to 1PG (3) *(Swansea)*.	1946 *****KIWIS** 1G, 2PG (11) to 1PG (3) *(Cardiff)*.

No caps awarded

480

APPENDIX III

FIVE NATIONS' CHAMPIONS

1883-84	ENGLAND	1919-20	ENGLAND / SCOTLAND / WALES	1952-53	ENGLAND
*1884-85	——	1920-21	ENGLAND	1953-54	ENGLAND / FRANCE / WALES
1885-86	ENGLAND / SCOTLAND	1921-22	WALES	1954-55	WALES / FRANCE
1886-87	SCOTLAND	1922-23	ENGLAND	1955-56	WALES
*1887-88	——	1923-24	ENGLAND	1956-57	ENGLAND
*1888-89	——	1924-25	SCOTLAND	1957-58	ENGLAND
1889-90	ENGLAND / SCOTLAND	1925-26	IRELAND / SCOTLAND	1958-59	FRANCE
1890-91	SCOTLAND	1926-27	SCOTLAND / IRELAND	1959-60	FRANCE / ENGLAND
1891-92	ENGLAND	1927-28	ENGLAND	1960-61	FRANCE
1892-93	WALES	1928-29	SCOTLAND	1961-62	FRANCE
1893-94	IRELAND	1929-30	ENGLAND	1962-63	ENGLAND
1894-95	SCOTLAND	1930-31	WALES	1963-64	SCOTLAND / WALES
1895-96	IRELAND	1931-32	ENGLAND / WALES / IRELAND	1964-65	WALES
*1896-97	——	1933-33	SCOTLAND	1965-66	WALES
1897-98	SCOTLAND	1933-34	ENGLAND	1966-67	FRANCE
1898-99	IRELAND	1933-35	IRELAND	1967-68	FRANCE
1899-1900	WALES	1935-36	WALES	1968-69	WALES
1900-01	SCOTLAND	1936-37	ENGLAND	1969-70	FRANCE / WALES
1901-02	WALES	1937-38	SCOTLAND	1970-71	WALES
1902-03	SCOTLAND	1938-39	ENGLAND / WALES / IRELAND	*1971-72	——
1903-04	SCOTLAND	1946-47	WALES / ENGLAND	1972-73	5-WAY TIE
1904-05	WALES	1947-48	IRELAND	1973-74	IRELAND
1905-06	IRELAND / WALES	1948-49	IRELAND	1974-75	WALES
1906-07	SCOTLAND	1949-50	WALES	1975-76	WALES
1907-08	WALES	1950-51	IRELAND	1976-77	FRANCE
1908-09	WALES	1951-52	WALES	1977-78	WALES
1909-10	ENGLAND			1978-79	WALES
1910-11	WALES			1979-80	ENGLAND
1911-12	ENGLAND / IRELAND				
1912-13	ENGLAND				
1913-14	ENGLAND				

*Matches not completed

APPENDIX IV

TRIPLE CROWN WINNERS

WALES 16 times — 1892-93, 1899-1900, 1901-02, 1904-05, 1907-08, 1908-09, 1910-11, 1949-50, 1951-52, 1964-65, 1968-69, 1970-71, 1975-76, 1976-77, 1977-78, 1978-79.

ENGLAND 15 times — 1882-83, 1883-84, 1891-92, 1912-13, 1913-14, 1920-21, 1922-23, 1923-24, 1927-28, 1933-34, 1936-37, 1953-54, 1956-57, 1959-60, 1979-80.

SCOTLAND 8 times — 1890-91, 1894-95, 1900-01, 1902-03, 1906-07, 1924-25, 1932-33, 1937-38.

IRELAND 4 times — 1893-94, 1898-99, 1947-48, 1948-49.

APPENDIX V

GRAND SLAM WINNERS

WALES 8 times — 1907-08, 1908-09, 1910-11, 1949-50, 1951-52, 1970-71, 1975-76, 1977-78.
ENGLAND 8 times — 1912-13, 1913-14, 1920-21, 1922-23, 1923-24, 1927-28, 1956-57, 1979-80.
FRANCE twice — 1967-68, 1976-77.
SCOTLAND once — 1924-25.
IRELAND once — 1947-48.

APPENDIX VI

WELSH MEMBERS OF BRITISH TOURING TEAMS
(* — uncapped at time of tour; † — replacement)

1888 in New Zealand and Australia
W. H. Thomas (Cambridge Univ.), A. J. Stewart* (Cardiff and Dewsbury)

1899 in Australia
E. Gwyn Nicholls (Cardiff)

1903 in South Africa
R. T. Skrimshire (Newport)

1904 in Australia and New Zealand
R. T. Gabe, P. F. Bush* (Cardiff), Teddy Morgan (Guy's Hospital), A. F. Harding (London Welsh), W. M. Llewellyn (Newport), T. H. Vile* (Newport), T. S. Bevan, W. F. Jowett (Swansea)

1908 Anglo-Welsh team in Australia and New Zealand
A. F. Harding (capt.), W. L. Morgan*, J. F. Williams (London Welsh), R. A. Gibbs, J. L. Williams (Cardiff), G. L. Williams* (Liverpool), R. K. Green* (Neath), J. C. M. Dyke (Penarth and Coventry), L. S. Thomas (Penarth), D. 'Ponty' Jones (Pontypool), J. 'Tuan' Jones* (Pontypool and Guy's Hospital), E. Morgan (Swansea), R. B. Griffiths* (Newport)

1910 in South Africa
Walter E. Rees (joint manager), J. Webb (Abertillery), A. M. Baker, H. Jarman, D. 'Ponty' Jones, R. C. S. Plummer*, P. D. Waller, Stanley Williams* (Newport)

1924 in South Africa
Harry Packer (manager), D. Marsden-Jones* (London Welsh), Harold Davies†, Vincent Griffiths (Newport), Rowe Harding (Swansea)

1930 in Australia and New Zealand
H. M. Bowcott (Cambridge Univ. and Cardiff), H. Poole* (Cardiff), Ivor E. Jones (Llanelli), T. E. Jones-Davies (London Welsh), J. C. Morley (Newport), Jack Bassett (Penarth), Dai Parker (Swansea)

1938 in South Africa
Ivor Williams* (Cardiff), A. R. Taylor (Cross Keys), W. H. Clement, Elvet Jones* (Llanelli), V. G. J. Jenkins (London Welsh), W. Travers (Newport), Eddie Morgan, Haydn Tanner (Swansea)

1950 in New Zealand and Australia
J. D. Robins (Birkenhead Park), W. B. Cleaver, Cliff Davies, J. Matthews, B. L. Williams, W. R. Willis (Cardiff), B. Lewis Jones† (Llanelli), E. R. John, J. R. G. Stephens (Neath), D. J. Hayward (Newbridge), R. T. Evans, K. J. Jones, M. C. Thomas (Newport), D. M. Davies (Somerset Police)

1955 in South Africa
D. E. Davies (Hon. Sec.). G. M. Griffiths†, C. I. Morgan, H. T. Morris (Cardiff), Alun Thomas, R. H. Williams (Llanelli), T. Lloyd (Maesteg), C. C. Meredith (Neath), B. V. Meredith (Newport), R. J. Robins (Pontypridd), R. C. C.Thomas, W. O. Williams (Swansea)

1959 in Australia and New Zealand
H. J. Morgan (Abertillery), W. R. Evans (Cardiff), Terry Davies, R. H. Williams (Llanelli), B. V. Meredith, M. C. Thomas (Newport), M. J. Price, Ray Prosser (Pontypool), J. Faull (Swansea)

1962 in South Africa
A. O'Connor (Aberavon), H. J. Morgan, A. E. I. Pask (Abertillery), K. D. Jones, K. A. Rowlands (Cardiff), D. Nash (Ebbw Vale), D. K. Jones (Llanelli), G. Davidge†, B. V. Meredith (Newport), Dewi Bebb (Swansea)

1966 in Australia and New Zealand
J. D. Robins (assistant manager and coach), A. R. Lewis, A. E. I. Pask (Abertillery), G. J. Prothero (Bridgend), D. K. Jones, C. H. Norris (Cardiff), Terry Price†, W. Delme Thomas* (Llanelli), B. Price, D. Watkins, S. J. Watkins (Newport), Dewi Bebb (Swansea)

1968 in South Africa
J. Young (Bridgend), T. G. R. Davies, G. O. Edwards, B. John, Keri Jones, J. P. O'Shea, M. C. R. Richards (Cardiff), W. Delme Thomas (Llanelli), W. H. Raybould, J. Taylor (London Welsh), K. S. Jarrett (Newport)

1971 in Australia and New Zealand
Carwyn James (assistant manager and coach), S. J. Dawes (capt.), T. G. R. Davies, T. M. Davies, T. G. Evans†, M. G. Roberts, J. Taylor, J. P. R. Williams (London Welsh), J. C. Bevan, G. O. Edwards, B. John (Cardiff), A. J. Lewis (Ebbw Vale), D. L. Quinnell*, W. Delme Thomas (Llanelli), R. Hopkins (Maesteg)

1974 in South Africa
Alun Thomas (manager), G. O. Edwards (Cardiff), P. Bennett, R. T. E. Bergiers, T. P. David, J. J. Williams (Llanelli), T. M. Davies, C. F. W. Rees, J. P. R. Williams (London Welsh), R. W. Windsor (Pontypool)

1977 in New Zealand
S. J. Dawes (assistant manager and coach), P. Bennett (capt.), D. L. Quinnell, J. J. Williams (Llanelli), J. D. Bevan, A. J. Martin, C. Williams (Aberavon), S. P. Fenwick (Bridgend), Brynmor Williams* (Cardiff), A. D. Lewis*† (London Welsh), H. Elgan Rees* (Neath), D. H. Burcher, G. L. Evans, J. Squire† (Newport), T. J. Cobner, A. G. Faulkner†, G. Price, R. W. Windsor (Pontypool), T. P. Evans (Swansea)

1980 in South Africa
A. J. Martin (Aberavon), W. G. Davies, T. D. Holmes, A. J. Phillips, S. M. Lane (Cardiff), R. W. R. Gravell, P. Morgan, D. L. Quinnell (Llanelli), G. Price, J. Squire (Pontypool), D. S. Richards, C. Williams (Swansea), H. Elgan Rees† (Neath), G. Williams*†, I. Stephens*† (Bridgend), Dr Jack Matthews (medical officer).

APPENDIX VII

SOUTH WALES CHALLENGE CUP AND W.R.U. CUP WINNERS

South Wales Challenge Cup

Note on scoring values:

Scoring values in the early years of the South Wales Challenge Cup varied with confusing frequency. This makes attempts to translate results into points a difficult and often unrealistic exercise. Between 1877 and 1880, a goal of any kind was worth 10 points, a try 5 points, and a minor, or touchdown in defence, 1 point. Those values had obviously changed by 1882, when Newport were reported to have beaten Llanelli in the Final (see below) by 7 points to 5. At that early juncture, therefore, the W.F.U. were anticipating future international practice by valuing the try at 3 points. But not for long: in the Final of 1886 Llanelli were reckoned to have accumulated 44 points in a score including 11 minors, for by then a converted try was worth 18 points, a dropped goal 12 points and a try 9 points. When the cup was revived for competition among smaller clubs and second teams in 1889-90, the try was worth 2 points in accordance with W.F.U. and I.B. rulings. From 1892-3, the W.F.U., believing two tries should be worth more than any kind of goal, revived their practice of a decade earlier and increased the try to 3 points, though the I.B. did not adopt this valuation until the following season.

1877-78	Newport beat Swansea by 1 goal to nil (at Bridgend)
1878-79	Newport beat Cardiff by 1 goal and 2 tries to nil (at Cardiff)
1879-80	Swansea beat Lampeter College by 2 tries to nil (at Ystrad, near Carmarthen)
1880-81	Cardiff beat Llanelli by 1 try to nil (at Neath, after extra time)
1881-82	Newport beat Llanelli by 1 try and 4 minors to 1 try and 2 minors (at Swansea, in a replay)
1882-83	Newport beat Swansea by 1 goal and 2 tries to 1 goal and 1 try (at Swansea)
1883-84	Llanelli beat Newport by 1 try to nil (at Neath)
1884-85	Newport beat Neath by 1 try to nil (at Cardiff)
1885-86	Llanelli beat Newport by 2 dropped goals and 1 try to nil (at Swansea)
1886-87	Swansea beat Llanelli by 1 goal to nil (at Newport)
1889-90	Penygraig beat Llanelli 'A' by 1 try (2 points) to nil (at Penygraig)
1890-91	Newport 2nds beat Swansea Harlequins by 3 tries (6 points) to nil (at Newport)
1891-92	Llandaff beat Llanelli 'A' by 1 goal and 2 tries (8 points) to nil (at Neath)
1892-93	Pontymister beat Neath 'A' by 1 goal and 3 tries (14 points) to nil (at Cardiff)

1893-94	Llanelli 'A' beat Pontymister by 2 goals (10 points) to nil (at Llanelli)
1894-95	Neath 'A' beat Crumlin by 1 goal (5 points) to nil (at Mountain Ash)
1895-96	Pontymister beat Llandeilo by 2 tries (6 points) to nil (at Llanelli)
1896-97	Llanelli 'A' beat Risca by 6 tries (18 points) to nil (at Neath)

(In 1901 the W.F.U. reintroduced the trophy as the South Wales Junior Challenge Cup. In order to promote 'local junior rugby football', the competition was closed to all current senior clubs and their second teams).

1901-02	Cynon Stars beat Neath Excelsiors by 3 tries (9 points) to nil (at Neath)
1902-03	Ystrad Stars (Rhondda) beat Felinfoel by 1 goal and 2 tries (11 points) to nil (at Bridgend)
1903-04	Halfway (Llanelli) beat Troedyrhiw by 3 goals (15 points) to 2 tries (6 points) (at Neath)

| 1913-14 | Aberavon beat Blaina by 2 goals (10 points) to nil (at Bridgend) |

W.R.U. Challenge Cup

(from 1976 known as the Schweppes/W.R.U. Cup;
all games played at the National Ground)

1971-72	Neath beat Llanelli 15 points to 9
1972-73	Llanelli beat Cardiff 30 points to 7
1973-74	Llanelli beat Aberavon 12 points to 10
1974-75	Llanelli beat Aberavon 15 points to 6
1975-76	Llanelli beat Swansea 16 points to 4
1976-77	Newport beat Cardiff 16 points to 15
1977-78	Swansea beat Newport 13 points to 9
1978-79	Bridgend beat Pontypridd 18 points to 12
1979-80	Bridgend beat Swansea 15 points to 9.

APPENDIX VIII

PRESIDENTS, SECRETARIES AND HONORARY TREASURERS OF THE W.R.U.

Presidents

1881 (March)-1881 (Sept.) C. C. Chambers
1881 (Sept.)-1885 Earl of Jersey
1885-1906 Sir J. T. D. Llewellyn
1906-1947 Horace S. Lyne
1947-1953 Sir David Rocyn Jones
1953-1954 Ernest Davies
1954-1955 W. R. Thomas
1955-1956 Major T. H. Vile
1956-1957 Glyn Stephens
1957-1958 Enoch H. Rees
1958-1959 F. G. Phillips
1959-1960 Lt. Col. P. R. Howells
1960-1961 D. Hopkin Thomas
1961-1962 D. E. Davies
1962-1963 J. W. Faull
1963-1964 D. Ewart Davies
1964-1965 Nathan Rocyn Jones
1965-1966 David Jones
1966-1967 T. C. Prosser
1967-1968 Glyn Morgan
1968-1969 Ivor E. Jones
1969-1970 V. C. Phelps
1970-1971 Kenneth M. Harris
1971-1972 Rhys E. Williams
1972-1973 Vernon J. Parfitt
1973-1974 Leslie M. Spence
1974-1975 Harry M. Bowcott
1975-1976 Handel C. Rogers
1976-1977 Hywel Thomas
1977-1978 T. Rowley Jones
1978-1979 D. Luther James
1979-1980 Gwyn Roblin
1980-1981 Cliff W. Jones

Secretaries

1881-1892 Richard Mullock
1892-1896 W. H. Gwynn
1896-1948 Walter E. Rees
1948-1955 Eric Evans
1956-1981 W. H. Clement

Honorary Treasurers

1881-1891 Richard Mullock
1891-1903 W. H. Wilkins
1903-1930 T. R. Griffiths
1930-1934 Sam West
1934-1945 E. Roberts
1946-1952 P. O. Evans
1952-   K. M. Harris

APPENDIX IX

WELSH REPRESENTATIVES ON THE INTERNATIONAL RUGBY FOOTBALL BOARD

Alex Duncan 1887-91
Horace Lyne 1887-1938
Richard Mullock 1887-89
W. D. Phillips 1887-1907
F. J. Carlyle 1888-89
W. H. Treatt 1891
A. J. Davies 1892-1904
R. Gould 1892
W. H. Gwynn 1892-95
W. H. Wilkins 1893-1902
Walter E. Rees 1896-1900
Tom Williams 1901-08
D. Harry Bowen 1908
Ack Llewellyn 1909-22
T. D. Schofield 1912-27
W. M. Douglas 1914

James Jarrett 1928-39
Dr D. Rocyn Jones 1925-34
Daniel Jones (Risca) 1946-53
T. H. Vile 1946-53
Glyn Stephens 1954-55
D. Hopkin Thomas 1954-57
Enoch H. Rees 1956-59
J. W. Faull 1958-61
David Jones (Blaina) 1959-63
Ivor E. Jones 1962-65
Rayner Jones 1964-65
Glyn Morgan 1966-68
K. M. Harris 1966-79
Hermas Evans 1969-
Gwilym Treharne 1980-

SOURCES AND BIBLIOGRAPHY

A. A Note on Sources

There are no official records relating to the South Wales Football Club or the South Wales Football Union or, indeed, the first decade of the Welsh Football Union. The hand-written minutes of the W.F.U. still extant begin in 1892. Illegibility slowly yields to type, and frustrating brevity to exhausting length. The earliest W.F.U. handbook we were able to consult dates from 1895. There is little in the way of correspondence until 1956. These categories — minutes, handbooks and correspondence — comprise the bulk of the W.R.U.'s archives, and they were placed completely at our disposal.

Newspaper coverage could at times prove exasperating, especially before 1900, but this was the richest vein we were able to tap, allowing us to piece the rest of the jigsaw together from contemporary journals, club histories, memoirs and intuition. It was only from the mid-fifties that the rising torrent of books, then our own eyes and memories, released us from a daily trudge through yellowing newspaper files. We consulted the *Western Mail* and *South Wales Daily News* (the latter merged with the former in 1928) comprehensively from the 1870s to the 1950s, and selectively thereafter. We also quarried innumerable local newspapers for particular periods and places, and among the most useful were the *Aberdare Leader, Amman Valley Chronicle, Brecon and County Times, Cambrian, Llanelly and County Guardian, Llanelly Mercury, Merthyr Express, Monmouthsire Merlin, Neath Guardian, Rhondda Leader, South Wales Argus, South Wales Daily Post, South Wales Evening Post, South Wales Football Echo, South Wales Graphic* and *South Wales Times and Star of Gwent.* The cuttings-books of international players were often invaluable and always fascinating, and we would particularly like to thank the Misses Joyce and Nesta Gabe, and Mr. A. J. Gould, for allowing us to use the scrapbooks of their illustrious fathers. We have leafed through match programmes from the first decade of this century, old photographs, club minute books, ticket-stubs, and trunk-loads of ephemera in order to seize, where we could, the time, the feel and the smell of vanished years. We hope some of that vitality has been recaptured in this book. For those who would like to pursue their own reading, we append this bibliography. It is not exhaustive and makes no claims to be definitive, but it is a list of those books, periodicals and articles which we found to be most relevant to the history of Welsh Rugby.

B. Bibliography

Note: In sections (v) — (x), place of publication is London, unless otherwise indicated. Arrangement is alphabetical, not chronological.

(i)   **The Social Background**
P. C. Bailey, *Leisure and Class in Victorian England* (London, 1978)
M. J. Daunton, *Coal Metropolis: Cardiff 1870-1914* (Leicester, 1977)
Hywel Francis and David Smith, *The Fed: A History of the South Wales Miners in the Twentieth Century* (London, 1980)
Graham Humphrys, *Industrial South Wales* (Newton Abbot, 1972)
E. D. Lewis, *The Rhondda Valleys,* (London, 1959)
Kenneth O. Morgan, *Wales in British Politics 1868-1922* (Cardiff, 1963; revised ed. 1970)
Alan Butt Philip, *The Welsh Question* (Cardiff, 1975)
David Smith (ed.), *A People and a Proletariat: Essays in the History of Wales 1780-1980* (London, 1980)
James Walvin, *Leisure and Society 1830-1950* (London, 1978)
Hywel Francis, 'The Anthracite Strike and the Disturbances of 1925' *Llafur* vol. i, no. 2, (May, 1973)
Brinley Thomas, 'The Migration of Labour into the Glamorganshire Coalfields 1861-1911', *Economica* X (1930)
Wales 1911-14 (ed. J. Hugh Edwards)
Wales 1937-59 (ed. Keidrych Rhys)
Welsh Outlook 1914-1933
Welsh Review 1906-1907

(ii)   **The Pre-industrial Scene**
Roy Denning, 'Sports and Pastimes' in Stewart Williams (ed.) *Saints and Sailing Ships* (Cowbridge, 1962)
Brian Howells (ed.), *Elizabethan Pembrokeshire: the evidence of George Owen* (Haverfordwest, 1973)
Howard Lloyd, 'Tri o hen chwaraeon Cymru', *Transactions of the Cymmrodorion Society,* 1960.
I. C. Peate, *Diwylliant Gwerin Cymru* (Caerdydd, 1942)
H. M. Waddington, 'Games and Athletics in Bygone Wales', *Trans. Cymmrodorion Soc.,* 1954.
G. J. Williams, 'Glamorgan Customs in the Eighteenth Century', *Gwerin,* vol. 1, 1956-7.

(iii)   **Club Histories**
J. Dolan (ed.), *Aberavon RFC 1876-1976*
A. Breeze (ed.), *One Hundred Years of Abergavenny RFC 1875-1975*
H. S. Lloyd (ed.), *Aberystwyth RFC 1947-1972*
Ammanford RFC 1887-1947: Sixty Years of Rugby

E. Slocombe (ed.), *Amman United RFC 1903-1953*

W. A. D. Lawrie (ed.), *Bridgend RFC: the First Hundred Years 1878-1979*

D. G. Jenkins (ed.), *Blaenavon RFC 1877-1977*

Barbara M. Evans, *Blaina Rugby Football Club 1875-1976* (Newport, 1976)

R. J. Boulton, *Brecon Football 1860-1880* (Brecon, 1969)

C. S. Arthur, *Cardiff RFC History and Statistics 1876-1908*

D. E. Davies, *Cardiff Rugby Football Club History and Statistics 1876-1975* (Cardiff, 1975)

J. B. G. Thomas (ed.), *Cardiff RFC 75th Anniversary 1876-1951*

J. B. G. Thomas (ed.), *Cardiff RFC Centenary Year Brochure 1976-77*

T. L. Evans (ed.), *Carmarthen RFC 1874-1974*

B. Jarvis, *The Origin of Chepstow RFC* (Chepstow, 1978)

J. B. G. Thomas (ed.), *Captain Crawshay's Welsh XV 1922-1972*

Ebbw Vale RFC 1880-1980, *Gwent Gazette* Centenary Season Souvenir Supplement, 20 September 1979

T. G. Cadwalladr, *The Glais Rugby Story 1896-1971*

J. Howell Rees (ed.), *A History of the Gowerton Rugby Football Club* (Gowerton, 1959)

H. Meurig Evans (ed.), *Hendy Rugby Football Club 1907-57*

Tony Lewis, *The Mules — A History of Kenfig Hill RFC* (Pyle, 1973)

Michael Samuel (ed.), *Lampeter Town RFC 1875-1979*

T. H. Lewis, *Llandybie RFC 1901-1951*

Vivian Jenkins (ed.), *London Welsh RFC 1885-1957*

Ivor Edwards (ed.), *The First 100 Years: the history of Mountain Ash RFC 1875-1975*

G. Evans and G. Thomas (eds.), *Maesteg Celtic RFC: Fifty Glorious Years 1925-1975*

R. Gethin, *Merthyr Rugby Football Club 1876-1976*

T. Dargavel (ed.), *Neath RFC 1871-1971* (Also for Neath, Douglas A. Jones collection in Nat. Lib. Wales)

W. J. T. Collins, *Newport Athletic Club: the record of half a century 1875-1925*

W. J. T. Collins, 'Newport Football', *South Wales Argus,* Oct. 1913 — Feb. 1914

Jack Davis, *100 Years of Newport Rugby* (Newport, 1974)

Penarth RFC 75th Anniversary Brochure 1879-1954

W. D. Jones (ed.), *Penygraig RFC: 100 Years of Valley Rugby 1877-1977*

H. Benyon (ed.), *Pontyclun RFC 1897-1972*

Desmond T. Jones (ed.), *Pontypridd Rugby Football Club 1876-1976*

E. Hammett (ed.), *50 Years of Rugby History: Pontypool RFC Jubilee 1901-1951*

Brinley E. Matthews, *The Swansea Story* (Swansea, 1968)

Ron Griffiths (ed.), *Swansea Cricket and Football Club 1874-1974*

A. J. Ormond (ed.), *Tenby RFC 50th Anniversary Brochure* (Tenby, 1948)

Desmond Barnett (ed.), *Treherbert RFC 1874-1974*

D. Rees (ed.), *Treorchy RFC 1890-1965*

Stanley Owen, *Vardre United RFC 1921-1971*

E. Bayliss and H. George (eds.), *Waunarlwydd RFC 1900-1975*

(iv) **Schools and Colleges**
T. W. Bamford, *The Rise of Public Schools* (1967)
J. Gathorne-Hardy, *The Public School Phenomenon* (1977)
B. Simon and I. Bradley (eds.), *The Victorian Public School: studies in the development of an educational institution* (Dublin, 1975)
R. J. Boulton, *Rugby Football at Christ College Brecon* (unpublished mss. 1979, courtesy of the author)
Iolo Davies, *'A Certaine Schoole', A History of the Grammar School at Cowbridge* (Cowbridge, 1967)
H. Barber and H. Lewis, *The History of Friars School, Bangor* (Bangor, 1901)
D. J. Davies, 'The Finest Rugby School?' (Gowerton) in Gilbert Bennett (ed.), *Something Attempted, Something Done* (Llandybie, 1973)
D. T. W. Price, *A History of St. David's College, Lampeter*, vol. 1 (Cardiff, 1977)
R. J. Tree, *Mens Sana in Corpore Sano* (unpublished mss., courtesy of Lampeter U.C. Library)
W. Gareth Evans, *The History of Llandovery College 1847-1971* (unpublished University of Wales M.Ed. thesis, 1972)
H. C. Toulouse, *Monmouth School Rugby Football Club 1873-1973* (Newport, 1973)

(v) **Player's Autobiographies, Biographies, Memoirs and Manuals**
Fred Allen and Terry McLean, *Fred Allen on Rugby (1970)*
A. Budd, C. Fry and others *Football* (1897)
Gerald Davies, *An Autobiography* (1979)
Mervyn Davies with David Parry-Jones, *Number Eight* (1977)
W. J. A. Davies, *Rugby Football and How to Play it* (1928)
John Dawes, *Rugby Union* (1975)
John Dawes, Gareth James and others, *Thinking Rugby, the London Welsh Way* (1979)
Gareth Edwards, *Gareth — an autobiography* (1978)
D. Gallaher and W. J. Stead, *The Complete Rugby Footballer* (1906)
D. R. Gent, *Rugby Football* (1932)
John Gwilliam, *Rugby Football Tactics* (1958)
Rowe Harding, *Rugby Reminiscences and Opinions* (1929)
Barry John, *The Barry John Story* (1972)
Brian Jones and Ian McJennett, *Rugby under Pressure* (1972)
Cliff Jones, *Rugby Football* (1937)
Elias Jones, *The Palmy Days of Welsh Rugby: reminiscences of a veteran Welsh rugby forward 1886-1895* (Llanelli, 1935)
Lewis Jones, *King of Rugger* (1958)
C. Laidlaw, *Mud in your Eye* (1973)
D. Lalanne, *Géants du Rugby* (Paris, 1970)
H. F. McDonald and J. Idwal Rees, *Rugger Practice and Tactics* (1938)
Cliff Morgan (ed.), *Rugby: The Great Ones* (1970)
Hennie Muller, *Tot Siens to Test Rugby* (Cape Town, 1953)
George Nepia and Terry McLean, *I, George Nepia* (1963)

E. Gwyn Nicholls, *The Modern Rugby Game* (1908)
J. E. Raphael, *Modern Rugby Football* (1918)
Gus Risman, *Rugby Renegade* (1958)
Haydn Tanner, *Rugby Football* (1950)
J. B. G. Thomas, *Great Rugger Players* (1955)
J. B. G. Thomas, *Great Contemporary Players* (1963)
Watcyn Thomas, *Rugby-Playing Man* (1977)
H. Vassall, *Football — Rugby Game* (1889)
Alex Veysey, *Colin Meads, All Black* (Auckland, 1974)
W. W. Wakefield and H. Marshall, *Rugger* (1927)
Eddie Waring, *Rugby League: The Great Ones* (1969)
David Watkins and Brian Dobbs, *The David Watkins Story* (1970)
Bleddyn Williams, *Rugger My Life* (1956)
Gerwyn Williams, *Modern Rugby* (1964)
Les Williams, *Rugby Skills, Training and Tactics* (1963)
J. P. R. Williams, *J.P.R. — an autobiography* (1979)
Ray Williams, *Skilful Rugby* (1976)

(vi) **International Rugby Histories**
England
  B. Bowker, *England Rugby* (1976)
  O. L. Owen, *The History of the Rugby Football Union* (1955)
  W. Reyburn, *The Men in White: the story of English Rugby* (1975)
  U. A. Titley and R. McWhirter, *Centenary History of the Rugby Football Union* (1970)

France
  H. Garcia, *Le Rugby* (Paris 1962)
  A. Potter and G. Duthen, *The Rise of French Rugby* (1961)

Ireland
  S. Diffley, *The Men in Green: the story of Irish Rugby* (1973)
  E. Van Esbeck, *One Hundred Years of Irish Rugby* (Dublin, 1974)

New Zealand
  Winston McCathy, *Haka! The All Blacks Story* (1968)
  Terry McLean, *Great Days in New Zealand Rugby* (Wellington, 1959)
  N. A. C. McMillan and R. H. Chester, *Men in Black* (Auckland, 1977)

Scotland
  R. J. Phillips, *The Story of Scottish Rugby* (Edinburgh, 1925)

South Africa
  D. H. Craven, *Springboks down the Years* (Cape Town, 1956)
  A. C. Parker, *Growth of South African Rugby* (Cape Town, 1955)
  A. C. Parker, *The Springboks 1891-1970* (1970)
  R. K. Stent, *The Fourth Springboks 1951-2* (1952)

Wales

    John Billot, *History of Welsh International Rugby* (Ferndale, 1970; revised ed. 1971)

    John Billot, *All Blacks in Wales* (Ferndale, 1972)

    John Billot, *Springboks in Wales* (Ferndale, 1974)

    J. B. G. Thomas, *The Men in Scarlet — the story of Welsh Rugby Football* (1972)

    J. B. G. Thomas and Rowe Harding (eds.), *Rugby in Wales* (Llandybie, 1970)

    Wayne Thomas, *A Century of Welsh Rugby Players 1880-1980* (1980)

    Terry McLean, *Red Dragons of Rugby* (Wellington, 1969)

(vii) **General Rugby Histories**

    F. P. Marshall, *Football — The Rugby Union Game* (1892)

    C. Rea, *Rugby: a history of Rugby Union Football* (1977)

    J. Reason and C. James, *The World of Rugby* (1979)

    W. Reyburn, *A History of Rugby* (1971)

    E. H. D. Sewell, *Rugby Football up-to-date* (1922)

    N. Starmer-Smith, *The Barbarians: the official History of the Barbarian Football Club* (1977)

    J. B. G. Thomas, *On Tour* (1954)

    J. B. G. Thomas, *Great Rugger Matches* (1959)

    J. B. G. Thomas, *Great Rugger Clubs* (1962)

    J. B. G. Thomas, *Fifty-two Famous Tries* (1966)

    J. B. G. Thomas, *Men, Matches and Moments* (1970)

(viii) **General Rugby Books**

    W. J. T. Collins, *Rugby Recollections* (Newport, 1948)

    D. Frost, *The All Blacks 1967* (1968)

    J. M. Kilburn, *In Search of Rugby Football* (1938)

    W. McCarthy, *Rugby in my time* (Wellington, 1959)

    G. Nicholson and W. John Morgan, *Report on Rugby* (1959)

    T. O'Connor (ed.), *How the Lions Won* (1975)

    K. Pelmear (ed.), *Rugby Football — an Anthology* (1958)

    J. Reason (ed.), *The Lions Speak* (1972)

    M. Shearman, *Football* (1885)

    J. B. G. Thomas, *Rugby in Focus* (1979)

    A. A. Thomson, *Rugger My Pleasure* (1955)

    Col. Philip Trevor, *Rugby Union Football* (1923)

    H. B. T. Wakelam (ed.), *The Game Goes On* (1936)

    W. Wooller (ed.) *Fifty Years of the All Blacks* (1955)

    G. V. Wynne-Jones, *Sporting Commentary* (1951)

(ix) **Rugby Periodicals and Annuals**

    The Field 1853 —

    Football Annual (ed. C. W. Alcock) 1873 —

    Playfair Rugby Annual 1947/8 — 1972/3

    Playfair Welsh Rugby Annual 1949/50

    Rothmans Rugby Year Book 1972/3 —

John Wisden's Rugby Football Almanack 1923/4 — 1925/6
Rygbi '78-79 (gol. J. Jenkins)
Rugby Football Annual 1926/7 — 1939/40
Rugby World 1960 —
Welsh Brewers' Rugby Annual for Wales 1970/1 —
Welsh Rugby (formerly *Rugger Sport*) 1961 —

(x)   **Miscellaneous**
C. W. Alcock, *The Book of Football*(1906)
Peter Corrigan, *100 Years of Welsh Soccer* (Cardiff, 1976)
J. H. Davies, *A History of Pontardawe and District* (Llandybie, 1967)
Diary of George Dixon, Manager of 1905 All Blacks (unpublished, courtesy
of T. W. J. Auty and R. H. Chester)
E. Dunning (ed.), *The Sociology of Sport* (1971)
E. Dunning and K. Sheard, *Barbarians, Gentlemen and Players* (Oxford,
1979)
C. Edwards, 'The new football mania', *Nineteenth Century*, Oct. 1892
J. de Fursac, *Un Mouvement mystique contemporain: le réveil religieux du
Pays de Galles 1904-5* (Paris, 1907)
C. H. Gadney, *The History of the Laws of Rugby Football 1949-1972* (1973)
A. Gray-Jones, *A History of Ebbw Vale* (Newport, 1976)
W. J. Hoare, *Schoolboy Rugby Football* (N.U.T., London 1938)
Geraint Jenkins, *Cewri'r Bêldroed yng Nghymru* (Llandysul, 1977)
R. Gerallt Jones, Huw Ll. Davies a Carwyn James, *Y Gamp Lawn 1977-78*
(Talybont, 1978)
George G. Lerry, *F.A. of Wales: 75th Anniversary 1876-1951* (Wrexham, 1951)
Howard Lloyd (gol.), *Crysau Cochion* (Llandybie, 1958)
Howard Lloyd, *Chwarae Teg* (Llandybie, 1967)
Keith Macklin, *The History of Rugby League Football* (1962)
F. W. Mandle, 'Games People Played', *Historical Studies* (Australia and
New Zealand), xv, April 1973
M. Marples, *A History of Football* (1954)
Howard Marshall, *Oxford v. Cambridge: the story of the University Rugby
Match* (1951)
Tony Mason, *Association Football and English Society 1865-1915* (1980)
R. M. (Dickie) Owen, article in *South Wales Football Echo*, 12 Nov. 1927
Reg Pelling (ed.), *Welsh Rugby Football Triple Crown Souvenir* (Cardiff,
1950)
Percy Royds, *The History of the Laws of Rugby Football* (1949)
E. H. D. Sewell, *The Rugby Football Internationals' Roll of Honour* (1919)
J. B. G. Thomas (ed.), *Official Souvenir of the Triple Crown 1893-1952*
(Cardiff, 1952)
J. Walvin, *The People's Game: a social history of English football* (1975)
E. Watts Moses, *A History of the Proceedings of the International Rugby
Football Board 1886-1960* (1960); *Supplement, 1961-1972* (1973)
Gareth Williams, 'Fields of Praise', *Planet* 14, 1972
Gareth Williams, 'Chwaraeon a Chymdeithas', *Taliesin* 32, 1976
Percy M. Young, *A History of British Football* (1968)

INDEX

Aberavon R.F.C., 27, 100, 105, 115, 178, 181, 183, 226, 265, 300, 330, 359, 360, 394, 396, 400.
Abergavenny, 22, 30.
Abergavenny R.F.C., 2, 11, 24.
Abertillery R.F.C., 105, 183, 265, 268, 282, 365-66.
Aberystwyth R.F.C., 331-332.
Aberystwyth, University College, 15, 67, 331.
Argentina, 388, 393, 432.
Arthur, Tom, 211, 212, 223, 224, 257, 264, 265, 267, 274, 276, 277.
Association Football, 7, 30, 31, 32, 58, 79, 139, 176-178, 181, 186, 224, 232-233, 297-298.
Australia, 46, 47, 148, 175, 187, 304, 306, 382, 389, 398, 399, 432.

Badger, Owen, 91, 106, 138, 263.
Bancroft, Jack, 195, 198, 206, 296, 383.
Bancroft, W.J., 64, 72, 82, 86, 87, 88, 90, 100, 113, 114, 117, 118, 123, 133, 141, 142, 198, 262, 350, 409, 446.
Bangor R.F.C., 40, 41, 43, 271, 332.
Barbarians R.F.C., 202, 295, 306, 364, 365, 377, 396, 429-430, 431, 460.
Barry, 102, 178, 257, 313, 334.
Bassett, Arthur, 280, 281, 297.
Bassett, Jack, 223, 253, 262, 264, 265, 266-67.
Bebb, Dewi, 332, 334, 363-364, 378, 381.
Bennett, Phil, 369, 397, 400, 401, 414, 426, 429, 430, 431, 441, 442, 443, 445-446, 447, 449, 452.
Bergiers, Roy, 421, 429.
Bevan J.A. (Cambridge Univ. & Newport), 7, 24, 39, 40.
Bevan, J.C. (Cardiff Coll. of Educ. and Cardiff), 407, 408, 414, 421, 430.
Bevan, J.D. (Aberavon), 414, 442.
'Big Five', origins, 216-217.
Biggs, Norman, 33, 82, 87, 88, 92.
Biggs, Selwyn, 33, 82, 113.
Blackheath, 38, 40, 43, 45, 50, 56, 57, 113.
Blackheath R.F.C., 3, 9, 10, 21, 35, 36, 57, 69, 70, 71, 80.
Blaenavon R.F.C., 11, 245.

Blaina, 7, 26, 377, 401.
Blaina R.F.C., 101, 105, 181, 226, 330-331.
Boon, Ronnie, 257, 261, 262, 263, 264, 265, 266, 273, 276, 277, 281, 302.
Boots, George, 137, 143, 151.
Boucher, Arthur, 33, 72, 81.
Bowcott, H.M., 240, 243, 251, 253, 254, 257, 262, 273, 276, 277, 368, 388.
Bowdler, F.A., 251, 257, 278.
Bowen, Harry, 2, 62, 138, 142, 193.
Bowen, W.E., 243, 270, 323, 353.
Boyce, Max, 443.
Brace, Onllwyn, 18, 352, 353-354, 355, 360, 367, 377.
Brecon, 2, 22, 31, 44, 355.
Brecon, Christ College, 20, 23, 43, 47, 176, 239, 241, 242, 269.
Brecon R.F.C., 2, 11, 40, 41, 43, 44, 53, 246.
Brice, A., 33, 115, 122, 138.
Bridgend, 2, 47, 62, 219.
Bridgend R.F.C., 11, 27, 394, 395, 457.
Bristol R.F.C., 10, 246.
British Lions, 213; (1930) 258-259; (1938) 296; (1950) 335-336; (1962) 367; (1968) 393; (1971) 413-414, 421, 433; (1974) 423, 433, 441; (1977) 433, 444, 449.
Brynamman R.F.C., 11, 219, 268, 361, 403.
Budd, Arthur, 35, 80, 90-91.
Bush, P.F., 25, 105, 133, 148, 149, 150, 151, 159, 160, 161, 167, 169, 188, 189, 192, 193, 194, 270, 307.

Cambridge University, 10, 25, 39, 40, 54, 239, 241, 244, 246-7, 249, 250-1, 279, 280-1, 288, 304, 318, 400.
Cardiff, 1, 2, 11, 25, 39, 40, 61, 63, 64, 66, 73, 81, 83-4, 93, 104, 116, 138, 141, 148, 155, 169, 187, 292, 374.
Cardiff Arms Park, 6, 9-10, 26, 60, 114, 129, 134, 139, 175, 177, 219-220, 262, 284, 286, 306, 314, 348, 349, 350, 357-58, 359, 370-373, 400, 405-406, 432.
Cardiff R.F.C., 1, 2, 3, 4, 6, 8, 9, 10, 11,

501

159, 160, 161, 162, 165, 167, 175, 188, 192-193, 194, 195, 196, 198, 199, 221.
Oxford University, 24, 27, 32, 39, 40, 45, 54, 58, 142, 253, 269, 278, 353.

Packer, Harry, 72, 207, 213, 216-217, 245, 246, 351.
Parfitt, F.C., 72, 81.
Parfitt, V.J., 369, 385, 417.
Parsons, C.E., 47, 48.
Pask, Alun, 361, 366, 378, 381, 382, 386.
Peake, Revd Edward, 7, 27, 38, 40.
Pearson, T.W., 81, 90, 143.
Pegge, E.V., 24, 78.
Pell, Arthur, 20, 21.
Penygraig R.F.C., 4, 11, 53, 92, 105, 187.
Phillips, Lou, 131, 132, 142.
Phillips, Percy, 72, 81, 87.
Phillips, W.D., 40, 52, 78.
Pontypool R.F.C., 2, 41, 43, 178, 183, 209, 255, 260, 359, 428.
Pontypridd R.F.C., 26, 37, 38, 39, 40, 49, 74, 100, 105, 178, 227, 394, 428, 457, 458.
Powell, W.C., 209, 221, 246, 247, 250, 251, 253, 254, 262, 263, 265, 266, 278, 282, 283, 360.
Price, Brian, 378, 381, 384, 386, 397, 398, 400, 402.
Price, Graham, 443, 446, 452.
Price, Terry, 378, 380, 381, 382.
Pritchard, Cecil, 211, 251.
Pritchard, Charles Meyrick, 151-152, 153, 162, 163, 188.
Pritchard, Cliff, 151, 160, 162, 165, 169.
Prosser, Ray, 359, 362-363, 443.

Quinnell, Derek, 429, 431, 444, 455.

Ralph, Raymond, 263, 264, 266, 269, 272.
Raybould, W.H., 392, 400-401.
Rees, A.M., 60, 287, 288, 289, 290.
Rees, T. Conway, 81, 82, 87, 88.
Rees, Dan, 124, 130, 141, 142.
Rees, J. Idwal, 241, 278, 280, 282, 289, 290, 291, 295, 313.
Rees, T.A., 31, 40, 47.
Rees, Walter E., 45, 51, 52, 53, 98-9, 112, 113-4, 116, 153, 175, 177-8, 193, 202, 205, 208, 214-5, 218, 219, 225, 228, 229, 285, 296, 309, 310-11.
Revival, Religious 1904-05, 120, 126-128, 186, 286.

Rhapps, Jack, 92, 106, 108.
Richards, David, 440, 442, 455, 459.
Richards, Maurice, 334, 381, 397, 399, 400.
Richardson, A.H., 31, 41, 42.
Richmond, R.F.C., 10, 57, 70, 94, 339.
Roberts, John, 246, 251, 252, 253, 254, 271.
Roberts, M.G., 402, 411, 422, 455, 456.
Roblin, Gwyn, 271, 456.
Rodney Parade, 9, 34, 47, 59, 73, 92, 104, 122, 333, 391.
Rogers, Handel, 327, 389.
Rowlands, Clive, 18, 341, 369, 376-377, 379, 380, 381, 382, 386, 388, 389, 391, 393, 399, 410, 432, 441.
Rugby (School), 20, 21, 23, 43.
Rugby Football Union, 14, 21, 30, 37, 39, 40, 41, 43, 46, 47, 50, 51, 53, 56, 73, 74, 94, 108, 109, 110, 111, 118, 201, 203, 208, 222, 230, 246, 257, 262, 277, 326, 433, 438.
Rugby League, 90, 96-97, 106, 107, 112, 124, 178, 180, 203, 208-209, 224, 225-227, 236, 269, 294, 297, 312-315, 317.
Rydal, 269, 273, 298, 345-6.

St. Alban's Band, 286.
St. Helen's, 13, 26, 43, 49, 57, 73, 114, 117, 133, 138, 139, 141, 142, 169, 196, 199, 209, 228, 229, 265, 285, 288, 294, 314, 349, 350, 391.
Schofield, T.D., 182, 208, 213, 215, 216, 218, 230, 251.
Scotland, 8, 9, 24, 32, 48, 50-64 passim, 73, 88, 89, 91, 104, 107, 114, 123, 138-141, 143, 150, 176, 184, 186, 194-197, 203, 212, 228-229, 241-249 passim, 252-254, 257, 262-263, 266, 282, 305, 324, 337-40, 350, 359, 364, 380, 400, 407-409, 441, 450-451. See also 'Wales v Scotland'.
Scottish Rugby Union, 14, 43, 208-209, 326.
Scrines, Fred, 115, 118, 125, 138, 169, 180, 193.
Seeling, Charles, 148, 157.
Shea, Jerry, 205, 208, 209.
Skym, Archie, 223, 224, 236, 251, 257, 267, 274, 282.
South Africa, 186-190, 265, 343-345, 359, 365, 367, 368-369, 376, 380, 400-406. See also 'Wales v South Africa'.

502

v Fiji (1964) 380.

v France (1908), 190-1; (1909), 191; (1912) 191; (1913) 191; (1928) 253; (1931) 263; (1946) 301-2; (1948) 349; (1950) 325-6; (1955) 334, 352; (1956) 351-2; (1965) 382; (1971) 410-3, (1978) 451; (1979) 452; (1980) 459.

v Ireland (1882) 63; (1884) 61, 63; (1891) 53; (1893) 89; (1894) 90; (1895) 90; (1898) 113; (1899) 114; (1902) 125; (1903) 138, 143; (1904) 124; (1905) 141; (1906) 176; (1907) 193; (1908) 194; (1909) 196; (1911) 171, 197; (1912) 191, 199; (1914) 199; (1920) 205; (1924) 214; (1926) 244; (1927) 250-251; (1931) 263-264; (1932) 266; (1936) 284-285; (1950) 324-5; (1952) 337; (1957) 353; (1965) 380-382; (1969) 397; (1976) 446; (1978) 451.

v Japan (1973) 432.

v New Zealand (1905) 145-169 passim; (1924) 217; (1935) 287-292; (1953) 347-348; (1963) 389; (1967) 390-91; (1969 tour) 398-99; (1972) 430; (1974) 430; (1978) 430-31.

v Romania (1979) 432-433.

v South Africa (1906) 186-187; (1912) 191; (1931) 265-266; (1951) 343-345; (1960) 365; (1964) 367-368, 376; (1970) 400.

v Scotland (1883) 57-58; (1884) 59; (1886) 60; (1888) 62-63; (1891) 53; (1893) 88; (1894) 89; 104; (1895) 91; (1899) 114; (1900) 123, 138; (1901) 141; (1902) 139; (1903) 138, 139; (1904) 124, 143; (1905) 139-141; (1906) 176; (1907) 184; (1909) 194-196; (1911) 196-197; (1924) 212; (1921) 228-229; (1926) 244; (1927) 241, 247-249; (1928) 252-253; (1929) 254; (1930) 257; (1931) 262-263; (1932) 266; (1935) 282; (1938) 296; (1947) 305; (1950) 324; (1951) 339-40; (1952) 337; (1953) 338; (1954) 350; (1959) 364; (1965) 380; (1970) 400; (1971) 407-409; (1975) 441; (1978) 450-451.

Walters, D. Gwynne, 354-355.

Watkins, David, 331, 377-78, 380, 381, 382, 390, 401.

Watkins, H., 136, 141.

Watkins, L. 40, 57.

Watkins, Stuart, 334, 378, 382, 390, 401.

Welsh Football Union, see Welsh Rugby Union.

Welsh Rugby Union, 4, 5, 9, 11, 14, 15-16, 19, 37, 38; (Founding & early years) 41-53, 56, 65, 74-75, 78-80, 83; (& the Gould Affair) 93-95, 108-111; (Growing Co-ordination in) 96-100; 101-103, 106-107, 112, 115-116, 119; (in early 1900s) 121-123, 25; (& W. v N.Z. 1905) 153, 154-155; (& National Ground) 175, 219-220, 357-358, 371-373, 448-449, (& Northern Union) 178-180, 227, 314-315; (& Schools Rugby) 176, 437-439; (& Junior R.U.) 181, 434-435; (& 1st World War) 201-204; (& Scottish R.U.) 207-209; (demands for reform) 213-214; (& Male Affair) 214-215; (Reform of Match Committee) 215-217; (effect of inter-war slump) 224-225; (& law changes proposals) 245-246, 358-359; (& discontent with selection) 259; (& W.W.R.U.) 260-261, 268; (change from W.F.U. to W.R.U.) 204, 293; (& sub-committee into decline of interest in Welsh Rugby) 298 (& 7-a-side) 298; (suspension during 2nd World War) 299; (resumption after 1945) 301; (& Youth rugby) 315-316; (& C.C.P.R.) 329; (& rugby in North Wales) 271, 332; (last international at St. Helen's) 349-350; (changes during 1960s) 368-370; (& coaching) 369-370; (& Development Committee) 371; (1964 Working Party) 385; (& Coaching Organizer) 384-389; (Installation of squad training) 397; (& 'B' internationals) 401; (& S. Africa) 402-405; (& Sunday fixtures) 119, 417; (Setting up of Centenary Committee) 417; (fostering expansion of world rugby) 432; (1968 Report on Structure & Organization) 434-435; (office in St. Mary's St., Cardiff) 435; (geographical reorganization) 435-436; (League System proposal & relaunching of Challenge Cup Competition) 436-437; (& televised rugby) 447; (& charitable fund) 459; (& 'Laws of the Game') 460.

W.R.U. Challenge Cup, 428, 436, 448.

W.R.U. Coaching Advisory Committee, 329, 385-387, 393, 435, 436.